LEARNING AND HUMAN ABILITIES

Learning and Human Abilities
Educational Psychology
THIRD EDITION

Herbert J. Klausmeier
The University of Wisconsin

Richard E. Ripple
Cornell University

Harper & Row, Publishers
New York, Evanston, San Francisco, London

Part-opening photographs from Monkmeyer Press Photos. Photographers as follows: Part I, Rogers; Part II, Zimbel; Part III, Shackman; Part IV, Zimbel.

Learning and Human Abilities: Educational Psychology, Third Edition.

Contents

Preface

Since the writing of the second edition of *Learning and Human Abilities* in 1965, much research and development have been done that, potentially, can have positive results in improving educational practices on a nation-wide scale. During the same five-year period, however, conditions have emerged that exercise a profound negative influence on education at all levels. Among the more important of these are the Vietnam War, racism, the use of drugs, intensified poverty of a minority of the population, an increase in violence, and a tax rebellion directed against providing more money for public education. Awareness of the influence of these and other social conditions on education puts current educational practices and the study of educational psychology in proper perspective. In other words, the principles set forth in a course in educational psychology will contribute to improved educational practices only if schools are operated and supported in such a way that the principles can be *applied*.

In Part I of this book, learning and human abilities are discussed, and a model of school learning is outlined. Many recent studies of learning have focused on understanding learning conditions in school settings. Also, human abilities that may be improved through education are being identified. Especially promising are the recent advances made in developing instructional materials and procedures designed to develop the creative abilities of students.

Not only in Part I but throughout the book, ideas about human learning and human development that are usually treated separately have been integrated in the concept of emerging human abilities. Also, a model of school learning has been formulated in order to identify and bring together related knowledge and practices dealing with learning, abilities, and instruction. This model provides the organizing framework for this edition and may also become the framework around which the student can organize his own information.

In Part II, we have brought together psychologically sound and practical information concerning components of a school learning system, including educational and instructional objectives, instructional materials and related technology, characteristics of students and provisions for individual differences, characteristics of teachers as individuals and groups, and classroom interactions and teacher leadership. The events and concepts dealt with include the increasing attention given to instructional objectives, the demise of teaching machines, the use of the computer, the mixed blessings of educational technology, the failure to make compensatory education work well for disadvantaged students, the emergence of organized teacher groups and the related collective negotiations and strikes, and the gradual abandonment of self-contained classroom teaching in favor of teams and other organizations for instruction.

Principles that describe conditions internal to the learner and parallel instructional guides that enable teachers to deal more effectively with external conditions are becoming more clear as teams of researchers, developers, evaluators, and school people work vigorously at generating knowledge that can be applied directly to improving educational practices. We are involved in these teams that are concerned with motivation, various outcomes of learning, and retention and transfer. Therefore, we have provided firsthand information in the part of each of the eight chapters of Part III that deals with principles of learning and the parallel instructional guides. We have come to many conclusions, and one of the most important is that independent reading and prosocial behaviors in low-achieving children of relatively low socioeconomic status *can* be developed through systematic instruction.

For several decades, little progress has been made in test development. Though the early IQ scales, educational achievement tests, and personality inventories of the 1920s and 1930s have taken on a modern look during the past 20 or so years, they have not been much improved. In fact, nearly everyone now recognizes that norm-referenced IQ and achievement tests are of little value to the teacher in deciding what a child may be ready to learn, in assessing his progress in learning during the school year, or in assessing his final level of abilities or achievements. The use of personality tests also has come under increasing scrutiny because teachers are unable to interpret the scores and because adults, aware that the scores might be stored by computer and not kept confidential, have become fearful of the invasion of their own and their children's privacy. We point to both the limitations of published tests and the proper uses that can be made of them in Part IV; we also discuss more recent trends in test development, evaluating student progress and instructional programs, and using statistical concepts.

In order to help the student in his study of the various chapters, we have inserted questions and activities at the end of each main section of each chapter. These study aids are intended to encourage the comprehension, application, and evaluation of information included in each chapter and at the same time to stimulate creative thinking and problem-solving. No answers or possible solutions are given for the questions and activities because applications to school settings and the solution of educational problems vary according to such factors as the objectives of instruction, the characteristics of the students, the curriculum area, the availability of instructional material, and the like. For the same reason, students may find that it is most valuable for them, when considering the questions and activities, to organize themselves in small discussion groups, each group consisting of students with similar interests in a curriculum area and level of schooling (e.g., social studies in high school or communication skills in elementary school). The instructor also may find the questions and activities useful in organizing a class into discussion groups formed on other bases.

Included in the suggestions for further reading at the end of each chapter are most of the readings that appear in a parallel volume prepared by Professor Richard E. Ripple, *Readings in Learning and Human Abilities: Educational Psychology*, second edition, Harper & Row, 1971. Additional readings, also suggested, are mainly from other books of readings, each of which is devoted entirely to the topics included in one or two chapters of this third edition of the text.

A *Student Guide* prepared by Ruth S. Nickse and Richard E. Ripple accompanies this third edition. Each chapter of the *Guide* consists of an outline of the chapter in the text, a multiple-choice self-test, discussion questions, and projects. Answers to all the self-tests, a list of relevant general books, and an annotated list of professional journals are also included. The *Guide* is intended to help students decide which are the most important concepts in the text and assess their own achievements. The questions and projects are particularly designed to encourage productive thinking and evaluation and, to a lesser extent, comprehension and recall.

We cannot properly register our appreciation of the assistance from all the persons who contributed ideas to this edition. We have given the usual acknowledgments for ideas used from published sources. We express appreciation to the many instructors using the first and second editions who offered oral and written suggestions for improvement and to the many hundreds of students in our own classes who gave helpful suggestions. Representing a variety of subject-matter interests and levels of schooling, these students identified some of the applications of psychological knowledge to educational practices outlined in this third edition.

Former Ph.D. advisees of the senior author have influenced his ideas and writing in many ways. Included are Ronald Ady, Joey Byers, John Check, J. Kent Davis, Zackaria Ethnathios, Christopher Flizak, William Franzen, Dorothy Frayer, Wayne Fredrick, John Gaa, Elizabeth Schwenn Ghatala, Gerald Gleason, Elmira Layague Johnson, Leo Loughlin, Daniel Lynch, Dean Meinke, Gerald Miller, Ralph Pippert, James Ramsay, Joe Scott, Terrence Snowden, Glenn Tagatz, and Suzanne Wiviott. In addition, Richard Ripple as coauthor revised Chapters 14 and 15, while John Feldhusen served as the substantive editor of the entire book.

Special recognition is due to the persons listed below, whom the senior author employed to carry out specific activities: Robin Chapman, who prepared a first draft of the section in Chapter 10 entitled "Learning To Read: A Psycholinguistic View"; John Feldhusen, who prepared a first draft of the section in Chapter 5 entitled "Computers in Education and Instruction"; Wayne Fredrick, who prepared a first draft of the questions and activities for seven chapters; Mary Quilling, who prepared a draft of Chapters 17, 18, and 19; and Dorothy Cullen and Arlene Knudsen, who assisted with the typing.

November 1970   HERBERT J. KLAUSMEIER
                                                                                      RICHARD E. RIPPLE

To the Student

Learning from a textbook is facilitated if an efficient strategy or plan for learning is developed and used. We had a strategy in mind when we wrote this book; in describing it here, we are offering our best suggestions for facilitating your learning. Consider our plan only as a suggestion, however. You may already have evolved a more effective one. Also, your instructor may make additional suggestions.

First, study the titles of the four main parts of the book and the chapter titles within each part. This helps you learn how the authors organized all the information. If the organization is meaningful to you (as we hope it is), it will serve as your master organization for selecting, acquiring, retaining, and using the information presented.

Read and study Chapter 1. It presents an overview and thus is an advance organizer for the rest of the book.

Turn to the opening page of the chapter in which you are interested. Study the outline on that page until you can remember all the main headings and are familiar with the subtopics. Read through each main section of the chapter consecutively and formulate answers to the questions and carry out the activities listed at the end of each main section. Some of the questions are designed to help you in comprehending, applying, and evaluating information provided in the chapter. Others are intended to encourage you to think creatively and to identify and solve problems. Since most of the questions have no right or wrong responses, answers are not provided. If you are unsure about your response, a good way to start clarifying your thoughts is to talk things over with your instructor or with other students—or both.

As you read and study the successive parts of a chapter, don't just ask yourself, "What is important for me to learn and remember?" It is far more valuable—and interesting—to think about possible *uses* of the information. Furthermore, as you respond to the questions and activities, don't stop with only one application to your personal or professional life; think of several. An instructor obviously cannot point out all possible applications to the personal and professional lives of his many students; therefore, you must make most of the applications yourself—and there are many to be made.

Some students do not give enough attention to the material in figures and tables. You should remember that the figures and tables are in the book for a very good reason—they present certain kinds of information in less space and in a more easily comprehended and remembered form than many sentences of text discussion. When you come to a reference to a figure or table, first read the entire paragraph containing the reference, which will give you a kind of orientation. Then turn to the figure or table itself and study it carefully. Often, an important point will suddenly become clear. (If you have difficulty in interpreting information presented in tables, graphs, or drawings, study the first part of Chapter 19. There you will learn how data are collected, analyzed, and reported.)

There is another type of study aid in the book. You will see that certain passages are set off from the rest of the text by blue brackets. These are passages that the authors believe should be particularly noted because they give important information in a concise form. You are likely to find that this "flagging" of some passages will be helpful to you, both when you study a chapter and when you review it.

All behavioral sciences necessarily include a certain amount of technical information, and educational psychology is no exception. Understanding the technical information in this book requires some understanding of measurement, evaluation, and statistics. Accordingly, there are instructors who start the course by discussing statistical terminology as described in Chapter 19 and by assigning also the reading of Chapters 17 and 18 on measurement and evaluation. Other instructors cover this material in the last weeks of the course; still others omit much of it entirely. No matter when this material may or may not actually be assigned, you will find it helpful. That is, when you encounter a reference to a type of test or a statistical procedure that is new to you, go first to the index or to the table of contents and then to the appropriate pages of Chapter 17, 18, or 19. Do not hesitate to consult the instructor or other students if you need help in understanding anything in those chapters. By its very nature, such technical information must be closely studied to achieve true understanding.

The suggestions for further reading at the end of each chapter have been selected with care to provide sources you can consult when you want to expand your knowledge about a particular topic. Many of the suggestions are drawn from Ripple, *Readings in Learning and Human Abilities: Educational Psychology*, second edition, Harper & Row, 1971. We have tried also to identify useful information in other books that are often purchased by a central library and put on reserve. Enough suggested readings are included to permit in-depth study of the kind that is reported in a term paper.

There is a *Student Guide* (Nickse & Ripple) which you may purchase and use as an aid as you study. The *Guide* is divided into 19 chapters that correspond with the chapters in the text. Each chapter consists of four parts: (1) an outline of the chapter in the text; (2) a multiple-choice self-test; (3) discussion questions; (4) projects. Answers to all the self-tests, a list of relevant general books, and an annotated list of professional journals are also included. The *Guide* is intended to help students decide which are the most important concepts in the text, carry out independent, systematic study, and assess their own achievements. The questions and projects, which raise provocative questions of vital concern to the beginning teacher, are particularly designed to encourage productive thinking and evaluation, and, to a lesser extent, comprehension and recall.

We hope that your study of educational psychology will have an important direct result—more effective learning by you. We also hope that it will have an important indirect result—more effective learning by your own students later. Many of our students, as they begin teaching, report that their study of educational psychology is indeed of great practical value to them. As you might suspect, some report otherwise. Do not conclude, however, that the difficulties of the latter group are the fault of educational psychology. As we noted in the Preface, certain conditions that impede the development of excellent instruction have become increasingly evident in our society as a whole. These societal conditions must be rectified if all children are to have reasonably adequate opportunities to develop their emerging abilities.

Part I The Nature of Learning and Human Abilities

these are the two main concerns of educational psychology: through research, to generate knowledge about learning and instruction and, through development, to put this knowledge into forms that can be used by school people in nurturing the abilities and other characteristics of children and youth. Until recently, generating knowledge about learning and instruction received far more emphasis than developing principles, materials, and procedures that teachers can use. The emphases have become more balanced, however, and a system of school learning that permits the educator to organize his knowledge about learning, abilities, and educational practices effectively has now been formulated. This system is described in this book.

Theories of learning that clarify the conditions that influence initial learning, retention, and transfer within the learner and within the teaching situation are of special interest to school people. The role of the teacher, as the central person in a system of school learning, is in turn clarified by these theories. The theories have led to statements of principles associated with purposeful learning, conditioning, observational learning and imitation, meaningful reception learning, and informational theory; these principles merit careful study and personal validation through practice, rather than uncritical acceptance or rejection.

Through learning, including learning in school, human beings develop their abilities over a period of many years. In the past decades, remarkable progress has been made in identifying cognitive and psychomotor abilities and also in discovering more about the feelings, values, motives, and other affective characteristics of individuals. Education can now be planned with more confidence that it will identify and nurture the abilities that characterize each individual student.

Chapter 1 The Scope of Educational Psychology

Primary Emphases in Educational Psychology

1. learning and human abilities
   association and cognitive viewpoints
   cognitive and psychomotor abilities
2. a system of school learning
   components of an educational system
   components of an instructional system
3. achieving learning outcomes
   motivation
   six classes of learning outcomes
   retention and transfer
4. measurement, evaluation, and research design

Other Concerns of Educational Psychology

human development
exceptional children
school psychology
counseling

Research and Development in Educational Psychology

naturalistic observation
correlational studies
controlled experimentation
variables: dependent and independent
development of products for school use

his book is about learning in schools. It ranges from the stating of educational objectives through measuring and evaluating the results of instruction. It is concerned with human learning in all its richness and variety — the learning that changes the helpless newborn baby into a thinking, doing, feeling adult of magnificent abilities. Learning culminates in a person who can use machines to do much of his physical work, who can organize ideas that influence not only his life but also the lives of others, who can create and perform in the fine arts, who can deftly remove a malignant tumor to restore health, and who, perhaps most important of all, has compassion and respect for his fellow man. Not everyone achieves so much. But this type of person is the ideal, and it is through learning that we do at times achieve the ideal.

This book outlines principles of learning and related conditions and procedures for improving educational practices. It presents a positive picture of what the teacher can do for children and young people and what education can do in general. This confidence is based on the results of recent research and development that show how the school environment can be modified to facilitate learning. It is also based on concrete information. For instance, 52 of the first 53 American astronauts had their early education in public schools, and many of them indicate that a teacher had an important influence on their lives (Editorial, *Phi Delta Kappan*, 1969).

The school can capitalize on the positive motives of students for learning, nurture students' intellectual and psychomotor abilities, help them to master subject matter and to acquire favorable attitudes, and help them to become confident and capable adults. All this schooling *can* do.

Despite continuing unresolved social problems and their unfavorable effects on many aspects of education, we predict that the quality of education will continue to improve for an ever-increasing number of children, youth, and adults. These problems are serious, however. Knebel, an able reporter, recently summarized his perceptions of the mood of Americans; all the problems he describes have implications for school learning and teaching:

> People are more disturbed, anxious and apprehensive than at any time in my memory, which embraces the cruel years of the Great Depression. Unlike the Depression era, when American concern centered on purely economic items, today's distress flows from a score of sources: the war in Vietnam, inflation, crime, the rebellion of the young, the welfare "mess," the mechanization and depersonalization of society, riots, the assault on almost every institution from the Roman Catholic Church to the American Medical Association, the proliferation of drugs, the lightning changes of attitudes toward sex, family, church, school and authority, the squalor and infirmity of the big cities, the clamor of the blacks for room at the top and/or revolution, a growing realization that the brave new American Empire must retrench and curb its missionary passion to remake the world in its own image, the immense lethal force and influence of the U.S. military machine, the fouling of the atmosphere, waters and soil, the lack of knightly leaders who summon their countrymen to quests for the Holy Grail, a new feeling that there are no Holy Grails, the decline and fall of craftsmanship and the enthronement of the shoddy, the horrors of atomic-, gas- and

germ-warfare preparations, the allied, deeply sensed fear that civilization can end at any moment, and, above all, a gnawing suspicion that modern society is a hostile, capricious force that can only be endured by seeking refuge in the smuggeries of the family and the self. (Knebel, 1969, pp. 24-25)[1]

There are limits to what education can do in dealing with these problems. Furthermore, their impact on many school systems is often harsh, with an increasing number of temporary disruptions. Nevertheless, the great majority of schools continue to make remarkable improvements. There will be even more rapid progress when greater financial support is provided, when the present generation of prospective teachers assumes leadership roles in education (they will be considered "the establishment" the day they begin teaching), and when research and development strategies are applied more broadly to the solution of educational problems.

The vital importance of research and development to man's understanding of his world and of himself can be seen in many areas. For example, the result of years of research in agriculture is the production of more than enough food for a sharply increasing population by a sharply reduced number of farmers. Man's transportation system kept him tied to this planet until very recently; first he conquered our atmosphere; now he lands on the moon; and next he will travel to the other planets. Research connected with learning and schooling has not yet produced such dramatic achievements—although illiteracy has decreased sharply during the past century and the average level of educational achievement has risen consistently. Nevertheless, increasing research efforts are accumulating conclusions which, when brought together, comprise a substantial body of scientific and practical knowledge of education. Principles of school learning based on research can now be stated with more assurance that, if they are properly applied, the result will be more purposeful learning by more students.

This emphasis on research applied to practice has been aptly described by Hilgard (1964): "We believe that the scientific psychology of learning has the obligation to go all the way from theory to practice, using criticized data in every step." Hilgard is an American, but Wiseman (1959) and Woodsworth (1965), an Englishman and a Canadian, are among the psychologists of other countries who agree that the main concern of educational psychology should be learning in school settings.

PRIMARY EMPHASES IN EDUCATIONAL PSYCHOLOGY

Educational psychology is the science that studies student behaviors in educational settings; that is, student behaviors and education set the boundaries of the content and methodology of the science. The content focuses on the nature of learning, the development of students' abilities, types of learning outcomes acquired by students, conditions within the student and within the school setting associated with efficient learning, and measurement of the outcomes of learning. As for the methodology,

---

[1]By permission of the editors. From the November 18, 1969 issue of Look Magazine. Copyright 1969 by Cowles Communications, Inc.

research in educational psychology is conducted in laboratories with school-age children or directly in schools. School subjects and other relevant topics receive major attention. The primary concern of educational psychology is to generate knowledge and to organize it systematically in the form of theories or systems, principles, and related information. In this sense, educational psychology is a *behavioral* science.

As teachers and others know, knowledge of theory and principles does not automatically produce better educational practices. Experimentation by educational psychologists and others must be done directly in school settings to validate and apply their theories and principles. One central aim of this experimentation is to learn how instructional materials, teaching methods, and student activities may be varied, and eventually controlled, to help students attain a higher measure of self-realization through learning.

Educational psychology, then, has a central role in generating theoretical knowledge and in finding applications that ensure transfer from theory to practice. Further, because educational improvement is directly dependent on the development of new and improved instructional materials, methods, equipment, tests, and the like, educational psychologists are also involved, along with educational practitioners and subject-matter scholars, in such development work.

This is an appropriate place to mention the differences between graduate programs to prepare educational psychologists as behavioral scientists and other courses or programs specifically intended for educational practitioners, such as teachers, guidance workers, and curriculum coordinators. Graduate programs in educational psychology, particularly at the doctoral level, emphasize theory formulation and critical analysis of information; also, research competence is developed over an extended period of time.

On the other hand, a single undergraduate or graduate course designed mainly for educational practitioners does not permit critical analysis of theories and the development of research competence. It does, however, emphasize the theories, principles, and related applications that appear to be most relevant in the actual modifying of student behaviors — the practical function that is the primary responsibility of the school. In other words, such a course gives the practitioner information that enables him to analyze teaching-learning situations more intelligently, to make wiser decisions as a teacher or other educational worker, and to start developing his own ways to improve educational practices. This book is intended for such a course. Therefore, a study of the primary emphases around which this book is organized will provide a better understanding of the role of educational psychology related to educational practice. The following four numbered sections of this chapter (pages 7-23), which correspond to Parts I, II, III, and IV, give a brief overview of topics that are treated in detail in the rest of the book.

1. Learning and Human Abilities

Learning is a process or operation inferred from relatively permanent changes in behavior that result from practice. On the other hand, relatively permanent changes in behavior that result from maturation and temporary changes that result from drugs, fatigue, and the like are not considered to be learning. When a baby about 6 months old for the first time grasps a small object between the thumb and forefinger (prehensile grasping), he is manifesting behavior that emerges with maturation. When a child first walks upright, runs rather than walks, or does any of the similar things that all children do without practice or instruction, it is maturation rather than learning.

These behaviors, however, are examples of learning: A 6-year-old child cannot recognize any of the 15 words in a book; he receives instruction and practices; six months later he recognizes all the words. Another child cannot play a selection on the piano; he receives instruction and practices; eventually he plays the selection. Finally, a 6-year-old shows no differential reaction to other children based on skin color; at age 10 he interacts at school only with children of his own skin color and avoids other children. In the interim, he has avoided certain children. We infer from observing the overt behaviors, before and after practice, that all three children have learned.

Educational psychology is vitally concerned with both the nature of learning and conditions affecting learning in school settings. In considering the nature of learning, psychologists divide themselves, broadly speaking, into two groups. The *association* theorists treat learning as an associative process that can be explained in terms of a relatively few principles that relate stimulus events and response events. The *cognitive* theorists infer that human beings manipulate, or operate on, concepts, perceptual images, and possibly feelings and that only the most elementary changes in behavior can be explained in terms of association. The two groups of theorists are united in attempting to clarify the learning processes and to identify the conditions within the organism and within the environment that influence learning.

Efficiency of learning is usually measured in terms of a criterion — the amount learned, the time spent in learning, or the number of errors made. For example, students who have not spoken or heard French try to learn a dialogue. One repeats it fluently after 10 minutes of practice; another requires 20 minutes to reach the same criterion. The first has learned more efficiently. Assume that two other students have practiced the dialogue for 10 minutes. In repeating it one makes only three errors in pronunciation; the other makes 10. Again, the first has learned more efficiently. Other criteria, such as the quality of the performance and the cost of the practice in terms of dollars or energy, are also used in assessing efficiency. Throughout this book, "efficient learning" is a shorthand term for the relatively permanent changes in behavior that occur at a rapid rate or with few errors or in terms of some other chosen criterion. (In Chapter 2, principles that are relevant to the learning of many outcomes are discussed.)

A *human ability* is a union of a process (or processes) and a content (or contents) inferred from relatively permanent changes in behavior. A child at age 5 speaks English words that enable him to be understood by others. He has thus developed the ability to speak (process or operation)

English words (content). The two main classes of human abilities are cognitive and psychomotor.

A *cognitive* ability is a mediator, a kind of trace or mechanism, that enables the individual to interact with or to interpret rather discrete environmental experiences. For example, the child who *comprehends words* spoken to him can both modify his actions and interpret the behaviors of others; thus the ability, verbal comprehension, is a mediator. More generally, verbal comprehension is positively associated with facility in dealing with a variety of verbal encounters or experiences. Students who score high on a test of verbal comprehension generally score higher on comprehension tests in specific subjects, such as English, social studies, and science, than do those who score low. In other words, consistencies in performance on specific tasks, for example, mastering the vocabulary of science and English, are accounted for by the more general cognitive ability.

An example of a *psychomotor* ability is manual dexterity, the ability to make skillful, directed arm-hand movements when manipulating fairly large objects rapidly. Persons high in this ability are able to perform well in a variety of specific tasks, for example, playing a musical instrument or using tools.

In recent years marked advances have been made in identifying and sorting human abilities. Nevertheless, the classification of human abilities has not reached the advanced state of the classification of chemicals, plants, animals, and many other physical and biological phenomena which scientists have been studying for centuries. One important outcome of recent efforts to classify human abilities is a reexamination of the nature of intelligence. An earlier notion that intellectual ability is synonymous with the ability to learn all subject matter in the cognitive and psychomotor domain is giving way to a more enlightened viewpoint — that intellectual ability, as measured by IQ tests, is positively, but far from perfectly, correlated with *certain kinds* of subject matter achievements. (Chapter 3 discusses the nature and organization of human abilities, the role of maturation and learning related to abilities, and relevant topics.)

1.1. Are you more concerned with identifying school conditions associated with the improvement of school learning or with finding explanations of how learning occurs? Why?

1.2. What is an ability? Are your own abilities developed more fully in the cognitive or psychomotor domain? What home and school conditions are associated with your developments?

2. A System of School Learning

As will be discussed more fully in the next chapter, contemporary learning theories are useful in analyzing individual and group behavior in school settings. Nevertheless, learning theories in themselves do not present an adequate basis for understanding or managing the many variables associated with learning in school settings. Nor do present theories of instruction provide such a basis.

Learning in school may be examined fruitfully in terms of a *system*. Johnson, Kast, and Rosenzweig (1967) define a system as an array of components designed to accomplish a particular objective according to a plan. There must be an objective or purpose that the system is intended to accomplish. Also, there must be a design or an established arrangement of components. Finally, materials, equipment, space, personnel, and information must be allocated within the system according to a plan. In the social sphere, we readily identify a system of federal government, a system of higher education, and a system of monogamous family living, each of which meets the preceding definition.

We frequently refer to a school system as a social system that operates within specified geographical or political boundaries, such as township, city, county, or state. Within the larger school system are school buildings. Each building's program may be treated as an *educational system*. There are many ways to divide the educational system of a building into subsystems. One set of subsystems may be classified as an *instructional system*. An instructional system may encompass anything from a single lesson for a day to a comprehensive program in a subject field at one or more school levels.

In this book, a *system of school learning* is formulated that includes as its main components those specifically of interest to educational practitioners; in other words, the components are those that will enable them to organize both a large amount of relevant information and their own educational practices. The school learning system is considered in the context of an educational system and also of related instructional systems within a given building. The system should not be regarded as a refined theoretical model or as a substitute for a theory of learning; rather, it should be treated as a means of relating and integrating important information about the many variables associated with raising the level of human abilities.

In this connection, *any* kind of school may be described in terms of the components of a school learning system. The components are as important in describing a child-centered school of the kind proposed by Neill (1960) in *Summerhill* as in a behavior-management school as described by Skinner (1948) in *Walden Two*. In point of fact, Neill and Skinner are equally prescriptive about the objectives to be sought, the nature of the student activities, the responsibilities of the teachers, and other components. Both of these men, however, outline a less responsible role for teachers than the role outlined in this book. We would have teachers and their students more influential, and such people as Neill and Skinner less influential, in determining the education of the particular students.

This brings us to a consideration of the educational system and the instructional system, their characteristics, and their interrelationships. Just as educational psychology itself is far from being an abstract concept as it affects the lives of people, so the educational system and the instructional system are not abstract concepts or mere words; they are actual ways to help people—to help them learn. You will become more aware of this through considering the more specific components of an instructional system and an educational system.

An Instructional System. Figure 1.1 outlines an instructional system. The instructional system provides the framework to conduct a day's les-

Fig. 1.1. Components of an instructional system.

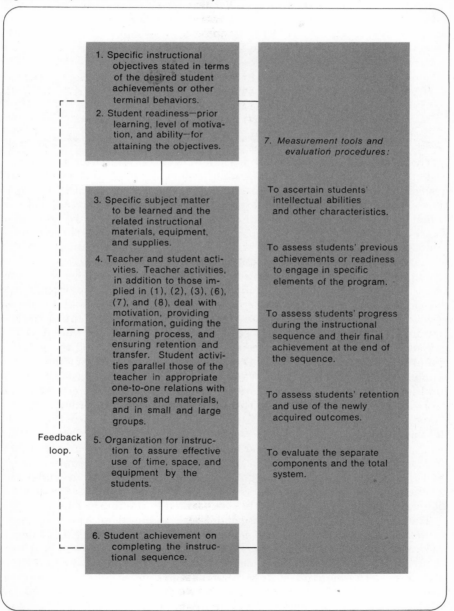

1. Specific instructional objectives stated in terms of the desired student achievements or other terminal behaviors.

2. Student readiness—prior learning, level of motivation, and ability—for attaining the objectives.

3. Specific subject matter to be learned and the related instructional materials, equipment, and supplies.

4. Teacher and student activities. Teacher activities, in addition to those implied in (1), (2), (3), (6), (7), and (8), deal with motivation, providing information, guiding the learning process, and ensuring retention and transfer. Student activities parallel those of the teacher in appropriate one-to-one relations with persons and materials, and in small and large groups.

5. Organization for instruction to assure effective use of time, space, and equipment by the students.

6. Student achievement on completing the instructional sequence.

Feedback loop.

7. *Measurement tools and evaluation procedures:*

To ascertain students' intellectual abilities and other characteristics.

To assess students' previous achievements or readiness to engage in specific elements of the program.

To assess students' progress during the instructional sequence and their final achievement at the end of the sequence.

To assess students' retention and use of the newly acquired outcomes.

To evaluate the separate components and the total system.

son, a unit of study, or a semester or year of work. Eight main components of the system have been identified in terms of the primary responsibilities of the teacher, or the team, or the students and instructional staff cooperatively. The amount of student participation in the various operations of the system varies according to the objectives to be achieved and the maturity of the students.

Such a system, or model, may be observed in use in many schools today. Inevitably, in actual practice, not all the components are carried out smoothly in all schools. The many references made throughout this book to school situations, however, refer to effective situations, rather than to ineffective ones.

A quick overview of the eight components shown in the figure will clarify their interrelationships. The components are numbered and italicized to aid the reader in relating to the figure.

The teachers, or teachers and students, determine the (1) *objectives* and state them in terms of the level of achievement, or other behaviors, desired of the students. (2) The students' *readiness* to attain the objectives is assessed. (3) The specific *subject matter*, the related *materials* in which it is incorporated, and the *equipment* and *supplies* are identified. There is, of course, a very close relationship among these three components—formulating objectives and assessing readiness cannot proceed without knowledge of the subject matter. (4) Teacher *instructional activities* and student *learning activities* are carried out to achieve the objectives. The more mature the students are, the more they participate in decision-making about the student activities. (5) An *organization for instruction* is needed so that time and the space and equipment of the entire building are used advantageously. (6) The students' final level of *achievement* and other behaviors are assessed on completing the instructional unit or sequence. Students participate in this assessment; for example, college students often take major responsibility for assessing their final level of achievement or other behaviors. (7) *Measurement tools and evaluation procedures* are used throughout instruction in order to assess the students' readiness, measure their progress while instruction is underway, and assess their achievements at the end of the program and later. (8) The information gained by measuring student progress, or lack of it, is used to provide *feedback*, which is necessary for students to learn well. The same information and other evaluative information enable the teacher to determine how effectively the components, such as the instructional materials and teacher activities, worked in the total system.

The instructional system described here is based on two important values: First, education is more a drawing out than a putting in. Children and youth have many abilities and can and should contribute to decisions about their own education. Their ideas need to be drawn out and their abilities need to be utilized as an integral part of the educative process. Second, education is a human and humanizing process, rather than a mechanizing process. Individual students participate in and are benefactors of instruction. The subject matter, the instructional materials, the equipment, and the management of the system exist to serve the students. In this connection, the use of computers, teaching machines, television, and other expensive hardware must be continuously examined to make sure that teachers and students are actually served by such use. This hardware assuredly can contribute to an excellent instructional system. It can also be used to prescribe the activities of the teachers and students too narrowly.

An Educational System Within a Building. Figure 1.2 shows the components of an educational system as it might function within an elementary or secondary school building or within a group of rooms of a very large building. The components involved in the system are: (1) the educational

Fig. 1.2. Components of an educational system within a building.

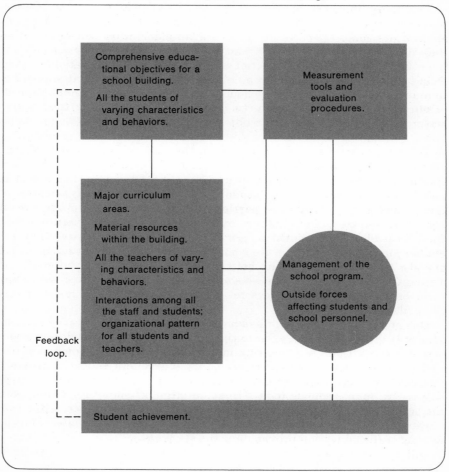

objectives of the school, (2) all the students, (3) the various curriculum areas, (4) all the material resources, (5) all the teachers and other instructional personnel, (6) the interactions of all the students and instructional personnel and the related organization for instruction, (7) the management of the entire school facility and educational programs, and (8) outside forces affecting the students and school personnel. (Students, teachers, and other educational personnel are included as components of a school system in the same sense that they are citizens in a democratic system of government.)

In this system, the building itself is the area of decision-making, rather than the central office of the school system as a whole or each individual teacher in the building. Thus the staff of the school building and the parents and others of the community can plan an educational program for and with the particular students within the context of the broad policies set forth for all the schools of the system. In turn, the staff of each school building and community personnel share in setting these broad policies that affect all the schools.

The main difference between the educational system and the instructional system is in the specificity of the components. For instance, an appropriate comprehensive objective for an elementary school might be that 75 percent of all students read at the level of literacy by age 9. On the other hand, specific instructional objectives would be stated for each child in terms of the specific reading skills to be mastered at successive time intervals. Similarly, the school would have a list of all its material resources and general procedures for their allocation, but the specific materials needed to reach each objective are components of the instructional system.

The two types of system also differ in the way they are managed. The administration of the educational system within a building must be more formal than the administration of an instructional system. For example, an elementary school of 700 students is organized into five teams, or units. Each team designs and carries out the instructional programs for about 140 children. The building principal, however, in cooperation with the unit leaders, must develop formal procedures and practices that will enable the five units to operate smoothly in a total building program. To achieve this, communications between the principal and the staff and among the staff must be open. This means that time during the school day must be arranged for teachers to plan, to study, and to make instructional decisions.

One of the components in the educational system is outside forces. This indicates the importance given to the home and neighborhood in the educative process. Close working relationships among school people, parents, and other community people are necessary if excellent educational opportunities are to be provided for the students. These desirable relationships do exist in many schools today. In some large school systems, however, the school people and the community people are embroiled in bitter controversies over the control of the schools, with unfortunate effects on the quality of the education provided for the students.

Outside forces also include broad cultural influences, such as those represented in the mass media; formal organizations of teachers and other educational personnel, such as teachers' unions and local education associations; and community organizations, such as private clubs and churches.

A system of school learning may now be conceptualized as the array of all the components of the educational system of the building and of the several instructional systems within it that are designed to bring about learning by each student according to a plan. Teachers and, to a lesser extent, students develop the plan for each instructional system. Teachers, the principal, other educational personnel, and some student representatives develop the plan for the building. Central office personnel, with representatives from the buildings, develop the plan for the entire school district.

It is obvious that providing an excellent learning environment for each student is a complex task, involving close working relationships among many people and requiring a large amount of specialized material and equipment. The complexities of the task will become even more apparent in the discussion of the following components of a school learning system: educational and instructional objectives; instructional materials and equipment; pupil characteristics; teacher characteristics; and interactions and organization for instruction. These topics are discussed in detail in Chapters 4 through 8. Types of learning outcomes and measurement and evaluation, also components of a school learning system, are treated in the last two parts of this book.

Educational and Instructional Objectives. Educational objectives are formulated and stated in general terms by national, state, and local groups. At the national level there seems to be some agreement that students should acquire knowledge, skills, and attitudes concerning quantitative relationships; communication; aesthetic development; the physical world; the social world; social relationships; ethical behaviors; individual social and emotional development; physical development and health and body care (Kearney, 1953).

The educational objectives for a school building are usually expressed in more detail in terms of subject-matter fields or curriculum areas. Schools, even schools within the same large city, vary greatly in their objectives. For example, in one high school the objective may call for 25 percent of the students to reach a certain level of achievement in mathematics; in another school, 75 percent may be the aim. Or in one elementary school none of the students may be expected to learn to speak a second language; in another school, all the students may be expected to acquire this ability. Thus the objectives for the school building determine the major thrusts of its educational program.

The instructional objectives are even more detailed descriptions of a school's objectives. They are expressed in terms of the level of achievement expected of students who participate in specific instructional programs, such as fourth-year mathematics or second-year shorthand. Such an objective may state that the student "writes the correct spelling of 50 words, drawn randomly from a 500-word list, when dictated at a rate of one word per 20 seconds." Note that this objective implies the subject

matter to be learned (the correct spelling of 500 specified words), indicates
a means for assessing the student's progress and final achievement (dictated timed tests), and indirectly implies conditions of learning (distributed practice on the 500 words).

A teacher should understand both educational and instructional objectives and the differences between them. He should be able to evaluate
educational objectives in terms of the characteristics of particular students, and he should be able to write instructional objectives related to
his major field of interest. Chapter 4 was written with these aims in mind.

Instructional Materials and Related Technology. Instructional objectives are not formulated in a vacuum; on the contrary, they must be related to the content and sequence of instruction or to the activities of
teachers and students. The best statements of instructional objectives
are those written by teams of subject-matter specialists, behavioral scientists, and practitioners. The best instructional objectives appropriate for
each particular student, however, are often selected or formulated by
each teacher or team and the individual students. Once the objectives are
determined, materials and, in some cases, related equipment must be
developed or identified which will help students to achieve the objectives,
that is, to attain the desired level of achievement. In developing such
materials, it should be remembered that they have a reciprocal effect on
the objectives; in other words, much of what students learn — and its sequence — is determined by the nature of the materials used to present
specific portions of the subject matter. Gagné (1965b) listed seven classes of
media for presenting content to students: objects and demonstrations,
oral communication, printed media, still pictures, motion pictures, sound
motion pictures, and teaching machines. Others divide the primary instructional media into three groups: printed, audio, and audiovisual instructional materials and equipment.

Each elementary school and high school constructed in recent years
usually includes an instructional resource center; a multimedia presentation room may be part of the center. Such a center contains not only
books and other printed materials, but also audio and audiovisual materials and equipment, computer terminals, individual study carrels, and
spaces for small- and large-group activities. Better materials and equipment, whether in central resource centers, libraries, science laboratories,
foreign language laboratories, or elsewhere, of course facilitate student
learning. Therefore, modern teachers keep informed of recent trends in
instructional materials and equipment. They also are ready to function as
members of instructional teams, so that audiovisual specialists and
others may make a maximum contribution to the school learning system.
Chapter 5 deals with the most promising recent advances in instructional
materials and equipment.

Learner Characteristics and Behaviors. The abilities and characteristics of the students must be considered, both when formulating objectives
and when developing and carrying out the instructional program. Almost
nothing can keep intelligent, healthy children from learning something.
Put 10 bright 6-year-olds in a room with appropriate reading and writing
materials, and they will learn to read and write without much assistance

from anyone. Put them in a swimming pool and each will probably learn to swim. With an excellent teacher, however, such children learn more efficiently. On the other hand, put 10 mentally retarded students of high school age in an algebra class, and even with the very best teacher and conditions, probably none will acquire a concept of algebraic equations. Put them in a shop class, however, and they might learn wholesome attitudes toward self, others, and work, and many might acquire a salable vocational skill.

In some schools today the objectives and related instructional programs are geared directly to the characteristics of the students. The instruction is set up to provide for individual characteristics by using all these procedures in appropriate ways and at appropriate times: one-to-one interaction between a student and a teacher or another student, small-group activities, class-size activities, and large-group activities, in addition to independent study, that is, one-to-one interaction with materials and equipment. It is obvious that the achievement of social objectives requires interacting with other human beings, not merely with materials or machines.

If the schools are to meet their challenges and responsibilities, it is important to recognize that students' attitudes toward themselves, school, and authority are changing as society changes. The problems of American society mentioned earlier permeate the lives of the young. According to two authorities, present-day teachers may expect more student behavior of this kind:

> Recently a sixth-grade class in a Midwest elementary school arose on a pre-arranged signal and walked out of the classroom and refused to return until the beginning of the next class. They were protesting the retention of a particular member of the faculty whose removal they had called for on two previous occasions—first by petition to the principal and second by a letter to the U.S. Supreme Court—asking for a definition of the rights of elementary students in a matter of this nature. For their action they received a double assignment of homework. When questioned as to the leadership behind the movement an eleven-year-old student replied, "We have no leaders, we are a cooperative movement." (Robertson & Engle, 1969, p. 7)

Gephart (1969) has pointed out that it is the academically apt, the logical thinkers, the articulate individuals—those who used to be called the "good" students—who make up the largest proportion of the groups who are demanding change in education and, in general, questioning the values of society. They are the ones who are organizing protest demonstrations and writing underground newspapers. Gephart quoted a sophomore high school student to illustrate his point:

> A friend of mine once suggested that the way we could best get the type of school we wanted would be to draw up detailed plans, petition the city for an experimental school, and use that school as a power base to force the city to make more changes. I cannot disagree with this idea more strongly. An administrative decision which would give us a freer atmosphere is no better than an administrative decision repressing a student newspaper. *We cannot be ordered into freedom.* What freedom we achieve must come from our own struggle. In order to change the ways in which people relate to each other, we must build a

community; a community of resistance. If we really wish to change people and not institutions, we will have to struggle, for conflict radicalizes us, and through it we may establish our own identities as human beings, and not numbers. The most radical demand we can make is the demand to be taken seriously. (Gephart, 1969, p. 2)

Chapter 6 treats characteristics of pupils in detail and also outlines ways to provide for differences among pupils.

Teacher Characteristics and Behaviors. How important is the teacher? In spite of the fact that there are some instructional objectives that can be attained by some students interacting only with materials and machines, in most situations the teacher greatly influences both the personal lives of the learners and what they learn. It follows that excellent teaching results in higher achievement, no matter how excellent the materials used.

Consider the contrasting characteristics of two music teachers. One knows music well, sings well, has great interest in teaching children to sing, is in excellent health, accepts himself and the pupils as worthwhile persons, and views his work as providing a challenging dual opportunity—to help learners develop their musical abilities and, in turn, to find self-fulfillment in successful teaching. The second teacher knows little music, sings poorly, and, in general, has negative attitudes toward teaching. Unless the pupils are unusually well behaved and have a burning desire to sing, they will not profit from instruction by the second teacher. Characteristics of the teacher, treated in more detail in Chapter 7, are very important.

Interactions and Teacher Leadership. Information and behavior patterns are acquired through interacting with people, as well as with instructional materials. (High-level intellectual skills, such as analyzing and evaluating information, typically are acquired in small discussion groups and seminars.) People within a school building interact with one another in three main types of relationships: students with other students, students with teachers, and teachers with administrators. The pupils, the teachers, and the administrators, however, are also members of peer groups that operate outside the school building, and these outside relationships may affect what happens within the building.

The school also operates in a social context—the homes and neighborhoods from which the pupils come. Home and neighborhood influences, particularly as represented by parents, are receiving increasing attention. The effect of difficult home and neighborhood conditions on the interaction between students and teachers can be profound. For example, a high school teacher reported:

These students have so many problems—home problems, personal problems, school problems. In many instances, there is no authority that they respect. And here at the school, this carries out exactly what's been happening in their home. In the past two years, I've had two students who tried to commit suicide. One was an honor student who had won a scholarship, but she found herself pregnant, and no one was aware of it for five months. And then, when she couldn't conceal it any longer, she tried suicide. I had another student, just a few months ago; I was having some problems with her, and I asked her mother to come into the school. I didn't know that her mother had just come out of a mental institution. This child was trying to conceal it, so while the mother came to the school, the child took pills at home in an attempt to commit suicide. I feel almost responsible here and have been involved with the whole situation ever since. You can't help but become involved, and you can't help but stay involved. (Havighurst, 1966, p. 48)

The functioning of an educational system rests on the assumption that educational personnel will cooperate in providing excellent instruction. Organization is intended to facilitate this cooperation. The traditional school building, divided into many rooms of the same size, each seating about 35 students, does not meet the educational needs of our modern society. The idea of each teacher in a building instructing exactly the same number of students in groups of about 30 is also obsolete. In both elementary schools and high schools new organizations for instruction, such as teaching teams, utilize space and various types of instructional media and equipment more effectively to promote student learning and personality development. Chapter 8 presents concepts from social psychology dealing with interactions and organizations that are particularly applicable to school learning.

1.3. What are the characteristics of a system? In what ways are an electric clock, a thermostat, a human being, and an instructional system alike in terms of the characteristics of a system? In what ways do they differ?

1.4. What is the relationship between objectives and the other components of a school learning system?

1.5. Based on your personal experiences, do the characteristics of the students or those of the teachers seem more closely correlated with how well students learn and how they conduct themselves in the classroom?

1.6. How are home and neighborhood conditions related to conditions of learning and instruction within the neighborhood school? In what kind of a school and neighborhood would you prefer to teach and live?

3. Achieving Learning Outcomes

It has been made clear that objectives, materials, student characteristics, teacher characteristics, and interactions are important components of a school learning system. Content or subject matter is also a primary component. In this book content is described in terms of a few main categories, called "outcomes of learning," rather than being treated in detail in terms of each subject field. Learning these outcomes is the primary educational objective of most schools.

What does a teacher do to help students to acquire a learning outcome—for instance, a concept (such as *deciduous*)? In capsule form, this is the sequence: The attention of the student is gained and subsequently maintained; instructional materials, teacher activities, and student activities are arranged in such a way that the students acquire information, think productively about the information, and arrive at the concept; finally, provisions for use of the newly acquired concept are made. Part

III, the largest single section of the book, is concerned with principles related to the learning of various outcomes, according to the sequence just outlined. Motivation is considered first, various learning outcomes are treated next, and, last, retention and transfer are discussed.

Motivation. Motivation is a general term referring to goal-seeking or need-satisfying behavior. The level, or strength, of motivation of an individual in connection with a task (any task, from conducting an experiment to playing the oboe) is judged by his attending and persisting behaviors. One who attends closely to instruction and persists until the task is completed is highly motivated. One who does not initially attend or who then does not persist is, obviously, less highly motivated. The level of motivation, then, is inferred from the individual's behavior, but this does not mean that the level cannot be influenced. In other words, another person, for example, a teacher, can arrange environmental conditions to secure student attention initially and to maintain persistent effort. Motivation must always be taken into account as one attempts to make an instructional system work smoothly. The following are some of the practical questions that must be considered every day: How may the attention of pupils be gained and then focused on learning tasks? How do goal-setting and feelings of success affect the level of motivation? Which prosocial behaviors should students learn, and how does the teacher get the student to want to learn them? When and how may rewards be used effectively? Principles concerning these and other aspects of motivation are discussed in Chapter 9.

Outcomes of Learning. A curriculum area, such as social studies or science, is a main component of the educational system of a building. The specific subject matter of a daily lesson, or a longer sequence, is a component of an instructional system. Whether considered in relation to a broad curriculum area extending from elementary through high school or in relation to the subject matter of a lesson, most of what students learn at all age levels can be classified into a relatively few categories of learning outcomes. Learning outcomes are relatively permanent *mediational units*, or mediators, inferred from behaviors, including written performances on tests and oral statements. Mediational units are lasting traces or impressions, primarily in the central nervous system, that act as intermediaries between the environment and behavior (as defined by Kagan & Havemann, 1968). These units consist of what is learned initially and then continually manipulated in thought as the individual remembers something or encounters a new situation and uses his earlier learnings.

The main learning outcomes in curriculum areas such as mathematics, science, social studies, English, and a foreign language are factual information, concepts and principles, and verbal, problem-solving, and creative abilities. Acquiring these outcomes involves coming to know, that is, cognizing, verbal or mathematical symbols and ideas. Mental processes in addition to cognizing are involved, but relatively little motor activity is. Thus, these outcomes are considered to be in the cognitive domain. Outcomes in the cognitive domain are dealt with in Chapters 10, 11, and 12.

The main learning outcomes in curriculum areas such as art, music, physical education, typing, and shorthand are psychomotor abilities and skills. Becoming proficient in any psychomotor skill requires practice involving motor activity. It also requires rapid feedback and correction of movements. This is possible only to the extent that there is accurate perception through the various senses. Thus, these outcomes are considered to be in the psychomotor domain. Outcomes in the psychomotor domain are the subject of Chapter 13.

Pupils may acquire attitudes, values, and motives both through their study of any subject matter and through their interactions with agemates and adults. Obviously, these outcomes of learning, far more than concepts and skills, involve feelings, such as liking and disliking, acceptance and rejection. But these outcomes, like all learning outcomes, are mediators. Attitudes, for example, are inferred from observing the approach and avoidance behaviors of individuals in connection with things, situations, and ideas. Because feelings are involved, these outcomes are considered to be in the affective domain. Outcomes in the affective domain are dealt with in Chapters 14 and 15.

Retention and Transfer. An outcome has been acquired when it is first incorporated into the learner's behavior pattern. For example, when a child first correctly spells a word or solves a problem, we say that he has acquired that particular outcome. When the child correctly repeats the performance later, we say that he has remembered or retained what he learned initially. Transfer of learning takes place when whatever is learned in one situation is used in a new or different situation.

To promote retention and transfer, the answers to questions such as these must be considered: What causes forgetting? What conditions facilitate retention? Which learning outcomes have the greatest possibility for transfer? What conditions facilitate transfer from the original learning situation? These and related topics are treated in Chapter 16, completing the discussion of efficiency in attaining learning outcomes.

4. Measurement, Evaluation, and Research Design

Measurement is the process of ascertaining the extent, dimensions, or quantity of something. The length of time to complete a task, the distance a ball is thrown, the height of an individual, and many other variables are subject to ordinary physical measurement. Measurement in education involves observing and then assessing the behaviors of an individual. We might wish to ascertain, for example, how much a child has learned and the level of his motivation. The frequency of behaviors, such as correct spelling of words and use of complete sentences, may be counted and summed. Sometimes performances cannot be counted and summed; if so, they often are ranked, from lowest to highest or from least to most effective or in some other way. The rankings may be assigned numerical quantities. Whether in research in a laboratory or in practice in a school learning system, accurate measurement of student characteristics and of what is learned is essential.

Evaluation is making judgments about the desirability or appropriateness of something in terms of a standard or criterion. For instance, we would evaluate a student's achievement in history as satisfactory if he had been expected to make a perfect score on a test and then did. We might evaluate a student's conduct as satisfactory even though he occasionally whispered and disrupted the work of others if we had decided that an appropriate standard for him must allow some minor lapses. As noted above, accurate measurement, or assessment, of each student's achievement and conduct is essential before evaluating can be done. Now it is apparent that the setting of standards is also essential for evaluation.

In the instructional system outlined in Fig. 1.1, measurement tools and evaluation procedures play a prominent role. Measurement is required at four points: early in the instructional sequence, to assess the student's current level of achievement and more general abilities related to the specific objective; throughout the instructional sequence, to ascertain the student's progress; at the end of the instructional sequence, to estimate the final level of achievement; some time later, to assess retention and possibly transfer.

Accurate information is needed especially to guide the learning process intelligently while instruction is in progress. A driver keeps his car in the proper lane of a highway only as he continuously senses where the car is going and corrects its path by proper steering. It would not help the driver much to find out, after his car had crashed, that a 20 percent error in his vision, in his steering, or in a mechanical aspect of the car had caused the crash. Similarly, if students are to learn, rather than fail, there must be continuous information feedback in school learning situations, so that corrections can be made rapidly and continually.

If instructional objectives have been written to include the desired level of achievement, then the standard stated or implied in the objectives is used in evaluating a student's progress and final achievement. In a reciprocal process, information about a student's achievements may also be used in evaluating various components of the system, including the instructional material. For example, a standard states that a student who studies certain material for a certain period of time under desirable conditions should score 85 percent correct on an achievement test. If one or a few students score only 65 percent, we make certain judgments about these students. But if many or most of the students score only 65 percent, we properly infer that the material is not doing what it should. Chapters 17 and 18 deal with measurement and evaluation.

To keep up with new knowledge through the study of research literature, comprehension of elementary statistical concepts is required. Statistics is the science that deals with the classification, analysis, and interpretation of numerical data. Also, statistical knowledge is applied in the design of research.

As noted later in this chapter, the methods of educational psychology include naturalistic observation, correlational studies, and controlled experiments. Before starting a study, a person must decide what data he will need and how he will analyze them in order to arrive at relevant findings and subsequent inferences. In other words, he must design the study before beginning data collection. Research design may involve any of the three standard methods just mentioned; these methods are used in planning many of the studies in educational psychology. Other methods are also often used. Chapter 19 is intended to aid the student in acquiring elementary concepts of statistics and research design.

1.7. What is the relationship between motivation and learning? Analyze your own recent college work or other experiences. Is how well you have achieved or performed more closely associated with motivation or with knowledge and ability?

1.8. Roughly estimate the proportion of your own high school education that was directed toward acquiring outcomes in each domain — cognitive, psychomotor, and affective. Was this a desirable balance? Why or why not?

1.9. A carpenter and a science teacher, both now aged 30, each took two years of Latin and one year of chemistry in high school. The carpenter now recalls scarcely any Latin and about half of the chemistry concepts and principles. The science teacher recalls about 15 percent of the Latin and about 99 percent of the chemistry. What conditions during high school instruction and after high school education might lead to these retention patterns? Would you recommend offering a high school course if you knew that most of the students would recall very little of it after 10 years? Why or why not?

1.10. Imagine that a school has no guidelines concerning the assessment of students' characteristics and performances. List in order of priority the kinds of information about the students you would try to get and how you would use the information.

OTHER CONCERNS OF EDUCATIONAL PSYCHOLOGY

The four primary emphases of educational psychology just discussed — those that comprise the four parts of this book — are treated in greater depth in many departments of educational psychology that offer graduate programs. Two other less extensive areas of graduate study are, first, human development and exceptional children and, second, school psychology and counseling. In this book the development of abilities and individual differences are discussed at appropriate places in most of the chapters, rather than being presented in separate chapters. The other topics mentioned are given only minor attention. Graduate programs in many major American universities, however, are organized around each of these topics.

Human Development and Exceptional Children

The study of human development for years emphasized the normative development of the individual from early childhood into adulthood. A typical sequence of four graduate courses in human development was infancy and early childhood, childhood, adolescence, maturity. Recently, developmental psychologists have been less concerned with describing developmental sequences. They are now studying cognitive processes, early childhood stimulation, attention, the shaping of behavior, and other phenomena related to learning. These are topics traditionally studied by psychologists and others whose main interest is learning. Thus, development and learning emphases appear to be merging along the lines outlined in this book, which treats learning and development as integrally related.

Closely related to human development is the area of exceptional children. Until very recently, most of the emphasis was given to children below normal rather than to those above. The main areas of investigation have concerned mental retardation, handicaps involving the various senses, orthopedic handicaps, emotional disturbances, and antisocial behavior and delinquency. Giftedness and creativity, however, have been making some headway as topics of investigation. Also, research concerning new methods related to teaching the disadvantaged is accelerating rapidly.

School Psychology and Counseling

Both school psychology and counseling in the public schools have shown remarkable growth and vitality in recent decades. School psychologists work mainly in the elementary schools; guidance and counseling personnel work in the high schools. The preparation of both groups of professional personnel is concentrated at the graduate level.

School psychologists do a considerable amount of diagnostic and therapeutic work with individual children and their parents. They work with teachers in outlining programs of education appropriate for the children being diagnosed or treated; they also participate in broader aspects of curriculum development and improvement of instruction. It is not uncommon in large cities for the chief school psychologist, who often holds a doctoral degree, to head the entire program of school testing and pupil guidance services, including those in the high schools.

Working usually in senior high schools, counselors do less individual testing and give more occupational guidance than do school psychologists in the elementary schools. Also, most high school counselors do less intensive diagnosis and psychotherapy than psychologists, primarily because they have not been prepared for this type of work. In many high schools, each student has an interview with a counselor twice during the school year. The situation is different in the case of elementary school children; many are not seen at all by a school psychologist, but some who have certain types of relatively serious difficulties are seen each week over an extended period of time.

In addition to varying amounts of graduate work in learning, development, exceptional children, measurement and evaluation, and statistics, both school psychologists and counselors gain clinical experience as interns in the schools.

RESEARCH AND DEVELOPMENT IN EDUCATIONAL PSYCHOLOGY

Research in educational psychology involves systematic inquiry into learning, student behavior, and the various components of a school learning system. Some research is directed toward the discovery of facts and principles and toward the formulation of theories, whereas other research is undertaken specifically to improve educational practices. Improvement of educational practice usually requires the development of new materials, tests, methods, equipment, organization, and other elements of a school learning system. Determining the cost, usability, and quality of a newly developed product is usually considered to be part of development. The development process is just as rigorous and essential as research designed to generate new knowledge. The point of view in this book is that most educational practitioners should do more development work in order to overcome readily observable deficiencies in educational practice. Therefore, development is discussed in this section, and suggestions to the student for producing or developing specific things are made throughout the book and in the accompanying *Student Guide*.

Research

To understand behavior, one must observe it carefully. To fail to do so, or to form an opinion too quickly on the basis of what may seem like common sense, can lead to beliefs that are contrary to the real facts. The methods of observing human behavior range from noting the behavior of an individual or individuals in a naturalistic setting, without any controls brought into the setting, to precise measurement in settings, usually laboratories, where all elements of the situation are controlled, so that one variable can be manipulated and its effects on other behavior noted.

Naturalistic Observation. Much knowledge is gained through careful observation of individuals, groups, and situations. Some excellent descriptions of changes in behavior have been done by psychologists who have observed, recorded, and interpreted the behavior of the same individuals at various ages, often from infancy into adulthood (two of these long-term case histories are summarized in Chapter 15). Following is part of a case history resulting from careful and sympathetic listening, as well as observation. As the girl dropout tells her story, some of the difficulties a student from a low socioeconomic class may encounter in school are vividly revealed.

> Bernice is living with her mother-in-law. I scaled a fifteen-foot muddy embankment up to this little run-down house. Apparently there is a more accessible route from the rear. Bernice required very little explanation. I asked her how long she had been out of school.
>
> "I quit two weeks before the end of school a year ago. I was only fifteen at the time but I talked to Mr. McCoy [principal]. He said that they wouldn't come get me because I would be sixteen before fall. I just didn't take the exams. I knew I wouldn't pass anyway because I didn't do any work except in typing. I

really loved typing. It seems I didn't like all of my teachers. I got kicked out of English six times. Me and the teacher couldn't get along. I don't think half the kids liked her. She talked about the same thing for about a week and you didn't learn anything. Then she would spend the whole period with one kid. I took a dislike to her the first two days. I guess I could have gotten along with her but after that I didn't try. And then I just didn't understand general math I suppose because I don't understand arithmetic. I love it but I don't get it. I just love fractions, but those reading problems, I could never get those all the way through school. I was really going to go all the way through Home Ec because I liked it, but then my schedule was changed so I could be in a different gym class. They said they wanted to break up a gang of us girls because we were beating all the other teams and smarting off a lot. Then I got changed to a gym class with a lot of these high class girls, as we call them. They think they are better than everyone else. They got a lot of money. They don't like us and we don't like them. When my class was changed, I didn't even dress for gym. So I failed that too."

"Bernice, what seems to be the rub with those high class kids?"

"Well, they seem to look down on us kids in this neighborhood. You know, they think we are scabs. You know, those kids always hung out on the east side of the building and us kids were always on the west side. Then in class, the rich kids always had their lessons. They never came without their lessons. Then if us kids didn't have ours, and we usually didn't, they would look at us. There were only two girls, Sally Clancy and Georgia Lane, that I could get along with out of that bunch. I guess it's a good thing I quit school because whenever there was any trouble, I was in the middle of it, street fights or anything else. It seems like it has been that way all my life. My temper gets me into trouble. I slap and ask questions later. That's the way my Mother and Dad were and I guess that's the way I am." (Havighurst, Bowman, Liddle, Matthews, & Pierce, 1962, pp. 13-14)

Behaviors observed to be typical of all children of the same age from various backgrounds become the age *norm* behaviors. The achievements of students in reading and other subjects at various age or grade levels have also been measured and interpreted; the typical achievement becomes the norm for the grade. The variations among individuals in reading and other behaviors are also observed. Such variations supply some of our best information concerning individual differences. Reports based on observations, including tests in natural school settings, are useful descriptions of behavior but usually do not explain why the behavior occurs or what behaviors are related.

Correlational Studies. Many events and conditions may be observed simultaneously in school settings, for example, the achievement level of the same students in several subject fields and their general intellectual ability. These observations take the form of scores on tests and may then be correlated. The method of correlation, discussed more fully in Chapter 19, is an excellent way to discover relationships among variables when some or all of them cannot be either controlled or manipulated. Correlating the scores tells us whether the same student tends to be at about the same level — high, middle, or low — on the various measures, or variables, that are correlated.

The coefficient of correlation (r) is the unit of measurement in correlational studies (in most studies the words "coefficient of" are omitted). To help interpret the correlational studies reported throughout the book, seven attributes of correlation coefficients are discussed here. A more complete account of correlational procedures is given in Chapter 19.

1. A correlation of +1.00 indicates a perfect positive relationship between two variables. If during each year of school attendance the number of words that students recognized at sight increased by a constant number, so that one could specify precisely the number of recognized words merely by knowing a student's year of school attendance, then years of schooling and word recognition would correlate perfectly, +1.00. This example, of course, is only hypothetical, but an example of an actual perfect correlation is the areas and the heights of a set of triangles with bases the same length. For instance, take three triangles with 10-unit bases and heights of 5, 10, and 18; their areas are 25, 50, and 90 square units. (The plus sign is usually not used with a positive correlation.) So long as the base remains constant, the r between various heights and areas will be 1.00.

2. A correlation of −1.00 indicates a perfect negative relationship between two variables. If the resale value of textbooks decreased by a constant amount with each year of use, then the correlation between years of use and resale value would be −1.00.

3. A correlation of .00 indicates no relationship. No correlation is expected between color of hair and level of reading achievement or between the number of permanent teeth of 8-year-olds and their level of achievement in any subject field.

4. A correlation between .00 and +1.00 or between .00 and −1.00 indicates an imperfect relationship. The higher the absolute value, that is, the closer the correlation is to +1.00 or −1.00, the greater the degree of relationship and the more accurately one can make a prediction from one variable to another. Thus, one can more accurately predict that students who do well in reading will also do well in science if the correlation between reading and science achievement is .60 rather than .40. Similarly, one can predict more reliably the resale value of his textbooks three years later if the correlation is −.80 rather than −.50.

5. A correlation is not a percentage; therefore, a correlation of .90 cannot be interpreted as being twice as high as .45 or three times as high as .30. Squaring an obtained correlation, however, does indicate in percentage terms the extent to which two or more sets of values have something in common. Thus, $.50^2 = .25$, indicating that 25 percent of what is measured can be considered a common factor; $.75^2 = .5625$, indicating a common factor of 56 percent; and $1.00^2 = 1.00$, which of course indicates 100 percent in common. The three values first mentioned can be assessed with more confidence by considering them as $.90^2 = 81$ percent in common, $.45^2 =$ only 20 percent in common, and $.30^2 =$ the still smaller amount, only 9 percent in common. In other words, there is much more spread between correlations than their numerical values seem to indicate, and this spread

is better shown by the values of their squares than by the values of the correlation coefficients themselves.

6. The extent to which a correlation coefficient is a relationship of importance depends not only on the size of the correlation coefficient but also on the number of cases on which it is based and the importance of the variables that are correlated. A correlation of .60 between reading achievement and social studies achievement is considered more accurate if it is based on 100 cases for each of three consecutive years than if it is based on 30 cases for one year. In any case, a correlation of .60 between reading achievement and social studies achievement might not be considered by school people to be particularly significant. However, if a correlation of .60 were obtained between the amount of schooling completed and lifetime earnings, it would be judged to be very significant. At the same time, a correlation may be so small that it is considered as not significant, regardless of what is being correlated.

7. Although two sets of scores may correlate positively, we cannot infer that one *causes* the other. For example, annual measurements of the length of shoes children wear during ages 6 to 12 correlate positively with the number of words they spell correctly during the same years; so also do annual counts of the number of permanent teeth and the measurements of their arithmetic achievement. Obviously, longer shoes do not cause better spelling, nor do more permanent teeth cause higher arithmetic performance.

Controlled Experimentation. Securing reliable information about cause-and-effect relationships (functional relationships) requires a special kind of observation in which one event can be determined as resulting in another. Psychologists have developed certain methods of observation and of controlling situational factors that are called *controlled experimentation*. In such experimentation in the laboratory, certain conditions are varied or manipulated, whereas everything else about the experiment is controlled, in order to determine the effect of one variable (the independent variable) on performance (the dependent variable). A variable is something that can have many different values, for example, amount of practice in minutes and speed of typing in words per minute. Thus, an experiment is set up to determine the effects on typing speed of five trials of 4 minutes each with 1-minute rest intervals (distributed practice) in comparison with one trial of 24 minutes (massed practice). If a significant difference in speed is observed that favors the distributed practice, one concludes that the performance was caused by or functionally related to the distribution of practice. (Most psychologists prefer to say "functionally related to" or "a function of" rather than "caused by.")

Although 20 different psychologists with 20 different students may get this result in the laboratory, we cannot be sure that 20 teachers, each with 30 students, will get the same results. So we also do controlled experimentation in classrooms. We select 50 teachers offering typing instruction to ninth-graders. We randomly divide them into two groups, one of which will use distributed practice and the other massed practice. We must make sure that the teachers use the same materials, methods, and so forth with the only difference between the two groups being distributed practice for one and massed practice for the other. At appropriate times during a year we determine the students' typing performance and observe the differences between the groups, if any. In spite of the obvious difficulties involved in conducting controlled experimentation in schools, it must be done. Generalizations drawn from the laboratory should not be applied directly to school situations without validation in school settings.

Development of Products

We have known for years that different people acquire the same ability, for example, reading independently, at different rates and that if individuals set their own goals they tend to persist until the goal is reached. Combine these two psychological principles. The implications for educational practice are clear: Set up a reading program in which each child sets his own goals and proceeds at a rate suitable for him. If this simple procedure were followed, it is possible that educational disadvantagement would disappear within a decade. Except in isolated instances, however, such reading programs do not exist today because relevant variables in school settings have not been taken into proper account, not enough specific instructional materials, methods, spaces, and time relationships have been developed, and instructional personnel have not been educated in the use of the materials that are available.

The relationship between the development of products and educational improvement has been described as follows (Gideonse, 1968): The object of development is to produce materials, techniques, processes, hardware, and organizational formats that accomplish specified objectives construed to be part of the broader goals of education. In other words, development builds on research; when a development activity is begun, the objectives are already known or established. These objectives for a development project are cast in the form of *performance specifications*—that is, what the students should become able to do—and all activities are geared to producing the necessary products and processes to meet these specifications. Once a development project has been undertaken to meet a clearly specified need or deficiency and the performance specifications have been established, the developer searches for research findings that may offer clues to carrying out the project. Any findings that seem relevant to the performance specifications are then incorporated in the project.

Schutz (1968) carried the developmental process further in terms of *educational specifications*, which he defined as a set of sequenced statements of desired instructional outcomes accompanied by other specifications. Once the educational specifications are established, the first step is to produce and try out in the laboratory methods and materials related to various parts of these specifications. When this first approximation has been judged to be successful, the next step is to prepare products—materials and procedures—for actual use in the classroom and try them out there. The attempt at this point is to produce a product that is attractive to pupils, manageable by teachers, takes as little time as possible to use, and can be made available at as low a cost as possible. Each of the preceding steps involves a repeated cycle: develop, then test, then refine to eliminate deficiencies in the product and increase its effectiveness. Such continuous evaluation of the product in terms of the stated objectives while in the formative or development stage is essential.

Klausmeier (1968) outlined the need for continuing large-scale development in education that takes into account all the components previously outlined in the system of school learning. Research and development, not merely research, have made it possible to bridge wide rivers, to erect 110-story skyscrapers, to transmit color pictures and sound via satellites, and to land men on the moon. Equally revolutionary achievements would be possible in many other areas of our life if efforts of a similar magnitude were made. But education remains the major underdeveloped institution in American society for lack of constructive development efforts by most of the thousands of people in higher education and most of the million or more schoolteachers and administrators. Poor instructional materials and inferior instructional procedures, management techniques, tests, and organizational patterns remain in use because, until recently, a system for development had not been formulated and implemented.

The Elementary and Secondary Education Act of 1965 did allocate a modest amount of federal money for educational development. Within less than five years it was demonstrated that educational improvement did result from this effort. We should realize, however, that to boost children's educational opportunities to a really significant extent (particularly in the large cities and rural areas), we need to spend at least as much money as was spent to land men on the moon.

1.11. What kinds of questions about learning and instruction can be answered through observation, correlation studies, and controlled experiments? Which type of study are you best prepared to undertake?

1.12. Why has knowledge about the nature and extent of individual differences among students and related educational provisions not been put into practice on a widespread scale during the last 50 years?

1.13. What is the role of research and development in improving educational practice?

1.14. What is the role of the educational practitioner in research and development? Have you developed, or tried to develop, any material or procedure that might improve learning opportunities for a student?

1.15. Basing your decision on your own assessment of deficiencies in various components of our schools of today, what would you judge should be given the highest priority for development?

SUMMARY

Educational psychology is concerned with identifying and describing principles of learning and related conditions and procedures for improving educational practices. Educational psychology involves the study of student behaviors in school settings. The content of educational psychology focuses on the nature of learning as it occurs during shorter time intervals and on the development of human abilities during longer time periods. An instructional system takes into account all the variables that affect learning and performance in school settings. Three major groupings are: (1) objectives, instructional materials, students and their characteristics, teacher activities, and organization for instruction; (2) outcomes of learning and related principles; (3) measurement of the outcomes of learning. Research in educational psychology is conducted directly in schools and in laboratories with school-age children. The laboratory studies of animals and adult human behavior outside school settings have some possible applications to education but are the primary concern of other psychologists and scientists.

Educational practitioners put their knowledge and skills to work in school settings. Because of the many variables that change from one school situation to another, teachers and other educational practitioners must continuously gather information and make important decisions based on this information in order to develop an excellent instructional program for each student. Excellent instructional programs are developed in the school by the teachers and students. They are not imported from outside sources. Concepts, principles, and skills learned in the study of educational psychology aid teachers in making decisions when dealing with the various components of an instructional system.

Until recently, research in education has been unorganized and of uneven quality. Most of it was done by graduate students to meet part of the requirements for a graduate degree. However, starting in 1964, a number of research and development centers and laboratories were established and funded, primarily with support by the federal government, to identify significant educational problems, to do research and development in the problems area, and to improve the related educational practices. Educators, psychologists, and others are slowly beginning to realize that the time has come when, rather than continuing to evolve more theories or identify more problems through research, solutions to chronic educational problems must be achieved. Research and development in education now hold much promise for contributing directly to the improvement of educational practice. Early results appear throughout this book. More important, teachers are finding means to contribute more directly to educational development and are taking more initiative for improving education.

SUGGESTIONS FOR FURTHER READING

BEHRENDT, D. Away with tradition. *American education*, 1970, 6, pp. 18-22.

In words and pictures an education writer for the *Milwaukee Journal* describes the status and promise of a system of individually guided education, based on observations made in multiunit elementary schools.

CARROLL, J. B. The future of educational psychology. In Ripple, R. E., ed., *Readings in learning and human abilities*. New York: Harper & Row, 2nd ed., 1971.

Carroll projects an Orwellian future for educational psychology. We may disagree about the future but the role of technology in education merits our serious consideration now.

CRONBACH, L. J., & SUPPES, P. *Research for tomorrow's schools: Disciplined inquiry for education*. New York: Macmillan, 1969.

Chapter 4, pages 115-169, describes conclusion-oriented inquiry, the purpose of which is to generate knowledge that may or may not influence educational practices. Chapter 5, pages 170-200, describes decision-oriented inquiry which is undertaken to improve educational practices directly.

EDITORIAL. The school behind masters of the moon. *Phi delta kappan,* 1969, 51, pp. 2-7.

The significant contributions of American public schools to space exploration are described.

GRINDER, R. E. The growth of educational psychology as reflected in the history of Division 15. In Ripple, R. E., ed., *Readings in learning and human abilities*. New York: Harper & Row, 2nd ed., 1971.

Study of the growth and development of educational psychology as a field of inquiry and as a division of the American Psychological Association, described in this article, provides a perspective for interpreting modern educational psychology.

HILGARD, E. R. Postscript: Twenty years of learning theory in relation to instruction. In Hilgard, E. R., ed., *Theories of learning and instruction*, National Society for the Study of Education, 63rd yearbook. Chicago: University of Chicago Press, 1964, part 1, pp. 416-418.

Hilgard summarizes the progress and changes in research and development concerning learning and instruction that occurred from 1944 to 1964.

JACKSON, P. W. *Life in classrooms*. New York: Holt, Rinehart and Winston, 1968.

The style and content of this short (177 pages) book on elementary schooling are reflected faithfully in the five chapter titles: "The Daily Grind"; "Students' Feelings about School"; "Involvement and Withdrawal in the Classroom"; "Teachers' Views"; and "The Need for New Perspectives."

JOYCE, B. R., & HAROOTUNIAN, B., *The structure of teaching*. Chicago: Science Research Associates, 1967.

Prospective and beginning teachers will especially enjoy the anecdotal and case-study materials in this short book of 252 pages.

KLAUSMEIER, H. J., & O'HEARN, G. T., eds. *Research and development toward the improvement of education*. Madison, Wisc.: Dembar Educational Research Services, 1968, pp. 132-163.

Persons may become acquainted with the earliest efforts of the U.S. Office of Education to improve educational practices through research and development by study of three articles by L. Bright and H. Gideonse, H. J. Klausmeier, and H. Gideonse, respectively. The emphasis here is on product development and decision-oriented research.

NEILL, A. S. *Summerhill: A radical approach to child rearing.* New York: Hart, 1960.

In this 392-page paperback, Neill describes his school and system of instruction in which unstinted love and approval, with a very minimum amount of constraint from any source, lead to happy, creative young adults. Failures of the school are noted.

ROGERS, C. R. The place of the person in the new world of the behavioral sciences. In Ripple, R. E., ed., *Readings in learning and human abilities.* New York: Harper & Row, 2nd ed., 1971.

Problems and choices connected with controlling human behavior through the skillful application of recently formulated psychological principles are made clear.

SKINNER, B. F. *Walden two.* New York: Macmillan, 1948.

In this 320-page paperback novel, B. F. Skinner presents his ideas of the utopia that would be possible if operant conditioning principles were put into effect in education, government, and other institutions. (Skinner and Neill present their divergent systems of educating with equal persuasiveness.)

Chapter 2 Learning Theories and Principles

Purposeful Learning

attending to a learning task
setting a goal
cognizing and organizing sequential components
practicing under desirable conditions
developing stable abilities and comprehensive knowledge

Classical and Operant Conditioning

classical conditioning
unconditioned and conditioned stimulus
unconditioned and conditioned response
first-order and higher-order conditioning
operant conditioning
positive and negative reinforcement
schedules of reinforcement
successive approximation or shaping

Observational Learning and Imitation

models: real life, symbolic, representational
exemplary models and prosocial behaviors
effects of observing: modeling, disinhibitory, eliciting
counterconditioning technique

Meaningful Learning

reception learning: meaningful, rote
discovery learning: meaningful, rote
subsumption: derivative, correlative
cognitive-structure variables
affective-social variables
achievement motivation
advance organizer

Informational Theory

information
contents
products
operations

What goes on inside the human being as he learns? What *internal conditions*, such as level of motivation and earlier experiences, are related to how well he learns? What *external conditions*, such as the type of subject matter or learning task and the amount of practice, affect how well he learns?

The efforts to find answers to these and similar questions have led to thousands of experiments in laboratories with both animal and human subjects and less formal research in school settings with school-age children. A main aim of many of these experiments is to generate a general theory of learning that will integrate existing information and permit reliable predictions about conditions that facilitate learning in individuals. Nevertheless, as Underwood (1965) points out, no single theory has yet emerged that is applicable to the wide array of learning outcomes in the many different settings in which learning occurs.

The combined efforts of the investigators, however, promise much for the eventual formulation of a comprehensive theory of learning. Experiments in both laboratory and school settings are constantly in progress. For instance, many psychologists are doing laboratory studies on specific phenomena, such as conditioning in animal and human subjects, associative processes in verbal learning, and cognitive processes in concept learning. Attempts are also being made to validate principles formulated in laboratories through experimentation in school settings. A third approach involves more or less the reverse of the second—experimentation in school settings for the purpose of generating principles and theory.

In the first part of this chapter, a synthesis of ideas drawn from functionalist and informational theory is outlined; these ideas, which describe *purposeful learning*, form the most adequate basis, from the authors' viewpoint, for interpreting learning in school settings, kindergarten through college. Four subtheories—those that treat *conditioning, observational learning, meaningful learning*, and *informational theory*—are then described briefly. These subtheories are discussed for two main reasons: First, it is instructive to understand divergent theories. Second, each theory has a number of proponents, and some educational practices are directly related to the principles from each theory.

Only a small part of the empirical research about each theory is presented, and because our purpose is to indicate only the main substance of each theory, the experimental methodology is not described. Some of the applications to school learning that have resulted from each theory are described. People differ in their reactions to these theories. A student may be more attracted by one than another, depending on his specific subject-matter field, such as physical education or social studies, and his specific age-level interest, such as kindergarten or junior college.

PURPOSEFUL LEARNING

Think for a moment about what you have learned with intent to learn. Purposeful learning is learning that occurs with intent. Much human learning is purposeful. At times it is controlled solely by the individual without instruction or guidance. At other times someone else is available to instruct the individual. We shall first describe a sequence in purposeful learning by an individual without instruction. Then, purposeful learning with guidance in a school setting will be described, taking into account variables associated with an instructional system, as outlined in Chapter 1.

Purposeful Learning by an Individual

Figure 2.1 shows a sequence in purposeful learning without instruction. This sequence describes how individuals acquire many of their intellectual and psychomotor abilities. In analyzing the sequence, which is now described in more detail, you might profitably think about your present learned behaviors and try to decide how closely the sequence applies to them.

Fig. 2.1. Sequence in purposeful learning without instruction.

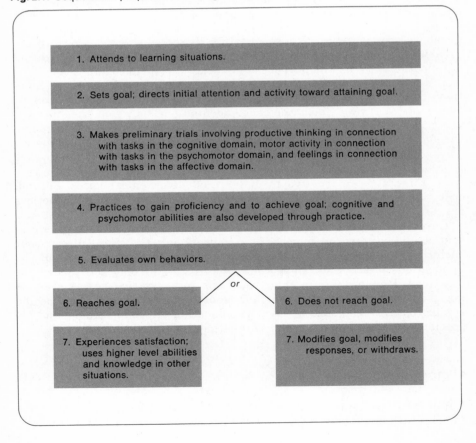

1. Attends to learning situations.

2. Sets goal; directs initial attention and activity toward attaining goal.

3. Makes preliminary trials involving productive thinking in connection with tasks in the cognitive domain, motor activity in connection with tasks in the psychomotor domain, and feelings in connection with tasks in the affective domain.

4. Practices to gain proficiency and to achieve goal; cognitive and psychomotor abilities are also developed through practice.

5. Evaluates own behaviors.

or

6. Reaches goal.

6. Does not reach goal.

7. Experiences satisfaction; uses higher level abilities and knowledge in other situations.

7. Modifies goal, modifies responses, or withdraws.

1. An individual at some stage in his maturation experiences a need, desire, or feeling of some sort and attends to the situation. He may be hungry or thirsty and want to satisfy these physiological needs. He may see a bright object and wish to know what it is. He may desire approval from an age-mate or adult. He may have a printed page in front of him and want to know what the printed page says. This state of need or arousal leads to attending closely to the situation.

2. Along with attending to the situation and experiencing heightened motivation, the individual perceives how his need or desire may be met and sets a goal. That is, he thinks about an end state or condition to be attained at some time in the future that will satisfy the desire or need. The extent to which the individual explicitly sets a goal varies. At times he may verbalize clearly to himself what he wants to attain, when it will be attained, and the means for attaining it. Many goals are not stated so explicitly.

3. While initially attending to the situation the individual may engage in some manipulative or exploratory behavior, preliminary to setting a goal. Once a goal is set, the intention or desire to attain it constitutes an initial and continuing motivational force (Miller, Galanter, & Pribram, 1960). The individual makes preliminary trials to attain the goal. If the goal is to compare various descriptions of utopia, to understand a mathematical concept, or some other phenomenon in the cognitive domain, productive thinking is involved. If the goal involves writing his name legibly, driving a golf ball 200 yards, or something similar in the psychomotor domain, motor activity is involved. If the goal is to convey a sense of trust in the child, feelings as well as productive thinking are important. Actually, feeling is involved in all goal-setting efforts, but the amount varies.

4. Redefinition of the goal in terms of raising or lowering one's expectations typically occurs after the preliminary trials. To reach most goals, practice, exercise, or activity is involved. Learning a second language or acquiring higher level concepts requires persistent mental activity and lesser physical activity. Learning to type or to play a musical instrument requires persistent practice of physical actions and lesser mental activity. It is the practice or exercise of partially developed initial skills and more general abilities that leads to their fuller development. In turn, skills and abilities developed while performing certain tasks enable the individual to pursue more complex or difficult related tasks later (Ferguson, 1956). For example, you can now learn to spell very complex words; at age 6 or 7, learning to spell even one-syllable words was difficult.

5. Individuals evaluate their own actions when seeking goals and when other individuals are not available to evaluate them. In connection with the sequence in purposeful learning the individual does not start evaluating here; he evaluates his actions and ideas from the outset. It is at this point, however, that an individual must assess his own performances in relation to whether the goal initially set has been attained. In the process of evaluation some knowledge and actions may be confirmed as satisfac-

tory, others may be judged to require modification, and still others may be rejected.

6. & 7. The individual does or does not reach his goal. If the goal is reached, satisfaction is experienced. Also, the knowledge and abilities are available for use in other situations. When an individual does not reach a strongly desired goal, frustration is experienced. The individual may lower his goal, modify his approach and renew his efforts to attain the same goal, set a substitute goal, or withdraw.

Two brief examples clarify the sequence:

Consider a young boy, Bill, who rides a tricycle well. Then he is given a bicycle. It is not surprising to find that he attends to it closely and enthusiastically and immediately sets as his goal (not using the word "goal," of course) to be able to ride it.

Bill makes preliminary trials almost immediately. These early trials, much like a person's early attempts at driving a car, are usually characterized by lack of such psychomotor abilities as precision, coordination, and flexibility. After several trials he will probably master the skills of starting, making a complete revolution first with one pedal and then continuing on to make the revolution of the other pedal. The next big task is to maintain and shift the body balance while returning to the pedal from which the ride started. Depending on his size and other characteristics, Bill may proceed quickly or he may try every day for weeks before he masters this part of the skill. After mastering this, Bill continues his trials. He drops the inappropriate responses and improves the ones he interprets as useful.

As soon as Bill feels that he is making progress or that he can actually ride the bicycle as well as he had originally set out to do, he experiences satisfaction — the affective component in the learning sequence. This component first entered when he originally wanted to learn and continues throughout the entire learning sequence. Bill is learning likes and dislikes and experiencing feelings of satisfaction and dissatisfaction in all his trying.

Suppose that despite his best and continued efforts, Bill cannot ride the bicycle as well as he would like, or perhaps cannot ride it at all. After repeated trials and feelings of failure, he may engage in one of a variety of behaviors. The behavior that might be most appropriate and likely to lead to future success would be to try to improve his performance with further effort. If he does not know how to make improvements, he may simply continue to try as he has in the past, with the possibility that such trying will lead to success. Bill may, however, quit. (It is not uncommon for individuals to quit after experiencing repeated failure despite their best efforts.) On the other hand, rather than quitting or trying the same or new responses, an individual without guidance may substitute a different goal if he is convinced that the present goal is unattainable. If Bill cannot learn to ride the bicycle, he may return to his tricycle and attempt to perfect his skills in riding it.

Learning to ride a bicycle takes many trials. In contrast, consider an example of purposeful verbal learning, without instruction, which may be accomplished with few trials and in a short time. Suppose that Mary, a fifth-grader, is reading about a basketball game at her school. She wants to understand the account fully. Then she encounters the following sentence and sees an unfamiliar word, "crucial": "John scored his lone point at a *crucial* moment."

Referring again to the sequence in purposeful learning in Fig. 2.1, examine how the sequence applies. Mary directs her attention to the unknown word and studies it in relation to the other words in the sentence in order to estimate its possible meaning from the context. Her preliminary attempts to pronounce the word occur almost simultaneously with the initial appraisal. In trying to get the pronunciation, Mary may look at the various letters in the word and try to sound them out. Or, she may try to divide the word into syllables and pronounce the syllables. If Mary has had good previous instruction in reading, she will probably attempt all three—getting the meaning of the word from the context, phonetic analysis, and structural analysis. Eventually she will evolve some meaning and some pronunciation of the word, correct or incorrect, or she may simply give up. Uninstructed, Mary accepts the meaning and pronunciation that make most sense to her, the ones that best complete her evaluation of the word. She may decide, from the context, that the word is "critical," rather than "crucial." Whether or not Mary pronounces the word as "critical" or "crucial," she has reached her goal and experiences satisfaction.

This is a difficult word for fifth-graders, and Mary might realize that she cannot read it. In that case, she would not reach the goal of getting full meaning, but she might have sufficient understanding of the word and quit without further effort. The frustration resulting from not knowing this one word might not be great enough to motivate her to try again or set a substitute or modified goal.

Purposeful Learning in a School Setting

Figure 2.2 shows the now familiar sequence in purposeful learning in the left column as learner actions; possible teacher actions are added in the right column. Nine principles that relate the student and teacher actions are now discussed. The principles are numbered according to the outline in Fig. 2.2 (two are subdivided in the discussion into two each). In each principle the learner's actions are stated and then the facilitative role of the teacher is sketched briefly. In studying the principles, you might find it helpful to consider them in terms of their value in explaining your own purposeful learning activities. It is important to remember that these principles constitute an overview of the conditions of learning that will be described in detail throughout Part III of this book.

LEARNER ACTIONS	TEACHER ACTIONS
1. Attends to learning situation.	1. Manipulates materials, activities, and other situational elements to secure and hold student attention.
2. Sets goal: directs initial attention and activity toward attaining goal.	2. Assists each student in goal-setting by discussing instructional objectives, tasks to be performed, and the like, and by outlining with the student specific goals to be attained.
3. Makes preliminary trials involving productive thinking in connection with tasks in the cognitive domain, motor activity in connection with tasks in the psychomotor domain, and feelings in connection with tasks in the affective domain.	3. Makes available instructional resources, such as models, materials, equipment, and supplies. Prompts and guides the student in the use of these resources and in the use of the student's own knowledge and abilities.
4. Practices to gain proficency and to achieve goal; cognitive and psychomotor abilities are also developed through practice.	4. Manages practice, study, discussion, laboratory, and other activities. Encourages the student to persist in goal-directed efforts. Prompts and guides the student in acquiring knowledge and in developing higher-level abilities and prosocial behaviors. Provides for differences among students in rate of learning, style of learning, type of ability, and level of motivation.
5. Evaluates own behaviors.	5. Assesses student's progress and makes results immediately available to the student. Corrects errors, praises or otherwise reinforces, and counsels with the student. Provides for review and additional practice as may be necessary to ensure retention.
6. Reaches goal.	6. Makes a summative evaluation with the student to ascertain the extent to which he has attained his goal.
7. Experiences satisfaction; uses higher-level abilities and knowledge in other situations.	7. Establishes conditions that make possible the use of recently acquired knowledge, skills, and abilities in further study in the same field, in other activities and fields within the school, and in situations outside the school setting.

Fig. 2.2. Sequence in purposeful learning with instruction.

1. *Attending to a learning task* is essential in initiating a sequence of learning activities. When introducing a lesson or unit, the teacher secures the attention of the students. Here the teacher appeals to more than one sense—for instance, to both hearing and seeing. Materials of instruction, other physical components of the room, the teacher's actions, and other social aspects of the situation may be organized to secure attention.

2. *Setting a goal* initiates and directs activity. Students need opportunity for and assistance in deciding what they will learn, how well they will learn it, and when it will be learned. Whole-class discussion, small-group discussion, and individual conferences are used to facilitate individual goal-setting by students.

3a. *Trying to attain a goal* involves interacting with persons and materials appropriate to the goal and to the student's characteristics. Many new responses are learned by observing and imitating real-life models, including teachers, and symbolic models in printed and visual materials. Thus a child learns to write by observing and imitating both the actions of the teacher and the model of letters provided in a chart or book. Also, information needed to attain goals is found in books, films, and other instructional materials. Increasingly, the school can do more to encourage purposeful and independent learning as the variety and quality of instructional materials increase.

3b. *Cognizing and organizing sequential components* is essential to goal attainment in the cognitive and psychomotor domains. Helping the student to identify meaningful relationships in verbal material and sequential activities in skill development is an important contribution of an effective teacher. If the student lacks knowledge about possible sequences and relationships among parts, he cannot get off to a good start or continue to final goal attainment.

4a. *Practicing under desirable conditions* is essential to goal attainment in both the psychomotor and cognitive domains and to improve performance in most subject-matter fields. Most practice usually requires both productive thinking and physical activity. To make practice effective, a teacher can provide for whole-part relationships, the length and spacing of practice sessions, knowledge of progress, and other facilitating conditions.

4b. *Learning in line with one's own abilities, style, and other characteristics* furthers goal attainment and learning more generally. Two practices that facilitate individualization are becoming increasingly common: (1) Students are grouped according to the objectives sought and the students' characteristics, rather than by age or grade; actually, such instructional groupings, now extended greatly in scope, have already been used for many years in music and athletic activities. (2) Materials, equipment, and spaces are arranged flexibly to encourage independent study; individual study carrels and a variety of instructional materials provide each child opportunity to learn according to his individual rate and style.

5. *Evaluating one's own performance* is essential in developing independence in learning and in attaining goals. Also, when the teacher informs a

student of his progress and helps him overcome errors, the student's goal attainment and his learning in general are hastened because he is encouraged to continue and his inadequate or incorrect responses are eliminated. Lack of progress and simultaneous failure in reaching goals are principal contributors to a student's losing his zest for learning and his interest in subject matter and in schooling.

6. *Developing stable abilities and comprehensive knowledge* requires productive learning experiences over an extended period of time. Systematic review of verbal material and spaced practice of skills are necessary for attaining long-range goals. One way of providing review and practice is to arrange for sequential tasks that call for students to use recently learned information and skills. This is far better than cramming immediately before a test or repeating the same tasks over and over.

7. *Applying newly acquired concepts, principles, skills, and other outcomes* increases their permanence. Helping students with applications to new situations facilitates both long-term retention and use. Verbal descriptions of possible applications are less effective than having students use newly acquired information or skills in actual situations. The great loss in learning from one year to the next and the inability to switch from one subject to another or from a school situation to an out-of-school situation result from the lack of opportunities to apply new knowledge and skills.

CLASSICAL AND OPERANT CONDITIONING

Principles of conditioning have been reasonably well established by laboratory studies on animal and human subjects. Their applications are now gradually being extended to school settings. Not everyone agrees with either the applications or the extensions. Nevertheless, it is important to understand the principles themselves. A clear presentation of these principles, along with samples of extensions to a wide range of human behaviors, is given by Staats (1968). Many of Staats's ideas are based on the earlier work of other psychologists (as is often true of research studies), but his work is followed closely in this section because it provides an authoritative basis for an attempt to present a concise overview of the principles.

Classical Conditioning

Figure 2.3 schematizes first-order and higher-order classical conditioning. In *first-order conditioning*, a *neutral stimulus*, in this case the tick tock of a metronome, is presented almost simultaneously with the *unconditioned stimulus*, food. The sight of food leads to the response of salivation in a hungry person or animal. After both have been presented again repeatedly and the food has been withdrawn gradually, the sound of the metronome alone eventually elicits the response of salivation. The metronome sound is now the *conditioned stimulus*, and salivation is the *conditioned response*.

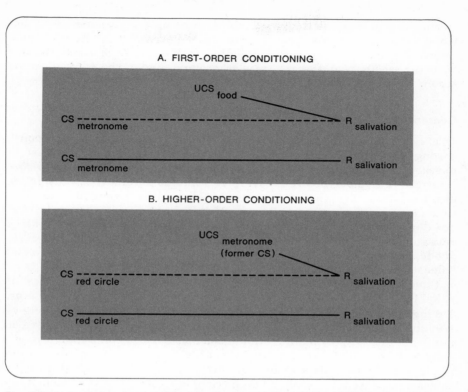

Fig. 2.3. *A*: In first-order conditioning, the association of the UCS, food, and the R, salivation, occurs before conditioning and is not learned. The association of the CS, metronome sound, and the R is learned. This occurs through pairing of the UCS with the CS followed by the R. *B*: In higher-order functioning, the former conditioned stimulus (CS) serves the same function as the UCS did in first-order conditioning.

In *higher-order conditioning*, the next step, the sound of the metronome, which produces the response of salivation, now serves the same function as did the previous unconditioned stimulus, food. When a new neutral stimulus, a red circle, is presented immediately before the metronome sound, the sight of the red circle alone, after repeated pairings with the metronome, eventually elicits the response of salivation.

Some psychologists explain all learning primarily in terms of associating two stimuli or stimuli and responses through first-order, or primary, and higher-order classical conditioning. For example, a child acquires his initial single-word vocabulary through associating names with their referents and later speaks in phrases and then in sentences through chaining, or associating consecutively, the words that comprise the sentences.

These principles of classical conditioning may be stated more formally. Whenever a stimulus that elicits a conditioned response occurs in close time proximity with a new neutral stimulus that does not, there is a resulting tendency for the new stimulus to elicit the response. Further, when the new stimulus, now the conditioned stimulus, elicits the conditioned response, it may be manipulated with another neutral stimulus with the result that the response is brought under the control of the second previously neutral stimulus.

Operant Conditioning

In classical conditioning, a previously neutral stimulus elicits a response through repeated pairing with an unconditioned stimulus. By contrast, in operant, or instrumental, conditioning, the response must be made *before* a reward is given or before an aversive stimulus is removed. Thus, in operant conditioning, when a response is followed by a reward, there is a tendency for the response to be repeated. For example, a hungry child at the dining table says "please" and is then given food. Each time this is repeated, the probability is increased that the child will say "please" to get food when he is hungry. Food serves as a positive reinforcer of the "please" response, or operant.

Children often experience aversive stimuli that involve feelings of pain. For example, a child touches an uncomfortably warm radiator. Taking his hand from the radiator (the operant) removes the aversive stimulus (heat) and removal of the heat strengthens the operant. (We do not deliberately apply painful stimuli, such as heat, to children, but physically painful stimuli are used in animal laboratories.) As a second example, a teacher isolates a child from others (aversive stimulus) until he copies a page from his book. When he completes the page, the teacher discontinues the isolation. Removal of the isolation condition strengthens the copying behavior.

There is little doubt that providing a positive reinforcement following a response usually increases the probability that the response will be made again. Also, the removal of an aversive stimulus strengthens the response that leads to its removal. This is different, however, from punishing for undesired behavior when the child has no opportunity to do something that will terminate the punishment. The effects of punishment following behavior that is unrelated to the termination of a punishment cannot be predicted reliably. Three effects are possible: When an adult punishes a child for an act and the child knows that he is being punished for having committed the act, there is a tendency for the child not to commit the act again. Thus, punishing for an act each time it is committed may lead to its extinction. Punishment may also, however, merely have a suppressing effect on the act in the presence of the punisher. The child may repeat the act in the absence of the punisher, particularly if the child has not developed another action to replace the punished one. The third effect is that the punisher may himself become an aversive stimulus for the child by becoming associated with the punishment.

In our discussion of classical conditioning we showed that higher-order conditioning is possible. This is also true in operant conditioning with both positive reinforcers and aversive stimuli. For example, when discussing positive reinforcers, we pointed out that presenting food to a hungry child who says "please" increases the probability of the child's continuing to say "please." In the next step, a neutral stimulus—for example, the words "good boy"—can be paired with the presentation of the food. After a number of times, the words alone have the same effect as the presentation of the food in maintaining the strength of the "please" response. The words "good boy" are now the *conditioned reinforcer* for the response, "please." Another important point can now be made. Such a secondary reinforcer, once its reinforcement property is established, may reinforce responses other than the one with which it was initially associated. Thus "good boy" may reinforce responses other than saying "please," for instance, sharing a toy willingly when asked or hanging clothes up neatly.

The main generalizations about operant conditioning may now be summarized. When a positive reinforcer closely follows a certain response, the probability that the response will occur again is increased. When a negative reinforcer is removed soon after a certain response that led to the removal, the probability that the response will occur again is also increased. Higher-order conditioning occurs in operant conditioning. When a neutral stimulus is paired with a positive reinforcing stimulus, the neutral stimulus, after repeated pairings, itself acquires reinforcing power. Secondary reinforcers are usually social. Among the positive social reinforcers are complimentary words spoken to another; physical or verbal responses of endearment; tokens, such as money, honors, and good grades; and approval of the group, in the form of applause, group laughter, or attention.

Higher-order negative reinforcers and conditioned aversive stimuli include disapproval by words or actions; threats and harsh tones; low grades; and group disapproval in the form of silence, booing, and the like. These become aversive stimuli through higher-order conditioning. For example, a child touches the television tube, the mother slaps the child's hand sharply and says "bad boy." This may be repeated. Eventually, "bad boy" has the same effect as the sharp slap.

Proponents of operant conditioning do not accept the idea that learning occurs merely through associating two events in close time contiguity. For example, the association of the word "milk" with actual milk is not learned merely by saying the word in the presence of milk. On the contrary, a child learns to call the proper liquid "milk" by having the word reinforced when said in the presence of milk and not reinforced when said in the presence of juice, water, or other liquids. Similarly, words chained into sentences as consecutive correct words are reinforced first by parents or other adults and later by the reward of improved communication.

Schedules of Reinforcement

If all the responses made are reinforced, the schedule of reinforcement is 100 percent. Many other schedules are possible and have been shown to have pronounced differing effects on behavior in experimental situations with animals; such experiments often involve reinforcement with food.

As might be expected, the effects are more clearly defined in laboratory experiments, where controls are more rigorously applied, than in school classrooms. Four main types of schedules have been demonstrated in the laboratory:

1. *Fixed ratio.* In this schedule reinforcement is given regularly after a specified number of nonreinforced responses of the same kind—for instance, after every three or every six or every 10 or every 100.

2. *Variable ratio.* In this schedule reinforcement is given after a certain number of responses, but with the numbers differing from one reinforcement to the next—perhaps after three responses, then after 10, then after 18, then three again, and so on (the numbers are often picked at random from a range). A variable ratio schedule tends to produce more rapid responding by a hungry animal than a fixed ratio.

3. *Fixed interval.* In this schedule reinforcement is given regularly after a specified time interval—for instance, every 15 seconds or every 30 seconds or every 60 seconds.

4. *Variable interval.* In this schedule reinforcement is given after irregular time intervals, differing from one to the next (the intervals are often picked at random). A variable interval schedule produces a rapid, stable rate of responding in animals.

According to the theory, the effects of various schedules of reinforcement are the same on human beings as on animals. Therefore, some programed instructional materials that are widely used in the schools permit the use of either a fixed ratio or a variable ratio reinforcement schedule (such materials are discussed in detail in Chapter 5). Also, teachers systematically manipulate reinforcements during experiments. In practice, they reinforce socially approved behaviors on an unscheduled, intermittent basis; so do parents, of course, and others in authority.

Successive Approximation

A response is made and in turn is reinforced. How is the response acquired in the first place? According to operant conditioning, the final behavior is shaped through a series of *successive approximations.* To achieve this, each act that gets closer to the final behavior is reinforced. In one experiment, human subjects were given score points as reinforcers in order to shape a variety of behaviors (Verplanck, 1956). One behavior chosen was scratching the ear. At first, the experimenter reinforced any movement of the subject; this strengthened the movement response. The next step was to reinforce any movement of the arms. Then movement of the hand toward the head and, finally, scratching movements were reinforced. This rough outline gives an idea of how the final scratching response was shaped by successive approximations. (The procedure is reminiscent of the familiar game in which one person is to find a hidden object within a time limit and the other players give "reinforcing" clues as "it" moves about the room—"you're lukewarm," "warm," "hot," "very hot," as the person comes increasingly closer to the hiding place.)

In another experiment, a number of college students were conditioned to make statements of opinion beginning with "I think," "I believe," "It seems to me," and the like (Verplanck, 1955). The students did not know an experiment was being carried out. The method used involved engaging each student in conversation on one of a variety of topics. In the first 10 minutes, the student was *primed* to talk by being asked questions. The number of his opinion statements was merely recorded inconspicuously. In the second 10 minutes, two reinforcement procedures were used: The opinion statements were reinforced with agreement—the experimenter said, "You're right," "I agree," or "That's so," while nodding his head or smiling. In the other reinforcement procedure, the experimenter repeated back to the student in paraphrase what he had said. The experimenter also at some time during the experiment ignored or disagreed with the opinion statements of the student. Every student increased his rate of stating opinions when reinforced by agreement or paraphrase (though the students varied greatly in the number of opinions they stated). Nonreinforcement and negative reinforcement resulted in fewer opinion statements.

Operant theory assumes that complex human behavior is gradually built up by *differential reinforcement* of more primitive behaviors. The theory further assumes that successive approximation succeeds only when the final behavior can somehow be achieved by the organism, that otherwise it could not be shaped; the two experiments just described illustrate this.

Forgetting and Conditioning

Psychologists who explain learning in terms of conditioning usually do not use the word "forgetting." They refer to the weakening of responses as *extinction*. As noted, responses strengthened through reinforcement may be weakened through nonreinforcement. For example, children who, after reinforcement, pull a lever in response to a red stimulus will eventually cease doing so if reinforcement is not given after the lever-pulling. This fact produces one of the primary difficulties in operant conditioning. Reinforcement strengthens a response. More important, a variable ratio schedule—reinforcing every second or third response—is more efficacious than a fixed ratio of reinforcing after each response. Practitioners constantly are faced with the problem: when and how can reinforcement be discontinued without producing extinction? Supposedly, as the response becomes stronger, the frequency of the reinforcements may be decreased. Eventually, the ability to perform the response well usually serves as a kind of self-reinforcement, so that external reinforcing is no longer needed. But there remains the problem of deciding *when* to decrease or discontinue reinforcements.

Drives and Conditioning

Some psychological scientists use the term *drive* instead of motive. A number of relationships are involved in the concept known as drive. First, deprivation, such as of food or water, has the effect of making an organism more active or aroused. Second, deprivation makes the appropriate stimulus reinforcing. For example, deprivation of food produces a hunger

drive that makes food a reinforcer for responses associated with securing
the food. The strength of the hunger drive is inferred from the duration
of food deprivation and the degree of arousal.

Primary drives, which are satisfied by primary reinforcers, are those
associated with the maintenance of life; they are not learned. Secondary
drives are learned by being associated with primary drives, as we have
noted in several connections. Deprivation of secondary drives may have
the same effects as the deprivation of primary drives, such as of hunger
and thirst. Thus a college student commits suicide after failing an exam
and a Vietnamese monk burns himself to death after being unable to
achieve certain religious values for his people.

The hunger and thirst drives have been manipulated in many lower-
form animals in psychological laboratories. As a matter of fact, principles
of both classical and operant conditioning were formulated initially in
laboratory experiments on animals at varying degrees of deprivation and
related arousal. For obvious moral and social reasons, deprivation of the
primary needs of students should not be manipulated in school settings.
Therefore, the concept of physiological drive has been rejected by most
practitioners and theorists, including the authors, as a basis for securing
the attention of students and then maintaining a high level of sustained
effort on learning tasks in schools. (The physiological drives of human
beings are manipulated at times, but only under carefully controlled conditions and by trained, experienced psychologists or clinicians. When such
manipulation is done for research purposes, selected volunteer subjects
are used. In addition, various governmental agencies now require that
specified minimum conditions be met in all experiments that use human
beings as subjects and in which aversive stimuli are used.)

Stimulus Generalization and Response Discrimination

What happens if a slight change is made in the conditioned stimulus in
classical conditioning or in the conditioned reinforcing stimulus in operant conditioning? The same response will be made to stimuli of the
same class. In this case, we say that *stimulus generalization* has occurred.
For example, children received 16 reinforced trials at pulling a lever
during a presentation of a one-colored visual stimulus (White, 1958); a
marble was used for each reinforcement. Later, the same experimental
situation was set up, but without the marbles, and the visual stimuli differed from one another in color, brightness, or both. The children responded to the varied visual stimuli with the same lever-pressing response, although with less frequency than to the original stimulus.
Stimulus generalization had occurred.

A young child may at first call his father and all other men "Daddy."
Later, he calls only his father "Daddy" and refers to other men by appropriate titles ("Mr. Smith," "Uncle John," "Grandfather"). He has learned
response discrimination, that is, to make different responses to different
stimuli. Go back to the first sentence of the previous paragraph. You
make a different response to each word or stimulus because you have
learned to discriminate among these stimuli. Stimulus generalization and

response discrimination are applicable not only to classical and operant conditioning but also to other theories of learning. Also, independent of specific theories, generalization and discrimination are involved in many learning tasks.

Application to School Learning

Application of conditioning theory may be viewed from the standpoint of the outcomes to which classical and operant principles are relevant, other phenomena associated with the theory, and the form in which the principles are actually used in school practices. Some psychologists and educators would like to base much more educational practice on principles of behavior modification that, in turn, are drawn from conditioning principles. Others believe, primarily for philosophical reasons, that any deliberate shaping of a student's responses through a system of rewards and punishments should be eliminated. Practitioners should study divergent theories in detail before accepting or rejecting any. Moral and philosophical judgments should be formed only on the basis of sufficient objective information. When they are so formed, however, they often present valid and compelling reasons for a person's course of action.

The learning of arbitrary associations and factual information can be accounted for in part by the principles of contiguity (two stimuli occurring almost or exactly simultaneously) and reinforcement. These principles should not be discarded because they originated in laboratories and can be used in *controlling* the behavior of others; rather, they should be studied as conditions that may facilitate the learning of certain outcomes by human beings. Learning the names of the numerals and the letters of the alphabet, the early associations between the correct pronunciation of a word and its printed form, the names of specific people and places, and other such facts are examples of learning that can be accounted for in terms of some combination of the principles of contiguity and reinforcement. Gagné (1967) described the learning of specific responses and chains of responses, two types of learning that correspond to learning the factual information that is part of any subject. He stated that these two types of learning also may be explained in terms of principles of classical and operant conditioning.

Other phenomena associated with conditioning theory include discrimination and generalization. These phenomena are included in the general fields of psychology and education—they are not unique to one theory; the same is true of reinforcement. Discriminating among discrete entities, or stimuli, and making the same response to things of the same class are central in the learning of factual information, concepts, and principles in any curriculum area. External reinforcement is at the heart of laboratory experiments in conditioning, but it also is studied in more general contexts. For example, Kennedy and Willcutt (1964) reviewed 33 articles covering 50 years of research on the effects of praise, a secondary reinforcer, and blame, a secondary aversive stimulus, on the performance of school children. They noted that praise produced higher achievement in all students except underachievers. If the definition of reinforcement is extended to include knowledge of progress and the self-reinforcement that comes with successful performance of a task, reinforcement is applicable to all outcomes of learning in all domains.

2.1. What gets associated in classical conditioning? What is the time sequence of the associations?

2.2. A rat presses a lever, which causes a food pellet to be released as a reinforcer. A child spells a word correctly and receives a smile. What is the operant in each case? What are the relationships between the operant and the reinforcement?

2.3. Give an example of an operant, or class of operants, in each domain — cognitive, psychomotor, and affective — that might be strengthened through reinforcement.

2.4. An animal cannot be told how and when its behavior will be reinforced, but a student can. How might this fact be related to the use of various reinforcement schedules in school settings?

2.5. What steps and procedures would be involved in teaching a child to read his first word (for example, "dog") if a combination of discrimination learning, successive approximation, and differential reinforcement were followed? (Differential reinforcement involves reinforcing correct responses and ignoring or punishing incorrect ones.)

2.6. Why might it be more difficult to extinguish a response when it has been learned under a variable reinforcement rate rather than a fixed rate?

2.7. Who controls what is learned in conditioning? Could students be taught to make independent and creative responses through the application of conditioning principles and procedures? Could other procedures and principles be used?

OBSERVATIONAL LEARNING AND IMITATION

A child suddenly notices that his father hugs his mother when the father comes home in the evening and that his mother and father seem happier. The next time the child comes into the house, he too hugs his mother. A teen-ager for the first time sees a singer making certain bodily movements. The teen-ager repeats the same motions as he sings a popular song. The first time a student hears a phrase in a foreign language, he tries to pronounce it exactly as the teacher did. Are these examples of learning by reinforcing successive correct responses and extinguishing incorrect responses through nonreinforcement?

According to Bandura and Walters (1963), new behavior units, or chunks of behavior, are learned initially through observing and imitating a model, rather than being shaped through successive approximations involving differential reinforcement. These psychologists think that enough laboratory experiments and field studies have been done to warrant an adequate description of learning through the observation and imitation of models. They are concerned especially with the learning of social attitudes and behaviors involved in aggression, dependency, self-control, and sexual relationships. In the next few pages, the most fundamental concepts and principles of Bandura and Walters related to imitation are discussed.

Models Imitated

The models children observe and imitate are classified as *real-life, symbolic*, and *representational*. At home, real-life models for younger children are parents and relatives. Teachers and other persons in the community are the real-life models for many school children. Models presented to children through oral or written instructions and pictures or through a combination of verbal and pictorial devices are symbolic. Models presented by audiovisual means, particularly television, are representational.

In the schools and in many homes much attention is given to *exemplary models*. Such models demonstrate prosocial behaviors, those that are considered desirable by the adults responsible for the education of the children. This socializing aspect of learning is probably more critical than is generally assumed. Much socialized behavior, and also antisocial and deviant behavior, is acquired through imitating models.

The Effects of Imitation

Bandura and Walters state that the initial acquisition of chunks of behavior, or responses, results primarily from the contiguity of events perceived through the senses, that is, seeing or hearing sequential behaviors in close time proximity. On the other hand, the subsequent strength of behaviors initially acquired by observing and then responding is dependent on the same differential reinforcement that has been described. The important contribution of this imitation theory, therefore, lies in its explanation of how responses are learned *initially*. The processes become more clear through considering three different effects of observation and imitation:

1. *Modeling effect.* By observing and imitating, the observer matches the behavior of the model with responses that are new to the observer, responses made for the first time. Obviously, the model must demonstrate behavior that is new to the observer, but it must also be behavior that the observer is capable of. For instance, some preschoolers were shown a film of a model performing various aggressive acts that the children had not previously exhibited. Figure 2.4 shows four scenes from the film and also the effects: without reinforcement of any kind, the young children demonstrated the same behaviors (Bandura, Ross, & Ross, 1963).

2. *Disinhibitory effect.* By observing and imitating a model, the observer may also weaken or strengthen inhibitory responses that the observer already has in his repertoire. Aggressive behavior is generally disapproved and, to some extent, usually inhibited. Observation of a model displaying aggressive behavior, however, weakens the inhibitory responses and thus tends to result not only in an expression of this partic-

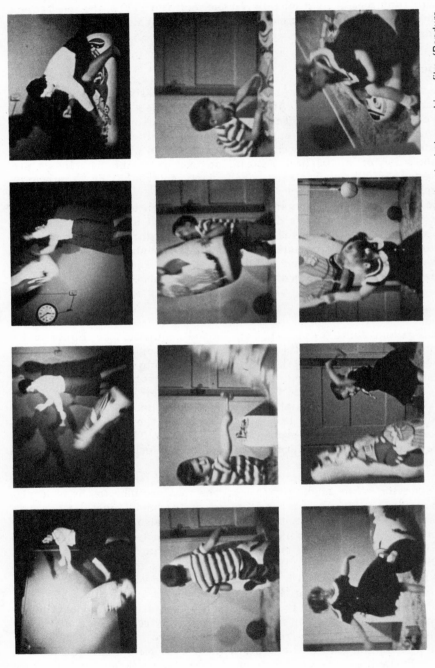

Fig.2.4. Photographs of children reproducing the aggressive behavior of the female model they had observed in a film. (Bandura, Ross, & Ross, 1963, p. 10)

ular aggressive behavior, but also in the release of other aggressive behavior that had been inhibited. Thus this is termed a disinhibitory effect—the strengthening of a whole class of behavior that is usually inhibited. Other forms of deviant behavior have also been shown to be disinhibited in individuals who have observed models displaying the behavior freely. The strengthening of inhibitory responses—the inhibition of behavior in the observer's repertoire—is most likely to occur under two circumstances: The model may be subjected to painful consequences as a result of his behavior. The observer then inhibits behavior that he perceives to be associated with the painful results. In other words, he fears he will be punished if he manifests the same behavior. The tendency of children to be fearful of some of the same events as their mothers is explained in this manner.

3. *Eliciting effect.* By observing and imitating a model, the observer matches the behavior of the model with responses that are already in the observer's repertoire. That is, the responses are elicited. (This effect can be demonstrated experimentally, though one can infer that it has occurred only if one knows the history of the observer.) Volunteering services or monetary contributions, pledging oneself to a course of action, and eating foods not ordinarily chosen are examples of behaviors that can be elicited through the presentation of appropriate models. A final note on the relationships among these three effects is interesting here:

> Modeling effects are possible only if the model exhibits responses that the observer has not yet learned to make, while disinhibitory effects can occur only if inhibitions have already been set up. However, in many cases of deviant behavior the model acts in ways which are both novel for the observer and socially disapproved; in such cases it is possible for the modeling, disinhibitory, and eliciting effects to occur simultaneously, and it is therefore virtually impossible to identify their relative contributions to the genesis of deviation. (Bandura & Walters, 1963, p. 81)

Some Factors Affecting Imitation

Many factors may be associated with imitation. One of these is the consequences of the responses to the model and to the observer. Another is the characteristics of the observer.

The consequences of the responses may be examined in terms of rewards and punishments. Imitation is facilitated when the model, in the presence of the observer, is rewarded for his behavior. Imitation is hindered when the model is punished. Further, if the observer knows that the model will receive either rewards or punishments, even though he cannot observe them, there are the same tendencies toward imitation or nonimitation. The effect of punishment, however, is not so predictable as that of reward.

Characteristics of the observer are also related to imitative behavior. The more imitative persons are those who lack self-esteem and competence because they have experienced too few rewards thus far; those who have previously been rewarded for exhibiting matching behavior; and those who have been frequently rewarded for conforming behavior and have thus become dependent. Others who believe themselves to be similar to the models in some attributes, rather than dissimilar, are also more imitative. Being emotionally aroused probably increases the likelihood of imitation. Such arousal can come through the stress of external situations or the use of drugs.

The continuing exposure to exemplary models and reinforcement strengthens socially approved behavior primarily through the dual operation of differential modeling cues, which elicit the responses and reinforcement of only these responses. Antisocial behavior, such as hitting and cheating, is also strengthened and becomes persistent when it is positively reinforced, even though the reinforcement may be intermittent. Similarly, the persistence of anxiety-motivated avoidance behavior, such as steering clear of low-grading professors, is accounted for by intermittent reinforcement through reduction of anxiety.

Forgetting Imitative Responses

Although the statements just made account for the strengthening of responses learned by imitation, they do not account for the forgetting or extinction of them. Bandura and Walters are concerned primarily with the extinction of behavior disapproved by someone or in some way harmful to the individual rather than with the weakening of behavior that is socially approved. Some means of extinguishing responses are: nonreward of responses; removal of a positive reinforcer through the deprivation of a privilege or possession that has previously served as a reinforcer; the use of an aversive stimulus, such as physical or verbal punishment; and counterconditioning by means of classical conditioning procedures.

Nonreward is not effective in extinction when there is a strong dominant response to be extinguished. The individual gains so much satisfaction from the activity that he continues it even though it is not rewarded. Punishment is often used to inhibit antisocial responses; removal of a positive reinforcer and the use of an aversive stimulus are both forms of punishment. Either of these techniques may work, particularly in the presence of the punisher, but either also may lead to other conditioned emotional responses, such as conditioned fear of the punisher. Also, the punished person may independently learn other responses that enable him to avoid the unpleasant or aversive stimulus.

Counterconditioning techniques involve the use of classical conditioning procedures. For example, in counterconditioning fear, a stimulus that produces the fear response is gradually introduced into the situation with a stimulus that does not produce fear. Thus, a child fears white-robed individuals after receiving innoculations at the pediatrician's office, but is comfortable with his mother. Situations are arranged whereby stimuli associated with the pediatrician are gradually introduced in the presence of the mother.

Application to School Learning

Bandura and Walters are concerned primarily with the learning of social behaviors. Their main contribution is the clear indication that chunks of social behavior are acquired initially through observing and imitating and that inhibitory and disinhibitory effects also come from observing and imitating. These findings imply that the real-life, symbolic, and representational models supplied, or not supplied, by the school can have a marked effect on the socializing role of the school. Undoubtedly, many disadvantaged and rebellious youth today are not finding exemplary models to imitate in school settings, in the home, or in any settings.

Observation and imitation also are important in the psychomotor domain. Cursive handwriting, throwing a football, playing the French horn, and other motor skills are acquired more efficiently in the presence of exemplary models. The development of vocal skills, such as speaking a second language, singing, and discussing, profits in the early stages from modeling. Thus, the potentially desirable effects of modeling appear to be relevant for many outcomes of learning at all levels of schooling.

Sarason (1968) reported two studies that applied modeling procedures to the treatment of juvenile delinquents housed in cottages at the Cascadia Juvenile Reception-Diagnostic Center (Tacoma, Washington). His graduate students first served as models. Then the delinquents each played model roles. There were 15 modeling sessions for each boy. Each session was explained as an opportunity to develop more effective ways of coping with problems that are important for people like themselves. Included were sessions on applying for a job, resisting temptation by peers to engage in antisocial acts, taking a problem to a teacher or parole counselor, and forgoing immediate gratifications in order to lay the groundwork for more significant gratification in the future. A practice problem-solving atmosphere was created during each session. The nature of the atmosphere and the modeling procedures may be inferred from the initial orientation that preceded the first meeting:

First, let's all introduce ourselves, starting with me. I'm Mr. – – – and this is Mr. – – – (boys introduce themselves). We are working with small groups of boys here at Cascadia. We are doing something new to show you some different ways of handling common situations and problems that will happen in your lives. The situations we'll work with and emphasize are often particularly important for fellows like yourselves. We say this because just the fact that you're going through an institution will have important effects on your lives, and we want to work with you to teach you better ways of handling some of these effects. In other words, we want to work together with you to teach you new ways to handle problem situations. These are situations which we feel will be of importance to you in the future. They are things that probably all of you will run into from time to time and we think that you can benefit from learning and practicing different ways to act in these situations.

The way we want to do this isn't by lecturing or advising you. Having people watch others doing things and then discussing what has been done is a very important way and a useful way to learn. It is easy to learn how to do something just by observing someone else doing it first. Oftentimes, just explaining something to someone isn't nearly as effective as actually doing it first while the other person watches. For example, it is easier to learn to swim, or repair a car, if you have a chance to watch someone else doing it first.

We think that small groups, working together, can learn a lot about appropriate ways of doing things just by playing different roles and watching others play roles. By role, we mean the particular part a person acts or plays in a particular situation—kind of like the parts actors play in a movie scene, only this will be more realistic. These roles will be based on actual situations that many young people have trouble with, like how to control your anger, or resist being pressured into doing destructive things by friends. Other roles are directly related to fellows like yourselves who have been in an institution. These are situations such as your review board, or the ways you can best use the special skills of your parole counselor to help you after you leave here. Things like this are things that not everyone can do well. We want to emphasize better ways of doing these things and coping with similar problems which will be important in the future for most of you. Everyone in the group will both play the roles for themselves and watch others playing the same roles. This is like acting, only it is realistic because it involves situations in which you might really find yourselves. We feel that the situations are realistic because they are based on the real experiences of a lot of fellows who have gone through Cascadia.

There are seven of us here at Cascadia who are working in these small groups. We are not on the Cascadia staff. We are here because we are interested in working with fellows like yourselves and in helping you improve your skills in how you approach the situations I've just described. Since we are not on the Cascadia staff, we do not have anything to do with the decisions made concerning you or where you will go after leaving here. We do not share any of our information with the regular staff. Everything this group does or talks about is kept strictly confidential and isn't available to or used by the staff in any way at all.

This group is one of several we have been working with here in – – – Cottage. Each group meets three times a week for about 40 minutes at a time. This same group will meet together each week during the time you are all here at Cascadia, but different ones of us will be with this group on different days. We will be playing different roles in different situations on each day. This is how we will do it. First, we will describe the situation to you. Then we will play out the roles that are involved. We want you to watch us and then take turns in pairs, playing the same roles yourselves. We will also discuss how everyone does and what is important about the particular roles or situations and how they may be related to your lives. We will want you to stick closely to the roles as we play them but also add your own personal touch to your role. As you will see, it is important that we all get involved in this as much as we can. The more you put yourself into the role you play, the more realistic it will be to you and to the rest of the group. We see these scenes as examples of real situations that you will all find yourselves in sometime, and it is important to play them as realistically as possible. We will outline each scene as we go along.

Also, each meeting will be tape-recorded. We use these tape-recordings for our own records of how each group proceeds. These tapes are identified by code numbers and no one's name actually appears in the tape. The tapes are confidential too, and will be used only by us. As we said, none of this information is used by the regular staff.

Before going any further, we want to give you an example of what we're talking about. Mr. – – – and I will play two roles which involve a scene that has really gone on right here in your cottage. This scene is based on information we got from a cottage counselor and other boys who have been in this cottage. This situation involves a common cottage problem and we will show you some things that can be done about it. (Sarason, 1968, pp. 259-260)

On completion of the first two studies, Sarason concluded that modeling was a potentially valuable behavior-modification procedure. The first groups of delinquents participating in the experimental modeling treatment were judged to have modified their attitudes in a desirable direction and to have learned some interviewing procedures and other sets of behaviors that would help them secure jobs and also meet other critical situations on leaving the center.

2.8. Assume that students are ready to start the initial learning of a set of responses, such as writing cursively, speaking a second language, or setting up a science experiment. What would be the differences in the teacher's procedures if instruction were based on (a) observational learning or (b) operant conditioning with successive approximation and differential reinforcement? Which would probably require more time? Which would probably be less applicable to instruction of a group?

2.9. Under what conditions might a white teacher serve as a model for black children and a black teacher serve as a model for white children? What would be the effects of reinforcing the child's imitations of the teacher's behaviors? What would be the effects of punishing rather than reinforcing?

2.10. What kinds of behaviors in your field of interest might best be learned through modeling? What kinds could not be learned in this way?

2.11a. You repeatedly demonstrate to a student the proper way to hit the bull's eye with an arrow, but when you give him the bow he misses. Why isn't modeling helping this student? What may be necessary?

2.11b. Being aroused or anxious will sometimes severely limit the responses you are capable of. Will you be more or less apt to follow modeled behavior? What if your anxiety level is such that a maximum number of responses is available to you?

2.12. In Sarason's experiment, graduate students modeled the desired sets of behaviors and then the delinquents played the model roles. Which one of the following do you infer that the delinquents lacked, with the result that the modeling was effective: motivation to succeed in adult life; desire to be independent of adults; the desired set of behaviors? Could more than one choice be correct if the answer is based only on the information presented in the quotation from Sarason?

MEANINGFUL LEARNING

Textbooks, reference works, sound films, and other instructional materials are used extensively in schools to present information. When students study the materials, they try to relate the information in them to what they already know. Ausubel (1963), a cognitive psychologist who infers mental processes and structures freely, called this *meaningful reception learning* and outlined a related theory of reception learning. Later, the theory was extended to include meaningful reception learning and meaningful discovery learning (Ausubel & Robinson, 1969). This section, which relies primarily on the latter source, is intended to clarify this theory.

Types of Learning

Two dimensions of learning processes are fundamental in this theory. One dimension relates to the two ways by which knowledge to be learned is made available to the learner. These two ways are *reception learning* and *discovery learning*. The second dimension relates to the two ways by which the learner may incorporate new information into his existing cognitive structure. These two ways are described as *meaningful* and *rote*. (The cognitive structure is the organized sets of facts, concepts, and generalizations that one has already learned and remembers.) It is assumed that the two dimensions are relatively independent. Therefore, four basic kinds of learning are proposed: meaningful reception, rote reception, meaningful discovery, and rote discovery.

In reception learning, the entire content of what is to be learned is given in its final form in the expository material. For example, in the preceding paragraph the two dimensions and the four types of learning formulated by Ausubel and Robinson are stated. No discovery process is required by the reader to identify these two dimensions and four types.

In discovery learning, not all of what is to be learned is presented in final form; some must be identified by the learner. That is, the learner gets some information independently. This information is then integrated into the existing cognitive structure and reorganized or transformed to produce a new or modified, cognitive structure. For example, according to the theory, if the reader is to form a concept of discovery learning without any further information, he must proceed independently.

Reception and discovery refer to the first stage of learning, in which information to be learned actually becomes available to the learner. In the second stage, the learner acts *on* the information in an attempt to remember it so that it will be available thereafter. If the learner attempts to retain the new information by relating it to what he already knows, meaningful learning occurs. If the learner attempts merely to memorize the new information, rote learning occurs. For example, memorizing the information presented so far about meaningful learning is rote, whereas relating it to what you already know is meaningful by definition.

Conditions for the four kinds of learning may now be stated. *Meaningful reception learning*: new, logically organized material is presented in final form and the learner relates it to his existing knowledge. *Rote reception learning*: material of any kind is presented in final form and is memorized. *Meaningful discovery learning*: the learner arrives at the solution to a problem or other outcome independently and relates it to his existing knowledge. *Rote discovery learning*: the solution is arrived at independently but is committed to memory.

The main thrust of the theory concentrates on meaningful reception learning, but some attention is given to meaningful discovery learning. The rest of this discussion, therefore, is directed toward clarifying these processes.

Internal Processes and Structures

Ausubel and Robinson view an individual's cognitive structure as pyramidal, with the most general theories or concepts forming the apex, the greater number of less general subconcepts forming the middle level, and the large amount of specific information forming the base. There can be many levels, depending on the number of phenomena in a specific superordinate-subordinate (general to specific) classification. For example, *learning, meaningful learning*, and *meaningful reception learning* form a superordinate-subordinate continuum (each successive concept is less inclusive than the preceding one).

As one acquires knowledge in several subject-matter fields, he develops a cognitive structure related to each. The principal way to get new information into the cognitive structure is to assimilate it as part of the existing structure in a process called *subsumption*. Subsumption is involved in relating a new idea to an existing one and at the same time modifying both, that is, giving meaning to both. There are two kinds of subsumption. When the new idea is a special case that supports or illustrates an existing idea, the process whereby the two are related and the learning occurs is called *derivative subsumption*. Thus, information presented in examples is related to existing concepts through derivative subsumption. When the new idea involves some transformation of an existing idea, the process whereby the two are related is called *correlative subsumption*. For example, an individual has already established a general concept of learning and encounters information related to meaningful learning; his initial concept of learning is extended and modified through correlative subsumption.

Subsumption does not account for the learning of superordinate concepts (such as learning) or the learning of new information for which a cognitive structure has not yet been developed. The theory of meaningful learning by subsumption admits that this is true, but does not attempt to explain how superordinate concepts and unrelated information *do* become incorporated in the cognitive structure initially.

Subsumption of new information is said to give it stability or resistance to forgetting. When first encountered, a new idea is anchored through subsumption to a superordinate concept. This provides the mechanism for remembering. For example, if the concept of learning was already established in the cognitive structure, the new information about meaningful learning became anchored to it, thus providing the basis for retention. As long as the characteristics of meaningful learning remain clearly distinct, or dissociable, from the characteristics of learning, they can be recalled. With the passage of time, the two concepts become less distinct if they are not used; that is, the characteristics of meaningful learning, including both reception and discovery, may again become subsumed in the general concept of learning and cannot be remembered as entities. According to the theory, the individual can recall for some time what he has learned but is not using; later he can only recognize it from among alternatives, but he cannot recall it; and still later he neither recalls nor recognizes it, though he can relearn it in less time than originally.

Variables in Meaningful Learning

Ausubel and Robinson (1969) outline two main sets of variables in meaningful learning of subject matter, *cognitive-structure variables* and *affective-social variables*. Under each of these categories more specific variables are indicated. The cognitive-structure variables and the treatment of practice are somewhat unique to this theory and are discussed below.

The cognitive structure of an individual is, as noted, his internalized, organized sets of facts, concepts, and generalizations. The existing cognitive structure purportedly provides the basis for the initial relatability and subsequent anchorage of new information. Therefore, the cognitive structure of relevant subsuming concepts for any new material is one important cognitive-structure variable. In other words, how well new material is learned depends on what is already known.

Two additional cognitive-structure variables are discriminability and the stability and clarity of the existing cognitive structure. The more the concepts and other content in the new material can be discriminated from those in the existing cognitive structure, the more likely to occur, presumably, are both efficient initial learning and retention. The hypothesis here is that new concepts, clearly discriminable from those already learned, are readily related or subsumed initially and also remain as distinct entities for an extended period of time. Stability and clarity of concepts and other content in the existing cognitive structure are defined in the theory only in a negative way—unstable and ambiguous concepts are undesirable. It does seem probable, however, that the more resistant to change (stable) and the more sharply delineated (clear) the existing structure, the more likely are both efficient initial learning and retention.

This is a good place to describe a valuable practical application of one of the important cognitive-structure variables. As noted, initial learning and subsequent retention of new material are hindered when relevant or appropriate subsuming concepts (subsumers) are not present. It follows that it would be logical, in teaching, to *provide* appropriate subsumers. A way to do this has indeed been worked out: appropriate subsumers, which in this context are called *advance organizers*, are carefully prepared; they are then introduced before the learner encounters new material. These advance organizers are not merely topical outlines of the new material. They are short expository passages that provide organizing elements for the new material; for instance, they may summarize superordinate concepts that are relevant to the new material or they may point out how previously learned related concepts are different from or similar to the new ideas to be presented. Advance organizers are discussed in more detail later in this section.

Practice in meaningful learning involves repeated presentations of the same learning material. Studying a specific paragraph or section of this chapter a second and a third time illustrates practice. The effect of practice is to increase the stability and clarity of the new material. *Distributed practice* purportedly facilitates retention of large amounts of potentially meaningful material. *Massed practice* appears to be more effective for the immediate retention of lesser amounts, particularly if the material can be mastered initially in one study session. To give an example that is quite relevant: This is a long chapter; therefore, most students will profit more from distributed study of it rather than from trying to master the content and to find applications in one study session.

Motivation and Meaningful Learning

Achievement motivation consists of three components, according to the theory. One component, *cognitive drive*, is associated with such internal states as the need to know, understand, and solve a problem. A cognitive drive arises in a reciprocal interaction process between the individual and the task. The individual becomes aware of the requirements of the task and attempts to master them. Until the task is partially or totally mastered, the drive state continues. Completing the task reduces the drive; no reinforcement or external incentive is required.

The second component of achievement motivation is *ego enhancement*. Ego enhancement is concerned with achievement as a source of primary or earned status. "Primary" here refers to what the individual ascribes to himself, whereas "derived" status refers to what others ascribe to him. The learner persists at a task, not to acquire knowledge or competence for its own sake, but to secure a feeling of status and prestige, which, in turn, generates feelings of adequacy and self-esteem. Fear of academic failure and the associated loss of prestige and status by the individual's own self-evaluation, rather than fear of the loss of approval of others, is thus an important element of the ego enhancement drive. Nevertheless, confirmation of status from sources external to the individual and task is suggested as necessary to reduce the drive or to satisfy the underlying need.

The third component of achievement motivation is the *need for affiliation*. This one, which is difficult to differentiate from ego enhancement, involves mastering school learning tasks in order to secure the approval of peers or superordinates from whom the individual obtains his derived status. The individual feels better toward himself when others show their approval of him, and he therefore does school tasks to secure this approval. In other words, in this case, the desire for approval is the primary factor.

Ego enhancement, in this theory, is thought to be the strongest component during the school years, in spite of the fact that the cognitive drive potentially is the strongest. This potential importance, however, is offset by extrinsic considerations. That is, the desires for self-esteem, anxiety

reduction, and career advancement become progressively more significant to individuals as they approach maturity. The progressive increase
is thought to be a result of our utilitarian, competitive, achievement-oriented culture.

Application to School Learning

Ausubel's theory gives comparatively little attention to discovery
learning. Therefore, it suggests few applications to younger children who
do not yet read well; such children probably acquire most of their basic
concepts more by discovery learning than by reception learning. Also, the
theory does not take into account the learning of .motor skills and outcomes in the affective domain.

Accordingly, Ausubel's theory primarily applies to older students who
can read reasonably well and who already have a fund of basic concepts
in a subject matter field—students who undoubtedly learn much organized information through meaningful reception learning. This is because
the theory primarily emphasizes the initial acquisition, retention, and
transfer of verbal and other symbolic material that is presented in final
form in textbooks and by other means; it also emphasizes the variables
related to this kind of learning.

As might be expected, therefore, attempts to validate various principles have been carried out frequently in university laboratories or classes
and only occasionally in school settings. Advance organizers have been
used in many of these studies in order to ascertain the effects of independent variables incorporated in them. Advance organizers that facilitate
learning can be written. For example, organizers designed to present
superordinate concepts were used successfully in these two cases: Unfamiliar scientific information presented to college students in a 2500-word
description of the metallurgical properties of steel was more easily
learned initially and retained better for 48 hours by the students when
introduced with a 500-word advance organizer (Ausubel, 1960). An advance organizer produced the same result with college students confronted by unfamiliar material dealing with endocrinology (Ausubel &
Fitzgerald, 1962). In another experiment, another type of organizer was
used: Expository material that discriminated between concepts of Christianity (already in the cognitive structure) and those of Buddhism (new
material) facilitated initial learning and later retention of the new material incorporated in a discussion of Buddhism (Ausubel & Fitzgerald, 1961).
This organizer is quoted on page 383.

The effects of advance organizers on transfer of learning have been
studied only in recent years. For example, Grotelueschen & Sjogren (1968)
found that both the type of material in an organizer and the sequence
(ordered or random) of the new material in it were related to initial learning and transfer. Introductory material containing principles facilitated
initial learning and transfer more than did either familiar or unfamiliar
concepts that did not include principles. Similarly, completely sequenced
new material, which apparently was easier to memorize, produced some-

what better initial learning but less transfer than did material that was only partially sequenced and could not be memorized.

This continuing research and development on advance organizers will probably have its greatest impact on school learning through its effect on the designing of curriculum materials, including textbooks.

Advance organizers are difficult to write, and it cannot be assumed that any one organizer will produce higher performance. Here is part of one that preceded 22 lessons of programed material designed to teach concepts of transformational and generative grammar.

> In order to describe something, we usually look at the whole thing and then look at the parts. Knowing the parts and how they fit together helps us in our description. If we are dealing with a number of things, we frequently put them into groups in order to make our description clearer and more organized. During the next two weeks, you will be using this approach in learning to describe English sentences.
>
> One of the first things you will learn is that all sentences can be described in terms of certain basic sentence patterns. There are nine basic sentence patterns in the English language. These nine patterns might be compared to the primary colors that an artist uses. All hues can be obtained from mixtures of red, blue, and yellow, which are the three primary colors. Similarly, every sentence you read can be described as taking the form of one of the nine basic sentence patterns, or as a combination or rearrangement of the nine basic sentence patterns. . . .
>
> In all nine basic sentences, the subject group is always a noun phrase. In other sentences, which are rearrangements or combinations of basic sentences, the subject group may or may not be a noun phrase; in basic sentences it is always a noun phrase.
>
> As you learn about noun phrases, you will discover that the last word in all noun phrases is a noun. What is a noun? Rather than depending on the traditional definition of noun as the "name of a person, place, or thing," you will learn to use the noun test-sentence. If a word fits in the noun test-sentence, it can be used as a noun. In a later lesson, you will be given other ways which will help you identify nouns.
>
> These pages you have just read are meant to give you a brief overview of today's lesson. Now that you have an idea of what you will be learning, you are ready to begin Lesson 1. (Blount, Klausmeier, Johnson, Fredrick, & Ramsay, 1967, p. 38)

A second area of related research does not use advance organizers; it is directly concerned with discovery and reception learning. Guthrie (1967) reported that a discovery method facilitated transfer, but not retention, in college-age students; expository instruction, on the other hand, resulted in better retention but actually impeded transfer. Worthen (1968) reported a study involving 432 children in fifth and sixth grades. The children were taught elementary mathematics through text-like sequenced programs introduced by classroom teachers instructed in both discovery and expository teaching procedures. Each of eight teachers taught a *discovery* and an *expository* class (careful observations showed that the two experimental teaching procedures were carried out reliably). The expository procedure yielded slightly higher initial learning; the discovery procedure showed slightly higher retention and transfer. Perhaps as important as the results is the fact that the teachers could learn to use two different instruction methods.

A third line of investigation deals with the distinction between rote and meaningful learning as independent types. King and Russell conducted a study dealing with this matter and concluded:

> It would seem that Ausubel's contention that S's [subjects] may learn meaningful material on a rote basis is, in general, correct. It should be noted, however, that there can be no sharp or clear-cut distinction between rote and meaningful learning, nor is it apparently easy to manipulate these learning processes by instruction. (King & Russell, 1966, p. 482)

2.13. In studying this chapter, you should have achieved certain results, including these three: (a) You should have learned bits of factual information, such as the association of Staats with principles of conditioning and the association of Ausubel with meaningful learning. (b) You should have learned or relearned concepts represented in words, such as conditioning and meaningful learning. (c) You should have applied the concepts to your own learning or to your role as a teacher. According to Ausubel's theory, categorize each of the three into one of the four types of learning — meaningful discovery, meaningful reception, rote discovery, rote reception. Aside from the theory, do you think that some discovery, or some reception, is involved in all three?

2.14. Teacher A is responsible for helping students to improve their composition skills. Teacher B is responsible for helping students to acquire prosocial behaviors, such as interacting on a friendly basis with children of a different race. Teacher C is responsible for helping students to understand and interpret the U.S. Constitution and other historical documents. If only limited time is available, which of the three teachers would you advise to study meaningful learning in greatest depth? observational learning? operant conditioning? Suppose the same teacher is responsible for all three tasks. Which of the three theories might be omitted first?

2.15. Three drives are associated with the concept of achievement motivation in Ausubel's theory: cognitive, ego enhancement, and need for affiliation. These drives, according to the theory, are experienced by all students. Under what conditions that a teacher might arrange would each of these drives become the strongest?

INFORMATIONAL THEORY

Guilford (1968) has developed an informational theory of learning that is useful in examining both what is learned and the cognitive operations involved in learning. In the course of developing his theory he has outlined a structure of intellect that has received much attention and much study, not only in this country but throughout the world. Students in many different fields find that Guilford's theories help them to analyze what they have learned and the operations involved. A brief outline of his ideas about learning follows.

Guilford defines *information* as "that which the organism discriminates." What the organism discriminates is described along two dimensions — *content* and *products*. Everything learned, according to Guilford, is a combination of a kind of content and a kind of product. In the third dimension, the individual acts on these combinations of content and product in one of five thinking *operations*. The structure of intellect is composed of these three dimensions. (See Fig. 3.2 for a diagram of the structure.)

Contents, Products, and Operations

There are four types of content that human beings discriminate: (1) *Figural content* is information in concrete form as experienced directly through seeing, touching, hearing, and so forth. The information does not represent anything but itself. Think of walking on campus. Everything you see, hear, feel, smell, and so on that is not embodied in signs or words is figural content. (2) *Symbolic content* is information in the form of signs that have no significance in and of themselves. Such information includes the letters of the alphabet, numerals, musical notations, and any other elements used in coding systems. Observe these letters: x, b, u, f, s; and these numerals: 3, 8, 4, 0. You are observing symbolic content. (3) *Semantic content* is information in the form of meanings attached to words and is thus most important in verbal communication and thinking. Reread and think about the last sentence. You are dealing with semantic content. (4) *Behavioral content* is essentially nonverbal information inherent in interactions with human beings, where awareness of the attitudes, moods, desires, intentions, perceptions, and so on of others and of oneself is important. The identification of abilities involving this type of content has not proceeded to an appreciable degree up to the present, and the precise nature of the abilities is problematic.

In Guilford's system, there are six products by which information in each of the four content areas may be classified: (1) *Units* are entities, each a relatively segregated or circumscribed item of information. For example, "2" is a symbolic unit, and "baseball" is a semantic unit. (2) *Classes* are sets of items of information grouped because of their common properties. Some concepts embody classes; for example, "birds" and "mammals" embody a large number of units, classified according to their common properties. (3) *Relations* involve recognized connections or associations between units of information. For example, "Meat and bread make a sandwich and the number set represented by 4 is larger than that represented by 2." We are expressing relations between semantic units in the first part of the sentence and between symbolic units in the second part. (4) *Systems* is the most inclusive category of the four — units, classes, relations, systems; it implies organized aggregates of information. The laws concerning the arabic numbers comprise a symbolic system. The laws or rules concerning the transmission of information in sentences comprise a semantic system. Now consider these examples of units, classes, relations, and systems in symbolic content: "3" and "8" are units; uneven numbers and even numbers are classes; "3 is to 6 as 5 is to 10" indicates a relationship; the associative and commutative laws are parts of a system.

The other two of the six products do not continue the hierarchy from units through systems: (5) *Transformations* involve making changes of various kinds in existing or known information or in usages of this information. For example, changing 65 in base 10 to 145 in base 6 involves transformation. Changing "the boy was hit by the man" to "the man hit the boy" also requires transformation. Writing a story requires transformation of the given information, the plot, into something else. (6) *Implications* take the form of predictions, statements of expectancy, known or suspected antecedents of events, consequences of certain actions, and other extrapolations of the given information. For example, identifying questions, the answers to which should help reach a decision in a conflict situation, involves implications from known information. Adding the detailed operations needed to make a briefly outlined plan succeed also illustrates implications with semantic content.

We are now ready to consider the five parts of the last set of the triad — operations. (1) *Cognition* refers to immediate discovery, awareness, rediscovery, or recognition of information that has been discriminated; synonyms for cognition are comprehension and understanding. If one could not distinguish figural, symbolic, semantic, or behavioral information, one could not cognize it. (2) *Memory* means the retention or storage of information in the same form in which it was initially learned and also the capacity for recalling or reproducing it. Tests of memory show whether or not an individual can recall or reproduce what he has learned; if he cannot, we assume that he no longer has the information in storage; he has forgotten it. (3) *Divergent production* refers to the generation of new information from given information, where the emphasis is on variety and quantity of output. Divergent thinking leads in different directions to responses that cannot be scored as correct or incorrect. For example, the task of giving clever titles to a story plot leads to responses that cannot be scored as right or wrong. The solutions or ideas produced through divergent thinking are novel to the producer, though not necessarily to others. (4) *Convergent production* implies the generation of new information from given information, where the emphasis is on achieving correct or conventionally accepted best outcomes. The given information determines the response that is accepted as correct. For example, "6 ÷ 4 = ?" requires convergent thinking. (5) *Evaluation* means reaching decisions or making judgments concerning the goodness, correctness, suitability, adequacy, or desirability of information in terms of criteria. The criteria might be consistency and goal satisfactions.

Principles in Informational Theory

Guilford has not worked out the details of his informational theory of learning; nor has he developed a systematic list of principles of learning.

His two main contributions are the formulation of the structure of intellect just described and the union of its three attributes—contents, products, and operations—into abilities; these abilities will be discussed more fully in the next chapter.

The statements that follow attempt to make explicit some of Guilford's main ideas about learning, all of which may be incorporated readily into the sequence of purposeful learning outlined earlier in this chapter.

1. The human being learns information. The information that he processes, stores, recalls, and uses is of many types; it is not merely one category, that is, associations of things.

2. Five different operations are involved in learning, and these operations vary with the type of information. For example, cognizing units and classes of figural content, as in the visual arts, is different from cognizing units and classes of semantic content, as in social studies or science.

3. Human behavior is self-corrective, or potentially so. Feedback is essential for self-corrective behavior. The ability of the individual to evaluate information makes self-feedback and self-corrective behavior possible. For example, evaluation of figural information makes it possible to secure the continuous feedback necessary to drive a car. Evaluation of combinations of products and contents makes possible self-corrective behaviors in the cognitive domain. This concept of evaluation covers the ideas of other theorists represented by such terms as "confirmation" and "self-reinforcement."

4. The observable actions of an individual are based on his cognizing, thinking productively about, and evaluating information. Engaging or not engaging in a particular action in a certain situation depends on the individual's cognition of the situation and whether or not he evaluates the action as suitable in the particular situation. In other words, the presence of a stimulus does not automatically elicit a response in human beings, nor is there an automatic chaining of stimulus → response sequences so that when the first stimulus is encountered the chain is elicited and run off automatically.

5. Remembering involves discovering, during initial acquisition, relations among items to be learned. For example, learning the letters of the alphabet involves a relationship of sequence. Neither mere repetition of responses nor repetition of responses when each is followed by a reward gives a satisfactory account of how human beings remember the vast amount of information they do remember.

6. Both the type of information that the individual can process and the nature of the operations change with development. The exact nature of these changes is not yet clear in Guilford's work. However, developmental psychologists indicate that with increasing age children handle systems, implications, and transformations with greater competence and that their productive thinking with symbolic and semantic content increases rapidly.

7. Individuals of the same age vary widely in the types of information they can deal with effectively and also in the speed with which they perform various operations. For example, some 10-year-olds deal with semantic content well and others do not; the latter may, however, deal with

figural content well. Similarly, some 10-year-olds are able to evaluate semantic content much more efficiently than others. Guilford's main contribution here is to specify many more abilities in which individuals might excel than most psychologists and school people had previously considered possible.

2.16. A 6-year-old is learning to write cursively. A college student is learning information from this book and is trying to apply it to his role as a learner or teacher. Which of the five operations are involved in achieving each goal? What kind of content is primarily involved in each case? What products are involved in each case?

2.17. Drawing from only one of the five theoretical approaches to learning outlined in this chapter or from any combination of them, identify a set of principles that you think could be most appropriately applied if you were trying to (a) teach a young child to accept Protestant or some other beliefs; (b) teach a 6-year-old to write cursively; (c) teach a 12-year-old to learn a concept such as "equation," "freedom," or "heredity"; (d) teach a prospective teacher to learn and apply principles of learning; (e) teach a prospective teacher to write a short sequence of programed instructional material for students.

SUMMARY

The main purposes of a learning theory are to explain learning operations and, to a lesser extent, to predict and control the course of learning. Earlier theories of learning advanced a few principles that purported to explain all operations and all outcomes of learning in all living organisms. The modern theories described in this book (except that of Staats) are less ambitious.

The theory of purposeful learning attempts to identify and describe conditions within the learner and the school setting that facilitate learning. The sequence of purposeful learning begins with attending to the situation and setting a goal; it ends with goal attainment and the use of acquired knowledge and abilities in other situations. The teacher's role is parallel to that of the student; it is viewed as facilitative and helping rather than as prescriptive and shaping.

Conditioning theory as set forth by Staats includes principles of classical and operant conditioning. These principles have been refined in animal laboratories and are now being extended to complex human behavior. The applicability of these principles to high-level mental processes, such as convergent and divergent thinking, is less well established than their applicability to lower-level processes, such as associating simple stimulus-response events. There are other principles that seem to be more applicable to human learning, such as that involved when a young child learns to speak the language of his parents. For example, Bandura and Walters offer observing and imitating as a better explanation for this type of learning.

Meaningful reception learning, which is based on the subsumption theory, is proposed by Ausubel as an explanation of the learning of most material that is presented to students in a final form in textbooks and by other means. Ausubel and Robinson have identified three other types of learning: meaningful discovery, rote reception, and rote discovery. The primary emphasis of the theory is on meaningful reception learning, which purportedly is the primary type engaged in by students who can read well and who have already formed basic concepts in the subject matter being studied.

Guilford is one of many information theorists. He is more inclined toward cognitive than toward association principles. One of his major contributions to learning theory is the description of five intellectual operations—cognition, memory, divergent production, convergent production, and evaluation. Of special interest is the emphasis he gives to the individual's seeking of information and to the continuous evaluating of the results of his mental operations and physical activities. Guilford views human beings as seeking, self-regulating organisms.

SUGGESTIONS FOR FURTHER READING

GAGNÉ, R. M. Learning hierarchies. In Ripple, R. E., ed., *Readings in learning and human abilities*. New York: Harper & Row, 2nd ed., 1971.

The transfer of specific intellectual abilities to consecutive learning tasks is discussed.

GLEASON, G. T., ed. *The theory and nature of independent learning*. Scranton, Pa.: International Textbook Company, 1967.

This 101-page book contains six essays, each of which makes an important contribution to clarifying the nature of independent learning.

GUILFORD, J. P. An emerging view in learning theory. In Guilford, J. P., *Intelligence, creativity, and their educational implications*. San Diego: Knapp, 1968, pp. 50-66.

This short chapter outlines Guilford's viewpoints about learning, including his criticisms of conditioning principles.

HARRIS, F. L., WOLF, M. M., & BAER, D. M. Effects of adult social reinforcement on child behavior. In Parke, R. D., ed., *Readings in social development*. New York: Holt, Rinehart and Winston, 1969, pp. 124-134.

The effects of an adult's nonattention and attention on the extinction of certain undesired behaviors in children and the strengthening of other desired behaviors were studied. Other articles in this book of readings deal with social reinforcement, imitation, dependency, independence and achievement, aggression, sex-role development, and moral development.

SHULMAN, L. S., & KEISLAR, E. R., eds. *Learning by discovery: A critical appraisal*. Chicago: Rand McNally, 1966.

The selections in this book present varying definitions of learning by discovery and also varying amounts of enthusiasm for it.

Siegel, L., ed. *Instruction: Some contemporary viewpoints*. San Francisco: Chandler, 1967.

In this book of 11 readings, written primarily for scholars, two of special interest to this chapter are A. D. Woodruff, "Cognitive Models of Learning and Instruction," pages 55-98; and R. M. Gagné, "Instruction and Conditions of Learning," pages 291-313. Both Woodruff and Gagné reject simplistic S-R views about learning.

Suppes, P. Modern learning theory and the elementary-school curriculum. In Ripple, R. E., ed., *Readings in learning and human abilities*. New York: Harper & Row, 2nd ed., 1971.

Applications of modern learning theory to children's instruction are discussed.

Chapter 3 Human Abilities

Identification and Organization of Abilities

abilities as mediators
abilities vs. skills
structure of abilities: general, group, specific
factor analysis in the identification of abilities

Cognitive Abilities

structure of intellect (SI)
   five operations of SI
   four contents of SI
   six products of SI
abilities of high school students
   general, group, specific
   stability and gains
Bloom's taxonomy of abilities

Psychomotor Abilities

abilities and perceptual motor skills
abilities and physical fitness
abilities and educational achievement

Affective Operations and Characteristics

receiving
responding
valuing
organizing values
characterizing value constellations

Our knowledge of human abilities has been accelerating rapidly in recent decades, and it is now substantial. Psychological scientists are systematically identifying and sorting abilities in their laboratories, and some large-scale studies in school settings have been completed. Equally important, excellent teachers and other educational workers are concentrating their efforts on developing students' abilities, rather than striving for mastery of content, particularly of factual information. In this chapter we first discuss how psychological scientists identify human abilities. The next sections of the chapter deal with cognitive abilities, psychomotor abilities, and affective characteristics.

IDENTIFICATION AND ORGANIZATION OF ABILITIES

The identification of abilities by scientific methods is a complex process that appeals to many psychologists, though not to some practitioners (especially those who are not interested in rather specialized mathematics). Nevertheless, as is true in so many areas of educational psychology, the scientists and the practitioners in effect form a team. That is, the practitioner is often able to *use* knowledge about human abilities more effectively than can the scientist who prefers to conceptualize and do research rather than teach. The nurturing of human abilities is, after all, the main objective of education, and it takes many years to accomplish. Because it does take so long, a teacher may at times feel somewhat like a production worker in a factory who has difficulty in seeing how his effort is essential for developing an interplanetary space vehicle; so a teacher may not see how his work contributes to the eventual development of a mature human being. In the next pages, therefore, the identification methods are discussed in the context of human development.

Performances of a High School Senior

A nine-point profile that summarizes some accomplishments and characteristics of a high school senior follows. The senior is 17 years old; she has been attending two public schools of a Midwestern city for 13 years, starting with kindergarten; she has had private instrumental music lessons since age 7 but no other private instruction. Music is her primary interest as a senior, although it did not become so until her junior year. She is planning a college major in music. This is her profile:

1. Expresses ideas clearly in oral and written form; takes part in discussions, chairs meetings, and makes oral presentations to small and large groups with ease and effectiveness; writes descriptions, reviews, essays, and short stories dealing with a variety of topics of 3 to 100 pages in length.
2. Solves daily problems involving quantitative concepts and arith-

metic operations readily; interprets mathematical ideas in textbooks and other instructional materials with ease.

3. Interprets everyday phenomena involving concepts and principles drawn from biology and chemistry; is concerned about the conservation of natural and human resources.

4. Interprets and criticizes current social and political events by utilizing concepts and principles from history, geography, sociology, economics, and political science; is strongly against the Vietnam war; is active in a church-affiliated youth group that is actively concerned with social ills; was vice-president of her class in her sophomore year.

5. Converses in French fluently; reads French newspapers and literature with ease and independence.

6. Plays the French horn well, the piano and flute less well; is first chair in the senior high school band; plays in a church instrumental group and in a larger state youth orchestra; sings in the church choir.

7. Types at about 40 words per minute with relatively few errors.

8. Swims, skates, water skis, and snow skis with much enjoyment and considerable skill; drives a car safely and well.

9. Enjoys life and is very active, averaging about 15 hours per week in musical activities outside school and about 5 hours in other group activities; attacks interesting school work with vigor and does many hours of homework and nonschool library research in connection with long-term projects; makes only a minimum effort to complete "dull" or "boring" teacher-made assignments.

Many other seniors attending the same public high school have a similar pattern of education and accomplishment. Each has a unique profile reflecting his own interests, home, neighborhood, and school influences. Naturally, there are also many high school seniors today who are somewhat less interested in school work and who may not have achieved as much, but a substantial number do have at least one area of highly developed accomplishment and are also well educated in several others.

The accomplishments and characteristics just outlined are not stated in terms of abilities. Nevertheless, abilities that have been developing over a period of many years are presumed to underlie each accomplishment. Our present knowledge about these abilities that may make each accomplishment possible is not sufficient so that we can specify with complete accuracy the specific abilities that are involved in, for example, playing the French horn, speaking French, or living with self and other people happily. Our knowledge is sufficient, however, to enable us to hypothesize the abilities, using theoretical frameworks as outlined by Guilford and Fleishman, to be discussed later in this chapter.

Attributes of Abilities

An ability, or configuration of abilities, such as speaking French fluently, is a *mediator*, identified through correlation and experimental research, that accounts for consistencies among separate performances. Thus, the ability to speak French well underlies the many separate encounters and experiences one has with others who speak French. In this sense it mediates, or helps the individual to interpret, the ideas and actions of others and also helps him to take action based on what they say.

Fleishman and Bartlett (1969), in a comprehensive review of research on human abilities, identified five important attributes of abilities:

1. Abilities are a product of maturation and learning. Much practice and learning are required, for example, to speak French well or to comprehend the concepts and principles of biology. The stage of development of the individual limits what he can learn. Thus, abilities develop at different rates from birth through adolescence. For example, verbal comprehension develops much more rapidly than arithmetic reasoning in early childhood.

2. Abilities are enduring and relatively difficult to change in adults. For example, manual dexterity is quite stable from year to year; it is resistant both to improvement and deterioration in adulthood.

3. The present abilities of the individual affect the rate at which he learns new tasks. Thus, the student high in spatial ability and arithmetic reasoning achieves higher in physics than one low in both, motivation and other factors being equal. Equally important, the study of physics will probably contribute to the further development of both abilities.

4. One ability may transfer to the learning of a greater variety of specific tasks than another. Arithmetic computation, an ability, facilitates only the learning of new tasks involving computation, whereas spatial ability facilitates the learning of broad classes of tasks in mathematics, science, engineering, and other areas.

5. Abilities are more general and inclusive than skills. The term *skill* refers to the level of proficiency on a unitary task or a configuration of tasks. Diving, swimming, flying an airplane, playing basketball, writing cursively, and typing are skills acquired at varying levels of proficiency. In acquiring each of these skills, the individual learns a sequence of activities and executes them rapidly and precisely. Each skill, however, can be described in terms of more basic abilities. Finger dexterity and finger speed are two of the more basic psychomotor abilities that underlie typing and handwriting; cognitive abilities are also involved.

Identification Through Factor Analysis

Without delving into the details of correlation and factor analysis, we may consider the relationship between factors and abilities and how they are identified.

Factors are derived quite precisely as unnamed numerical values through a statistical procedure called *factor analysis*. A factor is not identical with an ability, but an ability may be inferred from a factor. Abilities are inferred from factors and also from experimental studies. Persons who systematically attempt to identify and sort abilities first develop hypotheses about presumed abilities or a model set of abilities. They identify or prepare tests to sample the performances of individuals. The tests are administered and scores are obtained. The sets of scores are correlated. Then a factor analysis is performed on the correlations. When this procedure is followed and when the factors that emerge and their composition and nature are verified through additional experiments and are also related to what other investigators have found, the factors derived are given names and are called abilities. (Some factor analysis studies are performed to identify factors themselves, not abilities. However, most of the abilities discussed in this chapter have been inferred from factors derived from performances, measured by actual paper-and-pencil tests.)

We can now describe the meaning of a factor, as derived from analysis of test scores. Sets of scores from an IQ test and a test of reading comprehension correlate .70. What is common to the two tests is found by squaring the correlation. The result, .49, indicates that 49 percent of what is measured by either test can be regarded as representing a *common factor*. If we were operating from a model or theoretical framework, we might give a name to this factor and treat it as an ability underlying the performances measured by the two tests. (What is not common to the two tests can be obtained by subtracting the percentage figure from 100. Thus, 51 percent, $100 - 49$, of each test involves something distinct from and independent of the other test.)

Table 3.1 is a matrix showing the correlations obtained among seven sets of scores on the same boys. The boys ranged in general intellectual ability, from 65 to 146 on the Wechsler Intelligence Scale for Children. They were enrolled in several elementary schools of two large cities, many in regular classes, a few in classes for educable mentally retarded, and a few in classes for academically talented. The homes and neighbor-

Table 3.1. Matrix of Correlations Among Seven Variables

Variable	Weight	Carpal age	IQ	Arithmetic achievement	Reading achievement	Language achievement
Height	.75	.61	.40	.48	.44	.43
Weight		.66	.16	.19	.25	.19
Carpal age			.15	.19	.21	.16
IQ				.94	.94	.94
Arithmetic achievement					.93	.97
Reading achievement						.96
Language achievement						1.00

Source: Adapted from Klausmeier, Feldhusen, and Check, 1959.

hoods varied markedly, from inner city to suburb. The average chronological age of the boys was 10 years 5 months, and all had been enrolled in school for the same number of years. The study was undertaken in part to test the validity of the concept of organismic age, that is, the idea that rate of physical and mental growth is determined by some underlying common growth factor (Klausmeier, Feldhusen, & Check, 1959).

Two things are immediately apparent in the correlation matrix. The six correlations (in boldface type) among the four sets of scores in the cognitive domain—IQ, arithmetic, reading, language—are very high, ranging from .93 to .97. We infer that a large portion of the performances measured by these four tests is accounted for by a common factor that might be called *scholastic development*. Second, the three correlations (in italics) among the three sets of scores in the psychomotor domain—height, weight, carpal age—are fairly high, .75, .61, and .66. A *physical development* factor might be inferred as accounting for consistencies in these areas of development.

In contrast, note the correlations relating to carpal age, a measure of the stage of skeletal development (the extent to which cartilage has changed to bone) which is the best indicator of the rate of total bodily development. The highest correlation between carpal age and any of the four cognitive measures is only .21. Squaring gives .04, showing that carpal age and any measure in the cognitive area have no more than 4 percent in common.

Table 3.2. Factor Loadings Resulting from Analysis of Seven Measures

Variable	Factor I	Factor II
Height	.85	.23
Weight	.87	.00
Carpal age	.78	.00
IQ	.21	.95
Arithmetic achievement	.30	.94
Reading achievement	.27	.96
Language achievement	.25	.97

This correlation matrix was submitted to factor analysis, and two factors were extracted with *loadings*, not correlations, as shown in Table 3.2. Factor I is inferred from the three high loadings in column 1 and is interpreted as a physical development factor. Factor II is interpreted as a scholastic development factor on the basis of the four high loadings in column 2. Neither is treated as an ability, because the study was not related to a systematic model and was not designed to identify abilities. However, these results, along with other substantial information, were interpreted as not supporting the idea of a general growth factor underlying both physical and mental development.

In a simplified, nontechnical definition, a factor loading is the correlation obtained between each test and the new obtained factor. In Table 3.2,

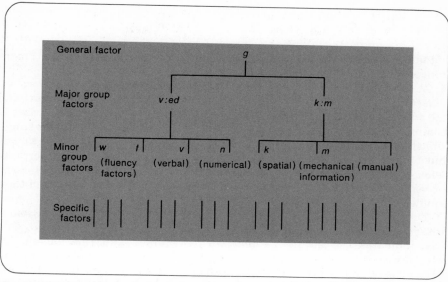

Fig. 3.1. Hierarchical structure of human abilities. (Adapted from Smith, 1964, p. 25. Used with permission of Robert R. Knapp, Publisher, San Diego, Calif., and the University of London Press Ltd.)

height correlated .23 and weight .00 with Factor II, whereas IQ and arithmetic correlated .95 and .94, respectively. Though oversimplified, we may think of Factor II as an average score of five measures—height and the four cognitive tests. The seven factor loadings are the correlations between each measure and the average of the five measures. The size of the factor loading indicates how much each test contributes to the common factor.

A Hierarchy of Abilities

After abilities are identified according to a systematic pattern, they may be related to one another. One set of relations is incorporated in the hierarchical structure treated next. Later in the chapter, a nonhierarchical structure of specific abilities is outlined.

Figure 3.1 outlines a hierarchical structure of factors or human abilities: a general factor, two major group factors, seven minor group factors, and an indeterminate number of possible but unidentified specific factors. Vernon (1950), a British psychologist, pioneered in the formulation of this model. Smith (1964) and Lovell (1965), both Englishmen, indicate that the general and group factors are widely accepted by British psychologists. Until recently, British psychologists have not given the specific factors serious consideration.

At this point we are considering the *structure*, not the nature, of the abilities outlined in Fig. 3.1. Furthermore, this discussion is not meant to

imply that the abilities as stated at any level in the hierarchy are themselves fully understood. There are unresolved differences of opinion about
how these and other abilities are manifested in the performance of individuals and about the effects of environment and heredity on their emergence.

According to Lovell (1965), the *g* ability, referred to also as *general in-*
tellectual ability or intelligence, is considered the basic ability underlying
all activities in the cognitive domain; it accounts for a part of what is
common to many specific tasks. It involves the ability to see relevant relationships between objects or ideas and to apply these relationships to new
but similar situations. As an example, in order to solve arithmetic problems, to conduct scientific experiments, or to communicate one's experiences in written form, relevant relationships must first be seen and then
applied to each specific situation.

There are two major group abilities. The *v:ed* ability is *verbal-numer-*
ical-educational and the *k:m* ability is *spatial-mechanical-manual*. The
v:ed indicates the ability to deal with meanings and relationships of
words in spoken and written form and to reason and compute with numbers. (The *ed* implies the ability to profit from a verbal type of education.)
The *k:m* subdivides into three components: spatial ability – the ability to
perceive and interpret form relationships; mechanical information –
knowing about things; manual ability – being able to use tools. The major
group abilities subdivide further if a sufficiently large number of more
specific tests is given and the analysis is continued.

We may now reexamine Table 3.2 to arrive at a better understanding
of general, group, and specific factors. The seven tests, as indicated before, yielded two group factors, but not a general or a specific factor. Consider the various factors that would have emerged had only certain combinations of tests been given. If only the IQ and the three achievement
tests had been administered, one general factor would have emerged.
(Note that the loadings for these tests are very high on Factor II, ranging
from .94 to .97.) If only the four cognitive measures and carpal age had
been obtained and analyzed, one group and one specific factor would have
been identified. (Carpal age loads .00 on Factor II.) Thus, factors that are
derived are directly related to the measurements that are secured and
correlated. For this reason, only a systematic approach to the identification of human abilities yields useful information about their nature and
organization.

An important and interesting practical aspect of the development of
the hierarchical model should be described here in a brief digression.
Smith (1964) concluded that too little attention had been given to spatial
ability and too much to verbal ability in the English educational system,
particularly in selecting some children to enter grammar schools, the only
route to the universities, and others to go to technical schools. He found
that spatial ability was the best single predictor of success in technical
courses for many classes of engineers and technicians and was also an
excellent predictor of success in advanced mathematics. On the other
hand, tests of verbal reasoning and English were not useful in predicting
success in these fields, but were useful in predicting success in linguistic
subjects such as English and modern languages, though spatial ability

was not. Despite this, the *g* ability is still relied on almost exclusively and the spatial ability scarcely at all in the selection and guidance of English children and youth. Smith's general conclusions, a few of which follow, question the uncritical acceptance of both the *g* and the *v:ed* in educational guidance:

> It is now apparent that far from being unimportant educationally, spatial abilities are necessary for the successful study of most practical and technical subjects and of the more advanced branches of mathematics, physics, and engineering. High spatial ability is essential in most scientific and technological occupations. For these studies and occupations verbal tests do not measure the appropriate abilities at all. . . .
>
> At the present time there is a developing educational crisis, because of the unsatisfied demand for personnel trained and qualified in all fields in which spatial ability is of fundamental importance. The technical revolution has put a premium on spatial ability at all levels, whether required for tile-laying or for topology. It is strange that in this situation there appears to be some reluctance on the part of educationists to accept the positive evidence for the value of spatial tests for educational guidance and selection; there is certainly tardiness in applying the findings in practice. . . .
>
> An explanation of the inertia of the educational system must be sought in the values which it inculcates; and it is likely that the resistance to spatial tests is at least due partly to a cultural tradition which values verbal abilities more highly than technical abilities. . . .
>
> The qualities which make for greatness in scientists and engineers are of a different kind; ability to think abstractly and analytically together with skill in visualizing spatial relations in two or three dimensions, and skill in manipulating objects with the hands. (Smith, 1964, pp. 298-300)

At present, a similar emphasis on verbal education probably holds in American schools, in spite of our different system. We require all students to go to high school on completing elementary school, regardless of their achievements, and we also encourage large numbers of high school graduates to go to college; that is, we do not have two official nationwide "tracks." Nevertheless, university students from our inner cities charge that the verbal emphasis is causing white racism to become institutionalized in our system of higher education, particularly in connection with admission into the graduate professional schools, such as those of engineering, law, medicine, and education. They base their charge on the fact that most of them are excluded from these schools by tests of verbal and numerical abilities and grade-point averages, all of which are geared to a verbal kind of education.

3.1. Name any ability that you have developed. Analyze it in relation to the five attributes of an ability to see whether the five attributes apply to it. (Do not be concerned if you have difficulty in discriminating between a skill and an ability. In some cases, the distinction can be made only through further research. Also, psychological scientists do not agree fully on the definitions of abilities and skills.)

3.2. How are an ability and a factor alike and different?

3.3a. Two tests correlate .60. What is the percentage of commonality between the two tests? What percentage is unique or distinct to each test?

3.3b. Under what conditions might what is common to the two tests be called an ability?

3.4. Suppose that a test of general intellectual ability is found to have a *loading* of .60 on a common factor associated with achievement in mathematics, science, English, foreign language, typing, and blueprint drawing. What percentage of the factor and the test is common?

3.5. A group ability test is found to load .80 on a mathematics-science factor. A different test is found to load .80 on an English-foreign language factor. Still another test is found to load .80 on a typing-blueprint factor. What percentages of the group factors and respective tests are common? Should these group tests be used in guiding high school students in connection with courses to pursue, or should the general intellectual ability test be used? Why? What practical conditions might lead a school to use only the test of general intellectual ability?

3.6. Which of the general, major-group, and minor-group abilities outlined in Fig. 3.1 do you think you have developed most fully? What educational experiences do you view as having contributed to them?

COGNITIVE ABILITIES

Three Methods of Identification

Cognitive abilities may be considered in terms of three methods used in identifying the abilities:

1. Abilities are identified systematically through programatic research carried out over a period of years by experimental and factor analysis methods, as described earlier. Here tests are specially developed to identify hypothesized abilities, and one set of studies leads consecutively to others until the system is completed. Many small-scale studies may be related to a larger model of this kind. For example, Guilford (1967) discussed his model of the structure of intellect briefly described in the last chapter. Within it he hypothesized 120 separate abilities, 24 of which are classified as divergent production. He and his associates developed at least two tests to measure each divergent production ability and then worked for about 15 years on identifying and describing these 24 abilities. At the same time, other researchers were using some of Guilford's tests, along with other tests, to investigate a smaller number of the abilities. Cuilford's structure of intellect is treated in detail in this section.

2. Abilities are identified through large-scale programatic research in school settings, using some tests not designed specifically to identify hypothesized abilities. In this case, the abilities are identified and classified (using factor analysis methods) with less assurance that a complete structure will emerge but with more assurance that a direct relationship with school tasks can be demonstrated. For example, a secondary purpose of Project Talent, to be described later, was to identify abilities related to the many achievements of high school students.

3. Abilities related to the various subject fields are identified by educators without engaging in research. Here individuals or groups survey the literature and formulate their models or hypotheses. Also, teachers identify students with the ability to read, the ability to spell, the ability to write lucid prose, and so on. An example of this informal approach is also given later.

The Structure of Intellect (SI)

Guilford believes that a concept of general intellectual ability is no longer tenable. His model (1967) is a foremost illustration of the systematic identification of human abilities and also of a structure of *specific* abilities. Figure 3.2. diagrams 120 possible human abilities in the cognitive domain, most of which have been identified (Guilford & Hoepfner, 1966; Hoepfner, Guilford, & Bradley, 1968; Hoffman, Guilford, Hoepfner, & Doherty, 1968). Five operations, four types of content, and six products comprise the basic components; therefore, there are $5 \times 4 \times 6 = 120$ projected abilities. As noted in Chapter 2, Guilford (1966) defines an ability as a union of an operation, a content, and a product. In summary form, the operations, contents, and products appear on pages 82 and 83.

Fig. 3.2. Model of the structure of intellect. (Adapted from Guilford & Hoepfner, 1966, p. 3)

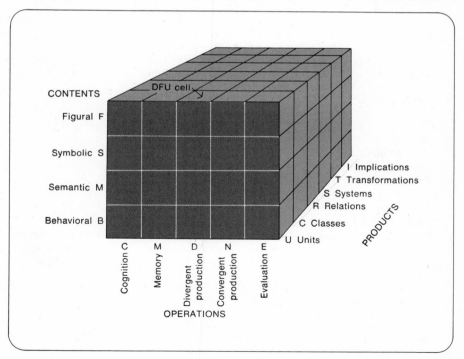

DEFINITIONS OF CATEGORIES IN THE STRUCTURE OF INTELLECT

Operations

Major kinds of intellectual activities or processes; things that the organism does with the raw materials of information, information being defined as "that which the organism discriminates."

C — *Cognition.* Immediate discovery, awareness, rediscovery, or recognition of information in various forms; comprehension or understanding.

M — *Memory.* Retention or storage, with some degree of availability, of information in the same form it was committed to storage and in response to the same cues in connection with which it was learned.

D — *Divergent Production.* Generation of information from given information, where the emphasis is upon variety and quantity of output from the same source. Likely to involve what has been called transfer. This operation is most clearly involved in aptitudes of creative potential.

N — *Convergent Production.* Generation of information from given information, where the emphasis is upon achieving unique or conventionally accepted best outcomes. It is likely the given (cue) information fully determines the response.

E — *Evaluation.* Reaching decisions or making judgments concerning criterion satisfaction (correctness, suitability, adequacy, desirability, etc.) of information.

Contents

Broad classes or types of information discriminable by the organism.

F — *Figural.* Information in concrete form, as perceived or as recalled possibly in the form of images. The term "figural" minimally implies figure-ground perceptual organization. Visual spatial information is figural. Different sense modalities may be involved, e.g., visual kinesthetic.

S — *Symbolic.* Information in the form of denotative signs, having no significance in and of themselves, such as letters, numbers, musical notations, codes, and words, when meanings and form are not considered.

M — *Semantic.* Information in the form of meanings to which words commonly become attached, hence most notable in verbal thinking and in verbal communication but not identical with words. Meaningful pictures also often convey semantic information.

B — *Behavioral.* Information, essentially nonverbal, involved in human interactions where the attitudes, needs, desires, moods, intentions, perceptions, thoughts, etc., of other people and of ourselves are involved.

Products

Forms that information takes in the organism's processing of it.

U — *Units.* Relatively segregated or circumscribed items of information having "thing" character. May be close to Gestalt psychology's "figure on a ground."

C — *Classes.* Conceptions underlying sets of items of information grouped by virtue of their common properties.

R — *Relations.* Connections between items of information based upon variables or points of contact that apply to them. Relational connections are more meaningful and definable than implications.

S — *Systems.* Organized or structured aggregates of items of information; complexes of interrelated or interacting parts.

T — *Transformations.* Changes of various kinds (redefinition, shifts, or modification) of existing information or in its function.

I —*Implications.* Extrapolations of information, in the form of expectancies, predictions, known or suspected antecedents, concomitants, or consequences. The connection between the given information and that extrapolated is more general and less definable than a relational connection. (Guilford & Hoepfner, 1966, p. 4)

Definitions and examples of the operations, contents, and products were given in Chapter 2. You may wish to review them. Table 3.3 lists certain specific tasks; the combination of operation, content, and product involved in each case; and the names of the abilities or factors. An example is given of each task that is thought to need clarifying.

Table 3.3. Illustrative Tasks, Operations, Contents, Products, and Abilities

Task	Operation	Content	Product	Ability
Finding correct synonym for word	Cognition	Semantic	Unit	Verbal comprehension
Selecting word in a set that does not belong to the class	Cognition	Semantic	Class	Conceptual classification
Selecting word to complete meaningful relationship	Cognition	Semantic	Relation	Semantic relations
Selecting solutions to problems with minimal arithmetic computation, maximum reasoning	Cognition	Semantic	System	General reasoning
Writing words containing a specified letter; e.g., *r*	Divergent production	Symbolic	Unit	Word fluency
Listing classes of uses for an object	Divergent production	Semantic	Class	Spontaneous semantic flexibility
Listing steps in appropriate order for completing a project, e.g., building a birdhouse	Convergent production	Semantic	System	Semantic ordering
Naming an object that could be made by combining two given objects; e.g., a coil spring and a beach ball to make a punching bag	Convergent production	Semantic	Transformation	Semantic redefinition
Indicating each digit in a row of 30 digits that is like the first one in the row	Evaluation	Symbolic	Unit	Symbolic identification
Judging whether symbolic conclusions are true or false based on given premises	Evaluation	Symbolic	Relation	Symbolic manipulation

Source: Based on Guilford & Hoepfner, 1966.

Three types of intelligence are associated by Guilford with the four types of content: *Concrete intelligence* pertains to abilities connected with figural content. Mechanics, operators of machines, artists, and musicians depend heavily on these abilities. *Abstract intelligence* pertains to abilities concerned with symbolic and semantic content. Learning to recognize words, to spell, and to operate with numbers involves abilities with symbolic content. Abilities with semantic content are required for understanding verbal concepts and ideas of all types. Present-day intelligence tests are heavily loaded with test items requiring the use of abstract abilities. *Social intelligence* pertains to behavioral content, understanding the behavior of others and oneself. Teachers, lawyers, social workers, politicians, and leaders are hypothesized to be high in social intelligence.

Substantial evidence is accumulating which indicates that specific abilities can be identified in children, youth, and adults. For example, six specific divergent-thinking abilities with semantic content that were discovered in ninth-graders and young adults (Gershon, Guilford, & Merrifield, 1963) were also identified in sixth-graders (Merrifield, Guilford, & Gershon, 1963). However, the chronological age at which the separate abilities become differentiated is not clear. For instance, abilities markedly different from those of the sixth-graders were found in children aged 4 to 6 (Meyers & Dingman, 1960); it seems likely that the semantic abilities are not yet clearly differentiated at ages 4 to 6. It is interesting to note that British psychologists find fewer abilities than American psychologists. This is in part because of differences in theoretical orientation and in part because of the statistical procedures used (Vernon, 1950).

The concept of abilities is most meaningful when considered in connection with outcomes of learning and broad subject-matter fields. In Fig. 3.3, the abilities connected with each type of content are related to outcomes and curriculum areas. For example, the ability to think productively with figural material is associated with performance in art and music and with certain aspects of the applied arts, such as home economics, agriculture, and industrial arts. As noted earlier, mathematicians and physicists also demonstrate high-level spatial abilities, which, in Guilford's system, involve figural content. An example of abilities involving symbolic and semantic content is productive thinking that leads to learning factual information, concepts, and problem-solving skills and to developing creativity in the English-language arts, social studies, science, mathematics, and other subject fields. Abilities with behavioral content are less clearly defined, but, as noted in Fig. 3.3, include understanding oneself and others and interacting in a group.

Divergent-Production Abilities

The most important contribution of the structure of intellect (SI) is a new way of thinking about the nature of intelligence. The fact that many relatively distinct abilities have been identified poses a direct challenge to the notion that all human beings can be placed from high to low on a single continuum of general intellectual ability and should be treated accordingly in educational and vocational settings. There are many intellectual

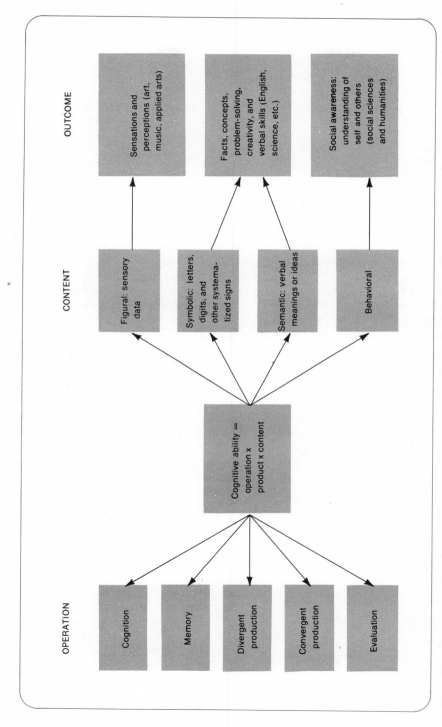

Fig. 3.3. Schematic arrangement of cognitive abilities and learning outcomes. (Based on Guilford, 1959, pp. 469–479)

Table 3.4. Matrix of the Divergent-Production Factors (D) Represented in the Structure of Intellect

Figural (F)	Symbolic (S)	Semantic (M)	
DFU	DSU	DMU	Units (U)
DFC	DSC	DMC	Classes (C)
DFR	DSR	DMR	Relations (R)
DFS	DSS	DMS	Systems (S)
DFT	DST	DMT	Transformations (T)
DFI	DSI	DMI	Implications (I)

Source: Adapted from Guilford, 1967, p. 139. Copyright 1967 by McGraw-Hill Book Company. Used with permission of McGraw-Hill Book Company.

abilities, and the same individual may be at quite different points on the various continua. Some students are much stronger in divergent- than in convergent-production abilities, and vice versa. In this connection, the identification of the divergent-production, or creative, abilities has already made some impact on educational policies and practices and should produce many more changes in the future.

Table 3.4 shows the 18 divergent-production abilities that have been identified or are projected for three of the contents and the six products (the divergent-production abilities related to behavioral content are not fully conceptualized or identified). Examples of the kinds of tests used to measure some of the divergent-production abilities follow (Guilford, 1967). Study them carefully with two purposes in mind. First, note that the items do not call for a single response to be scored as correct and, second, relate the content of the test items to kinds of assignments and activities that may be relevant for students as part of their regular instruction in schools.

Divergent production of figural units (DFU) is measured by a test called Sketches. The examinee is given a simple basic figure and is told to add just enough to it to make a recognizable object, as in Fig. 3.4. The number of sketches made is the score.

Fig. 3.4. DFU test item. Given a simple, familiar form, e.g., a circle, the examinee is to make as many real objects as he can with a minimum of addition of lines, as in the Sketches test. (Adapted from Guilford, 1967, p. 140. Copyright 1967 by McGraw-Hill Book Company. Used with permission of McGraw-Hill Book Company.)

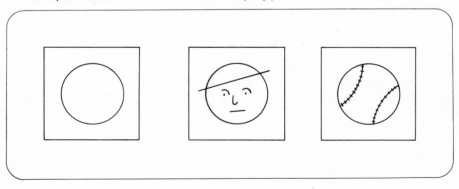

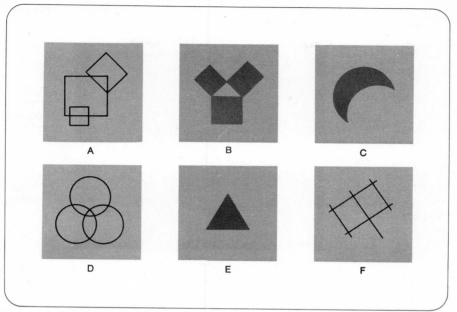

Fig. 3.5. DFC test item. Figural Similarities presents six figures each having a number of attributes. The examinee is to find as many classes, in sets of three figures each, as he can. Some classes are *BCE* (gray), *ABD* (three parts), *ABF* (straight lines), etc. (Adapted from Guilford, 1967, p. 144. Copyright 1967 by McGraw-Hill Book Company. Used with permission of McGraw-Hill Book Company.)

Divergent production of symbolic units (DSU), referred to also as word fluency, is measured by a variety of tests; for example, the examinee writes words with the first and last letters given (e.g., "r ____ m," "b ____ r") or lists words that rhyme with a specified word, e.g., "room." The meanings of the words are of no consequence; the number of words listed is the score.

Divergent production of semantic units (DMU) is also measured by several different experimental tests, the most effective type calling for the examinee to list things that call for two specifications, not one or three, such as "solid and soft" or "fluid and flammable," etc. In another kind of test, the examinee is not restricted in any way; he gives titles to a short story or lists possible uses of things, such as a common brick. The number of items given is the score.

Divergent production of figural classes (DFC) is measured by several tests, one of them called Alternate Letter Group. Here a group of letters such as "AHVTC" is given and the examinee is to form subgroups, each of which makes a class according to the figural properties of the letters. Illustrative responses are "AHT" (all having horizontal lines), "AHVT" (all straight lines), or "HVC" (open sides), etc. The Figural Similarities Test shown in Fig. 3.5 is excellent for adolescents but not for adults.

Divergent production of symbolic classes (DSC) is measured by different tests, one of which is called Name Grouping. A short list of names is given and the examinee is to classify and to reclassify them in different ways. A sample problem follows.

[**SAMPLE ANSWERS**]

1. Gertrude
2. Bill
3. Alex
4. Carrie
5. Belle
6. Don

1, 3, 4 (two syllables)
2, 4, 5 (double consonants)
1, 4, 5 (begins with consonant,
          ends with vowel)
etc.

Divergent production of semantic classes (DMC) is measured well by a number of tests, including Multiple Grouping. (Note that meanings are always involved in semantic content, but not in figural and symbolic content.) A sample item from this test is:

From the list of words at the left, make some small subclasses of objects.

[**SAMPLE ANSWERS**]

1. arrow
2. bee
3. crocodile
4. fish
5. kite
6. sailboat
7. sparrow

1, 2, 5, 7 (found in the air)
3, 4, 6 (found in the water)
2, 3, 4, 7 (animals)
3, 4, 5, 7 (have tails)
etc.

We have now presented six divergent-production test items, one each for figural, symbolic, and semantic *units* and one each for figural, symbolic, and semantic *classes*. Detailed information about other divergent operation × content × product abilities is given in Guilford (1967). We now give only a few more examples of divergent-production tests that deal with *systems, transformations*, and *implications*.

Divergent production of figural systems (DFS) is measured by the test, Making Objects. Figure 3.6 illustrates the kinds of items used in the test. Given two or more simple geometric forms, the examinee is to organize them to construct an object that is novel.

Divergent production of semantic systems (DMS) is measured by several tests, including Four-Word Combinations. In one form of this test, the first letter is specified; e.g., "w ____ c ____ e ____ n ____." Responses are of the type "We could exit now" or "Why can't elevators nod?"

Divergent production of figural transformations (DFT) is measured by a variety of match problems in which the given figures formed by the matches are transformed, or changed, in a specified way by the removal of some of the matches. This test calls for the subject to persist in trying something novel and also not to assume that the new figures should be of the same size. Flexibility for a change in direction is called for in the first instance and for relaxation of a restriction or revision of a rule in the second. Figure 3.7 is an illustrative test item.

Divergent production of semantic transformations (DMT) was for some time called "originality." As such, tests were designed to measure any of

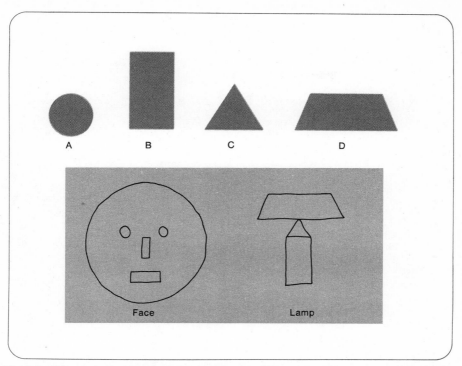

Fig. 3.6. DFS test item. Items as in the Making Objects test. The four simple figures at the top are to be combined in various ways to make named objects. Two examples of organized objects are shown. (Courtesy of the Sheridan Psychological Services, Inc.)

these three criteria: (1) ability to produce responses that are statistically rare in the population, (2) ability to produce remotely related responses, and (3) ability to produce clever responses. Judges are required to evaluate the responses produced according to one or more of the preceding criteria. Some success has been found for measuring remote associations with various items. In one type, two seemingly unrelated words are given and the response word must describe a similarity that they do have, e.g.:

nonsense-bed   (answer: bunk)
recline-deceive   (answer: lie)

In another type of test, the relationship is not confined to similarity, e.g.:

jewelry-bell   (answer: ring)
skin-conceal   (answer: hide)

The most commonly used test of cleverness presents a brief story and calls for the examinee to give titles. Nonclever titles are simply counted and the resulting score is taken as a measure of divergent production of semantic units, as noted earlier. Clever titles are counted and scored as divergent production of semantic transformation. A sample story and clever and nonclever titles follow.

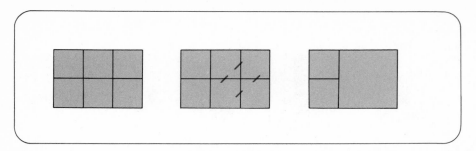

Fig. 3.7. DFT test item. Another item from Match Problems, calling for the removal of four matches to leave three complete squares. The solution requires the unusual resort to a square of larger-than-normal size. (Adapted from Guilford, 1967, p. 153. Copyright 1967 by McGraw-Hill Book Company. Used with permission of McGraw-Hill Book Company.)

A man had a wife who had been injured and was unable to speak. He found a surgeon who restored her power of speech. Then the man's peace was shattered by his wife's incessant talking. He solved the problem by having a doctor perform an operation on him so that, although she talked endlessly he was unable to hear a thing she said.

[**CLEVER TITLES**]   [**NONCLEVER TITLES**]

My Quiet Wife   A Man and His Wife
Doctor Quiets a Home   Medicine Triumphs
Yack, Yack, Hack   Never Satisfied

Fig. 3.8. DMI test item. In Possible Jobs, a test of divergent production of semantic implications, the examinee is given a symbol, such as an electric light bulb, to name groups of people or occupations for which the object could stand as a symbol. Some responses to the symbol given have been "electrician," "manufacturer of electrical appliances," "communication," "teacher," and "gifted students." (Courtesy of Sheridan Psychological Services, Inc.)

Divergent production of semantic implications (DMI) is measured by a test, Possible Jobs. Given a pictorial design, the examinee is to indicate what occupations or groups of people the picture might stand for. The response given by the examinee is an implication. Figure 3.8 illustrates this test.

Guilford is convinced that writers, planners, and scientists are strong in divergent production in the semantic area; that inventors and those in the visual arts are strong in the visual figural content; that mathematicians and mathematical scientists and cryptographers are strong in the symbolic content; and that musicians are strong in auditory abilities paralleling those of the visual. Guilford points out that any of the preceding might be strong in more than one area. As noted before, however, he states that a combination of specific abilities, rather than a general verbal ability, or several group abilities, underlies success in all these areas.

Use of SI Tests in Prediction

One of the important implications of the SI tests is their possible usefulness in predicting achievement in school subjects. Guilford (1968) recognizes that the tests developed to identify the abilities, or tests derived from them, must demonstrate predictive validity in order to be of high social significance.

A study was conducted to compare SI tests with other widely used standard tests in predicting achievement in basic mathematics, noncollege algebra, regular algebra, and accelerated algebra. Two specially constructed achievement tests, one in general mathematics and one in algebra, were used to measure the achievements of ninth-grade students enrolled in four kinds of classes — basic mathematics, noncollege algebra, regular algebra, and accelerated algebra. Sets of scores for no fewer than 73 nor more than 101 students were analyzed for each of the four kinds of classes. Scores were also obtained from the following tests: the California Test of Mental Maturity (CTMM) — a general intellectual ability test that yielded a language and nonlanguage score; the Iowa Tests of Basic Skills (ITBS) — an educational achievement battery that yielded a score on reading comprehension, arithmetic concepts, and arithmetic problem-solving; the Differential Aptitudes Test (DAT), which yielded a score on verbal reasoning, numerical ability, abstract reasoning, and clerical speed and accuracy; and a battery of 25 SI tests that yielded 13 factor scores.

Table 3.5 gives the multiple correlations for four combinations of tests with the two achievement tests. (A multiple correlation indicates the degree of correspondence between the sets of predictor tests and the criterion or achievement tests. The higher the numerical value, the greater is the predictive validity.) The CTMM correlations ranged from .18 to .40 with the achievement tests, the Iowa tests from .20 to .62, the DAT battery from .24 to .70, and 13 factor scores from 25 of the SI tests from .39 to .75. Thus, the DAT and SI batteries were about equally valid in predic-

Table 3.5 Multiple Prediction of Mathematical-Achievement Scores from Weighted Composites of Standard Tests and of Factor Tests

Prediction battery	Basic mathematics	Noncollege algebra	Regular algebra	Accelerated algebra
2 CTMM tests	.34	.40	.18	.37
3 Iowa tests (ITBS)	.53	.31	.20	.62
4 DAT tests	.57	.53	.24	.70
13 factor scores (SI)	.46	.45	.39	.75

Note: The coefficients of multiple correlations given are unbiased, i.e., corrected for shrinkage.
Source: Adapted from Guilford, 1968, p. 174.

tion. Both were better than the CTMM and somewhat better than the three Iowa tests.

Feldhusen, Treffinger, and Elias (1970) gathered information on seventh- and eight-graders in 1962 and on the same students as twelfth-graders in 1966 and 1967. Their main objective was to ascertain how useful various measures secured during junior high school years were in predicting school achievement in the senior year of high school. The 18 measures obtained during the junior high school years were as follows:

1. STEP Mathematics (1962)
2. STEP Science (1962)
3. STEP Social Studies (1962)
4. STEP Reading (1962)

5. SCAT Verbal
6. SCAT Quantitative

7. General Anxiety
8. Lie Scale

9. Originality
10. Flexibility
11. Fluency

12. Self-Rating
13. Self-Rating Conformity
14. Self-Rating Energy
15. Self-Rating Diffidence
16. Self-Rating Fluency
17. Self-Rating Flexibility
18. Self-Rating Total

Tests 1 through 4, Sequential Tests of Educational Progress (STEP), are educational achievement tests, and tests 5 and 6, School and College Aptitude Tests (SCAT), are tests of verbal mathematical ability. These may be considered as tests of convergent thinking, rather than divergent thinking. Tests 9, 10, and 11 are divergent thinking tests. Tests 7 and 8 are measures of personality, whereas tests 12 through 18 are self-ratings of various personality traits, including fluency and flexibility.

Five scores were obtained later on the seniors — achievement in mathematics, science, social studies, and reading was again measured by the Sequential Tests of Educational Progress, and IQ was measured by the Otis Quick Scoring Mental Ability Test. Separate multiple correlations were computed between the five scores in the senior year and the 18-measure predictor battery for each set of boys and girls as seventh- and eighth-graders. Thus, a total of 20 multiple correlations were obtained that indicated which measures of the predictor battery had turned out to be the most reliable. Nine of the 20 multiple correlations obtained were between .79 and .91; six were between .66 and .72; and five were between .37 and .57. The tests or ratings contributing most frequently to the prediction of achievement and IQ in the senior year as represented in the 20 multiple correlations were STEP mathematics, science, and social studies; SCAT verbal and quantitative ability; originality and flexibility; and the self-rating of fluency. Thus two of the three divergent-thinking abilities correlated positively with school achievement. Here we see better prediction based on the simultaneous use of convergent- and divergent-thinking tests than Guilford found using one or another type of test exclusively.

Cognitive Abilities of High School Students

Project Talent is a large-scale cross-sectional and longitudinal study of more than 400,000 students who were in grades 9, 10, 11, and 12 in 1960. The study is being carried out by the American Institutes for Research, and the intent is to follow up the same students at 5-year intervals after their graduation, for a period of 20 years.

Gains in Achievements and Abilities. Shaycoft (1967) reported a study done as part of Project Talent. In this investigation, about 3500 boys and 3600 girls who were freshmen in 1960 and seniors in 1963 in 118 different comprehensive and vocational high schools of the country were tested at both times. The students were given a comprehensive two-day battery of tests in 1960 and a one-day battery three years later. Scores from these tests were analyzed to find out more about what the students had learned during high school and also about their emerging and possibly changing abilities.

One of the most encouraging results of the study was the remarkable gain in achievement shown during the high school years. A second result was the substantial gain shown on most of the so-called aptitude, or ability, tests. Third, boys and girls showed different gain patterns on the various tests. These and other conclusions may be drawn from a careful study of the large amount of information in Table 3.6. Few other conclusions are reported here. Instead, comments intended to help in interpreting the table are made, and additional information, not included in the table, is given.

Fourteen tests (they are grouped in the lower half of the table) were developed to measure aptitudes, or abilities, whereas the others were intended to measure educational achievement. Gains were expected on the achievement tests, particularly on those relating to subjects taught every year in high school and taken for one or more years by most students, that is, the English and mathematics tests and some of the information tests. Smaller gains were expected on other information tests, and still smaller gains or no gains at all were expected on the aptitude tests. As will be noted later, the actual results on the aptitude tests were somewhat surprising. Further, when all the achievement and aptitude tests were analyzed, certain factors were found common to both types, and these factors were then called abilities.

The first row of information given in Table 3.6 dealing with Test R-102, Vocabulary I, may be summarized thus: There were 21 items in the test.

Table 3.6. Raw Score Gains, Grade 9 Standard Deviations, Ratio of Former to Latter, and Indication of Sex Differences in Gains

Achievement Tests	No. of items	Average raw score gain		Standard deviation of raw scores		Gain expressed as standard score	
		M (1)	F (2)	M (3)	F (4)	M (5)	F (6)
Information I							
R-102 Vocabulary I	21	2.60	2.67	3.80	3.86	.68	.69
R-103 Literature	24	4.33	4.64*	4.11	3.80	1.05	1.22
R-104 Music	13	.96	.97	2.87	2.82	.33	.34
R-105 Social studies	24	3.00	3.08	5.29	4.91	.57	.63
R-106 Mathematics	23	4.31*	2.11	4.03	3.61	1.07	.58
R-107 Physical science	18	1.58*	.53	3.69	3.51	.43	.15
R-108 Biological science	11	1.20	1.15	2.28	2.14	.53	.54
R-109 Scientific attitude	10	1.30	1.30	1.99	1.86	.65	.70
R-110 Aeronautics and space	10	1.33*	.88	2.35	1.64	.57	.54
R-111 Electricity and electronics	20	2.69*	.70	3.87	2.54	.70	.28
R-112 Mechanics	19	2.42*	1.61	3.28	2.72	.74	.59
R-113 Farming	12	.96	1.01	2.28	2.51	.42	.40
R-114 Home economics	21	1.55	1.95*	2.75	3.29	.56	.59
R-115 Sports	14	1.64*	1.31	2.94	2.27	.56	.58
Information II							
R-131 Art	12	1.37	1.48	2.46	2.44	.56	.61
R-132 Law	9	1.48	1.39	1.78	1.61	.83	.86
R-133 Health	9	1.18	1.22	2.04	1.95	.58	.63
R-134 Engineering	6	.49	.54	1.24	1.26	.40	.43
R-135 Architecture	6	.58	.52	1.25	1.19	.46	.44
R-138 Military	7	.96*	.75	1.38	1.14	.70	.66
R-139 Acct., bus., sales	10	1.57	1.73*	1.79	1.75	.88	.99
R-140 Practical knowledge	4	.47*	.40	1.04	.90	.45	.44
R-142 Bible	15	1.24	1.25	3.22	3.12	.39	.40

R-145	Hunting	5	.44*	.13	1.20	.89	.37	.15
R-146	Fishing	5	.42*	.09	1.23	.91	.34	.10
R-147	Outdoor activities (other)	9	.75	.70	1.87	1.81	.40	.39
R-150	Theater; ballet	8	.97	.92	1.61	1.61	.60	.57
R-162	Vocabulary II	9	1.44*	1.15	2.24	2.14	.64	.54

English

R-231	Spelling	16	1.67	1.93*	2.87	2.74	.58	.70
R-232	Capitalization	33	1.07*	.77	3.87	3.40	.28	.23
R-233	Punctuation	27	2.16	2.35	4.30	4.13	.50	.57
R-234	English usage	25	1.46	1.35	3.26	3.04	.45	.44
R-235	Effective expression	12	1.21	1.11	2.48	2.15	.49	.52

Mathematics

R-311	Arithmetic Reasoning (I)	16	2.16*	1.53	3.38	3.20	.64	.48
R-312	Intro. h.s. math (II)	24	2.67*	.77	4.06	3.87	.66	.20
R-333	Adv. h.s. math (III)	14	2.12*	1.15	1.63	1.51	1.30	.76

Aptitude Tests

R-212	Memory for Words	24	2.22	2.99*	4.79	5.18	.46	.58
R-220	Disguised Words	30	3.71	4.00	6.15	6.35	.60	.63
R-240	Word Functions	24	2.80	2.92	4.82	5.35	.58	.55
R-250	Reading Comprehension	48	6.31	5.99	10.56	10.07	.60	.59
R-260	Creativity	20	3.28*	2.78	3.77	3.50	.87	.79
R-270	Mechanical Reasoning	20	2.40*	1.59	3.93	3.41	.61	.47
R-281	Visualization in 2 Dimensions	24	3.04*	2.44	5.70	5.51	.53	.44
R-282	Visualization in 3 Dimensions	16	1.85*	1.23	3.21	2.92	.58	.42
R-290	Abstract Reasoning	15	1.40*	1.23	3.00	2.96	.47	.42
F-410	Arithmetic Computation	72	9.01*	6.04	20.14	16.21	.45	.37
F-420	Table Reading	72	5.48*	4.44	10.10	7.74	.54	.57
F-430	Clerical Checking	74	11.46	10.49	19.83	17.73	.58	.59
F-440	Object Inspection	40	4.83*	4.21	8.44	7.30	.57	.58

Note: The asterisks indicate significant sex differences in gains; see text. Source: Adapted from Shaycoft, 1967, pp. 5-7, 5-8.

Boys (M) made a gain of 2.60 points and girls (F) a gain of 2.67. Standard deviation, which is a measure of variation from the mean or average, is next. The larger the value, the more a score varies from the mean of the raw scores. Thus girls' scores varied slightly more from the mean than did the boys' – 3.86 in comparison with 3.80. The values .68 and .69 are obtained by dividing the mean score gain by the standard deviation (2.60 ÷ 3.80 = .68). These standard scores provide a way to compare the size of gains *between tests*, not to compare the difference in mean gains between boys and girls. The value for boys of .68 in Vocabulary I and 1.05 in literature shows that the boys gained relatively more in literature than in Vocabulary I. The asterisk following a mean score gain in column 1 or column 2 indicates that the difference between the mean gain of the two sexes was statistically significant at least at the .05 level. (A significance level of .05 means that the probability is 95 in 100 that this obtained difference is a true difference – that the probability is only 5 in 100 that the obtained difference is caused by chance factors.) Going down columns 1 and 2, observe that the boys' mean gain was higher than the girls' in mathematics, science, aeronautics and space, etc. Although not reported, the same sex showing the larger gain also had the higher mean score as freshmen, literature information being the only exception. You may find it interesting, before studying columns 5 and 6 further, to estimate the five tests on which each sex made the highest and lowest gains and then to compare your estimates with the values in the table.

At this point we digress briefly to indicate that large differences in mean gains of students were found among schools. The basis for these differences could not be determined precisely, but it was clear that some of the differences were caused by characteristics of the various communities in which the schools were located. The differences were not caused *solely* by differences in characteristics of the communities, however, nor by the number of course offerings in the various subject fields. One hypothesis offered by Shaycoft (1967, pp. 7-25) is that because of motivational and other factors, some students do not take the courses that could permit them to learn as they should; therefore, the mean gain for that school is lowered.

Organization and Stability of Abilities. As noted earlier, all scores obtained on a sample of the same students as ninth- and twelfth-graders were correlated and then submitted to factor analysis. One general ability, several group abilities, and many specific abilities were identified. Figure 3.9 shows a general verbal ability and four group abilities – mathematical, spatial, English, and technical information – that were identified from the ninth- and twelfth-grade scores. These abilities, except English, were common to both boys and girls. The names of the various tests loading relatively high on each factor are given in Fig. 3.9. The many specific abilities identified and some minor group abilities are not shown in Fig. 3.9, but are mentioned briefly later.

In the terminology of Shaycoft, the verbal factor is closest to what is variously called general verbal ability, general verbal intelligence, scholastic aptitude, or academic aptitude. It was found, as noted in Fig. 3.9, to

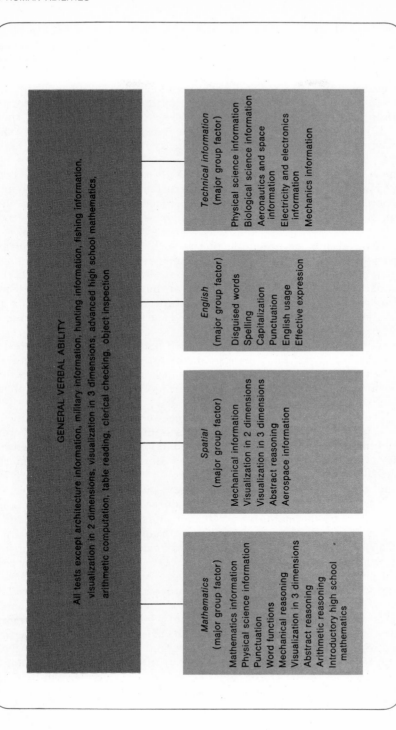

Fig. 3.9. General and major group factors common to grades 9 and 12 and to boys and girls: (Identified by Shaycoft, 1967)

load moderately high to high on the majority of tests. Also, it correlated substantially with the socioeconomic rating for both sexes. (The mathematics factor also correlated substantially with the socioeconomic rating for boys.) No cause and effect can be inferred from this correlation. However, in connection with general verbal ability, "boys and girls in the moderate-to-high socioeconomic bracket not only tend to have better verbal ability than those from a deprived background by the time they reach high school, but they are also somewhat more likely to be in the kind of environment that makes information available to them. . . ." (Shaycoft, 1967, p. 65).

The mathematics ability is related not only to the mathematics tests but also to mechanical reasoning, abstract reasoning, word functions, and punctuation. The kind of special ability needed in mathematics is also helpful in comprehension of grammar principles and the use of punctuation marks.

The spatial ability, as indicated in the earlier treatment of a hierarchical structure, might be related to engineering and some technical areas. It is possible, as Smith indicated, that this ability is not nurtured well because of the heavy emphasis on a verbal type of education. Further, the possibility exists that the substantial use of verbal tests in Project Talent to measure achievements did not permit better tapping of this ability.

The English ability was derived from a fairly limited range of tests, most of which measured the various aspects of formal English communication. The technical information factor had its highest loadings on information related to electricity, mechanics, aeronautics and space, and physical science.

Other group factors of lesser importance were identified, including a gain factor in English and another in general information, a rural factor, one in fishing and hunting, and one in common sense. Specific factors (those derived from a single test) included Bible information, memory, and about 20 others.

The fact that one general ability and several group abilities were extracted from both ninth- and twelfth-grade scores is of theoretical interest and also of practical interest. It identifies a tendency for students to maintain relatively the same positions throughout four years of high school. Those high, middle, and low on the various tests in ninth grade tended to be in the same relative position in the senior year. Another conclusion of practical importance is that the group abilities were extracted. This suggests that a general factor accounted for only part of what is common to the many tests and that each of the group abilities accounts for what is common to each of four classes of performances. Furthermore, although a group verbal factor was found, the presence of the group factors (and also of the specific factors) suggests that schools should not rely heavily on tests of general intellectual ability in counseling with students about courses or careers. These conclusions parallel those drawn by Guilford in connection with predicting mathematics achievement from various combinations of tests.

An Informal Approach to Cognitive Abilities

Bloom (1956) and others, basing their study on an analysis of literature, developed a statement of educational objectives in the cognitive domain in the form of a taxonomy. Six cognitive operations were described. These operations were implied as being applicable to the subject matter in various fields encountered by students at all school levels. The Bloom terminology differs from that of Guilford. Table 3.7 lists the operations in the two classification schemes. Let us examine the parallel terminology of Guilford and Bloom.

Table 3.7 Parallel Cognitive Operations from Guilford and Bloom

Guilford	Bloom
Cognition—discovery, rediscovery or recognition	Comprehension— understanding of communicated material without relating it to other material
Memory—retention of what is cognized	(Memory is assumed but not stated as an intellectual operation.)
Convergent production—arriving at one right answer or at a recognized best or conventional answer from known and remembered information	Application—using methods, concepts, principles, and theories in new situations Analysis—breaking down a communication into its constituent elements
Divergent production—arriving at a variety of unique responses not completely determined by known and remembered information	Synthesis—putting together constituent elements or parts to form a whole
Evaluation—arriving at decisions as to goodness, correctness, suitability, or adequacy of what we know, what we remember, and what we produce in productive thinking	Evaluation—judging the value of materials and methods for given purposes; applying standards and criteria

Sources: Based on Guilford, 1959, and Bloom, 1956.

"Cognition" and "comprehension" have the same meaning—becoming aware of and understanding information. Guilford proposed an operation of memory; Bloom did not list memory as an intellectual ability, but he did assume that memory is essential to the other operations. Guilford indicated two kinds of productive thinking—divergent and convergent; Bloom proposed three operations—application, analysis, and synthesis—without reference to the outcome produced. Nevertheless, Bloom's synthesis of information may lead to different and novel responses of the same type that result from Guilford's divergent production. Similarly, the application and analysis of information leads to the production of responses that may be judged as correct or incorrect; thus these operations are similar to Guilford's convergent production. Evaluation is very similar in both systems. Also, in both systems, problem-solving is considered to be a highly complex activity, not a single operation, dependent on a combination of many abilities.

How may schools move from these abstract statements of abilities to educational practices designed to develop these abilities in students? A good example is provided by the work of Sanders (1965) in the Manitowoc (Wisconsin) public schools. Sanders worked with teachers in improving their use of questions, problem-solving activities, and projects so that the students would acquire more of the higher-level abilities outlined in the Bloom taxonomy. His main approach was through a systematic consideration of teacher activities which require students not only to remember information, concepts, and theories but to *use* them.

In his early work with social studies teachers, Sanders clarified the terminology related to objectives with these examples:

> *Memory*: The student recalls or recognizes information. . . .
> *Application*: The student solves a lifelike problem that requires the identification of the issue and the selection and use of appropriate generalizations and skills. . . .
> *Analysis*: The student solves a problem in the light of conscious knowledge of the parts and forms of thinking. . . .
> *Synthesis*: The student solves a problem that requires original, creative thinking. . . .
> *Evaluation*: The student makes a judgment of good or bad, right or wrong, according to standards he designated. (Sanders, 1965, p. 3)

As teachers arrange activities to help students develop these abilities, they move from having students memorize information to having them use it in a variety of situations. In the process they contribute to the development of the higher-level abilities. A possible procedure that a teacher might use for each ability shows the relationship between the operations, the subject-matter content, and the teaching-learning activities.

> *Memory*: What is meant by "gerrymandering"? (The student is asked to recall the definition given to him earlier.) . . .
> *Application*: The mayor recently appointed a committee to study the fairness of the boundaries of the election districts in our community. Gather information about the present districts and the population in each. Determine whether the present city election districts are adequate. (The student is expected to apply principles of democracy studied in class to this new problem.)
> *Analysis*: Analyze the reasoning in this quotation: "Human beings lack the ability to be fair when their own interests are involved. Party X controls the legislature and now it has taken upon itself the responsibility of redrawing the boundaries of the legislative election districts. We know in advance that our party will suffer."

Synthesis: (This question must follow the preceding application question.) If current election districts in our community are inadequate, suggest how they might be redrawn.

Evaluation: Would you favor having your political party engage in gerrymandering if it had the opportunity? (Sanders, 1965, pp. 3-5)

It is easy to observe that the activities and questions after "memory" involve mental operations different from mere recall or cognizing. In this connection, let us examine an additional example of an activity intended to encourage synthesis of information. Here is an initial suggestion to teachers (not quoted in full) about how to stimulate with questions those students who are less creative or less motivated:

Directions: Which in this list do you believe are legitimate questions for collective bargaining?
A. How much should workers of various skills be paid?
B. How much should managers be paid?
C. How much vacation should workers have?
D. How fast should the assembly line move?
E. Is a particular worker incompetent and deserving of being discharged?
F. For what price should the products be offered for sale?
G. Who should be selected as officers of a company?
H. Should a new plant be constructed to expand production?
I. How much should be paid the owners of the company in dividends?
J. What new products should be produced?
K. How many laborers are required to do a certain job? . . .

. . . After studying this list, students are presented with this synthesis problem: *What principles or standards can you devise that would be helpful in determining which of the above questions should be decided by collective bargaining?* (Sanders, 1965, pp. 132-133)

Sanders notes that the synthesis problem could be presented for individual study or for group discussion. The following ideas resulted from a class discussion:

A. Workers should have the right to bargain on questions that immediately and directly affect wages, hours, and working conditions. Current law gives them this right.
B. Managers should make decisions in which there is little or no conflict of interests with workers.
C. Manager and workers should participate in those decisions in which they have a special competency that the other side does not possess or possesses to a lesser degree.
D. A principle of capitalism gives owners a right to initiate and operate a business. Under laissez-faire capitalism this right was almost absolute, but it has been limited to an indefinite degree. (Sanders, 1965, p. 133)

The students had not first read or heard these ideas. Instead, the ideas resulted from their synthesis of other information. (Sanders does not indicate, however, how much previous experience is needed to secure these responses.) Sanders cites many other examples of questions and activities that teachers in many subject fields and school levels, from primary through high school, can use to facilitate the development of the higher-level abilities.

3.7. Is Guilford's concept of concrete, abstract, and social intelligence more closely associated with the type of product or the type of content? Does any one or do any two of the five operations appear to you to be more important to all three types of intelligence than the others? Why?

3.8. How are divergent and convergent production abilities alike and different? How do both differ from the cognizing abilities?

3.9. Which type of content — figural, symbolic, semantic, behavioral — probably receives least emphasis in the elementary and secondary schools of today? Why?

3.10. Gains on 49 tests and differences between gains for boys and girls are shown in Table 3.6, and some conclusions about them were stated. What other main conclusions do you draw from studying the information?

3.11. In Table 3.6, the two largest information test gains made by boys were in mathematics (1.07) and literature (1.05); the largest gains for girls were in literature (1.22) and accounting, business, and sales (.99). Based on your own high school experience, would you predict the same results for boys and girls? Why or why not?

3.12. How does the hierarchical pattern of a general and four group abilities found in hgh school students of Project Talent compare with the general and major group factors discussed in the first part of the chapter? (You cannot deal with minor group and specific abilities, since they were not discussed in either structure. Also, a direct comparison cannot be made with Guilford's SI because of the different tests and methods used.)

3.13. Do the operations as defined by Guilford or as defined by Bloom appear more relevant to your professional interests? Why?

3.14. Sanders indicated that teaching procedures involving discussion, problem-solving, and project-type activities were more conducive to the development of the abilities to apply, synthesize, and evaluate information than were information-giving and testing for recall of the information. How does this conclusion compare with your own educational experiences?

PSYCHOMOTOR ABILITIES

So much attention is given to the rather specialized areas of interscholastic athletics and professional sports that it is easy to underestimate the importance of psychomotor abilities and physical fitness in the evolution of mankind and in the daily lives of individuals. There is a tendency to think of great literature, music, and art and the astonishing recent developments in medicine and science almost exclusively in terms of cognitive abilities. Obviously, however, the author, the composer, and the painter use their psychomotor abilities in developing their products. The remarkable modern advances in surgery of the brain and the heart also require the highest level of psychomotor abilities. Millions of people still make a living primarily through physical activity. Furthermore, each of us maintains better health and intellectual productivity through keeping physically fit. Every growing child has the potentiality to become a more effective individual through developing his psychomotor abilities.

A Matrix of Psychomotor Abilities

Guilford made a systematic and comprehensive survey of research completed in the field of psychomotor abilities and subsequently identified six psychomotor factors which he believed to be involved in many kinds of motor performances (Guilford, 1958). These processes, combined with parts of the body, may be called psychomotor abilities. The factors identified by Guilford are shown in Fig. 3.10. Though some of the terms are self-explanatory, others need defining.

Impulsion pertains to the rate at which movements are initiated from stationary positions; thus it is distinct from *speed*, which pertains to the rate of movements after they have started. The sprinter bounding from a stationary position illustrates impulsion and his running thereafter exemplifies speed. *Precision* has to do with the accuracy with which bodily positions can be held and with the accuracy of directed movements, once started. The tight-rope walker moves with precision. *Flexibility* is suggested as pertaining to the extent to which a part of the body is free to bend or to the scope of movement pertaining to a particular joint. The contortionist and the acrobat are flexible. In addition to these six major processes, muscular endurance, circulatory-respiratory endurance, and perhaps other psychomotor abilities are thought to be basic to vocal activities such as singing and speaking.

In the many perceptual motor skills taught in the schools—drawing, handwriting, typing, shorthand, the making of maps in social studies, and the manipulating of objects in home economics, agriculture, industrial arts, and other classes—a combination of several of the psychomotor abilities is used. A perceptual motor task, such as shorthand or playing a musical instrument, requires not only the physical movements but also the perception of words or musical notes that direct the physical movements. Here a combination of cognitive and psychomotor abilities is involved.

Other outcomes of learning in the psychomotor domain are motor sets. When an individual gets ready to hit a golf ball, to bat, to type, or to start playing a musical instrument, he has a feeling within himself about the stance and proper body attitude to assume. From observation of an individual's performances and from the individual's attempts to describe how he thinks as he prepares to do something, we have some knowledge of motor set. It is virtually impossible, however, for an individual to verbalize the motor set precisely; the many neural connections from the brain to the muscles and joints, although felt, cannot be described accurately.

Earlier we saw that cognitive abilities are improved through purposefully learning how to read, to solve problems, and the like. So also the psychomotor abilities are brought to higher levels through engaging in appropriate physical activities.

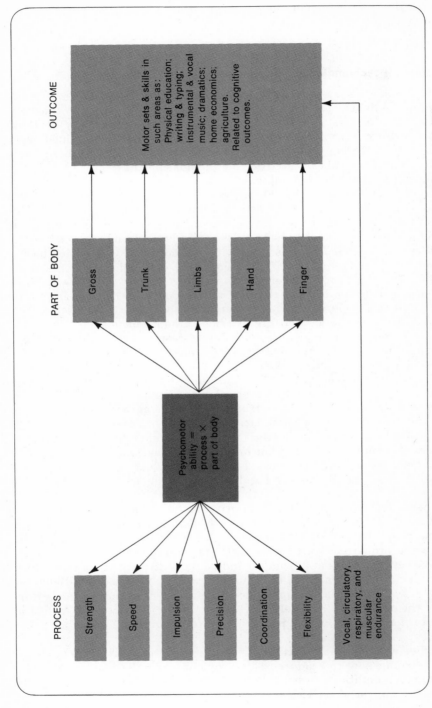

Fig. 3.10. Schematic arrangement of psychomotor abilities and learning outcomes. (Based on Guilford, 1958, pp. 161-174)

Abilities and Physical Fitness

In connection with a current concern of high interest, Fleishman (1964) reported an exhaustive study of the abilities underlying physical fitness. Eight abilities—a surprisingly small number—were found to be common to an entire battery of 60 activity-type tests. Proper exercise to develop and maintain these abilities supposedly contributes both to physical fitness and to excellent performance of a variety of vocational and avocational activities. Each ability is now described, along with part of the test activities recommended by Fleishman, to measure the ability in school settings.

1. *Static strength* is the maximum force that the individual can exert for a brief period, where the force is exerted continuously up to the maximum. Hand-gripping, pulling weights, and medicine-ball-throwing measure static strength with an arm-hand-shoulder emphasis, whereas pushing weights with the feet and pulling a trunk dynamometer measure static strength with a trunk emphasis.

2. *Dynamic strength* involves the exertion of muscular force repeatedly or continuously for a period of time, where muscular endurance and resistance to fatigue are critical. Pull-ups and push-ups are prominent in dynamic strength of the arms, and similar movements are involved in leg strength.

3. *Trunk strength* is dynamic strength that is limited primarily to the abdominal muscles. Activities involving leg, back, and abdominal muscles appear to be involved here.

4. *Extent flexibility* is the ability to flex or stretch the trunk and back muscles as far as possible with maximum force in a forward, lateral, or backward direction. Abdominal stretching and touching the toes with the fingers contribute to this ability.

5. *Dynamic flexibility* is the ability to make repeated, rapid, flexible movements in which resiliency of the muscles in recovery or strain is critical. Related activities are lateral bending, squatting, twisting, and floor-touching.

6. *Gross body equilibrium* is the ability to maintain body equilibrium, despite forces pulling the individual off balance. Balancing on one foot with the eyes closed, standing on one foot without closing the eyes, and rail-walking are high in this ability.

7. *Gross body coordination* is the ability to coordinate actions of different parts of the body simultaneously while making gross body movements. Physical activities commonly associated with this ability are not delineated. However, such actions as dribbling a ball with the hands while the feet are moving forward rapidly seem to be involved.

8. *Stamina* is the ability to continue maximum effort that requires exertion over a prolonged period of time. Jogging, stepping up and down until partial exhaustion is experienced, and treadmill-walking are proposed as tests of this ability.

The eight abilities are not a complete list of all the psychomotor abilities. The eight may be identified in the more complete scheme outlined by

Guilford, shown in Fig. 3.10. As with cognitive abilities, the exact number of psychomotor abilities and their organization is still under study. However, substantial correspondence between the work of Fleishman and Guilford may be noted in the strength, coordination, and flexibility abilities.

Psychomotor Abilities and Educational Achievement

Ismail and Gruber (1967) reviewed a large number of studies and did some themselves in which correlations were run between various measures in the psychomotor and cognitive domains. Height, weight, and similar physical measures, *which require no learning*, are uncorrelated with educational achievements and IQ. However, psychomotor abilities and particularly coordination, balance, and rhythm, *which require mental activity* as well as practice of motor acts in order to be developed, correlate low but positively with educational achievements.

Ismail and Gruber described a physical education program designed to achieve the following objectives: (1) organic development to be attained by developing muscular strength, muscular endurance, and cardiovascular endurance; (2) neuromuscular development to be attained by developing coordination, balance, rhythm, and kinesthesis; (3) personal-social interactions to be facilitated by including activities requiring cooperative efforts in order to achieve success.

The program was carried out for one year. Boys and girls in grade 6 who were put on the program achieved significantly higher academically than did a matched control group not put on it. The authors, though recognizing that the results are based on only one study, judged that instruction in physical education that is successful in developing greater coordination and balance will also improve educational performance in the usual elementary school subject matter. They concluded that physical education and academic education should be regarded as two conjugate approaches to the education of children, not as two separate areas.

Classifying abilities as *cognitive* or *psychomotor* does not indicate the relationship between abilities involved in performing many learning tasks. Two examples may clarify this. The main abilities involved in a child's learning to read are cognitive—the five operations combined with symbolic and semantic content. Nevertheless, psychomotor abilities are also involved in opening the book properly, sitting properly, and focusing on the printed page in a left-to-right and top-to-bottom sequence. Playing a musical instrument involves psychomotor abilities—speed, flexibility, precision, and coordination in combination with hands, fingers, and limbs. The reading of musical notes to guide the motor movement requires the development of cognitive abilities. Once note-reading is mastered, further improvement in performance results primarily from improvement of the psychomotor abilities. Similarly, once the motor aspects of reading become habitual, further improvement in reading requires the development of the cognitive abilities.

3.15. Which of the physical fitness abilities seem to be least well developed in persons of your age and interests? Is this a result of inadequate previous instruction in school or personal styles of living? Explain.

3.16. How might comprehension of the physical fitness abilities by the entire instructional staff of a building affect a program of physical education in the building?

3.17. Ismail and Gruber are confident that excellent instruction to develop the psychomotor abilities that require mental and motor activity will also produce better educational achievement. Do you share their confidence? Why or why not?

AFFECTIVE OPERATIONS AND CHARACTERISTICS

Included in Guilford's structure of intellect are 30 hypothesized abilities involving behavioral content; these abilities, however, are not so well identified at present as those involving figural, symbolic, and semantic contents. Furthermore, it is not clear in any case that behavioral content *can* be combined satisfactorily with the five operations—cognition, memory, divergent production, convergent production, evaluation—and the six products—units, classes, relations, systems, implications, transformations. In other words, it is not certain that what is learned and experienced in the affective or feeling domain can be categorized as abilities.

Krathwohl, Bloom, and Masia (1964) recently worked with a national committee that studied the literature on different kinds of affective behavior (feelings and valuing). The primary purpose of the group, however, was to identify educational objectives, not affective abilities. Accepting the concept of *internalization* as appropriate for dealing with such affective outcomes as interests, motives, attitudes, and values, they organized the objectives as a taxonomy. Internalization is the process of incorporating something into one's own behavior as one's own, not merely as accepting or conforming to the values of others. Internalization has more than the dimension of external to internal; it also has dimensions of simple to complex and concrete to abstract. These may be noted, in the order of headings from top to bottom, as set forth in the taxonomy of objectives in the affective domain:

1.0. Receiving (Attending)
    1.1. Awareness; e.g., the person is aware of the feelings of others whose activities are of little interest to him.
    1.2. Willingness to receive; e.g., the person listens to others with respect.
    1.3. Controlled or selected attention; e.g., the person is alert to human values and judgments on life as they are recorded in history.
2.0. Responding
    2.1. Acquiescence in responding; e.g., the person obeys the playground regulations.
    2.2. Willingness to respond; e.g., the person practices the rules of safety on the playground.

2.3. Satisfaction in response; e.g., the person enjoys participating in activities and plays according to the rules.
3.0. Valuing
    3.1. Acceptance of a value; e.g., the person accepts the importance of social goals in a free society.
    3.2. Preference for a value; e.g., the person assumes an active role in clarifying the social goals in a free society.
    3.3. Commitment; e.g., the person is loyal to the social goals of a free society.
4.0. Organizing
    4.1. Conceptualization of a value; e.g., the person judges the responsibility of society for conserving human resources.
    4.2. Organization of a value system; e.g., the person develops a plan for conserving human resources.
5.0. Characterization by a Value or Value Complex
    5.1. Generalized set; e.g., the person faces facts and conclusions that can be logically drawn from them with a consistent value orientation.
    5.2. Characterization; e.g., the person develops a philosophy of life. (Krathwohl, Bloom, & Masia, 1964)

Some general comments may help in interpreting the taxonomy, which is really a sequence for the development of a value system:

1.0. Receiving (Attending). Internalization begins with the individual becoming aware of something in his environment. After becoming aware he gives it his attention; and, in selective attention, he actually seeks the stimuli. For example, a person is aware of the feelings of others; next, he is willing to listen to others with respect; and then he gives selective attention to discussions of human values. This kind of receiving is the lowest level in the hierarchy.

2.0. Responding. Acquiescence in responding is close to selective attention in that the individual merely complies with the expectations of someone else. Then he willingly responds from inner motivation. At the third level of responding, satisfaction is experienced. The sequence is illustrated by acquiescence to playground regulations, overt practice of them, and then satisfaction in following them.

3.0. Valuing. The next level, valuing, implies increasing internalization. Acceptance of a value, for example, the importance of social goals, does not involve preference. However, preference for a value followed by commitment is exemplified by actively clarifying social goals and becoming loyal to them because one cannot live comfortably with oneself otherwise. Illustrative of the latter level of valuing is the behavior of the dedicated Peace Corps volunteers, religious missionaries, and students who participate in the registration of voters.

4.0. Organizing. As values become more internalized and more abstract, they also embrace more facets of experience. Organization is needed. Before there can be organization, however, conceptualization is required. Values ordinarily are put into words so that they can be manipulated readily in thought.

5.0. Characterization. After conceptualization and organization the individual's behavior is characterized by a value complex, the highest level in the hierarchy. The first behavioral step here is indicated by a generalized set; that is, the individual meets a large number of different situations in his daily life with a fairly consistent method of analyzing and responding to them. For example, when he hears diverse opinions and emotional appeals, he is willing to face facts and draw conclusions logically from them. As groups of organized values are internalized they form the individual's philosophy of life. Some elements of a philosophy of life may be inferred from a letter of a Peace Corps volunteer to his parents:

> The reasons why I am going into the Peace Corps are very personal and varied. The decision came as a result of thought and self-examination on many levels. Probably the deepest reason is that I wish to devote two years of my life at this time to other people through a program which will help men who are not as fortunate as I am. I have learned very much at Notre Dame during the last four years, and I have learned very much from you and others who are very close to me. The biggest thing I have learned is that one must be true to himself if he is ever to be happy in this world. Being true to oneself sometimes dictates that one do things which seem at first to be mistakes. But if that person truly knows himself and what he is capable of doing, the decision will be a correct one — no matter who might possibly try to point out weaknesses in the plan of proposed action. I have learned from many of the teachers whom I love and respect the most at Notre Dame that sacrifice and a certain amount of suffering are mandatory if one is to be sensitive to give and receive truth, love, and beauty in his life. On the deepest level, then, this is the sacrifice which I am now making.
>
> My ultimate goal in life is to be happy by helping to make it possible for others to be happy. I think that this can be done by me in teaching, public service, and maybe even politics eventually. I think that the two years of relative removal in the Peace Corps will enable me to make a decision on this which I can live with.
>
> One other reason for my positive decision on the Peace Corps is the nature of the country and project to which I have been assigned. I will be sent to Ceylon . . ., and I will be working in community development, public health education, and teaching. The country is plagued by a disease called filiariasis, which is a form of elephantiasis or a terrible swelling of the glands all over the body. The people in Ceylon are being grossly disfigured for the rest of their lives, and some are even dying. The real tragedy is that the disease can be eliminated by simple inoculation. This is what I will be doing there. I will be involved with the inoculating, but even more, with the program of public education which will tell the Ceylonese about the threat and about the solution to it. I will also work in the villages, helping to set up community projects and schools. All of this appeals to me very much, and the possibilities for helping these people are unlimited. Also, the possibilities for the Ceylonese to help me become a better person are unlimited. I think that I will be a much deeper individual for having experienced another culture and for having helped our brothers in Ceylon. (Hesburgh, 1969, p. 31)

3.18. Evaluate the sequence for the development of a value system according to two criteria: (a) it is sufficiently comprehensive to include all outcomes in the affective domain, including interests, motives, and values; (b) instructional procedures can be inferred directly from it.

3.19. To what extent do you think the development of a value system involves both divergent and convergent production?

SUMMARY

Abilities are developed over a period of many years of study and practice. They underlie performances of all kinds in the cognitive, affective, and psychomotor domains. Abilities are identified scientifically through controlled experimentation and factor analysis. Abilities are also identified through careful observation and analysis of the performances of many students.

Two main organizations of abilities have been hypothesized. One is a hierarchical structure involving a general ability that underlies many performances, group abilities associated with several kinds of performances, and either minor or specific abilities related to specific performances. The idea of a general intellectual ability, a group educational ability, and a group practical ability is in line with this kind of structure. The separate system of academic and vocational schools of Western Europe follows from this kind of conception, but in America we prefer the comprehensive high school.

Guilford's structure of intellect, in which 120 separate abilities are posited, recognizes neither a general ability nor group abilities. A system of education designed to identify and nurture different configurations of abilities in every individual follows logically from this conception. Two important contributions of this model to education, more important than the identification of the many separate abilities, are a different way of looking at the nature of intelligence(s) and an emphasis on the nurturing of divergent production, or creative abilities.

Other major efforts to identify and describe the cognitive, or intellectual, abilities that may be nurtured through education are illustrated in Project Talent and in a taxonomy of intellectual skills in the cognitive domain—memory, comprehension, analysis, application, synthesis, and evaluation. Both Fleishman and Guilford have made progress in identifying abilities in the psychomotor domain. A hierarchy of operations involved in the internalization of interests, values, motives, and other outcomes in the affective domain includes receiving, responding, valuing, organizing, and characterization. Thus, consistent progress is being made in identifying and cataloging human abilities and characteristics. The results of this work, in turn, provide a better foundation for organizing educational programs.

SUGGESTIONS FOR FURTHER READING

BLOOM, B. S., ed. *Taxonomy of educational objectives. Handbook I: Cognitive domain.* New York: McKay, 1956.

The statement of educational objectives is also an outline of abilities. Chapter 2, pages 25-43, has a good treatment of the nature of abilities.

CASPARI, E. Genetic endowment and environment in the determination of human behavior: Biological viewpoint. In Ripple, R. E., ed., *Readings in learning and human abilities*. New York: Harper & Row, 2nd ed., 1971.

Caspari discusses the relationship between biological and environmental determinants of behavior, stressing the uniqueness and dignity of the individual.

FLEISHMAN, E. A., & BARTLETT, C. J. *Human abilities*. In Mussen, P. H., & Rosenzweig, M. R., eds., *Annual review of psychology*. Palo Alto, Cal.: Annual Reviews, 1969, pp. 349-380.

Although this summary of research and theory is primarily for researchers, most of the discussion is nontechnical.

GUILFORD, J. P. *The nature of human intelligence*. New York: McGraw-Hill, 1967, pp. 2-20, 55-68.

In pages 2-20 Guilford presents a short history of the development of individually administered mental ability tests. In pages 55-68 he describes models of intelligence, including Spearman's, Burt's, Vernon's, and his own.

GUILFORD, J. P. Intelligence: 1965 model. In Ripple, R. E., ed., *Readings in learning and human abilities*. New York: Harper & Row, 2nd ed., 1971.

A structure of 120 specific intellectual abilities is outlined, and a model for problem-solving is presented.

HORN, J. L. Intelligence—why it grows, why it declines. In Ripple, R. E., ed., *Readings in learning and human abilities*. New York: Harper & Row, 2nd ed., 1971.

Fluid and crystallized intelligence are discussed; the limitations of the concept of a single general intellectual ability are implied.

JENSEN, A. R. How much can we boost IQ and scholastic achievement? *Harvard educational review*, 1969, **39**, pp. 1-123. Discussions of Jensen's article by Kagan, J. S., Hunt, J. M., Crow, J. F., Bereiter, C., Elkind, D., Cronbach, L. J., and Brazziel, W. F., are given on pp. 273-356.

The first article by Jensen generated nation-wide controversy concerning the relative influence of hereditary and environmental factors as causes of differences between blacks and whites in intelligence and educational achievements. Jensen drew controversial conclusions also regarding compensatory educational programs.

KLINEBERG, O. Negro-white differences in intelligence test performance—a new look at an old problem. In Wrightsman, L. S., ed., *Contemporary issues in social psychology*. Belmont, Cal.: Wadsworth, 1968, pp. 11-17.

In one of 33 readings with relevance to education, Klineberg concludes that there is no scientifically acceptable evidence for the view that ethnic groups differ in innate abilities.

KRATHWOHL, D. R., BLOOM, B. S., & MASIA, B. B. *Taxonomy of objectives. The classification of educational goals. Handbook II. Affective domain*. New York: McKay, 1964.

An outline is presented of affective development to be nurtured through education.

Part II Components of a System of School Learning

he objectives of education — what the schools should accomplish — are increasingly the concern of students, parents, taxpayers, and teachers. Once there is agreement on the main objectives, more specific instructional objectives may be formulated for each student or adapted to the characteristics of the student. Instructional programs may then be planned that provide for differences among students in both the rate and style of achieving the same objectives. Furthermore, variations in curriculum emphases must also be arranged, since not all students do pursue the same objectives.

Increasingly better instructional materials are being developed, and new media, including television and computers, are being adapted and refined for instructional purposes. Nevertheless, provisions for differences among students in rate and style of learning are still not adequate. Almost one-third of the total student population does not complete high school, while poverty and discrimination in the community and lack of resources and programs in the schools contribute to the disadvantagement of millions of children and youth. Preschool education, compensatory education during the school years, and special programs for dropouts, all of which have proved successful in a few settings on a small scale, have not materially improved educational opportunities for large numbers of the poor in our big cities and rural areas.

Teachers and others are well aware of present inadequacies. As a result, both the concept of teaching and the image of the teacher are changing. First, the idea of several teachers in a team contributing according to their strengths is replacing the idea of the generalist teacher who is expert in everything. Second, teachers are organizing in order to improve education, including learning conditions for students, as well as pay for themselves. New patterns in education thus are emerging. One of these patterns is called individually guided education; under this system, new roles are being established for educational personnel and better use is made of materials, time, facilities, and other components of a school learning system.

Chapter 4 Educational and Instructional Objectives

Attributes of Objectives

purposes or functions
kinds of outcomes included
explicitness of description
detail

Educational Objectives

guidance of educational decision-making
intellectual development
economic independence
citizenship and civic responsibility
social development and human relations
moral and ethical character
self-realization
comprehensive high school
social dynamite of the slums

Instructional Objectives

guidance of instructional decision-making
model for generating instructional objectives and
    related test items for dealing with concepts
  attributes of concepts
    examples, or instances, of concepts
      superordinate, coordinate, and subordinate concepts
instructional objectives for skill development in reading

much of what each student studies and learns in school is decided by persons other than teachers. The simple reason for this is that many teachers do not understand the nature of objectives and do not take sufficient initiative in formulating objectives. In this chapter, therefore, objectives, an important component of the instructional system outlined in Chapter 1, are considered in detail. First, the attributes of objectives are discussed, to clarify the different forms in which statements of objectives are written. Second, a few statements of educational objectives are presented, to indicate what some individuals and groups perceive as the overall objectives of public education. Third, instructional objectives are discussed, to aid those who are formulating these more specific objectives.

ATTRIBUTES OF OBJECTIVES

Objectives of schooling are formulated by many different individuals and groups, mainly philosophers who view education as an important part of the total human experience, laymen interested in education, and educational personnel other than teachers (Ammons, 1969). The objectives are formulated for various reasons; accordingly, there is not a single best way of stating them. Figure 4.1 shows how objectives can vary according to the following four attributes: purposes, outcomes incorporated in the objectives, explicitness, and detail. Each of these is now discussed.

Purposes of Objectives

Objectives are written for four main purposes: (1) to inform and influence various citizen groups; (2) to provide guidelines for making decisions about broad educational programs within a school system or a school building; (3) to provide guidelines for teachers in making decisions about an instructional program for a particular student or students; (4) to provide explicit information about the content to be incorporated in tests and instructional material, particularly programed material. These are all legitimate purposes of objectives and markedly influence how objectives are stated.

Some clarification of terminology is in order before considering the purposes of objectives. Some persons refer to the general objectives of education as *goals* or *aims*. "Goal" is also used to refer to the end state that an individual wishes to attain. Inasmuch as the terms "objective" and "goal" are often used synonymously, in many cases one can infer what an author means only by studying the context in which the word is used. As a further indication of this, some persons still state educational objectives in terms of what the teacher does instead of what the learner does. Thus, at a general level, "to teach communication skills" is used, rather than "to learn communication skills." The authors' preference is to state *instructional objectives* in terms of student behaviors and to use the term goal to refer to an end state sought by an individual.

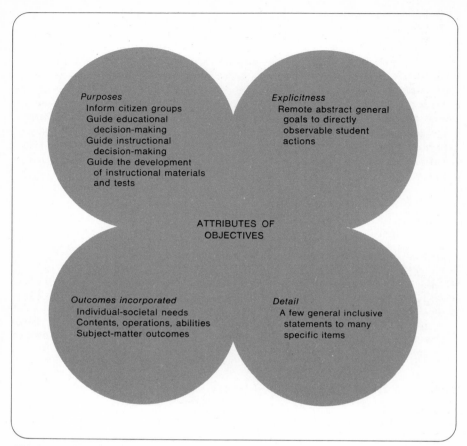

Fig. 4.1. Attributes of objectives.

Inform Citizen Groups. There are three main groups of people who are concerned with public education but who are not directly responsible for the instruction of any particular child or group of children. These three groups are: nonschool government officials who allocate the money for schools, parents whose main concern is what happens to their children, and educational personnel concerned with objectives other than those pertaining directly to their areas of interest. Objectives written for these groups are usually short statements that deal with broad interdisciplinary concerns.

At this level, objectives are stated in general terms and usually deal with one or all of the following:

Promoting the intellectual development of all children and youth,
Aiding each student to become economically independent,
Developing effective citizens,
Promoting social development and effective human relations,

Building moral and ethical character,
Helping each child and youth achieve individual self-realization.
(Bebell, 1968)

At this most general level, a statement of educational objectives may be clarified by providing additional information. For example, Recommendation 10, which follows, is one of 33 recommendations made by an NEA committee (1963). It deals with the role of the school in intellectual development, the first objective in the preceding list, but it describes more fully what is meant by intellectual development (the recommendation as stated is discussed in more detail in the NEA book from which the excerpt is taken).

RECOMMENDATION 10

Priorities for the school are the teaching of skills in reading, composition, listening, speaking (both native and foreign languages), and computation . . . ways of creative and disciplined thinking, including methods of inquiry and application of knowledge . . . competence in self-instruction and independent learning . . . fundamental understanding of the humanities and the arts, the social sciences and natural sciences, and mathematics . . . appreciation of and discriminating taste in literature, music, and the visual arts . . . instruction in health education and physical education.

Responsibilities best met by joint efforts of the school and other social agencies include: development of values and ideals . . . social and civic competence . . . vocational preparation.

The decision to include or exclude particular school subjects or outside-of-class activities should be based on: (a) the priorities assigned to the school and to other agencies; (b) data about learners and society, and developments in the academic disciplines; (c) the human and material resources available in the school and community. (NEA, 1963, p. 126)

Statements like the two just quoted are intended to indicate what certain people think the schools should strive for in the way of an ideal and also to secure support for public education from a broad segment of the population. One reason for not being more explicit in some cases is to gain more widespread support. All persons will probably agree, for example, that the school should promote the intellectual development of all children and youth. They may disagree, however, as to whether all students should learn to speak a second language fluently, master mathematics through trigonometry, and the like.

Provide Guidelines for Educational Decision-Making. Krathwohl (1965) outlined objectives at three levels of explicitness and detail that educators need. At the most abstract level are general statements of the kind made in Recommendation 10. These general statements are helpful to groups of educators in a school system who are thinking about programs of instruction for all the students from kindergarten through high school.

At the next level, more explicit objectives stated in behavioral terms are needed. In connection with Recommendation 10, more specific objectives in reading and mathematics to be achieved by each child early in his schooling might be:

Each child recognizes at sight 250 words.
Each child writes the numerals 0 through 100.

Teachers supposedly could organize instructional programs and develop tests or assessment procedures from careful analysis of objectives stated at this level of explicitness.

At the third level, explicit and detailed objectives are needed for persons who are not expert in the subject matter but who may be employed to write instructional materials and tests. For example, an expert in reading would have to identify the exact 250 words to be recognized at sight and would also need to specify the sequence in which they would be introduced in the instructional material. With this information a person less expert might be able to write instructional material or develop tests.

Provide Guidelines for Instructional Decision-Making. In Chapter 1 it was recommended that teachers and other instructional personnel working directly with the student should assume responsibility for the objectives of instruction for each student. Students may participate in formulating objectives at this level. But teachers need not start from scratch each school year to write a massive set of objectives for each student. On the contrary, a detailed statement of instructional objectives should be accumulating in each school building that each teacher studies and supplements. Each year each teacher should have contributed to the development of the statement. From this statement the teacher and student identify objectives appropriate to the student. For example, in social studies the student and the teacher may discuss, with the student making the final decision, whether to learn about the effects of the westerly winds on the climate of California or on that of North Dakota.

Otto and Peterson (1969), after securing ideas from teachers during a three-year period, outlined skills in reading and related objectives in a statement intended to serve as a guideline for use by the staff of a school building. One skill area is word attack, also referred to by some as word recognition. The first word-attack skill is, "Listens for rhyming elements"; the more explicit detailed instructional objectives are as follows:

I. Word Attack, Level A
  1. Listens for rhyming elements
    a. Words
       Objective
       The child is able to tell when (a) two words pronounced by the teacher (man-pan, call-bell, when-pen) and/or (b) the names of two objects, do and do not rhyme (i.e., "sound alike").

    b. Phrases and verses
       Objective
       1. The child is able to pick out the rhyming words in traditional verses (e.g., "Little Jack Horner Sat in a Corner") and nonsense verses ("Wing, wong, way/Tisha, loona, say") read by the teacher.
       2. The child is able to supply the missing word in a rhyming verse read by the teacher (e.g., "The big tall man/Fried eggs in a _____.").
       (Otto & Peterson, 1969, p. 25)

The preceding skill objectives are probably sufficiently explicit to help teachers in making decisions, but much freedom is also permitted and encouraged. Even more explicit statements would be needed in preparing instructional material or a battery of tests to assess the student's achievement of each objective, as will be discussed later in connection with the attributes of explicitness and detail.

Outcomes Incorporated in Objectives

In Chapter 3, outcomes of learning in the cognitive, psychomotor, and affective domains were discussed. A brief summary was presented of objectives in the cognitive domain as outlined by Bloom (1956). The objectives were stated so that they could be related to any subject-matter field, such as English, science, mathematics, or social studies. Objectives in the affective domain as formulated by Krathwohl, Bloom, and Masia (1964) were also outlined. The work of Bloom and Krathwohl illustrates how objectives may incorporate various outcomes of learning. In Chapter 3, various abilities were also described. They, too, provide a psychological basis for generating educational and instructional objectives that incorporate a certain kind of learning outcome.

A few statements follow that illustrate objectives from each domain. The statements vary in explicitness and detail. Blanks are left in parentheses to indicate where the reader may substitute something more closely related to his interests for the underlined examples. Each statement starts with a verb; the student is the assumed subject.

[A. COGNITIVE DOMAIN]

1. Learns how to learn (   ) *concepts pertaining to the natural sciences.*
2. Comprehends (   ) *concepts* of or about (   ) *the social world.*
3. Produces correct solutions to (   ) *mathematical exercises of the kind:* $5 - 3 =$ ____.
4. Produces a unique and different hypothesis regarding (   ) *the solution of the problems of poverty.*
5. Applies his ability (   ) *to count to 10 to adding integers with sums to 10.*
6. Selects two criteria from five given that he uses in judging the appropriateness of his (   ) *school conduct.*

[B. PSYCHOMOTOR DOMAIN]

1. Performs (   ) *everyday psychomotor activities with speed, precision, and coordination.*
2. Produces a (   ) *painting that expresses his own ideas.*
3. Plays (   ) *tennis* with rapid, coordinated movements.
4. Runs (   ) *2 miles* in 25 minutes.

5. Types (   ) *30 words per minute* with 2 errors or less for each 5 lines of typing.

[**C. AFFECTIVE DOMAIN**]

1. Values (   ) *the American way* of life.
2. Writes, in a two-page statement, what his responsibility is for attaining (   ) *economic independence.*
3. Talks daily with persons of a race different from his own and (   ) *states a preference for marrying a person of a different race.*

Scholars with high specialization in a subject field such as physics or history tend to be unfamiliar with recent advances in the knowledge of human learning and development. Also, they are only as familiar with educational practices as other well-educated parents who do not study education in depth. Many of these scholars, therefore, prefer to state objectives in terms of subject-matter content rather than explicit behavioral objectives. For example, they simply list the topics to be covered in a course without specifying more explicitly what the student should *know* or be able to *do* on completing the course.

In this connection, Eisner (1967, 1969), whose specialty is art, concedes that objectives in subject fields such as mathematics, languages, and the sciences can be stated explicitly. In these fields instructional objectives can be stated in such a way that they describe what the student who has learned the material well can *do*. Also, the objectives can be stated explicitly, so that the student's behaviors can be assessed to ascertain how well he has attained the objectives. Eisner points out, however, that in the arts, and perhaps in other subject matters where novel or creative responses are desired or where the students are to express their own ideas and feelings, the objectives in the form of student behaviors cannot be identified readily before instruction begins.

Explicitness and Detail

At the extreme pole from Eisner, Mager (1962) outlined procedures for developing explicit, detailed instructional objectives. Gagne (1965b), Lindvall and Bolvin (1967), and Popham, Atkin, and Raths (1968) similarly recommend explicit, detailed statements of objectives to provide the specifications for developing instructional programs. Mager (1962) summarized his ideas this way:

1. A statement of instructional objectives is a collection of words or symbols describing one of your educational *intents*.
2. An objective will communicate your intent to the degree you have described what the learner will be DOING when demonstrating his achievement and how you will know when he is doing it.
3. To describe terminal behavior (what the learner will be DOING):
   a. Identify and name the over-all behavior act.
   b. Define the important conditions under which the behavior is to occur (givens or restrictions, or both).
   c. Define the criterion of acceptable performance.

4. Write a separate statement for each objective; the more statements you have, the better chance you have of making clear your intent.
5. If you give each learner a copy of your objectives, you may not have to do much else. (Mager, 1962, p. 53)

Identifying and naming the overall behavior act, defining the important conditions under which the behavior is to occur, and defining the criterion of acceptable performance require brief explanation. Verb forms that involve doing are used to identify and name the overall behavior act. Mager indicated that verbs such as "to write," "to identify," "to compare," and "to contrast" were more explicit indicators of behavior than were "to know," "to appreciate," and "to believe." Thus, "to repair" a radio is more explicit, that is, easier to observe and evaluate, than is "to understand" or "to appreciate" how to repair a radio.

In connection with the conditions under which the final achievement is to be tested or observed, Mager gave examples including "without the aid of a reference," "given a standard set of tools," and "given a matrix of intercorrelations." A more complete example is as follows: "Given a linear algebraic equation with one unknown, the learner must be able to solve for the unknown without the aid of references, tables, or calculating devices" (Mager, 1962, p. 26). This specifies explicitly what the student does and the conditions under which it must be done.

Acceptable performance—the level of achievement—is also to be specified. For instance, the student is to get a percentage correct, such as 80 or 100, within a certain time limit, to complete the task perfectly, etc. An example that incorporates all three characteristics of an instructional objective is as follows: The student solves seven linear equations without the aid of any references within a period of 30 minutes.

In summary, we have indicated the need for objectives to be formulated and stated for various purposes, to incorporate a variety of outcomes, and to be stated at varying levels of explicitness and detail. Mager favored the greatest amount of detail so that the teacher and the student would know what is to be learned each day and would also have the means for observing and assessing how well it is learned. But the student and teacher also need to have a broader picture of where they are going and how they will get there during a semester, a year, or even longer.

Bloom's view of objectives, which is similar to that of Krathwohl outlined earlier, seems to be sensible:

> The point to be made is that not all purposes of education can or should be made explicit. However, . . . insofar as possible, the purposes of education and the specifications for educational changes (objectives) should be made explicit if they are to be open to inquiry, if teaching and learning are to be modified as improvement or change is needed, and if each new group of students is to be subjected to a particular set of educative processes. (Bloom, 1969, p. 30)

A further point is that many persons who can write reasonably well and know an area of subject matter well now have many avenues open to them for making significant contributions to the improvement of educational practice. One of the greatest needs today is for better instructional materials and related assessment procedures. Both for intellectual stimulation and as a practical exercise of potentially high social value, every person in education should learn to write objectives at different levels of explicitness and detail for at least two or three of the purposes given, including guiding the development of instructional materials — printed, audiovisual, and other types.

4.1. Assume that all the teachers of a certain school system accept the following as an educational objective of the school system: "Building moral and ethical character." Knowing this, which of the following do you think can be inferred about the large majority of teachers of the system?

 a. They agree on what is moral behavior for students.
 b. They set aside some time each week to give instruction regarding ethical character.
 c. They assess the moral development of each of their students as systematically as they do the intellectual development.
 d. They proceed as if the school did not have that particular objective.

4.2. Evaluate each of the following statements according to these criteria:

 a. It is ( ) is not ( ) sufficiently explicit to develop a test to assess when the student has attained the objective.
 b. It does ( ) does not ( ) name an observable behavior act.
 c. It does ( ) does not ( ) define the conditions under which the behavior is to occur.
 d. It does ( ) does not ( ) define the criterion of acceptable performance.

  1. Recognizes at sight 240 of the 250 words included in (exact name of a textbook).
  2. Develops effective oral communication skills.
  3. Tells when two words pronounced by the teacher do and do not rhyme.
  4. Values the American way of life.
  5. Recites the Gettysburg Address in one minute without error and without prompting.
  6. Writes instructional objectives that incorporate the attributes of objectives stated in this chapter.

4.3. Four purposes of objectives have been discussed in this chapter. Which of the purposes is best accomplished by each of the six objectives listed above (4.2)?

EDUCATIONAL OBJECTIVES

Educational and instructional objectives can be differentiated in terms of the four attributes of objectives in this way: The *purpose* of an educational objective is to inform citizen groups or to provide guidelines for developing an educational program for all the students in a school system or in a school building; the purpose of an instructional objective is to provide guidelines for making decisions about the instructional program of a student or a particular group of students. The *outcomes* incorporated in educational objectives merely provide broad indications of what students may learn; the outcomes incorporated in instructional objectives are precise descriptions of the processes, contents, etc. that a student or students are expected to learn. Educational objectives are stated in general terms; instructional objectives are statements of the *explicit, detailed behaviors* that students should demonstrate on attaining the objectives.

A few statements of general objectives of elementary and secondary education are partially outlined in this section. Various individuals and groups formulated the initial statements. All of the statements were developed in a context of *free compulsory education for all American children and youth*. That these are not merely words on paper may readily be inferred from the following:

> Public education in America is essentially free and is, in many respects, almost universal. Our concept of what these basic features are has been expanding for the past hundred years, and we strive to make the reality match the concept. In 1870, high school graduates composed only 2 percent of the population of 17-year-olds. This percentage has increased by leaps and bounds; by 1965 it was 72 percent. The numbers of graduates make interesting reading, too: In the year 1869-1870, it was 8,936; in 1964-1965, it was 1,337,000. In this period U.S. population increased less than fivefold, whereas the number of high school graduates increased 149 times.
>
> It is instructive to note how we compare with other nations in retaining youngsters through the final year of high school. The United States retains 70 percent of its age cohorts. Japan holds second place, retaining 57 percent. England and Germany retain 12 and 11 percent, respectively.
>
> These data hold considerably more meaning than the mere percentages suggest. Scholars have developed a retentivity index to show the relative chances that students from families with different occupational backgrounds will reach the last grade of the secondary school. This index shows that the United States is less selective or discriminatory than other nations. For example, more than two-and-a-half times as many pupils from working class families reach the final year of secondary school in the United States as in England. As a more extreme example, the same ratio for the United States and Germany is more than seven to one.
>
> Thus the United States provides education for a greater percentage of its young people than do most industrial nations. And it does so with the least social bias. (Polley, 1969, p. 13)

Nevertheless, it is common knowledge also that American education has a bias in terms of effects—it does least for the children of the poor. The passage that follows implies, however, that the difficulty lies not with the objectives, but with the practices:

> There is substantial evidence that the children of parents who are unskilled or semi-skilled—whether black or white—do not fare as well in schools as we would like. This is not a problem solely for the United States. It is indeed a world phenomenon. There is an irony here. The children who need education most appear to be most severely discriminated against in the educational process.

There are many reasons for this and many facets to the problem. But clearly, our educational system has the capability to address itself to the problem and effective measures can be taken to reduce or eliminate it. American schools will need the full support of the larger society and all its institutions in the campaign to remove this shortcoming—a shortcoming that undermines all the other commanding strengths of the American educational system and is therefore intolerable. (Polley, 1969, p. 15)

Elementary Education

One of the best statements of objectives of elementary education was prepared by the Mid-Century Committee on Outcomes in Elementary Education (Kearney, 1953). Figure 4.2 shows the objectives as organized in a three-dimensional framework. The first dimension is a growth scale dividing the first nine years of school into three equal time units. Although the detailed objectives for each time unit are not shown in Fig. 4.2, the committee did propose objectives that might reasonably be attained by most pupils toward the end of the third, sixth, and ninth grades.

Fig. 4.2. The behavioral continuum, showing broad curriculum areas intersecting major behavior categories. (Kearney, 1953, p. 38)

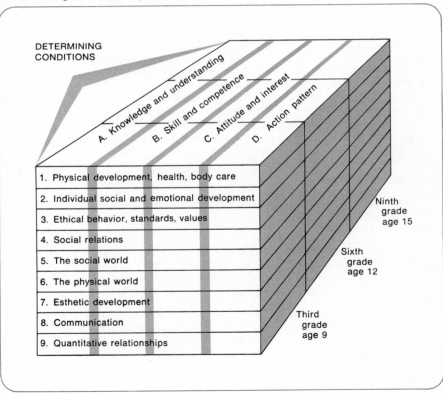

The second dimension includes the broad areas of elementary learning represented by the nine horizontal rows: physical development, health, body care; individual social and emotional development; ethical behavior, standards, values; social relations; the social world; the physical world; aesthetic development; communication; and quantitative relationships.

The third dimension gives the type of behavioral changes or outcomes expected: knowledge and understanding; skill and competence; attitude and interest; and action pattern. The *determining conditions* cannot properly be called "outcomes" in the same sense as knowledge, skill, attitude, and action. Determining conditions actually refer to the biological and sociological context in which children, teachers, and others in the school interact. It is possible that over a long period of time, perhaps two or three generations, these determining conditions might change because of more efficient pupil learning; that is, the nature of the students and of the environment itself might change.

When parents, other laymen, and subject-matter specialists first encounter these objectives, they are often perplexed because the objectives do not seem to fit neatly into separate subject fields. It is true that the communication area can readily be associated with reading, spelling, and English, quantitative relationships with arithmetic or mathematics, the physical world with science and geography, and so on. The committee did not specify, however, that the objectives had to be achieved in connection with any specific area of organized subject matter. Indeed, to achieve knowledge and skills in such objectives as social relations, ethical behavior, and individual social and emotional development, the student needs not only subject content but also many experiences with the teacher and other pupils.

Certain objectives can be achieved more readily in the school than others; for example, we can help children acquire communication skills and knowledge of the physical world more readily than we can help them achieve healthy emotional and social development. The home and neighborhood are more powerful determinants of emotional and social development than they are of communication skills and quantitative relationships. Nevertheless, the school can and should attempt to help each child progress in the directions implied by each of the nine curriculum areas.

Secondary Education

The launching of the first Russian satellite in 1957 provoked confusion and panic among many Americans, especially when American public education was used repeatedly as the scapegoat for losing this "race" to Russia. (The same sort of critics are still pointing with alarm at the schools, but they do not mention the great contributions our system of public education obviously has made to our recent space exploration, including the moon landings.) James B. Conant (1959), a former president of Harvard University and a distinguished organic chemist, responded constructively to the negative criticisms and the clamor to revert to a Western European pattern — academic high schools for some students and

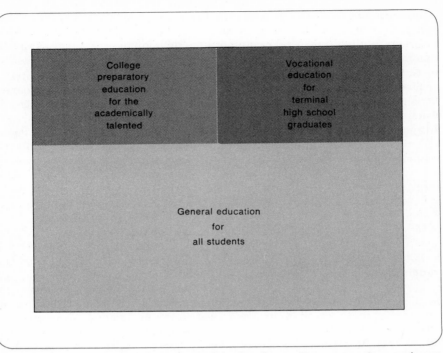

Fig. 4.3. Relative emphases given to general education, college preparatory, and vocational education in a comprehensive high school.

technical or trade schools for others. He made an exhaustive study of American high schools.

Conant recognized clearly the forces in American life that had produced our free public school system and the comprehensive high school in particular. All students in a community go to a comprehensive high school. All receive general education. However, there are some courses for students who go on to college and also some for those who go to work on high school graduation, as shown in Fig. 4.3. The proportion of the time given to the three segments varies among students, and, Conant said, there should not be rigid "tracks" or curricula.

Conant observed many examples of excellence in the comprehensive high schools he studied, as well as some deficiencies. Recommending that the fundamental pattern of comprehensive high school education should be continued, he thus summed up the role of such schools:

> . . . The three main objectives of a comprehensive high school are: first, to provide a general education for all the future citizens; second, to provide good elective programs for those who wish to use their acquired skills immediately on graduation; third, to provide satisfactory programs for those whose vocations will depend on their subsequent education in a college or university. (Conant, 1959, p. 17)

Conant made 21 recommendations for improving public secondary education. All should be studied, though none need be accepted, by anyone interested in education from kindergarten through graduate school. Actually, few besides Conant would agree with all 21 recommendations. For instance, he has been properly criticized for stating the objectives of general education simply as the number of years or semesters of various subjects required of all students for graduation. He did not specify what students of varying intellectual abilities were to achieve through taking the subjects, and he did not give his value system which led to this and other recommendations. The reasons for these criticisms are more apparent on studying the following two recommendations:

RECOMMENDATION 7: DIVERSIFIED PROGRAMS FOR THE DEVELOPMENT OF MARKETABLE SKILLS

Programs should be available for girls interested in developing skills in typing, stenography, the use of clerical machines, home economics, or a specialized branch of home economics which through further work in college might lead to the profession of dietitian. Distributive education should be available if the retail shops in the community can be persuaded to provide suitable openings. If the community is rural, vocational agriculture should be included. For boys, depending on the community, trade and industrial programs should be available. Half a day is required in the eleventh and twelfth grades for this vocational work. In each specialized trade, there should be an advisory committee composed of representatives of management and labor. Federal money is available for these programs.

The school administration should constantly assess the employment situation in those trades included in the vocational programs. When opportunities for employment in a given trade no longer exist within the community, the training program in that field should be dropped. The administration should be ready to introduce new vocational programs as opportunities open in the community or area. In some communities, advanced programs of a technical nature should be developed; these programs often involve more mathematics than is usually required for the building trades or auto mechanics programs. . . . the students enrolled in programs which develop marketable skills should also be enrolled in English, social studies, and other courses required for graduation. Furthermore, efforts should be made to prevent isolation from the other students. Homerooms may be effective means to this end. . . . (Conant, 1959, p. 52)

RECOMMENDATION 9: THE PROGRAMS OF THE ACADEMICALLY TALENTED

A policy in regard to the elective programs of academically talented boys and girls should be adopted by the school to serve as a guide to the counselors. In the type of school I am discussing the following program should be strongly recommended as a minimum:

Four years of mathematics, four years of one foreign language, three years of science, in addition to the required four years of English and three years of social studies; a total of eighteen courses with homework to be taken in four years. This program will require at least fifteen hours of homework each week.

Many academically talented pupils may wish to study a second foreign language or an additional course in social studies. Since such students are capable of handling twenty or more courses with homework, these additional academic courses may be added to the recommended minimum program. If the school is organized on a seven- or eight-period day (Recommendation 12), at least one additional course without homework (for example, art or music) may also be scheduled each year.

If as school policy a minimum academic program including both mathematics and a foreign language is recommended to the academically talented pupils and their parents, the counselors will have the problem of identifying as early as possible the members of the group. It may well be that, in the next lower 10 or 20 percent of the boys and girls in terms of scholastic aptitude on a national basis, there are a number who ought to be guided into similar but less rigorous programs. (Conant, 1959, p. 57)

Although Recommendation 9 appears to be a rigid prescription, another recommendation provides for individualized programs for each pupil, including the opportunity for academically talented students to take some work in the fine arts. Conant would not classify pupils according to various curricula or tracks, such as college preparatory, vocational, or commercial. In addition, if a talented girl had no interest in mathematics and disliked it strongly, she would not be required to take four years of mathematics. Likewise, Conant would not require an uninterested girl or boy to take the third year of science.

Schools for Slums and Suburbs

Conant continued his studies of American education, giving particular attention to schools in the slums of the large cities. As early as 1961, he pointed out that the problems of education in the slums and the suburbs are very different from those in small independent cities which are not part of a metropolitan complex:

> The task with which the school people in the slum must struggle is, on the one hand, to prepare a student for getting and keeping a job as soon as he leaves school, and, on the other hand, to encourage those who have academic talent to aim at a profession through higher education. . . . In the suburban high school from which 80 percent or more of the graduates enter some sort of college, the most important problem from the parents' point of view is to ensure the admission of their children to prestige colleges. . . . From the educator's point of view, however, the most vexing problem is to adjust the family's ambitions to the boy's or girl's abilities. (Conant, 1961, pp. 1-2)

According to Conant, neither the suburban nor the slum schools are truly comprehensive, although a far greater problem exists in the latter; in the slum schools we are allowing "social dynamite" to accumulate.

The social dynamite continues to accumulate. The Elementary and Secondary Education Act of 1965, which provided federal funds for education of the disadvantaged, was the first large-scale federal response to the problem. It is obvious, however, that a far greater effort is needed at all levels—by federal, state, and local governments and by individual citizens—to bring about significant and lasting improvement.

Education and Social Needs

At the same time that Conant was studying the problems of American secondary education, a task force set up by the National Education Association was studying all levels of education (NEA, 1963). The objectives they evolved that deal with critical individual and social needs are of special interest, as may be inferred from the six recommendations that follow (much of Recommendation 10 was quoted earlier in this chapter):

RECOMMENDATION 9

The instructional program should provide: (a) opportunities for developing the individual potentialities represented in the wide range of differences among people; (b) a common fund of knowledge, values, and skills vital to the welfare of the individual and the nation.

To achieve these objectives, the instructional program cannot be the same for all. Provision for individual differences should be made by qualified teaching personnel through diagnosis of learning needs and through appropriate variety of content, resources for learning, and instructional methods.

RECOMMENDATION 11

The schools can help to combat such serious national problems as youth unemployment and juvenile delinquency by: (a) evaluating the intellectual and creative potential of *all* children and youth in the schools; (b) identifying early the potential dropout and delinquent; (c) developing positive programs to challenge these young people to educational endeavor; (d) participating in cooperative programs with parents and with community groups and organizations— business and industry, labor, service groups, government agencies, and the many youth-serving agencies.

RECOMMENDATION 12

Rational discussion of controversial issues should be an important part of the school program. The teacher should help students identify relevant information, learn the techniques of critical analysis, make independent judgments, and be prepared to present and support them. The teacher should also help students become sensitive to the continuing need for objective reexamination of issues in the light of new information and changing conditions in society.

RECOMMENDATION 13

To help the student think critically about current issues, the curriculum should provide opportunities for adequate instruction concerning social forces and trends. Attention commensurate with their significance in modern society should be given to issues such as international relations, economic growth, urbanization, population growth, science and technology, and mass media.

RECOMMENDATION 14

The school curriculum should include a study of political and social ideologies focusing upon communism. The methods of rational inquiry should be stressed. The study should be set in the perspective of the modern world and be incorporated into the instructional program at appropriate points. If a special unit on communism is deemed desirable in the secondary school, it should supplement and complement earlier study of these topics.

As with other areas of the curriculum, decisions about *what to teach* and *how to teach* about these topics should be based upon policies developed by school administrators and teachers of the local school system. In the formulation and implementation of such policies, school personnel should utilize the resources of scholarship and be supported in their decisions by the school board and by an informed community opinion.

RECOMMENDATION 15

The school can provide and maintain a curriculum appropriately balanced for each student by offering a comprehensive program of studies, making early and continuous assessment of individual potentialities and achievements, and providing individualized programs based on careful counseling.

To avoid the imbalance that can result from limiting financial support to certain selected subjects and services, general financial support should be provided for the total program. This applies to local, state, and federal support. (NEA, 1963, pp. 125-129)

4.4. It is clear that education is least helpful to many children of the poor. To what extent do you think this condition is related to societal aspects of economics, politics, religion, and race? To what extent do you think it is related to preferences of teachers and other school people?

4.5. Write two or three instructional objectives related to any one of the nine broad areas of learning outlined by the Mid-Century Committee on Outcomes in Elementary Education.

4.6. Which of the recurrent emphases in general statements of educational objectives do you think should receive highest priority? Which should receive lowest priority? Are certain objectives more important than others for certain groups, say the rural poor? Try to arrange the objectives in a hierarchy of priorities from highest to lowest.

4.7. What emphases should be included in future statements of objectives? Worldwide outlook? Historical sense? Man in nature? Philosophy of life? Control of technology?

INSTRUCTIONAL OBJECTIVES

The teacher is a key figure in making decisions about instruction. He can formulate instructional objectives for a student or group of students when two conditions are met: (1) The more important *categories of outcomes* that students should learn related to the various curriculum areas require identification and description. For example, concepts and principles related to science, social studies, etc. that students of a particular age or school level might learn should be identified by specialists in the subject field, experts in learning, and teachers. (2) The different *levels* at which these outcomes might be attained by students also require identification and description. Thus your own concept of instructional objectives should be more clear as a result of your study of this chapter, so that you can now give examples of instructional objectives, state the attributes of instructional objectives, differentiate between educational and instructional objectives, and use your knowledge about objectives in formulating instructional objectives.

A model to help teachers and other educational workers generate objectives dealing with concepts has been developed and applied to some concepts in English, mathematics, science, and social studies (Frayer, Fredrick, & Klausmeier, 1969). It is presented and discussed in this section. One concept from mathematics and one from English are discussed. Later in the section some instructional objectives related to reading are presented.

Instructional Objectives: Concept Quadrilateral

A person must have considerable knowledge about a concept and other related concepts in order to formulate objectives and related assessment exercises and procedures. He should at least know the names of the attributes that permit different things to be put in the same class and also the attributes by which things in the same category are differentiated, e.g., rectangles and parallelograms are quadrilaterals, because both have four sides, but rectangles differ from parallelograms in relative size of angles. Also, this knowledge is important: instances and noninstances of the attributes, instances and noninstances of the concept, a verbal definition of the concept, the names of superordinate, coordinate, and subordinate concepts, one or more principles that embody the concept, and kinds of problems whose solution requires use of the concept or principle.

In connection with *quadrilateral*, specifically, it must be known, among other things, that squares, rectangles, parallelograms, rhombuses, trapezoids, and kites are quadrilaterals. All these quadrilaterals have the same four attributes; they are closed figures, plane figures, simple figures, and have four sides. The six kinds of quadrilaterals are differentiated from one another by the two attributes of relative size of angles and parallelness of sides. In order to formulate objectives and assessment procedures, 13 kinds of information about quadrilateral, including that just given, should be known, as now outlined:

1. Instances of the attributes of quadrilateral, e.g., closed figures:

2. Noninstances of the attributes, e.g., nonclosed figures:

3. Concept label: quadrilateral.

4. Instances of the concept:

5. Noninstances of the concept:

6. Attributes relevant for defining all quadrilaterals: closed figure, plane figure, simple figure, 4 sides (4 angles).

7. Attributes by which kinds of quadrilaterals are differentiated: relative size of angles, parallelness of sides. These two are *irrelevant* to determining whether a figure *is* a quadrilateral. Other attributes, such as the size of the figure and its orientation, are also.

8. Concept definition: a plane, closed, simple figure with 4 sides.

9. Superordinate or higher-level concept: polygon.

10. Coordinate concepts: triangle, pentagon, hexagon.

11. Subordinate or lower-level concepts: trapezoid, kite, parallelogram, rectangle, rhombus, square. (These are differentiated from one another in terms of the relative size of angles and the parallelness of sides.)

12. Use of the concept in a principle: The perimeter of a quadrilateral is equal to the sum of the four sides.

13. Use of the concept in solving a problem: Find the perimeter of a given quadrilateral.

Objectives, stated in *explicit behavioral* terms related to each of the preceding, are given shortly. One kind of objective requires the student *to select*, or *to identify*, one response as correct among a number of possible responses presented to him. The other requires him *to produce*, or *to supply*, a correct response to a cue or question. As noted earlier in the chapter, objectives may be stated at varying levels of explicitness and detail. The behaviors of selecting and producing are explicit; therefore, they do not include the cognitive operations, such as cognizing, analyzing, hypothesizing, inferring, and evaluating, that are involved in learning the concepts. Neither do they indicate how an instructional program should be organized so that students achieve the objectives.

In the model that follows, in the left column, objectives are given that are parallel to the 13 points already listed. The objectives are stated so as to apply to many concepts, not just quadrilateral. Those designated "a" require *selection* of the correct response and those designated "b" require *production* of the correct response. In the right column are test items related to quadrilateral. Items pertaining to the odd-numbered objectives are multiple-choice, requiring the student *to select* the correct response; those pertaining to even-numbered objectives require the student *to produce* the correct response.

| EXPLICIT OBJECTIVES (MAY BE APPLIED TO MANY CONCEPTS) | SAMPLE ITEMS (RELATED TO QUADRILATERAL) |

1a. Selects an instance of the attribute, given its name (closed figure).

1a. Which drawing is a *closed figure*?

A.   D.

B.   E.

C.

1b. Produces an instance of the attribute, given its name (closed figure).

2a. Selects the name of the attribute, given an instance of the attribute (closed figure).

2b. Produces the name of the attribute, given an instance of the attribute (closed figure).

2b. What term accurately describes all three figures?

3a. Selects an instance of the concept, given the concept name (quadrilateral).

3a. Which figure is a quadrilateral?

A.   D.

B.   E.

C.

3b. Produces an instance of the concept, given the concept name (quadrilateral).

4a. Selects a noninstance of the concept, given the concept name (quadrilateral).

4b. Produces a noninstance of the concept, given the concept name (quadrilateral).

4b. Draw a plane figure that is *not* a quadrilateral.

5a. Selects the name of the concept, given an instance of it (quadrilateral).

5a.   This figure is a

A. parallelogram
B. square
C. rhombus
D. quadrilateral
E. rectangle

5b. Produces the name of the concept, given an instance of it (quadrilateral).

$$\Big[\ \text{EXPLICIT OBJECTIVES (MAY BE APPLIED TO MANY CONCEPTS)}\ \Big]$$
continued

6a. Selects the name of the relevant attribute (4 sides) of the concept, given the name of the concept.

6b. Produces the name of the relevant attribute (4 sides) of the concept, given the name of the concept.

7a. Selects the name of the irrelevant attribute (4 right angles) of the concept, given its name.

7b. Produces the name of the irrelevant attribute (4 right angles) of the concept, given its name.

8a. Selects the name (quadrilateral) of the concept, given its definition.

8b. Produces the name (quadrilateral) of the concept, given its definition.

9a. Selects the definition (plane closed 4-sided figures) of the concept, given its name.

9b. Produces the definition (plane closed 4-sided figures) of the concept, given its name.

10a. Selects the name of a concept (polygon) superordinate to the one given.

10b. Produces the name of a concept (polygon) superordinate to the one given.

$$\Big[\ \text{SAMPLE ITEMS (RELATED TO QUADRILATERAL)}\ \Big]$$
continued

6b. List the characteristics which are true of all quadrilaterals.

7a. Not all quadrilaterals have
A. 4 right angles
B. 4 sides
C. closed sides
D. straight sides
E. 4 angles

8b. All plane closed figures with 4 sides may be called _____.

9a. All quadrilaterals are
A. plane closed 4-sided figures
B. plane closed 3-sided figures
C. plane open 4-sided figures
D. plane closed 4-sided figures with opposite sides equal
E. plane closed 4-sided figures with no sides equal

10b. Triangles and quadrilaterals may both be called _____.

11a. Selects the name of a concept (trapezoid) subordinate to the one given.

11a. Which is true?
A. All hexagons are also quadrilaterals.
B. All trapezoids are also quadrilaterals.
C. All circles are also quadrilaterals.
D. All triangles are also quadrilaterals.
E. All pentagons are also quadrilaterals.

11b. Produces the name of a concept (trapezoid) subordinate to the one given.

12a. Selects the principle that relates two concepts, given the concept names.

12b. Produces the principle that relates two concepts, given the concept names.

12b. What is the perimeter of a quadrilateral?

13a. Selects the correct answer by applying a principle to a given problem.

13a. Which is the correct way to find the perimeter of the quadrilateral below?

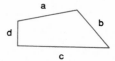

13b. Produces the correct answer by applying a principle to a given problem.

A. a × b
B. a × b × c × d
C. a + b + c + d
D. a + b
E. 2a + 2b

The objectives permit the generation of items other than the ones given. For example, items of types 1 and 2 may be written for all the attributes of quadrilaterals, specifically, and also for all the attributes of many other concepts. Similarly, additional items could be written for other kinds of quadrilaterals and relationships among them. Objectives 10 through 13 could be eliminated if one were concerned only with the initial learning of a particular concept and not with the relationship to other concepts, principles, and problem-solving.

Some concepts are not defined in terms of attributes. In this case, objectives 1, 2, 6, and 7 are not appropriate. For example, when a concept is defined in terms of synonyms or antonyms (beautiful-pretty, beautiful-ugly), the synonym or antonym may be substituted for the attribute.

Frayer (1969) used the preceding model of instructional objectives to prepare instructional material dealing with geometric concepts and also to assess the students' knowledge, or level of mastery, before and after instruction. (See Chapter 11, pages 420-421, for a discussion of this research and its results.) The same model is used to write items pertaining to concepts in other subject fields. A teacher who understands it fully and can also analyze concepts may greatly reduce the time involved in stating objectives and writing tests to assess students' mastery of the concepts.

Instructional Objectives: Concept Suffix

Objectives pertaining to the concept *suffix* and related multiple-choice items now follow. Here only the even-numbered objectives that call for *selecting* the correct responses are given.

[OBJECTIVES]

[RELATED TEST ITEMS]

2a. Selects the name of attribute (an addition to a word), given an instance of it.

In "Sadness is a lonely puppy," ness is called:
A. an addition to a word
B. a plural form
C. a contraction
D. a prefix
E. a root word

4a. Selects the noninstance of a concept, given the name of the concept (suffix).

Which of the underlined parts is *not* a suffix?
A. kitten   D. runs
B. slowly   E. walking
C. careful

6a. Selects the name of the relevant attribute of the concept, given the name of the concept (suffix).

Which of these is needed in order to have a suffix?
A. a root word   D. a capital
B. a form of *be*   letter
C. a period   E. a prefix

8a. Selects the name of the concept (suffix) given its definition.

The addition at the end of a word is called:
A. a suffix   D. a prefix
B. a closing   E. a singular
C. a helper

10a. Selects the name of a concept superordinate to the one given.

All suffixes are:
A. parts of words   D. modifiers
B. contractions   E. plural
C. prefixes

12a. Selects the principle which relates two concepts, given the concept names.

What is true about suffixes and plurals?
A. A suffix can be added to words to make them plural.
B. All plurals have suffixes.
C. All suffixes are plural.
D. Suffixes can be added only to plurals.

It is not anticipated that the student will learn all the preceding information about suffix during a unit of instruction or even during a year. Rather, it will be learned over several years. Cumulative learning of the concept suffix occurs from the earliest time at which a student observes a few different additions to root words and treats them alike until he properly categorizes all suffixes, defines suffix and related terms, and uses suffixes correctly. The same is true of quadrilateral. Wiviott (1970) found that no fifth-grade students scored perfectly on a longer test on quadrilaterals based on the preceding objectives; some, but not nearly all, eighth-graders did, and most, but not all, eleventh-graders did.

Instructional Objectives: Skills

Otto and Peterson (1969) outlined six skill areas in reading. The first three of the six are word attack, comprehension, and study skills. Each skill area was further analyzed into sequential levels of subskills. Instructional objectives were then formulated for the subskills. The instructional objectives were intended to be sufficiently explicit and detailed for teachers to use in developing an instructional program for a student and assessing his progress; they were not intended to be sufficiently explicit and detailed to prepare instructional material and tests. Earlier in this chapter, the objectives for "Word Attack, Level A: 1. Listens for rhyming elements" were given. The remaining objectives pertaining to three other subskills of level A follow:

2. Notices likenesses and differences
   a. Pictures (shapes)
      Objective
      The child is able to match key shapes with shapes that are identical in terms of form and orientation (e.g., ☐ + ⟋‾‾⟍).
   b. Letters and numbers
      Objective
      The child is able to pick the letter—upper or lower case—or number in a series that is identical to a key number or letter. (The child points to the letter or number that is the same as the first letter or number in a row: P: B T P K; s: s z e c; 9: 6 0 9 8.)
   c. Words and phrases
      Objective
      The child is able to pick the word or phrase in a series that is identical to a key word or phrase (e.g., *down*: wand/down/bone/find; *back and forth*: bank and find/back and forth/found it).
3. Distinguishes colors
   Objective
   The child is able to identify colors (e.g., blue, green, black, yellow, red, orange, white, brown, purple) named by the teacher. (The child picks from four choices the color named by the teacher, e.g., key word = *blue*, color choices = *blue* and *black*; the child chooses the proper crayon to fill in boxes with the color named by the teacher.)
4. Listens for initial consonant sounds
   Objective
   Given two common words pronounced by the teacher (e.g., bird-ball, boy-take, banana-dog), the child is able to tell when the words do and do not begin alike. (Otto & Peterson, 1969, pp. 26-27)

Lengthy detailed statements of instructional objectives are not needed to describe the desired final achievement of a student after a certain amount of instruction. For example, the following explicitly stated objective subsumes all of the preceding instructional objectives and many others: "Recognizes at sight the first 250 words included in the first three books of [a particular reading series]." Similarly, the achievements implied in the separate objectives concerning quadrilateral could be incorporated in a few short sentences. Thus, the *nature* of the final achievement desired can be stated in a few words. This does not, of course, provide the necessary detailed information concerning the steps in a sequence by which the final achievement is to be *reached*.

Also, it is not necessary to construct multiple-choice tests, or any other kind of written test, to assess whether a student has attained certain knowledge about a concept or any other outcome. Refer to any of the instructional objectives in this section. You will note that they are stated in such manner that the teacher can *observe* directly whether or not the student has acquired the information or skill. In most cases, indeed, the student will know independently whether or not he has.

4.8. Select a concept that categorizes a group of things in the same way that "quadrilateral" does. You might use the concept *instructional objective* or any other concept about which you have considerable knowledge. Then, as was done for quadrilateral, list the attributes of the concept, instances and noninstances, a definition, a superordinate and subordinate concept, if there are any, and a principle involving use of the concept. On completing this, write a set of instructional objectives that describe the behaviors of a student who has attained the concept at the level you desire. Select these from the 13 behaviors involving selecting and producing that were presented in the model or modify them as you desire. (The person who completes this exercise is able to analyze a concept and to write related instructional objectives at a level above that of most experienced teachers. Further, these abilities can be applied to most concepts. Do your best with this exercise now, but you may want to come back to it after studying Chapter 5, dealing with instructional materials, and Chapter 11, dealing with concepts and principles.)

4.9. It is difficult to determine the skills that are prerequisite to other skills. Do you think all subject matters can be explicated, as was done with reading? Which subjects seem to have such sequences of skills and subskills, and which do not?

SUMMARY

Statements of *educational objectives* are formulated at two levels by many individuals and groups. At a most general level, a statement of educational objectives is intended to inform the public and secure their support. At a less general level, another statement provides guidelines for developing an educational program for all the students of a school system or a school building. Some persons refer to these general statements as educational aims or goals. *Instructional objectives* are also formulated at two levels of explicitness and detail. At a less explicit level, instructional objectives are formulated so that a teacher who knows subject matter reasonably well can outline a related instructional program for a student or group of students and can also develop tests or observational schedules to assess students' attainments. At a more explicit level, instructional objectives may be stated in greater detail so that expert writers who are not specialized in the subject matter may prepare instructional materials and tests.

Groups in America assert that it is still reasonable to aspire toward providing a high quality of education for *all* American children and youth. Six objectives of schooling for all students, widely accepted—at least at the verbal level—are: intellectual development, economic independence and vocational opportunity, citizenship and civic responsibility, social development and human relationships, moral and ethical character, and self-realization. It is only too obvious that these objectives have not, by and large, been attained reasonably well so far in this century. Furthermore, it is now apparent that if we are to survive physically, we must see that both education and society in general give the highest priority to the elimination of war, poverty, and environmental pollution.

Instructional objectives specify the behaviors that the student will show on attaining each objective. These behaviors may be stated in terms of actions that can be observed directly, such as "states," "writes," "produces," "identifies," "performs," etc.; or they may be stated in terms of operations that can be readily inferred from test results or direct observation, such as "comprehends," "analyzes," "evaluates," "applies," "values." Instructional objectives can be stated explicitly and concisely. For example, here is an objective stated explicitly and concisely: "The student on a written test of 15 minutes' length spells 48 of 50 words correctly that have been drawn randomly from a group of 5000 words listed in the school's curriculum guide in spelling." One could also formulate 5000 instructional objectives, one for each word in the guide. Instructional objectives should be stated in sufficient detail so that both the student and teacher know what is to be learned. At the same time, one can get into so much detail that the teacher does not have time to write the objective and the student does not get a clear understanding of the larger instructional program. Thus, objectives must be formulated in terms of the purposes intended.

SUGGESTIONS FOR FURTHER READING

ASSOCIATION FOR SUPERVISION AND CURRICULUM DEVELOPMENT. *To nurture humaneness: Commitment for the 70's.* Washington, D.C.: The Association, 1970.

This 255-page yearbook has 22 short chapters in which persons from various occupations and disciplines give their viewpoints about the importance of the individual.

BLOOM, B. S., ed. *Taxonomy of educational objectives. Handbook I: Cognitive domain.* New York: McKay, 1956.

The statement of educational objectives is also an outline of abilities. Chapter 2, pages 25-43, has a good treatment of the nature of abilities.

GARDNER, J. W. *Excellence: Can we be equal and excellent too?* New York: Harper & Row, 1961.

In this 171-page paperback, an educational psychologist and a former secretary of Health, Education and Welfare discusses three competing forces in American society: hereditary privilege, equalitarianism, and competitive performance.

GARDNER, J. W. *Self-renewal: The individual and the innovative society.* New York: Harper & Row, 1963.

This 141-page paperback outlines the conditions in the individual and in society that are essential for continuous re-creation.

HEILBRONER, R. L. Priorities for the seventies. *Saturday review,* January 3, 1970, pp. 17-19, 84.

Priorities related to the *physical survival* of Americans and the peoples of the world are outlined. A changed emphasis on research and education in the universities is also proposed.

KLAUSMEIER, H. J., & O'HEARN, G. T., eds. *Research and development toward the improvement of education.* Madison, Wisc.: Dembar Educational Research Services, 1968, pp. 42-86.

Five scholarly articles are devoted to outlining research and development since 1950 in English, mathematics, reading, and science. Each author in this section has made a significant contribution to curriculum development.

KRATHWOHL, D. R., BLOOM, B. S., & MASIA, B. B. *Taxonomy of objectives. The classification of educational goals. Handbook II. Affective domain.* New York: McKay, 1964.

An outline is presented of affective development to be nurtured through education.

MAGER, R. F. *Preparing instructional objectives.* Palo Alto, Cal.: Ferron, 1962.

This short programed textbook is helpful to individuals who wish to learn to write highly detailed, explicit instructional objectives.

OJEMANN, R. H. Should educational objectives be stated in behavioral terms? In Ripple, R. E., ed., *Readings in learning and human abilities.* New York: Harper & Row, 2nd ed., 1971.

Ojemann distinguishes between overt behaviors in test-like and other situations, gives examples, and outlines measurement procedures.

POPHAM, W. J., EISNER, E., SULLIVAN, H. J., & TYLER, L. *Instructional objectives.* Chicago: Rand McNally, 1969.

This 142-page AERA monograph deals with kinds of instructional objectives and the explicitness and detail with which they are expressed.

Chapter 5 Instructional Materials and Related Technology

Types and Uses of Instructional Materials

evolution of instructional technology
quality control of instructional material

Instructional Television

present status
conditions favorable to ITV
principles to consider in use of ITV

Programed Instructional Materials

early promise for individualization
programed material: linear, branching, adjunct
unrealized expectations and reassessment

Computers in Education and Instruction

educational research
information storage and retrieval
computer-managed instruction
computer-assisted instruction
basic modes of CAI

It is often essential to give the same information to large numbers of students simultaneously. Among the methods that have been developed to do this are televised instruction, lectures, and sound motion pictures. It is also essential to provide for differences among students in three critical dimensions of learning—what each student learns, the means by which he learns it, and the rate at which he learns it. Other methods and systems have been developed to do this. One-to-one and small-group activities of various kinds obviously are necessary in providing for individual differences.

Any method of instruction, regardless of its objective, usually incorporates a combination of three variables—student activity, teacher activity, and instructional materials. The importance of the third component—instructional materials—has been increasingly recognized in recent years. It is not surprising to find, therefore, that in the last two decades major efforts have been made by educational personnel and many others—including psychologists, subject-matter specialists, engineers, and electronics specialists—to develop a variety of instructional materials and related devices and procedures. The resulting applications of principles of physics, electronics, chemistry, learning, and measurement to instruction are called *instructional technology*.

In this chapter, different kinds of instructional materials and their possible uses are surveyed. Then three of the methods that developers have successively concentrated on in recent decades—televised instruction, programed instruction, and computer-assisted instruction—are dealt with. The main purpose of the chapter is to provide information that is helpful in making broad decisions about which materials to use for which purposes of instruction. A secondary purpose is to encourage teachers themselves to devote more effort to the development of better instructional procedures and materials.

TYPES AND USES OF INSTRUCTIONAL MATERIALS

Instructional materials are constantly and rapidly increasing in both number and variety. One kind of high-quality material may work better to achieve certain objectives than another. Needless to say, however, not all material is of equally high quality; furthermore, it is very difficult to determine its quality except after purchase and use. To clarify these points, a historical note on instructional materials and related technology is given. Then types and uses of instructional materials are described. Finally, recent attempts to assure higher quality material before widespread promotion and sale are discussed.

Historical Note on Instructional Materials and Technology

Lumsdaine (1964) portrayed some of the contributions of the physical sciences, mathematics, and the behavioral sciences to the development of instructional materials and devices for use in instruction. He referred to these developments as educational technology. Figure 5.1 shows the interrelationships. Our main concern is to view the information in the figure historically. Running down the second column are these words: "paper," "ink"; "printing press," "movable type"; "lithography," "photography"; "projected still pictures"; "silent films"; "sound recording"; "sound films," "television"; "complex teaching machines (optical, elec-

Fig. 5.1. Some of the interrelationships among developments in physical and behavioral sciences related to educational technology. (Lumsdaine, 1964, p. 375)

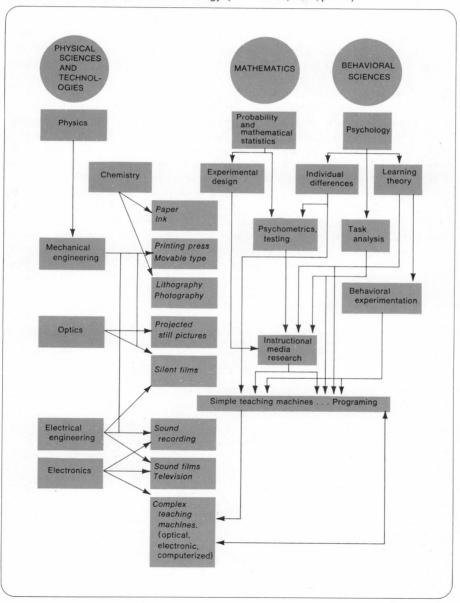

tronic, computerized)." The striking fact is that about half these were not invented until the twentieth century. Similarly, most of the contributions of mathematics and the behavioral sciences to instructional technology shown in the figure also originated in this century. Experimental design, psychometric testing, learning theory, task analysis, instructional media research, simple teaching machines, programing—all are products of the twentieth century. Obviously, there has not yet been much time to bring together the many possible applications to education from all these fields. Also, not much money and effort have yet been spent on evaluating the instructional applications that have been evolved. It does seem quite certain, though, that these recent developments can be extended to improve both the quality and the amount of instruction, not only for the people of this country but also for those throughout the rest of the world.

Uses of Various Materials

Persons experienced in teaching who have specialized knowledge of instructional materials and devices as well are sources of valuable information on what kinds of materials may be used for various purposes. Also, a substantial amount of research has been done to learn how certain materials perform, and comparisons have been made between different materials designed to achieve the same objectives. For instance, Allen (1967) reported his judgments of high-quality material in different media. He evolved a thumbnail sketch of media effectiveness in relation to broad objectives, which is provided in Table 5.1. Examine it carefully in terms of your own specific subject-matter and teaching-level interests. You may wish to come back and review the table after completing your study of this chapter and also after studying later chapters, especially as four later chapters deal with four of the learning objectives included in Table 5.1.

Table 5.1. Relationships Between Instructional Media and Learning Objectives

Instructional media type	Learning factual infor- mation	Learning visual identifi- cations	Learning principles, concepts, and rules	Learning proce- dures	Performing skilled perceptual- motor acts	Developing desirable attitudes, opinions, and motivations
Still pictures	*medium*	**high**	*medium*	*medium*	low	low
Motion pictures	*medium*	**high**	**high**	**high**	*medium*	*medium*
Television	*medium*	*medium*	**high**	*medium*	low	*medium*
3-D objects	low	**high**	low	low	low	low
Audio recordings	*medium*	low	low	*medium*	low	*medium*
Programed instruction	*medium*	*medium*	*medium*	**high**	low	*medium*
Demonstration	low	*medium*	low	**high**	*medium*	*medium*
Printed textbooks	*medium*	low	*medium*	*medium*	low	*medium*
Oral presentation	*medium*	low	*medium*	*medium*	low	*medium*

Source: Allen, 1967, p. 28.

Allen (1967) also summarized useful information about 11 kinds of equipment, the cost of each, the availability of facilities and equipment for its use, and aspects of production, shown in Table 5.2. Again, because of differences in quality among examples of the same kind of material, rapid changes in technology, and varying applications in various subject matters at different school levels, one should use the information only as a general guide. For instance, as noted under item 9 in the table, closed-circuit television is not normally available; nevertheless, many schools do have television receivers and thus can receive programs, even if they cannot produce them. Also, as item 10 implies, teaching machines are not being used much, but programed textbooks can be used as readily as any other books, and many are available.

Improving the Quality of Instructional Materials

Instructional materials, including textbooks, are purchased for use at a designated grade level with the expectation that students of average intelligence can read most of the words and that they can also learn new concepts from studying the textbooks. Some textbooks, unfortunately, do not meet this expectation. Recently, an advanced seminar conducted by the senior author identified single and compound words representing concepts in fourth-grade textbooks. Some of these words were then put on cards and tried out on fifth-grade children to see if the children could recognize (read) and comprehend the words. It turned out that there were many words in the fourth-grade books in mathematics and science that even the fifth-grade students of average and above-average reading achievement could not recognize and also could not comprehend when presented orally. Hilton (1969) noted that as university scholars in the subject fields have participated more in writing textbooks during recent years, the readability of the material and its difficulty for students have been given less attention. The result is that more students simply cannot read the textbooks well enough to learn from them.

Many people are concerned because instructional materials are not tested properly before being marketed. In this connection, the regional educational laboratories that were established by the Elementary and Secondary Education Act of 1965 have as one of their major objectives the development of curriculum materials. To a lesser extent, the federally funded research and development centers have the same objective. Both kinds of organizations are committed to developing new products and evaluating how well students of specified characteristics learn from the material before making the material available to publishers for final production and sale.

Lange (1967) outlined a repeating cycle of developing, testing, and revising programed instructional material in order to assure that the material is appropriate for the students for whom it is intended. The complete sequence is shown in Fig. 5.2 in steps A through J. Examine the steps from the standpoint of how you might proceed in developing a short set of printed material for students, such as a lesson for a day or several lessons. It need not be programed material of the type described later in this chapter. Without further study, you can probably identify appropriate content for lessons in terms of a subject field (A) and write some re-

Table 5.2. Cost and Other Considerations Related to Various Instructional Media

Instrument	Media used	Materials production considerations
1. Filmstrip or slide projector	35mm filmstrips or 2x2 slides	Inexpensive; may be done locally in short time
2. Overhead transparency projector	Still pictures and graphic representations	Very inexpensive; may be done locally in short time
3. Wall charts or posters	Still pictures	Very inexpensive; may be done locally in very short time
4. Motion pictures (projection to groups)	16mm motion picture (sound or silent)	Specially produced; sound film is costly and requires 6–12 months time
5. Motion picture projection as repetitive loops (8mm silent) to individuals	8mm motion picture film (silent)	Special production normally necessary; may be produced as 16mm film alone or locally at low cost and in short time
6. Magnetic tape recorder	¼″ magnetic tape	Easy and inexpensive; usually produced locally
7. Record player	33⅓, 45 or 78 rpm disk recordings	Need special recording facilities, usually commercially made
8. Display area	3-D models	May vary in complexity and in difficulty of production; component parts easy to obtain
9. Television (closed-circuit)	Live presentations, motion picture film, video tape recordings, still pictures	Normally requires large and skilled production staff
10. Teaching machines and programed textbooks	Programed material	Some programs available commercially; but will normally be specially prepared for course
11. System combinations	Television, motion pictures, still pictures audio recordings	Complex; probably will be done locally to meet specific requirements

Source: Allen, 1967, p. 31.

Availability of facilities and equipment	Equipment cost
Usually available; requires darkened room	Low
Available; may be projected in light room	Low
Available; no special equipment needed	Very low
Usually available; requires darkened classroom	Moderate
Not normally available; will need to be specially procured to meet requirement of instructional program	Low per unit, but moderate for groups
Available	Low
Usually available	Low
Available	Varies from low to high
Not normally available	Moderate to high
Not normally available	Low per unit, but moderate for groups
Not normally available	Moderate to high

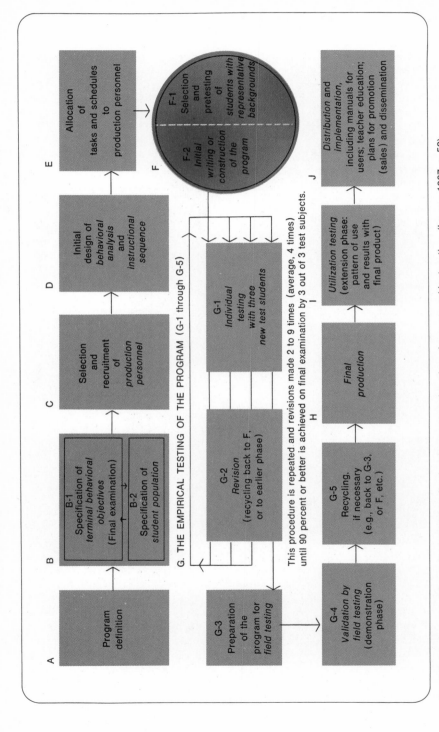

Fig. 5.2. A generalized flow chart showing the development and testing of programed instruction. (Lange, 1967, p. 58)

lated behavioral objectives (B-1) for students whose characteristics you can specify according to grade or age level and earlier level of achievement (B-2). (Assessment of student characteristics is dealt with in Chapters 17 and 18.) You are probably not concerned at this time with steps C, D, E, H, I, and J. Notice, however, that D calls for a behavior analysis and an outline of an instructional sequence to achieve the objectives. This means that you identify what students must learn or do to attain the terminal objectives that you have stated and the sequence that will be followed from beginning to end.

F-1 indicates that a population of students who will use the material should be identified. A small sample of these are pretested so that their characteristics are known. You might simply estimate their characteristics. Then you write an initial draft of the printed material and identify and develop the audio and visual materials and devices. Steps G-1 and G-2 indicate that this material is tried out with consecutive new groups of three students until all three score 90 percent or higher on the final test, which is designed to be a true measure of attainment of the objectives. (You might not wish to proceed beyond this point.)

When the material performs this well, it is prepared for field testing (G-3). If the material works as it should in several school settings in different regions of the country with a relatively large number of students, it goes to final production. If not, it is recycled as necessary back to G-3, F-2, or even D and B-1.

As noted, the preceding sequence outlines the developing and evaluating of programed instructional material. It appears equally relevant for other kinds of instructional material, except that subject-matter experts should be brought in at A and again at F-2 to validate the content, and more extensive field testing should be done. As part of the field test, the particular material being developed should be compared with other material also to see if one set performs better than another.

Considerable time and money are involved in this kind of development and evaluation of instructional material. Neither individual authors nor profit-making publishers normally engage in the extensive field testing that has been outlined. As noted before, however, the federal government is supporting this kind of development through laboratories and centers. Also, large curriculum projects supported by federal funds are gradually being required to evaluate their materials in the field and to report the results. Nevertheless, each school system or state still needs a materials evaluation capability to learn how effective various materials are with children of specified characteristics when used under clearly described conditions. So far, there are not enough expert evaluators and there is not enough money available both to guarantee the quality of material and also to learn to use it so that it produces the best results. Unfortunately, therefore, the evaluation of instructional materials by a school system is too often based on format and appearance, not on content, useability, and level of difficulty. School people have generally not been sufficiently concerned with ascertaining how well students learn from use of the material. Furthermore, there are teachers who actually prefer to have others decide what their students should learn.

5.1. Rate this textbook on the same bases that Allen used to rate various types of instructional media in Table 5.1. Compare your rating with his ratings of textbooks generally. Note also that Allen rated motion pictures much higher than textbooks for certain purposes. Would you also rate motion pictures so high for the same purposes? Why are motion pictures not used more in instruction?

5.2. Which media, other than printed books, might profitably be used in a course in educational psychology? To what extent can any media replace your direct participation, as a prospective teacher, in the instructional activities of a school?

5.3. What is the possibility that instructional technology will enslave, or manipulate, teachers and students? What would teachers have to be or do in order for this to occur?

INSTRUCTIONAL TELEVISION

There were great expectations when instructional television (ITV) started off during the 1950s. The early results were much less than promised, however, and the inevitable disillusionment set in. Nevertheless, with experience, better instructional programs and more effective use of programs by teachers came to characterize the late 1960s. Enough information has now been gathered by case studies and other research techniques so that conclusive statements may be made about student achievement under and attitudes toward ITV, general conditions favorable to ITV, some limitations of ITV, and the specific conditions that facilitate student learning through ITV. Also, two facts are now apparent: The teacher of students receiving television lessons can do much to make the learning more effective. In addition, there is an increasing number of opportunities for those who decide to become studio, or television, teachers.

Student Achievement and Attitudes Toward ITV

Students learn well from television instruction when certain conditions related to the television program and the teacher's use of the program are managed well. Also, students' attitudes toward ITV vary, depending on quite clearly defined conditions.

Student Achievement. Chu and Schramm (1968) reviewed 207 studies involving 421 separate comparisons between ITV and conventional teaching. The results of these comparisons are reported in Table 5.3. Of 202 comparisons made at the college level, 14 percent favored conventional instruction, 11 percent favored television instruction, and in the remaining 75 percent no significant differences in educational achievement were found. At the secondary school level, 13 percent of the comparisons favored regular classroom teaching and 20 percent favored ITV. At the elementary school level, only 6 percent favored conventional instruction and 16 percent favored ITV. Thus the comparisons of the significant differences show that ITV was more effective at the elementary and sec-

Table 5.3. Results of 421 Comparisons Between Instructional Television and Conventional Teaching

	No significant differences		Television more effective		Conventional more effective	
	Number	Percentage	Number	Percentage	Number	Percentage
Elementary	50	78	10	16	4	6
Secondary	82	67	24	20	16	13
College	152	75	22	11	28	14
Adults	24	73	7	21	2	6
Total Number	308		63		50	

Source: Chu & Schramm, 1968, p. 7.

ondary school levels than with college-age students. (Note, however, that there was no significant difference between ITV and conventional instruction in 67 percent of the comparisons at the high school level and in 78 percent at the elementary level.)

Although the differences among the three levels are small, Chu and Schramm gave their best judgments as to the factors contributing to these differences. One possible explanation is related to the fact that there is no immediate feedback to the student in televised teaching. The higher the grade level, the more complex is the material that is taught, and the more need there is for feedback. At the higher levels, then, student achievement under ITV is lower because the needed feedback is not provided. Another possible explanation of the greater effectiveness with elementary children is that during the 1950s and 1960s, the period during which the research was done, the younger children had had more experience with television in general than the older students. A third possible explanation is that the television teacher usually has a higher prestige value for younger children. Thus the younger children may learn more because they may attend better and also because they may imitate the television teacher more. Finally, elementary teachers have more favorable attitudes toward ITV than do college instructors.

Television instruction seems to be about equally effective in all subject-matter fields, as shown in Table 5.4. The television groups did as well as,

Table 5.4. Effectiveness of Television in Various Subject Fields

Subject	Number of comparisons	Percentage in which television groups did as well as or better than conventional groups
Humanities	45	95.5
Social studies	77	89.6
Mathematics	56	89.2
Languages	77	88.3
Science	100	86.0
Miscellaneous	40	75.0

Source: Chu & Schramm, 1968, p. 10.

or better than, the control groups in 95 percent down to about 86 percent of the comparisons involving five different specific subject fields. These results should not be interpreted to mean that schools can switch completely to ITV, as Chu and Schramm point out:

> However, this does not mean that instruction can be turned over entirely to television in any of these subject-matter areas. As we shall have occasion to point out later, almost nowhere in the world is television now being used seriously to carry the *entire* weight of teaching; it is always combined with classroom teaching, or supervised learning groups, or some other device to stimulate and direct learning at the receiving end. What the results do seem to mean is that television is not essentially subject-bound. It can contribute in many areas. Where demonstrations are needed or where expert teaching needs to be shared widely, it is strong. Where learning requires continuing interchange between student and teacher, it is not strong. But in almost any area of subject matter, if needed and if used well, it can contribute. (Chu & Schramm, 1968, p. 10)

Attitudes of School Personnel. The attitudes of teachers and other school personnel (in Hagerstown, Maryland) toward various aspects of television instruction are shown in Table 5.5. The rank order from highest

Table 5.5. Percentages of Different Groups of Teachers and Administrators Who Agreed with Certain Statements About Instructional Television (Hagerstown, 1965)

Statements	Admin- istrators	Primary teachers	Inter- mediate	Junior high	Senior high
Much or some help in teaching	83.3	76.9	80.9	62.5	40.9
Provides richer experience	98.7	98.4	96.4	90.0	76.3
Enriches and expands curriculum	91.1	94.2	90.7	77.8	76.0
Limits or reduces curriculum	3.8	3.3	6.4	15.3	18.6
Has no effect on curriculum	5.0	2.5	2.8	6.9	5.4
Improves curriculum planning	91.0	94.0	88.0	81.0	68.0
Improves quality of overall program	97.0	94.0	88.0	81.0	66.0

Source: Chu & Schramm, 1968, p. 62.

to lowest for valuing ITV is administrators, primary school teachers, intermediate teachers, junior high school teachers, and high school teachers. Even at the high school level, about 75 percent of the teachers felt that ITV provided a richer experience for the students and enriched and expanded the curriculum. The differences among the teachers in their attitudes toward ITV are presumed to be related to these five factors: (1) how they perceive the degree of threat to the role of the classroom teacher, (2) how they estimate the likelihood of mechanized instruction replacing direct contact with the students, (3) how they estimate the effectiveness of ITV, (4) how they see the difficulties connected with using modern techniques, and (5) whether or not they trust or distrust educational experimentation (Chu & Schramm, 1968).

Attitudes of Students. Chu and Schramm report that the attitudes of students toward ITV paralleled those of the teachers, as indicated in this summary:

> Thus there are few absolute guides in the research on attitudes toward instructional television. There is a tendency for attitudes to be more favorable toward teaching by television in the early grades than the later ones, but this is not always true. There is no good reason to doubt that instructional television may be either liked or disliked at almost any grade level and in almost any subject matter; and the way it is used, along with the conditions of its use, rather than grade level and subject, will decide what attitudes it draws forth. A student's attitudes toward teaching by television seem to relate closely to how he perceives the quality and interest of the course, how frustrated he is at having to wait until the end of the broadcast to ask his questions, how he perceives the alternative to being taught by television, and his feeling about the conditions of viewing. A teacher's attitudes seem to relate closely to his estimate of what television is likely to do to the classroom teacher's present status and future prospects, and his perception of how effectively it works in the classroom. If a teacher can be made to feel involved and if he can be helped to learn his new role, then his own improved attitudes are likely to be reflected in student attitudes, and he is more likely to integrate the broadcast into an effective classroom situation — which will make both students and teacher like it better. (Chu & Schramm, 1968, p. 72)

General Conditions Favorable to ITV

Schramm (1968) reported his experiences with ITV in some underdeveloped countries of the world in addition to the United States. If ITV is to contribute to its fullest potential to a student's learning, five general conditions must be present, since ITV works best (1) when solving a clearly-defined educational problem, (2) when fully integrated into a teaching-learning system, (3) when receiving adequate financial support, (4) when telecast to relatively large numbers of students, and (5) when planned adequately.

1. Solving a Clearly Defined Problem. ITV is not expected to carry the whole weight of instruction. However, when it is used only on an occasional supplementary basis, no measurable benefits above regular classroom teaching are usually found. In places where there is a complete television curriculum in a subject field, supplemented by live face-to-face teaching, excellent results are usually obtained. Following are five specific purposes for which ITV is used and a representative, not complete, list of places where it is used for each purpose: *upgrading instruction*: Colombia, Hagerstown, MPATI (Midwest Program on Airborne Television Instruction), Niger, Nigeria, Samoa; *teaching teachers*: Algeria, Colombia, Hagerstown, Italy, Nigeria, Samoa; *extending the school*: Chicago, Italy, Japan, Peru; *literacy and fundamental education*: Italy, Ivory Coast, Peru; *adult education and community development*: Colombia, Italy, Peru, Samoa (Chu & Schramm, 1968, p. 16).

A brief account of the situation in Hagerstown, Maryland, shows how ITV can contribute to upgrading instruction:

> *Hagerstown* was neither the best nor the worst among United States school systems when it went into television in 1956. It wanted to be able to offer science throughout elementary as well as secondary school; foreign language beginning early in the elementary grades; art and music expertly taught in all schools; some advanced work in mathematics and science in high school. Many of its elementary teachers were not prepared to offer up-to-date courses in science or to teach foreign languages; and it was very short of well-qualified art and music teachers, as well as others. To hire teachers for these places would have been a very large addition to the budget, even if they could have been hired. Furthermore, it was necessary to build new schools, and the question arose whether some space and money could be saved by designing the buildings around large areas for television viewing plus small rooms for group teaching and discussion. When the opportunity came to go into television, and share its best teaching more widely, Hagerstown jumped, and has since been amply satisfied with the results. (Chu & Schramm, 1968, p. 17)

2. Integrated into a Teaching-Learning System. ITV works best when it is part of an integrated teaching-learning system, that is, part of a team-teaching situation. The team is comprised of the studio, or television teacher, the regular classroom teacher, and perhaps a teacher whose work is incorporated in books or other instructional material. There is need for both planning and continuous discussion between the studio teacher and the classroom teacher. Schramm and others summarized the teaming operation in this way:

> In effect, then, by their very nature the new educational media enter into a kind of team teaching. It is not precisely the kind of teaching usually called "team teaching" in modern schools, where the term usually refers to the division of specialized responsibilities for a large group of pupils among a group of teachers and assistants. But the principle is the same. Each teacher has a special task which, supposedly, he can do best. In the case of the media, a teacher at the point of input, a teacher at the point of reception, perhaps another teacher speaking though textual or exercise materials, combine their efforts, each doing his own part of the task of stimulating students' learning activity. When the media are used for adult education (let us take agriculture as a possible subject area) the teacher at the transmitting end may be an extension specialist, the supervisor at the receiving end may be a forum chairman or village-level worker, and the materials may be prepared by a group at the agriculture research station. But the division of responsibilities is the same. Obviously, such a division and combination of responsibility requires a clear and common set of learning objectives, the will to work together, careful planning, and adequate training in the special skills required. (Schramm, Coombs, Kahnert, & Lyle, 1967, p. 97)

3. Supported Financially. In the early days of television instruction, it was thought that such instruction would markedly reduce the educational cost per pupil. However, it is now recognized that when ITV is used properly, it does not and should not replace the classroom teacher. Also, the pupil-teacher ratio should not be increased to offset the costs in installing and maintaining the television receiving equipment and the sending studio and of paying the staff to produce television instruction.

4. Telecast to Large Numbers. To keep costs at a reasonable level, the same television lessons must reach a relatively large number of students. For example, *Patterns in Arithmetic* (PIA), an instructional program covering six grades, cost about $500,000 to produce initially. During the first year after its development it reached about 500,000 children, mainly in inner cities and economically poor rural areas. Some additional costs, though not large ones, were incurred by the school systems using the program; in the case of schools already equipped for ITV, the costs were quite modest. *Patterns in Arithmetic* is a complete television course for grades 1-6 (Van Engen & Parr, 1969). Materials include 336 video-taped lessons, one student workbook at each grade level, and one teachers' manual at each grade level. Incorporated into each of the sequential courses are the most recent research studies done at the Wisconsin Research and Development Center for Cognitive Learning. The program uses one or two quarter-hour televised lessons each week to present basic mathematics concepts. Pupil exercises provide follow-up work for each telecast. Teacher notes review the objectives of the lessons and suggest activities related to the television program. The classroom teacher is an integral part of the teaching team. The program materials can be used in urban and isolated rural school systems within the reception range of an educational television station or in schools with a closed-circuit setup. PIA is particularly effective in situations where students are transient and where teachers are not well prepared to present modern mathematical concepts and skills. Furthermore, the students can learn from seeing and hearing; relatively less must be learned from reading.

5. Planned Adequately. Adequate planning for ITV means that time and effort are given to developing a production capability, to securing proper receiving equipment and assuring proper conditions in the school buildings, and to preparing the classroom teacher for the new role he must assume. The amount of time and effort that may be required varies with the level of sophistication of the instructional staff. In underdeveloped nations and in smaller low socioeconomic school districts of the United States, more effort is required than in well-developed localities where skilled teachers and other technical personnel are readily available.

Some Limitations of ITV

Even under the best conditions of instruction, television teaching is essentially a one-way communication used to present identical information in the same time interval to large numbers of students. Because the communication is one way and the instructor is talking to a camera rather than directly to his students, he obviously has no way of knowing, for example, whether he is going too fast or too slowly, whether he should elucidate certain points, or, indeed, whether the students are listening to him at all. Because it is one-way communication, the student cannot raise questions, ask for clarification, or engage in discussion until after the television presentation is completed. Similarly, the television teacher cannot provide informative feedback or reinforcement.

The second limitation of ITV is that the rate of information-giving is the same for all viewers. This, combined with the usual practice of reaching a relatively large number of students simultaneously, means that differences among the students in their ability to comprehend the information cannot be provided for.

In this connection, film has advantages over television, just as audiotape has advantages over radio in the hands of a skillful classroom teacher. The teacher can introduce the film at any time that may be appropriate, and the film can be shown again as necessary for one or more students (depending on the viewing arrangements). Similarly, the film can be stopped at any time for questions or discussion. Nevertheless, when reliable videotape recorders become as available to the classroom teacher as are film projectors, most of the advantages of films over ITV will disappear.

Specific Conditions That Facilitate Student Learning

Chu and Schramm (1968) drew 37 conclusions concerning what has been learned so far about ITV as an instructional medium. Most of these deal with production matters. For example, it seems to make no difference in student achievement if a large screen is used, rather than a small one; if color is used, rather than black and white; if animation is used, rather than nonanimation; and if a dramatic presentation is used, rather than an expository one. In considering the specific conditions under which ITV is received and *used* in the school setting, eight main principles were identified. (Most of these principles were drawn from research based on film or other presentations, rather than television directly, but they are fully applicable to television.)

1. Motivation. Studies connected with motivation and media are identical to those done on other instructional procedures. For example, students who are promised a monetary reward achieve higher than do those not receiving such a promise. Also, students learn more from viewing films in which they are more interested than those in which they are less interested.

2. Informative feedback. Though practically no research has been done to ascertain the effects of informative feedback on television instruction, a substantial amount has been done with films. This research shows clearly that students should get informative feedback as soon as possible to find out whether they have learned what was intended. A practical way for handling this is to administer a short test immediately after the television presentation and have the students score the test themselves.

3. Practice on the television task. A student may respond covertly or overtly during and after a television presentation. If he responds covertly, the teacher obviously has no way of knowing what the responses may be. Thus the teacher may decide to develop exercises to be completed or questions to be answered after the television lesson as a way to secure

overt student responses. In several experiments with films, practice on the task has been shown to increase student achievement. Further, practice with immediate feedback that enables the student to learn whether his responses are correct is more effective than mere practice without feedback.

4. Note-taking. Note-taking during a continuous presentation interferes with learning unless time is specifically provided for taking notes by means of pauses in the telecast. Note-taking probably has a more detrimental effect on ITV than on regular classroom teaching because the classroom teacher normally does slow down or pause when he sees students taking notes (the studio teacher, of course, does not see the students).

5. Teacher-directed follow-up. Attempts have been made to find out which procedure is associated with higher student achievement — showing the lesson a second time or follow-up by the classroom teacher. It was found that teacher-directed follow-up or discussion and providing clarifying information yielded better results than a second presentation of the television lesson. Even better results, however, were obtained when there was a first television presentation, then the teacher-directed follow-up, and then a reshowing of the television lesson.

6. Noise. Noise may originate from the receiving or sending equipment and from external sources. When what is to be learned is presented primarily by the auditory medium, noise has an interfering effect. Students learn to adjust quite readily to noise when the information to be learned is carried primarily by the visual medium.

7. Viewing angle. In any presentation where seeing the image or visual is an important part of learning, a wide viewing angle interferes with learning. A television image on a screen differs from the real object in many ways, one of which is dimensional. Because the television screen lacks a third dimension, the image appears slanted to students sitting at a wide angle. Thus when the television screen is relatively small, such as 18 inches, and individuals are sitting considerably to the right or left of the receiver, they get a distorted view.

8. Distance. Similarly, being too close or too far away from the television receiver interferes with vision. In other words, when detailed visual information is presented that must be discriminated, it is important to be at the proper angle and distance in relation to the receiver.

Chu and Schramm published their report in 1968. In 1970, another report, "TV Comes of Age in the Classroom," described "two remarkable strides forward in the use of television" during 1969 — "Sesame Street" and "Patterns in Arithmetic." A few excerpts from the article give the flavor and impact of the two programs:

"Sesame Street" is . . . a fast-moving, technically skillful blend of the Madison Avenue art: animation, brief and pointed skits, hand puppets, songs, and stories. But the repetitious "commercials" advertise the letters of the alphabet instead of soap or cereal, and the content of every item is carefully calculated to move toward educational goals. Even the guests—stars like Mahalia Jackson, Burt Lancaster, and Pete Seeger—are fitted into a scheme with teaching objectives carefully worked out in advance. . . .

By all present indications "Sesame Street" has been a huge success. A practical proof is the fact that John W. Macy, Jr., president of the Public Broadcasting Corporation, has proposed that another such experiment should get under way in another field of education, such as adult education or remedial reading, to show that "television, properly used, can be the most effective tool for mass education yet devised."

Still to be assessed is the long-range impact on the schools themselves if the idea should spread that good education, on the "Sesame Street" model, is also an enjoyable experience for the learner.

"Patterns in Arithmetic" is less obviously a break with the traditions of educational television, but may also have far-reaching effects. Its basic idea is that television could be used to introduce the new concepts of math into the schools and, at the same time, teach the concepts to thousands of school teachers. . . .

Again like "Sesame Street's" developers, the originators of "Patterns in Arithmetic" tried the first versions of their work on the actual users—in this case, between 30 and 100 teachers at each grade level in the Madison, Wisconsin, area during 1965-1966 and 1966-1967. Every few weeks the teachers met with the program developers to help evaluate the broadcast lessons, and on the basis of these sessions, the developers say candidly, some programs and lesson sheets were entirely rewritten. . . .

The two big successes of 1969-1970 in educational television thus offer a very hopeful prospect. Both techniques are obviously applicable to many other areas of education in addition to the ones they have tackled. And perhaps best of all they show that there is more than one way to break a path through the immense expense and complication of using the powerful electronic medium. (Editors, *Education U.S.A.*, 1970, pp. 50-55)

5.4. You have probably experienced commercial television since your infancy and also some instructional television. What do you learn or experience, if anything, from television that you do not get so readily from well-illustrated printed material? What are your objections, if any, to commercial and to educational television? Could television be modified or advanced to improve instruction?

5.5. Teachers have generally expressed more negative than positive reactions to television instruction even though students seem to learn reasonably well from television instruction. Chu and Schramm give several reasons for the teachers' negative reactions. Do you agree with the reasons given? Do you think television should be used more or less in American schools?

5.6. Do you feel the studio teacher, compared with the classroom teacher, has a more important, less important, or equally important role in television instruction? How might a teacher's answer to this question affect his reactions toward television instruction?

PROGRAMED INSTRUCTIONAL MATERIALS

The emphasis in this section is on programed instructional *materials*. Actually, however, *programed instruction*, or an instructional program, may include any kind of audio, visual, or audiovisual materials and many kinds of learner and teacher activities, as outlined in Chapter 1.

A brief historical overview of programed instruction is given first, followed by some earlier and later examples of programed material and related discussion. Enough information is provided so that the student might try his own hand at writing such material; or he might prefer to go to one of the supplementary readings for still more information. Finally, the status of programed instruction in terms of what students learn from it is discussed.

A Note on the Historical Setting

Programed instruction received its strong initial impetus in 1954 through an article by B. F. Skinner, "The Science of Learning and the Art of Teaching." Skinner, who had been active in evolving the principles of operant conditioning (discussed in Chapter 2), outlined the application of these principles to instruction in spelling and arithmetic by the use of programed instructional material managed by a teaching machine. The principles may be stated as follows: (1) Decide on the final behavior desired and identify the sequence of specific behaviors essential to achieve the desired terminal behavior. (2) Get the student to make the initial response through imitation or by other means, such as prompting and cueing. (3) Take the student gradually through a sequence of steps so that each of his successive behaviors, or responses, leads to the final terminal behavior. Here three conditions are important, according to Skinner: The student must respond overtly; the sequence of responses must lead to the final terminal behavior; the steps in the sequence must be small, to ensure that the correct responses are made. (4) Reinforce the responses by an appropriate schedule, so that the responses are strengthened. Skinner also noted that each student might need a somewhat different sequence of instruction, schedule of reinforcement, and size of step. That is, it was planned that students would go through a program at different rates, with the result that regardless of their cognitive abilities and other characteristics, they were all expected to learn the material equally well.

Pointing out that a teacher could not devise and manage an excellent program for one student, much less for 30 or more, Skinner invented a teaching machine that he thought would do this. In 1954, he was confident that operant conditioning would transform educational practices. He said:

> There is a simple job to be done. The task can be stated in concrete terms. The necessary techniques are known. The equipment needed can easily be provided. Nothing stands in the way but cultural inertia. But what is more characteristic of the modern temper than an unwillingness to accept the traditional as inevitable? We are on the threshold of an exciting and revolutionary period, in which the scientific study of man will be put to work in man's best interests. Education must play its part. It must accept the fact that a sweeping revision of educational practices is possible and inevitable. When it has done this, we may look forward with confidence to a school system which is aware of the nature of its tasks, secure in its methods, and generously supported by the informed and effective citizens whom education itself will create. (Skinner, 1954, p. 97)

Fourteen years later, however, although Skinner was still advocating application of the same principles and though his teaching machines had been widely introduced and tried out initially, research and experience with them had resulted in their virtual abandonment. Also, the applications of the principles in programed textbooks, although effective in some cases, had not brought about the large increases in student achievement that had been predicted, even in the many situations where enthusiastic attempts were made to do so. Thus in 1968 Skinner stated his expectations with much more realism:

> Both the basic analysis and the technology are, of course, incomplete, and that was to be expected. Human behavior is an extremely complex subject. An effective technology of teaching can scarcely be any simpler than, say, electrical engineering or medicine. We cannot circumvent a detailed analysis by extracting a few general principles. Just as we do not design a new radio circuit by applying a few general principles of electricity, or a new form of therapy by applying a few general principles of health, so the day has passed when we can expect to improve teaching by applying a simple common-sense theory of human behavior. The most effective techniques of instruction will be drawn only from the fullest possible understanding of human behavior, a goal toward which an experimental analysis slowly but steadily moves. (Skinner, 1968, p. 226)

Nevertheless, programed instruction, as now more broadly defined to include a reproducible sequence of instructional events designed to attain explicitly stated objectives, is still a powerful force in education; it will probably become more so if reasonable development and quality control are carried out before promotion and sale of the materials. Programed instructional material, like instructional television, should now properly be considered as being able to contribute significantly to a total instructional program for some students but not as the total program for all students or as a replacement for live teachers. Unfortunately, however, not only the early proponents but also some modern enthusiasts treat programed instruction as a complete self-instructional system for all students that can make teachers almost unnecessary.

As might be expected, early programed materials were developed in accordance with Skinner's ideas; these were called *linear* programs. Shortly thereafter, the idea of *branching* or *intrinsic* programs was evolved. *Adjunct* programs had been in use already. These three kinds of programing are now discussed. Actually, program developers now tend not to use any one of the original models in pure form, and new ideas are being tried out continuously.

Linear Programed Material

In a linear program a sequence of items, or frames, is written. Successive frames call for only small steps, or increments, in learning, so that the student will make few or no errors and will receive many reinforcements. The student is required to construct a response after each frame. If the response is correct, it is reinforced in order to strengthen it. Two other points should be made: Prompts and cues are provided to assure that the student will make the correct response. Also, the sequencing calls for review or use of earlier responses later in the sequence and the gradual fading out of the earlier prompts and cues.

An English Program. The 11 frames that follow are the first of 60 frames that comprise the first lesson of a set of 22 lessons designed to teach selected concepts from structural and transformational grammars.[1] Eighth-grade students of average and above-average intellectual ability learned the selected concepts well by using these lessons (Blount et al., 1967). This material is representative of modern linear programing except that more information is given in certain frames in a simple narrative style, and many of the other frames are designed more to facilitate practice and testing than to give new information in itself. Note particularly the amount and kind of information given in frames 1 and 10.

---

1. The English language has nine types of very simple sentences. These are called BASIC SENTENCES. They may be used alone, or they may be combined. All more complicated sentences which you read and write are combinations of these nine _____ sentences.

---

2. < Some pianists are women. > is an example of one of the _____ types of basic sentences. (How many?)   basic

---

3. < The umbrella is black. > is also a basic s_____.   nine

---

4. < Turkeys gobble. > is another _____ _____.   sentence

---

5. < The umbrella + is black. >   basic
   < Turkeys   + gobble. >   sentence
   These basic sentences have _____ main parts. (How many?)

---

6. How many main parts does this basic sentence have? < Our team + won the match. >   two

---

7. < The umbrella + is black. >   two
   < Our team   + won the match. >
   All English sentences, whether they are basic or not, have two main parts. In < Most rabbits eat carrots. > we would put a + after _____ to show the two main parts.

---

8. To show the two main parts of < Don looked happy. >, we would put a + after _____.   rabbits

---

9. < The chicken + seemed sick. > This basic sentence, like all English sentences, has _____ main parts.   Don

---

[1]These materials were developed by Professor Nathan S. Blount of the University of Wisconsin.

10. We would save a lot of words and time if we could refer to the   two
two parts by single terms, instead of saying "the part to the
left (or right) of the + sign." Let's call the part to the *left* of
the + sign the SUBJECT GROUP.
In < Two mice + were behind the stove. > *Two mice* is the

---

11. < Some of my books + are at home. >   subject
Here *Some of my books* is the subject _____.

A Program To Assist in the Teaching of Concepts. Markle and Tiemann
(1969) brought out audiovisual and printed material, the purpose of which
is to teach teachers how to analyze concepts, teach the concepts, and test
students' mastery of the concepts. The printed part is called a *Program
Book*. The *Program Book* of 37 pages contains response sheets and exercises written in a format similar to other programed books. Part 1 of the
program teaches the teacher or program developer an understanding of
concepts; Part 2 indicates the problems that students experience in connection with concept learning; and Part 3 describes how to analyze concepts in the detail required to prepare lessons or programed materials.
Space does not permit the inclusion of the longer exercises included in
the preliminary edition (many are more than a page long). However, in
each of the three parts there are exercises that enable the teacher or program developer to apply the information that he has gained through study
of the earlier frames.

The three kinds of problems that students experience in connection with
learning concepts, according to Markle and Tiemann (1969), are indicated
in frames 1-6 of Part 2 of their program. As you proceed through the
frames, decide whether these are the main kinds of problems.

---

1   1

A concept may be represented by a circle with
all members placed inside and
all nonmembers outside.

---

2   2

OVERGENERALIZATION: The student includes some
nonexamples as members.

---

3   **3**

Check which of these is the overgeneralization.

Child sees:	Says:	Overgeneralization?
Single boxcar on a siding	"Truck"	____
A square	"Rectangle"	____

4   **4**

UNDERGENERALIZATION: The student fails to recognize some true examples as members.

5   **5**

Classify the responses of a child learning "car" as:

Generalization = G   Undergeneralization = U
Discrimination = D   Overgeneralization   = O

Child sees:	Says:	Type of response
Convertible	"Car"	____
Delivery truck	"Car"	____
Antique car	"Not Car"	____
Pick-up truck	"Not Car"	____

6   **6**

MISCONCEPTION: A combination of undergeneralization and overgeneralization.

Only part of one of several exercises from Part 2 of the program by Markle and Tiemann follows. The exercises should enable you to decide whether you understand generalization, overgeneralization, under-generalization, and misconception. Naturally, if you are not familiar with the content in either exercise a or b, you cannot complete the exercises. In each exercise, one correct answer is indicated by an X.

Analyze the *pattern* of student responses on the following "tests" with respect to *each* of the concepts listed. Remember, an error may give you information about two of the concepts being tested. Classify the student's responses to each concept as:

Generalization—all responses correct, with no overgenerali-
zation or undergeneralization;
Undergeneralization—fails to identify an instance;
Overgeneralization—accepts a nonexample as an instance; or
Misconception—evidence of *both* undergeneralization and
overgeneralization.

a) *Grammar:*   Student will identify declarative, interrogative, exclamatory, and imperative sentence patterns.

NEW INSTANCE	STUDENT RESPONSE
Declarative	Declarative
Interrogative	Imperative
Interrogative	Interrogative
Exclamatory	Exclamatory
Imperative	Imperative

Concept: Declarative: G _X_   O ____   U ____   M ____
           Interrogative: G ____   O ____   U ____   M ____
           Imperative: G ____   O ____   U ____   M ____

b) *Language Arts:*   Student will identify figures of speech.

NEW INSTANCE	STUDENT RESPONSE
Metaphor	Metaphor
Simile	Simile
Personification	Metaphor
Simile	Simile
Metaphor	Metonomy
Metonomy	Metonomy
Synecdoche	Synecdoche
Personification	Personification

Concept: Simile: G ____   O ____   U ____   M ____
           Metaphor: G ____   O ____   U ____   M _X_
           Personification: G ____   O ____   U ____   M ____

Part 3 of the Markle and Tiemann (1969) program is intended to teach a detailed analysis of concepts. It assumes that the teacher has consider-able knowledge about concepts related to one or more subject fields. (Chapter 11 of this textbook was written specifically to enable you to get a better understanding of concepts.) Markle and Tiemann indicated five specific objectives of the teacher's or programer's analysis of a concept as follows:

---

6   6

SPECIFIC OBJECTIVES: Your analysis of a concept will:
1) Identify the obvious characteristics of typical examples so you can determine:
   a) the critical attributes shared by all members of the class; and
   b) irrelevant attributes of typical examples which might lead students to make errors; that is, to overgeneralize or undergeneralize.
2) Prepare a rational set of teaching examples and nonexamples. The lists should include *at least* a minimum set of nonexamples, i.e., those necessary to exclude *each* critical attribute, and a number of examples sufficient to vary *each* ir-relevant attribute.

3) Include an additional rational set of examples and nonexamples reserved for evaluating the student's attainment of the concept after instruction.

4) Rationalize *each* choice in steps 2 and 3; that is, identify the variation of irrelevant attributes incorporated in each example *and* the critical attributes excluded by each non-example. (Markle & Tiemann, 1969, p. 21)

After giving some examples of the critical and irrelevant attributes of a few concepts in Part 3, Markle and Tiemann then give a complete analysis of a few concepts. An analysis of a concept includes the critical and the irrelevant attributes of the concept, teaching examples and nonexamples of the concept, and examples and nonexamples that might be used in testing whether the student has formed the concept. The complete analysis of the concept of *pair* follows. Study it carefully and decide whether or not you think what is included is appropriate for preschool children, the level for which it is intended. Also, decide what changes in the attributes and the examples you would make if you were planning to teach the concept to 10-year-olds.

Preschool Concept: Pair

Attributes	Critical	Irrelevant
1. Includes exactly two members	X	
2. Members are matched in "function"	X	
3. Members belong to the same "narrow" class	X	
4. May be:		X
a) identical, or		
b) mirror images, or		
c) "functional pairs" that differ on some obvious attribute which is irrelevant to their "function"		
5. May be drawn from a variety of possible classes:		X
a) clothes		
b) other objects		
c) animals		
6. May be:		X
a) joined to each other		
b) free		

Teaching Examples   *Teaching Nonexamples*

		Rationale			*Rationale*
mittens		[4b,5a,6b]	Treys		[lack 1]
glasses		[4b,5b,6a]	fork & spoon		[lack 3 (& 2?)]
deuces		[4c (differ in suit), 5b,6b]	right-hand mittens		[lack 2]

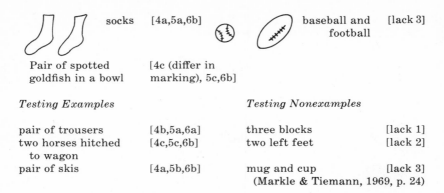

socks   [4a,5a,6b]   baseball and   [lack 3]
                                                    football

Pair of spotted   [4c (differ in
goldfish in a bowl   marking), 5c,6b]

Testing Examples   *Testing Nonexamples*

pair of trousers   [4b,5a,6a]   three blocks   [lack 1]
two horses hitched   [4c,5c,6b]   two left feet   [lack 2]
   to wagon
pair of skis   [4a,5b,6b]   mug and cup   [lack 3]
                                          (Markle & Tiemann, 1969, p. 24)

Markle and Tiemann (1969) departed markedly from linear programing principles as initially outlined by Skinner. Their program is intended to teach individuals how to analyze concepts in preparation for teaching the concepts. This involves a set of high-level intellectual skills that do not seem to be learned through proceeding by small steps. Instead, exercises have been developed that are designed to give practice in developing the skills. The person who completes the program will be able to analyze a concept, mainly through studying the excellent models and doing the exercises, which require his applying his newly acquired knowledge.

Branching or Intrinsic Programed Material

Branching programs, developed initially by Crowder (1963), differ from linear programs in four ways: (1) Small steps are not used. (2) The student selects a choice from among those given, rather than constructing a response. (3) Subsequent steps, or branches, that are to be taken depend on which choice the student has made. Linear programers strive for correct student responses, but intrinsic programers welcome student errors as an opportunity to branch out and thereby correct misunderstandings; a different branch might be possible for each of the three different choices a student might make. The choices for each item, or frame, are constructed in such a way as to serve a diagnostic function; in turn, the branches of the program are written in such a way as to provide for the student whatever instruction he needs. (4) More information is provided in the program in narrative form. Thus, fewer frames are used and less cueing is required in order to get the student to learn a certain amount of material. Intrinsic programers also tend to use a more informal and humorous style than linear programers.

Limitations of space prevent reproducing a large section of a branching program here. However, the first two pages of a semiprogramed introduction to verbal argument (Allen, Kauffeld, & O'Brien, 1968) and the first two branches, which follow, give an idea of the technique. Notice that a substantial amount of information is presented first in narrative style; then there are a few self-testing exercises calling for constructed responses; and at the end the student is given a summary test item. As is indicated, the student branches to either of two different answers, depending on which choice he makes earlier.

LESSON I

Ordinary Uses of Language

We live in a world of language. Each day we utter thousands of words and are bombarded by thousands more. Although our lives are immersed in language, seldom do we take time to think critically about ourselves as language users. In Lesson I, you will be asked to look at language, and at yourself as a language user, in a special way.

By the time a student becomes a young adult, he has been taught, with varying degrees of precision, to look at language according to certain rules of grammar and syntax. Given the sentence "John is a cowboy," most young adults can label "John" as a subject noun, "is" as a linking verb, "a" as an article or noun marker, and "cowboy" as a predicate noun. Although looking at language according to its rules of grammar enables us to compose proper sentences and criticize the grammatical literacy of the sentences of others, the grammarian's view is but one way of looking at language.

Apart from looking at language according to its consistency with the rules of grammar, we may also view language *functionally*. When language is viewed according to its *function* the question asked is "What *use* is being made of language?" Imagine, for example, that you overhear a small boy uttering the following sentence:

It's a gooder day than yesterday, ain't it?

How might you respond? If you view his utterance according to its consistency with rules of grammar you would probably correct him by saying "It's a *better* day than yesterday, *isn't* it?" But perhaps you might also respond "Yes, it's a lovely day." In the first case you looked at his language grammatically and found it to be an improper utterance. In the second case, you looked at his language *functionally* and responded to his *use* of language as a question by responding to the question.

In place of looking at language according to the rules of grammar, this lesson will look at language *functionally*, according to the *use* to which it is put.

Before continuing with this discussion of the functions of language, you will wish to consider the following questions. Before answering each question, you should cover the right hand column with an answer shield so you may check your response only after you have written your choice.

When we look at sentences from the standpoint of their use, we are looking at language f_____y.	functionally
———	
If we say that a sentence is being used to ask a question, we (are, are not) looking at the sentence functionally.	are
———	
If we say that a sentence contains a subject, a verb, and an object, we (are, are not) looking at a sentence functionally.	are not

------

If we view a sentence as asking a question,
we are looking at a sentence _____.   functionally

When we look at a sentence functionally we
are looking at language according to the _____
to which it is put.   use

Consider the following conversation:
  John: "When are we going to the parade?"
  Marty: "Tomorrow at 7:00 P.M."
In the above conversation, Marty reacted to John's sentence:
  A. According to the rules of grammar. . . . Turn to page 10 □
  B. According to the functions of language. . . . Turn to page 10 ○
(Allen, Kauffeld, & O'Brien, 1968, pp. 1-2)

□ Marty did not react to John's sentence according to the rules of grammar. If
Marty had looked at John's sentence grammatically, she would have reacted by
saying "That is a correct sentence" or "*We* is being used as a subject, *are going* is
being used as a predicate, and *when* is being used as an adverb." However, this
lesson is not concerned with the ability to evaluate the grammar of a sentence.
Throughout this lesson and this book you will be looking at language according
to its *function* or the *use* to which it is put. By responding to John's sentence as
a question, Marty is clearly concerned with sentence function or use rather than
sentence grammar. Return to page 2 and select the other alternative.

○ Your answer stated that Marty reacted to John's sentence according to the
functions of language.
    John: "When are we going to the parade?"
    Marty: "Tomorrow at 7:00 P.M."
Good. Why wasn't it viewed according to the rules of grammar? The answer is
that Marty did not respond by commenting on the grammatical correctness or
lack of correctness of John's utterance. Instead she reacted to John's sentence
functionally. She responded to how the sentence was *used*—as a question—by
responding with an answer—"Tomorrow at 7:00 P.M." Return to page 2 and continue with the lesson.
  (Allen, Kauffeld, & O'Brien, 1968, p. 10)

At present, branching programs are judged to offer better opportunity
for student learning than are straight nonbranching linear programs
(Stolurow, 1969a). It should be pointed out that present linear programs can
also have branches, even though only small steps and constructed responses are used in the linear program.

Adjunct Programed Material

Pressey is credited with devising the first teaching machine during the
1920s. He described the use of a simple machine to test the student and to
inform him of the correct answers (Pressey, 1926), the use of an apparatus

for automatically teaching drill material (Pressey, 1927), and the elements of a machine for scoring tests and tabulating by item. At that time he predicted that an "industrial revolution" might occur in education by means of mechanical devices which would free the teacher from routine tasks.

Pressey (1964) had serious misgivings about linear programing. Believing that linear programers were guilty of an unjustified application of an animal-based learning theory to meaningful human learning, he advocated the use of programs in an adjunct or facilitating role, rather than in a primary role. He used material as it was presented in a well-written textbook and then presented multiple-choice items, with answers, based on the material. The items were designed to focus on points of possible misunderstanding. Thus the student learned while studying the narrative material, discovered how much he had learned by taking the tests, and also ascertained what he had mastered and what might require further study. Many college textbooks now have adjunct programs in the form of self-administering tests in the student workbook that accompanies the text.

Student Achievement and Programed Instruction

Schramm (1964) reviewed 165 studies on programed instruction, nearly all of it linear and most of it incorporated in textbooks, rather than in teaching machines. These studies dealt with those characteristics of programed instruction that program developers felt were required by the Skinner operant conditioning model. Conclusions about these characteristics are now discussed briefly.

1. Ordered sequence. Early experiments showed that students learned about as well when the frames of shorter programs (up to 180 or so frames) were presented in a completely random order as when they were presented in a logical sequence. No programer would scramble frames intentionally, of course, but the conclusion is clear that one need not be too concerned about highly detailed aspects of sequence.

2. Step size and error rate. A satisfactory criterion of step size had not been identified for the many different kinds of instructional programs; therefore, neither the size of the step nor the number of errors that impede learning have been determined.

3. Constructed response. Most studies found no difference among three kinds of responding: writing the response, selecting the correct response from those given, and merely "thinking" it. Furthermore, in an additional test, Pressey rewrote 64 of the frames of an introductory psychology program developed by Holland and Skinner as good prose paragraphs. No significant difference was found in student achievement between the prose and the programed material; the prose material, indeed, required less study time.

4. Immediate feedback. A few studies reported better achievement when the student was told immediately whether or not his response was correct. Glaser and Taber (1961), however, reported no difference in the

students' achievement whether 100 percent, 50 percent, or 25 percent of their responses were accompanied by feedback. They suggested that when steps are so small as to ensure few errors, feedback is probably not important.

5. Pacing. Most experiments on the rate at which students proceeded through a program were carried out over only a short time period. Typically, no significant difference was found between the mean score of a classroom group that went through a programed lesson in a fixed time for everyone, e.g., 30 minutes, and one that went through a lesson at rates appropriate for each individual, e.g., 15 to 60 minutes.

Schramm (1964) concluded that students did indeed learn from linear programed instructional material, but that it was not clear that they learned better from such material than from studying other materials, including films, television lessons, and books. Feldhusen (1963), reviewing the research earlier than Schramm, concluded that teaching machines had proved to be ineffective and that students learned no better from linear programed material than from well-written narrative material. It is possible, however, that some programed material, such as the three examples quoted from earlier, is now developed more carefully than are many textbooks. (It is scarcely necessary to point out that students do not always learn well from some current textbooks, either.)

These negative conclusions about linear programs do not give a picture of the negative results as they affected the actual people involved—the bitterly disappointed children and teachers who had been led to believe that programed instruction would really work, that it would enable children to teach themselves. Some of the disappointments came simply because the teaching machines were not tried out in enough schools before being widely promoted and sold. Furthermore, the very scientific methods that Skinner used to evolve principles in the animal laboratory were not followed by him or by many others to learn whether the principles could really be applied to instruction for school children of varying characteristics. As Dale put it,

> Furthermore, programed instruction was introduced into education by psychology—in a technical language and in a format and with hardware more suitable to the research laboratory than to school or home. Introduced as a stranger and often poorly introduced, it came to education without visible evidence of ancestry. It has been handicapped, therefore, by the lack of historical perspective on the part of both psychologists and educators. (Dale, 1967, p. 31)

Dale also pointed out that actually each of the following ideas had been tried out in education before 1954: activity analysis and the specification of behavioral objectives, criterion tests of terminal behavior, feedback, individualized instruction, self-managed instructional materials and environment, and educational engineering. Skinner, however, was the first to bring all these conceptions together in an effective manner. As Dale described it, this was the primary contribution of Skinner and his followers:

We have recognized that programed instruction as we now know it received its present impetus from psychology and psychologists; and from this scientific tradition it has gained much of its experimental approach, its disciplined logic and empiricism.

Finally, we conclude in view of historical developments that programed instruction, by reason of its research emphasis, its empirical nature, its efficiencies, its exploitation of new materials, media, and technologies—and especially through its emphasis on the clarification of instructional objectives—will be a major force in educational innovations. (Dale, 1967, p. 54)

Stolurow, an early and vigorous proponent of linear programed instructional material, recently defined programed instruction, not only in the earlier sense of a tangible program but also as a kind of abstract model, or strategy, to achieve instructional objectives. The strategy may be applied to computer-assisted instruction, instructional television, and to any other instructional system wherein the student interacts with a machine, material, person, or combination of all of these to attain behaviorally stated objectives. Stolurow's conclusions about programed instruction in 1969 were much like those of Feldhusen (1963), Schramm (1964), and Dale (1967):

Current trends suggest that teaching machines are out, branching machines are used increasingly, and computer-based learning systems hold the promise of the future. Programed texts are the mainstay and will continue to be used. The concepts originally systematized in the development of programed instruction are beginning to influence the management of the classroom and the design and use of television and film. This trend, particularly in the use of feedback, will probably increase. The decisions to use programed instruction for education are not simple or easy, but any doubts about its permanence or effectiveness would have to stem from prejudice or ignorance. The only course for areas of application is how to use programed instruction most effectively, and the only course for research is how to improve upon what little we know now so that we can begin to understand teaching and learning as they take place in schools, universities, and training establishments. (Stolurow, 1969a, p. 1020)

5.7. Programed learning of a linear kind was an attempt to make teaching more a science, or technology, and less an art. Principles of learning developed in the animal laboratory were applied in the development of linear material and teaching machines. So far, linear materials and teaching machines have not produced better results than good narrative prose material. Which do you think are primarily at fault—the principles or their applications? Make this judgment for each of the principles.

5.8. What principles would you use as guides if you were writing instructional material? Do you think it is a worthy goal for a teacher to try to write material from which students can learn more effectively? Who should be writing the material that students study in the classes you teach?

5.9. Did you learn any of the content incorporated in the brief sets of material quoted from Blount, from Markle and Tiemann, and from Allen et al.? Can you recall it now? Could you learn that content more readily than the content in the regular part of this book? Why or why not?

5.10. Why do both branching and adjunct programing appear to be more promising now than straight linear programing?

5.11. Might the questions included in this chapter be classified as a kind of adjunct programing? How well do you learn from studying the questions? Do the questions call mainly for the recall of factual information or for application, synthesis, evaluation, and divergent production?

COMPUTERS IN EDUCATION AND INSTRUCTION

Computers are widely used in banking, transportation, manufacturing, and other industries; in these settings they perform certain functions very quickly, while at the same time not increasing costs; indeed, they often actually reduce costs. In providing better service without increasing costs, the computer replaces other machines or reduces the hours of human labor or both.

Computers are coming more slowly into education than into business and industry because they have not yet demonstrated a sustained capability to deliver certain instructional and other services at a reasonable cost. They are, however, being used extensively in educational research in universities. A computer of even moderate capability can perform in a few minutes a set of calculations that would require a researcher a week or more to complete with a desk calculator. Also, computers are used in the storage and retrieval of information in the central offices of large school systems. Using computers to help the teacher manage parts of a total instructional program may soon prove to be economically feasible. The extent to which computers will be used to interact on a one-to-one basis with the student to assist in day-to-day instruction is still uncertain. These four uses of the computer are discussed more fully in this section.

Computers in Educational Research

From about 1930 to 1960 educational research developed rapidly as a scientific enterprise. Empirical evidence came to take precedence over art and intuition as a guide to educational practice. On many college and university campuses and in many large-city public school systems, research bureaus sprang into existence specifically to work on problems of learning and instruction. Also, the federal government, through the U.S. Office of Education, the National Institutes for Health, and other agencies, began to offer financial support for educational research.

Along with the growth of interest and activity in educational research, new statistical theories and methodology emerged. The new statistical methods almost invariably called for much more elaborate calculations than did earlier methods. The emerging sampling theory in statistics also forced the researcher to use larger and larger samples, with the result that ever greater amounts of information were gathered on ever greater numbers of students—information that could not have been used effectively if the computer had not been available to store and process all of it very rapidly.

Finally, the rapid growth in the number of school-age children during the 1950s and 1960s led to new problems especially related to improving the *quality* of instruction. The schools increasingly looked to researchers for assistance in solving these problems. As researchers took on problem-solving projects in increasing numbers, they needed rapid and efficient processing of large amounts of information. The computer also met this need admirably.

In summary, throughout the 1950s and 1960s rapid progress was made in applying computer technology to educational research. For instance, Project Talent (mentioned in Chapter 3) is just one example of the type of research now possible. This project involved thousands of students; much information was systematically gathered on each of them, and a computer was then used to store and process all this information.

Educational psychologists characteristically emphasize the results of research in their courses in educational psychology. Such courses help the teacher to become a consumer of research, a participant in research, and even a performer of some research. As performers of educational research, teachers will increasingly use computers in order to save many tedious hours of calculating and to avoid errors. The computer can be used to answer important questions about teaching and learning at low cost if the right questions are asked and if the relevant information is gathered properly. These two things many teachers can learn to do; technologists can then do the actual information-processing by computer.

Computers in Information Storage and Retrieval

An urgent problem facing school people is to receive, store, process, call up selectively or retrieve, and/or transmit a vast amount of potentially useful information that will facilitate student learning, relieve the teacher of noninstructional functions, or both. There are thousands of new books, journals, magazines, and other documents in the library; hundreds of slides, filmstrips, films, television tapes, audiotapes, and records in the audiovisual section; thousands of test scores, grade reports, and similar items of information in the student personnel office; and great masses of data about students, courses, and classrooms which must be stored and used for scheduling and other purposes. The usual desk files and filing cabinets have become inadequate in recent years. Thus when only they are used, finding, or retrieving, information when needed and processing it quickly to arrive at wise educational decisions has become exceedingly difficult, often, indeed, impossible.

New techniques have been developed to solve this problem, including microfilming records, producing books on microfiche, and using the computer for a variety of tasks. Computers provide the most promising of the new ways to handle information; the rest of this section, therefore, describes the use of computers in information storage and retrieval in educational settings.

Information storage and retrieval systems must do the following:

1. Facilitate storage of large amounts of information.
2. Economize on space.
3. Facilitate selective and rapid retrieval of information.
4. Facilitate ready access to information for particular kinds of processing.
5. Transmit information from one place to another.

Grossman (1965) suggested the following as the major educational applications of computerized information storage, retrieval, and processing:

1. Receiving or preparing class lists or enrollment records.
2. Recording attendance, absence, and tardiness data.
3. Assigning marks for student achievement.
4. Reporting marks to students, parents, and others.
5. Posting marks to cumulative records.
6. Preparing honor lists.
7. Making mark adjustments.
8. Making special reports.

To this list should be added scheduling of classes, scheduling of individual students to classes, and daily assignment of students to instructional activities where modular scheduling is used. (The latter is a system for scheduling students for one-to-one, small-group, and large-group activities on the basis of student characteristics and needs, rather than on a fixed schedule for a semester or year.) Other additions to the list are information storage and retrieval in libraries and in guidance and counseling. In some school systems, the computer performs all the services listed; in others, computer service is available; and in still others, selective use is made of the computer.

Computer Operations in Information Storage and Retrieval. Van Ness (1966) outlined five functions of a computer system: input, storage, control, arithmetic, and output.

Input. Information is given to and accepted by the computer, frequently by means of the familiar punched IBM card. Cards, which are prepared on a card-punch machine that is similar to a typewriter, transmit numeric, alphabetic, and symbolic information to the computer via the card-reader. Data can also be fed into the computer via punched or magnetic tapes or directly from a keyboard without card or tape intervention. Direct reading of numeric, alphabetic, and symbolic material is also becoming possible with new optical scanning equipment. Specially devised characters that look essentially like normal ones are printed with magnetic ink and read directly into the computer. This Magnetic Ink Character Recognition is now widely used by banks.

Storage. Once information has been introduced to the computer, it can be stored internally. Many different kinds of storage are used by computers, including a magnetic core, tape, disks, drums, cards, rods, etc. A major problem in all computer systems is how to provide enough storage for the vast amount of information presented to the system. Most storage is based on the binary system — bits of information are stored as on-off functions of a magnetic unit.

Control. Control is the capacity of the computer to organize and execute internal operations according to a plan or program. In addition to the actual information, a program must be fed into the computer; this program is the control agent that directs the retrieval of stored information and the assembling of such information in a systematic fashion.

Arithmetic. Arithmetic refers to the capacity of the computer, and especially of the program, to act on numerical information by adding, subtracting, multiplying, dividing, etc. In information storage and retrieval this function is seldom used, but in research it is vital.

Output. Output refers to the various ways information stored or processed in the computer can be transmitted to a human receiver. The common forms of output include information on a magnetic tape or cards, printouts produced either by a high-speed printer or by a special typewriter activated automatically by the computer, and images formed by the computer on a cathode-ray tube (CRT). Several kinds of information, such as numbers, letters and words, symbols, and simple pictures can be viewed directly on the CRT, which is much like a television screen.

Hellwig (1969) described the memory of a computer and related structures. The total memory system is divided into numbered registers, each one called a location. The contents of a register are called bytes; four bytes are called a word. The central processing unit (CPU) performs two essential functions to and from the registers — store and fetch. When a word is committed to, or stored in, a register, it may later be fetched back by the CPU without destroying its existence in storage.

The overall operation of an information storage and retrieval system has been described as follows:

> Records are gathered or inserted into the collection in some orderly manner, possibly with indexing. A would-be user addresses a question to the collection. On the basis of the question a search of the collection is conducted and pertinent records are identified or retrieved. Note that the collection of records in a system has been created and organized *before* the specific questions it is to answer have been stated. In other words, the system is created in *anticipation* of needs that are not fully known. Yet the measure of adequacy of a system is its ability to satisfy its users' needs as they arise. (Lipetz, 1966, p. 177)

Such storage and retrieval systems have been set up specifically for educators. The most widely known of these is ERIC (Educational Resources Information Center), a national computerized information system (U.S. Government Printing Office, 1968). Through a network of specialized centers, each responsible for a particular educational area, ERIC makes available educational research results, research-related materials, and other resource information that can be used in developing more effective educational programs. The information is monitored, acquired, and evaluated; it is then abstracted, indexed, and listed in ERIC reference publications. Students who plan to use ERIC to get information on a specific aspect of education should consult the indexes and abstracts in the monthly issues of *Research in Education* and the annual cumulative indexes for relevant documents; also the *Thesaurus of ERIC Descriptors* (the guide to ERIC information retrieval). There are full collections of ERIC documents in many university libraries, state departments of education, local school districts, and other organizations involved in education throughout the country. (Documents not readily available can be ordered in hard copy or microfiche.) Hundreds of thousands of ERIC documents, a rich source of information for educators, are now available. New abstracts of reports and projects are constantly being prepared at the various centers.

Computer-Managed Instruction

In computer-managed instruction (CMI), a computer may be programed to perform three functions for many students that a teacher has difficulty managing even for a few students: (1) It stores a great deal of information about each student; (2) it stores a great deal of information about the instructional program—materials, objectives, test scores, etc.; (3) it relates student characteristics to the instructional program and informs the teacher of the relationship. For example, all the information that a teacher might gather on 150 students and all the information about the instructional materials and activities available might be entered and stored in a computer. The 150 students might then take a short test to assess their level of achievement and might also indicate their interests or choices of activities. This new information from each student can also be put into the computer, and in a few minutes the computer can print out information concerning possible activities that each student might undertake in line with his level of achievement and his expressed interests. A computer, of course, can also keep track of what each student has done, how he has performed, etc. In this computer-managed instruction, however, the student does not interact directly with the computer (as is the case in computer-assisted instruction). Two illustrations of CMI will clarify its features.

    Project PLAN. Project PLAN (Program for Learning in Accordance with Needs) is a major effort to implement CMI for grades 1 to 12. By 1969, PLAN had undergone some evaluation (Dunn, 1969; Rahmlow, 1969; Wright, 1969). Flanagan (1968) listed the *components* of the system as follows:

    1. A comprehensive set of educational objectives.
    2. Teaching-learning units which are the instructional material, and guidance on how to use them.
    3. A set of tests.
    4. Guidance and individual planning functions.
    5. Evaluation of the system.

Earlier Flanagan (1967) emphasized three critical aspects of PLAN: (1) It is a systematic, not a piecemeal, approach to educational innovation and improvement; all major aspects of a complex are considered. (2) It is a large cooperative enterprise involving many school districts and their personnel and several other agencies. (3) It is a major effort to focus on current problems in education and to utilize recent research in education.

Individualization of instruction under PLAN is accomplished in three ways: (1) Each child proceeds in an essentially ungraded fashion with material appropriate to his specific level of achievement. (2) For each unit of instruction, several alternative sets of materials and procedures are available. (3) Each unit is a two-week module, and the modules are arranged according to each student's level of achievement in each subject.

The *guidance* program under PLAN includes four main functions: (1) Units on occupational information are incorporated in the regular program. (2) Pupils are given experience in planning for their own education by making choices for themselves among the alternative activities and materials for each module. (3) Units of instruction designed to foster self-understanding are planned. (4) The student is encouraged to manage the total instructional program which he selects for himself.

The computer, of course, plays a large role in Project PLAN. Flanagan says that its function "is to handle the scoring, the record-keeping, the comparing of student and learning material, the scheduling, the making of recommendations for immediate steps, or long-range steps, which would enable a system like this to work within currently available budgets" (1967, p. 7).

Flanagan describes the operation of PLAN in practice as follows:

To give a final illustration of the way the system is intended to function, a sample student's activities will be described. Sammy has just entered Mr. Adams' Fifth Grade class. Of course "Fifth Grade" is just a convenient chronological designation because it is well known that there are students in the class studying material at the Second Grade level, and other students studying material at the Eighth and Ninth Grade levels. Although Mr. Adams has not seen Sammy before, he has received a detailed account of what Sammy knows, how Sammy learns, what Sammy's interests are, and what Sammy's potentials and plans are currently estimated to be.

Sammy will be assisted in setting tentative goals for the year in language arts, mathematics, social studies, science and subsequently in other fields on the basis of precise assessment of both his previous learning and his interests and longer-range plans. These tentative goals will usually be stated in the form of about 20 sub-objectives to be achieved during the year in each of the fields of instruction.

For each sub-objective, there will be lists for both the teacher and student stating as clearly as possible the behavior changes expected and the content to be learned. There will also be a performance test, or assessment procedure, for confirming the student's achievement of these objectives.

On the basis of his tentative goals and estimates of his present knowledge, Sammy and his teacher will receive descriptions of the two or three teaching-learning units in each of the various fields which appear best suited to his learning style, interests and special aptitudes. Together, the teacher and student will select the specific teaching-learning unit on which he will start the year's work in each field. They will then each receive a statement of the learning materials to be used and the knowledge and behavior changes to be learned.

The student's statement will suggest the reading to be done, the workbook and other questions and exercises to be completed and the audiovisual materials to be used. The teacher will be given suggestions as to desirable points to check student progress, possible difficulties, and some hints and suggestions for handling specific problems.

In about two weeks the student will take the performance standard test. This test will be scored by the computer through the terminal in the school building and the results sent back the next morning to the teacher and student where they proceed to plan the next work. (Flanagan, 1967, pp. 9-10)

Individually Prescribed Instruction. Cooley and Glaser (1969) hypothesized that the most important potential use of computers in schools is to individualize instruction. They asserted that efforts to improve instruction must be based on a model of learning and instruction; this they called individually prescribed instruction (IPI). The model they offered included the following sequence of operations:

1. State the objectives as observable student behaviors.
2. Begin instruction after assessing the student's capabilities relevant to the instructional objectives and program.
3. Offer alternative modes of instruction to the student.
4. Monitor and continually assess each student's performance.
5. Proceed with instruction in terms of how the student has performed thus far, what he is ready for next, and the available alternatives that may be pursued.
6. Use performance data and other information to monitor and improve the whole system.

The eventual operation of IPI may be inferred from the following quotation:

In Individually Prescribed Instruction, the entire curriculum in each subject area (mathematics, reading, and science) has been broken down into instructional units for subgoals of achievement. For example, the math curriculum has identified 430 specific instructional objectives. These objectives are grouped into 88 units. Each unit comprises an instructional entity which the student works through at any one time; on the average there are five objectives per unit, with a range of 1 to 14. A set of units covering different subject areas in mathematics comprises a level; levels can be thought of as roughly comparable to a school grade level. On entering the school, the student takes a placement test which places him in a particular unit. If his profile is scattered, he begins work on the lowest numbered unit. A unit has associated with it a pretest and a posttest, and each objective (or skill, as it is called in the subsequent printouts) within the unit has attached to it one or more curriculum-embedded tests. Following placement to a unit, the student takes the unit pretest which attempts to diagnose the student's profile within the unit. For example, he may have mastered objectives 1, 2, 4 and 5, but not 3, 6, 7 and 8; at this point, the teacher prescribes for him work related to the objectives he has not mastered. As a student works through a lesson, he takes, at the teacher's discretion, the curriculum-embedded test which assesses whether mastery has been attained on the objective and also to what extent some competence has been attained on the next objective.

When all objectives have been mastered, the unit posttest is taken. If 85 percent is attained on this test, the student begins the next unit; if not, he is reassigned to an appropriate objective in the unit until he masters it. Various discretionary powers are left to the teacher about whether to keep the student in a unit or to move him ahead. (Cooley & Glaser, 1969, pp. 578-579)

The computer operations related to IPI are called the management and information system (MIS), described as follows:

> There are four major functions which the MIS can provide in an individualized school; it can (1) collect data; (2) monitor student progress; (3) provide information as a basis for prescribing a course of instruction; and (4) diagnose student difficulties. These functions have two primary objectives: to increase the effectiveness of the model for individualizing instruction and to increase the productivity of the teacher operating the IPI system. (Cooley & Glaser, 1969, p. 579)

The MIS is still under development by the Learning Research and Development Center in Pittsburgh in cooperation with the staff of the nearby Oakleaf Elementary School. This process is time-consuming and expensive. As late as the school year 1969-1970, clerks, rather than a computer, scored the students' tests at the Oakleaf School and then told the students what to do, according to a set of guides based on the test scores. The clerks then provided the same information to the Pittsburgh Center for storage and analysis by their computer.

The first experimental material developed for IPI was mathematics (it was still being revised in 1970 and other curriculum areas were being designed). The relatively high cost of this experimental material, added to the cost of the clerks to score the tests, store materials, and perform other functions, substantially increased the cost of education per student. Two critics have questioned what they see as the rather premature widespread dissemination of information about the mathematics curriculum of IPI. They express their viewpoint as follows:

> IPI has made progress toward reaching *measurable* universal educational goals, through processes created by mass production and applied by mass production with rate tailoring to pupils grouped by the level of their attained behavioral objectives rather than by their chronological age. It is an experiment and valuable as such. It is not yet an important addition to current practice. As its originators and disseminators are first to stress, many complex questions of abstruse theory and of workaday practice still remain unanswered.
>
> IPI shows promise as an intelligent and bold experiment pointing toward significant and valuable improvements in *one* of the ingredients in the educational mix. (Oettinger & Marks, 1969, p. 149)

Computer-Assisted Instruction

Computer-assisted instruction (CAI) is probably the most imaginative of the new applications of the computer in education. In essence, CAI tries to use the computer as an all-knowing teaching "brain" in such a way that students can interact directly with it without the immediate mediation of a human teacher. The student communicates directly with the computer, in other words. For all current forms of CAI, however, human effort is required in massive amounts in preparing the system and the specific instructional material to be stored in the computer.

Experimental CAI has moved quite rapidly in universities and in business, but slowly in public schools. The main reason for this is that none of the installations are yet able to deliver instruction at a practical cost level. Nevertheless, the experimental installations have proved the operational feasibility of CAI. The growth of CAI has been facilitated by three factors, as suggested by Atkinson and Wilson (1969). These are the programed instruction movement of the late 1950s and early 1960s, the mushrooming of electronic data-processing, and the increasing federal support for innovation and experimentation in education. To this list should be added independent or self-instructional techniques and individualization of instruction. The latter two, of course, go hand in hand.

Stolurow (1969b) described five basic modes of instruction which can be classified as CAI: (1) tutorial, (2) drill and practice, (3) inquiry, (4) gaming, and (5) problem-solving. To this list is added (6) dialogue.

In all of these modes the student is seated at a terminal which provides his "interface" or connection with the computer. In some types of terminals, the student's response mode is limited to multiple-choice buttons. In another variety (Fig. 5.3), the student registers responses to the computer's typed messages by touching a cathode-ray tube with a special light pen. In addition to the computers that communicate with the student

Fig. 5.3. CRT used with a light pen. (Courtesy of the IBM Corp.)

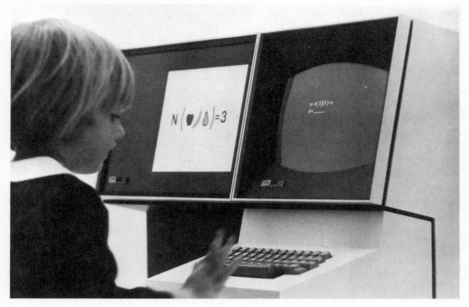

Fig. 5.4. CRT with messages printed on it. (Courtesy of the IBM Corp.)

by typing messages, there are some that print messages on the CRT, which is like a television screen (Fig. 5.4). It would be very costly, of course, if only one student interacted with the computer, using all of its power at a given time; actually, new time-sharing computers make it possible to operate a number of terminals simultaneously.

This general description of ways of interacting with computers leads us to each of the modes of CAI listed by Stolurow, with an illustration of each.

1. Tutorial Mode. In the tutorial mode the computer is programed by someone to act as a didactic instructor talking directly to the student and receiving communication from him, in both cases in natural language. The computer acts didactically in that it takes the lead as a tutor. The following is a dialogue implemented in this mode. In this case the instructor was trying to teach about three types of statistical relationships. ("C" identifies dialogue generated by the computer. "S" identifies one student's responses to the computer.)

C. Correlation coefficients which are positive show a direct relationship between two variables, those which are negative show an inverse relationship, and those which are zero show no relationship. Examine the following data and state the type of correlation shown.

Name	Height	Weight
John	54	69
Tom	63	91
Mary	58	74
Sue	60	80

S. *It is a negative correlation.*
C. No, that is not correct, try again.
S. *I guess it is a zero correlation.*
(Since the student missed twice, the computer now decides to branch the student to further explanation)
C. Here is a further explanation of correlation coefficients. In positive correlation when one variable gets larger the second also gets larger. In negative correlation the opposite is true. Now look at these data and decide what type of correlation seems to exist.

Name	IQ	Test Score
Ann	100	21
Tom	94	18
Sandy	110	28
Jean	82	14

S. *It is a positive correlation.*
C. Right. Now let's try some more problems.

In this illustration of CAI in the tutorial mode we see that the computer has been programed to perform the following operations: (1) present verbal and numerical instruction to the student; (2) present questions or exercises for the student to respond to; (3) accept and judge the adequacy of the student's responses; (4) perform instruction in a proper sequence; (5) make a decision to give further explanation when the student shows failure to understand; (6) reinforce the student when he performs correctly ("Right").

2. Drill and Practice Mode. In the drill and practice mode (Atkinson & Wilson, 1969) the computer is programed to present repetitive exercises designed to build skills in mathematics, English, or some other area. The exchange between student and computer may be as follows:

C.   67
     −32
    ‾‾‾‾
     ○□

S. $\boxed{5}$

     $\textcircled{3}$

C.   54
     −31
    ‾‾‾‾
     ○□

S. $\boxed{3}$

     $\textcircled{1}$

C. Try again.

S. $\boxed{3}$

    $\textcircled{2}$

C.   37
    −11
    ‾○□

S. $\boxed{6}$

    $\textcircled{2}$

C.   129
    +214
    ‾△○□

(The computer, after printing out the problem,
positions the typewriter to accept the first response in the box.)

(The fact that the computer goes on to a new
problem tells the student he answered correctly.)

In this illustration of drill and practice the computer was programed to
present several two-digit subtraction problems, to receive and judge the
student's responses, to call for correction when the student made an error, and to decide to go on to addition when the student seemed to perform correctly on the subtraction problems. In subsequent sessions the
computer checks the student's skill in subtraction of two-digit numbers.

3. Inquiry Mode. In the inquiry mode the computer is programed to
present a problem to the student, to allow him to decide what information
or sources of information he will use, and to answer his questions related
to the problem (Lyman, 1968, p. 3). The following is an inquiry exchange:

C. Today we would like to have you figure out why the snow in the picture seemed
     to be melting even though the thermometer in the picture shows 28. Which of
     the following would you like to do?
       A. Ask some questions.
       B. Examine the picture some more.
       C. Try giving an answer.
       D. Run an experiment in varying the temperature.
S. *D.*
C. OK, tell me what to do in the experiment.
S. *Decrease the temperature to 10.*
C. When the temperature is decreased to 10, the snow continues to melt.
S. *Decrease temperature to 0.*
C. When the temperature is decreased to 0, the snow stops melting.
S. *A.*

C. Now you wish to ask questions. Which one of the following would you like to ask:
  1. Is it a fahrenheit thermometer?
  2. Is it a centigrade thermometer?
  3. Is it real snow?
  4. What is the atmospheric pressure?
S. *1.*
C. No, it is not.
S. *C.*
C. Now you want to try giving an answer. Go ahead.
S. *The thermometer in the picture is a centigrade thermometer.*
C. That is correct but you need to explain more.
S. *The freezing point on the centigrade scale is 0.*
C. Correct. You have done very well. Now we will go on to another problem.

This illustration of the inquiry mode shows more versatility on the part of the computer and the teacher-programer in structuring a problem situation and in permitting some degree of dialogue between computer and student.

4. Gaming Mode. In the gaming mode a more complex problem confronts the student. This sequence is followed in gaming: (1) The computer is programed to simulate complex problem situations. (2) The student is required to make numerous decisions as a leader in the situation. (3) The computer is programed to react to the student's inputs or decisions and to modify the course of events in the game according to the sequence of student decisions.

Wing (1966) reported that the gaming method of teaching economics principles was as effective as conventional instruction in terms of amount learned and more effective than conventional instruction in that significantly less time is required. Here is a sample computer printout from the Sumerian game developed by Wing (1966):

C. Imagine that you have just been made Ruler of Lagash, a City-State of Sumer, in the year 3500 B.C. Twice yearly your Royal Steward, Urbaba, will report to you the economic condition of the kingdom. Guided by these reports, you will decide the use of your grain and other resources, trying to keep your population stable and well fed. Between reports, your court advisor will come to you with news of your kingdom.

The Steward will use the typewriter to report and ask for your decisions. When the "Proceed" light comes on, type your answer in figures and press "Return." (If you make a mistake, press "Cancel" instead and try again.) Good luck!

Initial Economic Report made to the New Ruler of Lagash by his Humble Steward:

Total population now	500
Total farm land under cultivation, acres	600
Total grain in inventory, bushels	900
one season old	900
two seasons old	0
three seasons old	0
Total grain just harvested, bushels	13000
Total resources, harvest + inventory	13900

You must now decide how to use your resources.
How many bushels of grain do you wish to FEED your people?
S. *4000*

C. How many bushels of grain do you want PLANTED for the next crop?
S. *9000*
C. This means that zero bushels must be removed from storage. Is this all right?
Do you wish to 1 — let your decisions stand or 2 — revise them?
S. *1*
C. Resulting inventory   900
The steward will execute the royal commands and return in 6 months.
Sir, I am sorry to report that 225 bushels of grain have rotted or been eaten by
rats this past season.

Economic Report of the Ruler's Steward for the SPRING Season in the year 1 of
Luduga 1.

Population at previous report	500
Change in population	−55
Total population now	445

The quantity of food the people received last season was far too little.

Harvest last season	13000
Harvest this season	14396
Previous inventory	900
Change in inventory	−225
Present inventory	675
Total resources, harvest + inventory	15071

You must now decide how to use your resources.
How many bushels of grain do you wish to FEED your people?
S. *5000*
C. How many bushels of grain do you want PLANTED for the next crop?
S. *9000*
C. This means that 396 bushels must be placed in storage. Is this all right? Do you
wish to 1 — let your decisions stand or 2 — revise them?

5. Problem-Solving Mode. In the problem-solving mode the student interacts with the computer by using it as a computer or calculator in such
course work as mathematics, statistics, and the sciences. For example,
here is an excerpt from a student-computer interaction in a program developed by Hesselbart, D'Arms, and Zinn (1968):

C. Which of the following samples do you want to work from?
    (1) entire population
    (2) random sample
    (3) stratified sample
S. *1*
C. You will be working with the entire population (211 students). Which test scores
do you want to use as data for your statistical calculations? Name one test and
grade level.
S. *SCAT, junior*
C. Which of these statistics do you wish to calculate from the test scores? Mean?
Median? Mode? Variance? Standard deviation? T-test (Comparing junior and
senior levels for your data)? Correlation (Specify 2nd test for correlation later)?
S. *Correlation*
C. Give the name and grade level of the test that you want to correlate with your
data.
S. *IQ score*
C. Mean = 271.60
Variance = 88.62
Mean = 110.17

Variance = 127.57
Correlation = 0.76
Which of the following do you want to do:
    (1) Change the psychological test you are using?
    (2) Change the sample of students you are working with?
    (3) Calculate another statistic from the same test scores for the same sample
    of students?
    (4) Stop?
S. *1*
C. Which test scores do you want to use as data for your statistical calculations.
    Name one test and grade level.
S. *SCAT*
C. Which of these statistics do you wish to calculate from the test scores? Mean?
    Median? Mode? Variance? Standard Deviation? T-test (Comparing junior and
    senior levels for your data)? Correlation (Specify 2nd test for correlation later)?
S. *Correlation*

The major feature of the problem-solving mode is that the computational
power of the computer is used. Such instruction is sometimes carried on
with no natural language dialogue between student and computer. That
is, printed materials, not in the computer, are used to direct the student
to problems and data. Then the student uses a computational language,
such as FORTRAN, to communicate with the computer to work various
kinds of numerical problems.

    6. Dialogue Mode. In the dialogue mode the teacher attempts to pro-
gram the computer to carry on a conversation with the student with perhaps no other limitation than the topic. Here, for example, is an illustration from a computer-student dialogue reported by Weizenbaum (1966, p.
36):

S. *Men are all alike.*
C. In what way?
S. *They're always bugging us about something or other.*
C. Can you think of a specific example?
S. *Well, my boyfriend made me come here.*
C. Your boyfriend made you come here?
S. *He says I'm depressed much of the time.*
C. I am sorry to hear you are depressed.
S. *It's true. I am unhappy.*
C. Do you think coming here will help you not to be unhappy?
S. *I need some help, that much seems certain.*
C. What would it mean to you if you got some help?
S. *Perhaps I could learn to get along with my mother.*
C. Tell me more about your family.
S. *My mother takes care of me.*
C. Who else in your family takes care of you?
S. *My father.*
C. Your father?
S. *You are like my father in some ways.*
C. What resemblance do you see?
S. *You are not very aggressive but I think you don't want me to notice that.*
C. What makes you think I am not very aggressive?
S. *You don't argue with me.*

C. Why do you think I don't argue with you?
S. *You are afraid of me.*
C. Does it please you to believe I am afraid of you?
S. *My father is afraid of everybody.*
C. What else comes to mind when you think of your father?
S. *Bullies.*
C. Does that have anything to do with the fact that your boyfriend made you come here?

The descriptions and the examples give a little of the flavor of experimental CAI as of the early 1970s. The field is changing rapidly. Thus a teacher should not base a decision either to accept or reject any use of the computer in instruction only on printed information, which does not give a reliable or complete picture of how well students learn or the dollar cost. In other words, the teacher should try to observe the computer in use in a school in the way he is considering using it.

Evaluation of Computers in Education

Morgan summarized the pooled conclusions of several federal agencies that have sponsored most of the recent research and development related to a variety of computer applications:

1. Of the several kinds of computer applications being researched, some should become operationally feasible before others.
2. With the existing hardware, many of the more exotic applications (CAI, CMI and computer-based guidance systems) would not become feasible for widespread school use unless significant reductions could be made in per student cost.
3. There are a number of non-exotic but useful functions which could be furnished to schools with the available technology.
4. Computer systems for schools should be developed to provide services currently available and be able to accommodate the expected newer functions at a future time with minimum disruption and systems modification.
5. The services provided by such a computer system probably should not increase the per student per year costs by more than 2 percent. In order to provide a range of services within this cost level it is reasonable to assume that a large central computer service with terminals extended to participating schools and school districts would be required. (Morgan, 1969, p. 4)

Feldhusen (1969) reviewed a number of evaluative documents dealing specifically with CAI and concluded that computers were being used experimentally to:

1. Secure, store, and process information about the student's performance before and/or during instruction to determine subsequent activities in the learning situation.

2. Store large amounts of information and make it available to the learner more rapidly than any other medium.

3. Provide programed control of several media, such as films, slides, television, and demonstration equipment.

4. Give the author or teacher a convenient basis for designing and developing a course of instruction.

5. Provide a dynamic interaction between student and instructional program not possible with most other media.

The cost of CAI, in comparison with conventional instruction, is not considered excessive in some university and business settings by Kopstein and Seidel (1968); they also see the possibility of low-cost CAI in school settings. The major obstacle is not in the machines—the hardware. There are two greater difficulties: Excellent instructional programs and related assessment exercises that can be incorporated in the computers must still be developed. Also, inexpensive communication systems are needed that will permit the individual to communicate with the computer orally, in handwriting, or by some means other than typing.

5.12. The computer has demonstrated its versatility in educational research where it saves hours of human drudgery in data analysis and simultaneously reduces costs. What are a few functions connected with instruction that teachers might like a computer to perform to reduce the drudgery in teaching?

5.13. What important things can teachers do for or with students that a computer will probably never be able to do?

5.14. Do some teachers produce negative effects by failing to do some things to or for students that a computer could do? Explain.

5.15. Some instruction is excellent; some is poor; little is as good as it might be. Suppose you had an unlimited amount of money for research and development to improve instruction. To what extent would you invest it in attempting to develop better teachers or other educational personnel, television instruction, instructional materials, or computer applications to education? Justify your investment.

SUMMARY

Principles and inventions from the physical sciences and engineering, mathematics, and the behavioral sciences are being used in developing a technology of instruction. The emerging technology is illustrated in television instruction, programed instruction and teaching machines, and computer applications to instruction. In turn, combinations of the machines and the instructional programs incorporated in them are being used mainly to reach larger numbers of students simultaneously or to individualize instruction. Nevertheless, in contrast to the authors' viewpoint expressed in Chapter 1, some complete instructional systems are now being developed outside the schools that are quite frankly designed to make a teacher a nonprofessional technician or to eliminate the teacher completely.

Televised instruction started with glowing promises during the 1950s, but disillusionment was widespread during the 1960s. By the 1970s, however, television instruction had reached early maturity characterized by a strong national educational television network and some excellent state and local programs. It is clear that television instruction can solve some clearly defined educational problems in America and in underdeveloped nations. To be successful, television teaching must be incorporated into a team-teaching arrangement, must be supported financially, and must be planned adequately. The adequate planning includes instructing the television teacher and the classroom teachers in how to use television teaching as part of the *classroom instructional program.*

Though the enthusiasts for linear programed instruction and teaching machines promised solutions for most ills in American education during the late 1950s, by the mid-1960s teaching machines were no longer used except in research. Branching (intrinsic) and adjunct programing had begun to move to the fore. Despite the demise of the teaching machine and the early rigid style of linear programing, a noteworthy residue remains. Many behavioral scientists, subject-matter experts, and educators are now developing and testing instructional materials, procedures, media, and systems that will enable students to learn better and teachers to perform at a more professional level. More rigorous research and development and a greater knowledge input from a larger variety of people are going into the improvement of instruction.

The use of the computer and related technology have moved educational research from the horse-and-buggy era to the jet age in about 15 years. Larger libraries, some large school systems, and other agencies are using the computer to store and retrieve vast amounts of information. Small but very promising beginnings have been demonstrated in school settings in using the computer to store and analyze information that assists the teacher in finding a better fit between the student's characteristics and his instructional program. Computer-assisted instruction received much fanfare and even outright propagandizing during the 1960s. Hopefully, the subsequent disillusionment has now begun to diminish. Interactive arrangements between students and a computer that promise to produce significant advances have been demonstrated. Particularly at the university level, in medical schools, and in engineering, the computer is being used effectively to assist in instruction. It is now clear that the computer cannot replace the human teacher for all instruction; nevertheless, the computer may eventually be able to handle some parts of a total instructional program as well as it now handles data processing in educational research.

SUGGESTIONS FOR FURTHER READING

ATKINSON, R. C. Computerized instruction and the learning process. In Ripple, R. E., ed., *Readings in learning and human abilities.* New York: Harper & Row, 2nd ed., 1971.

A computer-assisted instructional program in reading is described.

ATKINSON, R. C., & WILSON, H. A., eds. *Computer assisted instruction: A book of readings.* New York: Academic Press, 1969.

In this 362-page paperback 21 articles by the pioneering enthusiasts of CAI and computer-managed instruction are presented. Instructional programs in use are included in part 4.

KLAUSMEIER, H. J., & O'HEARN, G. T., eds. *Research and development toward the improvement of education.* Madison, Wisc.: Dembar Educational Research Services, 1968, pp. 87-117.

In one article, W. Schramm describes the use of instructional television around the world. In another article, L. Stolurow presents a theoretical-technical account of a computer-based instructional system.

LANGE, P. C., ed. *Programed instruction.* National Society for the Study of Education, 66th yearbook. Chicago: University of Chicago Press, 1967, part 2.

This yearbook contains some interesting accounts of the status of programed instruction. The selections by E. Dale, "Historical Setting of Programed Instruction," pages 28-54; and by S. Markle, "Empirical Testing of Programs," pages 104-138, are most closely related to this chapter.

PRESSEY, S. L. Autoinstruction: Perspectives, problems, potentials. In Hilgard, E. R., ed., *Theories of learning and instruction,* National Society for the Study of Education, 63rd yearbook. Chicago: University of Chicago Press, 1964, part 1, pp. 354-370.

The inventor of the first teaching machines discusses the problems encountered with Skinner-based machines and linear instructional programing.

STEPHENSON, H. W., & SIEGEL, A. Effects of instructions and age on retention of filmed content. In Ripple, R. E., ed., *Readings in learning and human abilities.* New York: Harper & Row, 2nd ed., 1971.

Differences in students of various ages in mode of processing information are identified.

TOBIAS, S. Dimensions of teachers' attitudes toward instructional media. In Ripple, R. E., ed., *Readings in learning and human abilities.* New York: Harper & Row, 2nd ed., 1971.

In a factor analytic study of teacher attitudes toward instructional media, a "threat of automation" factor is identified.

Chapter 6 Characteristics of Students

Characteristics in Which Students Vary

intelligence: general, crystallized, fluid
changes in IQ scores over time
limited value of IQ scores
divergent-production (creative) abilities
value of stressing creative abilities
level of educational achievement
practical uses of knowledge of educational achievement
psychomotor abilities and skills
level of motivation
sex roles and related behaviors

Disadvantaged Students and Impoverished Environments

major groupings of disadvantaged people
environmental contributors to disadvantagement
low socioeconomic status
impoverished homes and neighborhoods
unresponsive schools
characteristics of children from disadvantaged backgrounds

Educational Provisions for Disadvantaged Students

physically safe environment
preschool education
post-high school training
integration

Individually Guided Education for All Children

provisions for differences in learning rates
provisions for differences in learning styles
provisions for differences according to substance, or curriculum areas
attributes of IGE

during the late 1950s the race into outer space set off a national concern for identifying and providing for gifted students. During the 1960s the civil rights movement generated a national effort toward better education of the disadvantaged — the children of the economically poor. These newer concerns have added newer emphases to our continuing attempts to try to make education more valuable for children and youth who are neither exceptional nor in any way handicapped. In all these aspects of education, individualization is assuming even greater significance. Though psychologists and educators have been urging for the past half century that individual differences be taken into account, it is only in recent years that their plea has come to be widely acknowledged and heeded. We know that education cannot be mass education — the same 12 years of schooling for all, using identical instructional materials and activities. What this all adds up to is that we must improve educational practices now. This chapter is directly related to that goal.

The range of differences among students is outlined first. Then special consideration is given to characteristics of disadvantaged students. Provisions for the disadvantaged, including preschool education, are considered next. Finally, a system of individually guided education for all students is discussed. Study of these concepts and related practices should enable teachers and other educational personnel to understand what is needed to improve educational practices now. Obviously, however, we must be willing to abandon outmoded practices in order to put this knowledge to use.

CHARACTERISTICS IN WHICH STUDENTS VARY

Figure 6.1 shows categories of characteristics that affect an individual's readiness to start a particular learning task, his progress in learning tasks, and the upper limits he may reach. The five categories are: cognitive abilities and related characteristics, psychomotor abilities and related characteristics, affective characteristics, family and socioeconomic status, and sex. (Because family and socioeconomic status are closely associated with disadvantagement, they will be discussed later in the chapter rather than in this section.)

When one designs an instructional program for a student, as outlined in Chapters 1 and 4, variables associated with each of the preceding categories may be important. However, certain variables are more important for particular instructional programs than others. Also, a small amount of specific information is more useful than a massive amount of general information. Thus, knowing the child's present level of reading achievement and the specific reading skills that he has mastered is more useful in organizing an instructional program in reading than is knowing his sex, family background, IQ score, and psychomotor abilities. On the other hand, sex and psychomotor abilities are very important in organizing an instructional program in physical education for a 12-year-old.

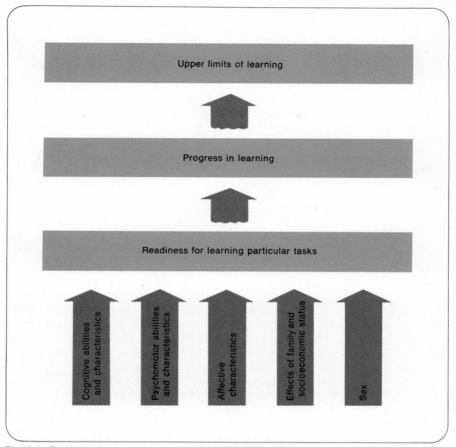

Fig. 6.1. Student characteristics and learning.

The characteristics of students also lead to differences in the amount they learn, even though initially they are equally ready. For example, at some point in time two youngsters run at exactly the same speed. Thereafter, one improves more rapidly than the other, and as time passes they draw further apart in running speed. The same thing happens in other learning activities. The characteristics that affect readiness also affect later progress and eventually the upper limits of performance, although the particular characteristics may be of lesser or greater importance as performance improves.

Intellectual Abilities and Other Characteristics

It is obvious that students of the same age vary in intellectual abilities and other characteristics. Naturally, this variability is related to the level of educational achievement that the students attain in many school tasks. Three of these variables that merit careful study are general intellectual ability, specific intellectual abilities, and earlier educational achievement related to the tasks. The nature and importance of these variables are under continuous study.

General Intellectual Ability. Scholars do not agree on the nature of intelligence (as noted earlier in Chapter 3). In studies of individual differences, however, IQ scores, as measured by tests of general intellectual ability, have been used for years. For this reason and because IQ tests are administered more systematically to students of school age than any other kind of test, much information is available on the kind of intelligence called general intellectual ability and its relation to other characteristics. We therefore discuss it in some detail now.

One of the more recent theories about the nature of intelligence is particularly relevant at this point because it postulates two kinds of intelligence, crystallized and fluid, that differ from the concepts of general intellectual ability and specific intellectual abilities discussed in Chapter 3. They are, however, somewhat analogous to the two major group factors described by Vernon (1950), which were also discussed in Chapter 3. In this recent theory, outlined by Cattell (1967) and Horn and Cattell (1966, 1967), the two kinds of intelligence are described as follows:

Crystallized intelligence has three main attributes: (1) It is associated with cognitive tasks characterized by stability and permanence; the abilities underlying the performance have become crystallized through practice and learning. (2) It is postulated to be heavily dependent on environmental conditions; that is, its development depends on the opportunities to learn and practice. (3) It is presumed to increase until age 30 or beyond; as the individual continues to learn, crystallized intelligence increases. *Fluid intelligence,* on the other hand, (1) is more involved in tasks that require the individual to adapt to new situations; (2) is more dependent on heredity; (3) is presumed to reach its peak at about 15 years of age.

The authors of this book accept the point of view that both heredity and environment determine how well an individual performs many tasks. Beyond that generalization, however, it is difficult to be specific about the nature of intelligence. Furthermore, it is virtually impossible to ascertain to what extent the various IQ tests to be mentioned in this chapter measure either crystallized or fluid intelligence — or any of the other theorized types of intelligence, for that matter. Nevertheless, as we have said, IQ tests, fallible as they are, do provide the most convenient way to discuss intelligence as it relates to many other variables in the learning process.

The qualities that are measured by intelligence tests are described in different ways according to the type of test and according to the use intended to be made of the results. Thus throughout this chapter the terms *general intellectual ability, intelligence, IQ,* and *academic aptitude* are used synonymously to refer to what is measured by individual and group intelligence tests. In this connection, an aptitude test is any kind of test or measure that is useful in predicting subsequent levels of performance or achievement. In other words, if an IQ test is used to predict the level of achievement in mathematics, English, and other academic subjects, it may be called an academic aptitude test. How much, if any, weight to give

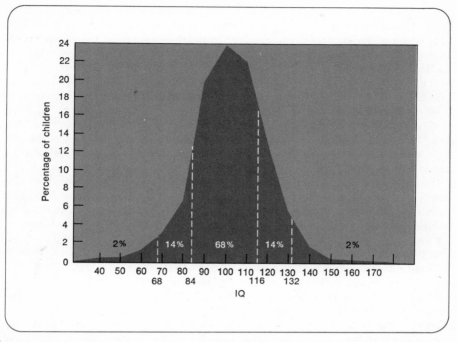

Fig. 6.2. Distribution of composite form L-M (Revised Stanford-Binet Intelligence Scale), IQs of standardization group, ages 2 to 18 (n=2904). (Adapted from Terman & Merrill, 1937, p. 37)

to the IQ score in organizing an instructional program for a child may be inferred from the following discussion of variation in IQ scores among individuals, variation in IQ scores in the same individuals, and the limitations of IQ scores in organizing an instructional program.

Variation in IQ Scores Among Individuals. In the standardization of the Revised Stanford-Binet Scale, one of the two individual intelligence tests most widely used in America, a range in IQ from below 35 to above 170 was reported, as shown in Fig. 6.2 (Terman & Merrill, 1937). The majority of the standardization group had IQs between 84 and 116, with slightly more than 68 percent of the total group in this IQ range. Approximately 14 percent had IQs between 116 and 132, 14 percent between 84 and 68, 2 percent above 132, and 2 percent below 68. (The average in Fig. 6.2 is actually slightly above 100.)

Variation in IQ Scores in the Same Individuals. The personality, familial, and physical correlates of the changes in intelligence from ages 3 to 12 were ascertained in a group of 140 children (Sontag, Baker, & Nelson, 1958). The Revised Stanford-Binet Scale was used to measure intelligence. Each child was rated on 14 personality dimensions, and anatomical measures were taken. Variations in IQ from one year to the next were found, with the highest degree of stability from ages 4 to 6 and again from 6 to 10. The median change throughout the study was 17.9 points, *and 52 percent of the children had changes of 15 points or more.* Children showing a high need for achievement, competitive striving, and curiosity gained more in IQ than did children not showing these characteristics. Those who gained in IQ also showed high independence and competitive inclinations rather than withdrawal behavior. Rate of physical growth and rate of mental growth were found not to be related; that is, there was no relationship between how rapidly the children grew physically and how rapidly they grew mentally.

Limitations of IQ Scores in Organizing an Instructional Program. Suppose that in a community all the children of school age are tested during September and their IQs are found to be distributed much the same as those in Fig. 6.2. We can assume that 50 percent will experience changes of 15 or more IQ points during subsequent years. Also, we know from the beginning that the IQ scores will be of very little use in assessing readiness of individuals for typing, art, music, physical education, and other activities that emphasize psychomotor abilities. Will the IQ scores be useful in assessing each child's readiness for particular learning, activities in mathematics, language arts, science, social studies, and though to a lesser extent, foreign language?

Let us first consider the 2 percent who have IQs below 68 and the same percentage with IQs above 132. We expect that children with IQs below 70 *who come from enriched homes and neighborhood environments* will not perform well in academic subjects. Further, those below 55 from enriched environments will probably not do well in *any* school tasks, including most of those heavily based on psychomotor abilities. We expect, further, that the children with IQs of 35 and below will not even attend school and will require much help throughout life with the simplest tasks of eating, dressing, keeping clean, and the like. Note that these comments do *not* apply to children from impoverished environments. At the top end of the scale, 145 and higher, we expect superior performance in all types of academic work. Those in the 130 to 145 range also are predicted to do very well. Occasionally, however, students in this 130 to 145 group do produce relatively mediocre performances. About 14 percent of the IQ group is shown in Fig. 6.2 to be in the 68 to 84 range and another 14 percent is in the 116 to 132 range. In some academic work a few in the lower group might achieve higher than a few in the higher IQ group, and vice versa. Among the 68 percent in the range of 84 to 116, we expect much variation in achievement; for example, those with IQs of 100 would vary widely in the level of reading and arithmetic achievement.

As may be inferred from the discussion thus far, the IQ score has limited value in planning instruction for a student for these reasons: (1) IQ scores change 15 points or more for more than half the students. (2) The largest number of students, about 65 percent, have IQs between 85 and 115, and the levels of achievement in reading, mathematics, and other academic subjects vary widely among students in this range, even among those who have the same IQ score. (3) Different IQ tests result in somewhat different IQ scores for the same individuals. (4) IQ tests have not been standardized adequately on any population of children, except Caucasian. (5) IQ scores correlate so low with psychomotor performances and affective characteristics as to be virtually useless in planning programs in these domains for *individual* students.

Categorizing children and youth as slow learners, disadvantaged, or unsuited for later college work on the basis of IQ alone and then not providing them with an enriched educational environment is probably the most serious misuse that can be made of intelligence testing; however, this unfortunate practice is still widespread. Misuse of the IQ comes from assuming that it is unchangeable or that there is a high relationship between achievement in all school subjects and IQ or that a particular IQ test is equally accurate and valid for measuring the intelligence of students from all types of homes and neighborhood backgrounds.

Specific Intellectual Abilities. A specific ability underlies performance of a limited range of tasks, rather than a broad range. Specific abilities are usually inferred from test results. Students of the same age vary in specific abilities, just as they do in IQ. You will remember that Guilford hypothesized 120 specific abilities, rather than a general intellectual ability (Chapter 3). We shall not enumerate the many abilities identified by Guilford or by others. Also, only a few applications to the schools are described here, as such applications were discussed in Chapter 3. It was noted there that the assessment of special abilities by means of extensive test batteries is expensive and is not widespread in the schools.

Several points may be recalled from Chapter 3:

1. Guilford (1968) found that a battery of special ability tests, including divergent production, correlated higher (.39 to .75) with achievement of several ninth-grade groups in mathematics than did the California Test of Mental Maturity (.18 to .37). Also, Feldhusen, Treffinger, and Elias (1970) reported that tests of originality and flexibility, administered to seventh- and eighth-graders, contributed to better prediction of their academic achievements in grade 12 than did tests of IQ or achievement alone. Smith (1964) concluded that spatial ability was more useful than IQ in predicting a variety of educational achievements, particularly those not requiring high verbal abilities.

2. Getzels and Jackson (1962) reported that various measures of creativity were useful in predicting achievement of students in academic subjects and that creative abilities did not correlate high with IQ.

3. Harootunian and Tate (1960) reported positive correlations between problem-solving and tests of divergent thinking. Each separate test of divergent thinking, as expected, did not correlate quite so high as did the single IQ test.

The preceding brief statements illustrate the relationships between tests of creative abilities and spatial ability on the one hand and academic achievements on the other. The use of a special ability test score in arranging instruction for individual students has the same limitations as does the use of the IQ score. However, as more and better specific ability tests are devised and validated, particularly in relation to creativity, the school will have better information to use in organizing instructional programs for individual students.

Level of Educational Achievement. Accurate information about a student's present level of achievement in any curriculum area, for example, in reading or science, is useful in predicting how he will do in the future in the same curriculum area. It is more useful, actually, than an IQ score or any special intellectual ability score. In addition, the teacher who knows what is needed for students to succeed on a task and who also is reasonably good in test development can write a test to ascertain what students know now in relation to what will be studied. Increasingly, instructional programs are being organized for particular students, not on the basis of IQ scores or other specific ability tests, but on the basis of the student's present level of achievement. The two main sources of information about level of achievement that are available to teachers in most schools are results of standardized educational achievement tests and teacher-made tests or other teacher-developed procedures. These are discussed more fully in Chapters 17 and 18.

Figure 6.3 indicates the correlations between achievement at each grade level and achievement at grade 12. The correlations reported by Traxler are based on his administering a reading comprehension test in grades 7 through 12 (Traxler, 1950). Hicklin secured his information by means of two different reading tests, one in grades 4 and 5 and the other in grades 6 to 10 (Hicklin, 1962). Scannell gave a test battery to students in grades 4, 6, and 8 and another battery to the same students when they were in grades 9 and 12 (Scannell, 1958). The correlations in Fig. 6.3 between an earlier grade and the twelfth grade range from about .75 in the fourth grade to above .90 in the eighth grade. These correlations are high, indicating that achievement in the same subject areas is stable over a long period of schooling. Shaycoft (1967) drew the same conclusion about achievements from grades 9 to 12. It is obvious that accurate information about each student's level of achievement in each subject field is very important and that teachers should secure it in order to teach well.

Because the present level of achievement is a good indicator of future achievement, it is interesting to note the extent to which 103 students, enrolled in *three seventh-grade classes*, differed in reading and in arithmetic achievement, as shown in Fig. 6.4 (Findley, 1963). The student lowest in reading achieved at a level of 3.7 (the midpoint between 3.5 and 3.9), whereas the highest achievers were at 11.2. The scores are equivalent to grade levels. For example, a seventh-grader scoring 3.7 is achieving at the level of the average of third-graders in the seventh month of the school year; one scoring at 11.2 is at the average of eleventh-graders in the second month of the school year. The range among the students in arithmetic achievement was not so wide, that is, from 4.7 to 9.7; the difference in range may be partly owing to the tests used, however.

The information in Fig. 6.4 is also interesting for comparing the achievement of the same students in reading and arithmetic. Note that Fig. 6.4 divides the students roughly into thirds in each subject. Of the 103 chil-

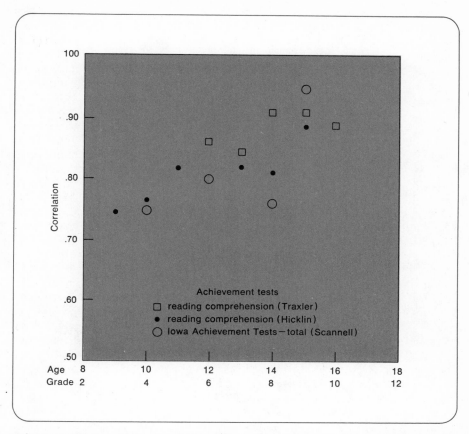

Fig. 6.3. Correlations between achievement at each grade and achievement at grade 12. (Adapted from Bloom, 1964, p. 101)

dren, 21 are in the upper third (approximately) in both reading and arithmetic, 16 are in the middle third in both, and 18 are in the lower third in both. Slightly more than half, 55, are in the same third in both subjects; the other 48 are not. Six students are in the top third in one subject and in the bottom third in the other. Four who are in the top third in arithmetic are in the bottom third in reading; two who are in the top third in reading are in the bottom third in arithmetic. Cases such as these six provide good evidence for not using the IQ score alone in planning an instructional program in reading or in mathematics for an individual or a group.

The most useful information produced by either a general or special intellectual ability test identifies students who may be considerably higher or lower than their achievement level in one or another subject. Further study of these children is warranted in planning an instructional program for them.

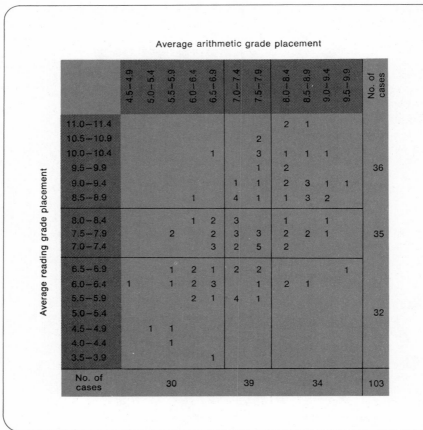

Fig. 6.4. Scatter diagram of achievement (grade placement) in reading and arithmetic, Stanford Achievement Test, Advanced, Form J, for pupils *in grade 7 in a school with average achievement.* (Adapted from Findley, 1963, part 2, p. 18)

Psychomotor Abilities and Physical Characteristics

Psychomotor abilities involving strength, impulsion, speed, precision, co-ordination, and flexibility were discussed in Chapter 3. These abilities in various combinations are essential to excellent performance in many activities, such as instrumental music, handwriting, typing, shorthand, the making of maps in social studies, and the making of objects in home economics, agriculture, industrial arts, and other classes. Individual and group sports also involve psychomotor abilities, as do talking, singing, and dramatics.

The wide range of performance in motor skills and the differences in physical characteristics found among students of about the same chronological age are shown in a representative study summarized in Table 6.1.

The range and the average, or mean, in six measures of 40 boys and 40 girls with IQs ranging from 62 to 146 are shown in the table (Klausmeier, Feldhusen, & Check, 1959). The chronological age ranges from 119 to 132 months, and the mean age is 125 months. The difference in strength of grip, a good indicator of vitality, between the strongest and weakest boy is 15.5 kilograms. (This measure of strength is obtained by giving the student a hand dynamometer which he squeezes as hard as he can.) The strongest boy scored about three times higher than the weakest girl. Carpal age in months is the best indicator of skeletal maturity currently available. (Carpal age is secured reliably by experienced radiologists who X-ray the hand and wrist and then compare the X-ray with norms already established. The principal criterion of carpal age is ossification of the bone.) The range in skeletal maturity ranges from 89 to 156 months — 7 years 5 months to 13 years. Handwriting speed of these children varied greatly, from 5.4 to 98 letters written per minute. It is obvious that at the time of these measurements, the children were far from being equally ready to engage in any lesson or activity that required the same amount of material to be written.

We correlated the measures above with achievement in reading, arithmetic, and language. Strength of grip and handwriting speed were found to be positively correlated with achievement in all subjects; however, four other physical measures were not, namely, carpal age, height, weight, and number of permanent teeth. Here skeletal development as inferred from carpal age was not positively related to rate of mental development. The same conclusion was reported at about the same time in another study (Sontag, Baker, & Nelson, 1958).

Thus the large differences reported in strength of grip and handwriting speed indicate unequal readiness for various activities and various subjects. In other words, each student's present achievement level in both cognitive and psychomotor domains must be assessed in order to arrange appropriate instructional programs for individuals.

Table 6.1. Means and Ranges for Six Measures of 40 Boys and 40 Girls, Normally Distributed According to WISC IQ at 125 Months of Age

	Boys		Girls	
Measure	Mean	Range	Mean	Range
Height in inches	55.10	47.9-60.8	55.24	50.8-60.0
Weight in pounds	77.22	49.3-113.3	75.36	55.0-115.5
Grip in kilograms	20.90	13.0-28.5	17.70	9.4-23.7
Permanent teeth	15.05	11.0-28.0	16.45	11.0-27.0
Carpal age in months	120.65	89.0-153.0	124.80	101.0-156.0
Handwriting speed in letters per minute	43.60	5.4-98.0	47.20	9.2-82.0

Source: Klausmeier, Feldhusen, & Check, 1959, p. 86.

Affective Characteristics

Students vary as much in affective characteristics, such as level of motivation and values, as they do in intellectual and psychomotor abilities. Therefore, the affective characteristics of students must also be considered when planning an instructional program for each student. In Chapters 9, 14. and 15, motives, attitudes, and personality integration are dealt with at length. Accordingly, the discussion that follows of motivation and prosocial values, two of many variables in the affective domain, is brief.

Motivation. Atkinson (1965) identified one pervasive motive as the need to achieve success and the related need to avoid failure. Individuals vary widely in these needs, and this variability markedly influences their tendency to undertake or to avoid activities. Thus, of two individuals faced with the same task—for example, writing a theme or playing a basketball game—one with a high need to achieve success and a low need to avoid failure enters the activity with vigor. The other may have a high need to avoid failure and puts off the task or does not participate at all for fear of experiencing failure. Individuals likewise vary in other needs—motives such as for love and belonging, for self-esteem, and for self-actualization (Maslow, 1943)—topics discussed at length in Chapter 9.

Values. Honesty is one of many prosocial values. The range of differences among students in honesty is probably about the same as in other values.

The honesty of children was the subject of part of a study called the Character Education Inquiry (Hartshorne & May, 1928). Tests that confronted pupils with temptation or with a conflict between their own pleasure and the good of others were devised. In one test, the pupil was asked to do as well as he could on an impossible task, such as putting dots in small circles while blindfolded. Obviously, any pupil who succeeded in this task certainly did so by removing or looking around his blindfold. In another test, the child was given a box of coins and had the opportunity to take some of the coins before returning them to the front of the room. The investigators could check whether or not the child actually took any coins. Ten tasks of this kind were arranged.

The distribution of ratio scores for cheating, i.e., the number of times in 10 opportunities to cheat in a large number of situations, is shown in Fig. 6.5. About 7 percent of the pupils had near perfect ratio scores (did not cheat at all) and about 4 percent cheated at every opportunity. The higher percentages fall between the high and the low ends, however, illustrating the tendency of individuals to be honest in some situations and dishonest in other situations. In point of fact, this distribution is fairly similar to the distribution of intelligence scores based on the Stanford-Binet scale shown earlier in this chapter (Fig. 6.2).

Many other studies and firsthand reports of teachers could be cited to show the wide variability among students of the same age in three other affective characteristics: identification with the values and practices of the older generation, or the establishment; attitudes and feelings toward self; and attitudes and feelings toward others of the same age. The teacher who disregards these affective characteristics will not be able to

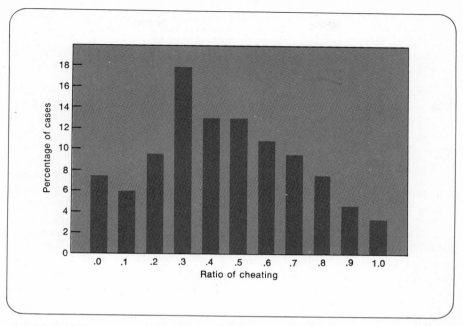

Fig. 6.5. Distribution of cheating ratios for children. (Adapted from Hartshorne & May, 1928, p. 386)

nurture the intellectual development of students fully. It has become obvious in recent years that even college students are demanding that greater attention be given to their development as feeling human beings, not as intellectual machines.

Sex Roles

The roles of males and females in American socity are not crystallized, to put it mildly. (Indeed, it is sometimes difficult to be sure, when viewing someone from a distance, whether the individual *is* actually male or female, because of the similar hair styles and clothing that have become fashionable.) Not only do people in general find it hard to define male and female roles with assurance, but scholars also disagree:

> This lack of consensus is the result of a rapid rate of social change and the presence of considerable subgroup differentiation. Negro wives are more likely than white wives to have power in the family, and lower-class wives are expected to be more subservient than middle-class wives; there are even regional differences in the willingness of girls to "play dumb" in order to please their dates. Role consensus is likely to be reduced as members of these diverse subgroups interact with one another. Perhaps the often-noted relationship between homogeneity of social background and marital success is a product of shared role perceptions.

Accordingly, there is so much uncertainty about which adult roles the child will play that anticipatory socialization is very difficult. It is impossible to socialize for all contingencies. All that early socialization can do is lay a foundation that is compatible with the most probable later experiences. (Maccoby, 1966, p. 210)

Despite this confusion about the role of males and females and the difficulty this poses for the growing child, there are differences in the *average* scores or ratings between boys and girls that are of significance to education. (You may refer back to Table 3.6 to note average differences between high school boys and girls in educational achievements.)

1. The average height and weight of boys is greater than for girls except at ages 11 to 15, when there is little difference because of the more rapid rate of maturation in girls. Girls, on the average, precede boys by 24 months in reaching puberty.

2. The average IQ for large groups of boys and girls is the same because tests have been constructed to eliminate sex differences. However, girls typically score higher on verbal items and boys on quantitative and spatial items in both intelligence and achievement tests.

3. Differences between the sexes in preference for play, games, and other activities become apparent in early childhood and increase with successive age levels into adolescence. Girls, for example, prefer reading and actually do more reading on the average at all school levels than do boys, whereas boys engage in more active games. Large differences appear in vocational interests at the senior high school age.

4. Males show a higher degree of aggressive and dominant behavior than females, with more boys than girls apprehended as delinquents, and a much higher incidence of males among adult criminals. Females are more cooperative than males; in school, girls tend to comply with the teacher's wishes more frequently than do boys.

These relatively small average differences between groups of males and females should not be permitted to overshadow the much larger differences among individuals of the same sex. The average differences between and among the sexes and also the range of differences in six measures observed for boys and girls at a mean age of 125 months are shown in Fig. 6.6 (Klausmeier, Feldhusen, & Check, 1959). The range in IQ of the boys is from 62 to 146, with a mean of 100.6; the range of the girls is from 63 to 135, with a mean of 100.8. It is not surprising that these ranges and means are much alike, simply because we selected these boys and girls to be of the same mean IQ and chronological age for our study. These were the only two measures used intentionally to produce groups similar in average scores, however.

On the first nonselective measure, strength of grip, the boys' mean score is 20.9 and the girls' is 17.7. Though this average difference is quite large, the differences within the sexes are also marked: 15.5 between the weakest and strongest boy and 14.3 between the weakest and strongest girl. The girls have, on the average, 16.5 permanent teeth and the boys 15.5; however, the difference among the boys in permanent teeth is 17.0 and among the girls it is 16.0. We did not find the higher achievement

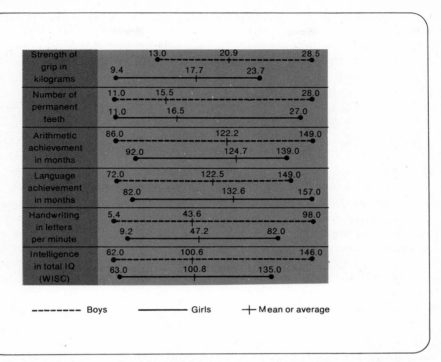

Strength of grip in kilograms	13.0	20.9	28.5
	9.4	17.7	23.7
Number of permanent teeth	11.0	15.5	28.0
	11.0	16.5	27.0
Arithmetic achievement in months	86.0	122.2	149.0
	92.0	124.7	139.0
Language achievement in months	72.0	122.5	149.0
	82.0	132.6	157.0
Handwriting in letters per minute	5.4	43.6	98.0
	9.2	47.2	82.0
Intelligence in total IQ (WISC)	62.0	100.6	146.0
	63.0	100.8	135.0

- - - - - - - Boys   ———— Girls   + Mean or average

Fig. 6.6. Range and mean score for strength of grip, number of permanent teeth, arithmetic and language achievement, handwriting speed and IQ; 40 boys and 40 girls; mean age: 125 months. (Adapted from Klausmeier, Feldhusen, & Check, 1959)

generally found and predicted for boys in arithmetic; the girls had a slightly higher mean score. In language and in handwriting speed, the average achievements are higher for girls than for boys, as expected. In all areas except language, however, it was a boy who had the *highest* score. In all measures the differences between members of the same sex are far greater than the differences between the averages of the two sexes. For example, the difference between the lowest and highest scores for the same sex in handwriting speed is about 25 times greater than is the difference between the average scores of the two sexes.

What do sex differences such as those reported mean in relation to a possible need for separating boys and girls for educational purposes? Boys and girls can probably remain together for all instruction through at least the fourth grade and for most instruction thereafter. There are some physical differences that should be taken into account, however. For instance, at the time of menarche in early developing girls it is probably wise to separate boys and girls for any strenuous activities. Further, at the time the male voice begins to change boys should be separated from girls for instruction in vocal music (unless our music teachers can somehow provide better instruction in mixed groups to boys whose voices are changing).

6.1. Two children at age 6 had Stanford-Binet IQ scores of 100. At age 12 one had a score of 84 and the other a score of 116, equivalent to about the sixteenth and eighty-fourth percentile, respectively. What percentage of students had changes in IQ this large in the Sontag, Baker, and Nelson study? Knowing that some, but not all, students show changes of this magnitude and larger, how much reliance would you put on the results of one IQ test in making judgments about either the readiness of a student to learn something, e.g., to read, and the upper limits of performance he will ever reach, e.g., in mathematics?

6.2. Guilford views intelligence as the interaction of any of five intellectual operations on any of four contents to achieve any of six products. How might this view of specific abilities account for an individual scoring differently on two different IQ tests given on two consecutive days? How might it account for different scores by the same individual on the same test at two different ages?

6.3. In Fig. 6.4 we see that almost half the students are not consistent performers in reading and arithmetic. Many are poor in one subject and mediocre in the other, or they are average in one and good in the other. Suppose reading achievement and social studies were compared; would you expect more or less consistency of performance? Why? How might arithmetic and science compare?

6.4. Which is more stable over a period of years, the level of educational achievement in a subject or the IQ score? Basing your judgment on the answer, what information would you like to have about seventh-grade students to predict their achievements as high school seniors?

6.5. The study of cheating by Hartshorne and May was reported in 1928. Do you feel the distribution of the percentages who cheat in various situations has changed significantly since then? Might cheating behavior vary also as a function of age? As you review your schooling, what was the general attitude of students toward cheating? What influenced your own behavior in this area?

6.6. Name two or three activities or learning tasks for which you might consider separating the sexes because of large average differences between boys and girls. In which, if any, activities or curriculum areas do the *majority* of girls show superiority over the highest boys?

6.7. Is being a male or a female particularly advantageous in certain teaching areas, e.g., kindergarten, high school physical education? Should a single woman with no dependents be paid as much as a husband and father with three dependents for the same teaching job, e.g., $8500 for the third year as a high school history teacher?

DISADVANTAGED STUDENTS AND IMPOVERISHED ENVIRONMENTS

The environment that contributes to the educational disadvantagement of students has three general characteristics or attributes: (1) The total environment—home, neighborhood, and school—does not provide opportunity for achieving a reasonable measure of self-realization and eventual economic independence as a young adult. (2) The home and neighborhood do not provide the essentials for a successful start in school as a young child. (3) The neighborhood and school contribute to lack of progress in school during childhood and adolescence.

Individuals from such an environment show a higher incidence of certain characteristics than do individuals from other more favored environments. Students who grow up in such an environment are now generally called *disadvantaged*. Terms that have been used in the past and are still sometimes used to designate children and youth from impoverished environments or the environments themselves are: culturally deprived, socially disadvantaged, underprivileged, low socioeconomic status, low social class, and economically poor.

Before considering the more specific aspects of disadvantaged environments and then the characteristics of the students who come from these environments, we should have a general picture of who the disadvantaged are. In one valuable study, Havighurst and Moorefield identified groups of disadvantaged people in terms of race, ethnic origin, and geographical location. They listed the poor and otherwise disadvantaged groups, in order of their number, as follows:

1. Urban whites. Children of Caucasian parents, some of them being old-American families who have been living in urban places for generations, while others are recent immigrants from Europe, and still others are recent migrants from rural areas to the cities.
2. Urban Negroes. Most of them are children of rural migrants to the big cities.
3. Rural Negroes. Most of them are living in the southern states.
4. Rural whites. They live about equally in the southern states and in the rural northern states.
5. Rural Spanish-Americans. Some are of long-established families in the southwestern states while others are children of recent immigrants from Mexico. These are Caucasians but are distinguished from the other "whites" by their Spanish origin.
6. Urban Puerto Ricans. They are mostly Caucasians, but are distinguished by their Puerto Rican origin and by their concentration in a few urban centers.
7. American Indians. Many Indians are well-established and well-adjusted on their tribal lands, but many of those who live away from the tribal lands are disadvantaged with respect to the labor market and the educational and social expectations of their new environment, especially if it is a big city. (Havighurst & Moorefield, 1967, pp. 19-20)

Environmental Contributors to Disadvantagement

Low socioeconomic status, impoverished home and neighborhood conditions, and unresponsive schools are the main environmental contributors to disadvantagement. The explicit discussions of each of these that follow will make their contributions clear. As shown in Fig. 6.7, these three basic conditions work in a kind of vicious interrelationship with certain characteristics (to be discussed in the next section); the environmental conditions tend to produce the characteristics, but the effect of the characteristics tends to perpetuate the conditions.

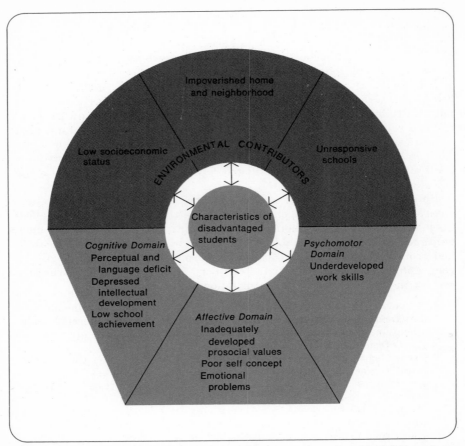

Fig. 6.7. Environmental contributors to disadvantagement and characteristics of disadvantaged students.

Low Socioeconomic Status. Socioeconomic status and social class are closely related. The lower the income, the lower is the social class, although other factors also contribute to defining social class. For example, some of the concomitants of social class in "River City" are shown in Fig. 6.8. (Here the young people from the upper and upper-middle classes are combined into one group.) Interest in church, amount of education, and socioeconomic rating as a young adult were lowest for the lower-lower social-class group, whereas the tendency of girls to marry under age and the incidence of delinquency in boys was highest in this same lower-lower class. This and other evidence make it clear that the opportunities and rewards in life are unequally distributed—more good things go to the children of higher-status families.

The difficulties that children of the poor experience in our educational system will be specifically described in the next section. Figure 6.9, however, summarizes the effect of these difficulties: the child who is either low in academic ability or is from a low socioeconomic status indeed has barriers to hurdle in order to achieve happiness and progress in school. But the plight of the child who is low in both academic ability and socioeconomic status is extreme; such a child falls in the "cell of double jeopardy"—his chances of attaining success and contentment in school are tragically slim.

Impoverished Home and Neighborhood Conditions. The factors that initiate, and perpetuate, the poverty-disadvantaged cycle are extremely varied and complicated, and the literature on each of them is voluminous. Fantini and Weinstein succinctly summarized some of the environmental factors that contribute to the plight of low-income families in this way:

> Low income forces a family to seek residence in low-rent areas where housing is bereft of the more comfortable aspects of American living and where landlords are not motivated to keep their buildings in good repair. In some cases, even the municipality bypasses these areas in regular maintenance programs, largely because middle-class taxpayers keep maintenance departments busy with pressure on the city to attend to details in their own "finer" neighborhoods. Consequently, the whole area becomes more and more run down, garbage

Fig. 6.8. Social class and facts about youth in "River City." (Havighurst, Bowman, Liddle, Matthews, & Pierce, 1962, p. 13)

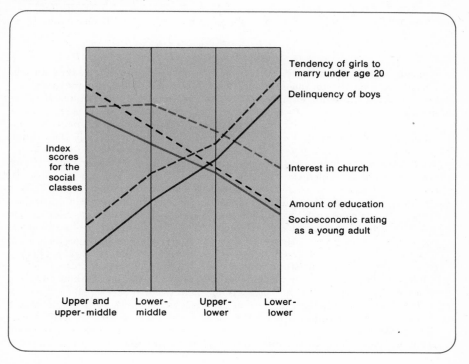

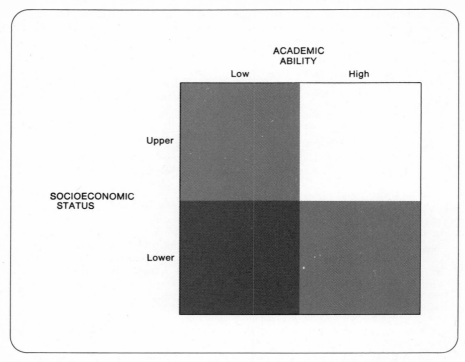

Fig. 6.9. Difficulty in adjusting to and succeeding in school (difficulty indicated by shading).

piles up, sewage drains clog, and rats and vermin move in with the tenants. The depressing, oppressive appearance of the slum neighborhood, along with general economic hardship, eats away at the aspirations and motivations of its inhabitants. The parents of children born into this environment may be away from home day and night trying to eke out a meager wage, or, unable to cope financially or emotionally, one or the other of the parents (especially the father) may flee home and neighborhood. Escapes are also available for those who remain: alcohol, frequent card or dice games on streets or in taverns, drugs, gossip, sex — to all of which the children are exposed at an early age as a natural part of their environment and as the accustomed way of adult living.

The severity of such conditions is well known and, in some communities, efforts at "slum clearance" have been made. However, the implicit, middle-class attitudes which underlie these remedial efforts have done little to improve the outlook and self-image of those for whom better housing conditions have been provided. In order to be accepted into a low-income housing project, applicants must answer — to the satisfaction of the housing authorities — a battery of personal questions that go far beyond the typical credit-rating information asked of middle-class applicants to privately sponsored housing. Moreover, once accepted, tenants must continue to meet the rules and regulations set up by the authorities. For example, if a family gains or loses a member, it is required to uproot itself — at its own expense — to move into a larger or smaller apartment, perhaps one which is in a distant and unfamiliar neighborhood. Imagine a middle-class family being required to pack up all of its belongings and move to another dwelling unit—one that they themselves have not chosen, and merely because a son or daughter has married and moved out of the household! (Fantini & Weinstein, 1968, pp. 14-15)

Unresponsive Schools. Warner, Havighurst, and Loeb (1944), studying social life in a New England community, concluded that the educational system was contributing to the crystallization of a social class system. That is, the educational system was making it possible for children of the middle and upper social classes to gain further advantages over the lower social class. There is considerable evidence that a quarter-century later many schools still are unresponsive to the needs of the poor and various disadvantaged groups.

For example, one of these groups is the Florida migrant workers. Kleinert (1969), outlining four attributes of the migrants, emphasized the effects of the schools on them: (1) They vary greatly in their characteristics; the one characteristic they have in common, however, is their migrancy. (2) Migrants as a group receive the least education of any group of workers in the national economy. (3) The only kind of help from society in which migrants themselves see any significance is direct financial aid. (4) The migrant child learns as soon as he begins school that he is an outcast from society. Kleinert points out that the migrant child is somewhat anxious about his new and unknown environment as he moves into each new camp. It is when he goes to school, however, that he experiences the full effects of discrimination:

> At school he finds that he is one of a disliked minority, disliked by the ones whose views are by far the most important to him—the other children. Although his skin color and language variations are commonplace to the other rural children of the area—those who live there year-around—he is quickly categorized as a migrant; he learns where he stands in the unique caste system rigorously observed by children. Except for migrant children, every child learns to cope with the caste system of his peers. He learns that there is mobility in this system, that yesterday's clown can be tomorrow's hero. The migrant child does not have this chance when in school he confronts the rest of the world for the first time.
>
> We have here, then, a situation which should present a challenge to the educational system in the migrant area, an opportunity for it to penetrate these deep and early sensitivities of children and throw light upon them. Whatever essential human values are associated with them can be reexamined and perhaps reordered. Unfortunately, the school finds itself hampered by the attitudes of the adults of the community, by the number of children each teacher must work with, and, most critically, by the limitations of its teachers' own backgrounds. So the greatest single effect the school could have upon migrant children is lost the first year it deals with them. It cannot make them feel wanted; therefore it cannot educate them. (Kleinert, 1969, p. 92)

The educational condition of minority groups in the United States is not dissimilar to that of Indians in Canada, according to Fisher (1969). He found that from 1959-1960 to 1962-1963, the welfare costs of the Indian population of Alberta more than doubled (from about $300,000 to $700,000). During the same time the number of schools and the number of years of schooling available to Canadian children increased. The Canadian Indian, however, failed to use these opportunities. In 1965, for instance, a study at the Blackfoot Indian Reservation in Alberta showed that 50 percent of the children had dropped out of school after 1961 and that 95 percent of the dropouts left school before they completed the ninth grade. In other words, the school showed no holding power from grades 5 to 9. Fisher summarized the difficulties in this way:

> In conclusion, these studies show that the expanded educational opportunities for Canadian Indians are not really opportunities at all. For what the school offers is an irrelevant set of values and training. Moreover, the school often comes into direct conflict with certain moral and cultural values of the student. Thus, it is the educational system that fails the student and not the student who fails the system. In trying to be a good and successful Indian, the Indian student must often be a bad and unsuccessful student. (Fisher, 1969, p. 33)

In the United States, the various sections of the Elementary and Secondary Education Act of 1965 provided more than $1 billion per year to improve the education of disadvantaged students. At this time it is too early to know how much these funds actually have increased the educational achievements of disadvantaged students and decreased the dropout rate. In general, some excellent programs have emerged, but many problems are also experienced in many cities.

Characteristics of Disadvantaged Students

In the first part of this chapter we indicated the range of differences among individuals in characteristics in the cognitive, psychomotor, and affective domains. Characteristics of disadvantaged students in these domains are now described. It should be immediately apparent that any individual who is classified as disadvantaged may be higher and lower on one or another characteristic, rather than uniformly low in all of them. Also, there are large differences in all characteristics among individuals in the various categories of the disadvantaged. Therefore, the relevant characteristics of each student from an economically poor background must be carefully assessed in order to plan an excellent instructional program for him.

Refer again to Fig. 6.7, which shows how the environmental factors we have just discussed contribute to — and are in turn influenced by — the various characteristics of the disadvantaged in the cognitive, affective, and psychomotor domains. Also, because a higher proportion of the racial and ethnic minority groups of this country, in comparison with the majority, are of low socioeconomic status, live in poor neighborhoods, and go to unresponsive schools, the disadvantaged can be considered to possess a fourth group of characteristics, shown in the figure as minority-group characteristics. These four areas are now considered.

Cognitive Abilities and Characteristics. The three most damaging effects of poverty as related to education are perceptual and language deficit, depressed intellectual development as measured by IQ tests, and low achievement in school. These discouraging effects have been thoroughly described in both professional and general literature in recent years; therefore, we discuss only a few specific studies here.

1. Perceptual and Language Deficit. Deutsch (1963) observed children in the slums of New York. These homes did not provide opportunity for young children to develop the auditory and visual discriminations needed for success in language arts, reading, and other school work. The children on the average were low in their ability to attend to situations of the kind encountered in school.

Bernstein (1961) made an extensive analysis of the language of disadvantaged children. His work has received widespread and deserved attention in planning educational programs. Bernstein designated the language of the disadvantaged as *restricted code* and that of other students as *elaborated code*. The characteristics of the restricted code are as follows:

> 1. Short, grammatically simple, often unfinished sentences with a poor syntactical form stressing the active voice.
> 2. Simple and repetitive use of conjunctions (so, then, because).
> 3. Little use of subordinate clauses to break down the initial categories of the dominant subject.
> 4. Inability to hold a formal subject through a speech sequence; thus a dislocated informational content is facilitated.
> 5. Rigid and limited use of adjectives and adverbs.
> 6. Infrequent use of impersonal pronouns as subjects of conditional classes.
> 7. Frequent use of statements where the reason and conclusion are confounded to produce a categoric statement.
> 8. A large number of statements and phrases which signal a requirement for the previous speech sequence to be reinforced: "Wouldn't it? You see? You know?" etc. This process is termed "sympathetic circularity."
> 9. Individual selection from a group of idiomatic phrases or sequences will frequently occur.
> 10. *The individual qualification is in the sentence organization: It is a language of implicit meaning.* (Bernstein, 1961, p. 169)

Both the overt speech and the thought processes are limited in explicitness and continuity. The speech is disconnected and repetitive, as shown by a 16-year-old boy of normal intelligence:

> It's all according like these youths and that if they get into these gangs and that they most have a bit of nark around and say it goes wrong and that and they probably knock someone off I mean think they just do it to be big getting publicity here and there. (Bernstein, 1961, p. 171)

The elaborated code has the following characteristics:

> 1. Accurate grammatical order and syntax regulate what is said.
> 2. Logical modifications and stress are mediated through a grammatically complex sentence construction, especially through the use of a range of conjunctions and subordinate clauses.
> 3. Frequent use of prepositions which indicate logical relationships as well as prepositions which indicate temporal and spatial contiguity.
> 4. Frequent use of the personal pronoun "I."
> 5. A discriminative selection from a range of adjectives and adverbs.

6. Individual qualification is verbally mediated through the structure and relationships within and between sentences.

7. Expressive symbolism discriminates between meanings within speech sequences rather than reinforcing dominant words or phrases, or accompanying the sequence in a diffuse, generalized manner.

8. It is a language use which points to the possibilities inherent in a complex conceptual hierarchy for the organizing of experience. (Bernstein, 1961, p. 172)

The *number* of words in the vocabulary does not differ for children of the same age and IQ level, whether they use the restricted or the elaborated code, according to Bernstein. However, children in homes and neighborhoods of higher socioeconomic status learn to speak their ideas in connected phrases and sentences. Also, in their thought processes they use words that stand for concepts and principles and relate them to one another. Individuals with a restricted code tend not to connect and relate concepts in their speech or thought. Thus, individuals with a restricted code tend not to conceptualize abstract ideas, including ideas about interpersonal relationships, according to Bernstein.

2. Depressed Intellectual Development as Represented in IQ Scores. An impoverished environment during infancy and early childhood, such as those found in our inner cities and other economically poor areas, might retard development of the individual to a point where he could not catch up later; an enriched environment might accelerate his development (Bloom, 1964). The early years are most critical, as shown in Table 6.2, which assumes that 100 percent of mature intelligence is achieved by age 17. Breaking this assumption down, Bloom estimated that 50 percent of mature intelligence is achieved by age 4 and that a deprived and an abundant environment can result in differences in intelligence scores of at least 10 points until age 4, as shown in the last column. Similarly, with 80 percent of mature intelligence being achieved by age 8, the difference resulting from the extreme environments can be at least 16 points; and at age 17 the difference can amount to at least 20 IQ points. In interpreting the change in IQ caused by environment, we assume an average IQ of 100, with about two-thirds of all individuals having IQs between 84 and 116. Thus, a change of 20 IQ points is considerable. For example, two indi-

Table 6.2. Hypothetical Effects of Different Environments on the Development of Intelligence in Three Selected Age Periods

Age period	Percentage of mature intelligence	Variation from normal growth in IQ units			Possible difference
		Deprived	Normal	Abundant	
Birth–4	50	−5	0	+5	10
4–8	30	−3	0	+3	6
8–17	20	−2	0	+2	4
Total	100	−10	0	+10	20

Source: Bloom, 1964, p. 72.

viduals at age 17 might have IQs of 120 and 100, the difference being ascribable to an enriched and an impoverished environment. The individual with the IQ of 100 would not be expected to complete the baccalaureate, whereas the one with 120 IQ would be expected to complete the baccalaureate and also graduate work in some fields. Actually, Bloom considered the possible difference of 20 IQ points because of environment to be a conservative estimate.

Hunt (1961) believed that an enriched environment in early childhood could make a still larger difference:

> It might be feasible to discover ways to govern the environments, especially during the early years of their development, to achieve a substantially faster rate of intellectual development and a substantially higher adult level of intellectual capacity. (Hunt, 1961, p. 363)

3. Low Achievement in School. The average educational achievements of children of low socioeconomic status and impoverished backgrounds are slightly below the median of all children in the first grade. Similarly, children from more favorable environments are above the median. With each additional year of schooling, the average of the students from impoverished backgrounds falls further below the median, and children from enriched environments move further ahead. This typical pattern is shown in Fig. 6.10.

Fig. 6.10. Hypothetical achievement of disadvantaged and other students with increasing education.

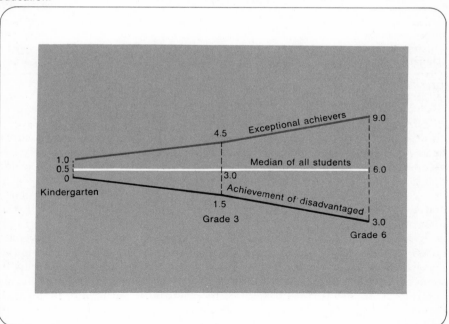

Wilson (1963) studied sixth-grade children in 14 schools of Berkeley, California. Berkeley has three fairly distinct living areas: the Hills, the Foothills, and the Flats. The low area around San Francisco Bay—the Flats—consists of working-class homes. The expensive homes occupied mainly by people in professional and white-collar occupations are in the high Hills area. The Foothills between are heterogeneous. Table 6.3 shows the average reading achievement scores of boys and girls according to the father's occupation and the location of the school in terms of Hills, Foothills, or Flats. The large difference in achievement is among the locations of the schools. For example, the boys from the white-collar and merchant groups have reading scores of 106, 93, and 81 in the Hills, Foothills, and Flats, respectively. There is also a substantial difference in reading achievement according to the father's occupation. For example, the boys in Foothills schools have reading scores of 100, 93, and 91, according to the three sets of occupations. (Notice that there are some exceptions to this general pattern, especially in connection with girls in the Foothills area. Also, in some large cities the difference in the mean achievement scores between inner-city and suburban-type schools is much larger than in Berkeley. The differences in socioeconomic status also are larger.)

Table 6.3. Mean Reading Achievement Test Scores of Sixth-Grade Students, Classified by Sex, School Strata, and Father's Occupation

Father's occupation	Boys			Girls		
	Hills	Foothills	Flats	Hills	Foothills	Flats
Professional and executive	107	100	—[a]	107	108	—[a]
White collar and merchant	106	93	81	102	69	81
Manual and artisan	—[a]	91	71	103	93	84

[a]Means are not reported for cells containing fewer than 10 cases.
Source: Wilson, 1963, p. 223. Reprinted with permission of Teachers College Press.

Affective Characteristics. The impoverished environment of the big city slum or the depressed area of Appalachia or the migrant workers' camp or the Indian reservation produces many children with inadequately developed prosocial values, poor self-concepts, and high anxiety and other emotional problems. Although some children from these environments do enjoy buoyant emotional health, economic poverty, in general, is associated with a higher incidence of children who are disadvantaged in the affective domain also.

1. Inadequately Developed Prosocial Values. Many persons have accused the schools of attempting to force on lower-class children middle-class values that are inappropriate to modern society. This may be true in some cases. However, Havighurst (1966) identified a set of values that are not related to social class but that are essential in an urban, industrial, democratic society. He listed the values and described the situation in this manner:

      Punctuality
      Orderliness
      Conformity to group norms
      Desire for a work career based on skill and knowledge
      Desire for a stable family life
      Inhibition of aggressive impulses
      Rational approach to a problem situation
      Enjoyment of study
      Desire for freedom of self and others

    These are values of an urban, industrial, democratic society. *They are not social class values.* It is misleading to speak of the school as a protagonist of middle-class values versus the inner-city homes and neighborhood as a nourisher of lower-class values, with resultant conflict. This talk has just enough basis in fact to worry an inexperienced teacher, but not enough to serve as a basis for a positive educational program aimed at reducing the value gap.
    A young Negro woman high school teacher had the following to say:

> *I want you to know I took time out of a very busy weekend to talk to you because I felt someone should know what is going on at our school. The violence and stabbing between the students, not the teachers but the students, is getting worse every day. In my opinion, this is taking place because of the weak position taken by the principal. We are now on our third principal in two years. The others were moved up to supervisory positions, I believe. The last two were Negroes, the first one was white. In every instance, the principal did not want to come to grips with the violence of the students. He might be blamed and that would stand in the way of his promotion. So it was better to ignore it and leave it up to the next principal. Since the students recognize the changing and weak administration, they feel there is no control over them, and they are getting out of hand. The climate is one of fear and intimidation, particularly of those students who want to learn. I don't know how anyone can learn in such a climate.* (Havighurst, 1966, pp. 47-48)

Havighurst indicated that this young woman was not talking about a conflict of social class values:

> She was talking about a disorganized, demoralized community in which the pupils want to do better but do not know how, and the parents do not know how to help. In this community it is not the school with value set A working against the neighborhood with value set B. It is the school without a coherent and effective set of values and without good leadership working in a neighborhood without a coherent and effective set of values. If the school were to state explicitly a program for teaching some such set of values as those listed above, and were to organize itself for this task, most of the parents in the neighborhood would support the school to the best of their understanding and ability. (Havighurst, 1966, p. 49)

2. Poor Self Concept. As one grows he identifies himself according to sex, race, physical appearance, achievements, and the like. He also evaluates himself. His self-description and evaluation comprise his self concept. In interviews with students from impoverished environments, Bowman found that they revealed their low self-evaluations. The despair and hopelessness that come early in life to such people are shown in these statements of youth growing up in this country.

I couldn't get along with teachers; that is the main reason I quit. I really didn't like any of them. In a way it seems better being out of school and in a way it don't. When you are in school, at least you have some place to go and pass the time.

I do wish I could have graduated from high school. I'd give a million for that. It makes you feel that you are something. People ask you what you have done. I really haven't done anything, but I would be somebody anyway if I finished high school. When I got kicked out I just sat down in the hall and cr¹ed.

[A composition] When I was a boy in fust grade I was slow in most everthing I did. I usual had to stay after school and finish my work. That was first time I flunk. The second and threeth grads went by and I didn't learn anything. Fourth grade I was flunk again. What was my trouble? I never couldn't learn to reade and no one saw to it that I did. I am seventeen and in the tenth grade and I still don't know how to read good. And when you can't read you soon get discouraged. And when I use your sentence "Finally I gave up the search in despair" I am talking of hope of learning to read. [A boy with IQ of 120] (Bowman, 1966, pp. 83, 84)

Proshansky and Newton (1968) summarized research showing that some young Negro children reject being black and prefer to think of themselves as white. This happens because the American Negro is forced to play an inferior, passive, servile role and eventually comes to believe that this role is the only one he can ever have. Not surprisingly, this belief is accompanied by a sense of powerlessness and frustration. Escape from these feelings is frequently sought through the excessive use of alcohol and drugs and compulsive gambling. The more subtle and devastating escape route leads to attempts to become white. Negro adults, particularly males, who recognize this situation are increasingly angry and resentful, but they also may show hopelessness and despair at the same time. These frustrations, along with miserable housing conditions, unemployment, and a dominant role played by the black mother who is frequently employed and absent from the home, produce a nonsupportive environment for the child. The child's parents symbolize degradation and deprivation in the larger society and are rejected by the child, who also then rejects his own skin color and his own race of people. Until recently, there has been little hope in the midst of poverty and despair. Some desirable change has occurred in the last few years, however, mainly because of more aggressive social and political activity by blacks, which may lead to healthier self concepts in young black children:

In the last decade, the American Negro's struggle has taken on a new, dramatic, world-wide significance. Spurred by the emergence of the African nations and the pervasive influence of the mass media, there has been a rediscovery of "Black culture" and a growing bond uniting black peoples throughout the world. In his own battle, the American Negro is able to achieve a new sense of kinship and feeling of purpose—a new, larger, black identity. The struggle of black men has become symbolic of the struggle of all oppressed groups to achieve dignity and respect in the face of bigotry and discrimination. (Proshansky & Newton, 1968, p. 215)

3. Emotional Problems. An environment that does not provide for the physiological and safety needs of young children is especially cruel and brutalizing in its effects. Children who habitually experience hunger, cold

in the winter and heat in the summer, untended cuts and burns, rat bites, and the like might well be expected to be anxious throughout the rest of their lives and also to labor under many emotional problems.

Figure 6.11 shows the incidence of emotionally disturbed children by grade. A sharp rise is seen from kindergarten to first grade. The percentage of disturbed children is about the same from first through seventh grade, with a rise again at the eighth grade. It is not surprising that the ungraded special classes for mentally retarded children show an even higher percentage than do the regular classes through eighth grade. Figure 6.12 shows the incidence of emotionally disturbed children by home condition. Emotionally disturbed children, more frequently than normal ones, come from broken homes, from homes where the mother is employed full time, from homes where there is serious neglect and deprivation of the child, and from homes in which a foreign language is spoken.

Psychomotor Abilities and Physical Characteristics. In general, motor activities are engaged in much more by children in impoverished environments than are intellectual and cultural activities. For example, Klausmeier, Feldhusen, and Check (1959) found that children of low IQ from impoverished inner-city environments did not differ much from children of average and high IQ in favored environments in a number of motor skills and physical characteristics.

Although children from impoverished environments show good motor development, they do not develop salable work skills. In part, this is be-

Fig. 6.11. Incidence of emotionally disturbed children by grade. (Adapted from Clancy & Smitter, 1953, p. 212)

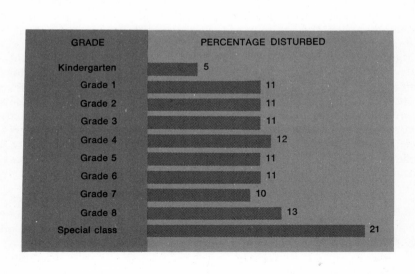

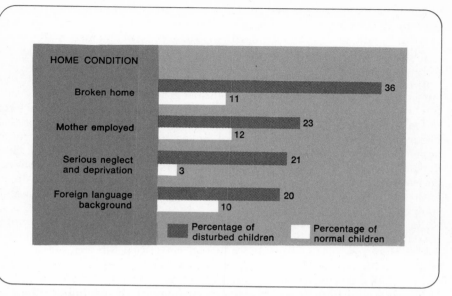

Fig. 6.12. Incidence of emotionally disturbed children by home condition. (Adapted from Clancy & Smitter, 1953, p. 214)

cause they do not learn to read and write well enough to perform a variety of jobs where simple instructions must be read and understood and where they must write reports. Further, many cannot get part-time jobs as teen-agers, and organized labor groups do not admit enough of them into apprentice programs. Attitudes in the home and neighborhood that cause difficulty in the school are also sources of problems in employment. As noted earlier, the same prosocial values that Havighurst described as essential for schooling are also essential in industry.

Racial and Ethnic Characteristics. As noted earlier, the disadvantaged represent all races and ethnic groups. Actually, the largest number are white; nevertheless, certain racial and ethnic groups have a higher *percentage* of disadvantaged than is the case for whites of Western European origin. Despite this concentration of disadvantaged among certain groups, great variability in all cognitive, psychomotor, and affective variables is characteristic of *all* races and ethnic groups. Exceptionally high achievers, fully committed to the advancement of human values, are found in large numbers among all the racial and ethnic groups.

6.8. Suppose a list of disadvantaged groups were drawn up on an international basis, rather than a national basis. Where would the various American groups identified by Havighurst rank in the international scene?

6.9. One problem of disadvantaged students may be not that they are unable to speak, but rather that they speak a language that simply is different from the white middle-class school dialect. If this is the case, should these students be taught the school dialect or should the school accept and use their language patterns in teaching?

6.10. With each succeeding year in school, the disadvantaged fall further behind relatively in school achievement and IQ scores. In addition to the disadvantaged home life, what might contribute to the relative decline in IQ scores?

6.11. Using Berkeley as an example, suppose that the population was not stratified by area of residence but that families of all socioeconomic status were randomly distributed throughout the city. What effect might this random mixing have on reading achievement? On civic pride?

6.12. The list of prosocial values (Havighurst) must be interpreted carefully. Which of the phrases seem most prone to a negative rather than a positive interpretation?

6.13. As you reflect on the self-concept of a disadvantaged youth, which right would you attempt to fulfill first, the right to read or the right to a minimum standard of living? Why?

6.14. Many children, perhaps the majority, rise far above their impoverished backgrounds and achieve well. What do you think are the most important determiners of the success or failure of a particular child from a poor socioeconomic background? Should the teacher ever treat any child as if he might not be able to learn to read well?

EDUCATIONAL PROVISIONS FOR DISADVANTAGED STUDENTS

Small efforts made in isolated segments of the present complex educational system will not greatly improve educational opportunities for disadvantaged children and youth. A reading program of an hour or two a week after school, a guidance counselor or social worker for each thousand or more students, a new set of reading books with black or brown children in the illustrations, a computer terminal for practice and drill — all these are examples of small efforts that no sensible group should advocate on the ground that they will solve the problem of educating the disadvantaged. Such efforts may, of course, produce token effects, but any real improvement will require massive innovations and reforms that simultaneously deal with *all* the components of a school learning system as outlined in Chapter 1. A few of these more inclusive and basic reforms — those connected with developing a physically safe school environment, preschool education, and post-high school training — are now considered explicitly. The approaches taken in preschool and post-high school training merit serious consideration by those interested in elementary and high school education who are still unaware of the major changes that are essential — or fearful of them if they are aware of them. The section ends with a brief discussion of integration.

A Physically Safe Environment

A Senate subcommittee on juvenile delinquency pointed out in a report — summarized in *Time* magazine (1969) — that violence in the schools is

common, especially at the junior high school level. The incidence of bur-
glary, larceny, and assault continues to increase at all school levels. For
example, in a single year, Chicago teachers were attacked by students
1065 times. In the Philadelphia school system, 116 incidents of attacks on
teachers were reported; New York City reported 180; and 87 instances
were reported in San Francisco elementary schools in a five-month period.

It is obvious that excellent instructional programs cannot be organized
and maintained in schools where teachers and students fear violent physical attacks. However, solutions to this problem are not reported in the
literature. Certainly, more force and more police are not the solution.
Possibly, school people fear the unfavorable publicity they think would
result if they brought the seriousness of the problem to public attention.
Nevertheless, the situation may *have* to be widely publicized, because
school people independently cannot solve the problem; a larger effort involving all segments of the community is required.

Preschool Education

Some preschool programs already have been started. Many more schools
for young children aged 3 to 5 are urgently needed. The objectives, programs, and procedures of present schools vary. One program that has
commanded widespread attention was developed by Bereiter and Engelmann (1966); it was based on five main points, as follows:

1. By the age of three or four, disadvantaged children are already seriously
behind other children in the development of aptitudes necessary for success in
school.

2. Disadvantaged children must somehow "catch up" in the development of
these abilities, or they will enter elementary school with handicaps that will
spell failure for a large percentage of them and a limited future for all of them.

3. If they are to catch up, they must progress at a faster than normal rate.

4. A preschool program that provides the usual opportunities for learning
cannot be expected to produce learning at above normal rates.

5. A short-term preschool program cannot be expected to produce above
normal gains in all areas of development at once; a "well-rounded" program is
therefore incompatible with the goal of catching up: selectivity is necessary.
(Bereiter & Engelmann, 1966, p. 19)[1]

Moving from these assumptions, Bereiter and Engelmann developed
an instructional program based on experimentation with small groups
over a period of three years. The main emphasis is on language development. Their observations indicated that the language deficiencies were
not in vocabulary and grammar but in failure to master certain *uses* of
language. The disadvantaged child has a language adequate in maintaining social relationships and meeting his material needs. He does not
use language, however, to obtain and transmit information, to monitor
his own behavior, and to carry on verbal reasoning. Further, he tends not
to use sentences that can be taken apart and recombined. Also, he fails to

---

[1]© 1966. Reprinted by permission of Prentice-Hall, Inc.

master the use of root words and inflections that are necessary for the expression and manipulation of logical relationships. With these and other considerations in mind, Bereiter and Engelmann outlined behavioral objectives of preschool education as follows:

1. Ability to use both affirmative and *not* statements in reply to the question "What is this?" "This is a ball. This is not a book."

2. Ability to use both affirmative and *not* statements in response to the command "Tell me about this _____ [ball, pencil, etc.]." "This pencil is red. This pencil is not blue."

3. Ability to handle polar opposites ("If it is not _____, it must be _____") for at least four concept pairs, e.g., big-little, up-down, long-short, fat-skinny.

4. Ability to use the following prepositions correctly in statements describing arrangements of objects: on, in, under, over, between. "Where is the pencil?" "The pencil is under the book."

5. Ability to name positive and negative instances for at least four classes, such as tools, weapons, pieces of furniture, wild animals, farm animals, and vehicles. "Tell me something that is a weapon." "A gun is a weapon." "Tell me something that is not a weapon." "A cow is not a weapon." The child should also be able to apply these class concepts correctly to nouns with which he is familiar, e.g., "Is a crayon a piece of furniture?" "No, a crayon is not a piece of furniture. A crayon is something to write with."

6. Ability to perform simple *if-then* deductions. The child is presented a diagram containing big squares and little squares. All the big squares are red, but the little squares are of various other colors. "If the square is big, what do you know about it?" "It's red."

7. Ability to use *not* in deductions. "If the square is little, what else do you know about it?" "It is not red."

8. Ability to use *or* in simple deductions. "If the square is little, then it is not red. What else do you know about it?" "It's blue *or* yellow."

9. Ability to name the basic colors, plus white, black, and brown.

10. Ability to count aloud to 20 without help and to 100 with help at decade points (30, 40, etc.).

11. Ability to count objects correctly up to 10.

12. Ability to recognize and name the vowels, and at least 15 consonants.

13. Ability to distinguish printed words from pictures.

14. Ability to rhyme in some fashion to produce a word that rhymes with a given word, to tell whether two words do or do not rhyme, or to complete unfamiliar rhyming jingles like "I had a dog, and his name was Abel; I found him hiding under the _____ ."

15. A sight-reading vocabulary of at least four words in addition to proper names, with evidence that the printed word has the same meaning for them as the corresponding spoken word. "What word is this?" "Cat." "Is this a thing that goes 'Woof-woof'?" "No, it goes 'Meow.'" (Bereiter & Engelmann, 1966, pp. 48-49)[2]

The specific strategies to guide the teacher in achieving the objectives related to the subject matter were also outlined. These are stated explicitly as follows:

1. Work at different levels of difficulty at different times.

2. Adhere to a rigid, repetitive presentation pattern.

3. Use unison responses whenever possible.

[2]*Ibid.*

4. Never work with a child individually in a study group for more than about 30 seconds.

5. Phrase statements rhythmically.

6. Require children to speak in a loud, clear voice.

7. Do not hurry children or encourage them to talk fast.

8. Clap to accent basic language patterns and conventions.

9. Use questions liberally.

10. Use repetition.

11. Be aware of the cues the child is receiving.

12. Use short explanations.

13. Tailor the explanations and rules to what the child knows.

14. Use lots of examples.

15. Prevent incorrect responses whenever possible.

16. Be completely unambiguous in letting the child know when his response is correct and when it is incorrect.

17. Dramatize the use value of learning whenever possible.

18. Encourage thinking behavior. (Bereiter & Engelmann, 1966, p. 120)[3]

Bereiter (1968) reported favorable results from the program. The level of achievement in reading, arithmetic, and spelling of one group of 15 children after one year of nursery school and one year of kindergarten and another group of 13 after one year of nursery school was very promising. The first group scored at or above the median of first-grade children in all three subject fields. After one year the second group was at about the beginning level of first-grade children and equal to a similar age group that had two years of experience in a Montessori school. All three groups had the same pupil-teacher ratio of five-to-one.

Post-High School Training

Who should educate the many high school dropouts and also the many high school graduates who remain functionally illiterate and thus are unable to secure gainful employment? How should it be done? There are no clear answers.

Some partial answers can be inferred, however, from the experience with Project 100,000, a military training program that sheds some light on the whole problem. Under the leadership of Secretary of Defense Robert McNamara, the armed services annually accepted 100,000 men who by earlier standards would have been rejected. One group of 100,000 men is compared with a control group in Table 6.4. The training program developed for this group included tutoring and counseling, repeating some basic learning activities, the formation of special training companies for the men, and remedial education. Greenberg (1969) found the program to be quite successful. The main ways this training was changed from that of other recruits, the controls, were the following:

Eliminating subject matter and theory found to be unrelated to the job.

Simplifying the reading levels of the materials. We used simpler words, shorter sentences, and added pictures, diagrams, and cartoons to increase comprehension.

[3]*Ibid.*

Table 6.4. Characteristics of Project 100,000 Men Who Received Special Training and Their Control Group

	Project 100,000 men	Control group
Percentage high school graduates	43.3	75.8
Number school grades completed (average)	10.6	11.9
Reading ability— median grade	6.1	10.9
Percentage reading below fourth-grade level	14.4	1.1
Percentage who failed or repeated school grades	47.0	Unknown

Source: Greenberg, 1969, p. 571.

"Hands-on" training was increased to allow more learning by doing, and lecture time was reduced.

More audio-visual aids were added and many of the training aids were improved. For example, in an eight-week automotive maintenance course we added 21 kinescopes, 50 new slides and charts, and five new simulators to better demonstrate the vehicle components.

Instructors were added to some courses to permit training in smaller groups.

Tests used in the courses were revised to make them relevant to the job the man would be required to perform. In some cases pencil and paper tests were replaced with performance type tests. (Greenberg, 1969, p. 573)

We do not mean to imply that these military training procedures should be adopted unchanged in schools. It is quite likely, however, that procedures *similar* to the military ones should be incorporated in high school programs for youth who exhibit characteristics similar to those of the Project 100,000 men, as listed in Table 6.4. Some of the procedures would probably be helpful also to other students who do not have so many difficulties but who do not plan to continue their education beyond high school.

Integration

Integration is, of course, related specifically to the education of disadvantaged black children. The complicated problems and controversial issues involved in attempts to achieve integration of the schools throughout the country do not, strictly speaking, fall within the scope of this book. Nevertheless, we feel we should point out that an increasing number of educational experts strongly believe that integration provides the only truly effective way to improve the education of disadvantaged black children. These authorities recognize that certain procedures aimed at improving the school environment and providing compensatory education—such as those we have described and many others—can be very helpful, but they maintain that, in the final analysis, integration is the only known educational mechanism that has a *significant* impact on the disadvantaged black child. The author of the well-known Coleman Report, a federal study of educational equality, is one of the most fervent advocates of this viewpoint. Coleman points out that so long as middle-class students remain in the majority in an integrated school, they establish the achievement tone of the school — and it is this atmosphere that enables disadvantaged students to make more consistent educational gains than by any other means. Coleman stresses that the achievement of middle-class children does not suffer in such a school. It suffers, he says, only when they attend schools in which the majority of the children are lower class, whether black or white (Coleman et al., 1966).

6.15. Which five of the 15 abilities in the Bereiter and Engelmann list that preschoolers are to develop do you feel are the most important? Which, if any, are surprising to you?

6.16. The 18 strategies that Bereiter and Engelmann suggest for teaching disadvantaged preschoolers are in some cases unique to such a group. Can you offer logical support for each strategy, basing your support on what you see are the needs and abilities of the disadvantaged preschooler? Do you disagree with any of them?

6.17. The military training program reported by Greenberg succeeded largely because nearly all the instruction was by example, by picture and demonstration, and by small-group interaction. With which students and tasks related to your area of interest might the same procedures work well?

6.18 What major changes in curriculum, methodology, school organization, etc., would you suggest to help disadvantaged students? Which, if any, of such changes might help the other students?

INDIVIDUALLY GUIDED EDUCATION FOR ALL CHILDREN

Individually guided education (IGE) is a system for formulating and carrying out instructional programs for individual students in which planned variations are made in what each student learns, in how he goes about learning, and in how rapidly he learns. It was developed cooperatively by personnel from the Wisconsin Research and Development Center for Cognitive Learning and from local school systems and other specialists. The first seven IGE schools started in 1967-1968 (Klausmeier, Morrow, & Walter, 1968). The variations are based on knowledge of the characteristics of each student and the educational objectives and program of the school. Thus, the explicit instructional objectives and the related program of instruction for each student take into account both the school's overall objectives and the characteristics of the student.

In attaining instructional objectives, each student normally participates in one-to-one relations with the teacher, aide, or other student; in one-to-one relations with instructional material, including during independent study; in small-group activities; in class-size activities; and in large-group activities. The amount and relative proportion of each of these kinds of activities for each student are dependent on the characteristics of the student, the objectives to be attained, the nature and quality of the instructional material, and the cost of the instruction. Each of these can be illustrated: (1) One student, because of emotional problems, a physical handicap, or some other characteristic, may require more one-to-one instruction from an adult than does another child. (2) Achieving certain objectives requires different kinds of activities. For example, learning to set a realistic goal is done best in a one-to-one relationship, developing communication skills is accomplished in small groups, and certain games are played only in larger groups. (3) Some instructional materials, more than others, permit students who can read and who have acquired basic concepts to learn with independence. Other important subject matter is not incorporated in instructional material, and students require much assistance from the teacher. (4) In connection with cost, the smaller the group led by the teacher, the greater the cost of instruction. Therefore, in order to keep costs at a reasonable level, larger groups are used whenever possible and differentiated staff, including lower-paid aides, are employed.

The principal and instructional staff of the school building determine the educational program for the building, taking into account any system-wide or state-wide guidelines. The instructional staff responsible for a group of children makes the decisions about each student's program. Each student participates in decision-making about his own program as he sets individual goals in consultation with the teacher. Careful assessment is made of each student's characteristics, progress in learning, and final performances. Thus, in individually guided education a complete instructional program comprised of many kinds of activities is developed for each individual student, and he is continuously guided by a professional.

In order to carry out a system of individually guided education, many modifications in the present practices of most schools are required. Starting with the first seven IGE schools, the modifications have been made in a number of elementary schools of the Midwest, particularly in Wisconsin. (These schools may be visited.) To make these changes clear, we now describe the typical elementary school and contrast it with the multiunit IGE school in terms of 15 attributes. You may not agree with the description of one or more of the attributes of the typical elementary school. We do feel that most elementary schools are as described, though we have not made a detailed survey to be certain of how many. The description of IGE schools is accurate within variations made to meet local school characteristics, but the number of such schools is still quite small.

1. Student Readiness or Entering Behaviors and Characteristics

Typical. Differences among students in readiness, or entering behaviors and characteristics, are not seriously considered; rather, students are expected to adjust to the existing instructional system with little attention to individual differences. For example, the same science or social studies textbook is used for students who vary widely in ability to read.

IGE. Entering behaviors and characteristics are assessed and are given consideration in relation to curriculum areas or more explicit learning tasks in this order: present level of achievement related to the task, level of motivation, and other more general abilities and characteristics. Instructional objectives and learning tasks are designed for each individual based on his entering behaviors and characteristics. This does not mean that students do not work or study together. For example, the readiness of 150 students aged 9 to 11 for particular reading skills and mathematics is assessed through administering group tests that may be scored rapidly. Students who are ready to attack the same reading skills using similar material are identified and put into 12 or more groups of eight to 20 students each. Similarly, students ready for like tasks and material in mathematics are put in other small groups. Periodically, and as often as every four weeks, the instructional groups are rearranged, based on the progress each individual makes. Within the smaller group some children get more individual attention than others. As individuals read with greater independence and also form basic concepts, they spend more time in independent study and less in group instruction in reading and mathematics.

2. Objectives

Typical. Either the school has no statement of its educational objectives, or an overall statement, developed by outside groups and inadequate for either program development and evaluation, is accepted as the school's objectives. Instructional objectives for individual students are implicit or nonexistent.

IGE. The educational objectives for the school building are developed in sufficient detail to guide program development and evaluation within the school building; instructional objectives are developed and stated explicitly for each student. For example, the particular reading skills and level of achievement expected of each student for the first semester of the school year are formulated during the first months of the school year, based on a careful assessment of the student's present achievements. As noted in Chapter 4, each school cumulates a bank of instructional objectives over a period of time.

3. Curriculum Content and Sequence

Typical. The instructional staff accepts a content and sequence recommended by others and usually incorporated in textbooks or system-wide curriculum guides.

IGE. The instructional staff of the building, in consultation with central office personnel and others and within local and state regulations, selects content and arranges sequence on the basis of such criteria as the structure of knowledge of the discipline, difficulty of the material for the students, relation to future and current study in school, and relation to out-of-school activities. Recommendations concerning the scope and sequence developed by the central office and outside agencies may be accepted tentatively but are tested for utility in the particular school building and for particular children. Appropriateness of the content and sequence is based on continuous assessment of student performance.

4. Materials, Media, and Supplies

Typical. Basic textbooks and supplementary textbooks are adopted system-wide and little additional printed information is available in a school building; a limited amount of audiovisual material, mostly sound films, is distributed from a central location; teachers lack time and competence to develop needed instructional material.

IGE. A large variety of printed material—textbooks, supplementary textbooks, programed material, library books, unit material—and audiovisual material—sound films, sound tapes, video tapes, slides, recordings, etc.—is adopted system-wide. From this system-wide selection the building staff chooses the ones that are appropriate for each student. Most of this material is kept within each building; additional material is distributed from a central location. Special material related to each subject field is available, some of which is developed locally; material is readily accessible to the children and instructional staff, and access to material outside the building is beginning to be managed by computer. Teachers are encouraged and given time to develop teaching materials and refine them.

The material is carefully selected and organized so that, for example, certain concepts may be introduced to a larger group by means of a film, the same concepts may be studied in a smaller group by means of slide films, and students may use printed and audiovisual material to study the same concepts independently. Various combinations of material usage, size of group, teacher activity, and student activity are used to provide for differences in *how* students learn, as well as in rate of learning.

5. Student Activities

Typical. Students are instructed in age-graded, class-size groups and receive identical assignments common to the group. Although small-group instruction in reading is common at the primary level, there is little one-to-one instruction or small-group instruction at other levels in the subject areas. Children in class-size groups encounter the same amount of material during a certain period of time.

IGE. The instructional program for each student permits planned variation among students mainly in the rate at which they learn and to a lesser extent in what they learn and how they go about learning it. For example, students take an unequal amount of time to reach a certain level of achievement in reading. Also, those who learn rapidly spend less time on reading and more on science, art, or some other curriculum area. Finally, because some students learn concepts better through seeing films and engaging in group discussions and others learn the same concepts better through reading and independent activities, appropriate adjustments are made.

6. Teacher Activities

Typical. Each teacher has equal responsibility for the total instructional program of about 30 children, except as there may be special art, music, physical education, or other instruction.

IGE. Activities of the instructional staff of a unit (see 10. Organization for Instruction) are differentiated in terms of the subject matter taught, the size of groups taught, the nature of the activities performed in terms of whether instructional or noninstructional, and the nature of the activities performed in terms of planning for instruction or actual teaching. These differentiations are made cooperatively by the unit staff on the basis of the preparation, experience, leadership, and interests of each staff member. (A more complete description of practices is given toward the end of Chapter 7.)

7. Use of Time and Resources

Typical. All children spend about equal time daily in connection with each curriculum area; e.g., 45 minutes in mathematics, 90 minutes in language arts. The time allocation is usually set by the central staff or a system-wide committee. Material resources are limited and not used well.

IGE. Each child's time is allocated in terms of his instructional objectives and program. Variation is found among children in the amount of time spent in connection with curriculum areas and also with respect to one-to-one, small-group, class-size, and independent study activities. The time of all instructional personnel is planned by each unit staff within the guidelines established by the building committee. Material resources are used flexibly to the maximum advantage of each student.

8. Terminal Behavior or Level of Achievement

Typical. Final achievement levels, or more explicitly stated terminal behaviors, that should be congruent with the instructional objectives for each student are not set for a year or for a shorter or longer period of time. All students in a class may thus study the same unit, achieve at very different levels, but still be passed along to the next unit without assessment of what they have learned and without attempting to overcome inadequacies.

IGE. Desired or expected final performances are indicated as the students' instructional objectives. In some curriculum areas great differences among students are anticipated, e.g., in art, music, speaking, physical activities, and some areas of social studies. In other curriculum areas, such as reading, mathematics, and possibly spelling, one set of outcomes in a sequential series is presumed to be essential before starting the next set. When the sequence is clearly defined the student attains the desired level before moving to a next unit or area of study. His achievement is carefully assessed. In turn, the level of achievement provides the essential feedback information for determining the next steps to take, e.g., whether to go to the next unit, review part of the last unit, start a new or different program, etc.

9. Assessment and Evaluation

Typical. Standardized and teacher-developed tests are used (1) to evaluate the comparative achievements or other characteristics of students, (2) to assign grades, or (3) to make comparisons among schools.

IGE. Standardized and teacher-developed tests and procedures are used systematically (1) to assess the child's entering behaviors and readiness related to each set of learning tasks so that each child may be properly placed initially, (2) to assess each child's progress, (3) to provide informative feedback to the child, (4) to provide information to the teacher for monitoring student progress, and (5) to improve the instructional system, including the components. Computers are being used in a few settings to manage a system of individually guided education. Computer management permits more pertinent information on each student to be gathered, analyzed quickly, and used to plan and carry out his instructional program.

10. Organization for Instruction

Typical. Age-graded, self-contained classrooms of 20-40 children are typical; occasional teams and nongrading are found. Time is not available during the school day for teachers to plan, or for the building principal to meet with those of his staff primarily responsible for formulating the building program. Ad hoc system-wide curriculum improvement committees develop printed curriculum guides.

IGE. Large nongraded instruction and research (I & R) units are comprised of 75 to 150 children, a unit leader or lead teacher, other certified staff teachers, an intern, and an instructional aide. The I & R unit replaces the age-graded, self-contained classroom. The children of each unit vary three or four years in chronological age. The nongraded vertical organization facilitates continuous progress of each student. The horizontal organization permits maximum opportunity for capitalizing on the capabilities and personal characteristics of each member of the instructional staff of the unit. Each unit meets for at least two hours weekly during the school day to plan and coordinate the activities of the unit.

A permanent Instructional Improvement Committee in each building, comprised of the unit leaders and building principal, with relevant central office personnel as consultants, makes educational decisions at the building level. The building committee meets at least one hour a week during school hours.

A permanent System-Wide Policy Committee, comprised of representatives of the central staff who have the relevant specialized knowledge and decision-making responsibilities, building principals, unit leaders, and teachers, sets system-wide policies for the multiunit schools. (This organization for instruction, including research on its effectiveness, is described in sections of Chapters 7 and 8.

11. Instructional Staff

Typical. The principal usually does not assume leadership for instructional improvement. Further, every elementary teacher is supposedly competent in all subject fields. Every teacher is certified to perform the same tasks at presumably the same level of excellence. There is an occasional instructional secretary and instructional aide. The special teacher or a supervisor in music, art, or foreign language usually proceeds independently of the total building program.

IGE. The principal's first responsibility is instructional leadership. Teachers have a specialty in one broad field of elementary education. Teachers are certified at four levels—professional or lead teacher, regular or staff, resident or first year, and intern as a replacement for current student teaching. (Certification was still in the planning stage in 1970.) Instructional secretaries and instructional aides in each building are certified according to previous training and experience. Special teachers function as part of the building staff, and their teaching activities are carried out in accordance with the instructional objectives for each child.

A teaching intern, an instructional secretary, and an instructional aide can be employed for about the same amount of money as can one experienced teacher with a master's degree. The aides can take over all the routine activities and can also work with individual students and small groups. The full-time intern performs professional teaching at a beginning level. These three, the lead teacher, and three staff teachers—a total of seven adults for 150 children—can make IGE work much better than can five staff teachers when other components are also properly functioning.

12. Other Educational Personnel

Typical. Central staff curriculum coordinators, school psychologists, research directors, home workers, audiovisual specialists, and others proceed relatively independently, working infrequently with groups of teachers on instructional matters during the school day. They do not instruct the children directly. Outside resource personnel from universities, state departments of education, and industry rarely consult with teachers except to present information to large groups outside regular school hours.

IGE. Central staff personnel work often during school hours with the building committee and unit leaders in interpreting and implementing system-wide policies and in designing an instructional program for each child. Resource personnel systematically work with unit leaders and other staff during school hours in connection with the instructional and other functions of the school. The number of high-salaried specialists not working with children is reduced as the unit staff performs more effectively directly with the children and the parents.

13. Decision-Making and Instructional Management

Typical. Few important decisions about major instructional components are made by the teacher. Only a few experienced teachers have the subject-matter competence and other capabilities to design and carry out a program of individually guided education.

IGE. The staff of the building makes the decisions about all the components of the educational program, within the local and state requirements. The staff of each unit cooperatively designs and carries out an individually guided instructional program for each child. Each certified teacher makes important decisions daily.

14. School Facility

Typical. A separate elementary school building houses 300 to 1200 children. Equal-sized, box-like classrooms with fixed walls accommodate about 30 children each. The larger building occasionally has one auditorium, a gymnasium, a lunch room, and a library; some have only one of these. Space is used inflexibly. Relatively little equipment is available; occasionally there are an overhead projector, tape recorder, slide projector, sound film projector, and some special equipment for science, art, and music.

IGE. Some buildings remain separate; others are incorporated as integral components of educational parks. Spaces of varying size and shape accommodate 75 to 150 children and permit one-to-one, small-group, class-size, and total unit activities. A large flexible space is designed for noisy and vigorous activities, such as music and gym. Large central instructional resource centers are used for computer terminals, audiovisual equipment, the library, and instructional materials of all types. Space utilization encourages maximum flexibility and an environment conducive to many types of learning activities. Audio, visual, and audiovisual equipment is available for presenting information. Integrated systems combine and coordinate the use of various materials and equipment, e.g., language laboratory, multimedia center.

15. Home and Neighborhood

Typical. A uniform educational program is formulated for all children throughout the system, independent of home and neighborhood backgrounds. Communication between the school and home is through report cards, supplemented by parent-teacher conferences. A PTA deals with peripheral problems, frequently only problems identified by school people.

IGE. Home and neighborhood characteristics are given major attention in connection with the entering behaviors and characteristics of each child. Unit leaders and teachers develop a systematic program of parent-school, teacher-home visits. Reporting involves teacher, parent, and child. Aides are drawn from the neighborhood. Parents are brought frequently into the Instructional Improvement Committee and into unit meetings to convey information, values, and feelings.

This brief description of individually guided education touches on several structural components that are required for successful operations. The actual components used are subject to some variations to fit local needs. The following process components, however, seem to be essential in all cases.

1. Whatever the number and size of the units of a building, the staff of each unit must plan, instruct, and evaluate *cooperatively*. A quasiunit, which meets only to become aware of individual teachers' plans, cannot accomplish IGE. Optimal unit operations are based on the cooperative exchange of expertise and the division of labor according to talents.

2. In IGE, important instructional decisions must be made by groups at the *appropriate level* in the organization. In the traditional school, where this is usually not the case, decisions about curricula are often made at the central office level and imposed without regard to differences among schools; or, at the other extreme, such decisions are made by individual classroom teachers, many of whom lack the depth of knowledge and experience to make them. In IGE, decisions with impact for a certain age range of children are made by the unit staffs, rather than by individual teachers. Decisions with building-wide impact are the responsibility of the Instructional Improvement Committee, and those with district-wide application are made by the System-Wide Policy Committee. This pattern of decision-making requires that some decisions traditionally made in the central office be decentralized and that some formerly made by individual teachers be centralized. Furthermore, the principle of group decision-making leads to a wider choice of alternatives, higher quality decisions, and more effective implementation.

3. Individually guided education presumes greater *role differentiation* and role clarity than is the case in the traditional school. The educational task, formerly assigned in its entirety to each teacher, is factored into its instructional development and its noninstructional parts. These, in turn, are assigned to personnel according to their competencies, that is, to the principal and the unit leader, the staff teacher, the resident and intern, and the nonprofessional aide. The consultant's role is redesigned for its original purposes, that is, to provide specialized knowledge (not to act as substitute teacher or critic) and to interpret system-wide policies. Central office personnel function as advisors and supporters of the building staff (not as mandators and monitors, as so often has been the case).

4. The multiunit organizational structure for IGE rests on a carefully designed *leadership structure*. In the traditional school, leadership is assumed to be the function of the principal. It usually fails in that setting for two reasons: (1) the principal is expected to lead too many persons without assistance, that is, his span of control is much too large; (2) nei-

ther the principal nor the staff have time during the day when the principal's leadership may be exercised. The multiunit organization provides formal leadership for each small group of personnel: the unit leader leads the aides and also the three to five teachers in his unit (more than seven slows down communication and effectiveness); the principal's leadership is exercised primarily with three to five unit leaders. Furthermore, each group—aides, the staff teachers, and the lead teachers in the Instructional Improvement Committee—meets with its leader regularly during school hours. There is time for leadership to have effect.

5. In a multiunit school, *communications flow* is more adequate than it can be in the traditional school. In the latter, communications are usually written, often authoritarian in tone, and are commonly vertical in direction. The work environment of the multiunit school provides oral communications as well, and horizontal and vertical channels open naturally. Thus there is healthy constructive criticism among the unit staff and also among other personnel.

The combination of all these features changes the school tone remarkably. The traditional, self-contained classroom school is a collection of isolated functionaries performing the same tasks and lacking either time or stimulation to alter their performance substantially. The situation is subdued and static. Individually guided education in the multiunit school, by contrast, is characterized by flexibility, cooperativeness, and a spirit of inquiry.

6.19. Which of the 15 attributes that differentiate IGE from traditional schooling do you consider major and which minor? Which changes will be especially appropriate for disadvantaged students? For advancing the profession of teaching?

6.20. Related to instruction in the field of your interest, try to determine which parts of it would be best handled by the unit leader, by specialized teachers, and by teacher aides. Are some components of the instruction most appropriately handled in one-to-one tutoring, small groups, large groups, or independent study? Do you have a preference for working with any particular type of student or size of group?

6.21. What special skills in addition to subject-matter competence must a unit leader possess? Do you think you would like to become a lead teacher even though there were no additional pay? Why or why not?

6.22. Discuss how and whether each of the following is changed or put to new uses in a system of individually guided education—standardized tests, grade levels, textbooks, the school bell.

6.23. Would IGE be implemented more easily with disadvantaged or nondisadvantaged schools? What do you think must be done so that IGE does not cost more than traditional staffing patterns?

SUMMARY

Students at any age vary widely in intellectual abilities and characteristics, psychomotor abilities, affective characteristics, health, and socioeconomic status. Also, their home and neighborhood conditions vary. All of these conditions are related to what a student is ready to learn at a point in time, to the progress he makes over a period of time, and to the highest level of achievement he eventually attains. Knowing a student's current level of achievement in a curricular area or related to a more specific set of learning tasks is the most useful information in the cognitive domain for predicting what the student is ready for next and how he will progress. IQ scores and more specific ability scores have limited value in working out an instructional program for an individual. They sometimes are misused because too much reliance is placed on their accuracy, stability, and usefulness in predicting a student's progress or his final level of educational achievement.

Low socioeconomic status, impoverished home and neighborhood conditions, and unresponsive schools produce disadvantaged children. Urban whites, urban Negroes, rural Negroes, rural whites, rural Spanish-Americans, urban Puerto Ricans, and American Indians are the seven main groupings of disadvantaged in America. The poor environments are associated with perceptual and language deficits in the children, depressed intellectual development, low school achievement, inadequately developed prosocial values, poor self-concept, and emotional problems. The vicious cycle of impoverishment during the preschool years, low school achievement, and further economic poverty, joblessness, or insecurity in adolescence and adulthood is repeated from one generation to the next. To break the pattern, massive changes are needed in all segments of society, including education.

Preschool education starting as early as age 3 may prove highly beneficial if the home and neighborhood conditions can also be improved. Regular education that enables some students to prepare for jobs and others for college is essential. Free higher education, further vocational education, and nondiscrimination in employment, housing, and social arrangements also are needed. Only the affluent and the large middle-class groups can make these conditions possible; therefore, it is they who must do it.

The massive changes needed in education to provide for all students can be observed in schools that recently started practicing the ideas embodied in individually guided education. Here all traditional arrangements that impede providing for differences among students in rate of learning, style of learning, and outcomes of learning are abandoned. Particularly, a new organization for instruction involving team teaching, differentiated staffing, and nongrading is imperative. More flexible use of space, materials, and time and better assessment of each student's abilities and characteristics permit an excellent instructional program to be developed and carried out for each student in one-to-one relations with a teacher, in small groups, in class-size groups, and in large groups.

SUGGESTIONS FOR FURTHER READING

BROWN, W. N. Alienated youth. In Frey, S. H., ed., *Adolescent behavior in school.* Chicago: Rand McNally, 1970, pp. 325-334.

This article is especially helpful to the teacher in understanding the underachievers, the potential dropouts, and those who rebel against society. (Many other articles in this book are of practical significance to high school teachers.)

CLARK, C. A., & WALBERG, H. J. The influence of massive rewards on reading achievement in potential urban school dropouts. In Ripple, R. E., ed., *Readings in learning and human abilities.* New York: Harper & Row, 2nd ed., 1971.

The positive effects of praise on the reading achievement of potential urban school dropouts are demonstrated.

DEUTSCH, M. The disadvantaged child and the learning process. In Borgatta, E. F., ed., *Social psychology: Readings and perspective.* Chicago: Rand McNally, 1969, pp. 168-179.

Deutsch discusses the environmental, psychological, and school conditions that contribute to slow intellectual development and lowered school performance.

DEUTSCH, M., KATZ, I., & JENSEN, A. R., eds. *Social class, race, and psychological development.* New York: Holt, Rinehart and Winston, 1968.

This scholarly volume includes several selections of interest to this chapter including H. Proshansky and P. Newton, "The Nature and Meaning of Negro Self-Identity," Chapter 5, pages 178-218; J. M. Hunt, "Environment, Development and Scholastic Achievement," Chapter 8, pages 293-336; and C. Bereiter, "A Nonpsychological Approach to Early Compensatory Education," pages 337-346.

ELKIND, D., & SAMEROFF, A. *Developmental psychology.* In Mussen, P. H., & Rosenzweig, M. R., eds., *Annual review of psychology.* Palo Alto, Cal.: Annual Reviews, 1970, pp. 149-238.

A scholarly review is presented of recent research and theory regarding development and learning during infancy, early childhood, middle to late childhood, and adolescence.

HAVIGHURST, R. J. Minority subcultures and the law of effect. In Ripple, R. E., ed., *Readings in learning and human abilities.* New York: Harper & Row, 2nd ed., 1971.

Havighurst states six propositions regarding the nature of rewards and indicates how rewards influence the course of learning. Specific applications to disadvantaged children are indicated.

HOFFMAN, L. W., & HOFFMAN, M. L., eds. *Review of child development research.* New York: Russel Sage Foundation, 1966.

Three of 11 selections are of special interest for this chapter: J. C. Glidewell, M. B. Kantor, L. M. Smith, and L. Stringer, "Socialization and Social Structure in the Classroom," pages 221-256; H. M. Proshansky, "The Development of Intergroup Attitudes," pages 311-371; J. F. Short, "Juvenile Delinquency: The Sociocultural Context," pages 423-468.

MARSHALL, H. H. Learning as a function of task interest, reinforcement, and social class variables. In Ripple, R. E., ed., *Readings in learning and human abilities.* New York: Harper & Row, 2nd ed., 1971.

The effects of material and symbolic rewards on kindergarten children of varying socioeconomic status are reported.

MEAD, M. Youth revolt: The future is now. *Saturday review*, January 10, 1970, pp. 23-25, 113.

A renowned anthropologist describes why people born before 1945 cannot understand the new world that the present generation feels and experiences.

ORNSTEIN, A. C., & VAIRO, P. D., eds. *How to teach disadvantaged youth.* New York: David McKay, 1969.

This paperback has 23 readings organized around three themes: Why do teachers of disadvantaged youth fail? How can teachers of disadvantaged youth succeed? What preparation do teachers of disadvantaged youth need?

STROM, R. D., ed. The inner-city classroom: Teacher behaviors. Columbus, Ohio: Merrill, 1966.

This 204-page paperback contains nine selections and a summary that provides practical suggestions to teachers and others concerned with educational improvement in inner-city schools.

WITTY, P. A., ed. *The educationally retarded and disadvantaged*, National Society for the Study of Education, 66th yearbook. Chicago: University of Chicago Press, 1967, part 1.

The 16 selections are written by various specialists and include descriptions of educational programs at four levels: preschool, elementary school, secondary school, and college.

Chapter 7 Characteristics of Teachers

Characteristics and Behaviors of Teachers

cognitive characteristics and teaching effectiveness
affective characteristics and teaching effectiveness
warm, understanding, friendly vs. aloof, egocentric, restricted behaviors
responsible, businesslike, systematic vs. evading, unplanned, slipshod behaviors
stimulating, imaginative, surgent vs. dull, routine behaviors

Differentiated Roles in Teaching

multiunit elementary school
instructional and research unit, or team
lead teacher
staff teacher
teacher intern
instructional secretaries and aides
Temple City differentiated staffing model

Characteristics of Teacher Organizations

National Education Association
American Federation of Teachers
collective negotiation
sanctions and strikes

I t is obvious that teachers are vital to education. Specifically, they occupy prominent positions in the school learning system outlined in Chapter 1 and in the system of individually guided education designed to meet the needs of all children, including the disadvantaged, outlined in Chapter 6. Nevertheless, to improve instruction in the many ways discussed in earlier chapters, it is also obvious that many more teachers are needed who are more capable as individuals, who take greater responsibility for identifying and filling new roles, and who work together in organizations at the local, state, and national levels to secure better educational opportunities for all children.

In this chapter, the characteristics of effective teachers are described first. Then, differentiated staffing patterns that call for varying amounts of education, experience, and leadership among the teaching staff are considered. Last, teacher organizations and their role in securing educational improvement are discussed. Thus, this chapter is concerned not only with characteristics of individual teachers but also with a changing pattern of positions in teaching and with characteristics of organized groups of teachers.

Table 7.1. Criteria of Effective Teaching

Criterion	Examples	How assessed
Product	Student gain in subject-matter knowledge and related abilities Student gain in psychomotor skills and related abilities Student gain in interests, attitudes, personality integration, and other affective characteristics	Directly with tests and performance ratings before, during, and after instruction
Process	Teacher behaviors, such as explaining, questioning, leading a discussion, counseling, evaluating Student behaviors, such as courtesy, industriousness, attentiveness, conducting an experiment, leading a discussion Student-teacher interactions, such as teacher-directed and student-directed exchanges, information exchange, warmth	Directly through observations of the teacher and students during instruction in the classroom
Presage	Intellectual abilities of the teacher, amount of college work completed in the teaching major, grade-point average in college, personal characteristics, and others	Indirectly from college records, tests, ratings outside the classroom

Source: Based on Mitzel, 1960, and Flanders, 1969.

Before turning to these main topics we shall look briefly at how the effectiveness of teaching is assessed. Three main types of criteria are used, as shown in Table 7.1 (Mitzel, 1960; Flanders, 1969). One of these is the *product*, or what is learned. Persons who prefer this criterion think that the best test of teacher effectiveness is in terms of how well students achieve. This includes achievement in all domains—cognitive, psychomotor, and affective. A second criterion deals with the *process*. Judgments about the teacher's effectiveness are made in terms of what the teacher does, what the students do, the interactions between teacher and student, or all three, but not in terms of student achievement. To use process criteria, observations must be made of the behaviors of the teacher and the students. The final criterion, *presage*, is, as its name implies, partly a predictive factor. Judgments are made about the teacher's present and probable future effectiveness on the basis of his intellectual ability, grades made in college, personal appearance, and other characteristics. The best means of assessing teacher effectiveness is to relate explicitly described process variables directly to the student behaviors, including achievement, that they are expected to produce.

CHARACTERISTICS AND BEHAVIORS OF TEACHERS

In this section the main concern is with relating presage variables to teaching effectiveness. Less attention is given to processes and interactions, as these are considered more fully in the next chapter. Also, only those characteristics that have been associated with effective teaching in a variety of situations are considered. Thus, only a few of many possible reports of teaching effectiveness are discussed.

Cognitive Characteristics

Three decades ago teachers who were rated excellent, even distinguished, had higher general intellectual ability than did those who were rated average or failing. The superior group had a higher grade-point average while in college. No difference was noted between the average and the failing groups (Shannon, 1940). More recently, academic grade-point average and the grade in student teaching were related positively and significantly to administrators' ratings of teachers on two criteria—preparation of subject matter and discipline. Faculty ratings of prospective teachers' appearance (a noncognitive characteristic, of course) also correlated significantly with three later ratings by administrators of the teachers' ability in preparation of subject matter, discipline, and tact with students (Simun & Asher, 1964). These two studies are typical of many that report a low but positive relationship between teaching effectiveness and general intellectual ability, academic grade-point average, and student-teaching grade. Some of the characteristics—for example, effort, ability, punctuality, reliability—that contribute to higher grades in college and in student teaching seem to be associated also with subsequent success in teaching.

Other information gathered during teaching has been related to teaching success. For example, eighth-grade teachers of English, mathematics, and social studies were divided into three groups, and a different procedure was carried out with each group (Hoyt, 1955). One group was given no information about the pupils. The second group was given only the results of an intelligence test for each pupil and achievement test results in English, social studies, and mathematics. The third group was given all the test information plus a pupil information blank; the members of this group were encouraged to discover all they could of significance about each pupil. Further, Hoyt helped the last two groups in understanding the information. No difference was found among the three groups in student achievement in any subject; however, the increased knowledge of the pupils among the teachers of two groups did result in improved attitudes of the students toward the teachers.

Slightly different results were obtained in a similar experiment carried out earlier by Ojemann and Wilkinson (1939). Considerable information about each pupil was given to an experimental group of teachers, and the investigator assisted the teachers in understanding the information. Teachers in the control group were given no information about their pupils. Students in the experimental group made a significantly greater academic gain than did the students in the control group. Further, the students in the experimental group showed better attitudes toward school and better general adjustment to school and to their classmates than did those in the control group. The teachers' knowledge of the students resulted in more effective guidance of academic learning and in better personality development in the students.

Turner (1965a, 1965b, 1967) for several years carried out programmatic research on teacher effectiveness. He treated teaching as a kind of problem-solving that can be taught and measured. His early work showed that the scores of prospective elementary teachers on simulated teaching tasks (problem-solving tasks) increased significantly from the beginning of a methods course to the end of student teaching. At the same time, teachers with one to three years' experience scored higher than did the prospective teachers. Further, higher scores on the simulated teaching tasks by the experienced teachers were associated with higher gains in arithmetic achievement by their students.

Later, Turner concluded that there also were personal-social characteristics associated with performance of the simulated teaching tasks and that the relationships among the personal-social characteristics, the problem-solving performance, and teaching success were affected by differences among school settings. The importance of school settings as related to student achievement was also discovered by Shaycoft (1967), as reported in Chapter 3. Thus, though problem-solving competence seems to be associated with teaching success in some situations, in others it is not. The same statement can probably be made for other characteristics of teachers; that is, the many uncontrollable conditions that vary widely from one school setting to another may lead to the same teacher being successful in one setting and unsuccessful in another. This is in line with the idea outlined in Chapter 1—that all the components of a teaching-learning situation must be dealt with simultaneously in order to provide excellent instruction for each student.

Intellectual ability, total grade-point average in college, subject-matter preparation, student-teaching grade, information of a professional nature about child development and learning, and problem-solving ability are related to teaching effectiveness. Nevertheless, when actual teaching success is correlated with these cognitive abilities and characteristics, the correlations are quite low; thus ratings on these abilities are useful primarily in an actuarial sense—in predicting the effectiveness, not of individuals but of *groups*. That is, teachers rated in the top half in several of these characteristics would have a higher average rating in various criteria of teaching success than would the lower half. Many teachers in the bottom half on several criteria would, however, be found to rate higher in teaching success.

Affective Characteristics

The range of differences among teachers in interests, attitudes, values, and personality integration is greater than that in general intellectual ability and other variables in the cognitive domain because college education is more selective on cognitive than on affective variables. Also, differences among teachers in affective characteristics are probably more important in determining success than are differences in cognitive characteristics.

Ryans (1960) did outstanding work involving more than 6000 teachers in 1700 schools over a period of six years to relate behaviors of teachers in the affective and intellectual domains. The more important results are summarized in Table 7.2. The results reported in the table correspond well with the results obtained by many earlier researchers and also by a smaller number who have continued in this field of inquiry. The personal qualities of the combined group of elementary and secondary teachers who were judged to be "high" in classroom behaviors associated with successful teaching are given in the right column of Table 7.2. They merit brief discussion:

The "high" group showed generosity in their appraisals of the behaviors and motives of others and expressed friendly feelings for others. They were social and sociable; teaching seems to require this. Also, as noted in part B of Table 7.2, the same teachers enjoyed their relationships with students and preferred nondirective to directive classroom procedures. This kind of teacher listens to the students, accepts the students' contributions, and draws ideas from them. These teachers are warm, friendly, and teach by drawing out rather than by lecturing and other more directive methods. In connection with warmth and friendliness, Kounin and Gump (1961) reported that elementary school children who had punitive teachers, compared with those having nonpunitive teachers, manifested more aggression in their misconducts, were less concerned with learning and school situations, and also were unsettled and in conflict about misconduct. It is probable that children who have punitive teachers do not acquire as much trust of school as do those with nonpunitive teachers.

The "high" elementary and secondary teachers, as noted in Table 7.2, also indicated a strong interest in reading, literary matters, music, paint-

Table 7.2. Personal Qualities That Appear To Distinguish Teachers Selected To Be High and Low with Respect to Overall Classroom Behavior

Elementary teachers	Secondary teachers	Elementary-secondary teachers combined
	Characteristics of "high" group teachers	
A. "High" group members more frequently (than "low"):	A. "High" group members more frequently (than "low"):	A. "High" group members more frequently (than "low"):
1. Manifest extreme generosity in appraisals of the behavior and motives of other persons; express friendly feelings for others.	1. Manifest extreme generosity in appraisals of the behavior and motives of other persons; express friendly feelings for others.	1. Manifest extreme generosity in appraisals of the behavior and motives of other persons; express friendly feelings for others.
2. Indicate strong interest in reading and in literary matters.	2. Indicate strong interest in reading and in literary matters.	2. Indicate strong interest in reading and in literary matters.
3. Indicate interest in music, painting, and the arts in general.	3. Indicate interest in music, painting, and the arts in general.	3. Indicate interest in music, painting, and the arts in general.
4. Report participation in high school and college social groups.	4. Report participation in high school and college social groups.	4. Report participation in high school and college social groups.
5. Manifest prominent social service ideals.	5. Judge selves high in ambition and initiative.	5. Judge selves high in ambition and initiative.
6. Indicate preferences for activities which involve contact with people.	6. Report teaching experience of 4–9 years.	
7. Indicate interest in science and scientific matters.	7. Report teaching-type activities during childhood and adolescence.	
8. Report liking for outdoor activities.	8. Indicate preference for student-centered learning situations.	
9. Are young, or middle-aged.	9. Manifest independence, though not aggressiveness.	
10. Are married.		
11. Report that parental homes provided above-average cultural advantages.		
B. "High" group members (compared with "low" group):	B. "High" group members (compared with "low" group):	B. "High" group members (compared with "low" group):
1. Indicate greater enjoyment of pupil	1. Indicate greater enjoyment of pupil	1. Indicate greater enjoyment of pupil

relationships (i.e., more favorable pupil opinions).
2. Indicate greater preference for non-directive classroom procedures.
3. Are superior in verbal intelligence.
4. Are more satisfactory in emotional adjustment.

A. "Low" group members more frequently (than "high"):
1. Are from older age groups.
2. Are restricted and critical in appraisals of the behavior and motives of other persons.
3. Are unmarried.
4. Indicate preferences for activities which do not involve close contacts with people.

B. "Low" group members (compared with "high" group):
1. Are less favorable in expressed opinions of pupils.
2. Are less high in verbal intelligence.
3. Are less satisfactory in emotional adjustment.

relationships (i.e., more favorable pupil opinions).
2. Indicate greater preference for non-directive classroom procedures.
3. Are superior in verbal intelligence.
4. Are more satisfactory in emotional adjustment.

Characteristics of "low" group teachers
A. "Low" group members more frequently (than "high"):
1. Are from older age groups.
2. Are restricted and critical in appraisals of the behavior and motives of other persons.
3. Indicate preference for teacher-directed learning situations.
4. Value exactness, orderliness, and "practical" things.
5. Indicate preferences for activities which do not involve close contacts with people.

B. "Low" group members (compared with "high" group):
1. Are less favorable in expressed opinions of pupils.
2. Are less high in verbal intelligence.
3. Are less satisfactory in emotional adjustment.

relationships (i.e., more favorable pupil opinions).
2. Indicate greater preference for non-directive classroom procedures.
3. Are superior in verbal intelligence.
4. Are more satisfactory in emotional adjustment.

A. "Low" group members more frequently (than "high"):
1. Are from older age groups.
2. Are restricted and critical in appraisals of the behavior and motives of other persons.
3. Value exactness, orderliness, and "practical" things.
4. Indicate preferences for activities that do *not* involve close contacts with people.

B. "Low" group members (compared with "high" group):
1. Are less favorable in expressed opinions of pupils.
2. Are less high in verbal intelligence.
3. Are less satisfactory in emotional adjustment.

Source: Ryans, 1960, pp. 360–361.

ing, and the arts in general. In addition, they reported participation in high school and college social groups. Schultz and Ohlsen (1955) also found that a successful group of student teachers showed higher intellectual and social service interests than did a less successful group.

The other qualities in which both the "high" elementary and secondary teachers excelled were that they judged themselves high in ambition and initiative, were high in verbal intelligence, and had more satisfactory emotional adjustment. Along similar lines, Symonds and Dudek (1956) found effective teachers to have superior personality organization, good judgment and reasoning, the capacity to relate to others, and low aggression.

Ryans (1960) also identified larger patterns of behavior related to variables such as school level, sex of the teacher, subject field, and community. The three main patterns of teacher behavior identified in his study, known as the Teacher Characteristics Study, were:

> TCS Pattern X_o: warm, understanding, friendly vs. aloof,
>   egocentric, restricted teacher behavior;
> TCS Pattern Y_o: responsible, businesslike, systematic
>   vs. evading, unplanned, slipshod teacher behavior;
> TCS Pattern Z_o: stimulating, imaginative, surgent or
>   enthusiastic vs. dull, routine teacher behavior. (Ryans, 1960, p.77)

The difference in the behavior patterns of teachers according to such variables as teaching level, subject field, and sex are worth careful consideration. Among elementary teachers in general, the three patterns of behavior were highly intercorrelated. In other words, warm, understanding, friendly behavior went along with responsible, businesslike, systematic behavior and also with stimulating, imaginative, surgent behavior. The comparisons for high school teachers included only teachers of English, social studies, science, and mathematics. The correlations among the three behavior patterns were not so high for these teachers as for elementary teachers. Among the high school teachers, men and women social studies teachers and women English teachers were high in Pattern X_o. Women mathematics teachers were highest in Pattern Y_o, and women social studies and science teachers surpassed other groups in Pattern Z_o.

Teachers at both the elementary and high school levels who were warm and understanding and more stimulating showed more favorable attitudes toward students and also toward administrators. Those judged to be warm and understanding in their classroom behavior—and, though to a lesser extent, stimulating and imaginative—expressed more permissive viewpoints toward education. Teachers who were more businesslike and systematic showed a slight tendency toward more traditional viewpoints about education. Elementary-level teachers who were judged to be warm and understanding in their classroom behavior—and, though to a lesser extent, stimulating and imaginative—also showed superior emotional adjustment. It is not surprising to find that, in general, teachers who demonstrated friendly and warm, organized and businesslike, and stimulating and surgent behavior were judged to be more effective teachers.

The preceding patterns of teacher behaviors were identified through observations made by persons with teaching experience who were instructed in how to observe the teachers' behaviors. In contrast with this procedure, Veldman and Peck (1963) had junior and senior high school students rate the behaviors of their student teachers immediately after the student teachers had completed their assignments. A total of 554 student teachers were rated. Table 7.3 shows the five clusters of behaviors, or factors, obtained from the student ratings and subsequent factor analysis.

Clusters 1 and 5, associated with "friendly, cheerful, and admired" and "democratic procedure," are similar to Ryans' Pattern X_o, "warm, understanding, and friendly." Clusters 2 and 4, associated with "knowledgeable, poised" and "strict control," describe the kind of competence represented in Ryans' Pattern Y_o, "responsible, businesslike, and systematic." Cluster 3, the "interesting, preferred" behaviors, corresponds more closely to the students' estimate of effective teaching than do any of the other clusters, according to Veldman and Peck.

The students' ratings of their student teachers were compared with the supervisors' ratings of the effectiveness of the same student teachers. A high positive relationship was found between the ratings of the students and the supervisors on Clusters 1, 2, and 4, but only a low relationship was found between the ratings on Cluster 5 and no relationship on Cluster 3. The supervisors rated the teachers, in connection with Cluster 3, on such traits as friendliness, poise, and control of the classroom, whereas the students rated the teachers on other traits they associated with effectiveness. Similarly, in connection with Cluster 5, the supervisors gave more weight to strict classroom control than did the students.

Not mentioned explicitly in the Ryans or Veldman and Peck studies is enthusiasm. However, Mastin (1963) reported that in 19 of 20 classes in 10 schools, teacher enthusiasm was associated with high student achievement. In addition, the students showed more favorable reactions to the enthusiastic teacher and to material that was presented with enthusiasm. The differences in student achievement and in attitudes were large and consistent. This suggests that enthusiasm may be a more powerful characteristic than many of those discussed earlier.

Other Characteristics

One other characteristic of teachers that seems to bear some relationship to teaching success in connection with particular components of a school is the sex of the teacher. Also, the socioeconomic background of the teacher warrants brief attention.

Sex. Sex differences in interests, attitudes, and values are revealed in the choice of level of teaching. Teachers in nursery school, kindergarten, and primary grades are almost exclusively female, with the percentage of male teachers rising progressively through the intermediate grades, junior and senior high school, and college teaching. Most of the superintendents of schools and a large percentage of high school and elementary

Table 7.3. Behaviors of Effective High School Student Teachers Inferred from Student Ratings

1. Friendly, cheerful, admired
   She is always friendly toward her students.
   She is good-natured and easy to get along with.
   She never seems to order her students around.
   She always seems cheerful and happy.
   She usually looks on the bright side of things.
   She smiles most of the time.
   You can tell that she really likes her students.
   She is always interested in hearing a student's ideas.
   You can depend on her to be fair with you.
   She is as interested in her students as she is in her subject.
   She seems to understand the problems students have.
   I would like to have her as a personal friend.
   She is admired by most of her students.
   She sets a good example for her students.
   She hardly ever gets flustered about anything that happens.
   I would like to be like her in some ways.
2. Knowledgeable, poised
   She knows a great deal about her subject.
   She doesn't get confused by unexpected questions.
   She must have studied hard to know so much about her subject.
   She is never stumped by a student's question.
   She seems to know more about her subject than just what is in the book.
   She always seems sure of herself in front of the class.
   She always seems to know just what she'll do next.
   She doesn't seem to be afraid of making mistakes.
3. Interesting, preferred
   She makes learning seem more like fun than work.
   She is the best teacher I have ever had.
   Her class is never dull or boring.
   I wish all my teachers were like her.
   She knows how to put her subject across in a lively way.
   She has made her subject alive and interesting for me.
   She doesn't try to cover the lesson too fast.
   She explains her assignments clearly and completely.
4. Strict control
   She doesn't let her students get away with anything.
   She expects a lot from her students and usually gets it.
   Students respect her because she means what she says.
   She doesn't let the class discussion get too far off the subject.
5. Democratic procedure
   Before she decides on a new project, she often asks the students what they think.
   She likes to give the students a choice of how to do an assignment.

Source: Veldman & Peck, 1963, p. 349.

principals are male. Teaching fields such as science and mathematics are heavily dominated by males, whereas other teaching fields, such as business education and English, have many females. Agriculture teachers are male and home economics teachers are female. Both biological factors inherent in the male and female and cultural factors that delimit appropriate roles for each contribute to the choice of teaching level and subject field.

More important than these general differences are problems that women teachers may experience in their treatment of aggressive behavior in boys. Meyer and Thompson (1956) studied teacher approval and disapproval of the behavior of boys and girls. Three classrooms with women teachers were observed. During the observations, the boys received more disapproval from the teachers than did the girls. Also, students of both sexes *said* that boys received disapproval more frequently than girls. The observations, corroborated by judgments of the pupils, led to relating the teachers' behavior to a theory of aggression. Boys are more aggressive than girls. Women teachers attempt to socialize boys by means of dominative counteraggressive behavior, but because boys are more aggressive toward their teachers than are girls, the teachers tend to counteract with a higher degree of aggressiveness toward the boys. In turn, the boys become still more aggressive, and the vicious cycle continues. Women teachers could, however, improve the situation:

> We feel that the consistent trends in our findings imply that teachers' negative attitudes towards their male pupils arise from a lack of appreciation for the term "normal" male child. In our culture, aggressive outgoing behavior is as normal in the male as quiescent nonassertive behavior is in the female. The teacher who attempts to thwart this behavior by means of threats and punishment can only meet with frustration, since the boy is confronted with a conflicting social code. A more reasonable plan to follow would seem to be one in which the excess energy and tensions of the male child could be discharged on some constructive activity. Planned physical education classes will do much to dissipate aggressive needs in a socially acceptable manner. Perhaps most important of all, however, is the knowledge that some degree of aggressive behavior is a normal part of development in both boys and girls and should be treated not as a personal threat to the teacher but as a sign of "normal" social and personality development. (Meyer & Thompson, 1956, p. 393)

Socioeconomic Status. Many prospective teachers come from farm and working-class homes; however, increasingly larger numbers come from homes where the father is engaged in a profession or business. Though the home background does influence attitudes and values, some young adults do diverge markedly from the value system of their parents. It is important for teachers to recognize their own attitudes and values and those of their pupils so that they accept, rather than discriminate inadvertently against, a child whose attitudes and values are different from their own. For example, Hoehn (1954) reported that teachers had more contacts with the higher-status and higher-achieving students in their classes than with the lower-status and lower-achieving students. These teachers very likely did not deliberately discriminate; nevertheless, the students of lower socioeconomic backgrounds probably profited less from attending school than did the other children because of their lack of contact with the teachers.

Accepting each child as he comes to school does not mean accepting antisocial conduct or permitting the highly withdrawn child to remain unattended. Regardless of the child's attitudes and values and their origins, the teacher cannot permit fist-fighting, cursing, stealing, vulgar language, destruction of property, and open rebellion against the rules and regulations needed to operate a school or classroom (Havighurst, 1966). The teacher can—admittedly, it is sometimes difficult—demonstrate regard for a student and treat him as a worthwhile human being and at the same time not condone his violation of generally accepted codes of conduct. Research has not yet shown clearly which teachers can be most helpful to the many boys and girls of lower-class backgrounds—those from upper-, middle-, or lower-class backgrounds. Apparently, the social-class background of a teacher is not nearly so important as his present attitudes, values, and skills.

In summary, general intellectual ability, grade-point average while in college, subject-matter preparation during the college years, and student teaching grade show low positive correlations with subsequent success in teaching. During actual teaching, knowledge of the subject matter, having and interpreting information about the students, ability to solve problems of teaching, and a preference for indirect teaching also show low but positive correlations with teaching success. Interest in verbal activities and the fine arts, a warm personality, good emotional adjustment, and enthusiasm for teaching have been reported as characteristics of the more effective teachers. Reviewing the research on teaching effectiveness, Gage (1965) reported that five characteristics were related to effective teaching: warmth; cognitive organization, including intellectual abilities and knowledge of subject matter; orderliness; indirectness; and problem-solving ability.

It is true in many areas of investigation that as soon as a number of research studies seem to agree and that therefore their conclusions might be generally accepted, other research studies—equally authoritative ones—are published that seem to disprove the conclusions. Research on variables and teaching success is no exception. Thus one can find at least one research study in which each of the preceding characteristics or abilities has been shown to bear no relationship or even to show a small negative correlation with teaching success as measured by student achievement or other student behavior or as measured by ratings of teachers' effectiveness. Nevertheless, such contradictory findings should be assessed in a balanced way. We do not interpret them to mean that we cannot identify very excellent teachers who are teaching particular students in particular situations. In any one school, parents, students, and school officials unanimously identify some of the excellent teachers, just as they also unanimously identify some of the poor ones. Obviously, parents and others disagree in some cases, for example, in the case of a teacher who works well with boys but not with girls, or vice versa.

Perhaps it all comes down to the fact that *good* teaching is so subjective, so intangible, so bound up with the nature of teachers as people that it will never be possible to reduce its components into factors that readily lend themselves to statistical analysis and conclusions. In this context, a fine teacher might be compared with a fine actor or a fine musician. It is often very difficult to say why any one of these three is superior to his colleagues, but we know he *is*. Commenting on the relationship of present research to good teachers, Hamachek (1969) expressed his thoughts with eloquence:

> It is, I think, a sad commentary about our educational system that it keeps announcing both publicly and privately that "good" and "poor" teachers cannot be distinguished one from the other. . . . I think we do know what the competent — or effective, or good, or whatever you care to call him — teacher is. . . .
>
> . . .
>
> 1. A good teacher is a good person. Simple and true. A good teacher rather likes life, is reasonably at peace with himself, has a sense of humor, and enjoys other people. If I interpret the research correctly, what it says is that there is no one best better-than-all-others type of teacher. Nonetheless there are clearly distinguishable "good" and "poor" teachers. Among other things, a good teacher is good because he does not seem to be dominated by a narcissistic self which demands a spotlight, or a neurotic need for power and authority, or a host of anxieties and tremblings which reduce him from the master of his class to its mechanic.
>
> 2. The good teacher is flexible. By far the single most repeated adjective used to describe good teachers is "flexible." Either implicitly or explicitly (most often the latter), this characteristic emerges time and again over all others when good teaching is discussed in the research. In other words, the good teacher does not seem to be overwhelmed by a single point of view or approach to the point of intellectual myopia. A good teacher knows that he cannot be just one sort of person and use just one kind of approach if he intends to meet the multiple needs of his students. Good teachers are, in a sense, "total" teachers. That is, they seem able to be what they have to be to meet the demands of the moment. They seem able to move with the shifting tides of their own needs, the student's, and do what has to be done to handle the situation. A total teacher can be firm when necessary (say "no" and mean it) or permissive (say "why not try it your way?" and mean that, too) when appropriate. It depends on many things, and good teachers seem to know the difference. (Hamachek, 1969, pp. 341, 343)

7.I. Which criterion — product, process, or presage — do you feel is best for rating teacher effectiveness? Why? If you were rated on your past, current, or forthcoming teaching, on which of the preceding criteria would you rate highest and on which lowest? What can one do to develop greater effectiveness?

7.2. The studies by Ryans and by Veldman and Peck imply that teachers weak in subject-matter preparation are often rated as poor teachers, whereas excellent teachers are generally conceded to have thorough subject-matter preparation. Also, understanding and working well with students, organizing effective learning situations, and other professional behaviors are critical. Review the college courses you have taken in your subject-matter field and also in education; then answer the following questions:

a. Has there been a proper balance between your subject-matter preparation and professional education courses?

b. Do you feel that all your professional courses in education have been worthwhile?

c. Do you feel that all your other courses have been worthwhile?

d. With what you personally know now of the requirements to become prepared to teach, structure what you feel would be an ideal college preparation program in your field. Be specific.

7.3. In most communities, teachers normally are part of the middle social class. Many of the teachers, however, originally came from lower-middle- or lower-class backgrounds. The suggestion has been made that the latter types of teachers might better relate to pupils from the lower class and thus should be assigned to schools in disadvantaged areas. React to this idea. Be specific.

7.4. Think of the best teacher you ever had. Check your description against the characteristics listed in Tables 7.2 and 7.3.

DIFFERENTIATED ROLES IN TEACHING

Corwin (1969) pointed to four developments that make the concept of a single teacher performing all instructional tasks effectively in a self-contained classroom setting obsolescent. (1) The knowledge explosion means that our structures of knowledge have become so complex that no one *occupation*, much less one person, can comprehend them all or treat them as a whole. (2) To achieve professional status, teachers must demonstrate that they have acquired specialized knowledge and abilities that other groups do not have. No one teacher can be expert in all facets of the curriculum, instruction, measurement, home-school relations, etc.; instead, specialization is required. (3) Many duties have been imposed on teachers that are not instructional, for example, collecting money, running a ditto machine, supervising lunch and play; these jobs deflect teachers from their primary instructional functions. (4) Technology, for example, instructional programing and management, multimedia presentations, and computer applications, is transforming education, particularly the self-contained classroom. Technology not only is creating new roles in the schools; it is also providing a means for separating nonteaching from teaching activities.

Two recent plans for differentiated staffing that incorporate the viewpoints of Corwin and others have received considerable attention nationally. The first plan (multiunit) was developed in cooperation with school personnel directly for the elementary school. (The various roles, or positions, and related programs to prepare large numbers of personnel for the roles were still being formulated during the early 1970s.) The second plan (Temple City), which will be discussed after the first one, is more pertinent to the high school than the elementary school.

Differentiated Roles in the Multiunit Elementary School

In Chapter 6 a system of individually guided education (IGE) at the elementary school level was outlined, with the primary emphasis on how the system is intended to help the students, particularly in providing for their individual differences. We noted in that chapter that IGE requires many departures from the present system of age-graded, self-contained classrooms, including a different kind of organization for instruction and also differentiated staffing. These changes are embodied in the multiunit school, which has been evolved as the best way to implement IGE. In this section the development of the multiunit school is described first, then the organization for instruction is outlined, and, finally, the new and changing roles of the staff are described.

The Emergence of the Multiunit Concept. In 1965 the Wisconsin Research and Development Center for Cognitive Learning (R & D Center) started research and development projects in seven elementary schools in an attempt to help schools become capable of a continuing program of self-renewing, elementary school education (Klausmeier, Morrow, & Walter, 1968). (By 1970, the effort had expanded to more than 200 schools.) These elementary schools initially had a few teaching teams, but were primarily organized as self-contained classrooms.

A careful analysis of the situation in the seven elementary schools revealed several deficiencies: (1) There was no time during the school day for teachers to engage in instructional improvement efforts. The teachers were involved with children throughout the school day and did not have time to share in identifying innovative or development activities or in planning, implementing, and evaluating them. There was a related factor: as the teachers (nearly all of whom were members of organized educational associations or unions) quite properly pointed out, little work could be done before or after school hours as an unpaid overload. (2) The teachers were not engaging in tasks that took into account differences in their interests, experience, and capabilities. Differentiated roles had not been worked out whereby one teacher could take more responsibility than another for working with larger or smaller groups of children or for instruction in mathematics or some other curriculum area or for research and evaluation, planning the instructional program, or any other activity. (3) No mechanism had been established in any of the schools that enabled the principal and teachers of a building to plan and carry out an educational program for the children of their building. For example, many inner-city schools in 1964-1965 were following the same curriculum guides and using the same instructional materials as were all other schools in the same large city.

Administrators and teachers working with the R & D Center staff and others attempted to develop a more effective total instructional system for an elementary school building, starting with the organization for instruction and the related differentiated roles. What emerged after several years of development, testing, and refinement is called Individually Guided Education in a Multiunit Elementary School (Klausmeier, Morrow, & Walter, 1968).

The Multiunit School Organization. The multiunit elementary school organization may be thought of as an invention that incorporates the best practices associated with team teaching, continuous pupil progress through nongrading, role differentiation involving professional and non-

professional personnel, group decision-making, and individualized instruction. The organization was developed explicitly to make possible individually guided education for all children.

Figure 7.1 shows the organization of a multiunit elementary school of
600 students. The organizational hierarchy consists of interrelated
groups at three distinct levels of operation: at the classroom level are four
Instruction and Research (I & R) units, at the building level is the Instructional Improvement Committee (IIC), and at the system level is the
System-Wide Policy Committee (SPC). Each of these is now described further:

The I & R Unit. The nongraded I & R unit replaces age-graded, self-
contained classrooms. We call it a "unit" rather than a "team" because it
includes the students and also because it has many other features, including nongrading, not usually present in team teaching. In the prototype shown in Fig. 7.1, each I & R unit has a unit leader, or lead teacher,
four staff teachers, one teacher aide, one instructional secretary, one intern, and 150 students. Thus, in the prototype there are five certified
teachers and three noncertified personnel for each 150 students. In actual
practice, some units have as few as 75 and others as many as 200 children.
Also, the number of instructional personnel in relation to students varies
from one school system to another, and within a school system it varies
from inner city to outer city. The number and proportion of certified
teachers, aides, secretaries, and teaching interns varies among units and
buildings.

The eight staff members of each unit meet once a week and more often
if necessary. Such a meeting may last from 30 minutes to half a day,
though at least two hours a week seems to be necessary during the first
year under the system. A variety of means have been used to secure this
time during school hours. The most widespread practice is to lengthen the
school day slightly for four days per week and dismiss all the students an
hour or two early on the other day.

The children are placed in units primarily on the basis of years of
school attendance; the range in age within a unit is about four years
when two usual grade levels are combined into one unit. There is some
interchange of students among units for part of the instruction. In the
prototype, grade lines are completely abandoned as children participate
in one-to-one, small-group, class-size group, and unit-size instructional
activities. In practice the teachers work with children of varying age levels, and groups are formed for instruction in reading, mathematics, social
studies, and the like, independent of grade level.

The unit staff is responsible for all the instructional, research, development, teacher-education, and other functions performed in its unit. Thus,
an instructional program for each individual student, as outlined in
Chapter 6, is carried out by the unit staff. Consultants from the central
office or elsewhere assist the unit staff in planning both the instructional
program and research and development projects. The consultants' time is

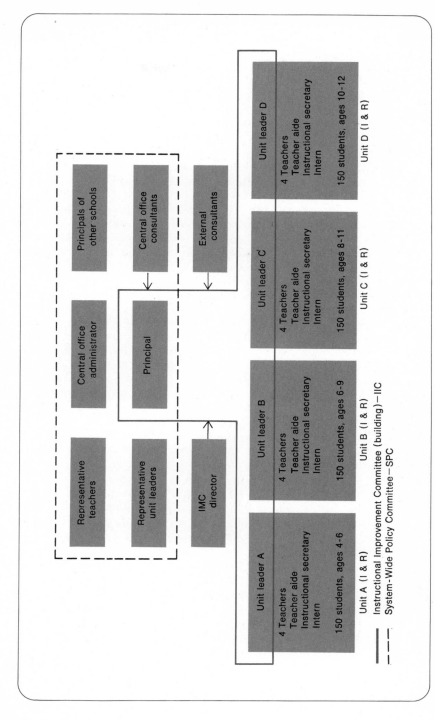

Fig. 7.1. Organizational chart of a multiunit elementary school of 600 students.

used efficiently in the unit, as the meetings are during regular school hours and for clearly defined purposes.

The Instructional Improvement Committee. At the second level of organization is the IIC of the building. This is a new organization that had not emerged in any elementary school of Wisconsin before 1966. It became possible, and also essential, when entire school buildings were organized completely into units. As shown in Fig. 7.1, the prototypic IIC is comprised of the building principal and the unit leaders. Also, other building staff, such as the director of the instructional materials resource center (IMC), meet quite regularly with the committee. Consultants from the central office meet with the IIC when a curriculum area such as reading or mathematics is given major attention in the building. The IIC meets weekly; the agenda for the meetings are formulated by the principal in consultation with the unit leaders.

The three main functions of the IIC are interpreting and implementing system-wide and statewide policies that affect the building program; developing the broad outlines of the educational program and other activities for the building; and coordinating the activities of the units, including the use of facilities, time, material, etc., that the units do not manage independently. It thus has developmental and coordinating, but not supervisory, functions. Supervisory functions remain with the principal and with the central office.

Decision-making is at an appropriate level within the building as it relates to each child's program in this way: (1) Teachers determine the program for each child within the broad limits of the unit. (2) Each unit determines the program for all the children of the unit within the building context. (3) Each building operates within the requirements of the whole school system and the state. The net effect is to reduce the influence of both central office personnel or other outside agencies and single teachers in determining the instructional program for a particular child and to increase the influence of the IIC of the building and the staff of each I & R unit in it.

The System-Wide Policy Committee. As shown in Fig. 7.1, the SPC, chaired by the superintendent or his designee, includes consultants and other relevant central office staff and representative principals, unit leaders, and staff teachers. It meets less frequently than either of the other groups, but its operation is important to the success of the multiunit school. Four responsibilities of the SPC concern identifying the functions to be performed in the multiunit schools of the system, recruiting personnel for each school, providing instructional materials, and providing relevant information within the system and community.

In connection with these responsibilities a decision may be made that one function of a multiunit school is to adapt and evaluate a new science program to ascertain whether it might be adopted by the entire school system. The staff of at least one multiunit school must share in this decision-making. After the decision is made, the SPC makes sure that the necessary science instructional materials and consultants are made available to the school and that the project is properly interpreted to the school board and community.

Staff Roles in the Multiunit School. A significant characteristic of the multiunit school is the changed roles of the building principal, unit leader, staff teachers, teacher interns, and paraprofessionals. Increasingly, the first-year teacher is regarded as a resident rather than as a fully qualified staff teacher.

Principal. The role of the principal is changed in the multiunit school in two ways. First, he organizes and chairs his building committee, arranges its meetings, and sets the agenda for them. Second, he assumes responsibility for three functions not common in the elementary schools. That is, he takes leadership in connection with the educational program of the building, managing the preservice and inservice teacher education activities in his building, and administering the research, development, and dissemination activities. The purpose here is not to define the administrative responsibilities of the principal, but to indicate that the building principal has a key role in a multiunit school. Actually, some building principals, even experienced ones, are unable to carry out these new responsibilities without some special inservice education.

Unit Leader or Lead Teacher. Defining the position of lead teacher represents the first large-scale attempt to establish a career teaching position in the elementary school. The unit leader is a career teacher, not an administrator or supervisor. He is the leader of the teachers, paraprofessionals, and students in his unit. He exercises leadership primarily through planning the instructional program of his unit, coordinating the activities of his staff, and being a model teacher of children. The responsibilities of the unit leader are now outlined in connection with instruction, research and related activities, and teacher education. Though the unit leader exercises primary responsibility for each task as stated, he cooperates with the building principal, the unit staff, central office personnel, including psychologists, social workers, special teachers, subject-matter consultants, and with others.

[**A. INSTRUCTION**]

1. Formulates, or plans, the program of individually guided education for his unit, giving attention to objectives, materials, equipment, activities, assessment, etc.
2. Coordinates the activities of the instructional staff, the placement of children in appropriate activities, the use of materials, time, space, etc.
3. Formulates and coordinates a program of home-school relationships involving the students of his unit.
4. Teaches from 50 to 80 percent of the time, or in other ways is directly involved with the children.
5. Utilizes a portion of the remaining 50 to 20 percent of the time (a) to

act as a liaison between the building principal and staff (and students) in his unit; (b) to meet with staff members in the unit to plan instruction and to enhance their understanding and direction of individually guided education; and (c) to meet with the Instructional Improvement Committee. (Unit leaders often leave the building for a day to participate in a workshop or seminar.)

6. Keeps abreast of advances in subject knowledge, instructional materials, and other components of a system of individually guided education.

[B. RESEARCH, DEVELOPMENT, INNOVATION]

1. Research
   a. Plans research activities of the unit with appropriate personnel of the unit, the building, the central office, and other agencies.
   b. Coordinates the research activities within the unit.
   c. Guides the administration of experimental treatments — instructional methods, materials, media — by subexperimenters (teachers and others) to ensure continuous adherence to the specified experimental design and to a schedule for collecting information.
   d. Guides the collection and, as time permits, the analysis of information collected.
   e. Keeps abreast of relevant research results and methods.
2. Development
   a. Plans the development activities of the unit with appropriate personnel of the unit, building, the central office, and other agencies.
   b. Coordinates the development of a system of individually guided education within the unit, including a statement of objectives, the assessment of the capabilities of students, the instructional program, and evaluation procedures.
   c. Participates directly in preparing instructional materials, diagnostic procedures, measurement instruments, etc.
3. Innovation
   a. Coordinates the introduction of novel instructional materials, measurement and evaluation tools and procedures, instructional methods, etc.
   b. Stimulates the invention of new instructional methods within the unit.
   c. Keeps abreast of innovations throughout the school system, the state, and nation through visits, conferences, and reading.

[C. TEACHER EDUCATION]

1. In-service
   a. Develops, cooperatively with the certified unit staff, the building principal, and relevant central staff, a building program of on-the-job training for the certified personnel of the unit, including first-

year teachers; carries out the relevant elements of the building program in the unit.

b. Develops and carries out a similar program for instructional secretaries and aides.

c. Coordinates the in-service education activities of the certified and noncertified personnel in the unit whereby capabilities of the aides are identified and improved and the certified teachers learn to work effectively with aides.

2. Preservice

a. Develops, with the certified unit staff, the building principal, relevant central staff, and representatives of teacher-education institutions, the building program for interns; implements the relevant elements in the unit.

b. Coordinates the placement of the intern in the unit and the instructional activities of the intern with the certified and noncertified personnel.

Rewards should follow the kinds of responsibilities enumerated, including a higher salary than a staff teacher of comparable experience and education. (In 1970, during the school year, unit leaders in four school systems received only from $250 to $500 above the regular salary schedule of staff teachers with equivalent experience and education.) Also, the unit leader should be employed for 11 of 12 months annually. His salary for 11 months should be about $3500 higher than that of a staff teacher who works for 10 months and about equal to that of a building principal of similar education and experience who works for 11 months. Career teachers should no longer need to move from teaching to administration in order to get higher pay.

Many teachers who are committed to a career of teaching could qualify as unit leaders if they wished to assume the additional responsibilities. In 1970, nine characteristics were being considered in discussions of possible certification of lead teachers:

1. Certification as a teacher.
2. Two or more years of successful teaching experience.
3. Master's degree, or progress toward one, for beginning unit leaders. (In each building an attempt is made to secure lead teachers each of whom represents high competence in a different curriculum area.)
4. Graduate education in human learning and development, curriculum and instruction, and research and development. A flexible program is recommended: the equivalent of 6-15 semester hours in human learning and development, measurement and statistics, and research and development; and 6-15 semester hours in a broad subject field and related instructional theory and methodology. Some practical work in unit operations is essential.
5. Commitment to a lifetime career in teaching.

6. Positive attitudes toward curriculum improvement, research and development, and teacher education.

7. Flexibility and inventiveness in the adaptation of methods, materials, and procedures.

8. Ability to recognize and utilize the capabilities of the unit personnel.

9. Ability to maintain effective interaction with all personnel of the unit, children and parents, the building principal, central office personnel, and other consultants in research and in teacher education.

Staff Teacher. The staff teacher teaches full time, except to attend unit meetings and to study or plan independently. He has one or more years of experience and usually has less formal education than the lead teacher. Many staff teachers are married women who prefer to spend more time with their families than do lead teachers. That is, the staff teachers are excellent in working with children but prefer not to take on the added responsibilities of the lead teacher. In each unit an attempt is made to get staff teachers each of whom is especially competent in a different curriculum area.

The main differences between the roles of the staff teacher in the unit and the teacher in the self-contained classroom are that the staff teacher plans with other members of the unit, works with many children and with other members of the unit rather than with a smaller number of children independently, and performs at a more professional level. The higher level of professional activity is shown in the participation in research and development activities and in dealing with high-priority instructional matters such as setting goals with each child, assessing each child's characteristics, developing an instructional program for each child, using new materials and equipment, and trying out new instructional procedures.

The most important rewards to the staff teacher in a unit are participating in all the instructional functions of the unit, engaging in decision-making about all components of the instructional program, making a maximum contribution according to his strengths and interests, being relieved of nonprofessional activities by aides and secretaries, and having a stimulating learning and teaching experience. Teaching in a unit is strenuous at times, but is always mentally stimulating and emotionally satisfying.

Teacher Intern. The one-semester intern is usually assigned to one unit for the entire semester. The two-semester intern is usually assigned to two units, changing from one to the other at the end of the first semester. This works best when at least two interns are in the same school. The intern engages in professional activities, not in routine or clerical duties (the latter are performed by the instructional secretary and aide). In connection with the instructional program, the objective is for the intern to engage at first in observation and minor participation, but to move rapidly to full responsibility at a level similar to that of a beginning certified teacher. A well-prepared intern who has had preservice participation in a school and in a workshop for the entire building staff before the opening of school may assume full responsibility for one-to-one, small-group, and class-size activities within two weeks after the opening of school. The intern does not assume decision-making responsibilities for the instructional program of the unit, as do the unit leader and experienced staff teachers. However, the intern participates in unit meetings.

Instructional Secretaries and Teacher Aides. The two main classes of noncertified members of units are instructional secretaries and teacher aides. The wise use of their abilities and previous background is the responsibility of the unit leader in cooperation with the building principal and the unit staff. The instructional secretary performs a number of clerical responsibilities such as keeping attendance records, collecting and keeping records of special money from the students, duplicating materials, making lists of pupil supplies, typing, and filing.

The precise responsibilities of teacher aides vary, partly because they are directly related to the background of training and experience of the aide. For example, the aide with a college degree in a subject field such as science will perform different functions than the high school graduate who has had no work in science beyond the ninth grade. Even though no common set of specific activities can be stated, there are some areas in which all aides participate effectively. An aide may perform many housekeeping chores connected with lighting, ventilation, cleanliness, instructional materials, supplies, chalkboards, plants, etc. Also, an aide may help children in caring for clothing, moving from one part of the building to another, or receiving attention from a specialist, such as a nurse or social worker. Lunchroom and playground activities may also utilize the service of an aide. In individually guided education, teachers have found aides especially helpful in working with children in one-to-one, small-group, and independent activities.

The differentiated staffing pattern just described is not yet accepted by some experienced self-contained classroom teachers who want more autonomy and also by some principals who prefer to assume less responsibility for the educational program of the school building. On the other hand, the pattern is regarded by some proponents of differentiated staffing as moving too slowly. In any case, during a short period of three years, from the time the first multiunit school was established until the first 100 or so were operational, literally hundreds of teachers, principals, central office, and other persons helped to identify and describe the roles and put them into daily practice. This was done with very little increase in the cost of education per pupil in the local schools. The early desirable effects of the program on teacher morale and other aspects of education are described in Chapter 8.

The Temple City Differentiated Staffing Plan

Rand and English (1968) described the model used in developing a differentiated staffing pattern for the schools of Temple City, a Los Angeles metropolitan-area community. Figure 7.2 shows the planning as of January 1968 (except at that time the positions of teaching research associate and teaching curriculum associate were being revised with the in-

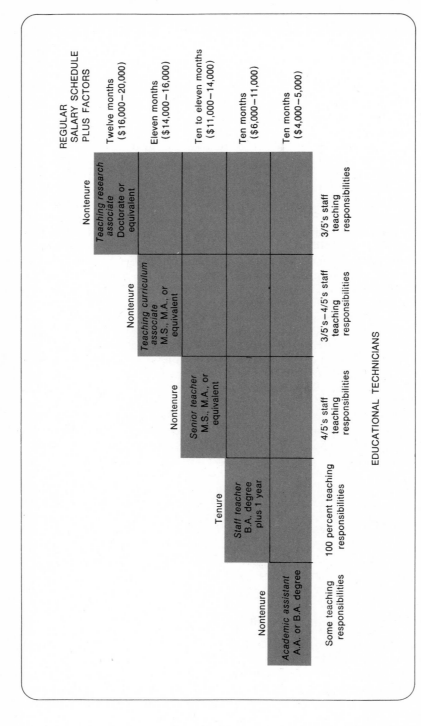

Fig. 7.2. A model of differentiated staffing: Temple City Unified School District. (Rand & English, 1968, p. 267)

tention of combining them into a single position; also, the salary figures were tentative). It should be noted that persons filling each position do some teaching of students, the proportion varying from 100 percent for the staff teacher to about 60 percent for the teaching research associate. A description of each position is now given.

Teaching Research Associate. The main job of the teaching research associate (TRA) is to introduce new concepts and ideas into the school system. He is specialized in research methodology and evaluation of curriculum materials and instruction. He does some research and evaluation, but his main job is to translate the results of recent research and curriculum development into a form that the teachers of this system can use. Thus, the TRA spends considerable time discussing and planning with others of the instructional staff. As shown in Fig. 7.2, the TRA is at the top of the hierarchy in salary and in amount of education. This is not a tenured position and assumes employment for 12 months.

Teaching Curriculum Associate. The teaching curriculum associate (TCA) may have lesser knowledge of research methodology but requires more expertise related to the curriculum. The TCA is expert in at least one curriculum area and keeps abreast of national and state curriculum studies. He takes the leadership in modifying national studies to meet local needs. The TCA is at the second level in the hierarchy. In the model only the MS, the MA, or the equivalent is required. Employment is projected for 11 months.

Senior Teacher. Rand and English (1968) describe the senior teacher as the "teacher's teacher," an acknowledged master practitioner, a learning engineer, and a skilled diagnostician of the learning process. The senior teacher is the first applier of curriculum and instructional innovations to the classroom setting. He directs a subject area, such as English, social studies, or science, and shares with the school principal the selection and evaluation of the staff teachers. In a team-teaching situation the senior teacher serves as the team leader. The senior teacher is employed for 10 months and also is nontenured. It should be noted that the usual position of head, or chairman, of a department in the high school, such as social studies, English, etc., is eliminated. In the Temple City model the senior teacher replaces the head of the department. (The senior author observed a modification of this model in a high school in Madison, Wisconsin. The teaching curriculum associate, rather than the senior teacher, performed the functions described here for the senior teacher. In turn, the building principal served as the instructional leader and research associate.)

Staff Teacher. The staff teacher spends full time with the students. He operates at the same level as do most teachers in typical school districts except that clerical and semiprofessional duties are performed by assistants. The Temple City plan calls for only the baccalaureate plus one year of further education and a projected salary of $6,000 to $11,000 for 10 months. This is a tenure position.

Academic Assistant. Academic assistants are of two kinds. One is a skilled paraprofessional; the other is a teacher intern. The academic assistant works directly with students and may instruct in his special area of competence. He may also assume responsibility for maintaining instructional materials, grading papers, and supervising resource center activities or student study. A baccalaureate is required and the projected salary is $4000 to $5000 for 10 months.

Educational Technician. Clerical and housekeeping tasks are performed by the technician. Typical of these tasks are keeping records, duplicating material, typing, supervising students' noninstructional activities, taking attendance, and the like. No direct instructional responsibility is given to the technician.

Other Roles and Relationships. In the Temple City model the senior teachers comprise the *academic senate*, which establishes policies related to the educational program in the school. Also, the senior teachers participate in "professionalizing and disciplining their own ranks" through the academic senate. As noted earlier, they recommend the hiring of staff teachers and also evaluate them.

The teaching research associates and the principals of the various buildings comprise an *academic coordinating council* headed by the superintendent. This council assures that broad educational policies are developed and carried out throughout the system.

The teaching curriculum associates are part of a *curriculum coordinating council* headed by the assistant superintendent. This council is responsible for curriculum development throughout the school system.

Thus under this plan, senior teachers and staff teachers do not participate in the system-wide academic or curriculum councils. Further, only senior teachers participate in the academic senate of the school building. In other words, the two levels of teachers are freed to *teach*.

A *school manager* is employed, rather than an assistant principal. This school manager takes over the business functions and daily operational matters; again the purpose is to facilitate *teaching* by freeing the principal for more attention to actual instruction. Indeed, the plan calls for the principal eventually to do some teaching.

There are other ways to achieve differentiated staffing, but these multiunit and Temple City plans were the most widely followed in practice in the early 1970s. Nevertheless, their long-term future cannot be predicted reliably. In point of fact, whether or not they actually succeed will be determined primarily by the reaction of teachers as organized groups. That is, they will have to accept three conditions: (1) at least two levels of professionalism in teaching; (2) noncertified personnel performing noninstructional functions; (3) relatively fewer high-paid specialists in the school system who do not directly teach students. It might seem that teachers would almost automatically accept the third point, but what it actually involves should be kept in mind: the teacher in the multiunit school and the senior teacher in the Temple City plan must assume responsibility for some of the curriculum development work, testing, counseling, and home-school relations that nonteaching specialists now perform.

7.5. The multiunit elementary school organization calls for lead teachers, staff teachers, and aides. The lead teacher is a career teaching position that

carries a higher salary than staff teachers. Aides perform noninstructional duties; the ratio of aides to certified teachers is as high as one to two in some
schools. In turn, this usually means a slight reduction in the number of certified teachers for the same number of students. Which school people do you
think might endorse the roles of the lead teacher and aides? Why? Who do
you think might oppose the use of the lead teacher, the aides, or both? Why?

7.6. The multiunit school organization requires cooperative team teaching,
nongrading of students, and flexible use of time, space, and student activities.
What advantages do you think might result from each of these?

7.7. How do you feel about the Temple City plan as reflected in the responsibilities of the various staff members, their salaries, and the tenure or non-
tenure of certain instructional personnel? Is the plan likely to work better at
the high school or the elementary school level?

CHARACTERISTICS OF TEACHER ORGANIZATIONS

During the first half of the twentieth century many occupational groups
organized successfully, gained power, and decisively influenced policies
that affected their members. Teachers, however, were not among these
groups in any effective way until the 1960s. During that decade, the existing organizations of teachers grew increasingly strong. Thus in very
recent years, teachers, too, have begun to exert power—indeed, they now
influence educational policies at the local, state, and national levels. They
have made remarkable gains in salary and improved working conditions
in many localities and states. But, more important, they have gained the
legal right of collective bargaining as government employees. This right
carries with it challenging opportunities, for, if properly exercised, it can
be used not only to improve salary and working conditions for teachers,
but also to improve the actual education of children.

These opportunities are not always acknowledged. As a matter of fact,
in a fallacy that is all too common, power is identified only with its
abuses; the general assumption is that power is used only for selfish ends.
Thus in connection with teacher power, there is a tendency to think only
that more power for teachers means more money and fewer hours of work
for them. The narrowness of this viewpoint is well stated by Lieberman:

> A group which is too weak to protect its immediate welfare interests will
> usually be too weak to protect the public interest as well. Teachers need power
> to protect academic freedom, to eradicate racial segregation in education, to
> secure more and better instructional materials, and to do many other things
> that have little or no relationship to teacher welfare. If teachers are weak, they
> cannot protect the public interest in education. This is why the weakness of
> teachers as an organized group is one of the most important problems in Amer-
> ican education today. (Lieberman, 1967, p. 38)

The advances that teachers have made have come through their collective efforts in two organizations—the National Education Association and
the American Federation of Teachers. Most teachers belong to one or the

other of these organizations, and most prospective teachers will become members during their first year of teaching.

National Education Association

The National Education Association (NEA) came into being in 1870, emerging from a 13-year-old organization called the National Teachers' Association (Dershimer, 1969). Its membership varied between 150 and 380 for the next 13 years, but in 1884 it rose to 2729 and then never again dropped below 1000. The membership grew to 52,850 in 1920, 87,414 in 1921, 118,032 in 1922, and about 900,000 in 1964, according to Dershimer. There are state and local education associations affiliated with the NEA, and though the strength of these state and local groups varies, the local, state, and national education associations together form a very strong network.

The militant thrust of the NEA during the 1960s and its role as the leader in setting objectives for the state and local associations are vividly reflected in a statement by the NEA's executive secretary in 1967:

> Last year NEA had 1,030,000 members; by the end of this year we will have at least 1,100,000. Within 10 years our membership will exceed two million, the great majority with undivided loyalties. They will be members of the profession at all levels—local, state, and national. Beginning now we are going to put our power and influence to work for the things that are really the most important. NEA will—
>
> Be unrelenting in seeking a better economic break for teachers in this affluent society.
>
> Become a political power second to no other special interest group.
>
> Insist that the profession at all levels have a voice in the formulation of educational policy, in curriculum change, and in educational planning.
>
> Have more and more to say about how a teacher is educated, whether he should be admitted to the profession, and whether he should stay in it.
>
> Expand and improve its program of economic benefits of membership.
>
> Stop the old argument within its ranks over welfare versus educational leadership; both are a necessary and vital part of our program and both will grow.
>
> Continue to defend and protect any teacher, principal, or superintendent in this country whose civil or professional rights are being challenged or denied.
>
> And finally, NEA will organize this profession from top to bottom into logical operational units that can move swiftly and effectively and with power unmatched by any other organized group in the nation. (Lambert, 1967, p. 36)

The more positive aspects of the NEA's aims—those dealing less with teacher welfare and more with improving educational opportunities for children—seemed to be receiving greater emphasis in 1969, after considerable success had already been experienced in negotiations for higher salaries. Excerpts from a few of the many resolutions adopted at the NEA's 1969 convention give the flavor of the newer NEA objectives: free public education for all from early childhood through adulthood, desegregated schools, greater use of paraprofessional and auxiliary personnel to free the teacher from nonteaching and routine duties, more flexible space and better instructional materials, higher quality instruction, greater federal support of education, higher salaries for teachers and better retirement provisions and fringe benefits, written personnel policies, and nondiscriminatory personnel policies (NEA, 1969b).

American Federation of Teachers

Dershimer (1969) also traced the rise of the American Federation of Teachers, which was formed in 1916 by nine local teacher unions meeting in Chicago. In 1940 it had only about 40,000 members, but by 1966 the total had increased to 130,000. More important than numbers, according to Dershimer, is the fact that in secret balloting against local NEA groups, the AFT has won the right to negotiate for all the teachers of many of our larger cities, starting with New York City itself in 1961.

Being an affiliate of the AFL-CIO, the AFT uses labor terminology and methods, including strikes. (In 1970, the affiliation became somewhat clouded as divisions within the AFL-CIO became more pronounced.) The AFT membership is concentrated in the cities. Also, unlike the NEA, it does not admit administrators into its membership; only teachers can be members. According to Dewing (1968), these members have always been predominantly from minority groups, including many Catholics, Jews, and Negroes. Further, like organized labor generally, the AFT has consistently been at the forefront of progressive educational reforms in the United States. Indeed, it preceded the NEA in attempting to get both better working conditions for teachers and desegregated schools, according to Dewing (1968). Nevertheless, in a recent controversy over control of the hiring and firing of teachers in New York City, the AFT there became involved in conflicts with ghetto residents (Zeluck, 1969).

According to Lieberman (1968), the AFT and the NEA were actually in close accord on most of their objectives toward the end of the 1960s. In fact, in 1968 the AFT invited the NEA to discuss a merger; by early 1970, however, the merger had not been effected, apparently because the NEA opposed it. Nevertheless, as is generally acknowledged, competition with the AFT for membership and power during the early 1960s does seem to have stimulated the NEA to become much more vigorous. Commenting on the proposed merger, Lieberman concluded:

> It seems to me that one of the most encouraging aspects of the present situation is the tremendous improvement in the quality of teacher leadership and in the likelihood that merger will strengthen the tendencies in this direction. If this is the case, teacher militancy will continue to increase and will be increasingly devoted to constructive public policy as well as teacher objectives. (Lieberman, 1968, p. 144)

Collective Negotiation

As mentioned, the major gain made by organized teacher groups during the 1960s took the form of the right of collective bargaining or negotiation. In this process, duly chosen representatives of employees negotiate with their employers on terms and conditions of employment and on other matters that the parties may agree to or be required to negotiate. Typically, representatives of the school board and its administrative staff and representatives of a teacher organization conduct the negotiations. According to Elam, Lieberman, and Moskow (1967), not a single state authorized or required collective negotiations between teachers and school boards before 1960. By the early 1970s, however, about half the states had legalized collective negotiations.

In collective negotiations a particular teacher organization is recognized formally as the exclusive negotiating agent of the teachers. The board of education is legally required to negotiate with this teacher representative, and in turn the representative must meet certain legal requirements. The scope of the negotiations and procedures to resolve an impasse are made explicit in the statutes. Though pay and hours of work are important points of negotiation, other matters that may more directly affect the quality of education may also be negotiated.

Sanctions and Strikes

When negotiations fail, the two primary means by which teacher organizations attempt to gain their objectives are the sanction and the work stoppage—the strike. The NEA expresses a preference for the sanction. The AFT, however, openly advocates giving teachers the right to strike, opposes antistrike laws, and opposes the use of injunctions in teacher-board disputes (Cogen, 1967). The use of either sanction or strike may engender massive public ill will, as might be expected. Nevertheless, their overall effects seem to have been beneficial thus far, as may be illustrated briefly.

Carter (1967) described two instances of the use of sanctions by the NEA. In May 1964 the NEA publicly censured the state of Utah for failing to raise its educational standards, including pay for teachers. The NEA then declared it unethical conduct for any teacher outside the state to seek a contract there, threatened to expel members who did, and informed accrediting agencies and teacher education institutions of its actions. The sanction was lifted in March 1965, after Utah had added $25 million to its biennial education budget.

Late in 1964, the Oklahoma Education Association called in its parent organization, the NEA, to investigate the state's school problems. The NEA's experts soon found that these problems had reached a "critical plane." In March 1965, therefore, the Oklahoma Education Association declared sanctions against the state, and the NEA followed suit two months later, shortly after the state's voters had turned down a one-cent increase in the 2 percent sales tax. The NEA then informed the major corporations and banks of Oklahoma's educational deficiencies. Also, it set up five "relocation centers" to assist teachers who might want to move from the state and provided an emergency fund for them to draw on if needed. The direct result was that on July 7, 1965, Oklahoma's governor signed a new education bill that added $28.7 million to the biennial budget for common schools and vocational education. This amount, an increase of 25 percent over the previous budget, resulted in a school budget that was by far the greatest in the history of Oklahoma. In these two cases, both against states, the use of the sanction was judged by Carter to have had a powerful effect on securing additional state funds for education.

Teachers' strikes, often called protests or boycotts, have become commonplace. Often, salary demands made by teachers that were angrily labeled unreasonable before a strike have been met or nearly met after it. Teacher strikes increasingly are directed against conditions judged to be causing poor learning opportunities for students. For example, when the Association of Classroom Teachers of Los Angeles, the NEA's largest local association (19,200 members), boycotted classes on September 18, 1969, its leaders announced that these were the conditions that required improvement:

> Classes range upwards of 38, 39, 40, and even 45 students.
>
> Teachers' salaries are steadily less competitive, contributing to an educationally disastrous 50 percent turnover each year in inner-city schools.
>
> Dropout rates in inner-city high schools average between 30 and 45 percent.
>
> Reading scores are well below state and national averages, and are falling a little more each year.
>
> There are major shortages of equipment, supplies, and textbooks and other instructional material, and much of what exists is ancient and in poor repair.
>
> Many of the district's ramshackle school buildings have safety hazards and unhealthy and unsanitary conditions; maintenance is cut back a little further each year. . . .
>
> In the face of all this, teachers have virtually no voice in the setting of district priorities, or in any aspect of the decision-making process. (*NEA Reporter*, 1969c, p. 1)

Conditions are very bad for both teachers and students in many of our inner cities and poor rural areas. Even more critical, they have been deteriorating steadily since World War II, and the trend has not yet been reversed. Many teachers have tried as individuals, without much success, to improve the conditions. Under such conditions, furthermore, simply improving one's own competence as a teacher in any of the areas outlined earlier in this chapter is not enough. Obviously, teaching competence alone — even when combined with true dedication — cannot make much difference in the achievement of students when other components of the school learning system — such as those outlined in Chapter 1 — are not functioning properly or have virtually broken down — as indicated in the Los Angeles teachers' demands just quoted. Teachers confronted by such school situations have no alternative but to organize and take *collective* action — not necessarily strikes and sanctions, but some kind of action to insure reasonable educational opportunities for many American students.

Although the NEA is very large and bureaucratic and the AFT carries a connotation of trade unionism rather than of professionalism, both are capable of responding to changing conditions, as can be seen in their performances during the 1960s. These organized teacher groups offer a real hope for education. Far more than school administrators, university professors, or parents, these groups have the capability for bringing about needed improvements in educational practices. Teachers themselves must make teaching a profession; no one else can do it for them.

7.8. What are the main differences and likenesses between the NEA and the AFT? Which do you prefer to represent teachers in collective negotiations? Why?

7.9. Under what circumstances, if any, would you as a teacher favor the use of sanctions? Work stoppages? Do you think the conditions as described in Los Angeles warranted a work stoppage?

7.10. How much education about, and practice in, group procedures to gain desired ends should be included in a program of teacher education?

SUMMARY

General intellectual ability, grade-point average during the college years, subject-matter preparation during the college years, and the grade made in student teaching show a low but positive correlation with subsequent teaching effectiveness. During actual teaching, knowledge of the subject matter, having and properly interpreting information about students, and the ability to solve teaching problems are also associated with teaching effectiveness. In the effective domain, being friendly and cheerful, responsible and businesslike, and enthusiastic are also associated with effectiveness.

Increasingly, and desirably, teaching is shifting from a cluster of independent undifferentiated overall tasks to cooperative teaming arrangements with differentiated tasks. Instruction has become far too specialized for one person to be expert in all its components. The multiunit elementary school developed in Wisconsin and the Temple City Differentiated Staffing Plan developed in California are two of the best conceptualized plans of the early 1970s. Characteristics of these more complex organizations have far-reaching implications for both teacher education and the various kinds of personnel who work in the schools.

Teachers during the 1960s organized and took actions as organized groups at all levels—national, state, and local. Collective negotiations, sanctions against states and other governmental units, and work stoppages became common. Both the NEA and the AFT demonstrated the capability to respond constructively to deteriorating school support, segregation, and other problems that are seriously weakening public education in America. Organized teachers should no longer shirk their responsibility to lead Americans in providing better educational opportunities for more students and for making teaching a profession.

SUGGESTIONS FOR FURTHER READING

CARTER, B. The teachers give Oklahoma a lesson. In Elam, S. M., Lieberman, M., & Moskow, M., eds., *Readings on collective negotiations in public education.* Chicago: Rand McNally, 1967, pp. 381-388.

This is a reporter's account of the sanction imposed by the NEA and OEA and its effects.

DERSHIMER, R. A. *Professional educational organizations.* In Ebel, R. L., ed., *Encyclopedia of educational research.* New York: Macmillan, 1969, pp. 1008-1016.

A concise history is outlined of educational organizations, including the NEA and AFT — a must for anyone interested in education as a career.

ELAM, S. M., LIEBERMAN, M., & MOSKOW, M., eds. *Readings on collective negotiations in public education.* Chicago: Rand McNally, 1967.

This book contains 41 articles written by proponents of NEA, proponents of AFT, impartial critics, experts in collective negotiations, and interested citizens and educators.

FULLER, F. F. Concerns of teachers: A developmental conceptualization. In Ripple, R. E., ed., *Readings in learning and human abilities.* New York: Harper & Row, 2nd ed., 1971.

Fuller identified changes that occur in the concerns of teachers during preteaching, early teaching, and late teaching.

HAMACHEK, D. E., ed. *Human dynamics in psychology and education: Selected readings.* Boston: Allyn and Bacon, 1968.

Readings 13 through 16 deal with classroom dynamics and teaching processes: D. Hamachek, "What Research Tells Us About the Characteristics of 'Good' and 'Bad' Teachers," pages 187-203; W. James, "Psychology and the Teaching Art," pages 204-206; W. J. McKeachie, "Students, Groups, and Teaching Methods," pages 207-215; and C. Rogers, "Personal Thoughts on Teaching and Learning," pages 216-218.

KOUNIN, J. S., & GUMP, P. V. The comparative influence of punitive and nonpunitive teachers upon children's concepts of school misconduct. In Ripple, R. E., ed., *Readings in learning and human abilities.* New York: Harper & Row, 2nd ed., 1971.

The effects of punitive and nonpunitive behavior of the teacher on children's concepts of school misconduct are indicated in this report of research.

TOLOR, A., SCARPETTI, W. L., & LANE, P. A. Teachers' attitudes toward children's behavior revisited. In Ripple, R. E., ed., *Readings in learning and human abilities.* New York: Harper & Row, 2nd ed., 1971.

This is a follow-up of a classic study done in 1928 by Wickman concerning the differences between teachers and clinicians regarding the behavior problems of children.

Chapter 8 Classroom Interactions and Teacher Leadership

Teacher-Student Interactions

interaction analysis
teacher talk: direct and indirect influence
student talk: initiating and responding
behaviors of liked and disliked teachers
microteaching to develop technical skills
self-instructional minicourses

Teacher Leadership of Students

authoritarian, democratic, laissez-faire
dominative, integrative
leadership and achievement of students
leadership and emotional security of students

Staff Interactions and Leadership in Instructional Teams

interdependence relationships
specialization of labor
authority, decision-making, and influence
operational goals of the staff
job satisfaction and environmental climate

Student-Student Interactions

group cohesiveness
personal attraction
task performance
group prestige

n the last four chapters, four components of a system of school learning have been dealt with successively: educational and instructional objectives, instructional materials and equipment, the readiness of students for learning and provisions for individual differences, and the characteristics of teachers as individuals and as organized groups. Throughout these chapters we have sampled the best research and practices of the past, and we have also made projections about the nature of school learning in the future. In this chapter we consider teacher-student interactions, teacher leadership of students, staff relationships and morale in teams, and student-student interactions. Again, we sample from the past and do some projecting into the future.

TEACHER-STUDENT INTERACTIONS

The teacher interacts with students by speaking, writing, and making actual physical motions. For example, in demonstrating how to solve a problem, the teacher may talk about it, write some or all of it on the blackboard, and gesture while speaking and writing. The music teacher may sing a song the first time with appropriate gestures and movements to convey the mood as well as the words and melody.

Students have some of the same means of interacting with the teacher as the teacher does with them. The teacher usually, however, controls the kind and amount of interactions. Thus when the teacher decides to lecture or to have the students study independently, there is no verbal interaction among the students or between the teacher and students. On the other hand, classroom discussions, panel discussions, question-and-answer sessions, and small-group activities call for much interaction.

As part of the continuing efforts by many researchers to develop information that will be helpful to teachers, attempts have been made in recent years to relate the amount and kind of teacher-student interaction to outcomes of learning. First, the behaviors of the teacher and the students, and particularly their verbal behaviors, are analyzed in great detail. Then the effects of different behaviors of the teacher are related directly to student achievements or other behaviors. The methods used in two of these recent investigations and their conclusions are now considered in detail; then other information that also may be helpful to the teacher in guiding his own interactions with students is presented.

Flanders' Analysis of Oral Interactions

Flanders (1968, 1969) developed a widely used system for observing, recording, and interpreting teacher-student interactions. This system is concerned only with oral behavior, on the assumption that the oral behavior of the teacher and students is an adequate sample of their total behavior. Also, oral *verbal* behavior—that is, talk—can be observed with higher reliability than can nonverbal behavior. Flanders' system is described at some length here so that the reader may become familiar with a scientific method for observing and analyzing interactions, with various patterns of classroom interactions, and with relationships between various interaction patterns and student achievements and attitudes. The other systems for observing and analyzing classroom interactions, which are about as complex, are not described here. Medley and Mitzel (1963) presented a detailed account of various methodologies, however, and Flanders (1969) reported the results pertaining to several different methods.

Categories of Interactions. In Flanders' interaction analysis system, all teacher talk is first classified as indirect or direct influence. Indirect influence, or response, maximizes student opportunity. Direct influence, or initiation, minimizes the opportunity for the students to initiate talk and respond. Student talk also is classified into two categories—responding to the teacher and initiating talk. A third classification, silence or confusion, is included in order to account for time that cannot be classified as teacher talk or student talk.

As shown in Table 8.1, teacher talk that demonstrates indirect influence (response) is further classified into four categories: accepts feelings, praises or encourages, accepts or uses ideas of students, and asks questions. The categories of direct influence (initiation) are lecturing, giving directions, and criticizing or justifying authority. A more complete description of Category 7 follows:

> *Category 7*: Criticizing or Justifying Authority. A statement of criticism is one that is designed to change student behavior from nonacceptable to acceptable. The teacher is saying, in effect, "I don't like what you are doing. Do something else." Another group of statements included in this category are those that might be called statements of defense or self-justification. These statements are particularly difficult to detect when a teacher appears to be explaining a lesson or the reasons for doing a lesson to the class. If the teacher is explaining himself or his authority, defending himself against the student, or justifying himself, the statement falls in this category. Other kinds of statements that fall in this category are those of extreme self-reference or those in which the teacher is constantly asking the children to do something as a special favor to the teacher. (Amidon & Flanders, 1963, p. 9)

As mentioned, only *oral* verbal behavior is categorized. In other words, if the teacher is talking (Categories 1 through 7), the students are assumed to be listening, and if the pupils are talking (Categories 8 and 9), the teacher is assumed to be listening.

Observing and Recording Interactions. Although this system of analyzing a classroom situation may seem complicated, it is really quite feasible. A tape recorder may be used to record a classroom period for later analysis, but, actually, a trained observer in a classroom is able to analyze the interaction more efficiently. Every three seconds the observer decides which of the nine categories of interactions has just occurred. Thus, for every minute of observed instruction, he records 20 category numbers.

A very brief example will show how this system works: A short time interval of 21 seconds might be recorded in an observer's notebook as 10-

Table 8.1. Categories of Interaction Analysis

Teacher talk and student talk

Teacher Talk
Response
  1. Accepts feelings: accepts and clarifies the feeling tone of the students in a non-threatening manner. Feelings may be positive or negative. Predicting or recalling feelings are included.
  2. Praises or encourages: praises or encourages student action or behavior. Jokes that release tension, but at the expense of another individual; nodding head, or saying "um hm?" or "go on" are included.
  3. Accepts or uses ideas of students: clarifying, building, or developing ideas suggested by a student. As teacher brings more of his own ideas into play, shift to Category 5.
  4. Asks questions: asking a question about content or procedure with the intent that a student answer.
Initiation
  5. Lecturing: giving facts or opinions about content or procedures; expressing his own ideas, asking rhetorical questions.
  6. Giving directions: directions, commands, or orders with which a student is expected to comply.
  7. Criticizing or justifying authority: statements intended to change student behavior from nonacceptable to acceptable pattern; bawling someone out; stating why the teacher is doing what he is doing; extreme self-reference.

Student Talk
Response
  8. Talk by students in response to teacher. Teacher initiates the contact or solicits student statement.
Initiation
  9. Talk by students which they initiate. If "calling on" student is only to indicate who may talk next, observer must decide whether student wanted to talk. If he did, use this category.

  10. Silence or confusion: pauses, short periods of silence and periods of confusion in which communication cannot be understood by the observer.

Note: No scale is implied by the numbers. Each number is classificatory; it merely designates a particular *kind* of communication event. Thus to write these numbers down during observation is to enumerate, not to judge a position on a scale.
Source: Flanders, 1968, p. 128.

9-3-3-3-4-8-10. What happened was that after a brief silence (10) a student proposed a new way to prove a geometric theorem (9), the teacher accepted and used the student's idea (3-3-3), the teacher asked a question applying the idea (4), and a student responded (8). The final 10 is added simply to show that the necessary series of observations is completed, for example, by the ending of a class period, the observer stopping, or a marked shifting in the kind of activities going on.

To give an overall picture of the interaction and to help the teacher analyze what happened, the observation numbers standing for the categories are rerecorded on a 10 × 10 matrix. To do this, the numbers are first listed in *pairs* formed by going through the series of observations one number at a time. In the example given, these pairs are: (a) 10-9, (b) 9-3, (c) 3-3, (d) 3-3, (e) 3-4, (f) 4-8, and (g) 8-10. The first number of each pair is the row index, and the second number is the column index. Thus, to record pair a, one marks a tally in the cell at the intersection of row 10 and column 9, pair b is marked in the cell at the intersection of row 9 and column 3, etc. The result of the recordings is shown in Fig. 8.1 (the letters of the interaction pairs are included in the figure merely for demonstration purposes — they are not normally used; also, several hundred interaction pairs are normally tabulated on a single matrix, rather than the seven used here for illustrative purposes).

Interpreting Interactions. Figure 8.2 shows how observations may be divided into special areas for interpretation. The special areas indicated in the figure, which are all of high interest to teachers, of course include many possible observations — many more than those reported in Fig. 8.1. Teacher talk Categories 1-4 are summed and recorded in Area A to indicate the percentage of time the teacher talks indirectly, in responding to students; the sum of Categories 5-7 is recorded in Area B to indicate the percentage of time the teacher talks directly. Similarly, the sums of Categories 8 and 9 in Area C and Category 10 in Area D indicate the percentage of time the students talk and the time spent in silence, pauses, and confusion.

Fig. 8.1. Flanders' matrix showing classroom interaction sequence. (Adapted from Amidon & Flanders, 1963, p. 27)

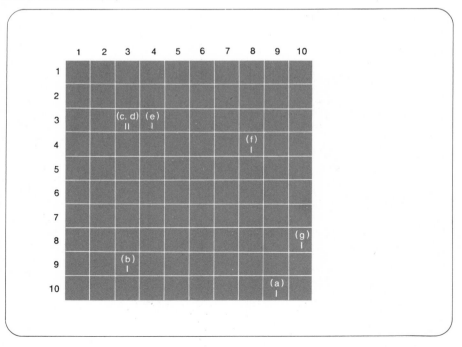

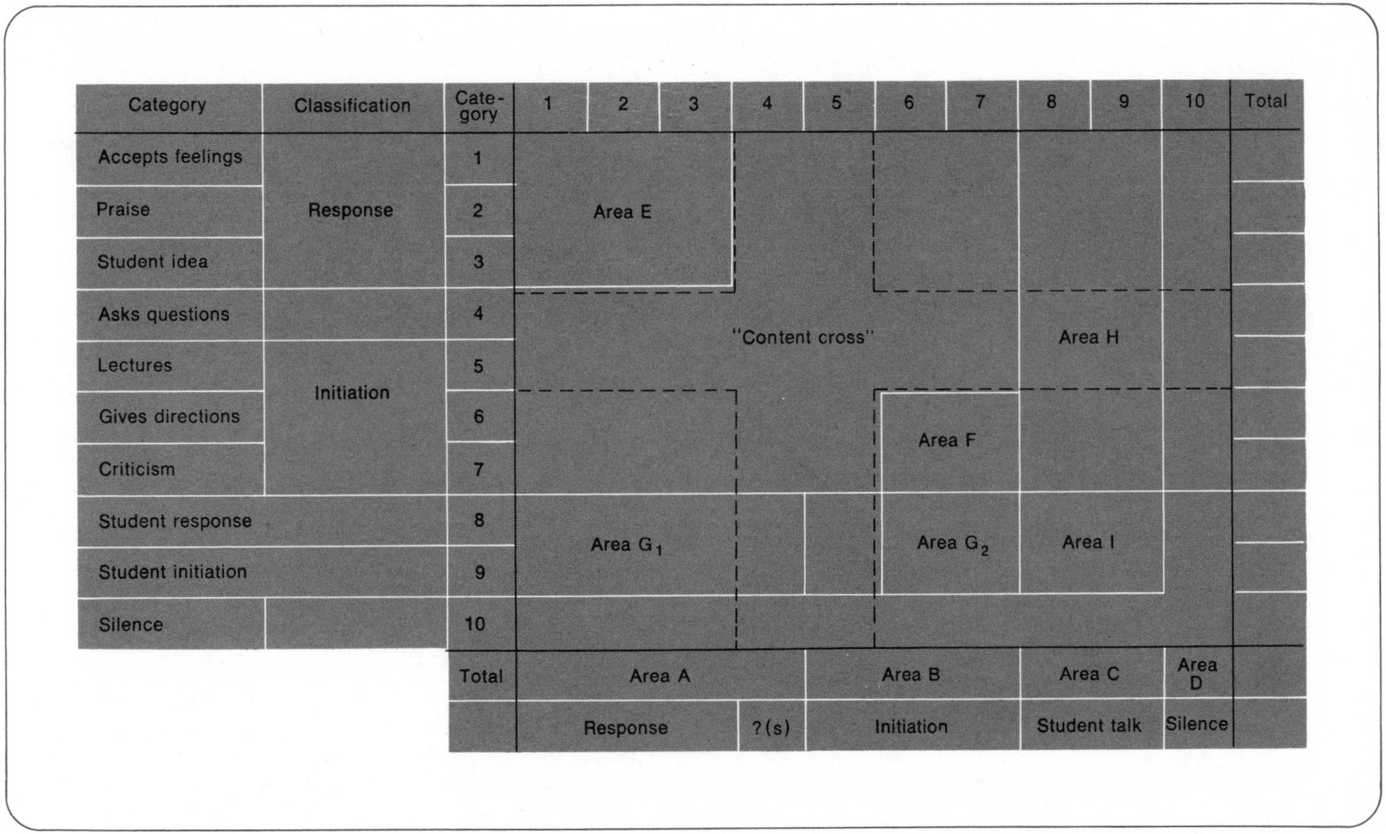

Fig. 8.2. Matrix of an interaction analysis and related areas for interpretation. (Flanders, 1968, p. 129)

Area E, incorporating all the tallies falling into Categories 1-3, indicates how much the teacher accepts feelings, praises or encourages, and accepts or uses the ideas of students.

Area F, incorporating Categories 6 and 7, indicates how much the teacher gives directions and criticizes. According to Flanders (1968), a concentration of tallies in this area indicates discipline problems. Particularly significant in this connection are the two transition cells. That is, tallies in the 6-7 cell, showing a shift from directions to criticism, indicate that the compliance of students with directions is judged unsatisfactory; tallies in the 7-6 cell, showing a shift from criticism back to directions, indicate that more directions are given to students after criticism.

Areas G_1 and G_2 show the teacher's responses immediately after the students stop talking. Tallies in G_1 indicate that the teacher accepts and uses the students' ideas and praises the students (Categories 1-3); tallies in G_2 indicate that the teacher guides and directs or criticizes following student talk (Categories 6 and 7).

Area H indicates teacher questions or statements that trigger student participation. One would expect that a teacher question (4) would trigger student responses (8) or student questions (9). Area I indicates sustained student participation of the kind that might go on in a student panel or in a lively discussion. It does not indicate which or how many students in a total group interact orally.

The total number of tallies in the central "content cross," when compared with tallies outside the cross, gives a very rough indication of the proportion of class time actually oriented around content.

Effects of Indirect and Direct Teacher Influences

It is quite obvious from the preceding discussion that one distinction that can be made between teachers is in their use of indirect and direct influences. A second distinction is in the amount of talking done by the teacher and by the students.

Flanders (1969) reviewed a large number of studies done during the 1960s dealing with differences among teachers in the use of indirect and direct influences. Most of the studies were carried out with elementary and high school teachers who were not instructed in the use of indirect methods; in a small number of cases, however, an experimental group was instructed in such methods. One of the most significant results of the studies is that, with only a few exceptions, indirect behaviors—those described by Flanders or other similar teacher behaviors—were associated not only with higher student achievement in the subject matter but also with more favorable student attitudes toward the teacher, the subject matter, or other aspects of the school situation.

In connection with the amount of teacher talk, Flanders (1969) also noted that many studies showed that teachers talk from 65 to 75 percent of the total class time. Furthermore, this teacher talk is usually of the kind that merely calls for the students to respond to the initiative of the teacher, rather than the reverse—that is, teacher talk that responds to the students in such a way as to cause them to take the initiative. Gallagher (1965), for example, showed that many student responses indicated that they were simply recalling something the teacher asked them to recall. Flanders summarized the effects of such direct teacher influence:

> Pupils' initiative and independent thinking are not encouraged in classroom discourse. Most of these studies provided evidence that teachers are more alike than they are different. The less effective teachers are more alike and less flexible and probably easier to identify than more effective teachers are. . . . The preponderance of evidence gathered so far would indicate that most currently practicing teachers could adopt patterns which are more responsive to the ideas and opinions expressed by pupils and realize a gain in both positive pupil attitudes and pupil achievement. (Flanders, 1969, p. 1429)

These conclusions lead to the question: What exactly is *indirect teacher behavior?* We now take a closer look at this behavior, which seems so likely to produce higher student achievement and more favorable student attitudes. The higher achievement comes partly because either the teacher *or* the students, through many oral interactions dealing with the subject matter, reinforce and confirm the correct or appropriate behaviors of the students. The behaviors of students can be reinforced in discussions, question-and-answer periods, and other activities involving student participation. For example, members of smaller groups within a class discuss an experiment that each has underway. As the members of each group discuss the project, large amounts of information are exchanged. Also, in teacher-led discussions, the students' answers are immediately reinforced or corrected, not only by the teacher but also by classmates. Board work, too, is sometimes effective because it gives the teacher the opportunity to see the results of a number of students' work, to reinforce whatever is correct, and to help them identify and overcome errors or difficulties immediately.

Producing favorable attitudes is directly connected with a theory that is almost universally accepted as fact—that most human beings need to give and to receive affection and to receive attention and approval. When given the opportunity, students satisfy these needs in the classroom in part through their oral interactions with other students. Furthermore, the effective teacher relies on oral interactions with students for satisfaction of some of his own social needs. To attain self-realization and to maintain a fairly well-integrated personality, the teacher must be assured that the students are actually learning under his guidance. This becomes possible when students participate actively in classroom activities and when the teacher thus can continuously observe their progress.

Providing feedback connected with either cognitive or affective aspects of learning is a two-way process. Students can be a source of information that is particularly useful to their teachers—when they are given opportunities to provide it. Tuckman and Oliver (1968) showed this in a rather dramatic way. In their study they assessed the effects of feedback on teachers from three groups: students only, vice-principals only, and both students and vice-principals. The feedback consisted of providing the teacher with the ratings and comments of his students, his vice-principal, or both. These ratings and comments related to 10 areas, including knowledge of the subject, ability to explain, ability to maintain discipline, degree of sympathetic understanding, fairness, and being interesting.

The effect of the feedback was judged by measuring the amount of change in the *students'* ratings of 256 teachers during a 12-week interval. Student feedback led to a positive change in the ratings assigned to a teacher. That is, in the opinion of the students, the teachers receiving feedback from the students changed in a desirable direction during the 12 weeks. Feedback from the students and the vice-principals combined also produced desired changes. However, feedback from the vice-principals alone produced a change in the opposite direction; that is, the sample of teachers receiving feedback from the vice-principals changed in a negative direction, as rated by their students. These effects have been interpreted in this way:

> It can only be surmised that teachers are defensive toward (or even hostile to) administrators who, in the absence of much basis for judgment, attempt to tell them how to teach. Of interest, though, is the fact that within the educational milieu, the only source of feedback to teachers, typically, is their supervisors. The data collected here indicate that such feedback is doing more harm than good, with the best source of feedback, students, overlooked. (Tuckman & Oliver, 1968, p. 300)

Other Interactions

Isaacson et al. (1964) studied patterns of behavior in college instructors. Asking college students to rate their instructors on a large number of items drawn from many inventories, he then identified six general patterns, or factors. The names assigned to them and a few examples of relevant behavior describe certain aspects of the behavior of college instructors (though these patterns of course also relate to teachers at all levels):

1. Skill. Instructor puts material across in an interesting way, stimulates intellectual curiosity of the students, explains things clearly, observes student reaction skillfully.
2. Overload. Instructor assigns difficult reading, asks for more than students can do, assigns a great deal of reading.
3. Structure. Instructor decides in detail what should be done and how to do it, follows an outline closely; everything goes according to schedule, activities are planned in detail.
4. Feedback. Instructor tells students when they have done a particularly good job, compliments students in front of others, criticizes poor work.
5. Interaction. Students in the class are friendly, feel free to express opinions, frequently volunteer their own opinions.
6. Rapport. Instructor listens attentively to students, is friendly, is permissive and flexible, explains reasons for criticism.

Isaacson did not attempt to relate these behaviors to instructor effectiveness in terms of how well the students learned or how they reacted to the instructors. You may find it interesting, however, to formulate such relationships in terms of your own experience—that is, decide which of the instructor behaviors would probably result in higher achievement for *you* and in more favorable attitudes toward the instructor. Comparing your judgments with those of others will help to determine the extent of agreement.

Leeds (1954) compared students' ratings of 10 most liked teachers and 10 most disliked teachers in a number of undesirable behaviors; he did two studies, one in 1946 and the other in 1951. Table 8.2 includes only those behaviors on which there were large differences between the two sets of teachers. For example, in 1946, only 4 percent of the students checked "scolds pupils a lot" as being undesirable behavior shown by the upper 10 teachers, whereas 71 percent checked this as undesirable behavior shown by the 10 most disliked teachers. As might be expected, the lower 10 teachers received much more disapproval in both years; nevertheless, the upper 10 teachers also were criticized by many students for scolding a student in front of others, for being easily annoyed or bothered, for detaining students during recess or after school, for punishing in front of other pupils, and for being uninterested in pupils' activities outside school. Although there are some fairly sharp differences on a few items between the teachers in 1951 and in 1946, pupils rated undesirable behaviors of best-liked and least-liked teachers with surprising consistency. Furthermore, the 1946 and 1951 studies were done in different states.

The Leeds study does not tell us how well the students actually learned subject matter under the best- and the least-liked teachers. Other studies, however, do relate student achievement and attitudes more precisely to classroom interactions and the organizational context. For example, Walberg and Anderson (1968) identified several aspects of *classroom organization*, such as speech constraint, goal direction, and democratic policy, and several aspects of *individual affect* in the classroom, such as satisfaction, intimacy, friction, and social heterogeneity. These factors were correlated with students' achievement scores in physics, with their understanding of science concepts, with their feelings about the physics course, and with certain student activities related to physics. The results are notable:

> Students who gained most on the Physics Achievement Test, for example, perceived their classes as socially homogeneous, intimate groups working on one goal; one might speculate that the goal is high achievement on physics tests. On the other hand, students who grew more in science understanding saw their classes as well organized, with little friction between their fellow students, and although the class is seen as egalitarian and unstratified, the students had a greater variety of interests. . . . Students who reported greater enjoyment of laboratory work perceived their classes as unstratified, democratic in policy setting, having a clear idea of class goals, and satisfying. Students who gained the most interest in physics saw their classes as well organized and unstratified. . . . Finally, students who reported engaging in more physics activities, because they were interested, felt more personally intimate with their fellow class members, less alienated, and less strictly controlled. (Walberg & Anderson, 1968, p. 417)

Table 8.2. Frequency of Pupil Reaction Toward Undesirable Behavior of the 10 Teachers Taken from Each End of the Distribution of Pupils' Ratings (1946 and 1951 Studies)

| | Percentage of pupil reaction | | | |
| | Upper 10 teachers | | Lower 10 teachers | |
Undesirable teacher behavior	1946 (n=281)	1951 (n=257)	1946 (n=265)	1951 (n=261)
Verbal Behaviors Implying Interpersonal Relations				
Scolds pupils a lot	4	7	71	50
Usually cross	3	4	59	20
Often "bossy"	2	4	58	32
Scolds a pupil in front of other pupils	44	23	91	80
Always "fussing at" the pupils	6	2	58	31
Talks too much	5	3	63	40
Nonverbal Behaviors Implying Interpersonal Relations				
Difficult to approach with problems	5	6	56	26
Difficult to please	7	4	64	33
Easily annoyed or bothered	17	11	70	61
Does not see things as children do	3	5	52	37
Behaviors Involving Work and Structure				
Does not participate in children's games	9	17	64	64
Uninterested in pupil's activities outside of school	33	9	63	39
Assigns "lots" of homework	5	8	54	55
Uses detention during recess or after school	16	30	69	87
Punishes whole class for one or two offenders	12	8	71	41

Source: Adapted from Leeds, 1954, pp. 31–32.

Technical Skills and Related Student Behaviors

Gage (1968) is among those who have pointed out that, despite research going back to the early 1900s, little has actually been known until recently about teaching methods and teaching effectiveness. Teaching methods — such as lecture, group discussion, Socratic or question-and-answer, laboratory, etc. — and also the effects of these methods in terms of teaching effectiveness, have been defined and accepted widely as, in a way, separate schemes, any of which can simply be "used on" students.

This approach has proved to be ineffective. Needed instead are explicitly defined teaching *behaviors* that can be related directly to explicitly defined, observable student *behaviors*. Gage called the teaching behaviors *technical skills*; he identified several skills in terms such as *using questions, recognizing and obtaining attending behaviors, providing feedback, employing rewards and punishments*, and *explaining*. The procedure for teaching the skills and also for observing them in use is called *microteaching*.

Microteaching. Microteaching, as defined by Gage, is a means of teaching the technical skills to a prospective or a practicing teacher. It is micro in that a specific skill is dealt with, an instructional session lasts only for 5 to 10 minutes, and no more than five students interact with the teacher. Each session is recorded on a videotape, and the teacher then sees and hears himself immediately after the session. The prospective teacher also receives comments and suggestions from his instructor. Then he teaches the same exercise or lesson to a new small group of students in an attempt to improve his skill. (The term microteaching now means a number of other things, too, because it is the term used by many persons who employ video techniques in other ways in their instructional programs for teachers and children.)

Explaining Ability. Gage (1968) observed that explaining, one of his technical skills, is widely engaged in by teachers at all school levels. Thus it merits some specific discussion here. As will be noted in Chapter 11 dealing with concepts and principles, a teacher may help a student understand a concept better by giving examples of the concept, indicating the attributes of the concept, presenting synonyms or antonyms of the word representing the concept, using the word representing the concept in a sentence or other context, or drawing an analogy. These are all examples of explaining behaviors.

Rosenshine (1968) related the explaining ability of 40 social studies teachers to student achievement in the material explained. For 15 minutes each teacher gave an explanation of something about Yugoslavia; judges rated the best and poorest explanations. The two behaviors that discriminated between the best and poorest were the extent to which the teacher described the how, why, or effect of something and the degree to which the teacher stated a concept or principle explicitly, gave examples of it, and then summarized in a series of illustrations at a higher level of generality than the illustrations themselves.

Minicourses. The Far West Laboratory for Educational Research and Development is attempting to go beyond the research on microteaching by developing self-instructional *minicourses* for experienced teachers. A minicourse, consisting of printed material and video tapes, attempts to teach a specific instructional skill in about four hours of instruction time. Minicourse 1, for example, consists of two self-instructional lessons in booklet form on conducting a class discussion, two video tapes that present a model class discussion for the teacher to observe, and two instructional tapes that more explicitly show how to conduct a class discussion. The course is designed to bring about changes in 12 specific teacher behaviors.

Borg (1969) studied the effectiveness of Minicourse 1 on 48 teachers. To determine whether or not the desired behavior changes occurred, first, each teacher received an instruction sheet for preparing a precourse discussion lesson. Then a 20-minute video tape recording was made of this lesson as the teacher presented it to his regular class. The teacher then took Minicourse 1. As soon as he had finished it, he received identical instructions for preparing a postcourse discussion lesson. This lesson with his regular class was also recorded on video tape. The video tapes from the precourse and postcourse lessons were then scored to assess the teachers' use of the specific skills.

Table 8.3 gives the results of the analysis of the precourse and postcourse video tapes for 10 changes brought about by Minicourse 1 that appeared to be large enough to be of practical as well as statistical significance, according to Borg (1969). Note especially these changes from precourse to postcourse analysis: the higher proportion of questions asked by teachers that called for higher-level cognitive responses by the students; the markedly lower percentage of teacher talk; the marked increase in the average number of words per student reply, indicating responses

Table 8.3. Results of Analysis of Minicourse 1 Precourse Tapes and Postcourse Tapes

Behavior compared	Precourse mean	Postcourse mean
Behaviors for Which Increases Were Sought		
Number of times teacher used *redirection*	26.69	40.92
Number of times teacher used *prompting*	4.10	7.17
Number of times teacher used *further clarification*	4.17	6.73
Length of pupil responses in words (based on five-minute samples of pre- and postcourse tapes)	5.63	11.78
Proportion of total questions that called for higher cognitive pupil responses rather than for factual responses	37.30	52.00
Behaviors for Which Decreases Were Sought		
Number of times teacher repeated his/her own questions	13.68	4.68
Number of times teacher repeated pupil answers	30.68	4.36
Number of times teacher answered his/her own questions	4.62	.72
Number of one-word pupil responses (based on five-minute samples of pre- and postcourse tapes)	5.82	2.57
Proportion of discussion time taken by teacher talk	51.64	27.75

Source: Borg, 1969.

other than "yes," "no," or a correct single-word answer; and the marked reduction in the number of one-word pupil replies. Other desired changes in behavior also occurred. One would expect that these changes would be accompanied by higher student achievement (though the research was not extended to a specific investigation of this point).

Further study of the effectiveness of Minicourse 1 by Borg (1969) indicated that it worked equally well with both male and female teachers, at all three grade levels involved in the study (4, 5, and 6), and in both low socioeconomic and advantaged schools. Also, the desired behavioral changes were found to be relatively permanent without further study or practice. (The term *minicourse* is now being applied by various college people to courses that carry less than one-hour credit. There is no relationship between some of these courses and the minicourses being developed by Borg and others at the Far West Laboratory.)

8.1. Verbal interactions between the teacher and students may serve several purposes, such as identifying and delimiting problems to be solved, setting goals to be attained, securing and directing attention, guiding thinking, assessing achievements and actions, and providing feedback. Describe a procedure for accomplishing one or two of these, first, with the teacher as the initiator and the students as receivers, and, second, with the students as the initiators and the teacher as receiver.

8.2. Which one or two things related to Flanders' interaction analysis do you think you can apply to your behavior as a teacher?

8.3. As a practice exercise, rate a college instructor as high, average, or low on each of the nine items of the Flanders system or on the six items that Isaacson proposed. Ask a fellow student to do the same. Compare your ratings.

8.4. Microteaching and minicourses are both directed toward identifying distinct instructional skills. Explaining and conducting a classroom discussion are two such skills. What are other skills related to your interests that might be handled through minicourses of about four hours' duration?

TEACHER LEADERSHIP OF STUDENTS

Authority may be defined as the power to make decisions that affect other people. The teacher, of course, has the authority to make decisions that affect the students. The ways in which the teacher as leader demonstrates his power and authority produce differing results, however, as will be shown later. In any case, authority is only one aspect of leadership. Stout (1969) indicated that an effective leader provides for interaction and communication among the group members. Also, Bowers and Seashore (1966) found that leaders are supportive of members, facilitate interaction among group members, facilitate work, and emphasize group goals.

Authoritarian, Democratic, and Laissez-Faire Leadership

Lewin and his associates, Lippitt and White, conducted a series of experiments to ascertain the effects of various forms of leadership on the individual and group behavior of 11-year-old boys in a club situation. Their procedures and results, reported in many articles and films, were best summarized by Lippitt and White (1958). Three forms of leadership—authoritarian (autocratic), democratic, and laissez-faire—were experimentally arranged; also, two atmospheres were found under authoritarian leadership: aggressive reaction (aggressive autocracy) and apathetic reaction (apathetic autocracy). The situations were so arranged that the groups of boys experienced each type of leadership, making possible comparisons of the leadership effects on the same boys. Now follow descriptions of the three leadership roles:

PLAN FOR AUTHORITARIAN LEADERSHIP ROLE

Practically all policies as regards club activities and procedures should be determined by the leader. The techniques and activity steps should be communicated by the authority, one unit at a time, so that future steps are in the dark to a large degree. The adult should take considerable responsibility for assigning the activity tasks and companions of each group member. The dominator should keep his standards of praise and criticism to himself in evaluating individual and group activities. He should also remain fairly aloof from active group participation except in demonstrating.

PLAN FOR DEMOCRATIC LEADERSHIP ROLE

Wherever possible, policies should be a matter of group decision and discussion with active encouragement and assistance by the adult leader. The leader should attempt to see that activity perspective emerges during the discussion period with the general steps to the group goal becoming clarified. Wherever technical advice is needed, the leader should try to suggest two or more alternative procedures from which choice can be made by the group members. Everyone should be free to work with whomever he chooses, and the divisions of responsibility should be left up to the group. The leader should attempt to communicate in an objective, fact-minded way the bases for his praise and criticism of individual and group activities. He should try to be a regular group member in spirit but not do much of the work (so that comparisons of group productivity can be made between the groups).

PLAN FOR LAISSEZ-FAIRE LEADERSHIP ROLE

In this situation, the adult should play a rather passive role in social participation and leave complete freedom for group or individual decisions in relation to activity and group procedure. The leader should make clear the various materials which are available and be sure it is understood that he will supply information and help when asked. He should do a minimum of taking the initiative in making suggestions. He should make no attempt to evaluate negatively or positively the behavior or productions of the individuals or the group as a group, although he should be friendly rather than "stand-offish" at all times. (Lippitt & White, 1958, p. 498)[1]

[1]Copyright 1947, 1952, © 1958 by Holt, Rinehart and Winston, Inc. Reprinted by permission of Holt, Rinehart and Winston, Inc.

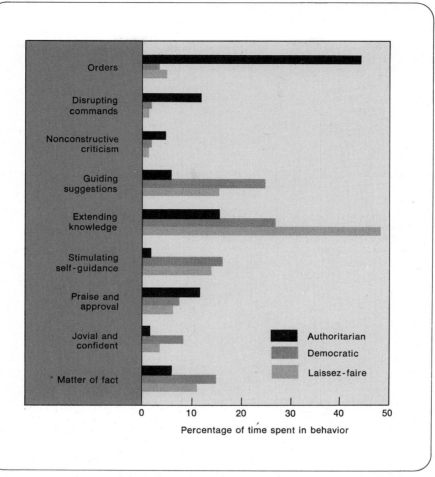

Fig. 8.3. Percentage of time given by authoritarian, democratic, and laissez-faire leaders to various behaviors. (Adapted from Lippitt & White, 1958, p. 499. Copyright 1947, 1952, © 1958 by Holt, Rinehart and Winston, Inc. Reprinted by permission of Holt, Rinehart and Winston, Inc.)

Figure 8.3 shows the behaviors of the leaders as actually carried out in the club situation. The authoritarian leader gave many more orders, disrupting commands, and nonconstructive criticisms. Guiding suggestions, extending knowledge, and stimulating self-guidance were much less frequent under authoritarian than under democratic and laissez-faire leadership. Praise and approval were engaged in most by the authoritarian leader, being jovial, self-confident, and matter of fact most by the democratic leader. Extending knowledge was the only behavior engaged in most by the laissez-faire leader. Thus with clearly planned procedures for producing differences in the leader behaviors, there were marked differences but also some overlapping of behaviors among the leaders.

Figure 8.4 gives the four patterns of reaction of the boys' groups to the three different styles of leadership. The boys' actions indicating dependence on the leader were much more frequent under authoritarian leadership than democratic or laissez-faire; critical discontent and demands for attention also were higher under authoritarian leadership. Friendly and confiding behavior and group-minded suggestions were highest with democratic leadership, as were out-of-club-field conversations and work-minded conversations. The asking of information was highest under laissez-faire leadership; 37 percent of all the boys' behavior toward the

Fig. 8.4. Four patterns of group reaction to the three different types of leadership. (Adapted from Lippitt & White, 1958, p. 502. Copyright 1947, 1952, © 1958 by Holt, Rinehart and Winston, Inc. Reprinted by permission of Holt, Rinehart and Winston, Inc.)

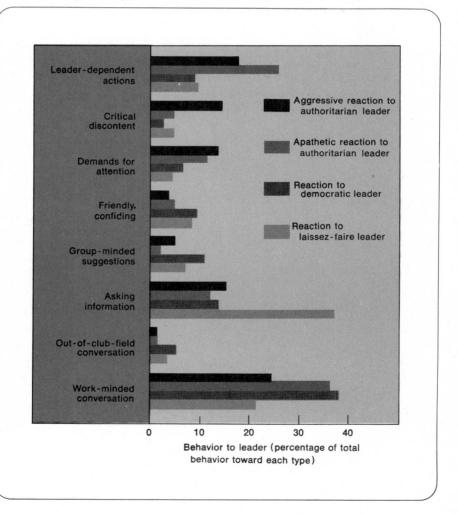

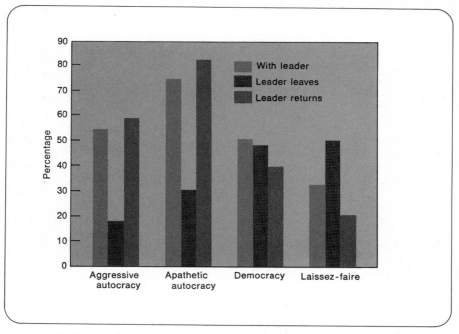

Fig. 8.5. Percentage of time spent in high-activity involvement. (Adapted from Lippitt & White, 1958, p. 503. Copyright 1947, 1952, © 1958 by Holt, Rinehart and Winston, Inc. Reprinted by permission of Holt, Rinehart and Winston, Inc.)

laissez-faire leader consisted of asking for information. It is interesting that about as much work-minded conversation took place in the apathetic authoritarian situation as in the democratic one.

Figure 8.5 shows the percentage of time spent in high activity involvement. In aggressive autocracy, for example, the boys were highly active for about 53 percent of the time when the leader was present, but only about 17 percent of the time when the leader left the group; the figure rose to nearly 60 percent as soon as the aggressive autocratic leader returned. The ratios were about the same in apathetic autocracy; however, the actual amount of time spent in high activity was much greater. Under democratic leadership, work activity was about 50 percent when the leader was present, but it dropped off very little when the leader left, and when he came back, it did not immediately pick up. With laissez-faire leadership the percentage of time in high activity involvement by the boys was lowest among the various forms of leadership when the leader was present. It was the highest, however, when the leader was out. Thus, when the adult leader left, other leaders from within the boys' group emerged to take over activities, and as a group they were sufficiently interested in the activity to go ahead on their own. It is especially significant that under authoritarian leadership, activity was much lower when the leader was out, but under democratic and laissez-faire leadership high activity involvement of the boys continued even though the adult leader left. With autocratic leadership, the boys did not know how to go ahead on their own and apparently did not want to go ahead, in any case.

Some of the more important conclusions reached by Lippitt and White other than those that may be inferred from the previous paragraphs are as follows:

> The adult-leader role was found to be a very strong determiner of the pattern of social interaction and emotional development of the group. Four clearcut types of social atmosphere emerged, in spite of great member differences in social expectation and reaction tendency due to previous adult-leader (parent, teacher) relationships.
>
> It was clear that previous group history (i.e., preceding social climates) had an important effect in determining the social perception of leader behavior and reaction to it by club members. A club which had passively accepted an authoritarian leader in the beginning of its club history, for example, was much more frustrated and resistive to a second authoritarian leader after it had experienced a democratic leader than a club without such a history. There seem to be some suggestive implications here for educational practice. (Lippitt & White, 1958, pp. 510-511)[2]

Though this study of leadership is one of the best from the standpoint of controlled experimentation, the authoritarian leadership was quite harsh and atypical of teacher leadership. One would not expect to find classrooms managed exclusively in an authoritarian or laissez-faire manner, as described in this experiment, except perhaps by beginning teachers or by experienced teachers in unusual situations.

Dominative and Integrative Leadership

Anderson (1943) measured three types of teacher-dominative and teacher-integrative behavior in two classrooms. After computing "mental health quotient" for the two classrooms, he found that domination by the teacher was accompanied by evidence of conflict between the teacher and pupils and tended to produce a low mental health quotient. Integrative behavior, on the other hand, was accompanied by evidence of teacher and pupils working together and produced a good mental health situation. Short examples of both dominative and integrative teacher behavior are now given to make the meaning of these terms clear:

DOMINATION WITH EVIDENCE OF CONFLICT

1. Teacher arbitrarily prescribes some activity: "Don't do it that way. I'll tell you what to do."
2. Teacher answers "No" when pupil asks if he can do something.
3. Teacher tells a child to go to another part of the room.
4. Teacher postpones something without giving any reason or setting a future date: "We can't do that now."
5. Teacher uses disapproval, blame, shame, obstruction, or interruption to secure different behavior from a pupil.

[2]*Ibid.*

6. Teacher uses warning, threats, conditional promises: "If you can't do what you're supposed to do, you'll have to go out in the hall."

7. Teacher calls to attention: "Jimmy, face this way, won't you?"

8. Teacher deprives children of specific materials, activities, rights, or privileges, sometimes practices corporal punishment, sending a pupil out of the room, keeping him after school, and sending him to the principal's office.

INTEGRATION WITH EVIDENCE OF WORKING TOGETHER

1. Teacher helps student to define, redefine, or make progress with the problem. The problem must have been stated and accepted by the pupil.

2. Teacher agrees with, approves of, or accepts the student's contribution. This is a response to spontaneous of self-initiated behavior; approval of the pupil's selection is given when several answers or new answers are possible.

3. Teacher extends invitation to go ahead in response to the pupil's wish, suggestion, or expression of need.

4. Teacher asks questions regarding the student's expressed interest or activity.

5. Teacher comments on such interest or activity.

6. Teacher accepts the responsibility for action by a child that is inconvenient, unjust, or unfair to another child; he also admits his own ignorance or incapacity. (Anderson, 1943, pp. 465-468)

The effects of different teacher leadership behavior on different types of students also have been determined. In a study of a group of women teachers, Heil and Washburne (1962) identified three teacher styles: Type A, turbulent, impulsive, and variable; Type B, self-controlling, orderly, and work-oriented; and Type C, fearful, anxious, and unsure of herself. The greatest difference was between Types B and C. The Type B teacher was warm and empathic with others; in contrast with Type C, she was not so fearful about how others felt toward her. The Type B teacher was self-severe; she set standards for herself and her pupils and then saw that they achieved these standards. The Type C teacher was lower in organizing and leading others, either directly or indirectly, and lower in social interests, but much higher in hostility and aggression.

Students gained most under Type B teachers, least under Type C, with Type A falling in between. Type B teachers were especially successful with children who seemed unsure of themselves. Type A teachers—turbulent, impulsive, and variable—obtained different results with different kinds of children. Uncertain children achieved low with Type A teachers; however, the children as a total group gained well in the subjects in which these teachers were interested. Type C teachers were not successful with any children.

What relationships can be predicted between type of teacher and pupils' feelings toward self and authority? Teacher Type B, goal-setting and work-oriented, was particularly effective with negative and hostile children. Toward the end of the school year, these children demonstrated more positive feelings toward authority, and their anxiety lessened. Apparently, the more hostile children developed better in an orderly, work-oriented environment than in a permissive environment. (It should be added that this last conclusion has not always been reached in other studies.)

Finally, the different types of teacher were reflected in the children's feelings toward one another. Children under Type B teachers became markedly more friendly toward each other than did children under either of the other two types of teachers. Apparently, the structuring and orderly tendencies of the Type B teacher developed a greater sense of security on the part of the children.

Comparison of Leadership Behavior and Outcomes

How do the various aspects of teacher leadership discussed throughout this chapter actually affect outcomes of learning? We may now relate teacher behavior to student behavior. Table 8.4 shows three dimensions of teacher leadership behavior — warmth, planning and execution of classroom behavior, and approach to student behavior and subject matter. As is often the case when considering psychological topics, we see teacher behaviors on a continuum, rather than as discontinuous and clearly delimited types. Thus the dimension of warmth extends from sentimental and personal through warm and understanding to aloof and egocentric. The planning and execution of classroom behavior extends from unplanned and slipshod through responsible to dominative. The approach of the teacher extends from impulsive and turbulent through stimulating to dull and routine.

It is not surprising to find that teachers characterized by behavior toward the middle of the continuum are most successful in securing high subject-matter achievement. The main reason is that they seem to be capable of selecting procedures in terms of objectives and student characteristics. Teachers characterized by the dominative type patterns secure reasonably adequate achievement in the outcomes emphasized by the teacher, except with rebellious students. In any case, when the dominative teacher remains aloof and uses power and coercion indiscriminately, this behavior in itself increases rebelliousness on the part of students. Unplanned, slipshod behavior produces inconsistent achievement, varying with the interests and abilities of the students. Insecure students and those of low ability should not be expected to accomplish much with teachers who show this behavior.

Emotional security is highest with warm, understanding teachers who are also businesslike. They are capable of maintaining a balance of direction and freedom in varied activities. On the other hand, the teacher who remains aloof from the students but who is also dominative produces low emotional security. Similarly, the sentimental, impulsive teacher, by focusing on some children and ignoring others, may produce low emotional security for most children but provide an adequate emotional outlet for those who receive his attention and who identify with him. Children rejected at home but accepted wholeheartedly and impulsively by the teacher might even find an emotional haven in the classroom with this type of teacher.

The generalizations just made were preceded by the statement that the behavior patterns are not pure types: actually, any teacher is likely

Table 8.4. Comparisons of Teacher Leadership Behavior and Learning Outcomes

Teacher Behavior	*Warmth*		
	Sentimental Personal identification with students	Warm, understanding, self-controlling Listens attentively Accepts feelings Accepts students' ideas Observes students' reactions skillfully Asks questions Praises and encourages	Aloof, egocentric Fearful, anxious
	Planning and Execution of Classroom Behavior		
	Unplanned, slipshod	Responsible, business-like Systematic Flexible Integrative Orderly, work-oriented Explains things clearly Rewards fairly Explains reasons for criticism	Dominative Prescribes arbitrarily Uses power and coercion indiscriminately Asks for more than students can do Uses nonconstructive criticism
	Approach to Student Behavior and Subject Matter		
	Impulsive, turbulent, variable	Stimulating, imaginative, surgent	Dull, routine
	Related Instructional Procedures		
	May handle one type reasonably well; perhaps independent study best	Effective with group discussion, lectures, recitation, and independent activities	May handle one type well; perhaps lecturing best
Student Behavior	*Related Subject-Matter Achievement of Students*		
	Inconsistent, varying with interest and ability of the students; insecure students do not learn well	High and consistent, when procedures are selected in terms of objectives and student characteristics	May be high in outcomes emphasized by the teacher; rebellious students do not learn well
	Related Emotional Security		
	Low for already unhappy children; might be high for a child who identifies with the teacher	High, when balance of direction and freedom is maintained in various activities	Low for most children

merely to *tend* to be toward one or the other pole on any dimension. Also, you will recall that, as Flanders and Gage both indicated, we are at the beginning of an era when more specific teacher behaviors will be related more directly to explicit student behaviors.

8.5. Think of two clubs or organizations (including a church, if that is applicable to you) of which you are a member. Can the leaders of each be characterized as more or less authoritarian, democratic, or laissez-faire? Compare the two organizations with respect to the incidence of behaviors listed in Fig. 8.3.

8.6. Compare Anderson's concept of integrative leadership with Flanders' indirect teacher behaviors.

8.7. Think of the teacher of a class in which nearly all the students seemed interested and achieved well. Go back to Table 8.4 and check the behaviors that were characteristic of this teacher and class.

STAFF INTERACTIONS AND LEADERSHIP IN INSTRUCTIONAL TEAMS

Instructional teams began to replace independent classroom teachers during the late 1950s; this trend accelerated during the 1960s and into the 1970s. The multiunit elementary school described in Chapter 7 is an instructional unit with differentiated staffing that was shown to incorporate the best practices of team teaching and also other practices that are essential for making a system of individually guided education effective for all children. In considering staff interactions in such a school, some research conducted in self-contained classes obviously is not directly relevant, because it does not relate to teams, or units, that involve differentiated staffing. Relevant research has been done recently, however. Its results are important because when a lead teacher, two or three staff teachers, a resident or first-year teacher, a teaching intern, and one or more aides work with a larger group of children, interactions among the staff become as important as interactions among the students. When one teacher is not completely responsible for a certain group of children, leadership is shared.

Some of this more recent research was done by Pellegrin (1969), who made the first report of a longitudinal study dealing with staff relationships in multiunit elementary schools. He studied three multiunit schools and three control schools in three different school districts. (The three control schools were primarily self-contained; however, the one reported on later in this section also had two teams.) Information was obtained from school personnel through structured interviews and a questionnaire. The first study concentrated on interdependence relationships among the instructional staff and the building principal; specialization of labor among the staff; authority, decision-making processes, and influence; the operational goals of the instructional staff; and job satisfaction and environmental climate.

Interdependence Relationships

Interdependence relationships, which refer to work-related patterns of interactions among people, are concerned with the particular interactions that affect people's abilities to get work done. According to Pellegrin (1969), a high rate of interaction, or dependence relations, facilitates the work efforts of a group. In order to identify two levels of interdependence relations in the multiunit schools and the control schools, lead teachers and staff teachers were asked:

1. List the names of those persons both within and outside your school (other than students) on whom you depend *most heavily* in order to perform your job most effectively.
2. Who are the persons listed above, if any, whose job is so closely related to yours that you believe the two jobs *must* be performed collaboratively in order for either of you to perform his work effectively?

Responses to these questions provided the raw information for this section of the results of the study. Figure 8.6 shows the interdependence relationships in a multiunit school of five units. A dotted line indicates a dependent relationship but not an essential one (question 1), whereas a solid line indicates an essential relationship (question 2). It may be seen that the staff of the five units of the school constituted a cluster of interdependence relationships. Thus, the members of a unit depended heavily on other members for the successful performance of their work. Also, the unit leaders were the focal points of the interactions within the units and also served as the connecting links between the staff teachers and the building principal. The principal, in turn, was perceived as having an essential relationship by three unit leaders and a dependent relationship by the other two. Most of the teachers expressed a dependent but not essential relationship with the principal. Interdependence relationships across units did not appear in the choices; that is, collaborative work effort was confined essentially within each unit.

Pellegrin found also that the interaction network within the units included instructional and clerical aides. Nominations of these aides by unit leaders and teachers were frequent, and the relationships were often considered essential ones. Aides were therefore important figures in the network of interdependence relationships within the units of these schools.

Figure 8.7 diagrams the interdependence relationships in a control school. The patterning of relationships was quite different from that of the multiunit school. The principal was the obvious focus of dependent relations, being mentioned by all but two of the 25 teachers, with 10 of these 23 relationships being essential. There were few interaction clusters among teachers, and essential relationships were the exception rather than the rule. The cluster of relationships at 10 o'clock on the chart is a team-teaching situation. Here the relationships of the staff teachers to the team leader are much like those in the units in the multiunit school. The three-teacher cluster at 6 o'clock involves a special un-

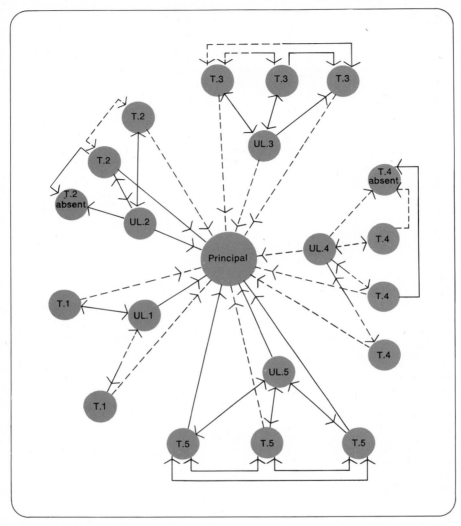

Fig. 8.6. Interdependence relationships in a multiunit elementary school. (Pellegrin, 1969, p. 28)

graded class for the educable mentally retarded to which all three teachers were assigned. With the exception of these two situations, interdependence relationships between teachers were few and rarely essential.

Pellegrin drew a few conclusions that extended beyond the two schools shown in the figures:

First, the pattern of relationships in the control school shown in [Fig. 8.7] is almost identical to that of the other control schools in our sample. Indeed, the pattern is very similar to that of other elementary schools we have studied elsewhere in the country. If anything, the control schools show more interdependence relationships than are usually encountered, owing largely to the presence of team teaching and other collaborative undertakings that are not found in the typical school characterized by the self-contained classroom. The fact is that the traditionally organized elementary school in the United States has a primitive division of labor and differentiation of functions in its professional staff. Grade

Fig. 8.7. Interdependence relationships in a self-contained elementary school. (Pellegrin, 1969, p. 29)

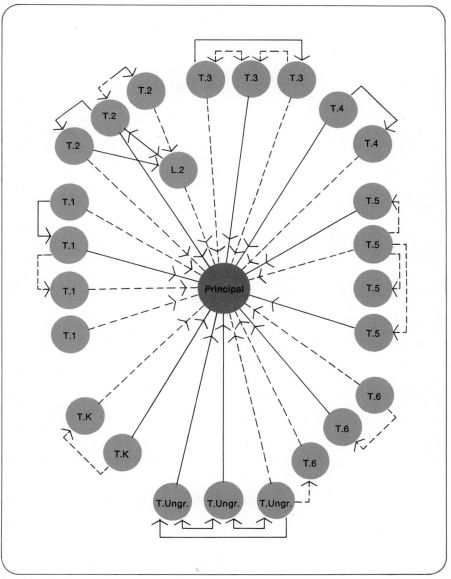

level is the only consistent basis for distinguishing among teachers. Emphasis is on the functions universally performed by teachers, not on the coordination of effort or any form of specialization. (Pellegrin, 1969, p. 6)

Specialization of Labor

Collaborative instruction, planning, and evaluation are called for by the multiunit system (as was pointed out in Chapter 7). In addition, the multiunit pattern calls for differentiation of roles between the lead teacher and the staff teachers and for more specialization of tasks by the staff teachers according to their knowledge, interests, and abilities. The specialization that Pellegrin observed in the multiunit schools may be summarized very briefly. A substantial amount of this specialization was conventional in nature; that is, teachers specialized by subject-matter areas. Also, in large units, with seven or more adults, there remained considerable specialization by grade level, and some teachers worked primarily with certain ability groupings or spent much of their time with small remedial classes. On the other hand, specialization in the multiunit schools was not confined to these conventional forms: new and often novel kinds of specialization were beginning to emerge in the units during their first year of operation. Three of these more novel forms are worth describing:

1. Some teachers devoted most of their time (75 percent) to working with individual pupils, whereas others spent about as much time working with small groups and class-size groups. A few teachers took special responsibilities for working with even larger groups than the usual class size, usually at the beginning or end of a unit of study.

2. In another kind of emerging specialization, some teachers served as advisers to their colleagues. The most obvious examples were teachers with special competence in some subject-matter field who served as the experts for their unit staffs. Even when specialized competence was lacking, a teacher was asked to, or volunteered to, take the responsibility for learning about developments relating to, for example, certain materials or media and for keeping his fellow teachers informed on the subject. Other teachers in the unit kept up with other topics.

3. Another type of specialization concerned special assignments not directly related to the instruction of children. In several units teachers were given special responsibilities for planning units of instruction. The logic of this procedure was extended in one instance to the entire instructional process; in one unit the teachers planned the different phases of the instructional units, with each staff teacher taking responsibility for one or more phases of the total process. According to Pellegrin, this type of division of labor offers ways to get jobs done that could not be worked out in a more permanent and fixed division of labor, such as in self-contained classrooms.

In connection with the specialized role of the unit leader, a staff teacher reported that the unit leader facilitated the work of the staff teacher by doing the following kinds of things.

Searching for, obtaining, and preparing new materials; scheduling the activities of the unit and arranging for necessary space and facilities; grouping students and making appropriate teaching assignments; handling reports; helping teachers keep up with new developments; discussing instructional problems of individual teachers; aiding teachers in their relationships with parents; keeping up teacher morale; and relieving teachers of routine chores. (Pellegrin, 1969, p. 12)

Authority, Decision-Making Processes, and Influence

Decision-making and influence are two important facets of leadership. Who makes the decisions is important in connection with instructional programs for individual children. Pellegrin investigated the roles the teachers played in the multiunit and self-contained control schools in various types of decisions. The decisions involved: (1) determining the teaching methods used in the classroom; (2) determining the scope and sequence of subject-matter content; (3) selecting the instructional materials other than textbooks; (4) deciding on pupil promotion; (5) scheduling daily classroom activities.

In the self-contained schools, each individual teacher made the decision, either in consultation with the principal or within limits prescribed by him. Few teachers were involved with one another in any group decision-making. The whole elementary school emerged as separate, relatively isolated classrooms, with the activities in each classroom being determined by the teacher, who, in turn, was monitored to a greater or lesser extent by the principal.

Pellegrin found that the multiunit organization showed marked differences from the self-contained classes in decision-making. Fewer teachers in the multiunit schools saw themselves as making decisions individually than was the case in the control schools. Most teachers indicated that decisions were shared with other teachers in a group decision-making process. Decisions were made by the unit leader and teachers, usually in a collaborative situation. Thus, decision-making was moving away from individual teachers and the building principal to the staff teachers and the unit leader. In all the multiunit schools the unit leader emerged as having influence on instructional matters at least equal to that of the building principal. Further, the principal's influence was less direct.

The Operational Goals of Teachers

Pellegrin identified which of the following operational goals teachers set for themselves: encouraging creativity among students; maintaining an orderly and quiet classroom; enriching the course of study or curriculum of the classroom; giving individual attention to students; experimenting with new teaching techniques; diagnosing learning problems of students; coordinating classroom activities with other parts of the school program; ensuring that students learn basic skills; solving personal problems of individual students; developing student ability in analytical reasoning and problem-solving; and developing the aesthetic potential of students.

Each teacher indicated the three that he considered most vital or important in his work as a teacher.

In the multiunit schools, the teachers ranked "giving individual attention to students" and "diagnosing learning problems of students" first and second in importance. In contrast, teachers in the control schools ranked "ensuring that students learn basic skills" first, followed by "developing student ability in analytical reasoning and problem-solving." In other words, according to the teachers, individually guided education and diagnosis of learning problems were the primary goals for teachers in a multiunit school.

Job Satisfaction and Environmental Climate

Pellegrin also assessed the satisfaction of the teachers with their work and work environment. In comparison with teachers in the control schools, those in the multiunit schools were more satisfied generally. In connection with seven aspects of their work, the multiunit teachers expressed significantly greater satisfaction. These seven aspects, together with the proportions responding "highly satisfied" in multiunit and control schools, are as follows: satisfaction with progress toward one's personal goals in present position, 26 percent and 15 percent; satisfaction with personal relationships with administrators and supervisors, 61 percent and 39 percent; opportunity to accept responsibility for one's own work or the work of others, 61 percent and 43 percent; seeing positive results from one's efforts, 36 percent and 15 percent; personal relationships with fellow teachers, 73 percent and 55 percent; satisfaction with present job in light of one's career expectations, 56 percent and 39 percent; the availability of pertinent instructional materials and aids, 60 percent and 27 percent. Also, 93 percent of the multiunit teachers and 60 percent of the control school teachers saw their school policies as encouraging freedom in experimenting with new teaching techniques; similarly, only 6 percent of the multiunit teachers but 32 percent of the control teachers viewed their school policies as encouraging close adherence to official course outlines and/or curriculum guides.

8.8. Is the lead teacher more or less dependent than the staff teacher on others for successful performance of his work? How do interdependence relationships differ in a multiunit school and a self-contained classroom setting?

8.9. Pellegrin noted that in multiunit schools some staff teachers took more responsibility than others for teaching certain subject matter; working with students in one-to-one, small, medium, and large-sized groups; serving as advisers to colleagues; and planning for instruction. Outline the responsibilities that you would prefer to assume in a unit, or team.

8.10. Many decisions about instruction must be made by the staff of a unit. Do you prefer to make decisions or to follow the suggestions of others? Which decisions about instruction do you feel capable of making?

8.11. Identify some characteristics and behaviors of teachers that would promote unit teaching. Which ones would destroy it?

STUDENT-STUDENT INTERACTIONS

Whether in a team or a self-contained classroom situation, most students communicate and otherwise interact with one another when given the opportunity. These student interactions may be guided to achieve useful educational objectives. A group may become cohesive and leadership abilities may be developed in many students. In turn, prosocial attitudes and values may be reinforced and social skills may be learned. On the other hand, students may organize along minority-majority patterns, socioeconomic status lines, and other undesirable bases when their interactions are not guided.

Group Cohesiveness

A cohesive group is one in which all of the members wish to stay in that group; in other words, the members are sufficiently attracted to one another or to the group activity so that they wish to stay in that particular classroom. Figure 8.8 shows a high school classroom group that is *not* highly cohesive. The circles at the far left represent a clique of four girls who gave mutual choices. When asked to list their five best friends in the class, these girls chose one another but, though given the opportunity, chose no one outside the group of four. In turn, only two girls from the entire class chose one of them as a friend and then as a fourth or fifth choice. The group at the lower right represents another clique of three girls and one boy (triangle) in which two of the three girls chose another boy outside the group. The two boys at the left of the diagram were isolated from the class; neither listed another member of the class as a friend, nor was either chosen as a friend by any member of the class. Thus, this class is characterized by some cliquism, a majority-minority pattern on an unidentified basis with resulting isolation, and one strong male leader, shown near the center of the diagram. It is not a cohesive group.

Personal attraction, performance of a task, and maintenance of group prestige were identified by Back (1951) as bases of cohesiveness. When cohesiveness was based on getting a job done, the members tried to get the job done quickly and efficiently, spending little time in conversation unrelated to the task. When cohesiveness was based on group prestige, the members did as little as possible to endanger their prestige status and acted cautiously, concentrating on their own actions and adjusting as best they could to the partners.

Along similar lines, a larger class was divided into groups of five people of the same sex (Lott & Lott, 1961). The group members who were congenial with one another were more accurate in perceiving the behavior appropriate to a task than were members of noncongenial groups. The cohesive groups communicated more effectively with one another and also conformed more readily to the dominant group opinion than did less cohesive groups. In a different situation, children were given different amounts of rewards in the presence of others (James & Lott, 1964). Those

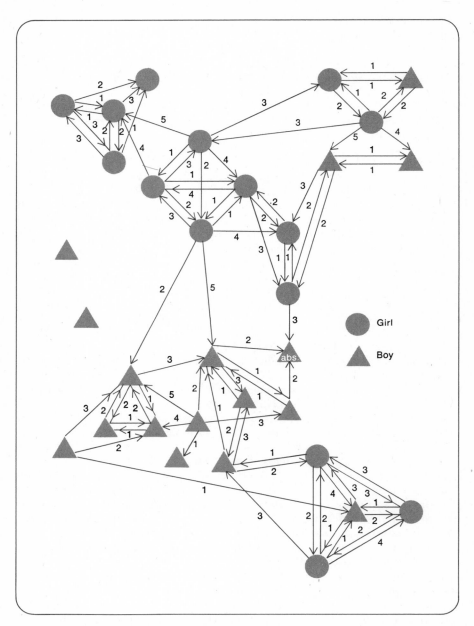

Fig. 8.8. Sociometric diagram of a high school classroom group. The numbers indicate rank order of choices. (Adapted from Klausmeier, 1958, p. 54)

who received the greatest rewards expressed more positive attitudes toward one another.

To establish cohesiveness within smaller groups, teachers may put students together who have an interest in the same activity or a common goal or put friends together in the same group. Also, the task or activity can be arranged so that the members experience success feelings or secure praise through doing the job well. Working with individuals and smaller groups within the class so that each member experiences a feeling of success is an excellent means of encouraging cohesiveness and securing high student achievement.

Student Leadership

Leadership characteristics emerge in children's groups in the primary grades. With teacher guidance, group activities can be arranged in which most children develop some leadership ability. This is in no way incompatible with the fact that all children should acquire excellent independent study habits and many individual skills.

One criterion of judging leadership is acceptance by others. Bonney and Powell (1953) reported that highly accepted young children showed more of the following behaviors than others: conforming more to classroom requirements and expectations, abiding more by the teacher's definition of appropriate behavior in the situation, smiling more frequently, engaging more frequently in some form of cooperative voluntary group activity, making more voluntary contributions to the group, and spending less time alone during free play or activity periods. Bretsch (1952) reported that highly accepted adolescents more frequently demonstrated ability to perform such social skills as dancing, carrying on a conversation, singing, playing cards, playing a musical instrument, swimming, playing tennis, and skating.

Cognitive abilities and other factors also are related to acceptance and leadership. For example, Hudgins, Smith, and Johnson (1962) found arithmetic achievement to be related to social acceptance. Gallagher (1958) reported that elementary school children of higher achievement and higher intelligence were somewhat more accepted than those of lower intelligence and achievement. However, living close together in the neighborhood was also an important factor; indeed, it was independent of level of intelligence and achievement.

Children and youth form groups on a variety of bases. Leadership in such groups is partly based on being known favorably and also on being helpful to the members. Children elect as class president a classmate who is well known and who the pupils think will be helpful to them. The high school football team elects a captain who they think will carry out his role efficiently and will be of mutual benefit to all. The prom queen elected in the high school or college is usually well known to both males and females, is attractive to them, and handles herself in such a manner that the majority feel that in this capacity she will be an excellent representative of the group. Leadership attitudes and skills developed in school transfer to life outside the school and are thus important objectives of schooling.

8.12. Do you agree that cohesiveness, rather than cliquism, is desired in the school? Are there any conditions under which a kind of pluralistic school, like pluralistic religious groupings in the community, is desirable?

8.13. Recall some of the cognitive and affective characteristics of students outlined in Chapter 6 and the characteristics of teachers outlined in Chapter 7 and in this chapter. Do you think it might be well to match teachers and students by computer, or by some other means, to get congenial persons together? Can you now describe your own characteristics and behaviors and relate them to the kind of students you would prefer to teach?

SUMMARY

Classroom interactions, teacher leadership, the instructional procedures used by the teacher, student achievement, and emotional security are all closely related. A balance is achieved between student-initiated and teacher-initiated talk as the teacher responds to student suggestions concerning activities, listens to students attentively, accepts student feelings, asks questions, and praises and encourages. A warm, effective environment can be maintained in an organizational or structural context characterized by a businesslike approach to instruction, orderliness, flexibility, and fairness. This kind of emotional climate and structure, combined with a variety of instructional methods, each to attain particular objectives, produces high student achievement, emotional security, and zest for learning.

Because of changing social conditions and increasing demands on the school from students, parents, and others, few teachers can independently be expert in several subject matters; plan and organize for instruction; use a variety of methods, media, and materials; develop effective home-school relations; and the like. Cooperative efforts and differentiated roles are essential. Also, time during school hours is needed for study and planning, and aides are needed to perform noninstructional tasks. The multiunit elementary school was developed to make possible all of these conditions, and, in fact, in these schools interdependence relations are increased, specialization of tasks is increasing, decision-making is shared, and teacher morale is high. Not all experienced teachers and principals can adjust to this kind of organization and environment; however, those who do find teaching more stimulating.

SUGGESTIONS FOR FURTHER READING

BEHRENDT, D. Away with tradition. *American education.* 1970, 6, pp. 18-22.

An education reporter for the *Milwaukee Journal* reports his observations and interviews regarding individually guided education in the multiunit school.

DEUTSCH, M. The effects of cooperation and competition upon group process. In Cartwright, D., & Zander, A., eds., *Group dynamics: Research and theory.* New York: Harper & Row, 1968, pp. 461-482.

This long chapter, which reports the testing of 34 hypotheses, has implications for teaching in teams and also for guiding interpersonal relationships of students.

GOLD, M. Power in the classroom. In Cartwright, D., & Zander, A., eds., *Group dynamics: Research and theory.* New York: Harper & Row, 1968, pp. 251-258.

The relative power positions of elementary school children, and the sources of their power, were identified tentatively through this research.

KLAUSMEIER, H. J., & O'HEARN, G. T., eds. *Research and development toward the improvement of education.* Madison, Wisc.: Dembar Educational Research Services, 1968, pp. 118-133.

Flanders describes his procedures for analyzing classroom interactions in one article. In the other, N. Gage describes how his research on microteaching contributes more generally to research on instructional methods.

MILLMAN, J., & JOHNSON, M. Relation of section variance to achievement gains in English and mathematics in grades 7 and 8. In Ripple, R. E., ed., *Readings in learning and human abilities.* New York: Harper & Row, 2nd ed., 1971.

The effects of grouping are examined in a research project. Suggestions are made concerning educational provisions for differences among students of the same grade level.

Part III Achieving Learning Outcomes

motivation is central to the learning of all outcomes. Eagerness for learning and high achievement can be expected when the teacher helps students to focus on the instructional program, set realistic goals, make progress toward their goals, and secure informative feedback and assistance in overcoming difficulties. Praise and other forms of reinforcement from the teacher are essential for some students and heighten motivation for most of them. As is the case with other learning phenomena, there are many differences in level of motivation among students, and individual guidance is needed.

One way of categorizing the outcomes of learning is: factual information and verbal knowledge, concepts and principles, problem-solving and creativity, psychomotor skills, attitudes and values, and personality integration. We now have enough knowledge so that principles applying to each of these sets of outcomes may be stated in terms of facilitating conditions internal to the learner. The practical applications of these principles are stated as parallel instructional guides external to the learner; the teacher may rearrange or modify these guides, according to the specific situation. The six sets of outcomes are all equally vital, regardless of the subject matter. A teacher, therefore, should not consider some of them to be more important than others.

The obvious objective for both students and teachers is long-term retention and use of what is learned in school. In this area also, principles and instructional guides have been formulated. The principles help in understanding the internal processes of retention and transfer; the related guides help in improving instructional practices.

Chapter 9 Motivation

The Nature of Human Motivation

human needs
Maslow's hierarchy of needs-motives
achievement-oriented activity
motive to achieve success
motive to avoid failure
exploration, manipulation, curiosity
goal-setting
overcoming the effects of failure
motivation and discipline

Instructional Guides

focus student attention
utilize the individual's need to achieve and other positive motives
help each student set and attain goals
provide informative feedback
provide real-life and symbolic models
provide for verbalization and discussion of prosocial values
use rewards and punishments as necessary
avoid the use of stressful procedures

A System of Individually Guided Motivation

entering behaviors and characteristics of students
objectives for each student
motivational program for each student
assessment procedures
feedback
procedures for development of prosocial behaviors
procedures for increasing independent reading

he school provides conditions that facilitate students' learning. They learn about the physical world, the social world, quantitative relations, language arts, foreign languages, the fine arts, and physical development. They acquire knowledge and skills connected with these and other curriculum areas. The school also takes some responsibility for the values students acquire. They must learn prosocial values; obviously, if they do not attend to learning activities and do not behave reasonably well, they will not learn subject matter. In other words, if the teacher has to spend much time on "discipline" problems arising from students' antisocial values, neither the teacher nor the students will achieve the main objectives of education. Because a certain amount of discipline is essential to instruction, motivation and discipline are integrally related. It follows, therefore, that the learning of prosocial values is central in motivation and that, in a reciprocal manner, motivation is central in the learning of both subject matter and prosocial values.

The nature of human motives and various forms of motivation are outlined in the first section of this chapter. Then, motivational principles and related instructional guides based on the theoretical and empirical information presented in the first section are identified and discussed. In the third section a system of individually guided motivation is outlined. Two projects involving procedures specifically developed to implement various motivational principles are described in some detail. The intention is to give the reader enough information so that he may learn to apply the principles to his own situation. In this chapter we discuss at some length these and other procedures developed and researched in recent years under the senior author's leadership. A detailed search of the current literature on motivation, including that in the *Encyclopedia of Educational Research* (Weiner, 1969) and the *Review of Educational Research* (Shaw, 1967), indicated that there is much theorizing about motivation; nevertheless, it appears that very little constructive development and testing of motivational procedures in school settings has been undertaken and reported, other than that described in this chapter.

THE NATURE OF HUMAN MOTIVATION

Literature, art, drama, music, religion—all reflect human motives. Literary, artistic, and philosophical thought often attempts to explain and interpret the "why" of life itself. At a less ambitious level, authors and artists portray the loves and hates of men and women, their striving for possessions and knowledge, their quest for love, security, peace—for all that we consider essential for happiness. These behaviors are intensely motivated, as we all know, but they are not well understood.

Some aspects of motivation, however, are quite well understood, and in this section we focus on them. That is, we are now concerned with the more restricted area of motivation in the schools, with human needs, interests, goal-setting, and the relationship of motivation and discipline as they all apply to school learning.

Human Needs and Interests

A motive is any condition within the organism that affects its readiness to initiate and continue any activity or sequence of activities. Thus, the experiencing of a need may serve as motive. Motivation is a more general term, applying either to the strength or duration of a motivational state (e.g., high motivation to study history) or to the regulation of other motives (e.g., the teacher motivated the students to attend to the situation). There is a tendency to classify motives as physiological and social or unlearned and learned. The tendency is also to refer to intrinsic and extrinsic motivation. These and related topics are considered in this section.

A Hierarchy of Needs-Motives

Physiological needs are inferred from physical states that indicate a lack of something. A person feels the need for food after not having eaten for a time, for liquid after not having drunk anything for a time, for warmth when the temperature goes below a certain level, for activity after rest, etc. Similarly, an individual desires or wishes to master things and ideas, to experience success, and to avoid failure. Also, the student sets a goal in consultation with the teacher and tries hard to attain it. Desires, wishes, and aspirations are also classified as needs-motives. Needs characteristically are experienced for a while, satisfied, and then experienced again. The duration or cycle of need-satisfaction-need varies greatly. The cycle for oxygen is very short; for food and water it is longer; and it may be much longer for success in business or a vocation.

Maslow (1943) sets forth a comprehensive theory of motivation that he intended to be useful in understanding the "why" of all human behavior and also the motivational states of individuals. He brought together many ideas that merit careful study by anyone who accepts the idea of human needs as being important in energizing and directing behavior. The six sets of needs Maslow listed are (1) physiological, (2) safety, (3) love and belonging, (4) esteem, (5) self-actualization, and (6) needs to know and understand.

1. *Physiological Needs.* Maslow listed as physiological needs only the major categories, e.g., oxygen, liquid, food, rest, and suggested that one could make an exceedingly long list, depending on the degree of specificity of description desired. The specific minerals and vitamins alone could comprise a very long list. He made two other important points related to the satisfaction of the physiological needs. First, an almost certain way of getting a distorted view of human nature and behavior is to make a person extremely and chronically hungry or thirsty. Extreme hunger or thirst dominates the individual's entire behavior and gives a very untrue picture of most of his higher motivations, including the social. Second, the individual's seeking to satisfy his social needs is far more critical in human motivation than is depriving him satisfaction of physical needs.

The physiological needs should be gratified, not deprived, so that the higher social needs and related goal-directed behaviors emerge.

2. *Safety Needs.* Safety needs in infants and children are demonstrated by their preference for some kind of routine or rhythm rather than disorder, their avoidance of various forms of perceived danger situations, and their withdrawal from strange and unfamiliar situations that elicit danger and terror reactions. In general, the safety need in children and adults is observed as an active and dominant mobilizer of the organism's resources in emergencies — war, disease, injury, natural catastrophes, and the like.

3. *Love and Belonging.* The love need is described as a desire or a hunger for affectionate relations with people in general and for a place in the group. The strength of this need is observed in the person who feels the absence of friends, wife or husband, children, or people more generally. This need is present and manifested in all mentally healthy human beings.

4. *Esteem.* The esteem need most clearly suggests seeking recognition as a worthwhile person. Satisfaction of the esteem need is accompanied by feelings of confidence, worth, strength, and usefulness. The thwarting of these needs produces feelings of inferiority, weakness, or helplessness. Coopersmith (1967) reported that a student's success in school is markedly affected by his sense of self-esteem.

5. *Self-Actualization.* The need for self-actualization is the need to be or to become the person one can be, that is, the tendency for the individual to become in actuality what he is potentially. Satisfaction of this need is expressed in various ways. One person becomes a homemaker, another an athlete, another a musician, another a teacher, and so on. The persons in whom these needs have been relatively well satisfied are the healthiest in our society.

6. *Needs To Know and Understand.* Maslow was not sure that the desires to know and to understand — cognitive needs — are as clearly established in all human beings as the others. Although curiosity, exploration, and the desire to acquire further knowledge can readily be observed, they are more evident in some persons than in others. Where the need is present and strong, it is accompanied by wanting to systematize, to organize, to analyze, and to look for relationships.

The serial order of the categories of needs is important, for they must normally be satisfied in the order given, that is, the physiological needs must be satisfied before there can be satisfaction of the safety needs; similarly, the safety needs must be met before the needs for love and belonging come into play. However, once the needs lower in the sequence are satisfied, the one higher up may energize and direct behavior. Maslow indicated how one need is more potent than another at any given time:

> These basic goals are related to each other, being arranged in a hierarchy of prepotency. This means that the most prepotent goal will monopolize consciousness and will tend of itself to organize the recruitment of the various capacities of the organism. The less prepotent needs are minimized, even forgotten or denied. But when a need is fairly well satisfied, the next prepotent ("higher") need

emerges, in turn to dominate the conscious life and to serve as the center of organization of behavior, since gratified needs are not active motivators.

Thus man is a perpetually wanting animal. Ordinarily the satisfaction of these wants is not altogether mutually exclusive, but only tends to be. The average member of our society is most often partially satisfied and partially unsatisfied in all of his wants. The hierarchy principle is usually empirically observed in terms of increasing percentages of non-satisfaction as we go up the hierarchy. Reversals of the average order of the hierarchy are sometimes observed. Also it has been observed that an individual may permanently lose the higher wants in the hierarchy under special conditions. There are not only ordinarily multiple motivations for usual behavior, but in addition many determinants other than motives. (Maslow, 1943, pp. 394-395)

Figure 9.1 visualizes the hierarchy of prepotency. The hierarchical aspect is shown by each successive need being built on the one below it. The prepotency idea suggests that at any given time the esteem needs, for example, might take precedence over the love and belonging needs or the safety needs. Similarly, if the lower needs in the hierarchy are temporarily satisfied, the self-actualization need would determine the goals of the individual.

These ideas have important implications for education. For example, the teacher wants the pupils to acquire certain knowledge, but a particular child's needs for love or esteem may not be satisfied. The child's goals

Fig. 9.1. Hierarchy and prepotency of needs. (Based on Maslow, 1943, pp. 370-396)

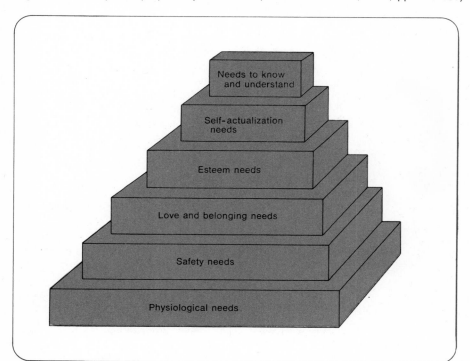

to satisfy these needs take precedence in energizing and directing his behavior. To give a more specific example, a disadvantaged child may have a much stronger need for love and belonging than a need to know and understand; therefore he directs his energy toward satisfaction of these needs rather than toward the learning task.

Achievement-Oriented Activity

All of the six sets of needs proposed by Maslow might possibly be related to a need to master some aspect of the physical or social environment, including self and self-other interactions. However, Atkinson (1965) has developed an outline for a theory of achievement-oriented activity which is more directly related to the need to achieve success and the need to avoid failure in learning tasks in school settings.

Atkinson proposed that the tendency to achieve success is a learned motivational disposition, not unlike Maslow's need for self-actualization and the desires to know and understand. The strength of this disposition is related to the individual's interest in more specific tasks and his performances related to them. This tendency to achieve success varies markedly among individuals and also in the same individual from situation to situation. The tendency to achieve success, T_s, in connection with any task or activity is a function of three variables: the motive to achieve success, M_s; the probability that performance of the task will be followed by success, P_s; and the relative attractiveness of achieving success, referred to as the incentive value of success, I_s. In other words, T_s is a function of $M_s \times P_s \times I_s$. The last three terms require further clarification.

1. Motive To Achieve Success. Individuals vary in the motive to achieve success and also in the corollary motive to avoid failure. Thus, two individuals may perceive the same difficulty level in a certain task; one, however, approaches the task with enthusiasm and vigor in order to experience possible success, whereas the other evades it in order to avoid possible failure. In the second individual the need to avoid failure is stronger than the need to experience success in the particular task. A strong need to avoid failure appears to be learned by experiencing repeated failures and by setting criteria or expectancies above what one really thinks he can accomplish. Similarly, the motive to attempt tasks that present the possibility of success or failure is learned by previous success experiences and by not setting criteria that are too high for success to be possible.

Being high or low on the motive for success, or need to achieve, is related to performance on a problem-solving task (French & Thomas, 1958). Figure 9.2 shows that among 47 subjects with high-achievement motivation scores, 25 solved a problem and 22 did not. On the other hand, there were only 14 solvers and 31 nonsolvers among 45 subjects in the low-motivation group. This result is similar to other reports of differences in achievement between students who score high or low on tests of achievement motivation.

2. Probability of Success. The tendency to achieve success when motivation for success is strong is greatest when the probability of success on a task is neither very high nor very low, that is, when the task is neither

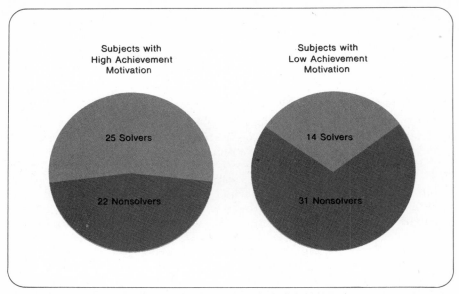

Fig. 9.2. Number of problem-solvers in high- and low-achievement motivation groups. (Adapted from French & Thomas, 1958, p. 46)

Fig. 9.3. Inverse relationship between probability of success and incentive value of success. (Litwin, 1958)

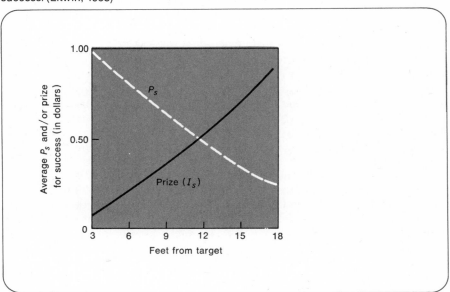

too easy not too difficult. As noted above, the tendency to achieve success varies among individuals. It varies most when the task is at an intermediate difficulty level. When the task is too easy, neither the individual with a high motive to achieve nor the one with a low motive to achieve experiences failure. Similarly, when the task is very hard and judged impossible to accomplish, neither the high-motive nor the low-motive individual perceives the possibility of being *able* to accomplish it; he thus does not perceive the possibility of either a success or failure experience.

3. Incentive Value of Success. Atkinson designated the relative attractiveness of success on a particular task as the incentive value of success. The incentive value or attractiveness of success is greater as the task becomes more difficult. In a simple but graphic experiment, Litwin (1958) asked one group of students to indicate how many times out of 10 they thought they could hit a target at distances of 3 to 18 feet from the target. Another group was asked to recommend a monetary prize for hitting the target at various distances. Figure 9.3 shows the results: As the probability of success decreased with increasing distance from the target, the prize recommended, or incentive value, increased. One presumes a similar situation in school tasks. For example, if a student can easily learn to spell 5 words correctly, learning to spell 10 correctly is likely to have more incentive value for him than learning to spell 6 correctly. Similarly, on a 50-item test, if a student can get 35 correct with only modest effort, it is presumed that he will find more incentive value in trying to get 45 correct than 40.

Atkinson described his approach to the study of motivation as follows:

> We study achievement-oriented behavior today assuming that all individuals have acquired a motive to achieve (M_s) and a motive to avoid failure (M_{af}). That is to say, all persons have some capacity for interest in achievement and some capacity for anxiety about failure. Both are expressed in any situation when it is apparent to the individual that his performance will be evaluated in reference to some standard. One of these motives produces a tendency to undertake the activity; the other produces a tendency to avoid undertaking the activity. There is what we traditionally call an approach-avoidance conflict. It is suggested by the conceptual scheme that we might better begin to think of this as a conflict between an *excitatory* tendency and an *inhibitory* tendency. It is assumed that the two opposed tendencies combine additively and yield a resultant achievement-oriented tendency which is either approach (excitatory) or avoidant (inhibitory) in character and of a certain strength depending upon the relative strength of motive to achieve success and motive to avoid failure in the individual. (Atkinson, 1965, pp. 34-35)

It is important to note that nothing that has been said should be assumed to imply that the strength of the tendency to achieve success cannot be modified in school children. On the contrary, anything that is done to modify a student's motive to achieve success or to modify the probability of his achieving success or to increase or decrease the incentive value — or any combination of these — will also increase or decrease the tendency of the individual to achieve success in connection with learning tasks.

Exploration, Manipulation, and Curiosity

The human being has other needs that are, in some respects, related to Maslow's desires to know and understand and Atkinson's need to achieve. Behavior described in such terms as *exploration, manipulation*, and *curiosity* belongs to a general class of behavior called *attention* (Dember & Earl, 1957). Attention is aroused by presenting stimuli different from the organism's expectations and is satiated by repeatedly presenting these originally discrepant or novel stimuli.

Even lower-form animals, when their physiological needs are satisfied, explore their environments and manipulate objects. In the presence of visual stimuli and in the absence of any reinforcement, monkeys actively explored their environment (Butler & Harlow, 1954). Rather than searching for food, the monkeys engaged in searching behavior of a kind similar to that caused by curiosity in human beings. Another manifestation of curiosity became apparent when the monkeys learned to make responses, not to secure food, water, or other rewards associated with physiological need deprivation, but to get the reward of being allowed to look briefly out of a window in their otherwise opaque cages (Butler, 1953, 1954, 1957). Evidence of this type contradicts the idea of motivation resulting primarily from the deprivation of food, water, and other things associated with biological needs. Monkeys do not learn best under extreme drive conditions (Harlow, 1953).

The relationship between curiosity and exploration is close. Maw and Maw (1965) reported years of research on curiosity in school children. They characterized a child as exhibiting curiosity to the extent that he (1) reacts positively to new, strange, incongruous, or mysterious elements in his environment by moving toward them, by exploring them, or by manipulating them; (2) exhibits a need or desire to know more about himself and his environment; (3) scans his surroundings, seeking new experiences; and (4) persists in examining and exploring. Marked differences in curiosity were found among boys and girls of the same age.

Maw and Maw (1964) indicated that curiosity is essential for learning, creativity, and mental health. The most important implication of the recent attention to curiosity is that much needs to be done to ascertain those events and objects about which pupils *are* most curious. This task may not be as simple as it appears at first glance. Consider the frustrated parent who spends many hours choosing and quite a lot of money buying a fascinating toy for his child, only to find that the child quickly discards the toy and instead persists obstinately in playing with the cardboard carton it came in.

Another implication of the recent attention to curiosity is that there is obviously a need to learn more about the classroom materials and activities and teacher practices which foster or inhibit curiosity and related creative activities. The work of Torrance (1965) and others, as described in Chapter 12, has been addressed to this problem.

Goal-Setting

Goal-setting in the classroom assumes that individuals are given the opportunity to set varying levels of performance on identical tasks or to complete tasks in varying lengths of time or to work at nonidentical tasks. Much goal-setting is done informally by students in connection with classroom assignments and activities. Thus, some students attend carefully to the assignment given by the teacher or participate in student-teacher discussion and subsequently decide when and what they will do and how well they will do it. Goal-setting can also be made more explicit and formal. In this case, the teacher and students discuss what each student will accomplish, how well, and by what time. Goal-setting capitalizes on the student's motive to achieve success. The teacher can markedly modify the probability that a student will achieve success in terms of grading and other teacher-imposed incentive values, so that more students set and *attain* goals in connection with school subject matters and prosocial behaviors. In the next pages the nature of goals and goal-setting is described.

Remote, Intermediate, and Immediate Goals. Remote, intermediate, and immediate goals are related to the developmental level of the individual. For a first-grade child, a remote goal might be something he wishes to achieve four weeks in the future, an intermediate goal would be achieved within a week, and an immediate goal within a few minutes or an hour. The college freshman sets a remote goal of becoming a successful teacher four or five years hence, an intermediate goal of completing the required courses in the freshman year, and an immediate goal of reading and understanding a chapter in a book in a two-hour period of study.

Setting Immediate Goals

Level of aspiration is the term generally used for an immediate goal. This term thus describes the level of performance in a familiar task that an individual tries for or thinks he can accomplish on the next performance. Table 9.1 shows the process of goal-setting and some of the terminology connected with level of aspiration. Imagine that Bill, Mary, George, and Susan are in a typing class. Their last performances are shown as 20, 30, 35, and 40 words per minute on a five-minute test. The teacher asks them to indicate how many words per minute they expect to type in a five-minute test two days later. They set their levels of aspiration or imme-

Table 9.1. Goal-Setting Terminology

	Last performance	Level of aspiration or goal	Goal discrepancy	Actual performance	Attainment discrepancy	Feelings of success or failure
Bill	20	40	+20	18	−22	Failure
Mary	30	33	+ 3	30	− 3	Failure
George	35	33	− 2	38	+ 5	Success
Susan	40	43	+ 3	45	+ 2	Success

diate goals as follows: Bill, 40, Mary, 33, George, 33, and Susan, 43. The difference between the last performance and the level of aspiration now set, *goal discrepancy*, can be positive or negative. Bill shows a positive goal discrepancy of 20 and George a negative goal discrepancy of 2. These students continue their class work and two days later take another test. Bill now achieves a speed of 18; Mary, 30; George, 38; and Susan, 45. The attainment discrepancy is again either negative or positive. Bill shows a negative attainment discrepancy of 22 and Mary of 3; George and Susan show positive attainment discrepancies of 5 and 2. If these students had all been ego-involved — if they had actually set the goals and tried to attain them — Bill and Mary would have experienced failure feelings.

In an actual experiment, fourth-, fifth-, and sixth-grade children were arranged in three experimental groups based on their previous success and failure experiences in school (Sears, 1940). The three groups were designated as success, failure, and differential. Children in the success group had shown both subjective and objective evidence of success in all academic subjects, including reading and mathematics; those in the failure group had the opposite experience; and the differential group had experienced success in reading but failure in mathematics. Each child was first given a familiar task in reading and in mathematics. Then the child's level of aspiration was ascertained by asking him to indicate how many seconds he would need to complete a *new* task in reading or mathematics.

Figure 9.4 compares the academically successful, failure, and differential or control groups in terms of goal-discrepancy scores — the difference between actual performance on the first trial and the level of aspiration set for the next trial. Most children in the success group set levels of aspiration in the reading task slightly above their past performances; however, the failure group set them erratically — three set goals below previous achievement and seven set goals above their previous achievement. The differential group was more like the success group in dispersion on the reading task. The pattern in mathematics showed the success group less widely dispersed than the failure group and the differential group in between. The success group set the most realistic goals in both tasks. After this initial work, failure and success feelings were induced experimentally in the three groups. Induced feelings of success in all three groups led to more realistic goal-setting; that is, the level of aspiration was set more in line with the past performance. Induced feelings of failure produced greater variability in subsequent goal-setting.

Byers (1958) replicated the previous experiment in an actual teaching situation in classes in U.S. history, except that there was no attempt to induce feelings of success or failure experimentally. The students were divided into two groups. One had experienced previous academic success, and the other had experienced lack of success as indicated by grade-point average. These students then set six consecutive goals throughout the academic year. The students with a record of previous academic success achieved higher and set goals more realistically (usually above previous performance), whereas those with previous failures achieved lower and set goals less realistically — sometimes above previous performance and sometimes below. The actual experience of success and failure in attaining

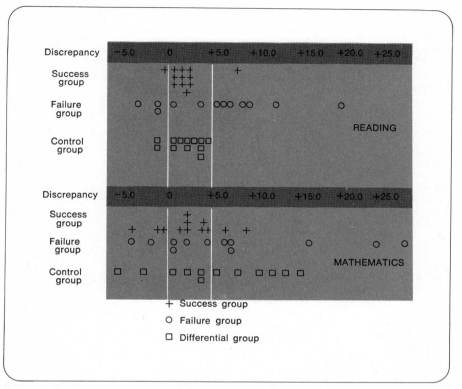

Fig. 9.4. Discrepancy scores of groups varying in past experience of success or failure. (Adapted from Sears, 1940, p. 511)

goals had similar effects on later goal-setting, as did the induced feelings of failure and success reported earlier. However, more eleventh-grade students than younger children who had experienced success tended to set the next goal lower.

Factors Affecting Goal-Setting

Present success and expectation of further success have a desirable effect on motivation, achievement, and subsequent goal-setting; failure has a definitely undesirable effect. Atkinson (1965) described the effects of success and failure on subsequent goal-setting for individuals in whom the achievement motivation is dominant. The solid curve in Fig. 9.5 indicates the tendency to achieve as the individual approaches a task with only his past experience influencing the strength of his expectancy of success on a task at various difficulty levels. The achievement-oriented individual, according to the theory, will choose to undertake the task when the probability of achieving success is .50. If he does so and succeeds, the change in expectancy of success on a next task will produce a change in motivation,

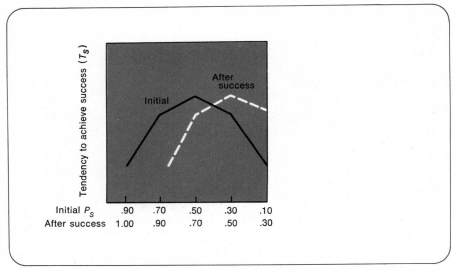

Fig. 9.5. Change in level of aspiration following success. (Atkinson, 1965, p. 49)

or in the goal set, as shown by the broken curve. What was initially considered of intermediate difficulty, at the .50 level, is now considered relatively easy, at the .70 level. That is, after success a higher goal will be set, with the 50-50 probability of achieving success.

The change in motivation, lowered goal, predicted when the individual experiences failure is shown in Fig. 9.6. After failure, the individual sets his goal lower in order to have an equal probability, 50-50, of achieving success. What was initially considered relatively easy, at the .70 level, is now considered of intermediate difficulty, at the .50 level. Atkinson concluded further that the effects of both success and failure generalize to other goal-setting activities.

Other factors affecting goal-setting include the nature of the task and various personality variables not directly associated with the task. Holmes (1959) analyzed 59 studies dealing with level of aspiration and drew five conclusions of importance to education: (1) A task can be so difficult that no student can realistically set a goal or hope to achieve success on it; also, a task can be so easy and accomplished with so little effort that no feeling of success is experienced. (2) Children who are realistic and confident and have comfortable feelings toward themselves and school set goals more realistically, and they strive more persistently to achieve those goals than do students with the opposite traits. (3) Low goal-setting is often accompanied by high need to avoid failure; some individuals protect their self-esteem by setting goals low enough to be achieved easily. (4) Insecure individuals experience a feeling of success by publicly setting high goals which they know they cannot attain; approval is generally given for "hitching to a star," even though one never rises from the smog. (5) The group influences goal-setting of members; after the goals of the entire group are known, there is a tendency for those with higher goals to lower them somewhat and those with lower goals to raise them somewhat.

Overcoming the Effects of Failure

Children of preschool age were placed in two experimental situations for 15 and 8 minutes and told to perform an attractive task involving a puzzle box; the task, however, was so difficult that they could not accomplish it readily, if at all, even with persistent effort (Keister & Updegraff, 1937). The experiment was arranged to induce feelings of failure. The responses of the children in the two situations showed considerable variation, and 15 of them demonstrated exceedingly immature behavior. In the second part of the experiment, 12 of those of immature behavior participated in a training program designed to ascertain the extent and the means by which the undesirable effects of failure could be overcome. In this experimental program, four similar but not identical attractive tasks were arranged according to level of difficulty, from quite easy to difficult but solvable with persistent effort. During the reeducation period the experimenter started with the easiest task, helped each child at times, encouraged him to continue at times, and arranged the situation so that the child could see his progress and was aware of his success with the

Fig. 9.6. Change in level of aspiration following failure. (Atkinson, 1965, p. 50)

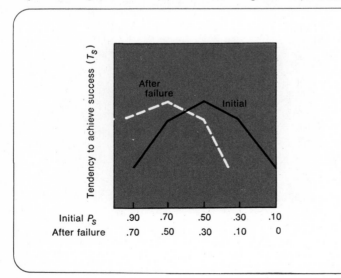

preceding task. Figure 9.7 shows the responses of the group on a task similar to the original difficult task, both before and after the experimental training. Marked improvement occurred in three kinds of behavior: attempting to solve the problem alone, amount of trying before asking another to solve it, and interest in the task. The training did not have much effect on the children's asking for help; however, on all other behavior the small differences show that the training did produce more desirable responses.

This analysis of goal-setting indicates that there are several ways a teacher may encourage the failing or low-achieving student to be persistent in his efforts. One way is to build the student's self-confidence so that he feels secure in striving toward a particular goal. Someone who is not afraid of being hurt by failure will be more willing to renew his efforts. A teacher should deliberately arrange pleasant learning situations in which the student feels successful. In addition to fostering self-confidence, this procedure will help him set realistic goals. Also, the student should be told when he makes progress, even if the amount of improvement seems small and insignificant to the teacher. These procedures are discussed in more detail in the last section of this chapter.

Fig. 9.7. Responses of trained group on puzzle-box test before and after training. (Keister & Updegraff, 1937, p. 246. By permission of the authors and the Society for Research in Child Development, Inc. Copyright 1937 by the Society for Research in Child Development, Inc.)

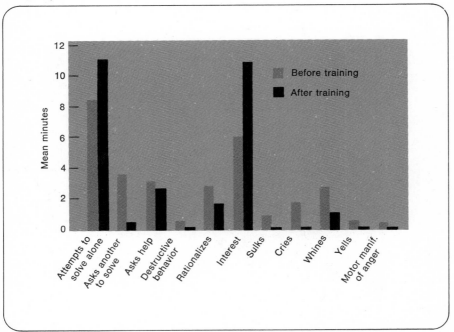

Motivation and Discipline

Sheviakov and Redl (1944) wrote one of the most widely studied treatises on discipline ever published in this country. Later it was revised by Sybil Richardson (1956). They describe the kind of discipline that they want and that, hopefully, most school people want as follows:

1. We want discipline which recognizes the *inherent dignity and rights* of every human being, rather than discipline attained through humiliation of the undisciplined.
2. We want discipline based on devotion to *humanitarian principles and ideals*. In a democratic society, loyalty to the principles of freedom, justice and equality for all rather than discipline based on a narrower, more egotistic affiliation with "*my* group" is essential.
3. We want *self-direction, self-discipline*, rather than discipline based upon unquestioning obedience to a leader.
4. We want discipline based on *understanding* of the goal in view rather than discipline based on taking someone else's word for specific appropriate behaviors. (Sheviakov & Redl, 1956, pp. 7-8)

This statement implies that students must learn values, described by such terms as freedom, justice, and equality, and also behaviors leading to and arising from self-direction and self-discipline. We assume that these values and behaviors must be learned, but we also assume that not all students want to learn them. Therefore, it is essential to develop motivational procedures in connection with these learnings. Further, the self-direction and self-discipline are to be based on understanding. This implies discussion and study, rather than blind conformity to teacher edicts or adult codes.

We accept these viewpoints and have made them central in the principles of motivation discussed in the next section and also in the treatment of the development of prosocial values in the last section of the chapter. The principles of motivation are as relevant to classroom discipline as they are to usual subject matter. Classroom discipline cannot be separated from the motivational procedures employed or from the rest of the school curriculum.

9.1. According to Maslow, one satisfies his safety needs before those involving love and belonging or the desire to know. There are times, however, when one risks his life to save a friend or to climb a mountain. Is Maslow's hierarchy incorrect in such cases?

9.2. What percentage of the time during a day do you spend in satisfying each need-motive, as listed by Maslow? Are the motives for all your activities easily classified according to Maslow's hierarchy?

9.3. Try to recall a task or activity that you have engaged in with vigor and another that you considered as possibly attractive but avoided. Do the need to achieve success and the corollary need to avoid failure explain your behavior in any way? Might some students' lack of commitment to certain assignments reflect a need to avoid failure?

9.4. How might manipulation and curiosity be factors in satisfying each of the needs-motives in the Maslow hierarchy?

9.5. Can you identify a remote, intermediate, and immediate goal related to your taking this course? How have teachers affected your goals?

9.6. Many persons say that learning subject matter is intrinsically motivating and that not learning it results in disinterest and avoidance. Can you explain this in terms of Maslow's hierarchy or Atkinson's tendency to achieve success?

9.7. Reflect briefly on the classroom behavior of many boys in junior high school: often they are rowdy and poorly disciplined (flying paper airplanes, pinching girls and pulling their hair, etc.). The same boys, when seen later as high school seniors or in college, listen attentively in class, are cooperative, and are attractive to girls. How do you account for this change in terms of motivation and self-discipline?

PRINCIPLES OF MOTIVATION

In this section a set of principles about motivation and learning based on research and theory and a corollary set of instructional guides are stated and discussed so that applications can be made to many settings. The principles here and in similar sections of later chapters are stated in a form that the individual reader may apply directly to his own study and learning. They may be thought of as internal conditions of the motivated individual. The instructional guides are statements designed to make more explicit the teacher's role. These guides may be thought of as external facilitative conditions. The principles and guides are offered as the best available hypotheses to be tested in school settings, rather than as prescriptions. The teacher might generate other principles and guides. Similarly, the principles may change as more research is done on motivation in school settings and as a more definitive theory of motivation in school settings emerges.

The principles listed here are related to the guides. The first four principles deal primarily with motivational concerns related to the learning of school subject matter—focusing attention, utilizing the need to achieve, goal-setting and goal attainment, and providing for informative feedback.

Principle	Instructional Guide
1. Attending to a learning task is essential for initiating a learning sequence.	1. Focus student attention on desired objectives.
2. Wishing to achieve control over elements of the environment and to experience success is essential to realistic goal-setting.	2. Utilize the individual's need to achieve and other positive motives.
3. Setting and attaining goals require learning tasks at an appropriate difficulty level; feelings of	3. Help each student set and attain goals related to the school's educational program.

Principle	Instructional Guide
continued	*continued*

success on current learning tasks heighten motivation for subsequent tasks; feelings of failure lower motivation for subsequent tasks.

4. Acquiring information concerning correct or appropriate behaviors and correcting errors are associated with better performance on and more favorable attitudes toward the learning tasks.

4. Provide informative feedback.

5. Observing and imitating a model facilitates the initial acquisition of prosocial behaviors such as self-control, self-reliance, and persistence.

5. Provide real-life and symbolic models.

6. Verbalizing prosocial values and behaviors and reasoning about them provide a conceptual basis for the development of the behaviors.

6. Provide for verbalization and discussion of prosocial values.

7. Expecting to receive a reward for specified behavior or achievement directs and sustains attention and effort toward manifesting the behavior or achievement. Nonreinforcement after a response tends to extinguish the response. Expecting to receive punishment for manifesting undesired behavior may lead to suppression of the behavior, to avoidance or dislike of the situation, or to avoidance and dislike of the punisher.

7. Develop and use a system of rewards as necessary to secure sustained effort and desired conduct. Use punishment as necessary to suppress misconduct.

8. Experiencing high stress and anxiety is associated with low performance, erratic conduct, and personality disorders.

8. Avoid the use of procedures that create temporary high stress or chronic anxiety.

The next two principles are more directly applicable to student conduct and discipline, dealing with the initial acquisition and subsequent conceptualization of self-direction, self-reliance, persistence, and other prosocial behaviors. The last two principles are equally relevant to motivation for acquiring subject matter and prosocial behaviors. The guides are now discussed in detail.

1. Focus Student Attention

When students come to school and encounter teaching-learning situations, they have interests and needs that may, at times, divert their attention from the instructional objectives. Therefore, in introducing a lesson or unit the teacher directs the students' attention toward the objectives. Before a teacher can thus direct the students' attention, however, he must formulate, state, or identify the objectives himself. The procedures for formulating objectives were described in Chapter 4. Here we merely emphasize that the teacher must know the objectives himself before he can communicate them to students. Though it seems obvious, it should nevertheless be pointed out that much instruction today is ineffective because neither the teacher nor the students know exactly *what* is to be learned. Mager and Clark (1963) and Miles, Kibler, and Pettigrew (1967) have shown that when teachers and students understand the objectives, achievement is increased markedly.

To secure and focus attention, the teacher appeals to more than one sense, usually both seeing and hearing and sometimes also smell, touch, and warmth. Properties of the environment that can be controlled to focus attention are change, movement, size, intensity, repetition, and vividness. Considering two possible environments arranged to focus the attention of many students, the advantage goes to the one of greater change from earlier experiences in it, greater movement of focal objects, and greater vividness of color, contour, or contrast. Recall some of the most fascinating motion pictures and compelling television commercials that you have seen. Both incorporate these features as a means of directing and holding attention.

These same procedures arouse curiosity. Curiosity is manifested in the looking, listening, smelling, and other attending behaviors which the individual directs toward new or infrequently encountered objects and events. In some instances also, children physically approach nonfeared objects and situations with which they are unfamiliar. When encountering a situation that differs markedly from his earlier experiences, the individual does not have immediately available responses to deal with it. He attends closely to the situation, possibly to identify relevant responses for dealing with it or possibly because attending is satisfying.

Here are illustrations of ways teachers can direct students' attention and arouse their curiosity:

Intermediate school children were introduced to the study of the "cold lands" in this way: The pupils arrived at school on a cold morning, the first day after the Christmas vacation. Eager to get in from the cold, the children hurried to their classroom. There, to their surprise, they found they were still cold. The teacher had arranged to have the heat in the room left at the low vacation level, with the result that the thermometer registered 55 degrees in the north side of the room. Still wearing their snowsuits, therefore, the children handled the totem pole and the walrus teeth that were displayed and examined photographs of Lapps with reindeer herds, laughing Eskimos on Baffin Island, Aleuts ice fishing, and many other relevant scenes, pinned to the bulletin boards. After spending a few minutes looking at all these things, some of the children began an intent scrutiny of library books that had been placed on tables. One or two others started to search for the cold lands on globes and maps. The novel appearance of the room and its unusual temperature were instrumental in arousing curiosity and directing pupil attention toward the study of the cold lands.

A beginning teacher focused pupil attention on the study of Japan in social studies as follows: On the first day of the unit, the students walked into an environment that was definitely Japanese. In the front of the room a wall map of Japan and a travel poster were hung. The bulletin boards were filled with pictures of Japan. But the most interesting things, some of the many products made in Japan, were spread out on a table. (The teacher had carefully included a number of unfamiliar objects.) Few students were in their seats when the bell rang. Most of them were still examining the products and eagerly asking the teacher about them. Instead of answering directly, the teacher asked more questions.

In addition to manipulating physical aspects of the environment, the teacher may also modify students' interests and needs through carefully chosen words:

In an English class studying mythology, one question proved especially fruitful in arousing curiosity: "Where do myths come from, and why were they told in the first place?" On discussing this question, the students realized that myths were created by people, people not so very different from themselves.

To get students interested in India, a teacher first held a class discussion, asking each student to tell whatever came first to his mind when he thought of India. Then each student wrote a "pretend" letter to a high school student in India, asking questions about what he most wanted to know. The letters helped the teacher to discover the preconceptions (and some misconceptions) the students had and to evaluate their existing interests.

A beginning history teacher found several techniques to arouse curiosity each day while the class was studying a unit on World War II. Two photographs were passed quickly around the room and then the students were asked what the photographs meant to them. For instance, one showed the monument erected in tribute to the people exterminated at Buchenwald; the other showed the burning chambers in which the bodies were cremated. Another item was an extra edition of the Washington *Daily News* with the huge headline, "Allies Invade France." Such presentations of photographs, news stories, journal articles, and editorials, always with a stimulating question, aroused much curiosity. These and many other procedures can be used in small-group, class-size-group, and large-group settings.

2. Utilize the Individual's Need To Achieve

Earlier, Maslow's hierarchy of needs-motives was discussed. Let us assume that few students experience deprivation of physiological and safety needs during school hours. We can then be concerned with their needs for love and belonging, esteem, self-actualization, and the desires to know and understand. Helping the students to satisfy these needs is a primary means of developing high motivation.

The need to achieve success, as discussed earlier, is closely related to the social needs and is present in most students. Some students do not manifest this need in school settings because of earlier unrewarding experiences. Students who want to achieve should be encouraged to do so, and special attention should be given to any student who does not show this need in connection with school work. The need to achieve is essential in setting and attaining goals that may be related to any area of school work and conduct. Detailed examples of this are provided in the last part of the chapter.

3. Help Each Student Set and Attain Goals

As noted earlier, goal-setting is defined as specifying some state of affairs to be attained by or for oneself at a specified future time; for example, spelling a group of 20 words correctly tomorrow, completing a report on India next week, and gaining first chair on the trombone a year from now. As is obvious from these examples, goals vary in the amount of time needed to achieve them and the specificity with which the final performance is defined. Also, a varying amount of initiative is taken by individuals in setting their own goals. Typically, the young child is expected to set specific goals of short duration with assistance from the teacher, but adolescents are expected to set goals of longer duration and with greater independence of the teacher or other adults. Though the teacher may suggest possible performances to be achieved at a certain time, the individual sets his own goal. The teacher's suggestions are merely words, not the child's goal. Goal-setting proceeds according to the nature of the task and the characteristics of the student.

How might individual goal-setting come about in a beginning typing class? All students start at the same point—not being able to type—and engage in the usual instruction and demonstration procedures, including distributed practice to increase speed and accuracy. Six or more weeks might be needed to reach this point. Once it is reached and each student knows his speed and accuracy, each sets the goal he expects to attain one week later in terms of number of words per minute and number of errors on a timed test. At the end of the week, the timed tests are used to ascertain the amount of progress toward the goal. After this first experience, the goal set for one week later should be more realistic. After several experiences in goal-setting at weekly intervals, more distant goals of two or more weeks in the future are appropriate. Along the way, both the teacher and the students acquire better estimates of the students' abilities, and the students' goals may be raised or lowered as the situation demands. At the end of the year, some students set and achieve goals in terms of speed twice to three times as high as others.

In the second week of a seminar for highly talented high school seniors, each student set a goal for the semester; all the goals were different.

One girl set a goal of writing children's literature. With professional guidance from her teacher, she identified a vast amount of children's literature during the first weeks and started to read and study it and to try out some selections on neighborhood children. On becoming better acquainted with the literature, she had to readjust her goal in the early part of the semester to complete more of the reading. After spending much time in these activities, she then started her first writing. In this case, the teacher helped her both to readjust her goal and to make progress toward achieving it. In the same seminar, another student set the goal of getting a better understanding of "protest" literature. After reading several novels, she found difficulty in understanding and evaluating them. The teacher then helped her develop criteria and locate critical reviews of the entire "protest" movement and of specific novels.

These examples from the typing class and the seminar show that class activities and discussions led by the teacher, smaller-group discussion led by the teacher or by designated pupil chairmen, and individual conferences between the teacher and pupil are essential for implementing purposeful and efficient learning based on goal-setting procedures.

4. Provide Informative Feedback

Students cannot always evaluate their own responses without help and need feedback in order to confirm correct or appropriate responses. For example, some students received their test papers back corrected and were given five minutes to go over the papers (Plowman & Stroud, 1942). Another group did not have their papers returned to them. One week later the test was again administered to all the students. The results were clear-cut and decisive. Students who had been given information about their performance scored considerably higher, one week later, than did those who had not seen their earlier papers.

In a study of broader scope, 74 teachers administered whatever test would next occur in the usual course of instruction for their own pupils (Page, 1958). The students, who were unaware that an experiment was in progress, were randomly assigned to one of three experimental treatments: the tests of one third were returned with no teacher comments; the tests of another third were returned with free teacher comments (that is, natural and appropriate for the particular students concerned); and the tests of the other third were returned with specified, but generally encouraging, teacher comments. All received the usual grades assigned to the paper. In the next objective exam, the free-comment group scored significantly higher than other groups and the no-comment group scored significantly lower. Thus, appropriate and natural informative comments by the teacher had a facilitating effect on student motivation and subsequent performance.

Another study was done in a natural classroom setting to ascertain the effects of informative feedback, including teacher comments, on both performance in and attitudes toward an English composition course (Sweet, 1966). Here the free comments, those made by the teacher in terms of how well the student had done but which also included encouragement to do better, resulted in higher performance and also more favorable attitudes toward English. Thus, receiving information about correct and incorrect responses and also a short comment which indicated the teacher's subjective estimates increased motivation. Feedback also may be given regarding oral contributions, physical actions, and other performances of the student in one-to-one settings, small groups, and large groups. Small-group discussions, question-and-answer sessions, and other group interchanges of information are valuable to the extent that informative feedback is provided to the various participants.

5. Provide Real-Life and Symbolic Models

A brief review of some of the information about observational learning outlined in Chapter 2 will aid in understanding this instructional guide and its subsequent application. The models children observe and imitate may be classified as real-life, symbolic, or representational. Teachers and older children are real-life models for children in school. There may also be other real-life models. Symbolic models are presented to children through oral or written material and pictures or through a combination of verbal and pictorial devices. The models presented in books and other printed material are important. Representational models presented by audiovisual means, particularly television, are also highly influential. In the schools much attention is given to exemplary models, models who demonstrate behaviors that are considered desirable by the adults responsible for the education of the children. Prosocial behaviors of the kind listed later in the objectives in Fig. 9.9 on page 343 are learned initially through imitation and are strengthened through the use of positive reinforcement.

Thus, a response may be made for the first time after observing a model. It is strengthened through reinforcement. For example, a student goes to his seat quietly after seeing a model do so. When the model praises the student for doing so, the strength of the response is increased. Even when reinforcement by an authority figure such as a parent or teacher is intermittent, rather than near 100 percent, it has a strengthening effect. On the other hand, removing positive reinforcers, such as taking away a privilege, or using an aversive stimulus, such as pinching the child, may lead to temporary inhibition of undesired responses.

Real-life models may be available to children in the school setting in one-to-one relations, in small groups, in class-size groups, and in large groups. Teachers and other members of the instructional staff are potential models for many students. In connection with motivation, their first responsibility is to portray the prosocial behaviors of the type described in this chapter and others they may identify. Further, they select other models and bring them into the school setting, making sure that children of all races, ethnic groups, and social classes may have adults and other children to imitate. These models then manifest desired behaviors. The teacher in the presence of the student and model shows approval of the model's prosocial behaviors and subsequently rewards the student for imitating the model.

6. Provide for Verbalization and Discussion of Prosocial Values

Student verbalization of prosocial values related to motivation serves three purposes: awareness, understanding, and acceptance.

1. Awareness. Being able to state the values gives some indication that the student recognizes them. At times, some students may simply not be aware of the prosocial behaviors generally accepted as essential for group living. If so, they may manifest behaviors that teachers regard as asocial or antisocial rather than prosocial, merely because they do not discriminate between prosocial and other behavior.

2. Understanding. Being able to verbalize the prosocial values permits discussion of them and reasoning about them. One of the objectives related to conduct is "Conserves own and others' property." A 7-year-old may describe conserving his own property in terms of subobjectives, such as "I put my hat and coat away," "I do not tear my clothes," "I do not mark or tear books." The child who still marks up books may wonder *why* he should not do so. Another who drops his boots or coat wherever he is when he takes them off at home may ask *why* he should always put them in a certain place at school. In discussion of prosocial behavior the child finds answers to such questions and learns how his actions may affect him favorably or unfavorably now and in the future and how they may affect others now and in the future.

3. Acceptance. Stating prosocial values and discussing and reasoning about them should lead to full acceptance of them by the individual. In turn, these values then comprise the individual's own motivational system so that, independent of adults or of other authority, he tries to learn well, sets realistic goals, commits himself to achieving the goals by socially approved means, continuously examines his own value system, and contributes to changing conditions in order to permit others greater opportunity for learning and self-realization. Thus, as the individual continues in school, he becomes increasingly self-directive in connection with learning and conduct.

7. Use Rewards and Punishments as Necessary

Punishment and threat of punishment are still widely used by teachers — all too often, improperly and ineffectively. Rewards are often used but frequently not with the students who most need positive reinforcement. If the principles and guides already outlined were always carried out effectively, very little rewarding and much less punishing would be needed. The primary reason for including and discussing this guide, therefore, is to indicate how more punishment may be eliminated and how positive reinforcing may be done more effectively.

A reward means, in this context, something given to one person by another person or group which brings pleasure or satisfaction to the recipient. When a student is rewarded immediately after some behavior and knows that the reward is given for the behavior, there is a tendency for the behavior to be strengthened. That is, the behavior is likely to recur when the situation is appropriate. Also, if a reward is promised for similar behavior, the probability is increased that the student will try to pro-

duce the desired behavior again. For example, one prosocial behavior is
"starts to work immediately." The teacher's rewarding a student for
doing so and then promising to reward him again increases the probability of the student's starting to work immediately. Similarly, saying
"good," praising the student, or smiling when he persists at tasks tends to
strengthen the persisting behavior of many students. In this way, rewards following certain responses serve as positive reinforcers of those
responses. From the standpoint of motivation, wanting to get the reward
or expecting to get the reward directs and sustains effort on the task.

An effective reward system does not require competition among children, nor should the higher-achieving, better-behaving children get
larger or more frequent rewards. On the contrary, the child who most
needs frequent rewards for starting work promptly is the one who does
not habitually start work promptly. He is rewarded the first time he does
start promptly, is promised rewards for starting promptly in the future,
and is rewarded when he does so. He is also reasoned with, and the
amount and frequency of rewards is gradually decreased as his behavior
improves. Through a combination of initial rewarding and reasoning, his
specific prosocial behaviors become stable. Similarly, the child who has
not read a book independently may profit from receiving rewards for
reading paragraphs and pages, rather than not being rewarded until he
does read a whole book. When he reads a book with relative ease, he may
then be rewarded only for reading an entire book. Further, when he enjoys
reading for its own sake, the earlier rewards will no longer serve as rewards. This is all true also of prosocial behaviors. For instance, at present
we know of no better way to encourage children who are antisocial to
demonstrate such behaviors as being friendly with students of other races
than by providing exemplary models, rewarding them whenever they show
friendly actions, and reasoning with them about why they should act in
this way.

In general, rewards are given more frequently at first and then are
gradually eliminated. But a careful balance must be maintained between
immediate rewards and promised rewards—and promised rewards must
actually be given when the conditions are met or the stipulated time has
elapsed. Furthermore, though it may seem an obvious point, rewards of
course apply throughout life. For example, most adults—including educational personnel—usually perform more and higher quality work when
promised additional pay, better working conditions, or even just recognition for work well done.

A punishment by definition brings pain or dissatisfaction to the recipient. Punishment takes many forms, including the withholding or withdrawal of anything that serves as a reward; expressing disapproval,
either verbally or in nonverbal ways; threatening, either verbally or in

nonverbal ways; giving low grades or other indications of unsatisfactory work or conduct; removal from a desired situation; and depriving of basic needs. Punishments may be administered by groups as well as by individuals.

Receiving a punishment immediately after a response may weaken the response; or it may lead to the recipient's temporarily suppressing the response or to his suppressing it only in the presence of the punisher; or it may result in evasion of or open aggression against the punisher. Being promised a punishment for not performing a task may lead to performance of the task, but it may lead to avoidance of the task, the punishment, and the punisher. Being promised a punishment if a specified antisocial behavior is manifested may lead to nonmanifestation of it, but it may lead to avoidance of the punishment and punisher while still expressing the antisocial behavior. In addition, punishment may result in undesirable anxiety in the child, negative feelings toward the punisher, and negative feelings toward school.

Punishment and threat of punishment are misused extensively, especially from the standpoint of the form of the punishment, the severity of the punishment, and the timing of the punishment. We now discuss these three aspects.

1. Form of Punishment. The performance of school tasks should not be used as punishment—doing additional work or extra assignments, staying in the building or classroom to do school work at times when other students are doing other things, and coming early or staying late to do school work. Using these forms of punishment results in an effect opposite from that intended (Mager, 1968). In other words, it creates a disliking rather than a liking for school and school learning tasks. Actually, these activities should be used as rewards rather than as punishments. Also, verbal insult, rebuke, and attack are used widely but ineffectively to curb aggressive behaviors. They are ineffective because they tend to reduce aggressiveness only in the presence of a strong authority figure but to increase it in his absence. Further, the punisher in the process of punishing models aggressive behaviors which the children may imitate and practice on other children.

The withdrawal or withholding of rewards, including privileges, serves better as punishment in school settings than does inflicting physical or psychological pain. For example, going to the instructional center to read, listening to a record, or using the tape recorder may be a privilege, or reward, for getting a certain task accomplished well. Not being able to do so may serve as a punishment; such a privilege can be readily withdrawn or withheld until the child manifests the desired behavior. Withholding or withdrawing juice or milk may also serve as a punishment for young children. The juice is withheld until the child exhibits the desired behavior, and then it is given to him, thus immediately reinforcing the desirable response. Saying words such as "good," "excellent," and "fine," smiling at the child, and making other gestures that serve as rewards may also be withheld as punishments. In general, if the teacher's approving and affectional behaviors toward the child reinforce his desired responses, then withholding or withdrawal will serve as a punishment or threat of punishment and can be used effectively to control behavior.

2. Severity of Punishment. The severity of a punishment is difficult to predict. Some acts intended as punishments do not result in either pain or dissatisfaction to the individual. On the other hand, a punishment may be so severe that it causes the child to feel continuing anxiety or permanent dislike of the punisher or both. When punishment is used, it should be sufficiently severe to cause temporary pain or dissatisfaction and yet not produce undesirable longer-term effects.

3. Timing of Punishment. To be effective, punishment should be administered before the start of an undesired response, or at its early inception, rather than immediately after or long after the undesired response has been completed. Once started, the punishment or threat thereof should continue until the child ceases the undesired response and, preferably, demonstrates the desired response. In turn, a reward is given when the child stops the undesired response or when he shows the desired response. The rewarding at this time has two important effects. It strengthens the desired response and dispels possible ill feeling which the child may have generated toward the punisher.

Extinction of responses is accomplished by nonreinforcement, by giving no form of reward or punishment following the response. Many teachers report that minor misbehaviors are best dealt with by the teacher's ignoring them, particularly when other students also ignore the misbehavior (Madsen, Becker, & Thomas, 1968). Ignoring, or withholding of attention or approval, may be interpreted by the child as a punishment rather than as a neutral condition. Further, if the teacher calls attention to the misbehavior, this form of attention—even though disapproving—may serve as a reward for some children, strengthening the misbehavior, rather than suppressing or eliminating it.

8. Avoid the Use of Stressful Procedures

Schooling presents some anxiety for most children. Mild anxiety probably heightens activity and facilitates learning. When anxiety becomes acute or chronic, however, it produces disorganization of cognitive responses (Ruebush, 1963). The anxious person does not concentrate well on learning tasks and does not perform as well as he might in other ways.

Trying to attain a goal is accompanied by some tension. Threat of loss of love is also accompanied by anxiety. Sometimes good students experience acute anxiety about not receiving "A's." Others become unduly anxious about not learning sufficiently well or not securing approval of a teacher or parent. In order not to produce acute or chronic anxiety, the school should identify children who seem to be unduly anxious and deliberately reduce, rather than increase, the stress of the school situation.

9.8. Principles based on learning theory and research are stated; they are considered as internal conditions directly associated with the level of motivation. Corollary instructional guides are also stated; they are considered as external conditions which may be modified or managed to increase a student's level of motivation. The guides are based on research and also on knowledge of what effective teachers do. Both the principles and the guides are difficult to formulate and to state explicitly. Does any one principle or guide appear not to meet the conditions just stated? Can you state it better? Could the number be reduced by combining one or more into a general statement?

9.9. What similarities and differences do you see between the concepts of focusing attention and advance organizers?

9.10. What are the characteristics of students whom you would expect to need the most help in setting goals?

9.11. Ideally, a student's learning is intrinsically motivated; that is, he is moved and directed by his own desires and goals rather than by external pressures. What is the possibility of feedback and modeling also having internalized aspects?

9.12. The actual act of punishment may in some cases not have to be carried out. For example, simply informing a conscientious student who has temporarily misbehaved that he deserves punishment may be sufficient. What assumptions about the student must be true for this procedure to be effective?

9.13. There are drawbacks inherent in using a system of concrete or material rewards in a school setting, but it is better to use incentives to motivate a student than to let him sit day after day after all other efforts to get him to learn have failed. It has been observed in recent programs with disadvantaged students that a material reward system has generated lively motivation and substantial learning, conditions not in evidence before the reward system was instituted. Often the student will identify the item for which he desires to "work." What is your opinion of the use of a concrete reward system? What effect might such a reward system have on the individual student? Consider both short- and long-term effects. From the standpoint of the community and society in general, what advantages and disadvantages might develop out of such a reward system? What similarities and differences do you perceive between rewarding a poor student to motivate him to learn and awarding a good student a college scholarship?

A SYSTEM OF INDIVIDUALLY GUIDED MOTIVATION

A system of individually guided motivation is outlined in Fig. 9.8. Here, as in the instructional system outlined in Chapter 1, the student's entering characteristics concerned with motivation are assessed, motivational objectives in the form of desired behaviors are decided with each student, a program designed to generate and maintain a desired level of motivation for each student is outlined and carried out, and the student's progress in attaining the objectives is assessed. On the basis of informative feedback, changes are made in the motivational program of each child. The components of the motivational program are based directly on the principles discussed in the last section. Motivational procedures used by the teacher are usually directly related to the instructional program in

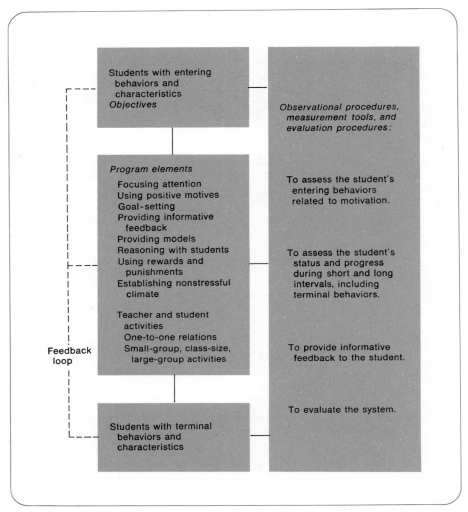

Fig. 9.8. Components of a system of individually guided motivation.

the various curriculum areas. For example, most of the motivational program is carried out in the same large-group, class-size, small-group, and one-to-one activities that are used in the instructional program. Thus, changes in the motivational program for a child usually require changes in his instructional program.

The 17 possible objectives of a motivational system, as listed here, merit brief attention. The behaviors are stated at two levels of generality. Four general objectives are stated that deal with motivation for learning subject-matter knowledge and skills, developing independence from adults in connection with motivation for school work, developing independence in connection with conduct, and conceptualizing a value system.

The more specific behaviors related to each general objective may be acceptable as the objectives of a school's system of individually guided motivation. However, each school must, in the final analysis, identify its own objectives. The objectives selected must be redefined in terms of the curriculum area within which the motivational procedure is utilized. Thus, in the case of the motivational procedure involving individual conferences in reading, certain of the preceding objectives were selected and redefined in terms of reading behaviors by a school staff (they are given later).

[**GENERAL OBJECTIVES OF A SYSTEM OF INDIVIDUALLY GUIDED MOTIVATION**]

A. The student starts promptly and completes self-, teacher-, or group-assigned tasks that together comprise the minimum requirements related to various curriculum areas.

1. Attends to the teacher and other situational elements when attention is required.
2. Begins tasks promptly.
3. Seeks feedback concerning performance on tasks.
4. Returns to tasks voluntarily after interruption or initial lack of progress.
5. Persists at tasks until completed.

B. The student assumes responsibility for learning more than the minimum requirements without teacher guidance during school hours and outside school hours. In addition to behaviors 1-5, the student

6. Continues working when the teacher leaves the room.
7. Does additional work during school hours.
8. Works on school-related activities outside school hours.
9. Identifies activities that are relevant for class projects.
10. Seeks suggestions for going beyond minimum amount or quality of work.

C. The student becomes self-directive in connection with use of property, relations with other students, and relations with adults.

11. Moves quietly within and about the school building during quiet periods and activities.
12. Interacts harmoniously with other students.
13. Interacts harmoniously with the teacher and other adults.
14. Conserves own and others' property.
15. Tells other students to behave in accordance with school policies.

D. The student verbalizes a value system consistent with the preceding behaviors.

16. When asked, gives examples of his own actions illustrative of behaviors 1-15.
17. When asked, gives reasons for manifesting behaviors 1-15.

No one motivational procedure can attempt to achieve all of these objectives with all students. Some selection from among the behaviors must be made in order to arrive at the objectives for a particular student, and the motivational program will also vary among students. The motivational procedures are clarified in the two more detailed discussions that follow; one describes a school-wide effort to develop prosocial behaviors; the other describes the use of short individual conferences to increase independent reading.

A School-Wide Effort To Develop Prosocial Behaviors

In line with the model outlined in the preceding pages, the staff of an entire elementary school participated in a combined development and research activity designed to encourage prosocial behaviors in children of elementary school age (Sorenson, Schwenn, & Bavry, 1970). The research was done to ascertain the effects of an adult conferring with children individually, in small groups of three or four, and in medium-sized groups of six or eight. In each conference the attempt was made to implement four motivational principles—goal-setting, reinforcement, feedback, and reasoning. So that each child would become more self-directive in setting and attaining his own goals related to prosocial behaviors, the conferences were conducted in a nondirective manner to the best of each teacher's ability.

The elementary school drew from the lowest socioeconomic area of Janesville, Wisconsin, a city of about 60,000. Approximately 35 percent of the children qualified as disadvantaged under provisions of the Elementary and Secondary Education Act of 1965. The school was organized for instruction on the multiunit pattern outlined in Chapter 8. The unit leaders, staff teachers, and the building principal participated with personnel of the Wisconsin Research and Development Center for Cognitive Learning in setting up the experiment and collecting information. The school staff assumed sole responsibility for carrying out the conferences.

Because the school functioned on the multiunit plan, the students were grouped in units, each headed by a leader, instead of grades; also, they were instructed by several persons, rather than by one teacher. Complete data were available for 628 students in the five units: 117 in Unit I (kindergarten), 102 in Unit II (first grade), 88 in Unit III (second grade), 166 in Unit IV (third and fourth grades), and 155 in Unit V (fifth and sixth grades).

Design. Before being assigned to the various treatment groups, all students rated themselves on the set of 20 behaviors listed in Fig. 9.9. As the chart shows, the students assessed themselves on various behaviors on a scale ranging from "you almost always have to be told to do the job" to "you almost always do the job yourself." Neither the students nor the teachers had access to these initial self-assessment sheets during the project period.

Teachers in each unit, at least two teachers in the smaller units and three teachers in the larger units, also independently assessed each child on the same 20 behaviors on which the students had evaluated them-

Name _____ Sex _____ Age _____ Date _____

Directions:

Put an X under column 1 if you almost always have to be told to do the job.
Put an X under column 2 if you usually have to be told to do the job.
Put an X under column 3 if you sometimes do the job yourself and sometimes have
          to be told to do the job.
Put an X under column 4 if you usually do the job yourself.
Put an X under column 5 if you almost always do the job yourself.

	1	2	3	4	5
1. I listen to the teacher.					
2. I begin schoolwork right away.					
3. I correct mistakes.					
4. I work until the job is finished.					
5. I work when the teacher has left the room.					
6. If I make mistakes, I still keep working.					
7. I work on learning activities in free time.					
8. I get to class on time.					
9. I do extra schoolwork.					
10. I do my share in class projects.					
11. I read during free time.					
12. I ask questions about schoolwork.					
13. I have pencil, paper, and books ready when they are needed.					
14. I move quietly to and from my classes.					
15. I listen to the ideas of others.					
16. I help my classmates.					
17. I pick up when the work is finished.					
18. I take care of my clothing, books, and other things.					
19. I take care of the school's books, desks, and other things.					
20. I follow directions.					

Fig. 9.9. Check list for student self-rating of prosocial behaviors.

selves. The ratings of the teachers were then averaged for each behavior to obtain the final value designated for each child on the teacher assessment form. Teacher assessment forms were filed in the central office and also were not accessible during the project period.

Within each unit all students were randomly assigned in approximately equal numbers to one of four conditions: (1) control group, which received no conferences; (2) group that received individual, or one-to-one, conferences; (3) group that received small-group (three to four students) conferences; (4) group that received medium-group (six to eight students) conferences. All conferences were held with a teacher from the unit. Each teacher was assigned six to eight students for individual conferences, six to eight students divided into two small conference groups, and six to eight for one medium conference group. At the end of the experimental period, each student again rated himself and the teachers also rated each student.

Conference Procedures. The control group did not receive conferences; however, they were in the same instructional groups with the children who had conferences and also were at times in the same rooms where the conferences were conducted. No effort was made to encourage the conference students not to show their self-assessment sheets to or to discuss the conferences with those in the control group.

At the first conference, regardless of the size of the group, each student received a second unmarked copy of the student assessment sheet (Fig. 9.9) to be used as his goal-setting sheet. During the conferences, the students were encouraged by the teacher conducting the conference to discuss the behaviors listed. The teacher endeavored to get the children to define the meaning of each of the behaviors through recalling or identifying everyday instances of the behavior. Each child was then encouraged to select a behavior or group of similar behaviors that he wanted to develop between conferences. The child checked where he presently ranked on that behavior and then set a goal for himself, another check on Fig. 9.9, to indicate where he would rate on the behavior by the next conference. At each succeeding conference each child reported on the progress he had made toward his goal and filled out another assessment sheet. Thus, the goal-setting was self-directed, with assistance from the teacher only on procedural matters. Not only did the children set their own goals but they assessed their own progress in achieving their goals.

Throughout the conferences the teachers attempted to be nondirective, accepting the goals as expressed by the child and also his estimate of progress. The main job of the adult was to ensure that through discussion the children understood what each behavior meant. The adult also tried to help the children realize that the behaviors could be related. In conducting the conferences the adults attempted to accept the children's responses and rework them to get at real problems. The sincerity of a child's response was never doubted overtly.

Within the larger groups the adult attempted to maintain the mood of the group as one of cooperativeness rather than competitiveness. The children in the group were encouraged to listen to each others' ideas and to build each other up rather than to criticize. The motivational principles used in the goal-setting conferences were related to goal-setting, rein-forcement, feedback, and reasoning. The goal-setting procedures just outlined were followed. Applications of the other principles are now summarized.

Reinforcement in terms of praise was administered by the adult when-ever a child showed progress toward his goal. In the group conferences, not only were children directly reinforced but they also observed others being reinforced for attaining goals.

Feedback was provided periodically by the adults to each child. The adult kept a conference comment card on each child so that progress and problems could be noted. The feedback consisted of telling the child how many goals he had attained and how, in general, he was succeeding in manifesting the behaviors as listed on his sheet.

Reasoning was involved when the adult attempted to elicit from the children their reasons for working toward manifesting the behaviors. The children discussed with one another and with the adult the consequences of their own behavior in various situations. In the group conferences the adult tried to guide the children to a consensus about the relative impor-tance of the behaviors to the individual and to the school as a whole. That is, the adult, in a nondirective fashion, led the children to verbalize and conceptualize the reasons behind their own behavior and why it was im-portant that they conform to certain rules and exhibit certain behaviors.

Scheduling of Conferences. All the children participated in four confer-ences. In Units II, III, IV, and V, the conferences were held every other week for an eight-week period. In Unit I, each child participated in the four conferences during consecutive weeks because the teachers felt that the younger children needed more frequent reinforcement and feedback.

All conferences at all unit levels were held during regular school hours, not during recess periods, noon hours, or after school. Actual hours of the day during which conferences were held depended on unit programing. Usually each unit staff scheduled their conferences at the beginning of a week. The medium- and small-group conferences lasted from 15 to 20 minutes. The individual conferences were from seven to 10 minutes in length.

Results. A pre- and postassessment checklist sheet and a teacher as-sessment form containing pre- and postevaluations were available for each student. In addition, the student goal-setting sheets, four for each student, and the teacher comment cards, one for each student, were also collected. One month after the completion of the project, a structured in-terview was held with the principal and unit leaders to obtain their evalu-ation of the project.

The average pre- and postself-assessment ratings of the students and the ratings of the students by the teachers are given for the four condi-tions in Fig. 9.10. It is immediately apparent that ratings of both the stu-dents and the teachers increased markedly and that the students rated themselves higher than did the teachers. This was true in all units. The conclusions that follow are based on an analysis of the information from all the units.

1. The gains from pre- to postassessment for the *combined* student and

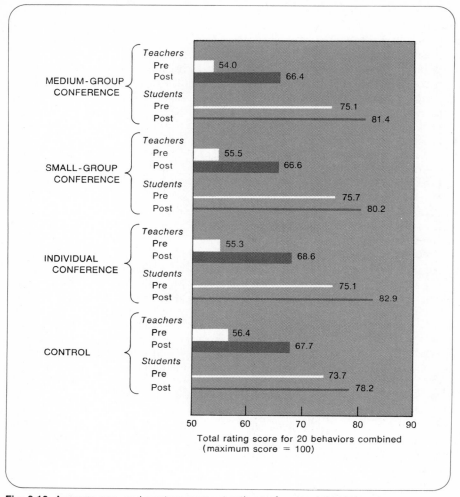

Fig. 9.10. Average pre- and postassessment ratings of prosocial behaviors.

teacher ratings were statistically significant and also of much practical significance. The control group gained significantly less than the three conference groups. Also, gains in the small- and medium-group conferences were significantly less than in the individual conferences.

2. The average gains for the four conditions from pre- to postassessment for the *student self-assessments* of their own prosocial behaviors were: control, 4.7; individual, 7.7; small group, 4.4; medium group, 5.8. The gain for the individual conferences was significantly higher than for the other types of conferences, which did not differ much from one another. Students participating in the small-group conferences had a mean gain lower than that of any other condition, including the control.

3. The average gains in the *teacher ratings* of the students' prosocial behaviors were: control, 11.7; individual, 13.5; small group, 11.7; medium group, 12.9. Again, of the three types of conferences, the individual conference was highest and the small group lowest.

4. The students consistently rated their prosocial behaviors higher than the teachers rated them, the difference being highly significant. In all units, at the end of the project period the students still rated their behaviors higher than the teachers did, even though the teachers' ratings had increased markedly, as noted above. The teachers' ratings changed more from pre- to postassessment than did the student ratings—the average change for the teachers was about 12. The average change in student ratings was about six.

At the end of the project, the unit leaders and principal responded to five questions during a structured interview. A few comments made by the leader of Unit V follow:

> Teachers are usually busy keeping the "lid on" in the spring. But with the conferences, the older students, normally sixth-graders, responded and kept up their academic work right to the last day of school, and discipline was no problem. Especially noticeable changes were seen in the "tomboy-type" girls, who responded enthusiastically to the conferences and seemed to become young ladies. Boys also seemed to take a more mature approach. Instead of bragging and getting a "swelled-head" from their success at the track meet and other competitive activities, for example, they accepted their successes as a responsibility and took on leadership qualities. Overall, the students were really serious about setting and reaching their goals.

Teachers preferred the medium-sized group of six to eight students from the standpoint of economy of time and lively group interaction. Leadership emerged in groups as the conference proceeded. The students also expressed a preference for group conferences. However, teachers felt that individual conferences might be more effective with certain types of children. Teachers could not observe differences in behaviors between the control and conference groups—they felt that children in the control group became caught up in the general spirit of the project.

All the teachers were enthusiastic about this kind of approach for this age level. It encouraged the idea of working together toward "more of a family situation . . . talking freely about behaviors." A few of the teachers in Unit V had had previous instruction and experience in this type of approach; others felt they would gain from more instruction in the technique.

The principal indicated that the conferences and the behavioral assessment sheets provided the teachers with a framework for viewing student behaviors positively. That is, instead of concentrating mostly on instances of misconduct by students, the teachers were encouraged to focus on positive behavior. Thus, the principal considered the greatest effect of the project to be in changing the direction of the teachers' thinking about student conduct. (The fact that the teacher ratings showed the greater shifts during the project period supports this observation.)

Although the goals pursued in this project were unlike the usual objectives of instruction, they nevertheless represent important behaviors which many adults want students to acquire. Most teachers are familiar with the way behavioral objectives in the cognitive domain serve as motivational devices. The objectives described in this project and the method of attaining them add an important dimension to the methods of classroom motivation.

Individual Conferences To Increase Independent Reading

Many children still do not learn to read well during the elementary school years. One reason for this is that many who try to learn to read in school have no idea that reading can be enjoyable. They think of learning reading as a chore—necessary, but still a chore. Thus they read only the material assigned in school. With these facts in mind, a combined research and development project was carried out on a school-wide basis to develop a procedure for increasing independent reading. The procedure involved an adult meeting for about 10 minutes each week with each child and implementing various principles of motivation outlined earlier. Another important part of the procedure was securing and making available to the children inexpensive but attractive books.

The elementary school where this project was carried out was in the inner city of Madison, Wisconsin, a city of about 200,000. The students were of racially different backgrounds, with about 35 percent classified as disadvantaged. In age levels they were equivalent to second-, fourth-, and sixth-graders. (The grade designations are used here, rather than age in years, on the assumption that most readers probably think in terms of grade levels.) Complete sets of reading and achievement data were available for 68 second-grade students, 58 fourth-grade students, and 49 sixth-grade students.

The following description of the procedures and results focuses on the procedures, so that the methods used to implement the motivational principles can be made explicit. The entire experiment was described in detail by Schwenn, Sorenson, and Bavry (1970); the procedures, including a list of the books used, were reported by Sorenson, Schwenn, and Klausmeier (1969).

Design. The number of books that each student in grades 2, 4, and 6 read during an eight-week baseline period early in the school year was recorded. Each student, with assistance and weekly reminders from the teacher, kept a record of the titles of the books he read and the dates when he completed them. The books read during the baseline period were classified as "above," "at," or "below" grade level, using standard reference catalogues. A value of 3 was assigned to above-level books, 2 to at-level books, and 1 to below-level books.

Students were selected to receive conferences based on the combined amount and level of reading done during the baseline period. Each student's reading-value score was simply the sum of the values assigned to the books he read. Students were placed in rank order according to this reading-value score. Those students with value scores in the top third were excluded from the experiment. This decision was based on the practical supposition that because the top third of the children were already doing a great deal of reading, motivational procedures to increase their reading would not benefit them as they would the lower groups. These top children were, however, considered to be an "ideal" group, and the others were compared with them later.

Reading achievement scores from standardized tests were obtained for each of the remaining students. Within each grade, students in the top half of their homeroom group were designated as high in achievement, and those in the bottom half were designated as low in the combined amount and level of reading (reading value) and additionally as either high or low in achievement. The goals of the adult-child conference, as well as the actual conference procedure, differed for students low in reading value and reading achievement, as compared with those low in reading value but high in reading achievement.

Within each homeroom, six groups were formed: Those students low in both reading-value score and reading-achievement score were randomly assigned to any one of three groups; also, those low in reading value but high in reading achievement were randomly assigned to any one of three other groups. There were thus two each of these types of groups: the control group, which received no conferences; the teacher-conference group, which had conferences with their homeroom teacher; the aide-conference group, which had all conferences with an instructional aide.

Conference Procedures. Three teachers in the second grade, three in the fourth grade, and two in the sixth grade conducted conferences. The same aide conducted the conferences in all three grades. (The aide was a mature, college-educated woman who had exceptional ability and great enthusiasm for working with children of low reading achievement.) All children, including those with high reading-value scores who were excluded from the sample, kept a list of the books they read and the date on which they completed each book during the project period. The conferences, which were held regularly, once per week, over an eight-week period, averaged 8 to 12 minutes in length. The locations of the conferences varied: a hallway, a small workroom, a carrel in a corner, a corner of a classroom, or at the teacher's desk. The conference activities of both adults and students depended on the objectives to be reached in the conferences with each child and the motivational principles employed in the conferences.

Behavioral Objectives of Conferences. Before the conferences were begun, a list of behavioral objectives for them was derived from the objectives of the total system of motivation, as outlined earlier. Specific objectives related to the conferences were classified into three areas, as follows:

A. Behaviors indicative of motivation which are general in nature and necessary for successful relationships to exist between the adult conducting the conference and the child. These behaviors include:
    1. The child comes to the conference on time.
    2. The child attends closely to the adult and other situational elements during the conference.

   3. The child begins his report promptly.
   4. The child reads from his book when asked.
   5. The child takes good care of books he is reading.

B. Behaviors related specifically to a child's reactions to reading. These behaviors include:
   6. The child expresses pleasant feelings about reading.
   7. When asked, the child tells about what he has read.
   8. When asked, the child tells why he reads.
   9. The child talks with other children and/or adults about his reading.
   10. The child reads on his own when adults are not present.
   11. The child goes beyond the minimum reading requirements for his group.

C. Behaviors related to improvement of independent reading skills and reaching achievement. These behaviors include:
   12. The child independently reads more books or longer books or more difficult books during school hours and/or outside school hours during the period following initiation of the adult-child conferences.
   13. The child reads more rapidly after initiation of the adult-child conferences.
   14. The child's word recognition skills and reading comprehension improve more rapidly during and after the initiation of the conferences.
   15. The child's preference for independent reading increases for a child who found reading low on his list of preferred activities and remains constant for a child who preferred reading as an independent activity.

The objectives were discussed with the eight teachers and the aide who were to conduct the conferences to be sure that they were clearly stated. During the conference period, systematic data were gathered on some of the objectives (C12 and C14) related to amount and quality of independent reading and vocabulary and comprehension skills. For other objectives, particularly those related to the child's attitudes toward reading and to the relationship between the adult and child (areas A and B), the adults noted progress on their conference comment cards.

Motivational Principles Implemented in Conferences. During the course of the conferences, the adults served as models of desired reading behaviors for the child to observe and imitate, reinforced desired reading behaviors and attitudes of the child, informed the child of his progress in reading, and helped the child select goals in terms of books of an appropriate difficulty level related to the child's current interests. Not all these were implemented in any one conference, but across the eight conferences each adult attempted to implement all of the principles with each child. For the purposes of the conferences, the motivational procedures were described as follows:

Modeling: doing such things as telling the child that he (the adult) reads frequently and likes to read; being engaged in reading when the child comes in for the conference and starting to read a book as the child leaves the conference. Modeling also includes such procedures as informing the child of the reading behavior of a possible model and indicating the value of independent reading to other persons who may serve as models for the child.

Reinforcement: smiling, nodding affirmatively, saying "good," "fine," etc., when the student shows that he has independently read a book or pages in a book. The adult also reinforces positive attitude statements about reading either made spontaneously by the child or in response to questions.

Feedback: informing the child of progress by telling him how many books or pages in a book he has completed. Feedback was also given on any improvement in word recognition or comprehension skills.

Goal-setting: helping the child select the next book of an appropriate difficulty level and length. The reading of the book or books then becomes the child's goal for the next conference.

During a child's first conference, the adult explained the purposes of the conferences and told the child how to keep his record sheet. The adult also pointed out to the child the books that were available in his homeroom and school library and told him how to check out the books he wanted. The rest of the first conference was spent in helping the child select his first book(s). In later conferences the child was encouraged to report on the books he had read independently between conferences.

For those students who were low in reading-value score but high in reading achievement, the adult emphasized the use of modeling and reinforcement to encourage independent reading. With students low also in reading achievement, much more emphasis was placed on improvement of reading skills by having the child read orally in the conference and by informal drilling on word recognition and comprehension skills. Feedback and positive reinforcement, along with goal-setting, played a major role in conferences with this type of child.

Materials for this project included a readily available supply of books in each homeroom, forms on which students could record titles of books read, and conference comments cards kept by the adults. About 70 paperback books covering a wide variety of subject matter and areas of interest and chosen over a broad range of difficulty were placed in each homeroom of about 25 students. All the students of the homeroom, including the high achievers not in the study, had access to the books during independent study time as well as before and after school.

Results. Table 9.2 shows the average numbers of books read during the baseline and project periods for each grade as a function of conference condition. The average gains are also given. For each condition, including the control, at each grade level there was a substantial gain in the number of books read from the baseline to project periods, 7.00 for the control condition, 9.95 for the teacher-conducted conferences, and 11.72 for the aide-conducted conferences. The mean gains were markedly and

Table 9.2. Average Number of Books Read During the Initial 8-Week Baseline Period and the 8-Week Project Period as a Function of Grade Level and Conference Condition

Grade		Conference condition			Average gain
		No conference	Teacher	Aide	
2	Baseline	3.36	3.88	3.06	
	Project	13.00	18.63	16.13	
	Gain	*9.64*	*14.75*	*13.07*	*12.49*
4	Baseline	3.75	3.85	3.77	
	Project	11.17	11.77	16.38	
	Gain	*7.42*	*7.92*	*12.61*	*9.32*
6	Baseline	4.00	3.75	3.40	
	Project	6.80	9.50	11.80	
	Gain	*2.80*	*5.75*	*8.40*	*5.65*
	Average gain	*7.00*	*9.95*	*11.72*	

significantly greater for the teacher- and aide-conference conditions than for the no-conference condition for each grade. Thus, children in all grades who received conferences increased their independent reading more than children who did not receive conferences, and it made little difference whether the conference was conducted by a teacher or the aide.

Table 9.3 shows the average grade-equivalent scores in reading achievement for the baseline and project periods for grades 2, 4, and 6. Scores for each grade are given separately for high- and low-achievement groups. The data for the teacher- and aide-conference groups were combined, because these groups did not differ.

In none of the grades was there a significant difference in amount of gain in achievement between the conference and no-conference conditions. This lack of difference between conditions was true for both high- and low-achieving students. More important than the lack of difference, however, was the remarkable gains made by the low-achieving students during an eight-month period from September through April. Students in the second grade gained more than a year in vocabulary. Students in the fourth grade gained almost two years in achievement. The gain for the sixth-grade low achievers was practically a year. This much gain is not ordinarily expected in inner-city or other schools where children are below grade level and tend to keep falling further behind with each successive year of schooling. Because the no-conference groups showed as much growth as the experimental groups, the gain obviously cannot be attributed solely to the reading conferences. It seems very likely, therefore, that the increased emphasis in all the homerooms on reading contributed to the high gain in achievement growth in both the control and the conference groups.

Data were also gathered on the independent reading of the "ideal" students in each grade who had been eliminated from the project because they already had done a large amount of independent reading during the baseline period. It proved to be very interesting to find out how students receiving conferences compared with these ideal students at the end of the experimental period. The comparisons made for the three grades are shown in Fig. 9.11; the low- and high-achievement students within the conference condition were compared separately with the ideal group for each grade.

Note that in grade 2, before the project period, that is, during the eight-week baseline period, the ideal group read an average of 13 books, whereas high achievers who later received conferences from the aide and teachers read 4 books and low achievers read 3 books. During the eight-week project period, the ideal students read an average of 19 books; the high achievers and low achievers receiving conferences read 17 and 18 books, respectively. To sum up, the students of both high and low achievement who later received conferences read significantly fewer books than the ideal group during the baseline period, but neither of these groups differed significantly from the ideal group at the end of the experiment. The conference groups gained much more than did the ideal group; actually, they almost caught up with the ideal group.

Similar results were obtained in grades 4 and 6, where the conferences almost eliminated reading differences between the high achievers in the

Table 9.3. Average Grade-Equivalents in Reading Achievement for the Initial Baseline and Project Periods in Grades 2, 4, and 6 as a Function of Achievement Level and Conference Condition

Grade	Achievement level		Conference condition	
			No conference	Conference
2	High	Baseline	2.0	2.2
		Project	2.9	3.3
		Gain	*.9*	*1.1*
	Low	Baseline	1.3	1.5
		Project	2.3	2.5
		Gain	*1.0*	*1.0*
4	High	Baseline	4.3	4.5
		Project	6.1	5.6
		Gain	*1.8*	*1.1*
	Low	Baseline	2.2	2.2
		Project	4.0	4.2
		Gain	*1.8*	*2.0*
6	High	Baseline	7.4	7.2
		Project	7.6	7.8
		Gain	*0.3*	*0.6*
	Low	Baseline	4.0	5.2
		Project	4.7	5.8
		Gain	*0.7*	*0.6*

Note: Scores for grade 2 from Gates-MacGinitie Reading Tests, Grade 2, Primary B; scores for grades 4 and 6 from Iowa Test of Basic Skills—Reading Skills Section.

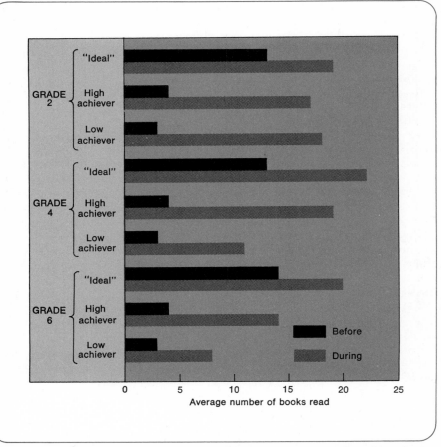

Fig. 9.11. Number of books read by "ideal" readers and by high and low achievers who received conferences, before project period (baseline period) and during project period.

conference condition and the ideal group. At these grade levels, however, the conferences were not sufficient to bring the low achievers up to the level of reading done by the ideal students. It is important to remember that the low-achieving students did, of course, increase their amount of independent reading over the low-achieving students in the no-conference group.

This study demonstrated that an inexpensive procedure was highly effective in increasing the independent reading of children. It is impossible to reach any definite conclusions about the relative contributions of any specific motivational principles to the obtained increases. Very probably, the individual attention, positive reinforcement, informative feedback, modeling of desired behaviors, goal-setting, and availability of attractive books all contributed in combination to increasing the students' motivation to engage in independent reading.

9.14. Four general areas are included in the objectives of a motivation system. Can you add other general areas? Should any one be deleted or modified?

9.15. How well did the conferences and related procedures implement each of the principles for developing prosocial behaviors? How important do you feel the additional personal contact between the teacher and student was?

9.16. What procedures might you set up in your field of interest to provide for systematic attention to the motivational level of students?

9.17. Low achievers in reading who also did little independent reading made remarkable progress during eight weeks in which individual conferences were held and also during the school year. Could all teachers implement the principles and carry out the other conditions of the conferences? Why might a school that has many low achievers not wish to use a 10-minute conference each week with each low-achieving student? Would some teachers quickly tire of this kind of conference?

SUMMARY

A hierarchy of needs-motives formulated by Maslow includes six categories: physiological, safety, love and belonging, esteem, self-actualization, and the desire to know and understand. This theory is intended to be useful in explaining the "why" of all human behavior.

In a more direct attempt to explain approach and avoidance behavior, Atkinson outlined a theory of achievement-oriented activity. Here, the need to achieve success and the need to avoid failure, along with the incentive value of success, are seen as powerful determinants of whether an individual will approach or avoid a task and also of his goal-setting behaviors. Exploration, manipulation, and curiosity also are positive, intrinsic motives.

These explanations of why some human beings are active, set goals, and strive are in line with the concept of purposeful learning set forth in Chapter 2 and also with ideas about classroom discipline, particularly as it pertains to the learning of prosocial values. Further, these theories and the related research provide the basis for several principles of motivation.

Eight principles of motivation are outlined. These principles are stated in such a way that they represent internal conditions of the motivated individual. Corollary instructional guides are stated as indicators of how external conditions in the school setting may be handled to increase student motivation.

A system of individually guided motivation is outlined that shows how to take into account differences among students. Giving students individual attention, modeling desired behaviors, reinforcing desired behaviors, providing informative feedback, assisting students in setting realistic goals, and using attractive materials and tasks appropriate for the particular student are shown to have highly desirable effects. A teacher who can control enough elements in a teaching situation and who also can

implement the principles need have little anxiety about student motivation, except perhaps with older students who are organized to disrupt
school or who are already strongly prejudiced against teachers and
schooling.

SUGGESTIONS FOR FURTHER READING

ATKINSON, J. W. The mainsprings of achievement-oriented activity. In Krumboltz, J.
    D., ed., *Learning and the educational process.* Chicago: Rand McNally, 1965, pp.
    25-66.

A theoretical account is presented of the need to achieve and the need to avoid
failure.

HAMACHEK, D. E., ed. *Human dynamics in psychology and education: Selected read-
    ings.* Boston: Allyn and Bacon, 1968.

Chapter 2, pages 48-118, has three sections on motivation: R. W. White, "Motivation Reconsidered: The Concept of Competence"; J. M. Hunt, "Experience and the
Development of Motivation: Some Reinterpretations"; R. E. Farson, "Praise Reap-
praised."

KUHLEN, R. G., ed. *Studies in educational psychology.* Waltham, Mass.: Blaisdell,
    1968.

Chapter 4, pages 80-119, has a short overview and four sections dealing with moti-
vation: R. W. White, "Motivation Reconsidered: The Concept of Competence"; E. R.
Keislar, "A Descriptive Approach to Classroom Motivation"; M. C. Shaw and J. T.
McCuen, "Age of Onset of Academic Underachievement in Bright Children"; W. J.
McKeachie, "Motivation, Teaching Methods, and College Learning."

MASLOW, A. H. Self-actualization and beyond. In Hamachek, D., ed., *Human dy-
    namics in psychology and education. Selected readings.* Boston: Allyn and Bacon,
    1968, pp. 173-183.

In this short essay, Maslow gives a clear picture of how self-actualization energizes and directs the behavior of a mature human being. Students probably respond
with enthusiasm to a self-actualizing teacher.

McCLELLAND, D. C. Toward a theory of motive acquisition. In Ripple, R. E., ed.,
    Readings in learning and human abilities. New York: Harper & Row, 2nd ed.,
    1971.

McClelland describes how the need to achieve is learned and how it may be modified.

SEARS, P. S., & HILGARD, E. R. The teacher's role in the motivation of the learner. In
    Hilgard, E. R., ed., *Theories of learning and instruction,* National Society for the
    Study of Education, 63rd yearbook. Chicago: University of Chicago Press, 1964,
    part 1, pp. 182-209.

The authors blend research, theory, and practical applications.

SHEVIAKOV, G. V., & REDL, F. *Discipline for today's children and youth.* Washington,
    D. C.: Association for Supervision and Curriculum Development, 1956.

Thousands of teachers have found this short book to help much in dealing with classroom discipline.

WEINER, B. Motivation. In Ebel, R. L., ed., *Encyclopedia of educational research.* New York: Macmillan, 1969, pp. 878-888.

Research on motivation, little of which was done in school settings during the 1960s, is summarized.

Chapter 10 Factual Information and Verbal Knowledge

The Nature of Factual Information

associations of low meaningfulness
verbal knowledge
knowledge of specifics
knowledge of means of dealing with specifics
knowledge of universals and abstractions

Developmental Trends

language development
seven-step sequence in verbal development
a psycholinguistic view of reading
oral language skills and reading
reading as decoding
errors in oral reading
letter-sound correspondence
reading failure

Instructional Guides

help the individual to identify appropriate learning units
help the individual to identify meaningful relationships
provide for proper sequencing of material
arrange for appropriate practice
encourage independent evaluation

he learning of factual information and verbal knowledge is an important educational objective from kindergarten through graduate study. The learning of information is essential to the learning of other outcomes. Figure 10.1 outlines a sequence of outcomes in the cognitive domain. The arrangement is intended to indicate that each outcome precedes the one to the right of it: Nonverbal information, cognized through sensing objects and events directly, and factual and verbal information, cognized by hearing others and by reading, are essential for attaining most concepts. In turn, concepts are essential to forming principles, and both concepts and principles are essential in solving problems and in creative thinking.

A similar sequence of outcomes, designated as end products of learning, and related conditions of learning and instruction were discussed by Brownell and Hendrickson (1950) and Thorndike (1950) in a classic work on learning and instruction. Brownell and Hendrickson dealt with information, concepts, and generalizations; Thorndike described problem-solving.

In the first edition of this book, Klausmeier (1961) carried the sequence of outcomes in the cognitive domain further than the work just referred to by adding creativity. In this edition, principles of learning, in connection with each type of outcome, are considered as internal conditions; instructional guides, parallel to each principle, are considered as external facilitative conditions. This approach, which was discussed in Chapter 9 in connection with motivation, will be described further and related to an instructional system in the last part of this chapter.

Gagné (1965b) outlined a similar hierarchy of learning outcomes and gave considerable attention to the learning of the elementary associations — referred to in the next section of this chapter as *arbitrary associations* — and also to chains of associations of the kind represented in putting words together in sentences and in integrating separate motor activities in a skill such as typing or handwriting. At the top of Gagné's hierarchy are concepts, principles, and problem-solving.

In this chapter, the focus is on the learning and teaching of factual information. The nature of factual information, developmental trends in acquiring information verbally, and instructional guides related to factual information are discussed. In Chapter 11, the learning and teaching of concepts and principles are considered. In Chapter 12, problem-solving and creativity are dealt with.

THE NATURE OF FACTUAL INFORMATION

Information is anything that is discriminated by an individual (Guilford, 1967). Information may be gained directly through sensing environmental objects and events; for example, a child gains nonverbal — in this case, preverbal — information about a pet cat by seeing, touching, and hearing it. Information may also be gained verbally by hearing what others say

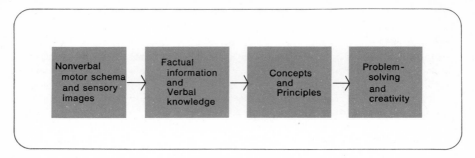

Fig. 10.1. A hierarchical sequence of learning outcomes in the cognitive domain.

and by reading. Thus, as the child grows older, he will gain more information about his cat and cats in general by hearing what others say and by reading about cats and other animals.

Factual information is information that is discriminated by many individuals who share the same cultural background and that is also accepted as correct or appropriate. A vast amount of factual information has been accumulated in all the subject-matter fields taught in the schools. This is information that is accepted as accurate by the teachers, the textbook writers, and others who know the subject matter.

Factual information is classified for illustrative purposes in this chapter as (1) associations of low meaningfulness, (2) specific information, and (3) verbal knowledge. Study of these classes of factual information and of the relationship of factual information to other outcomes of learning, particularly concepts, should enable the reader to identify types of factual information related to his own subject-matter interests. Such study should also help the teacher or curriculum worker in deciding how much emphasis to give to factual information in the curriculum.

1. Associations of Low Meaningfulness

Although you now have a large vocabulary and properly name things, you had to learn both the names and their associations with whatever they represent—their referents. If you had been born and raised in Russia or Japan, you would have learned a different set of names for many of the same things. In this sense, the three English words "letter," "page," and "book," which you learned long ago and the associations of them that you have made with the things for which they stand are of *low meaningfulness*. You did not ask about the origin of the words or why others had given the names to the things. No one explained why the things were named as they are. You accepted each name and its association with the thing.

The correct spelling of each word is also accepted factual information of low meaningfulness. Only one spelling is accepted as correct English usage (with a very few exceptions), and the correct spelling may be found in a standard dictionary. The nonphonetic spelling of so many English words is totally arbitrary, or at least of very low meaningfulness. Note, for example, a few of the different ways the "sh" sound is spelled in these words: "fission," "conscious," "facial," "mansion," "nation," "anxious," "mustache," "charade," "sure."

In learning a second language, the student learns some words or phrases in the second language that represent the same things or events as the English words or phrases he already knows. Because of differences in cultures, there often is not an exact correspondence between the two sets of words. Despite the frequent lack of perfect correspondence, the English-speaking student must develop a second vocabulary that can be used to represent the objects and events that he experiences. In other words, he must learn the vocabulary of the second language and associate it with either the corresponding English words or their referents. In either case, many of the associations are of low meaningfulness. Examples of these from French are: "book"-"livre," "dog"-"chien," "female teacher"-"maîtresse," "house"-"maison." In learning these associations, the student need not be taught why the word in the second language is equivalent. It will, however, help the student if he can find some device for associating the sets of words or phrases (for example, "door"-"portal"-"porte"), rather than proceeding by rote memory. In addition, all sources of possible relatedness, such as words having a common derivation and form, should be used.

The illustrations just given relate to languages. Other examples of associations of low meaningfulness can be identified in all subject fields. Thus, the labels associated with the numerals and other symbols in mathematics and with the symbols used in the sciences and music are of the same class. The labels associated with the colors and forms in art are, also. Students must learn many labels and what each is associated with if they are to use this information in attaining concepts and principles and in solving problems. Children who do not learn to speak the labels and make the associations before entering school are at a serious disadvantage in learning to read and to acquire basic concepts.

2. Specific Information

Specific information is of higher meaningfulness than are associations of the kind just described. One way of looking at specific information and relating it to educational objectives is in terms of the past and the present. In every subject field, not only in that called history, there is a continuously accumulating body of information that describes what was or has been. Thus, Neil Armstrong stepped onto the moon on July 20, 1969. This bit of historical information will be important to successive generations of Americans, perhaps as important as the fact that Columbus discovered America in 1492 or that the Declaration of Independence was signed on July 4, 1776.

Current information about many human, technical, and scientific matters was needed to get Armstrong and his companions to the moon. Thus, much information was assembled before the moon landing about human adaptability to weightlessness, the requirements for materials and equipment to be subjected to extreme temperatures and speeds, and the climate of the moon. You and I do not need to know all this information, but a number of people did need to know it for Armstrong to reach the moon. This information was all part of the vast body of information then known about man's adaptability, space machines and equipment, and the nature of the moon. The trip to the moon added still more information to what was known.

Another way of looking at descriptive information and relating it to various school subject-matter fields is in terms of substance. Many factual accounts focus on people, events and dates, and places or locations. (The dates are considered in connection with people and events.) A few examples of historical and current information of these different types may be helpful:

[PEOPLE]

Walt Whitman was an American poet.
Renoir painted in the impressionist era of the late 1800s and early 1900s.
Leonardo da Vinci was a famous Italian painter of the fifteenth century.
J. P. Guilford is the author of *Three Faces of Intellect*.
Edward Kennedy is the last of four Kennedy brothers (as of 1970).
Louis Armstrong is a famous jazz trumpet player (as of 1970).

[EVENTS AND DATES]

The Protestant Reformation occurred during the sixteenth century.
The Salk vaccine, introduced on a widespread basis in 1953, greatly reduced the incidence of poliomyelitis.

[PLACES AND LOCATIONS]

Philadelphia was the capital of the United States from 1790 to 1800.
Madison is the capital of Wisconsin.
The northern boundary of Montana is at the forty-ninth parallel.

3. Verbal Knowledge

Notice that each of the examples just given refers to one specific thing or event, not to a number of similar things or events. Also, each item of information stands by itself, and the different items cannot be related readily to one another. This kind of factual information is the first of three types of knowledge on a continuum of specific to general proposed by Bloom (1956). Bloom defined knowledge in the following way.

1.00 KNOWLEDGE

Knowledge as defined here includes those behaviors and test situations which emphasize the remembering, either by recognition or recall, of ideas, material, or phenomena. The behavior expected of a student in the recall situation is very similar to the behavior he was expected to have during the original learning situation. In the learning situation the student is expected to store in his mind certain information, and the behavior expected later is the remembering of this information. Although some alterations may be expected in the material to be remembered, this is a relatively minor part of the knowledge behavior or test. The process of relating and judging is also involved to the extent that the student is expected to answer questions or problems which are posed in a different form in the test situation than in the original learning situation. (Bloom, 1956, p. 62)

The three main categories of knowledge described by Bloom and the subcategories follow in outline form. Test items related to some of the subclasses are included to help you identify what may be considered as factual information related to your field of interest.

A. KNOWLEDGE OF SPECIFICS

Specific terminology — vocabulary of the fine arts, science, mathematics, and other subject fields.

A synapse can best be described as
(a) a lapse of memory caused by inadequate circulation of blood to the brain.
(b) the pairing of maternal with paternal chromosomes during maturation of the germ cells.
(c) the long cylindrical portion of an axon.
(d) the point at which the nervous impulse passes from one neuron to another.

Specific facts — dates, events, persons, places, sources of information, etc.

About what proportion of the population of the United States is living on farms?

(a) 10% (b) 20% (c) 35% (d) 50% (e) 60%

B. KNOWLEDGE OF WAYS AND MEANS OF DEALING WITH SPECIFICS

Conventions as embodied in correct form and usage in writing and speech, in common rules of etiquette, and in standard representational devices in maps and charts.

Which one of the following should not be classified as payment for the services of labor?
(a) The commissions earned by a real estate salesman.
(b) The fee paid a justice of the peace for performing a marriage.
(c) The dividend paid the owner of preferred stock.
(d) The salary of a United States senator.

Trends and sequences with respect to time.

The stages in the life history of the housefly are, in order,
(a) larva-egg-pupa-adult.
(b) pupa-larva-egg-adult.
(c) pupa-egg-larva-adult.
(d) egg-larva-adult-pupa.
(e) egg-larva-pupa-adult.

Categories into which specifics are grouped.
An engineer who designs houses is called
(a) a carpenter.
(b) a civil engineer.
(c) an architect.
(d) a draftsman.
(e) a mechanical engineer.
Criteria by which facts may be evaluated.
The criterion Darwin used to distinguish the more variable species from the less variable species was
(a) number of individuals in the species.
(b) frequency of individual differences in the species.
(c) number of varieties in the species.
(d) number of closely related species.
(e) number of different climatic conditions tolerated by the species.
Methods and techniques.
One use of the Periodic Table has been to
(a) determine the solubility of gases.
(b) find the degree of ionization of many compounds.
(c) predict undiscovered elements.
(d) determine molecular weights of compounds accurately.

C. KNOWLEDGE OF UNIVERSALS AND ABSTRACTIONS IN A FIELD

Principles and generalizations.
If the volume of a given mass of gas is kept constant, the pressure may be diminished by
(a) reducing the temperature.
(b) raising the temperature.
(c) adding heat.
(d) decreasing the density.
(e) increasing the density.
Theories and structures. (Bloom, 1956, pp. 62-88)

Categories B and C of course involve factual information; but they also involve concepts, principles, and problem-solving techniques—outcomes that, as noted earlier, are quite different from factual information. In this context, however, the emphasis is on the factual information—the verbal knowledge to be learned—in these two categories. As the test items indicate, the knowledge could be learned by memorizing, rather than by the search and study that lead to understanding of the concept, principle, or theory. In far too much schooling today, students are still led to acquire verbal knowledge solely by memorizing.

10.1. The name given to each of the 50 states, its capital city, the year that each became a state, the number of representatives and senators in the state legislature, and the area of the state are kinds of available information. Which of the five do you consider to be of lowest meaningfulness? Explain. Which, if any, do you think high school graduates should know?

10.2. Identify a few items of factual information related to your subject-matter major that you think every high school graduate should know. Check with your classmates, or others, to find out if they agree.

10.3. The amount of factual information is increasing at a very rapid rate, and only a little of it can be learned before high school graduation. Can you propose two or three criteria for deciding which factual information to include in a particular curriculum area or in the total school curriculum?

DEVELOPMENTAL TRENDS

Cognitive development during the early years of life involves comprehending the language others speak, speaking comprehensibly, and learning to read. In turn, these abilities enable a person to learn factual information and verbal knowledge.

The first part of this section is an overview of this development. A more detailed description of verbal learning follows. Next, the language and direct sensory experiences that precede initial concept formation are outlined. Finally, the developmental trends in reading as viewed by psycholinguists are traced. This emphasis on language is not intended to discourage the use of nonverbal means of presenting and securing information. The next chapter discusses in detail the need for direct experiencing in acquiring most concepts.

An Overview of Language Development

A developmental sequence related to language activities and their interrelations is shown in Fig. 10.2. The interrelations are now described.

Shortly after birth, the infant responds to objects and events in his environment. He hears, he sees, he touches. His experiences and increasing maturation provide the background for organizing sounds, sights, and feelings into patterns whereby various words are eventually distinguished, associated with experiences, and spoken with meaning. Noticing objects and events and listening to words that accompany them are necessary for the development of vocabulary and speech, which proceeds rapidly during the preschool years.

A fund of meaningful concepts, the ability to distinguish likenesses and differences among objects and sounds, and the ability to speak clearly and correctly are among prerequisites for beginning reading instruction, usually during a child's fifth or sixth year. The child who is ready to read is soon ready for writing. A rich background of manipulatory experiences provides the basis for beginning writing. Because the child is most interested in writing words that he says frequently and may have learned to read—his name, for example—he soon begins to spell some of the words. Some children scribble in imitation of adult writing or are even able to write their own names before they can do other writing. Spelling and writing facilitate reading through reinforcement, just as reading is enhanced by listening which broadens experience.

By the time they are 9 or 10 years old, many children are mature enough and have acquired enough proficiency in reading, writing, listening, and speaking so that they make rapid progress in these areas during

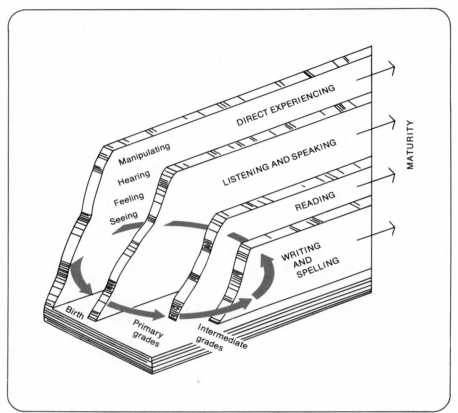

Fig. 10.2. Developmental sequence in language activities and their interrelations.

the intermediate grades and are able to apply them to other areas of study. Further growth in the language arts may be expected, provided instruction in school is planned for that purpose—that is, the children must be stimulated to continue their progress and must be given adequate guidance and assistance.

In relation to the above sequence, we should keep three points in mind when working with children: (1) For the child to use increasingly difficult abstractions—words—in reading and writing, some direct experience with the qualities or characteristics for which the words stand is essential, and such work needs special attention. For example, the child may encounter new words in his work in science, music, or any other area that he cannot understand fully unless their close connection with his direct experience is made clear. (2) Children may not develop language abilities exactly as indicated above; there are exceptional children in language development, as well as in other areas of development. (3) Not all children reach a given point in development at the same chronological age; one child does not read as well at age 9 as another does at age 8.

Verbal Development

Jensen (1968) described seven consecutive sets of behaviors that are characteristic of children, from early responding to words with motor responses through manipulating ideas in solving problems. He related these to seven types of learning. Here we are concerned with the developmental sequences in acquiring the labels or names, associating the names with the things for which they stand, and then associating words with other words. Therefore, only the behaviors are stated; each is followed by examples and then a short discussion to clarify the behavior. Jensen pointed out that each preceding behavior may be continued through the next levels; thus the behaviors overlap.

Jensen, like Staats (1968), as noted in Chapter 2, uses S-R terminology and treats concepts as mediators. However, he freely infers covert verbal behavior, also referred to as implicit behavior or speaking silently to oneself. In the following discussion the strict S-R terminology and interpretations are abandoned so that the developmental trends may be emphasized.

1. Responding nonverbally to the speech of others.
   Examples: Making a nonword sound when the word "milk" is heard.
   Smiling when the word "Mother" is heard.
   Pointing the arm when the mother points and says "Daddy."

Before the infant can speak he responds to the words spoken by others. The motor actions, of course, are limited by the level of development. The important point is that the word spoken by another person serves as a mediator between the infant's hearing the word and his motor response. Already at the age of 1 year words are more important to the child than any other form of auditory stimulation.

2. Making verbal responses to stimuli but without awareness of the responses implied by the word.
   Examples: Calling the bottle when seen "milk."
   Calling the person when seen "Mama."

This phase starts as soon as the infant can say words. The early responding to things with the name is at the same level as responding with motor responses insofar as mediation is concerned. The spoken word does not have any regulative feedback; that is, the child's speaking the word has no more effect on his subsequent behavior than does earlier smiling or pointing. But, being able to respond with a word is a developmental milestone in two ways. The sound attracts the attention of another person, such as the parent. In turn, the parent may smile, attend to the child, or in some other way reinforce the child's speaking. This tends to strengthen naming activity by the child.

3. Controlling one's own behavior by his own verbalization or responding with controlled behavior to the verbalization of others.

> *Examples*:   The child thinks of the word "run" and starts running.
> The child thinks "don't" and stops touching the television set.

At this level the child's own verbalizations influence his own overt behavior. He has now passed from merely responding to the speech of others with motor actions and verbal responses of a naming kind. At this level he can say a word to himself, such as "press," and respond by pressing an object in an experimental setting. He can say "one, two" and will press after saying each word. Similarly, he will respond by pressing after each "one, two" said by another person. At the two earlier levels he could not do these.

4. Experiencing verbal and nonverbal events which give rise to covert or overt verbal responses that in turn guide behavior.

> *Examples*:   Seeing a dark cloud, saying correctly "rain" and hurrying home.
> Hearing the teacher say "Give me an example of a quadrilateral," responding covertly, and then drawing a square.

This behavior emerges in some children as early as age 5 and is predominant at age 9 to 10. There is not an exact age, or even a clearly discriminable time, when this level begins. It emerges from a combining of the earlier two behaviors—naming many things and events properly and responding to external and internal verbalizations with both covert and overt behaviors. At this higher level, of which lower-form animals are incapable, the child uses words to manipulate concepts in thought.

5. Associating two words.

> *Examples*:   Hearing the word "salt" and thinking "pepper" or "hot" and thinking "cold" or the first name of a friend and thinking the last name.

During elementary school years there is a steady increase in word associations made according to form class—that is, nouns with nouns, verbs with verbs, and so on. Children also become more alike with respect to the words that get associated, and they form associations more rapidly with increasing age. At this level, the second word that becomes associated with the first, as well as the first, mediates between stimulus events and overt and covert behaviors.

6. Organizing and remembering ideas in phrases and sentences and in other ways relating two sets of verbal events.

> *Examples*:   Learning verbal material in usual sentence form more efficiently than in unrelated lists of words.
> Using mnemonic devices to organize and recall lists.

This level overlaps the preceding one. In the preceding only two verbal units were associated. Here, strings of symbols and words are associated, such as when associating things with consecutive letters of the alphabet and when forming sentences covertly to organize and remember the events of the day.

7. Organizing and remembering in a hierarchy of verbal associations and relationships.

>*Examples*: Associating "table" with "chair" but not with "bed" until all three are associated with furniture. Organizing and manipulating knowledge about increasingly larger bodies of related information of the kind incorporated in a taxonomy, the arabic number system, Guilford's structure of intellect, etc.

Knowing the words that stand for hierarchical concepts permits the organizing of the words and the concepts into hierarchical patterns of the kind outlined earlier in this chapter. Also, words get put into sentences as part of the thought processes, or mental operations, and permit the solution of problems. This final level begins during elementary school years and continues at an increasingly complex level as long as one acquires more information about relatable sets of human experiences.

The preceding outline shows that a child acquires names and associates the names with the things for which they stand. Also, names are acquired for behaviors, such as pointing and running, and are associated with the relevant behaviors. Subsequently, words are associated with other words. This naming and associating, acquired through observing and imitating others, illustrates acquiring factual information of low meaningfulness. As Jensen points out, having names and associations permits the subsequent learning of concepts. When the child has acquired names, associations, and some concepts, he talks to himself, thereby voluntarily guiding and controlling his own behavior, including that involved in problem-solving.

Development Preceding Initial Concept Formation

Figure 10.3 shows the relationships among preverbal motor and sensory experiences, naming objects and securing information about them (corresponding to Jensen's stage 2), and the first level of concept formation (corresponding to Jensen's stages 3 and 4). We have already used a child and his cat as an example. This illustration develops the example more fully.

A child has a pet cat. As an infant he saw and touched the cat, but could not speak the word "cat." Some internal representation of the cat probably developed in the form of a motor schema from his touching the cat, and an image developed from seeing it. The child matured, heard others say "cat" in the presence of the cat, and saw what they did with the cat. Eventually, and probably through observing and imitating, the child learned to say "cat" and to associate the word with the object. Re-

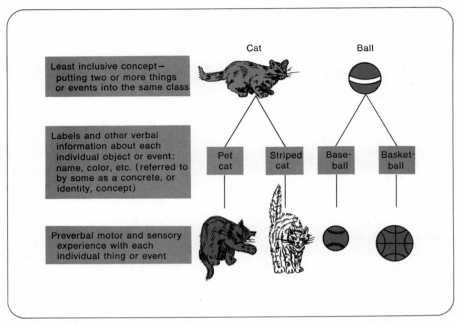

Fig. 10.3. Relationships among preverbal information, verbal information, and subordinate concepts.

gardless of whether the cat was walking, lying down, or drinking milk, the child also learned to treat it as the same pet cat. (This may have preceded the child's actually speaking the word "cat" comprehensibly.) When the one cat was treated in the same way, the child had formed what Woodruff (1962) referred to as a concrete concept and what Bruner et al. (1956) designated an identity concept.

Assume now that another cat is brought into the house and the child gains familiarity with it. When the child calls this new entry a "cat" and in other ways responds to it as he does to the pet, he has formed a class concept of cat. Through direct sensory experiences and through observing and imitating other persons, the child acquired information about both the first cat and the second cat—appearance, sound, movements, the name "cat," etc.—so that he now responds to both cats as if they belonged to the same class. In the terminology used in Chapter 2, the child has *discriminated* properties of the two cats, has acquired the name "cat," has associated the name with the thing, and has made the same response to the two cats (stimulus generalization). The conditions of learning are contiguity of sensory experiences, observation and imitation to learn the name and associate it with the cat, practice or use, and feedback. (You may wish to review this terminology in Chapter 2.)

Once an individual forms some concepts and has also developed language for representing the concepts, he may use the words to state descriptive information about objects and events. If he knows the words and the concepts "flag," "red," "white," "blue," he may say, "That flag is red, white, and blue." If another person also knows these same words and concepts, he will know what the first is talking about. Thus, cognizing information is essential to the learning of concepts. Some information is acquired through direct sensory experiences with things and events, some is acquired through observing other people, and some is acquired in oral discourse with others and by reading.

Older children and adults must also secure information in order to form concepts. The order in which they get information is often like this: acquiring the label or name for something, identifying or being given examples or instances of the concept, and then having direct sensory experiences with examples or instances of the concept. Books can provide the first two categories of information, but not the last. Thus, this book does attempt to carry out the first two; the student, however, must seek the direct experiences himself.

Learning To Read: A Psycholinguistic View

Learning to read is a complex developmental process that requires the child to learn factual and conceptual information about the relationship of the written English language to the oral dialect of the English he already speaks. It appears that the child must also bring to the reading task a variety of prereading skills and concepts or acquire them incidentally in the context of instruction. After he achieves some skill in the reading task itself, he must learn to read for a variety of purposes. Reading is vitally important, of course; it is through reading that much of the learning of all other subject matters is accomplished.

In this section we will consider reading in some detail from a psycholinguistic viewpoint. We will ask what reading is, what sorts of factual and conceptual information the child might profitably bring to the reading task, what information is acquired in learning to read, and why children fail to learn to read. Similar analyses of the content and acquisition of other subject matters, for instance, mathematics, can be made; reading is discussed here at length because, even in the space age, it is still our most-used educational tool.

What Is Reading? The first-grader stumbling aloud through "Run, Spot, run" and the college student silently studying this page are both said to be reading; clearly, there are long years of experience and skill separating the two performances. There is a different purpose in each case, as well; the child is practicing reading itself, whereas the adult is putting reading to use in getting information. Common to the two actions, however, is this: *Both readers are translating written symbols into that form of language from which they already derive meaning.* The adult may accomplish this translation with greater sophistication by using many more levels of information and swift, practiced integration of that information; but the translating, or *decoding*, process stands at the core of reading. This decoding process must be learned in early school years and later shaped to a variety of purposes in learning other subject matters, skimming newspaper headlines, looking up names in the telephone directory, amusing oneself with a murder mystery, or reviewing recent research in one's field.

Learning to read, then, can be defined as learning to translate from written symbols (the writing system, or *orthography*, of the language) into that form of language from which the child already derives meaning, most often, the spoken language (Venezky, Calfee, & Chapman, 1968). If this definition seems complicated, it is because it has a threefold purpose: (1) to focus on reading as a decoding process; (2) to focus on the child's already extensive mastery of the basic communication system, spoken language; and (3) to exclude certain skills that have traditionally been included in reading instruction. These three foci will be taken up in reverse order in the following paragraphs.

What Is Excluded by the Psycholinguist's Definition? The following are among the objectives that are not part of the teaching of reading: comprehension (in the sense of understanding utterances or drawing inferences from them), new oral vocabulary, organizational skills, and critical thinking. These are all legitimate — even crucial — instructional objectives, but they are properly considered objectives in their own right, rather than part of reading, according to psycholinguists. This in no way denies, however, the fact that the same elementary school teacher instructs the children in all these skills, whether they are designated as part of the instructional program of the school in reading, language arts, communications, or some other curriculum area. Assuredly, comprehension and thinking skills can contribute to the level and organization of information retained from reading; reading, in turn, may serve as one context in which these skills are acquired. The basic point, however, is that learning to read is not the same as learning to think; thus an ideal measure of the child's progress in reading would relate his understanding of a written text to his understanding of the same passage presented orally. Evaluating interpretations is one way to do this. Two children may interpret the written sentence "The grass is always greener on the other side of the fence" quite differently, and we may consider one interpretation more advanced than the other. But the question of interest for the *reading* process is whether each child interprets the written sentence as he would the spoken sentence.

Development of Oral Language Skills. Implicit in the psycholinguist's definition of reading is the assumption that the child's oral language skills are relatively well developed by school age; recent research supports that assumption (Ervin-Tripp, 1966). The learning of spoken language involves the learning of at least three basic systems of the language: the sound system (*phonology*), or what sounds belong to English and how they are put together in words; the grammatical system (*syntax*), or how words are put together into sentences; and the meaning system (*semantics*), or what words stand for. For each of these systems the child must master both speaking and listening skills.

The psycholinguist's account of oral language acquisition differs in part from the developmental learning account of Jensen, outlined earlier. In particular, Jensen does not discuss learning of the phonological system, and his account of the acquisition of syntax is disputed by the psycholinguist. The latter sees the child as learning general *rules* of sentence formation, rather than acquiring word-to-word associations; this is an area of disagreement among theorists. The S-R theory, however, seems less satisfactory than a "rule" theory in some respects; for instance, a child does say "mouses" or "goed," words that he has never heard adults say but that he could be expected to produce through overgeneralization of rules.

Setting aside the theoretical controversy over how language is learned, the data gathered on children's linguistic accomplishments give us the following picture of language development (Bellugi & Brown, 1964; Ervin-Tripp, 1966; McCarthy, 1954; Smith & Miller, 1966). The acquisition of phonology, syntax, and semantics, in that order, is discussed.

1. Phonology. The infant's earliest sounds are cries of discomfort; cooing increases in frequency in the first two months. Babbling, or repetition of sound sequences, usually appears by the fourth month, increasing in quantity and variety to a peak at about 8 to 11 months. Unlike crying and perhaps cooing, babbling serves no discernible communicative function. Linguists have reported hearing speech sounds characteristic of many different languages in the young child's babbling; it seems likely that the child's physiological capacity to make speech sounds, including those of his native language, is realized in infancy. A longer developmental span is required, however, for the child to learn to produce some intended sound sequence. The child's first words, appearing between 12 and 18 months, show considerable variability in the actual sounds used. For instance, "dada," "tata," and "papa" may all be produced for "da-da." Most sounds of English can be produced in at least some words at age 3 and 4, though the child may still persist in certain sound substitutions, e.g., "wed wabbit" for "red rabbit." This shows a failure of production, however, rather than perception: such a child is likely to reject an adult's repetition of "wed wabbit," furiously insisting that he said "wed wabbit." By 7 or 8, children produce sounds correctly in essentially all phonological environments, as adults do (Templin, 1957).

2. Syntax. The child's acquisition of syntax may be said to begin with the utterance of two-word sentences; this happens when the child has acquired 50 or so words of vocabulary (18 to 24 months). Even at this primitive two-word stage of sentence production, the child does not put together just any two words; rather, some few words occur frequently in either first (or second) position, followed (or preceded) by most other words in the child's vocabulary. This kind of construction is called a *pivot structure*; examples are "all-gone car," "all-gone milk," "there car," "there milk." From pivot structures the child progresses to *telegraphic* speech, so-called because the sentences sound like those adults might construct in writing telegrams (e.g., "milk on table"), leaving out function words such as prepositions, articles, and auxiliary verbs.

During the years 2 to 4 the child makes giant strides in mastering the intricacies of English syntax. He learns to use regular inflections marking tense and plurality (even saying "goed" and "mouses" for a while); to indicate agreement in number between subject and verb; to use and inflect auxiliary verbs ("I was going." "You will be going."); to place auxiliary verbs properly in question and negative constructions ("Was I going?" "Aren't you going?" "Won't you go?"), and to form the negative, the passive, many different kinds of question constructions, and their combinations. The child does not produce these constructions correctly from the outset, adding to his repertoire; rather, he seems to begin with simple rules that may seldom govern adult forms (e.g., placing "no" or "don't" at the beginning of sentences for all negatives), with intermediate stages that are consistent though often abbreviated or incorrect versions of the adult construction.

   3. Semantics. The child's acquisition of vocabulary during preschool years is equally as impressive; by the time he is 6, his spoken vocabulary can be estimated in thousands of words, his comprehension vocabulary in thousands or tens of thousands. Concrete nouns predominate in the child's early word learning, followed by verbs; adjectives appear relatively late (2 to 3 years). Interestingly enough, the referents for the early nouns appear to be generalized attributes, rather than unique objects; so, for instance, all adult males may be called "daddy" and all four-legged animals "doggie." As the child's vocabulary increases, specificity of reference increases and the meaning system more closely resembles the adult model.

   The child entering school, then, has mastered an extensive portion of his native language. The sounds, sentence structures, and words he produces are those of the dialect of English spoken around him; as dialects of English differ, so will the spoken language of 6-year-olds. There is no evidence as yet, however, that one dialect is less systematic or complex than another; nor is there good evidence that children of a particular culture and dialect—e.g., an inner-city-core—are retarded in the acquisition of their own dialect. Some constructions of English are still to be mastered, of course; for example, subjunctive clauses such as "if I were grown up" and nominalizations such as "the man who came to dinner" are relatively infrequent in 6-year-olds' speech, and if-then sentences, even if produced, are not interpreted as logical statements in the way adults understand them. The striking fact remains that children entering school are remarkably competent in their native language, despite wide variability in cognitive functioning and linguistic environment. Thus, we can expect that in teaching the child to read, we do not additionally have to teach him how to talk, unless we insist on trying to teach him to read words not already in his vocabulary or sentence structures which he does not normally produce or understand.

   To summarize, learning to read is neither learning how to talk nor learning how to think; rather, it is learning how to translate from written symbols into that form of language from which one already derives meaning. The ability to understand and produce the spoken language is the foremost of the prereading skills, in the sense that reading is derivative of spoken language; it is also the ability that children, with rare exceptions, bring to the classroom.

   Reading as Decoding: Component Skills. The psycholinguistic definition of reading implies several kinds of information which the child might profitably bring to first grade. Learning to decode the printed word requires either the *rote association* of a vocabulary word with its printed configuration or the rote association of sounds of English with the letters most often representing those sounds. The latter associations, called *letter-sound correspondences*, allow the child to sound out new words, discovering matches with his oral language. Such learning, of course, greatly reduces the memory load imposed by whole-word decoding methods. Either form of learning, however, is dependent on certain skills which the child must bring to the reading task or acquire therein. Letters or letter configurations must be recognized as the same or different and remembered. Even if the kindergarten child or beginning reader can match and discriminate shapes, the crucial fact of orientation on the page and left-right ordering may escape him completely. A cup is still the same cup, whatever orientation the child sees it in; he must learn, however, that a "b" is not a "d," nor a "p" a "q." A collection of blocks is still the same set of blocks when it is rearranged; "ab," however, is not the same as "ba." Letters and words must be processed in left-right order from line to line if letter-sound correspondences are to lead to recognition of words and whole-word correspondences are to lead to sentences. This processing order is not innate for a child; there are, of course, languages that are written from top to bottom (Chinese) or right to left (Hebrew).

The spoken word which the child must associate with the printed word is usually already available to him; but it is not clear that the child attends to the *individual* sounds of words which must be associated with *individual* printed letters in learning letter-sound correspondences. That is, the child does not necessarily come to first grade recognizing that "moon" and "mother" begin with the same sound.

The components of the decoding process just discussed can be listed as follows: matching, discrimination, and identification of a single letter and letter sequences, including attention to orientation, grouping, and ordering; left-right processing of information; matching and discrimination of single sounds; and the association of symbols with sounds.

The best single predictor of reading achievement in the early grades is the child's ability, in kindergarten, to name or recognize letters of the alphabet. Though this measure may simply reflect characteristics of the home, there is evidence that alphabet-naming continues to predict reading achievement even when factors expected to operate in the home (amount of reading to the child, mother's education, etc.) are controlled (deHirsch, 1966). There are several reasons why this may be so, if we consider the listing of component skills and concepts above. A child who can name the letters of the alphabet has had to learn much of the information just described: differentiation of same and different letters, including attention to orientation; possibly, left-right processing of a sequence of letters; and the association of nonsense sounds with letters—nonsense sounds which, within groups, differ only in the single sounds that generally correspond with the letter ("b," "t"; "f," "s"). Alternatively, the ability to learn alphabet names without explicit instruction may reflect ability to learn rote associations, or factual information, in general.

Information of a more general kind may also prepare the child for learning to read. A notion of the "reading game," or recognition that writing is a way of recording what we say, may be important. Familiarity with books—holding them, turning and inspecting pages—may be very helpful. Finally, familiarity with the situations and experiences described in beginning reading texts may enhance interest and motivation in reading. Such general knowledge may be expected to vary with cultural and socioeconomic background more directly than the specific sorts of information discussed above, and far more directly than oral language acquisition appears to vary.

Reading Acquisition. We have discussed component skills which the child might profitably bring to the reading task; if he lacks them, they must be acquired in the context of reading instruction. The primary content of early reading acquisition is the learning of factual information. We may regard the stimulus in every instance (word or letter) as being of low meaningfulness; the response to be learned can vary in meaningfulness from a concrete noun to a single nonsense sound. Letter-sound correspondence learning is more difficult, because the associations are of minimal meaningfulness; at the same time, such learning reduces the memory load involved in remembering and learning word-word correspondence. There is evidence that when illiterate adults are taught to read by the whole-word method, the better readers *acquire* letter-sound correspondences. Whether or not children who are better readers know more letter-sound correspondences is a topic that will soon be examined.

When we investigate what children actually learn during the first years of reading, we should consider not only letter-sound correspondences but also errors in reading made in the classroom. In addition, we can ask whether there is a developmental sequence to the information acquired. These topics will be taken up under the headings, *errors in oral reading* and *letter-sound correspondence learning*.

Errors in Oral Reading. One question that can be answered by examining children's oral reading errors is whether or not they make use of sentence context in identifying particular words. When children are asked to read sentences containing words that they have missed in reading word lists, they get most of the words right, indicating that they are using sentence context (Goodman, 1965). Older children get a higher proportion of the formerly missed words right in sentences than younger children: error rates decrease from 38 percent for first-graders to 18 percent for third-graders. Older children, then, can make increasingly correct use of sentence context.

Even first-graders reflect their knowledge of the oral language in the reading errors they make. Weber (1968) analyzed errors according to whether the sentence read, up to and including the error, remained grammatically and semantically acceptable. That is, she asked whether the reading error created an ungrammatical or nonsensical sentence beginning. Of the errors 91 percent were grammatically acceptable; and of these, 92 percent were semantically acceptable, indicating a remarkable fidelity to language constraints. No differences in these figures were found for good and poor readers.

Another study of reading errors made by first-graders indicates a developmental sequence of error types. Biemiller (1970) classified errors as belonging to one of three categories: dependence on sentence context, failure to respond, or dependence on graphic information (the first letters of the written and spoken word matched). He found three major stages of development during the school year: At first, the majority of children's errors depended only on context, showing no graphic relation to the written word. For instance, a child may have read "He went home" for "He went to school." Some children in the study continued to make such errors all year; in general, these were the poorest readers. A second phase was identified in which the majority of errors were failures to respond; on encountering an unknown word, the child simply waited to be told. The earlier in the year a child entered this phase, the more likely he was to be a better reader at the end of the year. Some weeks or months after the emergence of this error pattern, a third stage appeared. Errors of commission again dominated, but with this difference: When the child was reading easy material, the few errors he made (5 to 10 percent) were context-related; when reading difficult material, however, the child made errors that tended to reflect graphic information as well, for instance, reading "He walked home" for "He went home."

Two important generalizations can be drawn from these studies: (1) Children do not guess words at random in reading, but select a guess from the subset of words which would be grammatically and semantically appropriate at that point in the sentence. This is true of both better and poorer readers. (2) The better reader learns earlier to suppress an incorrect guess and begins to use letter-sound correspondences earlier in determining a guess. We now turn to the latter type of learning.

Letter-Sound Correspondence Learning. It has long been recognized that English orthography is not a one-letter-one-sound system. G. B. Shaw once observed that "ghoti" could spell "fish"—if the "gh" was pronounced as in "enough," the "o" as in "women," and the "ti" as in "nation." Irregularities in the pronunciation of letters are not so numerous as this example implies, however. Many letters do correspond to a single sound most of the time; other letters and letter sequences have invariant pronunciations when they occur in particular positions in a word. These may be termed simple letter-sound correspondences. There also are conditional correspondences, in which a letter has two major pronunciations, but the choice of pronunciation is regularly determined by following or preceding letters. For instance, the letter "c" is pronounced as both "k" and "s" at the beginning of words, but the "k" sound always occurs when "c" is followed by "a," "o," and "u" (e.g., "cake," "coke") and the "s" sound when "c" is followed by "e," "i," and "y" (e.g., "cell," "city").

Letter-sound correspondence learning can be studied by constructing synthetic words (e.g., "cofe") and asking children or adults to pronounce them; when this is done, we find that better readers give more appropriate pronunciations than poor readers. This is true of second- through sixth-graders and on through high school. In addition, mastery of the conditional, or complex, correspondences increases with age (Calfee, Venezky,

& Chapman, 1969). When simple correspondences are investigated (e.g., "f" is usually given the "f" sound), even second-graders show extensive mastery of them. Appropriate pronunciations are given 95 percent of the time by the best second-grade students and 75 percent of the time by the poorest; by sixth grade the poorest students are giving correct pronunciations 94 percent of the time (Chapman, Venezky, & Calfee, 1970). The children participating in these studies had been taught reading by a variety of methods; the better readers in each school and grade, regardless of method, showed greater mastery of letter-sound correspondences. As might be expected, mastery of simple correspondences occurs much earlier than mastery of conditional correspondence.

This account of reading in the early grades indicates that the beginning reader uses his knowledge of the oral language in attempting to decode texts; the better readers soon learn to use letter-sound correspondences in decoding as well. In the beginning reader these decoding strategies emerge sequentially, with an intervening phase in which the child waits for words to be supplied; in the older, better reader these strategies and many others may be available for getting meaning from the page. Such flexible strategies cannot emerge, however, until the child has acquired extensive information about the relation of orthography to language.

Reading Failure. The number of children who experience difficulty in learning to read, or who never advance beyond the fifth-grade reading level, is estimated at 15 to 30 percent of the school population. These children can be identified with some success as early as kindergarten or first grade; initial difficulty in learning to read is evident, and the gap widens each successive year. The causes and cures of reading disability are variously described and prescribed. Some attribute reading failure to minimal brain damage or malfunction of the visual perception system, some to lack of maturational or intellectual growth. Severe emotional problems have been cited as the cause. Use of the wrong teaching method or the use of texts which fail to match the child's oral language or cultural experience are also candidates. Finally, deficits in independent component skills have been suggested as a source of difficulty.

The appropriate remedy for reading failure depends on the judged cause: specific neurophysiological or perceptual training, given brain damage or malfunction; delayed, slowed, or intensified reading instruction, given lack of reading readiness, psychiatric therapy, given emotional problems; the use of a different teaching method or text, given inappropriate methods or materials; or early detection and remediation of component skill deficits, should they prove sources of difficulty.

Much research remains to be done in the prevention and remediation of reading failure; its importance is underlined by a declaration of the Office of Education that the elimination of reading failure by 1980 would be a national goal. At present, the literature on remediation indicates no single technique that is universally successful except, perhaps, a very simple one: spending extra time working with children. Different remedies may be appropriate for different children, in any case. What is clear is that *prevention* of reading failure is much better than remediation; the cost of years of failure is too great. (In this connection, the Wisconsin Research and Development Center for Cognitive Learning is developing and testing a design of reading and prereading instruction in which each child is taught systematically the component skills that he needs to attain successively higher levels of reading competence.)

10.4. "I read and write English." Trace how you yourself learned to say each of those five words for the first time and then learned to combine them into a sentence for the first time, in terms of the stages outlined by Jensen.

10.5. What is the distinction between an identity and a class concept? What additional information and abilities are needed to form a class concept?

10.6. How does the psycholinguist define reading? What is excluded from this definition that others have often included?

10.7. Some children read at age 5. Others are not reading at age 9. What conditions within the child and within the environment, including instruction, might be associated with these differences in achievement?

10.8. To what extent is making letter-to-sound correspondence meaningful or rote learning? Should the teacher try to explain to children why a letter or combination of letters sounds the way it does? Should the teacher try to explain to children why they should learn the letter-to-sound correspondences? Explain. What procedures are used in "Sesame Street"?

10.9. Information may be secured by: (a) having direct experiences with things, conditions, and events; (b) listening to someone; (c) reading; (d) hearing and seeing a television presentation or sound motion picture; and (e) discussing. Related to this course in educational psychology, indicate when and for what purposes each of these might be carried out.

PRINCIPLES PERTAINING TO FACTUAL INFORMATION

In Chapter 1, eight operations in an instructional system were outlined. The relationship of the instructional system to the teaching of factual information is now summarized in seven concise statements. Then, guides pertaining specifically to teaching-learning activities are identified and discussed at greater length.

1. State the objectives in terms of the factual information the students should know at the end of the instructional sequence. Here it is important to decide whether the main objective is the acquisition of factual information or whether factual information will be acquired primarily in connection with attaining other outcomes in the cognitive, psychomotor, or affective domain. Also, one must decide whether the instructional sequence should be designed to get all students to the same level of achievement or to encourage differences in final achievements. Each approach is appropriate for particular courses and units. Both the students and the teacher should know and accept the approach that will be used in the particular course or unit. (Chapter 4 deals with instructional objectives.)

2. Assess each student's readiness for learning the factual information.

A pretest that samples from everything the students are to learn will indicate their present level of knowledge. Securing information about students' past performances in the same or a related field will provide some indication of their readiness for the present program. (Chapters 17 and 18 discuss standardized and teacher-made tests and evaluation procedures to assess achievements and abilities.)

3. Identify the specific subject matter to be learned and the related instructional materials in which it is incorporated. In some situations the teacher will take the initiative in identifying all the instructional materials. In others, the students will assume much responsibility. As students grow older they normally can identify and use a wide variety of printed and audiovisual material and can secure information directly from observing, interviewing, etc. (Chapter 5 deals with instructional materials.)

4. Organize the teacher and student activities to promote learning. The instructional guides outlined in the next pages deal primarily with this component of the instructional system. (Chapter 8 deals with organization for instruction.)

5. Outline a pattern for the effective use of time, space, and equipment by the students and also by the instructional staff of the team or unit. This is especially important when equipment and spaces, such as foreign language laboratories and instructional resource centers, are used by many students to acquire information during or outside regular class periods. (Chapter 8 deals with organization for instruction.)

6. Assess student achievement throughout the instructional sequence and on completing it. The amount of factual information that is learned from the beginning to the end of a sequence can be determined quite accurately through the use of carefully constructed pretests and posttests which sample from all that should be learned, as discussed in Chapters 17 and 18.

7. Arrange for appropriate feedback to the students so that they may identify progress and overcome difficulties. In general, the students must participate directly in this, as will be pointed out in an instructional guide.

The principles that follow were derived from empirical research and theory, as reported earlier in this chapter and in Chapters 2 and 3. The instructional guides, in turn, are related to the principles and to the instructional system just described. Research identified as dealing directly with the instructional guides is also reported. Thus, the principles and guides might be treated as a heuristic aid in organizing additional information and also in generating hypotheses. Much of the information presented about each guide (and those related to other outcomes in later chapters) thus stems primarily from a careful analysis of the theoretical and empirical information; much also comes, however, from the authors' extensive experience as teachers, at the elementary, high school, and college level and their continuous work with school people in cooperative research and development activities. The guides are now discussed in detail.

Principle	Instructional Guide
1. Identifying an appropriate learning unit facilitates the acquisition of verbal knowledge.	1. Help the individual to identify appropriate learning units.
2. Cognizing relationships between new information and what one already knows and between components of a whole facilitates the learning of the new information.	2. Help the individual to identify meaningful relationships.
3. Cognizing and organizing sequential components is essential to the mastery of complex material.	3. Provide for proper sequencing of material.
4. Practicing, or using, is essential for attaining a high level of mastery of information and subsequently remembering it.	4. Arrange for appropriate practice.
5. Evaluating the adequacy and accuracy of one's information is essential for attaining independence in learning factual information.	5. Encourage independent evaluation.

1. Help the Individual To Identify Appropriate Learning Units

Suppose that an older student wants to learn a list of 25 unrelated items. How might the 25 items be handled? Miller, Galanter, and Pribram (1960) indicate that about 4 or 5 unrelated words, elements, items, chunks, or thoughts are about all the average person will reliably recall after one encounter. A student might thus divide the 25 items into 5 sets of 5 items and try to learn 5 items at a time; thus he treats each of the five sets as a single unit. To remember the order of the five sets, he might give a different name to each set. The five names might comprise an unusual sentence that would be easily recalled. If the individual can make these associations, all he has to do is to recall the 5-word sentence and he can then recall all 25 items. The same authors indicate that the longest unorganized list that most of us ever learn is the 26 letters of the alphabet.

When college students are asked to learn long lists of meaningless nonsense syllables during experiments, they make sentences. In turn, they can remember the sentences. For example, Miller, Galanter, and Pribram (1960) reported that a student faced with "BOF," "XAJ," "MIB," "ZYQ" developed this sentence: "BOF exaggerates his misery because he is not sick." A sentence like this is much easier to recall than are the disconnected syllables. Some students apparently are capable of devising their own mnemonic devices of this kind. Others, however, impose brutal repetition on themselves when they try to master long lists of material that is of low meaningfulness to them.

Analysis of the errors made in spelling clarifies the difficulty of one

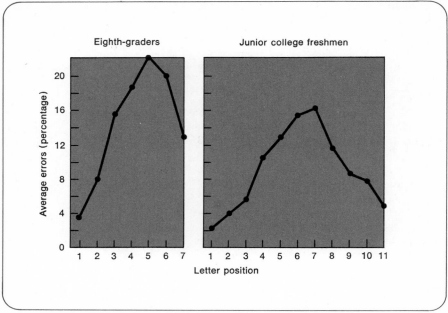

Fig. 10.4. Serial-position curves for errors in 7- and 11-letter words. (Jensen, 1962, p. 107)

type of potentially meaningful material (Jensen, 1962). Figure 10.4 shows the letter position at which errors were made in 7-letter words by eighth-graders and in 11-letter words by junior college freshmen. The peak error rate is at the fifth letter in 7-letter words and at the seventh letter in 11-letter words. Incidentally, no easy solution to eliminating spelling errors is apparent. Students who have difficulty in spelling do not seem to be able to devise, on their own, a way of dividing the words into two parts, practicing each part, and then remembering the parts. Also, when the missed letters are emphasized for study, fewer errors are made with them, but there is an increase in errors on the letters not emphasized.

2. Help the Individual To Identify Meaningful Relationships

One mark of a good teacher is the ability to help students find relationships among the informational items within the same subject field and across subject fields. The foreign language teacher relates some personal experiences or the experiences of others in the foreign country to the dialogues to be learned and points out associations between the English vocabulary and the foreign language vocabulary. Similarly, the history teacher relates the political facts of an era to the art, music, and literature of the era. When these relationships are identified consistently by the teacher, the students themselves find more relationships and thereby are enabled to organize relatively discrete information into meaningful patterns.

Another way to help students acquire new information is through providing a set of concepts — an advance organizer (described in Chapter 2) to which the new information can be related. Learning a few new concepts of higher generality and inclusiveness than the new information provides an organizational framework for the new material and facilitates learning. Obviously, however, if the new concepts are to provide an organizational framework, they must be directly related to the new information. For example, in one experiment, college students who did not know the subject matter at all were asked to learn some facts about the *endocrinology* of pubescence presented in a specially prepared passage (Ausubel & Fitzgerald, 1962). A control group was given a 500-word introductory passage dealing with the *behavioral* aspects of pubescence among different cultures. This material related to the new information only in a very indirect way. The experimental group was given a 500-word introductory passage — an advance organizer — dealing with the primary and secondary sex characteristics. The advance organizer was pitched at a higher level of abstraction, generality, and inclusiveness than the subsequent new material. The experimental group receiving this appropriate advance organizer learned the new material better.

The preceding example shows how an advance organizer works when the learner has little or no previous knowledge of the new material. The advance organizer may also be used to relate new information to that already learned (Ausubel & Fitzgerald, 1961). For instance, a comparative type of organizer was used that briefly described the main similarities and differences between new information to be learned about Buddhism and existing knowledge about Christianity. The students who studied the comparative material learned and remembered the new information on Buddhism better than did students who studied an introduction that outlined the history of Buddhism. In other words, the learning and retention of the unfamiliar verbal information was facilitated when the unfamiliar information was discriminated from previously learned material. This comparative advance organizer follows:

ZEN BUDDHISM

Recently you studied a form of Buddhism known as Mahayana Buddhism. The material presented here introduces you to a sub-school of Mahayana Buddhism called Zen Buddhism, which you will study shortly.

As you recently learned, Buddhism in general while not denying the existence of God, asserts that knowledge of such a Being is beyond man's comprehension. Whereas the concept of a Deity is fundamental to Christian theology, Buddhism places no value on things beyond this world. For the Buddhist, all that exists, exists within *this* world at *this* moment.

In Christianity salvation is gained through the intermediary, Christ. Buddhism, on the other hand, is a process of self-salvation which emphasizes the insistent present. In Christianity the source of authority is the Bible, in Buddhism it is the individual. The Buddha was a great prophet but not a divine Being, and the doctrines derived from his teachings are merely guides to the individual in his search for enlightenment (salvation).

In the passage explaining the principles of Mahayana Buddhism it was pointed out that salvation for the Mahayana Buddhist is achieved by reason and not, as in Christianity, by faith. Zen Buddhism, although an outgrowth of the Mahayana school, dispenses with both the "faith" of Christianity and the "reason" of its parent religion and stresses the need for direct intuitive experience as the means to enlightenment.

Zen, being a form of Buddhism, has no specific philosophy of its own except what is usually accepted by the Buddhists of the Mahayana school. What makes Zen unique is its *method*. The process of Zen is a leap from thinking to knowing, from second-hand conceptual experience to direct intuitive experience. For the Zen Buddhist to achieve enlightenment, a new faculty is needed, i.e., the power of immediate perception, the intuitive awareness which comes when the perceiver and the perceived object are merged in one. The technique of Zen is the development of this faculty.

Although the Mahayana Buddhist is less conformity-bound than is the Christian, both religions prescribe either the best (Mahayana Buddhism), or the *only* (Christianity), path to salvation. In contrast, Zen ridicules conformity and emphasizes the *creative* expression of the individual in his search for Nirvana.

Zen Buddhism is, in the last analysis, not so much a religion as it is a pointing to the religious life itself. It does not attempt to defend a point of view or to propagate a set of formal beliefs *about* the absolute basis of life, but rather to provide a method for grasping intuitively the nature of life itself. (Ausubel, unpublished)

The advance organizer, then, gives the learner a general overview of the more detailed information that follows. It also provides organizing elements to which the particular information to be learned can be related. How frequently should advance organizers of this type be used? There is no final answer. However, if one thinks of the material for a semester or year as being organized into a series of related units, one would probably start the instruction with an advance organizer and also start each unit with a comparative advance organizer that would enable the student to differentiate the ideas in the unit just completed from those in the one to be studied (Ausubel, 1962).

There are times when meaningful relationships among items cannot be found, as noted earlier in the chapter in the discussion of material of low meaningfulness, including letter-sound correspondences. Mnemonic devices are sometimes helpful in these cases, as was pointed out earlier.

Some students have difficulty in recalling more meaningful material; an example that is quite relevant is the set of principles pertaining to factual information. You will remember that these principles were stated only once, in tabular form near the beginning of this section, along with the guides; then the guides are restated in this discussion section. If you have difficulty recalling the principles from the single encounter with them, you might identify one or two key words in each principle and organize them into a sentence. Study of the principles indicates this sequence, which seems logical to the authors: *identify* an *appropriate* unit, *relate* the units, *organize* them into a *sequence*, *practice*, and *evaluate*. There are five principles. Some device such as "five-dive into factual information" might help to recall these principles. (There were eight principles of motivation. A device such as "eight-too late to motivate" might help to recall the motivational principles, provided again that one had put the key words into a sentence or some other string of words that could be recalled.

As a matter of fact, being able to recall the principles—although not necessarily in the identical form as stated — is helpful in relating the main ideas of Chapters 9 through 16 and eventually reorganizing these ideas into a smaller number which the reader can use in his own learning and later in teaching. Further, if one can recall the principles, he can probably reconstruct the instructional guides or formulate his own statements of them.

3. Provide for Proper Sequencing of Material

Earlier in the chapter, broad sequences in learning language and reading were described. Programed instructional material also gives careful attention to the sequence in which specific information is presented to the learner. Authors of textbooks are less concerned about sequence. This book has been written in such a way that it is desirable, but not essential, to proceed consecutively through the chapters. For example, one might proceed directly from the end of Chapter 3 to Chapter 9 and return later for Chapters 4 through 8.

Three general problems involved in sequencing subject matter revolve around the regularity of the structure of the material, the responses available to the learner, and the similarity and dissimilarity of different stimuli (Glaser, 1965).

Regularity of structure refers to the precision with which the concepts of the subject matter are differentiated. In some subject fields, certain information or abilities clearly must be learned before that which follows can be mastered. This is apparent in mathematics. Thus, Frayer (1969), in connection with learning geometric concepts of quadrilateral, square, rectangle, and other quadrilaterals, found this order, from easier to more difficult: cognizing instances and noninstances of the concept, cognizing a verbal definition of the concept, and cognizing superordinate-subordinate relationships among a set of concepts.

The readiness of the learner to make the required responses is another important consideration in the sequencing of instruction. When information is presented orally, the student must have the concepts for which the words stand. When information is presented in printed form, the student must not only have the concepts but must also be able to read the words. When the students cannot read the material, the main job of the teacher is to teach the children to read, not to acquire new information. Many current textbooks and programed instructional materials call for reading responses which the student is incapable of making without instruction in reading. For example, we recently found that many fifth-grade children from favored environments could not read the words standing for the mathematical concepts introduced in three sets of fourth-grade textbooks used in their school the year before. (Obviously, they had not learned the concepts from the books the year before.) The teachers in many schools, particularly in those where the children are of a low socioeconomic status and low educational achievements, must continuously check printed instructional material to be sure that the students can read it without further instruction in reading or can be taught to read it with reasonable effort and time.

The amount of similar and dissimilar material introduced into the sequence of instruction also is important. Students discriminate dissimilar material more readily than similar material, whether letters, words, symbols, or other forms. For instance, brown and white are more readily discriminated than are beige and cream. In music, we can readily make the distinction between a symphony and an opera, but not between an opera and an operetta. Instruction is more effective when it starts with clearly discriminable material to facilitate initial gross discriminations and then proceeds in the direction of greater similarity to facilitate increasingly finer discriminations than when it does not. Much remains to be learned about the sequencing of subject matter, especially in fields where instruction starts in the elementary school and continues into high school. There is great loss of student and teacher effort because of lack of continuity and sequence. You can probably recall many instances when you suddenly encountered some learning tasks for which you were not adequately prepared and others when you found that the tasks were mainly review of earlier work. Gagné (1965b) attempted to identify learning sequences that may be applicable to various subject matters. His efforts are described more fully in Chapter 16 in connection with transfer of learning.

4. Arrange for Appropriate Practice

The primary effect of practice is to increase retention of the new information that has been learned, or to prevent forgetting. When retention is better, further learning of new information is facilitated because the individual has more knowledge to which he can relate the new information. Practice in connection with factual material involves not just repetition but actually using the material in a subsequent situation. For example, the child uses recently learned spelling words in actual writing activities, rather than reviewing the same list of words repeatedly. Thus, practice or use in context facilitates the retention of factual information. Three subprinciples dealing with practice are now discussed:

1. Establish a learning set (sometimes called a *strategy*) so that the student attempts to find relationships. This is usually accomplished through discussion with students. The teacher indicates some relationships and the students identify others.

2. Provide for systematic use and review of verbal material. As noted earlier, practice in context is more effective than mere repetition. Use is, however, essential.

3. Provide for distributed rather than massed practice. The information in all subject fields is comprehensive and is not learned during any one year of schooling. This, then, requires that the information be organized into units of some type and that it be studied periodically, rather than only once. Any daily practice or study session should be long enough so that students master the new information; poorly mastered information will be forgotten quickly. At the same time, the session should not be so long that it produces low motivation, fatigue, and other conditions that

result in inefficiency. The length and spacing of instructional periods varies with the type of subject matter and the characteristics of the learners.

5. Encourage Independent Evaluation

A student takes part for the first time in a short conversation in a foreign language. Listening to the teacher say the same dialogue may enable the student to identify his appropriate and inappropriate responses. If not, the teacher gives more attention to the specific errors. Another student recalls the events associated with the First Continental Congress. He needs to know which events he recalled accurately and which he did not. These and other students require feedback to assess the adequacy or correctness of the information they have acquired.

Again turn to classroom learning of factual information, such as the correct spelling of words, the correct pronunciation of words, specific information about various objects and phenomena, and the location and size of cities and countries. A principal role of the teacher is to help the learner develop methods for evaluating his own responses, so that he may become independent in learning on his own. Feedback is required for independence, and the means for securing it can be taught to students. Thus, as soon as children can use a dictionary they can also check the correctness of the pronunciation and spelling of words. Encyclopedias, atlases, and maps can be made available for securing and checking factual information. The high school graduate should already have developed the abilities required to locate and check sources of factual information. He should also have developed considerable independence in deciding *which* facts are important for him to learn.

While acquiring independence in self-evaluation, many students also need reinforcement in addition to informative feedback. That is, most students demonstrate higher motivation to continue to study when told occasionally that they have done well. Acquiring large amounts of information, such as the table of chemical elements or the vocabulary of a second language, is difficult and time-consuming for many students. Many studies have shown the beneficial effects of praise, attention, and other forms of positive reinforcement.

10.10. A large amount of information is presented in this chapter and others. Knowledge of the five principles pertaining to factual information and verbal knowledge should enable you to learn the material better, provided you can apply them. Are certain principles more difficult than others for you to apply? Why?

10.11. Which of the principles (of course stated in appropriate terminology) do you think could be discussed with students of elementary school age in attempting to assist them in learning factual information? Which with high school students?

10.12. Which of the instructional guides appear to be the easiest to carry out in daily teaching?

10.13. Review the components of the instructional system outlined in Chapter 1. Over which one or two of the components does the individual teacher seem to have most control? Which of the instructional guides are related to these components?

10.14. How might a teaching-learning situation be arranged so that the students and teachers would take joint responsibility for carrying out most of the instructional guides?

SUMMARY

Factual information is information that is discriminated by individuals who share the same cultural background and is also accepted by them as correct or appropriate. Factual information is categorized in this chapter as associations of low meaningfulness, specific information, and verbal knowledge. This kind of information is essential to learning to speak, to read, and to write and also in forming concepts and in problem-solving.

The development of oral language starts in infancy and continues into adulthood. One interesting field of study is the identifying of conditions by which words get associated with experiences and then are manipulated in thought to guide the individual's own behavior. Being able to speak comprehensibly and to understand what others say is essential for learning to read, which for many individuals starts around age 5 or 6 and continues to age 10 to 15 before a high measure of independence in reading is gained.

Recently, psycholinguists have been studying the nature of language learning, including reading. Their emphasis in the teaching of reading is on decoding or translating from written symbols (the writing system or orthography of the language) into that spoken form of the language from which the child already derives meaning. To learn to read the child must already have extensive command of the spoken language and he must also be able to discriminate among printed symbols and be able to associate sounds with printed symbols. Many associations of low meaningfulness, much specific factual information, knowledge about means of dealing with specifics, and some principles are required in order to become proficient in reading. (This is also true in other fields, such as in foreign-language learning.) In turn, being able to read enables one to get factual information from many sources.

One's learning of factual information is facilitated through being able to identify appropriate amounts, or units, of factual information that he can learn readily; finding relationships among sets of facts; organizing sets of consecutive units, or segments, into larger wholes; practicing or using the information to ensure permanence; and evaluating the adequacy or correctness of one's information. Instruction may be given to students and instructional materials and conditions may be organized to put these principles to work in daily classroom practice.

SUGGESTIONS FOR FURTHER READING

CARROLL, J. B. On learning from being told. In Ripple, R. E., ed., *Readings in learning and human abilities.* New York: Harper & Row, 2nd ed., 1971.

Carroll discusses the relationships between psycholinguistics and educational psychology. He is of the opinion that meaningful verbal discourse is a primary instructional process.

CARROLL, J. B. Words, meanings, and concepts. In Ripple, R. E., ed., *Readings in learning and human abilities.* New York: Harper & Row, 2nd ed., 1971.

The relationships among words, their meanings, and the concepts represented by words are treated in the first part of this selection. In the second part, this information is applied to the teaching of concepts from several subject fields.

ERVIN-TRIPP, S. Language development. In Hoffman, L. W., & Hoffman, M. L., eds., *Review of child development research.* New York: Russell Sage Foundation, 1966, pp. 55-105.

This chapter outlines the development of language in considerable detail.

MARCKWARDT, A. H., ed. *Linguistics in the schools,* National Society for the Study of Education, 69th yearbook. Chicago: University of Chicago Press, 1970, part 2.

In "Language Development in the School Years," chapter 7, pages 215-242, R. E. Hodges discusses development during the elementary school years and N. S. Blount treats the high school years. In "Contributions of Linguistics to Reading and Spelling," chapter 8, pages 243-274, S. Ives and J. P. Ives discuss linguistics and reading and R. L. Venezky discusses linguistics and spelling. Study of the two chapters brings one up to date regarding recent contributions of linguistics to language learning.

NATIONAL SOCIETY FOR THE STUDY OF EDUCATION. *Learning and instruction,* 49th yearbook. Chicago: University of Chicago Press, 1950, part 1.

The information in chapter 4, pages 92-129, "How Children Learn Information, Concepts, and Generalizations," by W. S. Brownell and G. Hendrickson, and in chapter 13, pages 336-348, "The School as a Learning Laboratory," by G. L. Anderson, G. Whipple, and R. Gilchrist, is as timely today as it was in 1950.

Chapter 11 Concepts and Principles

An Analysis of Concepts

words, meanings, and concepts
denotative and connotative meanings
bases for defining words that represent concepts
attributes of concepts
psychological meaningfulness
structure
transferability

Developmental Trends

Piaget's stages in cognitive development
sensorimotor stage
preoperational stage
concrete operations
formal operations
Bruner's modes of internal representation
enactive
ikonic
symbolic

Instructional Guides

emphasize the attributes of the concept
establish the correct terminology
indicate the nature of the concepts to be learned
provide for proper sequencing of instances of concepts
encourage and guide student discovery
provide for use of the concept
encourage independent evaluation

he learning of *concepts* is an important educational objective at all
school levels. Accordingly, teachers, curriculum experts, and the
designers of instructional materials are involved in identifying
the concepts that students may learn at successively higher levels;
they also regularly work on the development of materials and procedures to teach concepts. *Principles*, too, are important outcomes of
learning. A principle is defined as a statement of relationships among two
or more concepts. In other words, if one has already learned the needed
concepts, one's task in forming a principle is to learn the relationships
among the concepts. The learning of concepts themselves also involves
the learning of relationships, in this case among attributes and rules (as
will become apparent later in this chapter). Thus the internal and external conditions that are essential for learning either concepts or principles are thought to be much alike. It seems logical, therefore, to concentrate on the learning of concepts in this chapter.

Many psychologists in recent decades have studied how students learn
concepts. Subject-matter specialists in the various disciplines have focused much attention on identifying the concepts that students *should*
learn. It might be expected that the divergent approaches of subject-matter experts and psychologists would have produced information that would
be very useful in facilitating the learning of concepts by school children.
Unfortunately, however, these hopes have proved to be rather optimistic,
mainly because of communication problems. For instance, psychologists,
subject-matter experts, and other experts in concept learning were brought
together in an attempt to pool their knowledge. However, these groups had
difficulty in communicating within their own groups and even greater
difficulty when trying to convey their ideas across groups (Klausmeier &
Harris, 1966). Furthermore, a survey of textbooks in mathematics, science,
and other subject fields revealed wide differences, even among texts in
the same field, concerning what concepts are and how they presumably
are learned. The central problem seems to be that individuals do not agree
on the *nature* of concepts. Each individual tends to focus on a certain attribute of concepts that is dominant for him while failing to perceive what
is dominant for others.

The analysis of concepts that follows, then, is intended to clarify the
whole situation—to provide a definition of concept that will make the several attributes of concept clear. Study of this detailed analysis of concepts
is essential also in understanding the two topics discussed in the last two
parts of this chapter: trends in cognitive development and principles and
instructional guides pertaining to concept learning.

AN ANALYSIS OF CONCEPTS

As more information is gained about the moon through space exploration,
the concepts of moon, earth, and planet all change. Similarly, the concept
of concept changes as the result of many studies that constantly yield
new information about the learning and teaching of concepts. Recent in-

formation about the nature of concepts is summarized in the following discussions of the relationships among words, meanings, and concepts; four bases for defining words that represent concepts; and a concept of *concept*.

Words, Meanings, and Concepts

Carroll (1964), discussing relationships among words, meanings, and concepts, indicated that human beings early in life have direct experiences with the *referents* of concepts. As they learn labels, or words, they associate the words with the objects or events, the referents for which the words stand. Words thus come to represent the concepts that the individual has. In a reciprocal manner, instances of a particular concept when experienced evoke the relevant word, and the word when encountered evokes the concept that one has attained. As an example, when one sees or hears a cat he thinks "cat," and when one hears or reads the word he thinks of or recalls some of his own experiences with cats. In this way, words and concepts are intimately related: Words represent concepts, and instances of particular concepts evoke the corresponding words overtly or covertly.

Words and concepts are related in another way. Human beings live in close physical and social proximity. They have many similar experiences with instances of particular concepts, thereby acquiring similar information, and they also learn the same language. Having the same language results in giving the same name to a particular class of things, or concepts, as noted before. Equally important, a common language makes possible the verbal diffusion and sharing of information on which concepts are based. Thus a person gains information and forms new concepts, or extends existing ones, from hearing what others say and from reading. In this second way, then, words and concepts are related: Much concept learning occurs through the use of words.

It is the similar information acquired nonverbally and verbally about things, qualities, and events that results in individuals acquiring similar concepts. So people throughout the world attain similar concepts of moon and sun. The words of a language common to a people, such as English, also acquire nearly the same standard speech form (with minor dialect differences) and are spelled identically, and sentences and paragraphs take the same form.

These common experiences and language lead to widely accepted *denotative* meanings of words of the kind found in standard, unabridged dictionaries. Here several techniques are used. Verbal equivalents or synonyms of the entry word are given, various examples of the use of the word are noted, and a formal definition is stated. A formal dictionary definition indicates what the concept represented by the word has in common with other related concepts and in what respects—attributes or other properties—it is different. *Barium*, for example, is defined thus:

> A silver-white malleable toxic bivalent metallic element of the alkaline-earth group that tarnishes rapidly in air, that occurs only in combination, that is made by reduction of barium oxide or by electrolysis of a fused salt, and that is

used in the form of alloys chiefly as a getter in electron tubes — symbol *Ba*. (See table of elements.)

Denotative meanings of words, the societally standardized meanings, are accepted routinely in school settings. (Makers of dictionaries, however, spend much effort keeping the definitions current.) Even though the denotative meaning is widely accepted, each of us has unique experiences with many concepts. For example, each of us has had different experiences with a mother, the mothers of others, or as a mother; thus each of us has a unique concept of *mother*.

The unique meanings or associations that the individual possesses constitute *his* concept and correspond to the *connotative* meaning of a word. Affect or feeling, as well as cognitive information, is embodied in the individual's concept and in his connotative meaning of the word representing the concept. Figure 11.1 shows the relationships among experiences, words, concepts, and meanings. Note particularly the relationship among an individual's experiences with the referents of the concept, his own concept, the word representing the concept, and the connotative meaning of the concept. The point at which the individual's network becomes related to other people's networks for the same concept is at the denotative meaning of the word.

Carroll summarized the relationships among words, meanings, and concepts in this way:

> Perhaps it is useful to think of words, meanings, and concepts as forming three somewhat independent series. The words in a language can be thought of as a series of physical entities — either spoken or written. Next, there exists a set of "meanings" which stand in complex relationships to the set of words. These

Fig. 11.1. Relationships among experiences, words, concepts, and meanings.

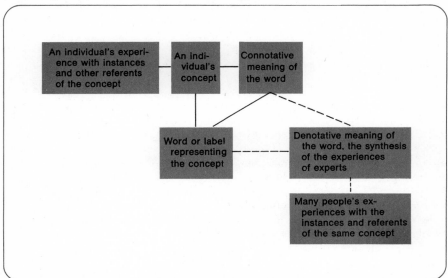

relationships may be described by the rules of usage that have developed by the processes of socialization and communication. A "meaning" can be thought of as a standard of communicative behavior that is shared by those who speak a language. Finally, there exist "concepts": the classes of experience formed in individuals either independently of language processes or in close dependence on language processes.

The interrelations found among these three series are complex: almost anyone can give instances where a word may have many "meanings," or in which a given "meaning" corresponds to several different words. The relationships between societally-standardized "meanings" and individually-formed "concepts" are likewise complex, but of a somewhat different nature. It is a question of how well each individual has learned these relationships, and, at least in the sphere of language and concepts, education is largely a process whereby the individual learns either to attach societally-standardized words and meanings to the concepts he has already formed, or to form new concepts that properly correspond to societally-standardized words and meanings. A "meaning" of a word is, therefore, a societally-standardized concept, and when we say that a word stands for or names a concept it is understood that we are speaking of concepts that are shared among the members of a speech community. (Carroll, 1964, pp. 186-187)

Carroll also gave a useful account of the relationship of parts of speech to concepts:

Many words or higher units of the linguistic system come to stand for, or name, the concepts that have been learned pre-verbally. Certainly this is true for a long list of words that stand for particular things or classes of things, qualities, and events. For the English language, these categories correspond roughly to proper and common nouns; adjectives; and verbs of action, perception, and feeling. It is perhaps less clear that "function words" like prepositions and conjunctions, or grammatical markers like the past tense sign can represent concepts, but a case can be made for this. For example, prepositions like *in, to, above, below, beside, near* correspond to concepts of relative spatial position in a surprisingly complex and subtle way; and conjunctions like *and, but, however, or* correspond to concepts of logical inclusion and exclusion, similarity and difference of propositions, etc. (Carroll, 1964, pp. 185-186)

The foregoing discussion might lead you quite properly to infer several characteristics of a *class concept*: (1) A class concept is an abstraction that represents a set of things, events, or ideas. The class concept is not a specific thing or idea; the latter is called an instance, or example, of the concept. For example, *book* represents a concept, a class of things, and the one you are reading is an instance of the class of things. (2) A class concept usually has a verbal name or symbol. One can have a concept of something without knowing the name or label for it. A young child, for instance, can feel intense *jealousy* without being able to name the feeling. More mature people, however, associate the name with the feeling. In general, then, a person who can see, hear, and speak does associate a name or other symbol with each concept that forms part of his own experience and way of life. (3) As the last point implies, the words representing many concepts have definitions that are accepted by mature people who speak the same language. Younger children do not know the definitions of many concepts, but they gradually learn them. (4) The particular meanings one associates with one's own experiences are one's concepts. An individual's concept of something may be very similar to the concept held by others, or it may vary markedly. To the extent that it varies, the individual has difficulty in communicating with others. Therefore, when a mature person is not understood by a child, it is often because the older person assumes the child has the same or similar definitions and experiences.

We shall discuss these and other attributes of concepts in more detail in the next two parts of this chapter. Before continuing, though, try this exercise: A few instances of identity concepts (IC), class concepts (CC), factual information (FI), and principles (P) are listed. Using the initials, indicate to which category you think each belongs.

1. Noun phrase. (   )
2. Precede. (   )
3. Richard Nixon. (   )
4. Equal. (   )
5. United States. (   )
6. A noun phrase normally precedes a verb phrase in a sentence. (   )
7. The angle of incidence is equal to the angle of refraction. (   )
8. Prices of products rise as supply decreases. (   )
9. Richard Nixon followed Lyndon Johnson as President. (   )
10. Man first set foot on the moon in 1969. (   )
(The answers are: 1.CC, 2.CC, 3.IC, 4.CC, 5.IC, 6.P, 7.P, 8.P, 9.FI, 10.FI.)

If you had difficulty answering the 10 questions, it might be well to review this chapter and also the first parts of Chapter 10. If further review and study are not productive, discussion with other students or faculty might be helpful. In any event, understanding the concepts that represent the outcomes of learning is essential for understanding and applying the principles and instructional guides that pertain to the outcomes treated in Chapters 9 through 15.

Four Bases for Defining Words That Represent Concepts

Four fairly common ways of defining words are in terms of (1) perceptible or readily measurable attributes; (2) synonyms, antonyms, and other semantic means; (3) logical relationships and axioms; (4) the use made of the things. These correspond to the types of definitions of words one finds in an unabridged dictionary. Examples of the bases are given in Table 11.1.

Type 1 definitions are in terms of the perceptible or readily measured attributes of the concepts represented by the words. These attributes are abstracted as being the same in otherwise dissimilar things or events. For example, the perceptible attributes that permit *oranges* and *lemons* to be classified as citrus fruit but also different from each other are size,

Table 11.1. Four Bases for Defining Words That Represent Concepts

Basis of definition	Examples of concepts	Denotative meaning
1. Perceptible attributes	Dog, orange, sentence, barium	*Dog* — domesticated, carnivorous mammal of the family Canidae
2. Semantics	Polite, pretty, liberal, up	*Polite* — marked by an appearance of consideration, tact, or deference; by a lack of roughness or crudity
3. Logical relationships and axioms	Straight line, equal, number, point	*Straight line* — a locus of points whose coordinates depend on a single independent variable
4. Use or function	Strawberries, bread, hammer, pencil	(Denotative meanings are not given in a dictionary solely in terms of use)

color, shape, and taste. Many living and nonliving things have been studied by naturalists and scientists. On the basis of observed attributes these things have been given names, assigned to classes, and organized into taxonomic systems, for example, the animal kingdom, the plant kingdom, the solar system, and the table of chemical elements. Words representing the concepts in these taxonomies are defined in terms of attributes.

Type 2 definitions are formed in terms of synonyms, antonyms, and other semantic means. Thus, *polite* is defined as marked by an appearance of consideration, tact, or deference; by a lack of roughness or crudeness. There are not widely agreed on specifiable instances of this concept, and other concepts of this type, from which the attributes may be abstracted. Many words representing concepts that are part of the general cultural heritage, rather than being related to a subject field, are defined in this manner.

Type 3 definitions are in terms of axioms or other theoretical statements that do not specify attributes directly. The label and the definition are encountered in close time proximity. Thus, a *straight line* is defined nonmathematically as the shortest distance between two points. Neither the line nor the points can be seen, but they can be defined in words. They can also be represented as a continuous mark and two dots; but these representations of line segments are not the concept or even precise representations of it, according to mathematicians (Fehr, 1966). Words representing concepts for which there are neither perceptible instances nor reasonably good representations and which cannot be defined semantically are often found in mathematics. Students who cannot read or understand the definitions can, however, learn to categorize representations of the instances, for example, graphical representations of line segments, squares, negative numbers.

Type 4 definitions are formulated in terms of use or function. Only young children define and classify primarily on the basis of the use made of things. Older children and adults define and classify primarily on the first three bases but may also ascribe a "use" attribute to a concept. Some categories based on use gain wide social acceptance. For example, *strawberries*, *bread*, and *ice cream* are all used as food by Americans. An individual also classifies things according to use in a manner unique to the individual. Thus, a *nail*, a *metal clamp*, a *cord*, and *glue* may all be classified by an individual as things to hold two pieces of wood together.

It should not be inferred that any word is defined on only one of the preceding four bases, that all individuals use the same basis for formulating their concepts, or that an individual uses the same basis for either defining or classifying throughout his life. Nevertheless, those who know most about a particular concept would probably agree on one of the first three bases as the primary basis for defining the particular word that represents the concept.

A Concept of *Concept*

One's own concepts are continuously changing, and ever increasing knowledge is changing the denotative meaning of many words (Deese, 1967). To provide a common frame of reference from which psychologists, subject-matter specialists, and educators may proceed, a definition of concept, or denotative meaning, is now given in terms of attributes. The three attributes are psychological meaningfulness, structure, and transferability.

Psychological Meaningfulness. The individual's *connotative* meaning of a word corresponds to that attribute of a concept here called *psychological meaningfulness*. Bruner, Goodnow, & Austin (1956, p. 244) emphasized the individual or idiosyncratic nature of concepts in their definition of concept as a "network of sign-significate inferences by which one goes beyond a set of *observed* criterial properties exhibited by an object or event to the class identity of the object or event in question, and thence to additional inferences about the *unobserved* properties of the object or event." Also, stimulus-response psychologists who accept the notion of mediation refer to a concept as the associative meanings, or implicit mediating responses, that the *individual* has formed between stimulus and response events whereby he treats otherwise dissimilar objects or events as belonging to the same class (Staats, 1968). Regardless of the definitional preference, it is apparent that individuals of the same age vary widely with respect to "the network of inferences," or the "implicit mediating responses" held about any concept. For example, concepts of *reading*, *school*, and *time* vary considerably among 7-year-olds as a result of differing learning and maturational conditions. Similarly, there is great variability among college students in the level of comprehension of more complex but common concepts, such as of *force*, *number*, and *structure of knowledge*.

The attribute, psychological meaningfulness, may also be inferred from the change that occurs in the concepts held by the same individual. An individual's concepts change with increasing experience with instances of the concept, including additional verbal information about the concept. Consider your own concepts of *pleasure* and *space* now and compare them with those you had when you were 10 years old. According to Inhelder and Piaget (1958), distinct changes occur in the mental operations that individuals can perform. These changes, in turn, result in increasingly higher-level, more abstract concepts. In essence, then, each individual has his own concepts, based on his nonverbal and verbal experiences. Thus, as already noted, this attribute of concept, psychological meaningfulness, corresponds to the connotative meaning of a word that represents a concept.

Structure. A second characteristic of concept is *structure*. Four primary structural components deal with the attributes that define the concept, the rules by which the attributes are joined, the hierarchy in which the concept fits, and the instances of the concept.

1. Attributes. As noted, the properties by which things may be categorized and by which the related labels may be defined are perceptible or readily measurable attributes, semantic meanings, or axiomatic and logical statements. Much research has now been done on concepts that are formed in terms of attributes, and a related structure is identifiable. (Further research and analysis are necessary to evolve structures of other concepts. Therefore, the rest of this discussion is limited to concepts defined by attributes.)

Attributes of concepts vary in number, relevance, and discriminability. The number may range from one to many for different concepts; certain attributes may be relevant and others irrelevant for a particular concept; and attributes may range from high to low discriminability. To illustrate the ideas of number and relevance, we recognize that the four relevant attributes of *quadrilateral* are closed figure, plane figure, simple figure, and four sides. The same four attributes and two others—equal size of angles and equal length of sides—are used in defining *square*. Thus the size of angles and equal length of sides are relevant for *square* but not for *quadrilateral*. The size of the figure, the position of the figure, and the way in which it is represented are irrelevant for identifying instances of squares; they are similarly irrelevant for identifying instances of quadrilaterals.

Discriminability refers to the extent to which the attributes are attended to and cognized. One can make attributes discriminable by various means. For example, *size* can be made more discriminable by using both small and large examples. Discrimination of the *number* of sides in triangles and quadrilaterals can be facilitated by holding size as constant as possible and using heavy lines to represent the sides. One can also tell individuals what to look for. (In general, as the discriminability of the attributes decreases, concept attainment becomes more difficult.)

2. Rules for Joining Attributes. Different rules for joining attributes are illustrated in concepts represented by the words *red, mammal, older,* and *strike* (Bruner, Goodnow, & Austin, 1956). (1) *Red* is a simple *affirmative* concept comprised of one property or dimension. (2) An animal that simultaneously, or *conjunctively*, has three attributes—warm-blooded, mammary glands, bearing live offspring—is classified as a *mammal*. (3) A 5-year-old child is *older* than one aged 4, but younger than a 6-year-old; *older* is a *relational* concept. (4) A *strike* in baseball represents a concept where attributes are joined by a *disjunctive* rule—and/or; a strike may be a ball thrown in the strike zone and called by the umpire or it may be a pitch swung at and missed or it may be a foul.

Most of the concepts encountered in school subject matter are either conjunctive or relational. However, only a careful analysis of various subject fields will identify the different kinds of concepts according to the rules for joining the attributes. The relative ease in attaining concepts defined by different rules is in this order: affirmative, conjunctive, relational, disjunctive (Bourne, 1966).

3. Hierarchical Patterning. Frayer, Fredrick, and Klausmeier (1969) outlined a procedure for analyzing concepts in order to prepare related instructional materials and to test the level of mastery that an individual has of a concept. The example already given of the defining attributes of a *quadrilateral* was drawn from that source. Figure 11.2 shows how *quadrilateral* fits into a hierarchical structure comprised of superordinate, coordinate, and subordinate concepts. It may readily be inferred that all instances of quadrilaterals are polygons (as are triangles, pentagons, etc.) and that all instances of trapezoids, kites, parallelograms, rectangles, rhombuses, and squares are instances of both quadrilaterals and polygons.

Figure 11.3 shows how *man* fits into a classification system—*vertebrate, mammal, primate, Hominidae, Homo sapiens*. Note that as one goes down the list in this order, each concept increases in number of defining

Fig. 11.2. Hierarchical position of the concept *quadrilateral.*

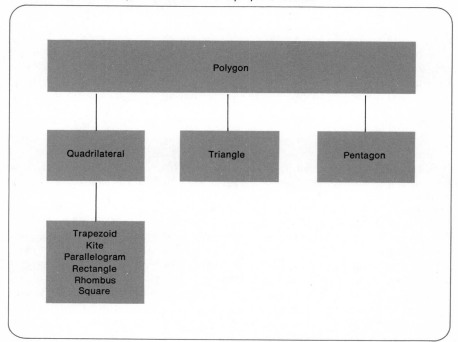

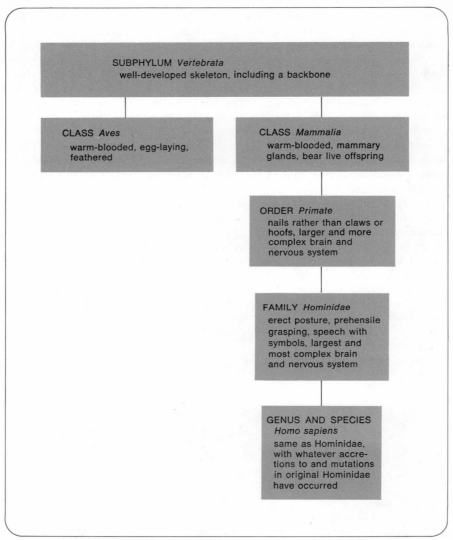

Fig. 11.3. Hierarchical position of the concept *Homo sapiens*. (Man is the only living survivor of the family Hominidae.)

attributes. In other words, each concept successively is defined by the relevant attributes in the higher-order concept and also by the additional ones required to differentiate among the various groups in the same overall classification. One of these differentiations is shown in two coordinate class concepts—*Aves* and *Mammalia*. Birds are warm-blooded, as are mammals, but they do not have mammary glands, nor do they bear live young. The subordinate concepts then continue from mammals only. Thus the successive concepts (read up the figure) are increasingly abstract and inclusive—just as quadrilateral is more abstract and inclusive than trapezoid and, in turn, polygon than quadrilateral.

4. Instances. The instances of concepts may vary from one to an indefinite number. As noted in the last chapter, a young child typically forms a concrete or identity concept, e.g., *dog,* before forming a class concept of *dog.* There are many concepts for which there is or was only one instance, e.g., *the moon, the earth, Abraham Lincoln,* and *the United States.* Other identity concepts have many instances, all of which, however, are identical. For example, *inch, yard,* and other units for measuring length; *pound, ounce,* and other units for measuring weight; *comma, period,* and other punctuation marks, and similar units in other fields have instances that are identical. No matter where they are encountered, instances of *inch* are identical in length and instances of *period* are identical in form. On the other hand, the instances of many concepts are infinite; for example, the instances of *numerals* are infinite, as *grains of sand* and *drops of water* also seem to be.

Instances also vary according to openness to sensory experiencing. At one pole are the instances that are available to sight, touch, hearing, and other senses simultaneously. At the other are concepts that are very difficult to represent. There are many things that cannot be seen, such as *atom* and *genetic code,* that are, therefore, difficult to represent.

Finally, instances may be positive or negative, and there are also noninstances. Positive instances possess the attributes of the concept. A negative instance has some of the same attributes as the positive instance, but not others. A *rectangle* is a positive instance of *quadrilateral* but a negative instance of *triangle.* It is a noninstance of *animal* and of all other concepts that are not geometric forms.

Transferability. Once a concept has been acquired, there are four possibilities for use in, or transfer to, other situations: (1) One categorizes other instances, when first encountered, as belonging to the concept; also, one can categorize other instances when first encountered as not belonging to the concept. (2) One can more readily cognize other concepts as superordinate, coordinate, or subordinate. (3) One can use the concept in forming and understanding a principle and in solving problems where the concept is applicable. (4) The learning of one concept facilitates the learning of other concepts.

1. Instance Recognition. Assume that a child has first learned to call correctly a number of figures "squares" and that he also cognizes, but not necessarily states, that a square is a closed, plane, simple figure that has four sides of equal length and four angles of equal size. Having acquired a concept of *square* at this level should enable him to categorize properly other square figures that might be encountered and also to treat them as squares rather than as rectangles or other four-sided figures.

2. Superordinate-Coordinate-Subordinate Relations. A child may have fairly well-established concepts of *square* and *rectangle* and beginning concepts of *quadrilateral* and *pentagon.* Having these concepts should enable him to cognize more readily that a pentagon is coordinate with quadrilateral and that square and rectangle are subordinate to quadrilateral.

3. Principle Formation and Problem-Solving. A principle is defined by Gagné (1966) as a relationship between two or more concepts. A problem is encountered when one does not have a solution, a method, or both to deal with a situation that one must resolve. According to Gagné, concepts are essential for the cognizing of principles and the solution of problems. Again, to illustrate with geometric figures, the student may have learned concepts of *triangle, equilateral triangle*, and *right triangle*, and of *quadrilateral, square*, and *rectangle*. Knowledge of these concepts will enable him more readily to acquire the principle that a concept higher in the hierarchy (superordinate) has fewer relevant attributes than one lower in the same hierarchy (subordinate). Similarly, knowledge of the particular geometric concepts will enable the student to find the perimeter and area of each more readily when problems of this kind must be solved.

4. Learning to Learn. Archer, Bourne, & Brown (1955) demonstrated that human beings have the ability to learn how to learn concepts. Later, this phenomenon was observed routinely in a series of laboratory and school experiments (Klausmeier, Harris, Davis, Schwenn, & Frayer, 1968). In these experiments the students learned consecutive concepts that were of the same type but that differed from one another—coordinate concepts. Both the amount of time required for learning and the number of errors decreased as successive concepts were attained. To return to the geometric figures, although we have not done the specific experiments, we are confident that students require decreasing amounts of time to acquire each of these coordinate concepts consecutively: *quadrilateral, triangle, pentagon.*

We are now ready to present a definition of the word "concept." A concept is a mental construct, or abstraction, characterized by psychological meaningfulness, structure, and transferability that enables an individual to do the following: (1) cognize things and events as belonging to the same class and as different from things and events belonging to other classes; (2) cognize other related superordinate, coordinate, and subordinate concepts in a hierarchy; (3) acquire principles and solve problems involving the concept; (4) learn other concepts of the same difficulty level in less time. Operationally, a concept may be defined as the level of mastery at which an individual has attained the concept, not merely whether he properly categorizes two otherwise dissimilar stimuli as belonging to the same class; this level of mastery is inferred from observation, including performances on tests. The most complete denotative meanings of words that represent concepts are found in books and articles written by experts (for example, physicists define *atom*, theologians define *religion*); the societally standardized meanings of concepts, not necessarily those held by experts, are found in standard unabridged dictionaries.

In line with the preceding definition and also with the analysis of concepts presented in this section, 30 concepts each in mathematics, English, science, and social studies were identified and analyzed; then tests were constructed to measure the level at which each concept had been mastered by 200 girls and 200 boys who had just completed the fourth grade. The same kind of analyses should be carried out by teachers, curriculum workers, and developers of instructional materials to help them in deciding what might be appropriate to teach children at various developmental levels.

The analyses of the concepts *equivalent sets* and *delta* follow. The attributes and instances are intended to be appropriate for children of the fifth grade. Notice that there are no "use" or "semantic" attributes included in the analyses. These were omitted intentionally because not enough research has been done to make a proper analysis using these attributes.

ANALYSIS OF THE CONCEPT *EQUIVALENT SETS*

1. Target concept label:
   Equivalent sets. (This concept is drawn from a set of concepts related to *set theory*.)
2. Definition that gives the name of the supraordinate concept and the criterial attributes of the target concept:
   Equivalent sets are two sets which have the same number of members.
3. Supraordinate concept(s):
   Sets
   Subsets
4. Coordinate concept(s):
   (None)
5. Subordinate concept(s):
   Equal sets
6. Criterial attributes that identify the target concept within the selected supraordinate concept (or coordinate concepts if a supraordinate has not been identified):
   a. have the same number of members
   b. two or more sets
7. Other attributes that are relevant but not criterial for the target concept include the following (attributes of the supraordinate need not be specified):
   Other attributes relevant to equivalent sets are those of its supraordinate, *subsets* or *sets*.
8. Irrelevant attributes of the target concept (attributes which vary among instances of the target concept) include the following:
   a. how many members: e.g., 3 members
   b. kind of members: e.g., animals
9. Concept examples include the following:
   a. {2 apples} and {2 oranges}
   b. {4, 5, 6} and {7, 8, 9}
   c. {cat, dog} and {ball, bat}
10. Concept nonexamples include the following:
    a. {1, 9, 10} and {8, 9}
    b. {mouse, rat} and {cat}
    c. {1, 2, 3} and {4, 5, 6, 7}
11. Relationship with at least one other concept. (This relationship should preferably be a principle. It should definitely *not* be a direct supraordinate-subordinate relationship, a relationship involving a criterial attribute, or a relationship involving an example.)
    If the number of members from two *equivalent sets* are *subtracted*, the answer is 0. (Romberg & Steitz, 1970)

ANALYSIS OF THE CONCEPT *DELTA*

1. Target concept label:
   Delta. (This concept is drawn from a set of concepts related to *geographic region*.)
2. Definition that gives the name of the supraordinate concept and the criterial attributes of the target concept:
   A delta is a river mouth which has some land which was formed when soil was deposited at the mouth of that river.

3. Supraordinate concept(s):
   River mouth
4. Coordinate concept(s):
   River mouths where deltas were not formed
5. Subordinate concept(s):
   Deltas where crops can be grown
   Deltas where crops cannot be grown
6. Criterial attributes that identify the target concept within the selected supra-ordinate concept (or coordinate concepts if a supraordinate has not been identi-fied):
   a. is newly formed land in the process of growing
   b. is found at the mouth of a river
   c. is found where the river joins a larger body of water and stops
   d. is made of land formed by soil carried by the river
   e. divides the river into several branches around the land
7. Other attributes that are relevant but not criterial for the target concept include the following (attributes of the supraordinate need not be specified):
   Other attributes relevant to delta are those of its supraordinate, *river mouth*.
8. Irrelevant attributes of the target concept (attributes which vary among in-stances of the target concept) include the following:
   a. the type of soil
   b. which river it is a part of
   c. the location
   d. how quickly it is formed
   e. its exact shape
9. Concept examples include the following:

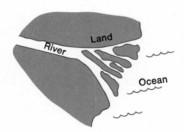

10. Concept nonexamples include the following:

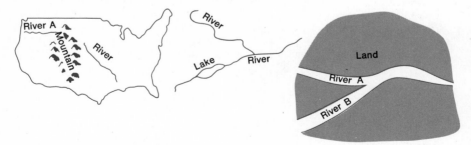

11. Relationship with at least one other concept. (This relationship should prefer-ably be a principle. It should definitely *not* be a direct supraordinate-subordinate relationship, a relationship involving a criterial attribute, or a relationship involving an example.)
    A *delta* can change a *coastline*. (Tabachnick, Weible, & Frayer, 1970)

11.1. According to Carroll, education is largely a process whereby the individual learns either to attach societally standardized words and meanings to the concepts he has already formed or to form new concepts that properly correspond to societally standardized words and meanings.

    a. Do you think the statement is equally applicable to all school levels—elementary, secondary, and college?

    b. Do you think the statement is equally applicable to mathematics, science, social studies, and other subject fields?

11.2. Think of your own concepts of *geometry* and *parent*. Which shows a closer correspondence to the denotative meaning of the word? Why?

11.3. Define *bird, beautiful, parallel lines, thermometer*.

    a. To what extent do you tend to define each in terms of perceptible attributes, synonyms, axiomatically, and use?

    b. For which of the four can you readily give verbal illustrations or instances?

11.4. What is the relationship between psychological meaningfulness of a concept and the connotative meaning of a word that represents the concept?

11.5. Analyze the concepts of *mammal* and *sun* in terms of attributes, hierarchical patterning, and instances.

11.6. You have now acquired a more complete concept of *concept*. How does this enable you to analyze the subject matter of science, history, or some other subject field in which you are interested?

DEVELOPMENTAL TRENDS

Developmental trends in concept learning have been clarified by a number of researchers. Indeed, as a result of the many investigations that have been done, our knowledge of conceptual development is now substantial, and, as the research continues, it is constantly increasing.

The research into concept learning has followed a number of paths, but two of the most important lines of research—both of which are discussed in this section—are complementary. First, Jean Piaget, the Swiss psychologist who is perhaps the most influential theorist of intellectual development of this century, laid the foundations for much later work when he identified qualitative changes that occur in cognitive development from infancy to maturity (as interpreted by Flavell, 1963, and translated in Ripple & Rockcastle, 1964). Along the same lines, Jerome Bruner and his associates at Harvard traced the changes in the conceptual development of children, reporting their results in the more familiar terminology of American psychologists (Bruner, Olver, & Greenfield, 1966).

Another line of pioneering research is being carried out at the Wisconsin Research and Development Center for Cognitive Learning under the direction of the senior author. In this programmatic research, concepts that are taught in the elementary school are identified. Each concept is analyzed as just shown, pages 403-404. Then instructional material, with visualizations, is prepared that presents information about the concepts in line with the analysis. One or another element of the analysis—for instance, the number of examples of the concept, the amount of repetition

of the same attributes, or an inductive-deductive sequence – is varied
through writing two or more versions designed to teach the same concept,
or set of concepts. The various versions of the material are assigned randomly to children regularly enrolled in school. To ascertain which version
does the better or best job, tests are constructed along the lines outlined
in Chapter 4. The same test is administered to all the children and scored.
In this manner, one can decide exactly which kind of information contained in the instructional material results in higher concept attainment.
Also, one can study the responses of the children to the various items to
learn where difficulties are being experienced. The long-range goal is to
formulate guidelines for developing better instructional material, which,
with good teacher utilization, will enable children to acquire concepts in
the various curriculum areas more effectively. In the process, we shall
learn much more about how children acquire concepts with increasing
experience and instruction. (This does not rule out the need for or importance of direct experiences with some of the referents of some concepts.)
An example of this line of research is the work of Frayer (1969), who
identified differences among fourth- and sixth-graders in their level of
mastery of geometric concepts.

Piaget's Stages in Cognitive Development

Jean Piaget has spent much of his life studying the cognitive development of children at his institute in Geneva. His ideas were ignored in the
United States for many years, partly because of his methods of research
and partly because the climate of opinion here was unfavorable toward
the ideas. Now, however, Piaget's findings and the related research of
many others in America and in England are considered vitally important
by individuals and groups preparing curriculum materials and instructional programs. Flavell (1963) and Baldwin (1967) have summarized
many of the publications of Piaget. The ideas that follow are drawn
largely from the interpretations of these two psychologists. In Piaget's
theory, cognitive processes are organized into four definable stages. Although these stages are identified with certain age ranges, the ranges are
by no means precise and binding, merely approximate. They also are continuous; one should not assume that one stage of development ends and
then another begins but that at each stage other capabilities are beginning to be actively acquired. Thus, there are *qualitative* changes in cognitive processes at successive stages. Graphically, we should look at the
four main stages like this:

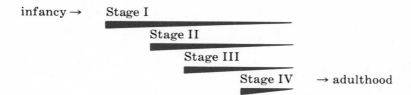

not like this:

infancy →   Stage I
_____

             Stage II
             _____

                  Stage III
                  _____

                       Stage IV   → adulthood
                       _____

From infancy to adulthood, the child is assimilating data from the world around him, accommodating to the world around him, and organizing his knowledge and experiences into a system or structure. Piaget stresses this active organizing as the most important force in the child's cognitive development. Other recognized forces are: maturation, experiences with the environment, and direct teaching by other people. *Equilibration* is the term Piaget gives to this active internal process of organizing and coordinating one's own intellectual development. Through the process of equilibration — a form of self-regulation — the organized system, or cognitive structure, is constantly changing, enlarging, and reorganizing as more experience with the world and with himself presents the child with ideas and events that must be assimilated or accommodated to. The four stages of cognitive development are useful in explaining the various levels at which a child operates as he builds this organized system.

Stage I: Sensorimotor Period. During this period, corresponding roughly to the first two years of life, the infant progresses from a reflex state in which he and the world around him are entirely undifferentiated to a relatively complex level of sensorimotor actions in a world just beginning to be organized systematically. A remarkable amount of adaptation is required to get from the neonate stage, when the infant has no awareness of his body, sensory relationships, and environment, to the time when he can successfully grasp an object, move toward a goal (perhaps using simple tools), and imitate sounds and actions. During this stage the child begins to organize visual images and to control his motor responses. At first, bodily actions are randomly uncontrolled, and indeed the child is unaware that it is his body that is moving. He then begins to coordinate different sensory experiences — sight, sound, touch, and taste — and to relate them to the same source, rather than to different sources. He gradually learns to look at what he hears, to touch what he sees. He learns to hold a toy still so that he can look at it and, eventually, to coordinate two hands and a body so they may work together to pull himself up or to grasp a toy. At the end of this period, physical responses are sufficiently coordinated so that the child begins to smooth out sequences of physical motions. For example, to pick up a kitten, he needs to do several things simultaneously: to bend his knees, still retaining his balance, to reach toward the kitten, and to grasp it in a suitable fashion. If he has not estimated correctly what is required of him, he may have to try again, perhaps grasping its body, rather than its tail or ear, and perhaps now expecting that the kitten will be heavier than a plastic toy. (The kitten's reaction is not a factor here!)

In addition to coordinating sensory impressions and controlling his physical motions, the infant begins to organize his environment. Instead of seeing his surroundings as one image that changes at times, he begins to differentiate separate objects. He sees the world as a relatively permanent place that is not dependent on his perception of it. A very tiny baby is helpless when he has dropped a toy next to him. Because it has left his field of vision, for him it exists no longer, and he finds it only if he happens on it by chance. As he begins to perceive the external world in a less limited way, he learns that things exist even when he cannot see them. He will be able to search for the lost toy because he realizes there is some stability in his physical environment. Piaget gives the label of *object concept* to the child's ability to see objects not as mere sensations or images that are pleasing to look at but as stable, permanent things that exist in themselves, that endure even when outside his field of vision, and that exist in a spatial field which also includes himself. The child knows where he is in relation to space and objects around him. He can deliberately hit the mobile hanging above him in his crib and know that it will move and please him.

Toward the end of the sensorimotor period, the child is able to follow a sequence of actions to reach a goal or to use a simple tool to reach an object. He can see that he will be able to get his toy by moving the pillow on which it is lying. But his thinking is still limited to immediate sensory experiences and is closely bound to motor actions, with a minimal amount of symbolic activity.

Stage II: Preoperational Period. This stage in development, representing roughly the five years between the ages of 2 and 7, is mainly a transitional period, not as fully understood as many of the others. Stage 2, unlike the others, is not characterized by the child's reaching any specific level of stability. It is that uncertain period when the child is learning labels, or names, for objects, when he is beginning to operate on a simple conceptual level while continuing to refine his sensorimotor abilities. As names for objects are acquired, he begins to form ideas of the sameness of things and to make some general categories of objects. Also, the child begins to form gross relational concepts such as *bigger, older, taller*, and *too much*.

In spite of his seemingly sophisticated behavior at times, a child at this stage is more often inconsistent and contradictory than not. At one moment he might say that one object is bigger than another, and several statements later reverse his decision completely, not realizing that the two are incompatible. He lacks the ability to think about what he is thinking or to plan much ahead. He is still operating nearly entirely on perceptual experience, using sensory cues rather than logical thinking to judge relations. To a very young child, an object seen from different viewpoints *is* actually different; that is, the child is egocentric, viewing the world from his own momentary perspective. An older child, who can bring more experience and knowledge to bear, will know conceptually that the characteristics of an object remain the same in spite of changing perceptions or viewpoints of it. In one well-known test, for example, a young child correctly stated that the length of two sticks, one positioned above the other, was the same; yet, when the top stick was merely moved to the right a little distance, the child stated incorrectly that now the top stick was longer. Thus, in Piaget's terms, the child is unable to conserve quantity and responds merely to perceived properties of objects and events.

Piaget proposes that the roots of conceptual thinking lie in the construction of mental images and symbolic processes. The first step, constructing mental images, is an internal process independent of overt physical action. A mental image is a "representation of a specific action or event" (Baldwin, 1967, p. 231). These images are still quite specific, not generalized. A child can imitate an adult after the actual model is gone. The little boy who picks up his toy lunch box and leaves the house for "work" is doing just that kind of imitating. The kinds of symbolic processes that develop at this stage are perhaps more obvious in children's play. In pretending, actions represent reality, but are definitely distinct from it in some way. And occasionally the child himself confuses the symbolic nature of his play with reality when he begins to play for "real" or when he actually believes his pretense.

Another important kind of symbolic process is that involved in the child's constructing verbal schemas. Words themselves play an important role in the development of concepts. Their arbitrary nature forces us to define them in some way in order to use them correctly. This need for definition helps us to create various class concepts. (The importance of classes in cognitive development will be considered at the next stage.) Piaget believes one must realize that, in spite of the importance of words, a child's use of them in this second stage does not necessarily indicate that conceptualization is taking place. A child uses labels in a much more limited way than adults do. The word *car*, for instance, may be used to mean anything moving, whether it is what adults call a car, truck, bicycle, wagon, or train. Words are gradually used in representative ways, and eventually a child will have little difficulty identifying and labeling a chicken. Yet *chicken* will still not be a concept in the way it is for adults. Thus, as he walks around a yard full of chickens, the child may call each one "the chicken," thinking that each time he sees a chicken it is the same chicken. For obvious reasons, Piaget calls this kind of concept a *preconcept*.

Little or no understanding of superordinate-subordinate classes is manifested. For example, in an experiment often described, a child is shown a box containing many wooden beads; some are brown, fewer are white. The child agrees that all the beads are wooden and that some are brown, some white. When he is asked whether there are more brown beads or more wooden beads, he will usually say there are more brown ones. And why are there more brown than wooden? "Because there are so few white ones." He cannot consider more than one characteristic of the beads at one time. For the time being, he can center on either color (brown, white) or composition (wooden), but not both. Gradually, the child at this stage gains the experience and maturity needed to allow him to decenter, to retain several bits of information, to consider simultaneously more than one aspect of a problem.

Stage III: Concrete Operations. Between 7 and 11 years of age a child's thinking begins to stabilize in the sense that internal actions and perceptual schemes are beginning to be organized into logical, operational systems. The child begins to be able to think out the consequences of possible action ahead of time, rather than learning by physical trial and error. Toward the end of this period, he has a fairly successful understanding of the conservational principles – changing the shape of a piece of clay does not necessarily change the weight or tearing a piece of bread does not reduce the total amount. Also, he begins to handle the more difficult concepts of time, space, quantity, and number, although the problems of volume remain a little too sophisticated.

Piaget has applied the term *operations* to cognitive actions closely organized into a strong system or network. The operations of this developmental period are still integrally connected to concrete objects and actions and quite generally involve the process of classification, the problems of learning to classify, to arrange previous classes on the basis of new information, and to build new classes. In relation to this problem of classification, Piaget has coined the term *grouping*, based on the mathematical concept of group as a set of elements having several similar characteristics related by some rule or law. A grouping is a set of operations that may not comprise a group as formally defined but that have several of the properties of a group.

Piaget theorizes nine groupings of operations: one simple equivalence grouping that pervades all others; four groupings related mainly to logical classes as abstractions not representing actual physical collections of objects; and four infralogical groupings concerning the relationships of parts of an object to the whole or of members of a class to the entire class. A child learning to classify experiences or concepts should acquire these grouping processes, which in a broad sense are different ways of logically organizing information about the external world.

The first grouping – grouping equalities – is perhaps the easiest of the nine to explain and understand. The child should first of all grasp the idea of equivalent sets by recognizing and grouping objects exactly alike in all respects. Mathematically, this process is represented like this:

$$x = y$$
$$y = z$$
$$x = z$$

This is a very simple equivalence in which the objects of a set are alike in every respect, and the child must logically realize that if x is identical to y and y is identical to z, then x must be identical to z. He must recognize that all elements are equivalent.

We will not discuss in detail the other eight groupings involving classes – they are shown as Groupings I-VIII in Fig. 11.4. In any case, some, which have not yet been subjected to extensive research, are hypothesized solely as the next logical step in a sequence. Nevertheless, because Grouping I, the inclusion of a subclass within a class, seems to have been the most thoroughly studied, it can readily be described:

A child, confronted with an array of different objects and asked to group those together which belong together, will respond differently at

GROUPING I:	Inclusion of a subclass within a class (hierarchical classification)	trees		
		deciduous		evergreen
		elm oak		pine juniper

GROUPING II:	Alternate divisions of the same class	buildings	
		houses	nonhouses

GROUPING III:	Division of a group of objects into 4 classes using 2 or more criteria	puppies	black	brown
		male	black male	brown male
		female	black female	brown female

GROUPING IV:	A special class of Grouping III in which for some reason one combination of criteria is impossible		grass	nongrass
		tree	X	tree, nongrass (elm)
		nontree	grass, nontree (crab)	nongrass, nontree, (rosebush)

GROUPINGS V through VIII concern relationships using different kinds of criteria:

GROUPING V:	Asymmetrical criteria	taller−shorter heavier−lighter $2 > 1$ and $1 < 2$
GROUPING VI:	Symmetrical criteria	Joe is Bill's brother; Bill is Kyle's brother; Joe is Kyle's brother.
GROUPING VII:	2 or more asymmetrical criteria	
GROUPING VIII:	2 or more symmetrical criteria	John is Pete's father; Pete is Don's cousin; John is Don's uncle.

Fig. 11.4. Groupings based on Piaget's theory of cognitive development.

different ages or developmental levels. Suppose we have a box containing triangles and squares that are large or small, white or blue. According to Piaget, here is how various children will react:

1. The youngest child arranges the objects in a "graphic" collection or geometrical form, rather than in a "logical" collection based on size, shape, color, and so on. He may put the objects in a single uneven line, but the line will have no logical sequence. The arrangements will please him, but will show little organizational pattern.

A slightly older child may make more complex geometric designs, like arranging the objects in a circle or triangle or making a symmetrical or representational design.

2. Next is a transition level in development at which the child either sorts objects into nongraphic collections, with some assorted items remaining, or divides them into many small classes, perhaps with only one object each.

3. A child a little older makes simple subclass arrangements. He may divide the entire array into two classes on the basis of one criterion, such as form.

4. In the final stages, the child can sort larger classes and arrange separate elements within the classes, according to size, form, and color—differentiating small from large, white from blue.

Other characteristics of this stage of concrete operations besides experience in classifying objects are numerous. The child is gaining more experience with the concepts of space and the relations of objects to each other, including himself in the relationships. He begins to understand changing points of view, the appearance of objects from other vantage points. By the end of this period, he no longer believes that a winding path and a straight path are the same length if they begin and end at the same point. Also, 7- to 11-year-olds are developing their concepts of quantity, of number, and of distance. A very young child at Stage II believes that there are fewer marbles in a cluster than in the same cluster spread out to cover a larger area. Gradually, through Stage III, the child can keep in mind more than one aspect of a problem. He can see that though the marbles when spread out enclose a larger area of space, their actual count has not changed at all. It is important to realize, however, that in this stage the child is still limited mainly to concrete objects, things that he has been able to perceive and manipulate. Although he is able to do very simple logical operations, he can think only about that which he has experienced concretely. He cannot imagine the "possible" in any organized way.

Stage IV: Formal Operations. At this most advanced stage of cognitive operations, the child older than 11, now an adolescent, becomes able to deal with more than the real, concrete situations of the last stage. He can conceive of possibilities existing only in the mind. He is more able to organize a situation or problem. He begins to reason correctly, to make logical inferences, and to understand causal relationships. In short, he is now at the level where he is improving his problem-solving abilities, his abilities for scientific reasoning. This kind of development needs not only the understanding of interclass and intraclass relationships characteristic of Stage III but also those classifications that are possible, though they are not necessarily concretely represented. In other words, the adolescent is now carrying out hypothetical thinking in which he can mentally (without relying on real-world representations) consider all possibilities or combinations, hypothesize the results, and establish an organized and logical sequence of procedures. An often-cited example of this kind of abstract thinking is found in the following study:

Four bottles containing colorless liquids are put before the child. The experimenter takes a smaller bottle containing another colorless liquid, x, and adds some of it to the liquid in a sixth bottle, causing it to turn yellow. He then asks the child to produce the same color, using the four bottles in front of him and the liquid x. Characteristically, a child at the stage of concrete operations will not go beyond the simple combinations of, for example, x with bottle 1, x with 2, x with 3, x with 4, thinking that he has done everything possible. When it is suggested that he try several bottles at once, he will do so randomly and may or may not hit on the correct combination. If, when he does produce the yellow color, the experimenter asks him to do it again, he becomes confused, forgetting what he has already done. The adolescent, however, will approach the problem systematically, first trying the simple combinations and then the more complicated ones in an orderly, organized way: 1 with 2 with x, 1 with 3 with x, and so on. After finding one solution to the problem, he will also continue to look for other possibilities and may offer hypotheses about the nature of the liquids in bottles 2 and 4, one of which destroys the yellow color.

In solving combinatorial problems of this sort, the adolescent will show the capability of holding several factors constant while varying another. He can handle the groupings of Stage III with greater flexibility and facility; he continues to refine his hierarchies of classes, while at the same time realizing the relationships between classes on a much higher, more abstract level than that of concrete operations.

At a conference at Cornell University in 1964, Piaget presented his main ideas in four relatively concise papers. (Duckworth translated the papers and the related oral comments.) The papers outline Piaget's theories as they have been somewhat modified during the past decades; they constitute his most recent formulations and thus merit careful attention. A few key definitions and Piaget's synthesis of the four stages, incorporated in the following quotation, provide an appropriate summary for the preceding discussion.

> To understand the development of knowledge, we must start with an idea which seems central to me—the idea of an *operation*. Knowledge is not a copy of reality. To know an object, to know an event, is not simply to look at it and make a mental copy, or image, of it. To know an object is to act on it. To know is to modify, to transform the object, and to understand the process of this transformation, and as a consequence to understand the way the object is constructed. An operation is thus the essence of knowledge; it is an interiorized action which modifies the object of knowledge. For instance, an operation would consist of joining objects in a class, to construct a classification. Or an operation would consist of ordering, or putting things in a series. Or an operation would consist of counting, or of measuring. In other words, it is a set of actions modifying the object, and enabling the knower to get at the structures of the transformation.
>
> An operation is an interiorized action. But, in addition, it is a reversible action; that is, it can take place in both directions, for instance, adding or subtracting, joining or separating. So it is a particular type of action which makes up logical structures.
>
> Above all, an operation is never isolated. It is always linked to other operations, and as a result it is always a part of a total structure. For instance, a logical class does not exist in isolation; what exists is the total structure of classification. An asymmetrical relation does not exist in isolation. Seriation is the natural, basic operational structure. A number does not exist in isolation. What exists is the series of numbers, which constitutes a structure, an exceedingly rich structure whose various properties have been revealed by mathematicians.

These operational structures are what seem to me to constitute the basis of knowledge, the natural psychological reality, in terms of which we must understand the development of knowledge. And the central problem of development is to understand the formation, elaboration, organization, and functioning of these structures.

I should like to review the stages of development of these structures, not in any detail, but simply as a reminder. I shall distinguish four main stages. The first is a *sensory-motor*, preverbal stage, lasting approximately the first 18 months of life. During this stage is developed the practical knowledge which constitutes the substructure of later representational knowledge. An example is the construction of the schema of the permanent object. For an infant, during the first months, an object has no permanence. When it disappears from the perceptual field it no longer exists. No attempt is made to find it again. Later, the infant will try to find it, and he will find it by localizing it spatially. Consequently, along with the construction of the permanent object there comes the construction of practical, or sensory-motor, space. There is similarly the construction of temporal succession, and of elementary sensory-motor causality. In other words, there is a series of structures which are indispensable for the structures of later representational thought.

In a second stage, we have *preoperational* representation—the beginnings of language, of the symbolic function, and therefore of thought, or representation. But at the level of representational thought, there must now be a reconstruction of all that was developed on the sensory-motor level. That is, the sensory-motor actions are not immediately translated into operations. In fact, during all this second period of preoperational representations, there are as yet no operations as I defined this term a moment ago. Specifically, there is as yet no conservation, which is the psychological criterion of the presence of reversible operations. For example, if we pour liquid from one glass to another of a different shape, the preoperational child will think there is more in one than in the other. In the absence of operational reversibility, there is no conservation of quantity.

In a third stage the first operations appear, but I call these *concrete operations* because they operate on objects, and not yet on verbally expressed hypotheses. For example, there are the operations of classification, ordering, the construction of the idea of number, spatial and temporal operations, and all the fundamental operations of elementary logic of classes and relations, of elementary mathematics, of elementary geometry, and even of elementary physics.

Finally, in the fourth stage, these operations are surpassed as the child reaches the level of what I call *formal* or *hypothetic-deductive operations*; that is, he can now reason on hypotheses, and not only on objects. He constructs new operations, operations of propositional logic, and not simply the operations of classes, relations, and numbers. He attains new structures which are on the one hand combinatorial, corresponding to what mathematicians call lattices; on the other hand, more complicated group structures. At the level of concrete operations, the operations apply within an immediate neighborhood: for instance, classification by successive inclusions. At the level of the combinatorial, however, the groups are much more mobile. These, then, are the four stages which we identify, whose formation we shall now attempt to explain.

What factors can be called upon to explain the development from one set of structures to another? It seems to me that there are four main factors: first of all, *maturation*, in the sense of Gesell, since this development is a continuation of the embryogenesis; second, the role of *experience* of the effects of the physical environment on the structures of intelligence; third, *social transmission* in the broad sense (linguistic transmission, education, etc.); and fourth, a factor which is too often neglected but one which seems to me fundamental and even the principal factor. I shall call this the factor of *equilibration* or, if you prefer it, of self-regulation. (Ripple & Rockcastle, 1964, pp. 8-10)

Bruner on Cognitive Development

Jerome Bruner's main interests in cognitive development that are of concern to us center on the means by which human beings internally represent their experiences and how they organize and store these representations for future use (Bruner, Olver, & Greenfield, 1966). Piaget and Bruner most closely approach each other in their descriptions of the developmental stages or gradients in the internal representation of experience.

Bruner emphasizes three ways of knowing something: through doing it, through seeing a picture or image of it, and through a symbolic means such as language. The terms he uses to denote these ways of knowing, or representing, experience, are *enactive*, *ikonic*, and *symbolic*. Bruner's conception of enactive corresponds somewhat to Piaget's sensorimotor, ikonic to Piaget's preconceptual, and symbolic to both Piaget's concrete and formal or hypothetic-deductive stages. Bruner, while recognizing with Piaget that qualitative differences may occur in thought corresponding roughly to Piaget's stages, insists also that human beings represent experiences enactively and ikonically throughout their lives, not just during certain earlier years or stages. Note that the three modes may be related not only to representing experiences internally, but also to operating *on* one's environment, as follows: acting on the environment: enactive representation; sensing the environment: ikonic representation; acting on the environment through language: symbolic representation. As the individual matures and becomes capable of the three successive modes of behavior, they, in turn, are interrelated, rather than being discontinuous from one age to the next. Excerpts from Bruner's explanations of the three modes of representation will clarify the modes themselves and permit inferring the interrelationships among them.

> We can talk of three ways in which somebody "knows" something: through doing it, through a picture or image of it, and through some such symbolic means as language. A first approach to understanding the distinction between the three can be achieved by viewing each as if it were external—though our eventual object is to view representations as internal. With respect to a particular knot, we learn the act of tying it and, when we "know" the knot, we know it by the habitual pattern of action we have mastered. The habit by which the knot is represented is serially organized, governed by some sort of schema that holds its successive segments together, and is in some sense related to other acts that either facilitate it or interfere with it. There is a fair amount of sensorimotor feedback involved in carrying out the act in question, yet what is crucial is that such a representation is executed in the medium of action.
>
> Representation in imagery is just that: the picture of the knot in question, its final phase or some intermediate phase, or, indeed, even a motion picture of the knot being formed. It is obvious, yet worth saying, that to have a picture before one (or in one's head) is not necessarily to be able to execute the act it represents, . . . A picture is a selective analogue of what it stands for, and only in a trivial sense is it a "copy" of its referent, . . . Yet it is not arbitrary. One

cannot fathom the word for something by looking at the something. One can learn to recognize an image of something just by looking at the something . . .

The representation of a knot in symbolic terms is not so readily stated, for it involves at the outset a choice of the code in which the knot is to be described. For symbolic representation, whether in natural or mathematical "language," requires the translation of what is to be represented into discrete terms that may then be formed into "utterances" or "strings" or "sentences," or whatever the medium uses to combine the discrete elements by rule. Note, too, that whatever symbolic code one uses, it is also necessary to specify whether one is describing a process of tying a knot or the knot itself (at some stage of being tied). There is, moreover, a choice in the linguistic description of a knot whether to be highly concrete or to describe *this* knot as one of a general class of knots. However one settles these choices, what remains is that a symbolic representation has built-in features that are specialized and distinctive. (Bruner et al., 1966, pp. 6, 7)

Related to these modes and of high interest to the teacher and curriculum worker is the clarification of the bases by which children of various ages classify things as belonging to the same class, that is, form concepts of equivalence (Bruner et al., 1966, pp. 68-85). Individuals aged 6, 9, 12, 13, 16, and 19 were given the same tasks. Initially, the subject was asked how two things represented by the words *banana* and *peach* were alike and different. Additional items—*potato, meat, milk, water, air, germs*—were added consecutively, and the same question was asked, to a total of eight. A final contrast item, *stones*, was presented and the subject was asked only how it differed from the preceding items. (Two sets of experimental items were used.) Although the eight successive items were perceptibly more diverse, all could be put into the same category on the basis of an equivalence property. Five modes of responding to the tasks were identified as the bases on which items were classified as equivalent: perceptual, functional, affective, nominal, and fiat. The definitions of the bases or modes of classifying follow:

Perceptual. The child renders the items equivalent on the bases of immediate phenomenal qualities such as size, color, shape, e.g., they are both green; or on the basis of position in time or space, e.g., they are both on the ground.

Functional. The child bases equivalence on the use of the items, e.g., they make noise (this is denoted intrinsic functional); or what can be done to them, e.g., they can be thrown (this is called arbitrary functional).

Affective. The items may be rendered equivalent on the basis of the emotion they arouse, e.g., I dislike both; or on the basis of the child's evaluation of them, e.g., they are valuable or important to me.

Nominal. The child may classify the items by giving a name that exists in the language; e.g., they are or are not peaches, all are fruit.

Fiat. The child states that the items are the same or different without giving further information as to the basis of the classification, e.g., banana is the same as plum, the two are the same thing really.

Figure 11.5 shows the percentages of groupings based on various modes. Six-year-olds classify according to perceptual properties more than do older children, but, equally important, all age groups thereafter still do some classifying on the basis of perceptual attributes or proper-

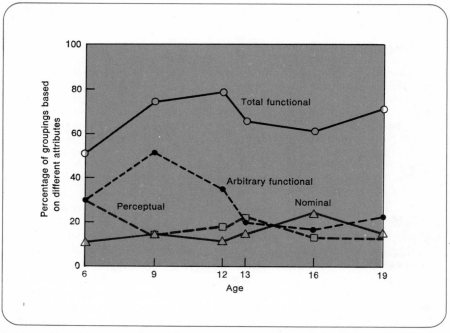

Fig. 11.5. Percentages of students using different modes of classifying, or grouping. (Bruner, Olver, & Greenfield, 1966, p. 73)

ties—colors, sizes, shapes, and places of things. After age 9, a sharp decrease occurs in arbitrary functional classification. However, total functional classification, which includes both intrinsic and arbitrary, increases to age 12, drops off slightly, and then increases to age 19. In other words, as arbitrary functional decreases, intrinsic functional increases, resulting in a total functional increase from about 49 percent of all responses at age 6 to 73 percent at age 19. The increase in classifying on the basis of the intrinsic functions, what the object does, reflects the child's lesser use of the more immediate, perceptible attributes of things in favor of more mature forms of grouping.

Another important characteristic of development is in the type of grouping structures employed with increasing age, as shown in Fig. 11.6. In superordinate grouping, the category or concept is formed on the basis of the common attributes characterizing the items. For example, *banana*, *peach*, and *lemon* are put into the same class because they all have skins or all can be eaten. Complexive grouping is at a more primitive level in which the common attribute is only partially identified or subsequently utilized to form a superordinate grouping. For example, a *bell* is silver, a *horn* is brown, and a *television set* is black, so they can all be grouped together. Or a *banana* and *peach* are both yellow, a *peach* and *potato* are both round, and a *potato* and *meat* are eaten. Note in Fig. 11.6 that while superordinate and complexive groupings are used by about 52 percent and 48 percent, respectively, at age 6, the comparable percentages are about 78 and 22 at age 9.

Bruner summarizes his position on the preceding and other matters as follows:

> Our point of departure is, then, a human organism with capacities for representing the world in three modes, each of which is constrained by the inherent nature of the human capacities supporting it. Man is seen to grow by the process of internalizing the ways of acting, imaging, and symbolizing that "exist" in his culture, ways that amplify his powers. He then develops these powers in a fashion that reflects the uses to which he puts his own life. The development of those powers, it seems to me, will depend massively on three embedded predicaments. The first has to do with the supply of "amplifiers" that a culture has in stock—images, skills, conceptions, and the rest. The second consideration is the nature of the life led by an individual, the demands placed on him. The third (and most specialized) consideration is the extent to which the individual is incited to explore the sources of the concordance or discordance among his three modes of knowing—action, image, and symbol. (Bruner, Olver, & Greenfield, 1966, pp. 320-321)

Bruner, more than Piaget, properly emphasizes the role of schooling, or education more broadly, on the child's development. In this connection, however, he has overgeneralized—stated the case too broadly: "Any subject can be taught effectively in some intellectually honest form to any child at any stage of development" (Bruner, 1960, p. 33). Still, the point that Bruner was making is that children can learn subject matter *that can be experienced nonverbally* at an earlier age than many have assumed. Moreover, on the positive side, Bruner's viewpoint has led to an

Fig. 11.6. Percentages of students using two types of grouping structures. (Bruner, Olver, & Greenfield, 1966, p. 77)

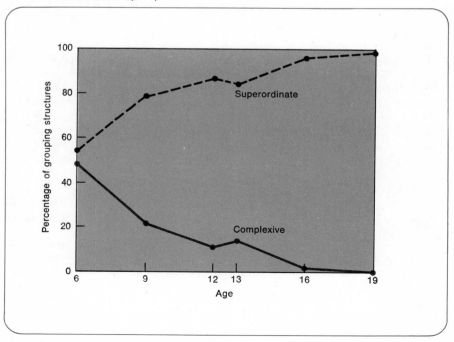

increase in the attempt to use nonverbal or nonsymbolic instruction to teach concepts to children at a younger age than previously. On the negative side, many people have ignored this part of Bruner's statement: "in some intellectually honest form." Bruner included action and imagery, as well as symbols, as intellectually honest forms. Many who prepare instructional material for young children forget the other forms and attempt to introduce difficult concepts through symbols only—to the complete frustration of children.

Development of Geometric Concepts

Frayer (1969) identified developmental trends among fourth- and sixth-graders in the level of mastery of seven geometric concepts: *quadrilateral, kite, trapezoid, parallelogram, rectangle, rhombus, square.* Programed instructional material was prepared to teach the concepts, the material was studied by the students, and then their mastery of the concepts was tested. Five types of production (completion) questions were written for each concept to assess each student's ability to produce (1) attribute values of the concept examples, (2) examples and nonexamples of the concept, (3) relevant attribute values and irrelevant attribute values for particular concepts, (4) a definition of the concept, and (5) related concepts in a hierarchy. Multiple-choice questions requiring cognition of the correct answers were also used. The instructional material was based on the model of instructional objectives presented and discussed at some length in Chapter 4 (Frayer, Fredrick, & Klausmeier, 1969).

Four programed lessons were given on consecutive days to fourth- and sixth-graders who had not had formal instruction in geometry. After all the lessons had been given, the children were tested. The results of the five production-type items dealing with *parallelogram* are shown in Table 11.2.

It is not surprising that the sixth-graders had higher average scores on each type of question than the fourth-graders. Of more interest, however, is the fact that there was a general increase in the difficulty of the questions for both fourth-graders and sixth-graders from Type 1 to Type 5, except that Type 4 proved to be more difficult than Type 5. In Table 11.2, then, are the results of a study (the first one, according to a literature search) that identified developmental trends in the level of mastery of concepts according to an analysis of the specific abilities involved, as represented in the test item types.

11.7. What, according to Piaget, are the main differences between the sensory-motor and preoperational periods in (a) how the child's world is represented internally and (b) the intellectual operations in which the child engages?

11.8. What are the main differences between operations in the concrete and the formal stages?

11.9. Taking as an example a concept such as *dog*, indicate the kind of experiencing and internal representation that are typical of each of Piaget's suc-

Table 11.2 Development of the Concept of *Parallelogram* According to Grade Level and Type of Information Possessed About the Concept

	Percentage correct	
Question	Grade 4	Grade 6
1. Attribute values How many pairs of parallel sides does this figure have?	55	88

	Grade 4	Grade 6
2. Examples and nonexamples Using a ruler, connect as many points as you need to finish the figure to make a quadrilateral that is not a parallelogram.	41	57

	Grade 4	Grade 6
3. Relevant attribute values All parallelograms have something special that not all quadrilaterals have. Parallelograms have ____ pair(s) of ____ sides.	31	54
4. Definition No matter what kind of angles they have or how long the sides, *all* quadrilaterals with two pairs of parallel sides may be called ____.	12	21
5. Relationships between concepts Give the name of one geometric figure that is a special kind of parallelogram.	23	41

Source: Based on Frayer, 1969.

cessive stages. What are the implications of the child's stage of development for instruction?

11.10. Bruner indicated that the concept of *knot* might be represented internally in any of three forms—enactively, ikonically, and symbolically. Describe the same representations for another concept, e.g., *book, skill.* Can all concepts be represented equally well in all three forms? If not, can all concepts be introduced to children at the same early age?

11.11. To what extent does classifying change with age? Does the change appear to be gradual, as Bruner hypothesizes, or according to definite stages, as Piaget hypothesizes?

11.12. Review the specific changes that occurred from fourth to sixth grade in the cognitive operations associated with mastery of the concept *parallelogram*. Does it appear that this kind of knowledge will be more usable by textbook writers or by teachers? Why?

PRINCIPLES PERTAINING TO CONCEPTS

The principles of concept learning, like those for the learning of factual information outlined in Chapter 10, are stated as internal conditions, or as operations that can be performed by the individual to facilitate his learning of concepts. The parallel instructional guides have been formulated to aid the teacher in organizing teaching-learning activities. (Other components of an instructional system, as outlined in Chapter 1, are not discussed here.)

In the last chapter and in this chapter so far, it has become apparent that securing information is essential for learning concepts and that information about concepts and their applications may be acquired through reading and studying printed material. College students, for example, extend their concepts markedly through reading. They can do this easily because they can bring their many direct experiences with the referents of the concepts to their reading and study. Students of school age, however, when starting their study of a new subject field or a new unit, generally have not had the necessary direct experiences; nor do they have a fund of necessary terminology and more basic concepts that are needed to acquire new concepts merely by reading and related study of printed material. Furthermore, some do not yet have the basic ability to read well. The principles and guides given here, then, are particularly relevant to school-age students who are acquiring their initial basic concepts in a subject-matter field. The guides are now discussed in detail.

Principle	Instructional Guide
1. Attending to likenesses and differences among things, qualities, and events is essential to subsequent classification.	1. Emphasize the attributes of the concept.
2. Acquiring the names of concepts, attributes, and instances facilitates the initial learning of concepts.	2. Establish the correct terminology for concepts, attributes, and instances.
3. Cognizing the definitional basis and the structure of concepts to be learned facilitates concept learning.	3. Indicate the nature of the concepts to be learned.

Principle	Instructional Guide
continued	*continued*

4. Cognizing the attributes, or other properties, and the rules that define the concept is facilitated through encounters with positive and negative instances of the concept.

4. Provide for proper sequencing of instances of concepts.

5. Inferring a concept inductively or deductively requires cognizing the defining attributes and rules, remembering information, and evaluating information.

5. Encourage and guide student discovery.

6. Cognizing other instances of the concept; cognizing other concepts as coordinate, subordinate, and superordinate; and using the concept in forming principles and in solving problems extend the individual's concept.

6. Provide for use of the concept.

7. Evaluating the adequacy of one's concepts is essential for independence in concept learning.

7. Encourage independent evaluation of the attained concept.

1. Emphasize the Attributes of the Concept

Suppose that one wishes to have children acquire the concepts *triangle* and *square*. One could present three instances or examples of equilateral triangles of the same size and three instances of squares of the same size. Children at a certain developmental level would readily separate the three identical triangles from the three squares. How effective would this be in helping the children to identify the relevant attribute, number of sides, and the values, three or four, in differentiating triangle and square? One cannot be certain. In any case, this procedure might work better: One could present three equilateral triangles of *different* sizes and three squares of *different* sizes. The attribute, number of sides, would be more obvious, because relative size and area could be seen as not relevant. Frayer (1969) found that specifically pointing out the relevant attribute also resulted in better concept attainment.

The usefulness of arranging instructional activities so that students can directly observe instances of the concept is shown in many ways. For example, children are taken on field trips to a turkey farm, an evergreen forest, and a natural history museum. Specimens are brought into the classrooms and laboratories. These realistic experiences with instances of classes have been shown to be helpful to children in forming basic concepts. Now, however, we go beyond merely providing opportunities for sensory experiences. In other words, we try to help the students in identifying the *attributes* by which things are classified. Thus, rather than going to a turkey farm to see, hear, smell, and feed many turkeys, only one class of *poultry*, we also show pictures of a few turkeys, chickens, geese, and ducks and have children identify their common attributes, as well as the attributes that differentiate them.

Helping children to identify attributes has caused us to move beyond not only direct experiences with actual objects but also certain types of pictorial representations of them. Actual objects and the usual photographs or drawings often include details that are distracting and that prevent cognizing the *defining* attributes. If you brought a live snake and a live snail into the class to help children discriminate between *reptiles* and *mollusks*, the distractions associated with the live animals might keep many students from learning the defining attributes. Similarly, photographs of flocks of turkeys, chickens, geese, and ducks in barnyards might contain so much distracting detail that children would have difficulty attaining the concept *poultry*. Special drawings or animated moving pictures in which the defining attributes are clearly shown are more helpful in establishing a desired concept. Indeed, there is mounting evidence that too much detail in audiovisual material distracts attention from the defining attributes and hinders efficient learning (Travers, McCormick, Van Mondfrans, & Williams, 1964).

2. Establish the Correct Terminology

As indicated earlier in this chapter, Carroll (1964) described a close relationship among words, meanings, and concepts. Along the same lines, Johnson and Stratton (1966) proposed that teachers could use five methods in teaching concepts: (1) present verbal or other instances from which the concept is inferred, (2) provide definitions of the word representing the concept, (3) use the word in a sentence, (4) give synonyms for the word, (5) use combinations of the first four methods. Johnson and Stratton demonstrated that college students could learn concepts to a higher level of mastery by any of these methods. The various single methods worked about equally well, but the combined method was superior to any of the single methods. Archer (1966) and Byers (1967) also reported experiments that showed that knowing the names of the concepts aided in attainment of the concepts.

The implication of this guide is that the student must have the name of the concept, the names of some of its defining attributes, and the names of some of its instances in his speaking vocabulary in order to learn from an oral presentation or a class discussion. As noted earlier, the words are essential for mediating our own experiences and also for mediating the experiences of others as represented in their oral or written accounts. The student needs to have the same terminology in his reading vocabulary in order to learn more about the concept from reading and related study. The teacher can profitably use some class time to make sure that the students *can* read the essential words. In this connection, it is commonly observed that a main difficulty encountered by inner-city children at all school levels is not being able to read, on the average, as well as many other children. In other words, a teacher should place the highest priority on making sure that *all* his students can say and read the necessary words when they are to learn concepts from reading. This in no way denies that having a nonverbal image of a series of processes or a final output, such as in connection with handwriting, playing the piano, and other psychomotor performances, is helpful (Ranken, 1963).

3. Indicate the Nature of the Concepts To Be Learned

The two preceding guides are intended to be taken into account early in the instructional sequence, and this one is, also. That is, when a unit of study is first started, the teacher can take steps to assure that the defining properties of the concepts to be learned will be emphasized, that the necessary terminology can be spoken and read, and that students understand the nature of the concepts that will be learned.

Earlier in this chapter it was shown that the difficulty of concepts is in this order: affirmative, conjunctive, relational, and disjunctive. It was also indicated that concepts are defined in terms of perceptible attributes, semantic associations, axioms, or use. In a series of experiments, Fredrick (1968) and Kalish (1966) found that describing to the students, before each experiment, the nature of the concepts to be attained resulted in better performance. Implementation of this guideline in school settings will probably require that teachers give more attention to the nature of the concepts than is done at present.

4. Provide for Proper Sequencing of Instances

Many studies involving the use of programed instruction and many experiments in laboratories have been done on the sequencing of material. In both these types of research, a great deal of time is spent in working out an effective sequence. The teacher, on the other hand, usually does not have much time to plan a sequence of instruction. Nevertheless, implementing any of the following ideas about sequence would probably achieve beneficial results.

The greater the amount of irrelevant information presented along with the relevant information, the more difficult it is to attain the concept (Archer, 1962; Haygood & Bourne, 1964). An analogy based on the classification scheme in zoology may be appropriate. In teaching the concept *mammal*, a teacher could present instances of vertebrates, including small numbers of mammals and nonmammals. Only a sufficient number of instances for learning the concept should be presented, and the defining attributes for each class of mammals and nonmammals should be emphasized. Details in either oral form or pictures that do not deal with the attributes should be avoided.

Concepts of high dominance and concepts embedded in instances of high dominance are attained more readily than are those of low dominance (Coleman, 1964; Wallace, 1964). A high-dominance attribute stands out clearly from those of low dominance—it is discriminated more readily. On these pages, for example, the words and phrases in italics are probably more dominant for most people than are other words and phrases. Similarly, the number of sides of a geometric figure is probably more dominant than is the number of angles.

A combination of positive and negative instances of the concept, rather than all positive or all negative instances, produces more efficient learning (Huttenlocher, 1962). For example, in teaching children the concept *equilateral triangle*, it is better to present mostly instances of equilateral triangles (positive instances) and a lesser number of right triangles (negative instances). The exact proportion of positive and negative instances is not known and may vary for individuals as well as for concepts. Frayer (1969) used an equal number of positive and negative instances and found two of each to be as effective as four of each.

A simultaneous presentation of instances of the concept is more effective than a successive presentation of instances (Cahill & Hovland, 1960; Kates & Yudin, 1964). Presenting several instances of the concept simultaneously permits discrimination of the attributes more readily and also reduces the memory load. If a child is presented with a triangle, a square, and a pentagon simultaneously, he can compare them better than if he dealt with each one of them at different times. Of course, if many instances are to be presented, there must be a successive presentation of single instances, or sets of four to five instances.

5. Encourage and Guide Student Discovery

In recent years there has been a marked trend away from rote learning in favor of so-called discovery learning. Widely used curricula, such as those of the University of Illinois Committee on School Mathematics (Beberman, 1964), the School Mathematics Study Group (Wooton, 1964), and the Chemical Education Material Study (Campbell, 1964), include textbooks, films, and other instructional material that encourage students to discover generalizations and concepts. Millions of dollars are being spent on the preparation of other instructional materials and teaching methods that are to assist students in discovery. These programs, however, are in no sense intended to enable the student to proceed without instruction. On the contrary, a higher quality of instruction is demanded. At least three features are usually incorporated into these and other programs: (1) presenting students with a problem that is real and meaningful, (2) encouraging and guiding students in gathering information, (3) providing a responsive environment in which students get accurate feedback promptly so they can ascertain the adequacy of their responses (Suchman, 1964). Further, the attempt is made to sequence the instructional material so that students are guided into arriving at a socially accepted concept or principle.

The curricula mentioned were developed on an intuitive basis without presently available knowledge of the more specific mental operations involved in learning concepts. For example, it has been quite clearly established that for a person to arrive at a concept inductively, he must be able to cognize the defining attributes and rules in instances of the concept (Fredrick, 1968), remember the information gained from the successive encounters (Miller & Davis, 1968), and evaluate the information as relevant or irrelevant (Jones, 1968). These operations can be carried out more efficiently with some instruction in what information to search for and how to evaluate it in arriving at the concept.

Guiding the discovery process by giving students some information about the structure of the subject matter and about a strategy or a principle to use in securing and evaluating information from positive and negative instances resulted in better concept learning (Klausmeier & Meinke, 1968). In this case, briefing the students about what they would learn and how to go about it proved highly successful. Giving students information about a principle for use in solving problems and for understanding material has had a long and consistent record of securing better *initial* learning than having the students proceed completely independently (Craig, 1956; Judd, 1908; Kersh & Wittrock, 1962; Kittell, 1957). *Long-term* retention and transfer are better, however, when the student arrives at the principle with only sufficient assistance to make sure that the desired concept *is* learned.

Tagatz (1967) demonstrated that giving elementary school children instructions in what to look for facilitated their attaining of concepts. Here the students were instructed, before starting to learn the concepts, to examine positive instances of the concept in order to ascertain the attributes, or values, common to the positive instances. Each student was given only one brief practice exercise in carrying out the instructions. The results of the instructions were favorable. Similar results were obtained later with college-age students (Tagatz, Walsh, & Layman, 1969). Davis and Klausmeier (in press) also reported that giving high school students cues to help them discriminate relevant from irrelevant information facilitated their attaining of concepts inductively.

Establishing more precise guidelines for the amount of direction to give students will require more experimentation by researchers; but it also requires—and always will require—the use of good judgment by the teacher. Previous knowledge of each student, his strategies or methods of learning, and his attitudes toward independent learning; the subject-matter field; the general climate for learning in the school; and the methods of the teachers—all are related to the extent to which independent discovery operates effectively (Wittrock, 1965). A good balance must be maintained between giving too much information and direction and giving too much freedom and responsibility. How much to help, when to help, and in what way to help require decision-making by the teacher in each immediate situation.

6. Provide for Use of the Concept

In the earlier definition of a concept, one attribute was designated *transferability*. Four uses that a learned concept serve were identified as: cognizing new instances of the concept without further learning; cognizing other coordinate, subordinate, and superordinate concepts that belong to the same hierarchy; using the concept in forming principles and in problem-solving; and learning to learn other related concepts in less time (Klausmeier & Frayer, 1969). Enough specific examples of these uses were provided earlier so that none need be given here. But it is important to remember that the teacher cannot *assume* that students will automatically transfer or apply their newly formed concepts without assistance, particularly if the students have had verbal rather than direct experiences with the referents of the concepts. The following discussions—the first directly relevant to the reader—will help clarify this point:

A number of concepts have been given verbally in this chapter that should help in the teaching of concepts. On the pages of this book the concepts, as represented in words, are merely blotches of ink. If presented orally by an instructor to students, they are merely a series of sounds. In either case, the reader or listener can memorize the information without getting the meaning intended. On the other hand, experienced teachers, reading or hearing both the concept names and the examples and thinking about them, can hardly help coming up with ideas about how the concepts applied in their previous teaching and how they might be applied in future situations. It follows that students without experience as teachers will probably have more difficulty at first in getting the intended meanings and then in attempting to find applications to future teaching situations. Nevertheless, even the student without teaching experience has many experiences to draw on, both as a student and as a learner of concepts. The point here is that an instructor can take some definite steps to help prospective teachers to utilize the experiences they have had and to encounter new experiences that will help them in finding applications. Opportunities for observation in regular classroom settings while enrolled in a course in educational psychology might be arranged. Also, sound films and closed-circuit television offer many possible ways to help the prospective teacher to acquire and apply the concepts.

A second example of the application of concepts takes on a broader aspect:

> What does it mean *to live* anything that is to be learned? What does it mean, for example, *to live persistence*? Can we not agree that actually to *live* persistence in any instance means (1) that one faces a life situation which itself calls for persistence; and (2) that one does then in his own heart accept the idea of persisting; and (3) accordingly does indeed so persist? When all these three things concur, then one has on that occasion *lived* persistence. If with this positive instance we contrast a negative one, the meaning may come clearer.
>
> Certain pupils were asked to write out the words of their morning flag salute. Among the various replies received, the following were noted: I perjur legens; I plaig alegin; I pledge a legion; to the Republicans; one country invisable; one country inavisable; with liberty and jesters.
>
> Is it not at once clear that these pupils did not adequately *live* the meaning of the words used in the salute? Whatever else they may or may not have lived, it stands clear that they did not in any full or adequate degree *live* the meanings which the words were supposed to carry.
>
> It may be added that we can live things in many different degrees. Take feelings, for example; some we may live so slightly that we hardly think of them at the time, and soon forget all about them. Others we live so deeply and poignantly that we can hardly banish them to give due attention elsewhere needed. (Kilpatrick, 1946, p. 535)

Now refer again to one of the guides for facilitating the learning of concepts: "Encourage and guide student discovery." In terms of Kilpatrick's analysis, what does it mean to have fully understood and learned this guide? The person who understands it fully actually *lives* it in teaching-learning situations in which he finds himself: He faces the situation by encouraging and guiding his students to seek and search and by persistently seeking and searching in his own personal and teaching behavior patterns.

7. Encourage Independent Evaluation

This guide carries the identical meaning that it did in the last chapter when proposed for facilitating the learning of facts. It is also applicable to other learning outcomes to be treated in later chapters.

Self-evaluation of the adequacy of one's concepts is one of the most important attitudinal and cognitive learnings that individuals can acquire. Many individuals seem to develop an attitude of inquiry almost automatically; others do not. We have not yet found specific environmental influences that would enable us to answer this general question precisely: Why do some individuals continually seek to evaluate not only their concepts but also their methods for acquiring them? Obviously, however, when concepts are taught merely as definitions of words to be memorized, opportunities to encourage self-evaluation are lost. It is essential both to create the atmosphere of seeking and searching that has been discussed and to help learners to find ways to evaluate their own concepts.

11.13. The length of the sides and the size of the angles are the relevant attributes for differentiating geometric figures of the same class, e.g., squares from parallelograms and right triangles from isosceles triangles. Outline two or three procedures that a teacher might use to help students recognize these relevant attributes.

11.14. Teachers realize that some students are unable to read some of the words of a particular textbook and therefore cannot acquire the desired information and concepts. Which of the following procedures, or a combination of them, appears to be most appropriate to use with such students?
   a. Identify the difficult words and teach the whole class to read these words.
   b. Have each student identify the words he cannot read and have another student who reads well help each one who has difficulty.
   c. Make available to those who cannot read well other books that include similar information but are more easily read.
   d. Present sound films and other visual aids to the whole class that give the same information and concepts.
What other procedures might be used?

11.15. In many textbooks a definition of a word is presented and then one or two examples or positive instances of the concept are given. What other procedures might be followed by the textbook writers, or by teachers in supplementing the textbook, to provide better opportunity for learning a concept through reading and studying printed material?

11.16. In the discovery, or inquiry, method of teaching concepts, the approach is to make available to the students actual instances of the concept or verbal descriptions of instances, to have the student raise questions about the instances or observe them carefully to identify the defining attributes, and to get the student to attain the new or more complete concept inductively. In the expository method of teaching concepts, the approach is to give the concept name, then a verbal discussion and definition in terms of defining attributes or synonyms, and then instances in which the students observe the defining attributes. Under what conditions associated with (a) the level of maturity of the students, (b) the amount of knowledge the students already possess, and (c) the nature of the concepts to be learned, might each of the methods be appropriate?

11.17. How might experience as a teacher facilitate transfer of the instructional guides to actual teaching situations?

11.18. Which one or two of the seven principles of concept learning seem to be the easiest to carry out in increasing your own ability to learn concepts? Which one or two appear to be most difficult?

SUMMARY

Much of man's cumulative experience is embodied in concepts and principles, most of which are expressed in verbal and mathematical symbols. A concept is a mental construct, or abstraction, characterized by psychological meaningfulness, structure, and transferability, that enables an individual (1) to cognize things and events as belonging to the same class and as different from things and events belonging to other classes; (2) to cognize other related superordinate, coordinate, and subordinate concepts in a hierarchy; (3) to form principles and to solve problems involving the concept; and (4) to learn other concepts of the same difficulty in less time. Concepts are usually represented in single and compound nouns, adjectives, and verbs of action, perception, and feeling. Some prepositions and conjunctions also represent concepts.

A principle is a statement of relationship between two or more concepts. Statements that indicate a relationship between specific facts are not principles. Similarly, statements may be made that give an instance of a concept, an attribute of a concept, or a definition of a concept. These also are not principles. The learning and teaching of concepts and principles are presumed to be identical, except that learning the relationships among concepts requires a higher level of abstraction than does the learning of relationships among instances and attributes of concepts.

Piaget has traced an orderly progression in the development of internal operations in terms of sensorimotor and preoperational periods and concrete and formal operations. He indicates that qualitative changes occur in how children think and that these changes are heavily dependent on maturational factors. Bruner discusses development in terms of internal and parallel external operations — enactive, ikonic, and symbolic. Bruner sees more continuity in development than Piaget and also places more emphasis on the environment, including instruction, in the unfolding of the operations.

At present, many teachers and scholars cannot differentiate among factual information, principles, and concepts. They talk about a structure of knowledge in science, mathematics, and other subjects as if it were a reality, but they cannot specify what the total structure and its components are. Many also are not familiar with internal and external conditions of learning, as applied to concepts and principles.

One can improve his learning of concepts by applying seven principles of concept learning: attending to likenesses and differences among things and events; acquiring the names of concepts and their attributes; learning verbal definitions; cognizing the attributes that define the concepts; inferring the concept inductively or deductively, depending on the available information; cognizing other concepts as coordinate, superordinate, and subordinate, when the concept fits into a hierarchy; and evaluating the adequacy of his own concepts. If one can use these principles in his own learning of concepts, he can probably also apply them in guiding the instruction of others, provided other external conditions permit him to do so.

SUGGESTIONS FOR FURTHER READING

ALMY, M. *Young children's thinking: Studies of some aspects of Piaget's theory.* New York: Teachers College Press, 1966.

In this 153-page paperback Almy gives the results of research from 1957 to 1965 with young children and the educational implications of the research.

BRUNER, J. S., OLVER, R., & GREENFIELD, P. *Studies in cognitive growth.* New York: Wiley, 1966.

Chapter 3 on equivalence by R. Olver and J. R. Hornsby, pages 68-85, deals directly with the changes that occur with age in classifying. Chapters by J. S. Bruner are also excellent.

FREDRICK, W. C. How significant concepts are attained in high school subjects. *North Central Association quarterly*, 1966, **40**, pp. 340-345.

Fredrick shows how the results of recent research on concept learning are applied to teaching concepts at the high school level.

JOHNSON, D. M., & STRATTON, R. P. Evaluation of five methods of teaching concepts. In Ripple, R. E., ed., *Readings in learning and human abilities*. New York: Harper & Row, 2nd ed., 1971.

This is a report of an experiment to ascertain the effects of five different techniques for teaching concepts.

KLAUSMEIER, H. J., & HARRIS, C. W., eds. *Analyses of concept learning.* New York:
Academic Press, 1966.

This scholarly book consists of 16 papers. Five chapters are of special interest to
teachers: R. M. Gagné, "The Learning of Principles," pages 81-95; J. M. Kagan, "A
Developmental Approach to Conceptual Growth," pages 97-115; C. P. Deutsch,
"Learning in the Disadvantaged," pages 189-204; H. F. Fehr, "The Teaching of
Mathematics in the Elementary School," pages 223-237; and J. D. Novak, "The Role
of Concepts in Science Teaching," pages 239-254.

LOVELL, K. *Developmental processes in thought.* In Klausmeier, H. J., & O'Hearn,
G. T., eds., *Research and development toward the improvement of education.*
Madison, Wisc.: Dembar Educational Research Services, 1968, pp. 14-21.

Lovell interprets the work of Piaget and describes its educational implications.

PHILLIPS, J. L. *The origins of intellect: Piaget's theory.* San Francisco: Freeman,
1969.

In this 149-page paperback Freeman gives a nontechnical, general summary of
Piaget's theory of cognitive development. Also, implications for teaching as seen by
Freeman are given with a few interesting examples.

PIAGET, J. Development and learning. In Ripple, R. E., ed., *Readings in learning and
human abilities.* New York: Harper & Row, 2nd ed., 1971.

Here Piaget gives an overview of the relationship between development and learning based on his studies of development.

PIAGET, J. The development of mental imagery. In Ripple, R. E., ed., *Readings in
learning and human abilities.* New York: Harper & Row, 2nd ed., 1971.

The internal representation of experiences is described in this essay.

RIPPLE, R. E. American cognitive studies: A review. In Ripple, R. E., ed., *Readings
in learning and human abilities.* New York: Harper & Row, 2nd ed., 1971.

American studies in cognitive learning and development are summarized.

TAGATZ, G. E. Effects of strategy, sex, and age on conceptual behavior of elementary
school children. *Journal of educational psychology,* 1967, **58**, pp. 103-109.

This is one of the best studies done on concept learning in a school setting.

Chapter 12 Problem-Solving and Creativity

The Nature of Thinking and Problem-Solving

reflective thinking
productive thinking
convergent and divergent thinking
sequence of steps in problem solving
hierarchical arrangement of problem-solving abilities
effects of success and failure on problem solving
group problem solving

The Nature of Creativity

creative abilities
fluency, flexibility, originality
productivity
principles for rewarding creative expression

Instructional Guides for Improving Problem-Solving Abilities

identify solvable problems
help students in stating and delimiting problems
help students in finding information
help students in processing information
encourage the stating and testing of hypotheses
encourage independent discovery and evaluation

Instructional Guides for Encouraging Creativity

encourage divergent production in many media
reward creative efforts
foster a creative personality

hinking, solving problems, and producing things and ideas that are novel to the individual are the most complex of human activities; they also are closely related. A problem cannot be solved without thinking, and many problems require solutions that are novel to the individual or to a group. In turn, producing things and ideas that are novel to the individual—that is, creating—involves problem-solving.

These observations are not intended to diminish the importance of factual information and concepts. As noted in the preceding chapters, acquiring information is essential to concept attainment, and both separate items of information and specific concepts must be remembered and manipulated in thought during problem-solving and creative production. Similarly, the cognitive abilities as outlined in Chapter 11, which are essential to concept learning, are also essential for problem-solving.

It is not true that there are some fortunate people who simply possess problem-solving abilities. On the contrary, as is the case with all other abilities, each ability required for solving problems is present to some degree in all human beings of the same age. In other words, every human being is capable of solving some problems. This is the point of view that pervades the treatment of the main topics in this chapter: (1) the nature of thinking and problem-solving; (2) the nature of creativity; (3) principles and instructional guides for improving problem-solving abilities; (4) principles and instructional guides for encouraging creativity. The chapter is intended to provide information that will be helpful not only in working with students but also in developing one's own higher-level cognitive abilities.

THE NATURE OF THINKING AND PROBLEM-SOLVING

Problem-solving enables mankind both to adapt to the physical environment and to change parts of it. Everyone (except perhaps mentally deficient persons and very young children) can think and solve problems, but it is obvious that there are wide differences in these abilities among individuals at all age levels. Our primary concern here, however, is: what can be done to help *children* think more clearly and solve problems more efficiently? As we consider this topic, we will encounter questions, some of which cannot yet be fully answered. In any case, the best way to familiarize ourselves with the present scope of knowledge of the field is to start by studying ideas about thinking that have been evolved over many years.

The Nature of Thinking

Thinking has interested human beings for a long time, partly because although they can do it, they cannot observe it directly. Learning also can be done but not observed. In fact, thinking may be considered as mental activity that is essential to learning most outcomes. Nevertheless, although learning evolves from thinking, thinking itself is as complex as learning. Many attempts have been made to describe thinking, but our knowledge of the process and therefore of how to improve thinking remains incomplete. As you study the different ideas about thinking, try to discriminate among them and to identify some common attributes.

Reflective Thinking. Dewey identified five phases or aspects of reflective thinking:

> (1) suggestions, in which the mind leaps forward to possible solution; (2) an intellectualization of the difficulty or perplexity that has been *felt* (directly experienced) into a problem to be solved, a question for which the answer must be sought; (3) the use of one suggestion after another as a leading idea, or hypothesis, to initiate and guide observation and other operations in the collection of factual materials; (4) the mental elaboration of the idea or supposition . . . ; and (5) testing the hypothesis by overt or imaginative action. (Dewey, 1933, p. 107)

Dewey stressed particularly that thinking involves a state of doubt, perplexity, or felt mental difficulty in which the thinking originates and, in addition, an act of searching, hunting, or inquiring to find material to resolve the doubt and to settle and dispose of the perplexity. Dewey's concept of thinking serves as a basis for problem-solving and is widely accepted as such. For example, the thought processes in problem-solving have been summarized thus:

> While the course of thinking out the solution of a problem varies somewhat for different cases, in general, examination reveals the following characteristic stages in the process: First, a difficulty is felt; second, the problem is clarified and defined; third, a search for clues is made; fourth, various suggestions appear and are evaluated or tried out; fifth, a suggested solution is accepted or the thinker gives up in defeat; and sixth, the solution is tested. (Kingsley & Garry, 1957, pp. 421-422)

Productive Thinking. Wertheimer summarized his ideas about productive thinking:

> . . . in the desire to get at real understanding, requestioning and investigation start. A certain region in the field becomes crucial, is focused; but does not become isolated.
>
> A new, deeper structural view of the situation develops, involving changes in the functional meaning, the grouping, etc., of the items.
>
> Directed by what is required by the structure of a situation for a crucial region, one is led to a reasonable prediction, which—like the other parts of the structure—calls for verification, direct or indirect. (Wertheimer, 1945, p. 167)

Probably you now agree that "What is thinking?" is an important question. In formulating your own answer, you attempt to organize your present and past experiences into some sort of *focus*. This becomes the crucial "region in the field," in Wertheimer's terminology. If you then find that you are satisfied with the way the organization of your experiences fits the meaning you already had for "thinking," no productive thinking will occur. If you are dissatisfied, however, you will attempt to fill in the parts of the whole, to bring the separate ideas into a new total organization. Direct or indirect verification of your new concept, *thinking*, will be required. In this process of acquiring a complete pattern with sufficient meaning to be satisfying, the emphasis is on structuring and restructuring of one's cognitive field.

Convergent and Divergent Thinking. Guilford introduced fruitful ideas about thinking, as shown in Chapter 2 (Guilford, 1967). Although Dewey and Wertheimer treated thinking as processes and did not specify the content of thought, Guilford differentiated among contents, products, and operations. He proposed five intellectual operations, including convergent and divergent production (as noted in Chapter 2). He wrote:

> Cognition means discovery or rediscovery or recognition. Memory means retention of what is cognized. Two kinds of productive-thinking operations generate new information from known information and remembered information. In divergent-thinking operations we think in different directions, sometimes searching, sometimes seeking variety. In convergent thinking the information leads to one right answer or to a recognized best or conventional answer. In evaluation we reach decisions as to goodness, correctness, suitability or adequacy of what we know, what we remember, and what we produce in productive thinking. . . .
>
> The unique feature of divergent production is that a *variety* of responses is produced. The product is not completely determined by the given information. This is not to say that divergent thinking does not come into play in the total process of reaching a unique conclusion, for it comes into play wherever there is trial-and-error thinking. (Guilford, 1959, pp. 470, 473)

It may be helpful for you to review the discussion of the divergent production abilities in Chapter 2. Guilford (1967) pointed out that parallel abilities are involved in convergent and divergent production. The convergent abilities are those involved in producing (converging on) *one* correct answer to a problem or exercise that specifies only one solution or answer as correct, but the three main divergent abilities are fluency, flexibility, and originality.

Levels of Thinking

Taba (1965), an educator with a strong interest in improving instruction in the social studies and language arts, identified levels, or types, of thinking involved in concept formation, in the development of generalizations and inferences through the interpretation of raw data, and in the application of principles. Her analysis merits study and comparison with the ideas presented earlier in this chapter and in the preceding one. It is especially noteworthy that Taba and Bruner et al. (1956) are among those who stress thinking in concept attainment. The levels of thinking proposed by Taba are outlined in the following quotation:

CONCEPT FORMATION

> In its simplest form, concept development may be described as consisting of three processes or operations. One is the differentiation of the properties or characteristics of objects and events, such as differentiating the materials of which houses are built from other characteristics of houses. This differentiating involves analysis in the sense of breaking down global wholes into specific properties and elements.

The second process is that of grouping. This process calls for abstracting certain common characteristics in an array of dissimilar objects or events and for grouping these on the basis of this similar property, such as grouping together hospitals, doctors, and medicine as something to do with health care or according to their availability as an index to the standard of living. Naturally, the same objects and events can be grouped in several different ways. For example, hospitals, X-rays, and surgical equipment can be grouped together as health facilities, as types of services, or as indices of standard of living, depending on the purpose of the grouping.

The third process is that of categorizing and labeling. This process calls for the discovery of categories or labels which encompass and organize diverse objects and events, such as evolving the concept of a unit measurement from measuring with a cup, a yardstick, a plain stick, and a rubber band. It also involves the process of super- and subordination; that is, deciding which items can be subsumed under which category.

In classrooms this cognitive task occurs in the form of enumerating or listing, such as identifying a series of specific items noted in a film or reported by a research committee, then grouping similar things, and finally, labeling the groups.

INTERPRETATION OF DATA AND INFERENCE

Essentially this cognitive task consists of evolving generalizations and principles from an analysis of concrete data. Several subprocesses are involved. The first and the simplest is that of identifying specific points in the data. This process is somewhat analogous to the listing or enumeration preceding grouping. The second process is that of explaining specific items or events, such as why ocean currents affect temperature, why Mexico employs the "each one teach one" system in eradicating illiteracy, or why the way of life in California changed when its harbors were opened for free trade. This process also involves relating the points of information to each other to enlarge their meaning and to establish relationships.

The third operation is that of forming inferences which go beyond that which is directly given, such as inferring, from the comparison of the data on population composition with data on standards of living in certain Latin American states, that countries with predominantly white populations tend to have a higher standard of living.

Interpretation of data and formulation of inferences takes place in the classroom whenever the students must cope with raw data of one sort or another, such as comparing the imports and exports of several countries or analyzing and synthesizing the factors which determine the level of technological development in a given culture by examining the tools and techniques used in the production of goods.

APPLICATION OF PRINCIPLES

A third cognitive task is that of applying known principles and facts to explain new phenomena or to predict consequences from known conditions. For example, if one knows what a desert is like, what way of life it permits, and how water affects the productivity of the soil, one can predict what might happen to the desert way of life if water became available.

This cognitive task requires essentially two different operations. One is that of predicting and hypothesizing. This process requires an analysis of the problem and of the conditions in order to determine which facts and principles are relevant and which are not. Second is that of developing informational or logical parameters which constitute the causal links between the conditions and the prediction and, in fact, make a rational prediction or explanation possible. For example, if one predicts that the presence of water in the desert will cause cities to be built, one needs also to make explicit the chain of causal links that leads from the availability of water to the building of cities. These chains may consist of logical conditions, such as that the presence of water is the only condition to make the soil productive, or from factual conditions, such as whether the desert soil contains salt or not. (Taba, 1965, pp. 536-537) [1]

Common Ideas About Thinking

What are the common elements in these theories of thinking? (1) Thinking involves mental activity which originates with a *feeling of perplexity*, doubt, or dissatisfaction as the individual perceives something in his environment that is not completely satisfying or meaningful. (2) For the thinking to be productive, rather than aimless reverie or daydreaming, there is a *focusing* on a problem or on perceived elements of the environment. The situation or problem is intellectualized, formulated, or stated in such a way that it is relatively clear to the thinker. In mathematics, in painting a picture, in composing a song, in writing a short story, the individual must have a reasonably clear idea of what the problem is in order to focus on it and to think productively toward reaching some type of solution. (3) Once the problem is intellectualized, thinking is directed toward the *solution*. In some problem situations the solution comes quickly; in others the individual may continue his efforts intermittently for months and years. (4) After a solution is tentatively accepted, it is *tested* or evaluated. The present information and methods one has, his hypotheses about the solution, and the particular social or other context of his efforts are all related to the testing or evaluating aspect of thinking.

There also are at least two directions of thinking. One is toward acquiring a solution or closure to a problem for which there is a known or a generally accepted answer. *Convergent thinking, logical thinking, critical thinking*, and *reasoning* are terms used quite generally to describe this direction. Another is involved in seeking a new (at least to the thinker) or not generally accepted solution. This direction of thinking, called *divergent thinking* by Guilford, has been termed by others *creative thinking, imaginative thinking*, and *original thinking*.

The preceding viewpoints suggest that thinking is necessary for problem-solving, but do not imply that thinking and problem-solving are synonymous. In this connection, the three sets of operations Taba outlined in defining thinking are significant: (1) *concept formation*—discriminating, grouping, and labeling things and events; (2) *interpretation of data and inference*—identifying elements, relating or explaining the ele-

[1]Reprinted with permission of the National Council of Teachers of English.

ments, and inferring conclusions; (3) *application of principles*—hypothesizing solutions and deducing relationships or solutions. Thus, Taba, more than other writers, gives thinking a central place in concept formation.

The Nature of Problem-Solving

An individual is confronted with a problem when he encounters a situation where he must respond but does not have immediately available the information, concepts, principles, or methods to arrive at a solution. For example, a child encounters a situation where he must use long division to arrive at a solution, but he does not know the needed methods. Problem-solving activity in line with a sequence outlined in Table 12.1 is needed.

Table 12.1. Steps in Problem-Solving and Creative Production as Proposed in Four Research Studies

Rossman (1931)	Dewey (1933)	Merrifield et al. (1960)	Klausmeier (1971)
Need or difficulty observed	Sensing a difficulty	Preparation	Attending to and cognizing difficulties
Problem formulated	Locating and defining the problem	Analysis	Cognizing and stating the general requirements → methods → solution → dimensions of the problem
Information gathered			Recalling existing knowledge and acquiring new information and methods
Solutions formulated	Suggesting possible hypotheses	Production	Applying substantive and methodological information Inferring possible solutions and predicting consequences of each
Solutions tested	Testing hypotheses; accepting one as correct	Verification	Evaluating the quality of the accepted solution
New ideas formulated New ideas tested and accepted		Reapplication	Transferring newly acquired solutions and methodology

Note the parallel terminology in Table 12.1. In the first part of the sequence we have these parallel operations, reading the top part from left to right: *need or difficulty observed, sensing a difficulty, preparation*, and, finally, *attending to and cognizing difficulties*. Other operations that are parallel are shown, though the number of operations is not identical in the four sets. Just as it is not necessary to have the same number of operations in the sequence because of the different degrees of inclusiveness of the terms, we do not need to think that problem-solving always follows the sequence from top to bottom. On the contrary, there is moving back and forth among the various steps, particularly when trying to solve complex ideational and social problems. For example, problems involved in educating the disadvantaged were identified years ago, and many solutions were hypothesized and tried out. However, we are still defining the problems more precisely and are engaging in other problem-solving operations in order to find better solutions.

In part the differences among the problem-solving sequences of Table 12.1 are related to the methods the various authors used for their research and the purposes for which it was intended. Rossman (1931) studied the activities of 710 inventors in arriving at his detailed steps. The exact sources of the ideas of the eminent John Dewey (1933) are not known in this case, but the fact that he started his career as a psychologist and later turned to philosophy and education (including establishing a laboratory school at the University of Chicago) is relevant. He was a keen observer of children and also a brilliant theoretician. Merrifield et al. (1960) based their sequence on factor analytic studies. The operations in the fourth column are based on some original research with children by the senior author but more on analysis and synthesis of the research of others. Note that the operations in the right column are combined with content, as will become apparent later in the principles for teaching problem-solving; these operations represent the senior author's best current estimates of the specific problem-solving abilities that can be nurtured by excellent education.

Even though there are differences in the exact terminology, we agree that problem-solving is at the apex of human learning. On what is problem-solving based? What must precede it? In Chapters 10 and 11 it was shown that information is needed to attain concepts and that principles, or generalizations, are essential for solving problems. In addition, there may be quite specific methods that are not readily classified as principles.

Gagné (1967) proposed seven types of learning and analyzed each of them. Three of these, which are particularly relevant to the present discussion, are shown in Table 12.2. Column 1 gives the overt types of performance that may be observed as individuals engage in various activities. Column 2 delimits each of the performances more precisely in terms of defining criteria. Column 3 gives a positive instance, or example, of each performance type. Column 4 indicates the internal capability inferred from the observable performances. Column 5 indicates, for each kind of performance learned, the internal conditions presumed to be necessary for learning. Column 6 gives the external conditions presumed to be useful in bringing about the learning. Gagné's report of the relationship between classifying and rule using, or applying principles, provides further clarification of the learning types and the external conditions presumed to facilitate the learning.

CLASSIFYING

Example: Learning the botanical classification *tuber* and the verbal classification "tuber."

The table indicates that previously learned discriminations must be recalled. In the example at hand, these discriminations pertain to the physical appearance of plant stems on the one hand and of roots on the other. Following this recall, a *variety of examples* is presented, illustrating the appearance of tubers as enlarged stems. In each case, there is reinstatement of a chain such as *potato* (or pictured potato)-*tuber*-"tuber." In order to emphasize the distinction, a similar set of examples may be presented for *root*.

RULE-USING

Example: Learning the rule "Pronouns which are the subjects of sentences are in the nominative case."

According to the table, the first concern is with the recall of previously learned concepts. External conditions must be arranged to supply verbal cues to stimulate such recall. Verbal cues may be in the form of questions, such as "Which of the following are pronouns? Which of these words is the subject?" These concepts having been aroused, it is then a fairly simple matter to use their names as verbal cues for the rule to be learned; in other words, to state the rule: "Pronoun subjects are nominative." But it is also important at this point to insure that such a statement is not learned merely as a verbal sequence. The next step in arranging external conditions, then, is to require a number of specific applications of the rule, such as "Supply the first-person pronoun for the following sentence: '_____ students like football games.'" A suitable variety of examples of rule application, of course, needs to be provided. (Gagné, 1967, p. 303)

Table 12.2 indicates one person's conception of a hierarchical arrangement of cognitive abilities. How does the ability to solve problems relate to other high-level cognitive abilities? Table 12.3 gives the correlations between problem-solving and seven other high-level abilities. The higher positive correlations are with reading (.73), judgment (.71), IQ (.68), and problem recognition (.62), which are considered to be primarily convergent thinking abilities. Positive but lower correlations are shown between problem-solving and word fluency (.42), closure (.40), and ideational fluency (.29). These are associated more closely with divergent thinking.

Although high positive correlations are noted between problem-solving and other high-level cognitive abilities, we should not infer that problem-solving can be done only by older persons who can read. Simple problems are solved by children at a relatively young age. For example, 3- and 4-year-olds successfully manipulated strings leading to subgoals in a simple succession that would allow reaching the major goal; these nursery children were capable of inference (Kendler & Kendler, 1956). To give another example, elementary school children use their concepts of geometric figures, such as rectangle and square, and their knowledge of the principle, area = length × width, in solving problems involving computation of areas.

Insight, Trial, and Confirmation. Two different points of view have been expressed about the means of solving problems. One is that the solution

Table 12.2. Three Types of Learning and Related Internal and External Conditions

1	2	3
Performance type	Definition	Example
Classifying	Assigning objects of different physical appearance to classes of like function	Distinguishing various objects as "plant" or "animal"
Rule-using	Performing an action in conformity with a rule represented by a statement containing terms which are concepts	Placing "i" before "e" except after "c" in spelling various English words
Problem-solving	Solving a novel problem by combining rules	Raising an automobile without using a jack

Source: Adapted from Gagné, 1967, pp. 299, 301.

to a problem is arrived at suddenly after some initial effort. In the other point of view, a problem gets solved through gradually eliminating errors and putting together correct responses. There has been considerable controversy over which is the correct interpretation. However, Harlow has arrived at a rational interpretation of the situation. More trial and confirmation and less insight are typical when a given *class* of problems is first encountered (Harlow, 1959). Subjects of low mental ability were presented a series of simple discrimination problems, such as selecting the larger of two stimuli, whether shown on the right or left. They displayed trial-and-error behavior, taking many trials to go through a series perfectly. After several hundred problems of the same class, however, the subjects would make the correct discrimination when each problem was first presented. These later performances seemed like insight learning, that is, suddenly getting the problem correct. In fact, the subjects had learned in previous trials how to learn the class of problems. They acquired what Harlow

Table 12.3. Correlations Between Problem-Solving and Other Variables

Variable	Problem recognition	Word fluency	Ideational fluency	Closure	Judgment	IQ	Reading
Problem-solving	.62	.42	.29	.40	.71	.68	.73
Problem recognition		.40	.56	.30	.55	.52	.60
Word fluency			.46	.33	.37	.40	.49
Ideational fluency				.17	.28	.32	.36
Closure					.27	.36	.35
Judgment						.54	.64
IQ							.56
Reading							

Source: Harootunian & Tate, 1960, p. 331.

4 Inferred capability	5 Internal (learner) conditions	6 External conditions
Concept	Previously learned multiple discriminations	Reinstating discriminated response chain contiguously with a variety of stimuli differing in appearance, but belonging to a single class
Principle (or rule)	Previously learned concepts	Using external cues (usually verbal), effecting the recall of previously learned concepts contiguously in a suitable sequence; specific applications of the rule
Principles plus "problem-solving ability"	Previously learned rules	Self-arousal and selection of previously learned rules to effect a novel combination

called a *learning set*. In more common terms, they acquired a method of learning that transferred positively to other problems of the same type. What is important here is that Harlow feels he has shown an orderly progression from trial and error to seemingly insightful learning. He states the idea thus: "Generalizing broadly to human behavior, we hold that original learning within an area is difficult and frustrating, but after mastery, learning within the same area becomes simple and effortless" (Harlow, 1959, p. 511).

To recapitulate, it is most likely that insight is possible only after previous experience with the class of problems. Also, some problems lend themselves to seeing means-end relationships more readily than others. Also, other things being equal, an older and more intelligent person solves a problem with less fumbling and fewer errors than a younger and less intelligent child. Further, teachers can arrange learning situations to facilitate achieving the correct solutions with fewer errors.

Success and Failure. The effects of success and failure in problem-solving are similar to the effects with other outcomes of learning. Repeated failures result in giving up, substituting a different goal, or showing other forms of unproductive behavior. The problem-solving processes of students after failure on initial attempts to solve problems are significantly inferior to those of students who were successful in their initial attempts (Rhine, 1957). Success and failure produce differential effects at different points during problem-solving. Students who withdraw from the problem-solving situation before achieving a solution set higher goals originally, use fewer alternative solutions in attempting to solve the problem, and perform less effectively than do those who achieve solutions (Schroder & Hunt, 1957). The differences between children of high and low intelligence who solve problems with different degrees of success will clarify these points.

Figure 12.1 shows differences in behavior involving problem-solving

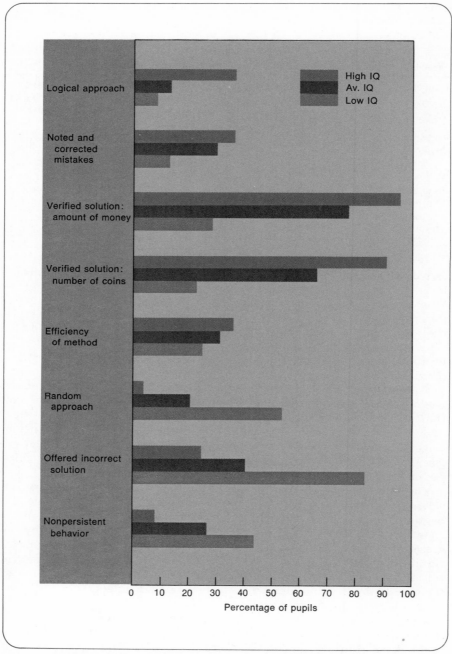

Fig. 12.1. Percentages of pupils of three IQ levels showing effective and ineffective problem-solving behaviors. (Adapted from Klausmeier & Loughlin, 1961, p. 149)

among children of high, average, and low IQ at an average age of 125 months. There were 40 children in each IQ grouping. On all the behaviors, the children of low IQ were less effective than were those of high IQ. More important, the differences in behavior give clues as to why failure was experienced more frequently by the children of low IQ. For example, more children of high than low IQ used a logical approach, noted and corrected mistakes, and verified solutions. More children of low than high IQ made random approaches to the problem, offered incorrect solutions, and did not persist in attempts at solving the problem. Actual descriptions of the performances of a high-IQ boy and a low-IQ boy may help in visualizing some of these differences:

Richard, who had a WISC IQ of 138, used 585 seconds to solve the problem: "Make $9.77, using 12 bills and coins." He studied the situation and during the first 3 minutes made a first attempt at solution, getting the amount correct but using 13 instead of 12 bills and coins—9 one-dollar bills, 1 half-dollar, 1 quarter, and 2 pennies. He checked the amount and number of coins and started over. During the next 3 minutes he made his second and third tries, each time starting with a five-dollar bill. On the second he had 12 bills and coins but an incorrect amount; on the third try, neither was correct. Each time he checked amount and number of coins. During the third 3 minutes he made his fourth try, but made a mistake in adding the amount. Checking through his solution at the beginning of the fourth 3-minute period, he found the error and after 45 seconds offered as a correct solution 1 five-dollar bill, 4 one-dollar bills, 1 half dollar, 1 dime, 3 nickels, and 2 pennies. Richard made 25 separate moves, but only 6 were needed, as shown in the final solution. Therefore, his efficiency ratio was 6/25, or .24.

Michael, one of the more able low-IQ boys, had a WISC IQ of 73; he used 805 seconds to "Make 46¢, using 4 coins." Ten coins of each denomination—penny, nickel, dime, and quarter—had been placed on the table before him. (In a pretest it had been established that he had the requisite skill in adding and knowledge of coins to solve the problem.) Michael, as Richard, restated the problem correctly prior to attempting a solution. During the first 3 minutes, Michael took 3 dimes and 10 pennies from the supply, then returned to the supply 3 pennies, one at a time, and offered the remainder as a correct solution. Upon being told that it was incorrect and with all coins returned to the supply, he studied the coins and offered 1 quarter and 2 dimes as a second solution during the second 3-minute period. During the third 3 minutes, he withdrew from the supply 1 quarter, 1 dime, 1 nickel, and 1 penny and offered this as correct. When told it was incorrect and the coins had been returned, he again studied the coins, and during the fourth 3 minutes withdrew 1 quarter, 1 penny, 1 dime, then put the quarter back. During the fifth 3 minutes he again withdrew the quarter and another dime from the supply, thus having 1 quarter, 2 dimes, and 1 penny. This he offered as correct without observably checking accuracy of amount or number of coins. He made a total of 16 coin movements when only 3 were needed; his efficiency ratio was .188. At no point was it necessary to encourage Michael to continue or to keep at the task; however, like the majority of low-IQ children, he offered incorrect solutions and did not verify amount of money nor the number of coins. (Klausmeier & Loughlin, 1961, pp. 150-151)

As noted in these descriptions, Richard was markedly superior to Michael in verification and reapplication, eventually arriving at the correct solution. Other children of low IQ, different from Michael, did not persist when informed that their solutions were wrong. After two or three such experiences, they manipulated the coins without producing a close approximation of the final correct solution. In this experiment we did not attempt to teach any child how to overcome his errors. In regular teaching situations, however, we feel that time can profitably be spent in teaching children of all IQ levels methods for solving problems, rather than giving them solutions or letting them fail repeatedly.

Set and Problem-Solving. Set is usually defined as a predisposition to react to a situation in a certain way. Instructions are frequently used to establish a set. For example, four functions of instructions in problem-solving are: (1) to identify the terminal performance required, (2) to identify parts of the problem situation, (3) to recall relevant abilities, and (4) to guide thinking (Gagné, 1964). When instructions achieve these purposes, the student receiving them behaves differently in the problem situation from the way he would without the instructions. In other words, each type of instruction establishes a set or predisposition concerning how to proceed or how to interpret the situation. (Instructions may also be used to increase motivation, arouse curiosity, induce stress, and the like.)

That set influences problem-solving has been demonstrated in a number of situations. Instructions to identify the attributes of a concept according to a systematic procedure resulted in improved performance on problems of the same class (Klausmeier, Harris, & Wiersma, 1964). However, when individuals were taught to solve a series of related problems by one method, they persisted in using that method in solving different problems even when they were repeatedly unsuccessful (Luchins, 1942; Schroder & Rotter, 1953). To generalize, persons taught by a single method and having experienced success repeatedly with it in solving a series of *related* problems cling to the method even when repeated trials with it are found not to work in solving *new* problems of another class. In other words, the method leads to *positive transfer* with problems of the same class but to *negative transfer*, or interference, with problems of another class.

The best examples of negative transfer resulting from set are found in connection with using various items in solving problems (Birch & Rabinowitz, 1951). For example, each member of one group was given an electric relay and trained in using it to close an electrical circuit. In another group, each was given an electric switch and trained to do the same thing. Then each person in these two groups and each one in an untrained control group was given both a relay and a switch. All three groups were then presented with a problem that involved using one or the other of the two pieces of equipment in a novel way—as a pendulum weight. The results were as follows: The group who had been trained earlier with only the relay all used the switch as a weight. The group who had been trained only with the switch preponderantly used the relay in the new problem. The control group, with no experience with either, used the switch and relay about equally as a weight. In other words, earlier use of the relay or the switch in closing an electrical circuit resulted in *functional fixedness*; that is, the equipment used for a particular function in one task was not used for a different function in a different task. The subjects were in effect clinging to the method (equipment) used in the earlier task. Thus they experienced *interference*, or, stated differently, negative transfer occurred.

The degree of influence a set or predisposition has on an individual is determined partly by the extent of his flexibility or rigidity when confronted by a particular type of problem. Flexibility and rigidity are not generalized personality traits (Johnson, 1955). That is, within individuals there is considerable variability in approaching problems with flexibility or rigidity, depending on the inherent nature and content of the problem. Thus either rigidity or flexibility may be a fairly consistent characteristic of an individual in meeting a series of *similar* tasks (Goldner, 1957). When an individual is presented with *varying* types of problem-solving tasks, however, he may be rigid on one type but quite flexible on another. For example, a student may show flexibility in dealing with social problems in his fraternity, but he may demonstrate extreme rigidity in dealing with professional matters in a psychology course.

Problem-Solving by Groups

Teachers generally work with groups as well as individuals. How do groups perform on problem-solving in comparison with individuals? Here we shall consider initial learning first and transfer later. Most researchers since 1950 have found that the initial performance of small groups is superior to that of individuals (Fox & Lorge, 1962; Hall, Mouton, & Blake, 1963; Hoppe, 1962; Lorge & Solomon, 1960; Tuckman & Lorge, 1962). However, a minority of researchers report that individuals do better than groups (Duncan, 1959; McCurdy & Lambert, 1952; Moore & Anderson, 1954). In particular, Duncan (1959) stresses that the best individuals exceed the averages of groups. It is possible that group members would more consistently perform better after more experience in working together and after instruction. Fox and Lorge (1962) in fact reported that groups that had received six months of instruction and practice in group problem-solving did outperform individuals.

Although individuals do not perform as well as small groups in most initial learning situations, how do they fare in transfer situations? Groups of four who did better initially than individuals were studied in three different transfer situations (Hudgins, 1960; Klausmeier, Harris, & Wiersma, 1964; Wegner & Zeaman, 1956). In two of the three experiments, those who had learned well initially as members of quartets performed less well in a transfer situation when working alone. In the third experiment, there was no difference (Hudgins, 1960).

Why is the average performance of small groups superior to that of individuals in most initial learning situations? During initial learning the members of small groups collectively arrive at an understanding of the problem more quickly than individuals, secure information more rapidly, cognize information more effectively, remember the relevant information better, bring a larger variety of methods to bear on the solution, pose more solutions, and verify the solutions more reliably (Klausmeier, Harris, & Wiersma, 1964). When working as individuals later on new transfer problems, however, some of those who initially were group members performed the functions just listed less well, apparently because they did not participate actively initially. That is, the task *required* each person when working alone initially to search actively and arrive at a solution if possible. It follows that over a short period of time probably a higher percentage of individuals who initially work alone learn better than do members of a group; none can sit back and not participate, as is the case in groups. Over a longer period of time all the individuals in small groups might participate actively and learn well.

12.1. Which of the steps in reflective thinking as outlined by Dewey is most difficult for you? Does the difficulty depend on the specific problem? What steps can groups perform better than an individual?

12.2. Explain the roles of facts, concepts, and principles in problem-solving.

12.3. Why do you imagine such diverse thinking games as crossword puzzles, mathematical games, anagrams, acrostics, chess, and bridge remain popular? Does thinking provide some kind of intrinsic gratification?

12.4. What kinds of skills appear to be common to problem-solving and reading?

12.5. You observe that a certain problem has been solved by others in various ways, and you have only to choose from among the many solutions available. How would you categorize the thinking involved?

12.6. When is "set" a positive factor in problem-solving, and when does it hinder solution?

THE NATURE OF CREATIVITY

Barron (1969) studied creativity in living adults over a period of several years and arrived at an overall concept of creativity. Consideration of his overview here will lead to a later treatment of specific creative abilities, productivity, variables associated with creativity, and school emphasis on creativity.

According to Barron, the making of thoughts is the most common instance of psychic creation; the making of a baby is the most common instance of material creation. Either a thought or a baby is absolutely unique, but both also are typical of the creations of mankind generally. Thus, a man may think a thought that is new for him, yet it may be one of the most common thoughts when all human beings are taken into account. This common thought is original for the thinker but not for mankind. Although the study of thinking in general is important to the research on creativity, Barron and other researchers are more interested in creativity of the kind implied in this quotation:

... All of us are both creatures and creators, but we vary both in our quality as a creation and in our power to create.

Great original thoughts or ideas are those which are not only new to the person who thinks them but new to almost everyone. These rare contributions are creative in perhaps a stronger sense of the term; they not only are the results of a creative act, but they themselves in turn create new conditions of human existence. The theory of relativity was such a creative act; so was the invention of the wheel. Both resulted in new forms of power, and human life was changed thereby.

Creative power of an outstanding order is marked by the voluminous production of acts which can claim a notable degree of originality, and the occasional productions of acts of radical originality. It is instructive to read in a good encyclopedia the history of the basic scientific disciplines; one soon finds the same names cropping up in field after field, for it is the nature of genius to range with fresh interest over the whole of natural phenomena and to see relations which others do not notice. (Barron, 1969, p. 19)

Creative Abilities

Table 12.4 lists the names of creative abilities, the intellectual processes and the products, and the types of task used to measure the ability. Although only semantic content is given in the table, there are parallel abilities for figural and symbolic content. You may recall from the discussion in Chapter 3 that figural abilities are thought to be more closely associated with performance in the visual arts and in the musical and architectural areas, whereas semantic content is more closely associated with performance in literature, science, mathematics, and the social sciences.

As indicated in Table 12.4, divergent-production abilities and other abilities involving transformations underlie creative performances. Note, however, that cognition and convergent production are also involved. Furthermore, one must remember information in order to use any earlier experience in a current creative performance. For example, Pollert et al. (1969) found positive correlations between children's scores on creativity tests and their ability to recall (1) a list of commonly used words presented orally, (2) the verbal details of a story presented orally about a visit to the zoo, and (3) specific objects and colors in four colorful pictures presented visually by means of an overhead projector.

We shall not elaborate on the types of tasks given in Table 12.4 except to note that all of them require the person to *produce* something, rather than to recognize something as being a correct or appropriate response. Further, the scoring of such tasks is not done on the usual right or wrong basis. Rather, the scores or ratings are usually in terms of number of responses for fluency, cleverness for originality, and ability to produce ideas in different categories for flexibility. You will find it interesting to carry out the tasks and to compare your responses with those of others.

We have now discussed some of the intellectual or cognitive factors in creativity. Nearly everyone working in the field accepts fluency, flexibility, and originality as being associated with creativity.

The adults whose creativity Barron (1969) studied were living writers, mathematicians, architects, and scientists. Highly creative individuals were compared with others who had an equal amount of education but were judged to be less creative by their contemporaries. Large differences in personality variables were found among the more creative individuals

Table 12.4. Creative Abilities Involving Semantic Content

Ability	Intellectual process	Product	Type of task used to measure ability
Conceptual foresight	Cognition	Implications	List as many as six different ways to accomplish a certain task.
Ideational fluency	Divergent production	Units	Write names of things fitting broad classes; e.g., things that are white and edible.
Semantic spontaneous flexibility	Divergent production	Classes	List uses for a wooden lead pencil.
Associational fluency	Divergent production	Relations	Write synonyms for each of several words; e.g., for the word "hard."
Expressional fluency	Divergent production	Systems	Construct a variety of four-word sentences, given four initial letters, no word to be used more than once; e.g., "W_____ f_____ r_____ d_____." (Possible answer: "Who found Rover dead?")
Originality	Divergent production	Transformations	(Clever) Write titles for a short story. (Remote) Give remote (distant in time or in space or in sequence of events) consequences for a specified event.
Semantic elaboration	Divergent production	Implications	Add detailed operations needed to make a briefly outlined plan succeed.
Semantic redefinition	Convergent production	Transformations	Name an object that could readily be made by combining two given objects.

Source: Based on Guilford & Hoepfner, 1966.

within the same group and a few differences were found between the creative groups. Here are the descriptive statements most common to the creative individuals:

Appears to have a high degree of intellectual capacity.
Genuinely values intellectual and cognitive matters.
Values own independence and autonomy.
Is verbally fluent; can express ideas well.
Enjoys esthetic impressions; is esthetically reactive.
Is productive; gets things done.
Is concerned with philosophical problems; for example, religion, values, the meaning of life, and so forth.
Has high aspiration level of self.
Has a wide range of interests.
Thinks and associates to ideas in unusual ways; has unconventional thought processes.
Is an interesting, arresting person.
Appears straightforward, forthright, candid in dealings with others.
Behaves in an ethically consistent manner; is consistent with own personal standards. (Barron, 1969, p. 70)

Productivity

Anyone may have daydreams and do a great deal of thinking of the divergent sort. Nevertheless, if there is no closure, if the thoughts are not developed into a *product*, the creative ideas do not become evident. This is true at all school levels, kindergarten through graduate school, and with all adults, including teachers.

The well-known long-term study of a group of gifted people carried out by Lewis Terman is an excellent source of information about productivity. After identifying children with IQs of 140 and higher during the early 1920s, Terman did several follow-up studies. When the males in the group were 25 years old or more, the 150 rated highest in success as measured by productivity (not income) and the 150 lowest were compared according to a number of criteria on which they had been rated during their childhood. In the elementary school years the high- and low-success groups had been much alike, with about the same grades and test achievements. Early in high school the groups had begun to draw apart, with the success group getting higher grades. A far greater percentage of the successful adult group had finished college. The most spectacular differences, however, showed up between the two groups in 1940, when they were 25 years old or older. The productive group, far more than the less productive, was superior in these personality characteristics: persistence in the accomplishment of ends, integration toward goals as contrasted with drifting, self-confidence, and freedom from inferiority feelings. The successful group appeared to have a much stronger drive to achieve good all-around mental and social adjustment and was relatively free from severe emotional tensions that bordered on the abnormal (Terman, 1954).

Other Cognitive Variables in Creativity

We have indicated in previous chapters that the concept of general intellectual ability (IQ) is not in harmony with the concept of many specific intellectual abilities. Although this is the case, tests of general intellectual ability do sample a composite of abilities that underlie broad classes of performance. Therefore, we might expect a positive correlation between general intellectual ability and creative performances, although the correlation would be far from perfect. When children representing the entire range of IQs from very low to very high were included in a sample, moderate positive correlations were found between IQ and measures of specific divergent thinking abilities (Ripple & May, 1962). In another study, children of low IQ were found to be consistently lower than children of average and high IQ in divergent thinking; also, as expected, they were still lower than the high-IQ children in *convergent* thinking abilities (Klausmeier & Wiersma, 1965).

Although we and others have discovered moderate positive correlations between divergent thinking and IQ, the correlations are not high enough to justify using intelligence tests to identify students who are high in creativity (MacKinnon, 1962; May, 1961; Torrance, 1965). Students of high IQ vary markedly in creativity, and highly creative students vary markedly in IQ. This point of view has been clearly stated: ". . . It is com-

monly observed that many children who are very high in intelligence as
measured by IQ are not concomitantly high in such other intellectual
functions as creativity, and many children who are high in creativity are
not concomitantly high in intelligence, as measured by IQ" (Getzels &
Jackson, 1962, p. 3). Here is a similar point of view: "The best conclusion
at present is that intelligence, as measured, accounts for only a minor
portion of the variation in creative performance and, by itself, is by no
means an adequate measure of creativity" (Taylor & Holland, 1962, pp.
93-94).

Just as intelligence test scores and creativity do not correlate highly,
neither do creativity and the grades assigned to students (Taylor, Smith,
& Ghiselin, 1963) nor ratings of creativity by teachers and scores of creativity (Holland, 1959; Klausmeier, Harris, & Ethnathios, 1962; Yamamoto,
1963). In this connection, the National Merit Scholarship administrators
made 25 scholarships available each year to candidates who could not
qualify on high school grades or on standard scholastic aptitude tests but
who had manifested a high level of creative ability in the sciences or the
arts. The following behaviors were recognized as having importance quite
apart from grades or test-measured achievement:

CREATIVE SCIENCE SCALE

1. Presenting an original paper at a scientific meeting sponsored by a professional society
2. Winning a prize or award in a scientific talent search
3. Constructing scientific apparatus on own initiative
4. Inventing a patentable device
5. Having a scientific paper published in a science journal

CREATIVE ARTS SCALE

1. Winning one or more speech contests
2. Having poems, stories, or articles published in a public newspaper or magazine or in a state or national high school anthology
3. Winning a prize or an award in an art competition (sculpture, ceramics,
   painting, and so forth)
4. Receiving the highest rating in a state music contest
5. Receiving one of the highest ratings in a national music contest
6. Composing music that is performed at least once in public
7. Arranging music for a public performance
8. Having at least a minor role in plays (not high-school or church-sponsored)
9. Having leads in high-school or church-sponsored plays
10. Winning a literary award or prize for creative writing
11. Having a cartoon published in a public newspaper or magazine (Barron, 1969,
    pp. 129-130)

The inferences to be drawn from the work thus far done in relating
creativity to other cognitive abilities are reasonably clear. We should not
expect children of low and average IQ to be as creative as children of high
IQ. At the same time we must not confuse IQ and creativity. There is a
wide variation in creativity among children of the same IQ level. The
same inferences hold for grades made in the various school subjects as
related to creativity.

Emphasis on Creativity in the Schools

As noted in Chapter 2, Guilford, a leading theoretician and psychologist, identified and related divergent thinking abilities to other abilities in a model of a structure of intellect. His work also renewed interest in the development of creative abilities as an instructional objective. Torrance is an educational psychologist and developer who has conducted pioneering research and development studies during the past two decades aimed at getting ideas about creativity into educational practice. As he summarized them, his efforts have focused on the following tangible applications: (1) experimental instructional materials for use by elementary and junior high school students; (2) books that report or synthesize his original research and the research of others; (3) articles in popular magazines that are nationally circulated; (4) actual teaching of regular courses and institutes on creativity and giftedness; (5) tests and other assessment procedures for studying creative behaviors; (6) scholarly papers and speeches at professional meetings and conferences; (7) articles in professional journals. Torrance (1967) indicated that these aspects of his work had influenced educational practices in the United States and other countries in the order given, ranging down from most to least influence. Others in research and development also recognize that translating ideas into forms that students can use directly is an important way to influence educational practices. A quick overview of Torrance's work—the kind of experimental instructional materials put into the hands of students and recommendations to teachers for encouraging creativity—will illustrate the most direct methods now being used in dealing with creativity as an educational objective. This overview will be followed by a brief outline of a different approach to teaching creativity under development by Davis (1969).

Experimental Instructional Materials. The two major developments evolved by Torrance, his graduate students, and colleagues are *Imagi/Craft* materials (Cunnington & Torrance, 1965) and *ideabooks* (Myers & Torrance, 1965a, 1965b, 1966a, 1966b). The Imagi/Craft materials consist of a set of 10 record albums with teacher guides. Great moments of scientific and geographic discovery, invention, and fantasy are dramatized in the recordings. The two main objectives are: (1) to help children learn about the nature of creative processes, the value of creative achievements, and the struggles of creative people and (2) to engage the children in creative thinking experiences similar to those presented in the recordings.

The ideabooks have been used in experiments and in regular practice in the primary and intermediate grades and in junior high schools. Each booklet (50 to 100 pages long) briefly tells the student what to do first and then provides space for the student to respond. The following instructions to students at the beginning of *Invitations to Speaking and Writing Creatively* indicate the student attitudes that the authors consider to be important and also give an overview of the booklet:

TO THE STUDENT

This ideabook is yours. Please regard it as your personal possession. On every page you are invited to express yourself—never to imitate someone else. The main purpose of INVITATIONS TO SPEAKING AND WRITING CREATIVELY is to help you to discover yourself. The authors believe that every individual can enjoy a richer, happier life if he recognizes and develops his abilities.

The ideabook's plan. Each of the twenty-one units in this ideabook consists of an exercise and some suggested activities. The activities are the "invitations." They are *only* invitations, however, and you need not feel obligated to accept them if they do not interest you. On the other hand, we believe that the more activities you engage in the more you will discover about yourself — and the more fun you will have with this ideabook.

Don't stop here! If you can think of other things you would like to do in connection with any of these units, try them out. The exercises are really only starting points. We hope you won't restrict yourself to the invitations on these pages.

Keep an open mind: Although some solutions to the problems in the exercises may be considered preferable to others, there are no "right" answers. Anyone using this ideabook must be willing to accept the fact that there may be many possible solutions to problems such as those presented here. In fact, the world is beginning to learn that there are few, if any, permanent solutions to its problems. By keeping an open mind and respecting the other person's ideas, you can gain considerably more from your experiences.

Starting with the first page, we invite you to learn as much as you can about the world and about yourself — and have fun! Nothing is more fun than learning. (Myers & Torrance, 1965b, p. iv)

In other words, the development of creative abilities calls for students to produce ideas that may be discussed but cannot be scored right or wrong. These ideas may be novel to the teacher as well as to the students.

One way to encourage originality may be inferred by studying Fig. 12.2, which is a reproduction of the first exercise in one of the ideabooks. The next "invitations" based on this situation, to which the student responds on two pages provided in the book, are these:

Use the space below to jot down ideas about your drawing. If you have created an original animal or plant, describe it. If you have drawn a machine, explain how it works.

What quality or ability do you like best about the thing you have drawn? Does it have one feature which is particularly pleasing or useful?

If it didn't possess this valuable characteristic, would there be fewer of these things? Why or why not? (Myers & Torrance, 1965b, pp. 2, 3)

Principles for Rewarding Creative Expression. A main problem in developing the creative abilities of students in school settings is that their expressions of creativity often are punished rather than rewarded. Torrance (1965) identified five principles that teachers should implement in order to reward the creative behavior of students. Indicating his realization that the principles might seem too obvious to merit serious attention, he added that, nevertheless, they are not that obvious, for the large majority of teachers either do not understand them or do not practice them. The principles are as follows:

1. Be respectful of unusual questions.
2. Be respectful of imaginative, creative ideas.
3. Show your pupils that their ideas have value.

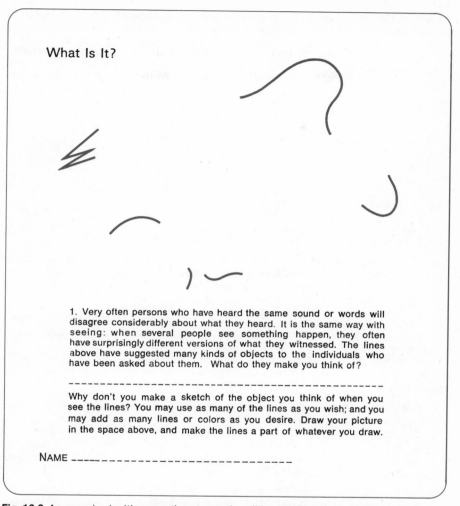

What Is It?

1. Very often persons who have heard the same sound or words will disagree considerably about what they heard. It is the same way with seeing: when several people see something happen, they often have surprisingly different versions of what they witnessed. The lines above have suggested many kinds of objects to the individuals who have been asked about them. What do they make you think of?

Why don't you make a sketch of the object you think of when you see the lines? You may use as many of the lines as you wish; and you may add as many lines or colors as you desire. Draw your picture in the space above, and make the lines a part of whatever you draw.

NAME _____

Fig. 12.2. An exercise inviting creative expression. (Myers & Torrance, 1965b, p. 1)

    4. Occasionally have pupils do something "for practice" without the threat of evaluation.

    5. Tie in evaluation with causes and consequences. (Torrance, 1965, p. 43)

Table 12.5 shows how well some teachers followed these principles in actual practice. It is obvious that respect for student questions and for unusual ideas caused these teachers the most problems. Here are some of the questions the students raised:

    1. How do we stay on the earth?

    2. Do rocks grow?

    3. Could our club have a code?

    4. What becomes of men salmon when females go upstream to spawn?

Table 12.5. Manifestation of Respect or Reward for Creative Thinking of Pupils in Applying Five Different Principles for Rewarding Creative Thinking

Principle	Respect/Reward		Lack of respect		Mixed/Indeterminate	
	Number	Percentage	Number	Percentage	Number	Percentage
Respect for questions	36	58.0	18	29.4	8	12.6
Respect for unusual ideas	29	51.8	15	26.8	12	21.4
Showing ideas have value	57	91.9	2	3.2	3	4.9
Unevaluated practice	54	96.4	0	0.0	2	3.6
Cause-and-effect relation	34	68.0	7	14.0	9	18.0

Source: Torrance, 1965, p. 50; © 1965. By permission of Prentice-Hall, Inc.

5. Why isn't the plural of cat written as kittens—because if you have more than one cat, you would have kittens, wouldn't you?
6. Does a baby have a smaller number of bones than we do?
7. Why didn't I get paid for how good I was? (in a variety show)
8. Where does the water on the blackboard go?
9. Why don't people like Negroes?
10. How far does space go and what comes after space? (Torrance, 1965, p. 51)

The following responses by a fourth-grade teacher indicate what Torrance judged to be unsatisfactory implementation of the principle about respecting questions:

1. *What was the question, who asked it, and what were the general conditions under which it was asked?*
The question asked dealt with sex; we had a rabbit in our room and discussion was centered around it. All of the class was very much interested in the discussion; a boy asked, "Why do you need two rabbits to have little rabbits?" Everyone joined in and wanted to know.

2. *What was your immediate reaction?*
My immediate thought was: "Can't teach sex in school." My action was to laugh and casually change the subject.

3. *What was the immediate reaction of the class, if observable?*
There was keen interest in the question. I observed that a couple of pupils drew a little color.

4. *In what way was respect shown for the question?*
I told the class that many questions that are asked are good, but too hard to answer without going into research.

5. *What, if any, were to observable effects (immediate and/or long-range)?*
Everyone sort of shrugged it off with a teacher-doesn't-know-anything attitude. (Torrance, 1965, p. 53)

These responses by a first-grade teacher show a more satisfactory approach:

1. *What was the question, who asked it, and what were the general conditions under which it was asked?*

"Where does the water on the blackboard go?" This was asked when the board was being washed. The teacher then asked the question of the class. One child thought it soaked into the blackboard.

2. *What was your immediate reaction?*
Return the question to the class. Get their opinions.

3. *What was the immediate reaction of the class, if observable?*
Many children said, "Oh, no—it goes into the air." The boy who answered the question looked embarrassed.

4. *In what way was respect shown for the question?*
I said that it did look as though water seemed to soak into the board and thought we would find out what did happen.

5. *What, if any, were the observable effects (immediate and/or long-range)?*
Discussion of evaporation. Experiments on causes of evaporation—heat, air, etc. We fanned a wet blackboard and saw evaporation take place more rapidly. This all led to a study of water, clouds, rain, fog, etc. (Torrance, 1965, pp. 53-54)

A Direct Approach to Teaching Creativity. Davis (1969) reported a strategy for teaching creativity that he developed during 1965-1968. The strategy is incorporated in Davis and Houtman (1968), *Thinking Creatively: A Guide to Training Imagination.* This 150-page book is intended for junior high school students. Humorous written material, cartoons, and a continuous plot involving several characters are used in developing favorable attitudes toward creative production and also in developing skill in four methods of generating novel ideas. Through understanding and doing exercises based on the methods, the students are to develop underlying creative abilities of the kind identified by Guilford and others. The material is intended to be more self-instructional than the usual expository textbook; nevertheless, when an excellent teacher stimulates the students to engage in the tasks and rewards their creative expressions throughout the school day, there are far better results than when the material is used by itself.

The four methods of generating novel ideas that are taught to the students are called: Part-Changing Method, Checkerboard Method, Checklist for Finding Ideas, and Find Something Similar. Each of the four methods is an adaptation of a procedure that has proved successful in generating new ideas in large industries. A first tryout of the methods as incorporated in *Thinking Creatively: A Guide to Training Imagination* showed that they also were successful with eighth-grade students who read fluently and who had encouraging, rewarding teachers. On the other hand, the material did not work well with eighth-graders who could not read well and whose teachers did not assist them with problems of word recognition, vocabulary comprehension, and the concept of creative production.

The following exercises are each based on one method from the book for junior high students. These exercises (there are many more in the book itself, of course) give enough information so that the reader can start to carry out the instructions and thus gain a more complete concept of each method.

Part-Changing Method. This is the first method introduced in the book. Common objects are used as the basis for inviting students to identify the parts, or attributes, that might be changed. This is one exercise:

1. Three parts (or qualities) of common classroom *chalk* are color, shape, and size. (Surprise! These are the same qualities Dudley found with buttons.) Invent some new kind of chalk by listing 15 different *colors* (and don't forget striped chalk, like the striped toothpaste), 10 different *shapes*, and 5 *sizes*. Try to think of *different* ideas, and don't worry about whether or not they are any good. (Davis & Houtman, 1968, p. 12)

(How many different "kinds of chalk" will one get from all possible combinations of 15 colors, five shapes, and five sizes?)

The ideas the authors want the students to generate from the instructional material and exercises dealing with the part-changing method may be inferred from the review of this method given in the book:

REVIEW

1. If you want to change something, just list the main parts and then think of different ways to change each part.
2. The PART-CHANGING method for thinking of new ideas can be used with many different kinds of problems.
3. Thinking of *perfect* (or *ideal*) problem solutions, even if they sound ridiculous, can lead to good ideas.
4. Use your imagination.
5. Look for new combinations of things. (Most new ideas are combinations of old ideas.)
6. Look around you for ideas.
7. Good ideas may (and usually do) come from nutty ones.
8. Don't criticize wild ideas of other people. They might turn into good ideas or else help you to think of good ideas. (Davis & Houtman, 1968, p. 24)

Checkerboard Method. The checkerboard method involves making a checkerboard figure with spaces for entering words or phrases on the vertical and horizontal axes. Properties or attributes are then identified and listed on the vertical axis and another set on the horizontal axis. Then one examines the intersection or combination of each set of two things or attributes. (The senior author of this book has used this by inviting persons who have completed internship, or student teaching, to identify and list along one axis all their own attributes that might be related to success in teaching and along the other all the attributes of a particular teaching situation. This exercise carried out during one class period and discussed in small groups yields new and welcome ideas for most of the students.) Here is an exercise from Davis and Houtman:

Your gym teacher has decided to give you a final exam in which you have to make up a new sport or game. Use a *Checkerboard* to help you do this by putting materials or equipment along the top and things the players do (running, batting, kicking, etc.) down one side. (Davis & Houtman, 1968, p. 40)

Checklist Method. One uses or develops checklists to make sure that something is not left out or forgotten. Davis and Houtman developed a checklist of only seven items that can be applied readily to many situations by junior high school students. Here is the checklist: Change color, change size, change shape, use new or different material, add or subtract something, rearrange things, identify a new design. One can apply this checklist to any objects, for example, to books, autos, television sets, or classroom desks.

Find-Something-Similar Method. In this method the student is encouraged to come up with new ideas by thinking of other things in the world that do the same things we want done. Here is an exercise:

> Imagine your school has a parking problem (which it probably does). Let's find ideas for solving this problem by thinking of how bees, squirrels, ants, shoe stores, clothing stores, and so on "store things." (Davis & Houtman, 1968, p. 96)

Davis and Houtman are concerned not only with the frequency of ideas generated but also with quality. In the later part of the book students are invited to identify the ideas that they think are best. The same book also outlines a problem-solving strategy: clearly understanding the problem and stating it generally, finding main types of solutions, finding specific ideas for each main solution, and choosing the best ideas. The students are encouraged to use any of the four idea-generating methods in evolving types of solutions and specific ideas. Figure 12.3 shows how this process is applied in the book to a problem that is familiar to most of us.

Feldhusen, Treffinger, & Bahlke (1970) reviewed the two preceding programs and two others. One of these was a series of programed lessons intended for fifth or sixth grade. The other was a series of 15-minute radio broadcasts on creative thinking which were presented once a week for 28 weeks to children in grades 3, 4, and 5. The children receiving the broadcasts scored significantly higher than a control group on all four tests of creativity administered to both groups. Further, the children receiving the creative instruction also scored significantly higher on a language achievement test. The best results were obtained with fifth-graders. Thus, substantial evidence is accumulating that creative abilities can be improved through instruction at the elementary school level.

12.7. Although a computer may be said to solve problems, it cannot "think." What steps in problem-solving can a computer not perform? In creative thinking?

12.8. Give a few examples of fluency, flexibility, and originality. Do you find these common in your own daily activities?

12.9. Try using the checkerboard method to create some new ideas. Notice when you have to be fluent and original and when you have to evaluate. Does it help to separate evaluation from the other processes?

12.10. Suppose you invent a new product but nothing ever comes of it. No prototypes are made, no development of any kind occurs, and the product is forgotten. Where does creativity end, and what is the responsibility of the creative person toward his creation?

12.11. Does creativity appear to be something that one can turn off or on? What experiences suggest that it might be? What kind of "set" is involved in creative behavior?

PRINCIPLES FOR IMPROVING PROBLEM-SOLVING ABILITIES

Here, as in earlier chapters, principles and related instructional guides are given. These principles and guides are intended to be treated as a heu-

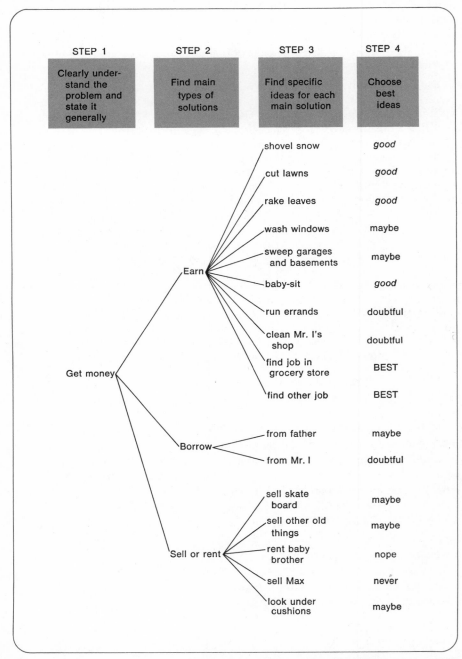

STEP 1	STEP 2	STEP 3	STEP 4
Clearly under-stand the problem and state it generally	Find main types of solutions	Find specific ideas for each main solution	Choose best ideas

shovel snow — *good*

cut lawns — *good*

rake leaves — *good*

wash windows — maybe

sweep garages and basements — maybe

Earn — baby-sit — *good*

run errands — doubtful

clean Mr. I's shop — doubtful

find job in grocery store — BEST

find other job — BEST

Get money

Borrow — from father — maybe

from Mr. I — doubtful

sell skate board — maybe

sell other old things — maybe

Sell or rent — rent baby brother — nope

sell Max — never

look under cushions — maybe

Fig. 12.3. A four-step sequence in creative problem-solving. (Davis & Houtman, 1968, p. 126)

ristic for finding applications to instruction at all school levels and for generating additional hypotheses. The focus is on helping the teacher deal more effectively with those situational elements most directly under the control of the teacher. (Other components of an instructional system as outlined in Chapter 1 are dealt with elsewhere in this book.) The guides are now discussed in detail.

Principle	Instructional Guide
1. Attending to and cognizing self-situational difficulties is essential to identifying a problem.	1. Identify solvable problems.
2. Cognizing the requirements → methods → solution → dimensions of the problem permits an initial attack on the problem.	2. Help students in stating and delimiting problems.
3. Recalling existing knowledge—information, concepts, principles, and methods—and securing new knowledge are essential for arriving at a solution.	3. Help students in finding information.
4. Applying knowledge to the problem situation is essential for generating possible solutions (hypotheses).	4. Help students in processing information.
5. Inferring possible solutions and predicting consequences lead to more permanent solutions.	5. Encourage the stating and testing of hypotheses.
6. Evaluating the adequacy of one's methods and solution facilitates independence in problem-solving.	6. Encourage independent discovery and evaluation.

To clarify each of the six guides, applications will be drawn from two sources in this manner: (1) Each guide will be followed by a description of its implementation in a class in educational psychology. (2) At the end of the section, a lesson in ninth-grade biology will be presented.

The class in educational psychology consisted of 25 university seniors. During the first five weeks of the semester, prospective teachers took an educational psychology class, methods classes, and one class in their major field. These classes met five days a week, each for 50 minutes. The students then went from the university campus into public high schools and did their student teaching for seven weeks. They were in the school throughout the school day, five days a week. After the student teaching, the students returned to the campus for the last four weeks of the semester, their classes meeting daily as before their student teaching.

1. Identify Solvable Problems

On the first day of the class, the instructor passed out a mimeographed outline divided into three parts: an introductory statement, a list of problems that student teachers and teachers in service frequently experience, and a short reference list. In drawing up the list of problems, the instructor had first studied the applicable research in order to identify the main problems actually experienced by student teachers and teachers in service. He had then picked from the many problems described by researchers 18 that he decided were most appropriate for this particular course. The short introductory statement presented to the class follows:

> Every attempt will be made by the instructor to conduct this course in line with what he thinks to be desirable conditions for promoting maximum efficiency of learning. In this connection, he assumes that
>
> 1. every student in this class wants to learn about human abilities and the nature of learning in order to become a successful student teacher;
> 2. the student will identify significant problems in order to learn efficiently;
> 3. the student will actively engage in finding solutions to his problems;
> 4. the resources among the students, the instructor, and the university are sufficient to enable each student to learn efficiently;
> 5. the student can learn through reading, discussing, thinking, and doing;
> 6. every student who is willing to accept the related responsibility should be given a wide degree of freedom in assuming direction of his own learning problems;
> 7. every student who is willing to accept the related responsibility should be treated as a mature individual and a beginning member of the teaching profession.

These ideas were discussed briefly during the first session, and then the instructor asked the students to consider the list of problems presented in the second part of the outline. After some discussion of these problems, the students proposed a few others.

As presented and first discussed, the problems were simply words for some of the students. Whole-class and small-group discussions clarified what they meant or might mean when the student was actually engaged in student teaching. The instructor and most of the students concluded during the first week that here were significant problems that could be partially, if not completely, solved during the semester.

2. Help Students in Stating and Delimiting Problems

The students and instructor spent most of the first week in discussing possible delimitations of the problems in terms of the situation. Each student chose one of the 18 problems that was of immediate concern to him and on which he would like to work before going into student teaching. The class was then organized into six groups, according to the first problem choice of each student. These six problems as finally stated by students were:

1. What are the attributes of a successful teacher?
2. How can I attain an orderly work situation in the classroom, free from disruptive incidents?
3. How can I provide for differences among pupils in rate of learning?
4. How can I encourage all pupils to want to learn?
5. What is the general course of purposeful learning?

6. What can or should I do to help pupils acquire well-integrated personalities and character?

During the first four weeks, when the students were not actually working on the problems, the instructor presented his analysis of two other problems: (1) What principles would help me in teaching students psychomotor abilities in typing, sewing, swimming, and the like? (2) What principles would help me in teaching students knowledge and related cognitive abilities, such as comprehending, analyzing, evaluating, creating?

In attempting to solve the problems before going out for student teaching, the class agreed to do three things. (1) Each group secured information about its problem, mainly through reading. An annotated bibliography was developed by each group and eventually distributed to the entire class, with recommendations. (2) After each individual had acquired some information through reading and class discussions, a list of principles was developed by each group as the tentative solution to the problem. These principles also were distributed to the rest of the class before the students left for student teaching. (3) During regular class periods in the fourth and fifth weeks of the semester each group demonstrated and then discussed one or more of its principles. (This, of course, took six class periods.) The instructor encouraged the students to use this opportunity to get first-hand experience in teaching by trying to make their demonstration sessions as realistic as possible. Also, he led the rest of the class in trying to help each demonstrating group have a successful experience by making constructive comments about the "teaching" and asking constructive questions during the discussion time.

In this situation, then, there was delimitation of the problem in two steps. The first was to find out what the statement or problem really meant in practice and to state it in such a way that there would be reasonable opportunity for making progress toward a solution during the semester. The second step was to decide the form in which the solution to the problem might appear. Three forms were agreed on: (1) a statement of principles; (2) a demonstration of one or more of the principles in class; (3) testing and evaluating these principles during the student teaching.

In the first three weeks, at least half of the class periods were used by each group in stating and delimiting the problem, in discussing information-gathering procedures, in analyzing information, and in organizing the principles. Also, individuals met with the instructor outside of class, and each of the groups met with him at least twice to consider various aspects of the problem-solving situation. It can be seen that delimitation of the problem did not occur suddenly but started in the first week and continued well into the third week. A considerable amount of the delimiting, of course, started after the students began securing information about the problems.

3. Help Students in Finding Information

Once individuals had selected problems and then organized themselves into groups, they needed information. Methods for getting information were devised by the groups, and procedures for bringing together and analyzing information were worked out. The minimum reference list the instructor had given the students was composed of one basic textbook, a supplementary textbook, and five books of readings. However, this list did include a number of selections pertaining to each of the problems. To this extent the instructor gave help, but he did not refer the students to any specific selection or group of selections that might be related to a particular problem. Students were helped in identifying various guides for use of the library, including the location of the current periodicals room and various reserve rooms. Only when individuals or groups asked for further specific help on sources of information did the instructor give such help. From the start the students in each smaller group were encouraged to draw on and contribute information from their previous experiences and knowledge about the problem.

In most groups it was relatively easy to apportion responsibility for examining the list of references in the course outline. Each group then developed procedures for going beyond the reference list. With occasional help, they developed ways to record their findings, and they evolved a fairly uniform system for writing the annotated bibliography. These bibliographies contained from 18 to 35 different entries. In checking these entries, the instructor found that about 60 percent of them were the same as those he had used in an earlier topical outline of the course before attempting this problem-solving approach to instruction. The other 40 percent were new entries, most of them excellent, of which the instructor had not been aware. Most of the new entries were drawn from the professional journals and from methods books in the major fields.

4. Help Students in Processing Information

When the students brought in information and started to write the principles in the small groups, considerable help was needed. Several class periods and meetings outside class with the instructor were required to develop the first draft. As many as three out-of-class meetings were needed with some groups before a fairly well-organized statement of principles was evolved.

One of the main difficulties that had to be faced in interpreting and analyzing information was this: When each group of three to six students started comparing what they had gathered, parts of it did not agree or, at least, needed to be analyzed in terms of the larger problem. The critical point came when the diverse information was to be incorporated in a fairly economical list of principles. The first list of principles tended to be exceedingly long, with 35 to 40 entries. When each member of the group had a typed copy of these, careful analysis started. Overlappings and discrepancies were found. At this point the instructor volunteered help and was called on frequently. If there had been more time, most of the groups would probably have analyzed and organized the information reasonably well themselves.

Now follows the list of principles (they are more properly called instructional guides) which a group of four students developed:

How Can I Attain an Orderly Work Situation in the Classroom, Free from Disruptive Incidents?
1. Take it for granted that the class is well intentioned and expect good behavior from them.
2. Do whatever is necessary and appropriate to get a reasonable amount of order, especially in the first meeting with the class.
3. Let the pupils know what is expected of them and make sure the expectations are reasonable and appropriate, for example, with respect to (a) standards of conduct, (b) class assignments and activities, (c) homework and other out-of-class activities.
4. Teach and illustrate, giving due consideration to the students' interests and backgrounds, such as learning ability, age, home background.
5. Maintain an active class with a variety of projects—not a monotonous routine.
6. Be consistent and impartial.
7. Be courteous to students—avoid the use of sarcasm and ridicule.
8. Promise only what can be carried out.
9. Arrange the situation so that crises are avoided.
10. Investigate the causes of misconduct carefully and take appropriate action, since the purpose of discipline is correction, not punishment.

This economical list of principles was based on information from 35 different sources and represents only a small portion of the many facts and concepts acquired by the students while searching for a solution.

A second group of students had as their problem to provide for differences among pupils in rate of learning in skill subjects. Although the instructor had originally stated the problem in broad terms not restricted to skills, these students delimited the problem to their specific interest. Their introductory statement and principles are as follows:

How Can I Provide for Differences Among Pupils in Rate of Learning in Skill Subjects?

Up to the present time, extensive pretesting has not been used to determine different rates of learning ability in skill subjects. Therefore, we will make two assumptions:
1. Skill classes are heterogeneous.
2. The teacher will have to deal with individual differences within the classes.

The aim of the teacher in handling individual differences is not to mold every student to the same pattern, but to assay the assets and liabilities of each student and to work with the individuals and groups so that members of the class, both individually and collectively, show a net profit at the end of the school year.

A. Dealing with individual differences within the classroom:
1. Ask questions which in general vary from easy to more difficult, so that all will have an opportunity to respond successfully.
2. Motivate the learners through praise and encouragement each day.

3. Enliven your class by having each student keep his own daily personal progress chart.
4. Give directions slowly, clearly, and simply.
5. Organize groups within the class into ability levels and work with these individually with the help of audio aids.
6. Let the fast learner occasionally help the slow learner. An example of this in a shorthand class would be to let the accelerated student dictate to the slower students and demonstrate shorthand outlines at the board.
7. Use audiovisual aids, such as tape recorders, movies, and records, for supplementary demonstrations.
8. Encourage the pupil to set his own goals, try for them, and decide for himself how good the results are.
9. Manage practice so that the learners as individuals or in small groups can proceed at appropriate rates.
B. Dealing with individual differences outside of the classroom:
1. Assign homework with different levels of difficulty that will be in line with the different interests and purposes of the major groups in the class.
2. Have a classroom library with materials of several levels of difficulty relating to the skill subjects.
3. Provide opportunities and facilities for students to improve their skills through purposeful practice in their spare time.
4. Have out-of-class sessions to determine the root of trouble for any student encountering difficulty.

The two groups of principles represent the students' best generalized conclusions about reasonable solutions to each problem before student teaching. The instructor privately evaluated the students' work as excellent, especially considering that the statements were drawn up within a four-week period.

5. Encourage the Stating and Testing of Hypotheses

As soon as a student first identified a problem and started thinking about it individually and discussing it in his group, hypotheses were already being formulated. Thus, there were usually three stages in hypothesis formulation and testing: (1) securing information and drawing up a list of principles; (2) demonstrating one or more of the principles; (3) actual student teaching. A considerable number of hypotheses were accepted and others were rejected—including, perhaps, some good ones. Thus each list of principles was in fact a list of hypotheses which the students first tried out in discussions and later in the demonstration before the class. The demonstration provided the first main test of one or more of the principles. Until students began planning for the demonstration, the principles did not carry the meaning which a principle should. However, when the students began deciding which one or more of the principles *could* be demonstrated in the classroom, the testing of the principle or hypothesis took form.

In the case of providing for differences in skill subjects, a very skillful demonstration was arranged in a business-education laboratory. One student acted as a teacher and dictated shorthand at a moderate speed to a second student while two other students took dictation from tape recorders, one at a low speed and the other at a high speed. The demonstration clearly showed that with sufficient equipment, shorthand dictation could be given at speeds suitable to the rates of at least three different groups of learners within a classroom.

6. Encourage Independent Discovery and Evaluation

This situation in educational psychology obviously encouraged independent discovery and evaluation. Only those students ready for student teaching during the semester were permitted to enroll, and during the five weeks before and the four weeks after student teaching, a relatively small number of other classes was taken. The arrangement enabled each student to plan his study and work schedule more efficiently than did the usual schedule of five or six classes; in turn, the student had more time outside class meetings to gather information independently, to meet with other members of his group, and the like. Further, the students perceived themselves as full-time student teachers. Their motivation for identifying and solving problems was high.

The instructor generally withheld direct evaluation of the students' statements of principles and their demonstrations. He did not tell the students that anything was definitely right or wrong, that anything was complete or incomplete. Instead, he raised questions. The raising of questions, along with discussions, helped the students arrive at conclusions independently. Furthermore, the instructor had and has as one main *instructional goal* the encouragement of independent discovery and evaluation by students so that, when they are on their own in teaching positions later, they will not fall into monotonous teaching methods or, indeed, a monotonous way of life. The goal, if achieved, leads the students to seek better ways of improving problem-solving abilities of their pupils. They will not be satisfied by being told what, when, and how to teach by someone else.

On the basis of the instructor's day-to-day evaluation of this classroom situation, the independent discovery and evaluation by the students yielded excellent results. Under an earlier instructional arrangement in which students took the class without doing student teaching, they had memorized principles and tried to associate as much meaning as possible with them. In the present situation, however, the student did not have to memorize the principles he and his group developed, for they were already incorporated quite well into his total pattern of meaningful learning. Also, the principles drawn up by the other groups were demonstrated and discussed and appeared to be as useful for guiding practices during student teaching as did those proposed by the instructor for the two problems he discussed. A small minority of students indicated that they would have preferred the instructor's handling all of the problems by presenting information and demonstrations and leading whole-class and small-group discussions. More than 80 percent of the students indicated that this was the first time they had been expected to accept the responsibility for their own learning. In addition some of them for the first time used the various library tools that had been available and waiting for their use throughout the first three and one-half years of their university life. They felt that their skill in identifying and using sources of information was an important one which could be applied in their subsequent teaching careers.

Implementation in a Biology Class

Consider how some of the guides were implemented by a beginning science teacher:

> I taught in a junior high school. The lesson I am about to describe was for my ninth-grade biology class which was composed of 13 high-ability students. The specific topic being considered was the salivary digestion of starch. These instructional materials were used: 14 test tubes, 14 medicine droppers, starch suspension, dilute iodine solution, and Benedict's solution. All of these materials were available at the school.
>
> When the class was asked, "What effect has saliva on starch?" the ready answer was, "It changes starch to sugar." When asked how this could be verified, the students were less responsive. They were then instructed to carry out the test for the verification of the presence of starch. This test amounted to putting 5 milliliters of starch suspension in a test tube and then adding one drop of the iodine solution. If starch was really present, a dark blue color should result from the addition of the iodine. The test was positive.
>
> The opening question was repeated and then I asked how to verify the answer given that saliva changes starch to sugar. One student proposed that some saliva be added to each test tube. All the students accepted and executed the proposal. Instructions were given to shake the tubes and to warm them in the fist for two minutes. During the hiatus, the reasons for the shaking and the warmth were discussed.
>
> Observations disclosed that the blue-colored contents of the tubes had become colorless or nearly so. This quickly led to possible theories to explain the change. One student proposed that the iodine had been used up. He suggested that we add more iodine solution in order to test his theory. Each student did so, but no color change occurred. As expected, someone said that the starch had been changed to sugar. (Sugar suspension does not form a dark blue color with iodine solution.) At this point I explained that this might be so, but that the explanation should be regarded as a tentative one, subject to verification. Someone then suggested that we test for sugar with Benedict's solution, so this test was carried out and it was positive — sugar was present.
>
> Henceforth the class seemed complacently satisfied until I asked, "How can we explain the presence of the sugar?" Of course the forthcoming answer was, "The starch changed into sugar; saliva caused it." A classmate objected, "Maybe there was sugar in the starch suspension." It took but a moment to test the stock bottle of starch suspension for sugar. The test was negative, whereupon the following questions were raised. "Is it possible that there was sugar in our saliva? Perhaps there was sugar in the iodine solution." Tests were carried out; the results were all negative.
>
> Since no other objections were presented, the findings were reviewed and listed on the blackboard as follows:

1. The bottle labeled starch suspension contained starch. It did not contain sugar.
2. There was no sugar in the iodine solution.
3. There was no sugar in the saliva.
4. After two minutes, the warmed mixture of starch and saliva gave a positive test for sugar.

Conclusions were called for and evaluated by the answers to the question, "If we had not tested each substance for the presence of sugar, how would our conclusion have been affected?"

12.12. Do you think the principles for developing problem-solving skills are equally applicable to all subject matters? Should they be?

12.13. After a search for information, it might be necessary to restate the problem. What effect might this restatement have on the students engaged in the problem-solving?

12.14. What kinds of decisions are necessary when involved in processing information?

12.15. Do you think it important for *each* student to solve the problem at hand? To reach the same solution? What kinds of opportunities for individual differences exist in the problem-solving situation?

PRINCIPLES FOR ENCOURAGING CREATIVITY

All of the principles related to problem-solving are applicable to developing creative abilities. In addition, three principles are inferred from research and development on creativity, as outlined earlier in this chapter. The principles and guides given here are intended to be applicable at all school levels. The guides are now discussed in detail.

Principle	Instructional Guide
1. Expressing oneself by figural, verbal, or physical means is essential for the production of novel forms or ideas.	1. Encourage divergent production in many media.
2. Experiencing success in creative efforts is associated with a high level of creative expression.	2. Reward creative efforts.
3. Thinking and behaving in divergent ways, in addition to accepting and conforming to some existing standards, are essential to creativity.	3. Foster a creative personality.

1. Encourage Divergent Production in Many Media

If original expression in many media—written language, oral language, rhythms, music, and art—is to emerge, there must be opportunity in the school day for instruction directed toward this end. *Each* teacher must try to encourage creativity, rather than assuming some other teacher will do the whole job. The typical school curriculum, filled primarily with assignments and other activities through which the students are to learn and reproduce what mankind already knows, does not encourage original expression. Indeed, all too often, not only is creative expression not encouraged—it is actually stifled so that students may devote more time to learning material that is not new even to the learner.

Fluency, originality, and flexibility in producing ideas and forms are three of the main divergent production abilities (Guilford, 1967). These abilities develop over a period of many years. Their initial manifestation in young children may take the form of free expression in spontaneous play, singing, finger-painting, and other activities. Here the quality of the output and the level of the technical skill shown are unimportant. Later, in the theme, dance, speech, or painting produced by the elementary and high school student, quality and technical skill are somewhat more important. In the synthesizing done by the inventor or engineer, quality and skill are even more important, without, however, any reduction in originality or flexibility. Starting a new mode of art expression, writing a novel, or conceptualizing a new design for housing or a new theory of human behavior—types of creative expression accomplished by only a few adults from a large population—require the highest quality and skill capable of mankind of a given generation.

In view of all this, it is apparent that a teacher cannot simply tell students that in a given length of time they are to "create" something. He cannot stand before a class and say, "Now write a poem" or "Get out your art materials and, before the period ends in 30 minutes, give me something to display on the bulletin board." From the idea to the finished product, time and effort are essential. In other words, throughout the school years there must be a continuing program for developing creative abilities—an active program, implemented by *all* the teachers.

Many larger elementary and high schools now sponsor annual art exhibits of students' work, arrange programs that include musical compositions by students, produce small volumes of their poetry and other literary work, print students' poems, short stories, and essays in the school newspaper, and stage students' plays. These are a few of the useful means for encouraging student creativity and for opening up opportunities for them to continue to produce after they finish school. Such programs and activities also, of course, do much to further the aim of encouraging creativity on a continuing basis throughout the school program.

A better perspective of the time sequence involved in creating something may be inferred from the original work of Wallas (1926) as interpreted by Johnson (1955). Wallas studied the intellectual activities of artists and poets, and the related time patterns are graphically portrayed in Fig. 12.4. Notice that the artists and poets spent a great deal of time in early preparation. Then there was a considerable increase in the time given to formulation of the idea, whatever it was. As the preparation fell off from the third to the fourth quarter, revision increased markedly. There are, of course, great differences in the total length of time required

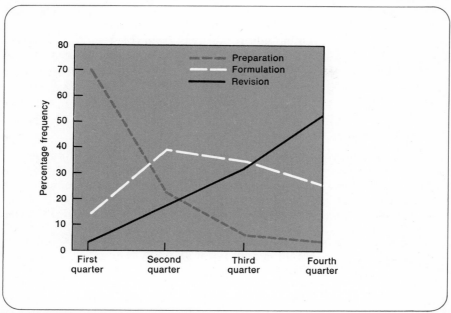

Fig. 12.4. Intellectual activities of poets and artists during four quarters of a creative enterprise. (Adapted from Johnson, 1955, p. 30)

to bring forth a poem or a painting. Some poets and artists spend years on a major work; lesser or shorter works are produced in a shorter time. Some novelists take as long as five or more years from the time they have the first ideas about a novel to bring it to completion; others finish a novel in less than a year.

2. Reward Creative Efforts

Earlier in this chapter five principles for rewarding creative behaviors as developed by Torrance (1965) were discussed. These will not be reviewed here (although the reader should review them). Instead, we will discuss a procedure that thwarts creative efforts.

Teaching and rewarding only one method as correct have done much to inhibit creativity in students. The history of athletic records provides a good analogy. Many athletic records stood for years simply because coaches generally agreed that there was only one proper or correct form for such things as putting the shot, shooting a basketball, or running the mile. Fairly static top limits were expected — and not exceeded — for decades. Then a young man and his coach devised a new way to put the shot, and soon the record went up markedly. When basketball players were encouraged to start shooting one-handed, they obtained much higher accuracy, and basketball scores went up. Running the mile in under four minutes, long thought to be virtually impossible, is now common. The breakthroughs in the arts make the point perhaps even more strikingly in connection with most teaching. For example, for many years a fairly uniform content and methodology of oil painting was rewarded. Eventually, some nonconforming individuals broke away from this tradition, and soon radically different forms of painting evolved. In music, American composers followed the style of the composers of Western Europe for many years. Once a break was made, however, new forms of uniquely American music emerged.

3. Foster a Creative Personality

In the discussion so far we have emphasized cognitive abilities. These abilities do not develop in a vacuum, however; they develop in an interrelationship with the personality of the individual. Because Chapter 15 is devoted entirely to personality integration, we shall indicate here only a point of view about personality traits that should be nurtured rather than discouraged.

Adjectives such as "conforming" "conventional," and "dependent" do not appear in the research as traits of creative individuals. "Impulsive," "sensitive," "self-confident," "independent," and "unconventional" do. Teachers and parents need to examine their own attitudes toward the behavior of children and try to decide honestly which of these characteristics in children are associated with warm and accepting behavior by adults. It is clear, too, that creative individuals are not law-breakers, seeking to destroy values and mores that have been decades, even centuries, in building. They are, however, more questioning of traditions, less inclined to consider all the possible outcomes before acting, and less concerned about how others regard them. If this kind of student is to feel relatively comfortable in the school, we probably must approve, or at least not condemn, a wider range of behavior patterns than we do at the present time.

Implementation in an English Class

A description of the attempts of an English teacher to encourage creativity follows. Try to decide which guides for encouraging problem-solving and creativity were implemented:

> When I first told my classes [high school English] about April 23, the four-hundredth anniversary of William Shakespeare's birth, I gave them a list of approximately 14 projects from which they could choose. They were to select the one which interested them most and have it ready for April 23, which would be set aside for our celebration. The following is a list of some of these suggestions which could be done individually or in small groups:
>
> 1. Dramatizing a scene from *Macbeth*
> 2. Making a bulletin board display
> 3. Writing a poem in commemoration of Shakespeare
> 4. Drawing a character or scene from *Macbeth*
> 5. Designing a costume for one of the characters
> 6. Constructing or drawing a model of the Globe Theatre
> 7. Writing a report on some aspect of Shakespeare

8. Giving an oral report
9. Making a diorama of a scene from *Macbeth*
10. Memorizing a speech and presenting it before the class
11. Presenting a panel discussion

From the above list alone, students were given a variety from which to choose. The selections ranged from designing costumes which called for much creative imagination to writing reports which could be merely factual expositions. I did, however, tell them that they need not feel restricted to that list. I was certain that they would be able to think of other projects, and I wanted them to feel perfectly free to carry out their own ideas.

Flexibility, however, was more important in the actual carrying out of the projects. Students questioned me as to specific directions which they were to follow. For instance, students giving written or oral reports wished to know if they had to be a specific length. Those memorizing passages wondered if they could choose any speech, or if I required a certain number of lines. The four groups that worked on bulletin board displays asked if there were certain requirements which they had to meet. I set no specifications of this kind. In the case of reports, I merely said that they should be well developed. I had learned that if you require a student's written work to be 500 words long, for example, he spends most of his time counting the words. Because he does not have enough to say to equal 500 words, much of the work is superfluous.

Three of the students wrote poems in commemoration of Shakespeare. I had, of course, told the classes that I would give them all of the help that I could, and these three students sought help often. One of them brought four poems in after school and wanted my advice as to which was the best and should be read on April 23. By means of my questioning him, he decided which one was the best. He told me that he enjoyed writing poetry very much but just never had much occasion to do so. I suggested that he submit his poem to *Patterns in Print*, a publication of student work, which he did. It was accepted and will appear in this year's edition. The critical point is that he was interested enough to continue to produce until he was completely satisfied.

Another student enjoyed the projects so much that she worked on three of them, a bulletin board display, a written report, and a costume for Lady Macbeth.

Two days before the deadline, one of the students brought in a model of the Globe Theatre which she had made out of sugar cubes. A tremendous amount of time and talent was involved in its construction. The most rewarding aspect of this incident was that this girl was extremely withdrawn and previously had not volunteered. If I called on her, she would keep her eyes on her book and never offer an answer.

I had another student who also never took part in the discussion. However, he did not even listen to me or to his classmates. I had tried every imaginable means to get him interested in the class, but I was not successful. His project was three drawings of Macbeth which showed much artistic ability. I felt that he had perhaps learned something and enjoyed doing it.

One of the students designed and made a costume for Lady Macbeth which was itself an expression of creativity, but the colors she chose for it were even more so. The majority of the costume was black as she felt that Lady Macbeth played the part of an evil character. She used white trim, however, as she believed Lady Macbeth really had a pure heart.

12.16. How might creative problem-solving be developed in students of the age level in which you are most interested?

12.17. In what situations might you wish to engage in creative thinking? Might there be times when you do not try to produce original ideas or solutions?

12.18. Does it help you to know the kinds of abilities that are necessary to be creative? Does this in itself encourage creativity?

12.19. What kinds of reward situations might be devised in school settings for the purpose of fostering creative effort?

SUMMARY

Thinking, problem-solving, and creating always occur in a situation or context, not as abstract processes. Thinking is about something, problem-solving is directed toward solution of a problem, and creativity involves expressing something in some form. Cognitive processes directed toward finding an already accepted or logical conclusion are usually designated by such terms as *convergent thinking, reasoning,* and *critical thinking.* The type of thinking, directed toward finding new or novel conclusions, methods, or forms of expression is called *divergent thinking, creative thinking,* and *imaginative thinking.* Some convergent thinking is involved in divergent thinking, and vice versa.

Problem-solving requires purposeful activity. The solution to some problems occurs suddenly with insight; in other problems, there is a continuing process of posing possible solutions, rejecting, and finally confirming one as most appropriate or correct. Problem-solving abilities of children and youth are improved by using these guides: (1) identify solvable problems, (2) help students in stating and delimiting problems, (3) help students in finding information, (4) help students in processing information, (5) encourage the stating and testing of hypotheses, and (6) encourage independent discovery and evaluation.

Developing new and better methods for solving problems and inventing new and better forms for expressing human experiences require divergent thinking. The school and society generally must identify more reliably and nurture more successfully the creative abilities of children and youth. Because little has been done in this area, particularly in social affairs, guides for improving creative abilities are necessarily tentative: (1) encourage divergent production in many media, (2) reward creative efforts, and (3) foster a creative personality.

SUGGESTIONS FOR FURTHER READING

BARRON, F. *Creative person and creative process.* New York: Holt, Rinehart and Winston, 1969.

In this 212-page paperback, Barron gives a nontechnical report of his work on creativity in adults extending over several decades. His ideas about educational experiences to increase creativity are indicated.

DAVIS, G. A. The current status of research and theory in human problem-solving. In Ripple, R. E., ed., *Readings in learning and human abilities*. New York: Harper & Row, 2nd ed. 1971.

This review of the research on problem-solving includes both traditional and modern viewpoints.

GOWAN, J. C., DEMOS, G. O., & TORRANCE, E. P., eds. *Creativity: Its educational implications*. New York: Wiley, 1967.

This book, comprised of 36 readings, brings together many of the shorter essays, reviews, and research reports dealing with creativity. Eight selections by Torrance include many concrete suggestions for teachers.

MacKINNON, D. W. The nature and nurture of creative talent. In Ripple, R. E., ed., *Readings in learning and human abilities*. New York: Harper & Row, 2nd ed., 1971.

In this essay, MacKinnon draws on his extensive research results and also on observations conducted over a period of many years.

RIPPLE, R. E., & MAY, F. B. Caution in comparing creativity and IQ. In Ripple, R. E., ed., *Readings in learning and human abilities*. New York: Harper & Row, 2nd ed., 1971.

Positive correlations are reported between IQ and creativity scores in a group of students who varied widely in IQ scores.

TORRANCE, E. P. Applying principles for rewarding creative thinking. In Torrance, E. P., *Rewarding creative behavior*. Englewood Cliffs, N. J.: Prentice-Hall, 1965, pp. 41-74.

A few principles are clearly stated and teachers' attempts to put them into practice are described. The anecdotal reports of the teachers' and students' questions, responses, and activities are presented clearly.

WALLACH, M. A., & KOGAN, N. A new look at the creativity-intelligence distinction. In Ripple, R. E., ed., *Readings in learning and human abilities*. New York: Harper & Row, 2nd ed., 1971.

The distinguishing characteristics of children high in both creativity and IQ scores, of those high in one and low in the other, and of those low in both are described.

Chapter 13 Psychomotor Abilities and Skills

The Nature of Skilled Performance

voluntary to involuntary control
rapid differentiation of cues
rapid feedback and correction
coordinated movement patterns
stability under various circumstances
three-phases in skill learning

The Nature and Types of Psychomotor Abilities

physical fitness abilities
manipulative abilities
changes in abilities with improved performance
genetic and environmental conditions

Developmental Trends

typical performances
individual differences and variability

Instructional Guides for Improving Skills

analyze the skill in terms of the learner
demonstrate the correct response
guide initial responses
arrange for appropriate practice
provide informational feedback and correct inadequate responses
encourage independent evaluation

psychomotor skills and physical fitness are important to students of all ages. The development of skills in the fine and applied arts, in the business education field, in individual sports, group games, and other areas starts early in life and continues through the college years for many students. The study of English, mathematics, foreign languages, science, and social studies contributes little to the development of psychomotor abilities and skills. Nevertheless, the physical fitness of students is important to excellent performance in these curriculum areas and also to the development of a wholesome personality.

The present group of students will soon be adults. Many will have jobs that depend on their psychomotor skills. This is true of typists and others in clerical positions, skilled craftsmen, unskilled and semiskilled workers, farmers, and some professional people, including dentists, surgeons, architects, artists, and musicians. Further, as our society changes and fewer jobs require manual labor, adults are increasingly participating in skiing, camping, boating, golfing, and the like. Increasingly, those in sedentary occupations are engaging in programs of physical fitness in order to maintain health and mental productivity. Thus, knowledge about psychomotor abilities and skills may contribute significantly to a better life for most teachers, as well as for most adults in general.

THE NATURE OF SKILLED PERFORMANCE

Skills that are learned in school vary in the amount of motor and perceptual involvement, as shown in Fig. 13.1: (1) Skills with high motor and low perceptual involvement include walking, dancing, running, swimming, bicycling, and gymnastics. (2) Skills with a considerable amount of both perceptual and motor involvement include playing a musical instrument and taking shorthand. Here the individual sees or hears the stimuli that, in turn, guide his motor responses. (3) Another group of skills has low motor and high perceptual involvement. In silent reading the motor component is low but includes focusing the eyes from left to right across the page, moving from top to bottom as successive lines are read, grouping the words to achieve a fast rate, and the like. However, the main component of reading silently is cognitive, that is, recognizing words and associating meanings with them. In this chapter we are concerned with skills relatively higher in the motor component and intermediate or lower in the perceptual component.

A complex psychomotor skill is characterized by highly organized *receptor-effector-feedback* processes. Thus, a skilled performance, in comparison with one less skilled, is accomplished with (1) less attention to the specific movements, (2) better differentiation of cues, (3) more rapid feedback and correction of movements, (4) greater speed and coordination, (5) greater stability under a variety of environmental conditions.

The excellent typist, in comparison with the beginner, gives little or no conscious attention to hand and finger movements, simultaneously hears or sees more relevant cues to guide sequential movements and ignores

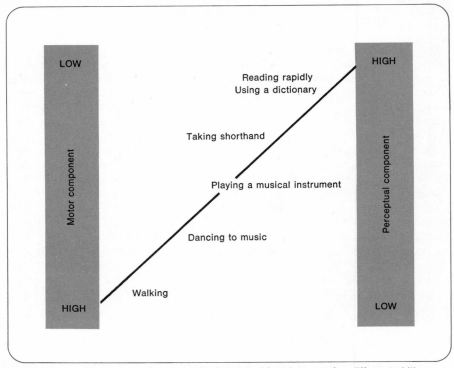

Fig. 13.1. Relative amount of motor and perceptual involvement for different skills.

the irrelevant, responds more quickly to internal and external sources of information concerning the typing movements, moves rapidly in a rhythmic, unbroken pattern, and types consistently under a variety of environmental circumstances. The level of proficiency achieved by an individual in an activity such as typing indicates the skill he has attained. Thus, we define a skill operationally as *the level of proficiency attained in carrying out sequences of action in a consistent way*. The five characteristics of a skilled performance just enumerated are now described more fully.

1. Voluntary to Involuntary Control

Miller et al. (1960) provide an interesting account of the changes in the cognitive control of skills. In the early phase, the movements are slow and unsure, each one controlled by a distinct voluntary plan incorporated in verbal statements. The beginning golfer, for example, thinks about how to grip the club, including the placement of the fingers and the thumbs. He probably verbalizes to himself such things as "grasp the club firmly in the left hand, have both thumbs pointing down the shaft, and put the right small finger over the left index finger." In the later phase, the actions are rapid and precise, a series of movements controlled by an involuntary, hierarchical plan that is not verbalized as the movements are carried out. Thus the skilled golfer takes a club from the bag and grasps it without internal verbalization or thought about how to do so. Extensive practice has brought him to the point where his gripping actions are automatic, or involuntary. The plan for driving a golf ball may be thought of as a *program* that controls the sequence by which the movements are carried out.

As an analogy, a phonograph has a program built into it for changing and playing records automatically. When the needle arm comes near enough to the spindle, the arm rises and gets out of the way, a new record is released and drops into place, and the arm returns the needle to the outer rim of the new record to start playing again. Engineers built the program into the phonograph.

Miller et al. (1960) show how a program or plan is related to a complete cycle of receptor-mediator, effector, and feedback events: as *receptor*, receiving sensory impressions, then acting on, or *mediating*, the impressions mentally; energizing and carrying out, or *effecting*, a physical action; acting mentally on the results of the physical action to determine its appropriateness, then using this *feedback* in deciding whether to modify the previous action, repeat it, or discontinue it. The plan controls the entire cycle in a hierarchical manner. Thus one might have an overall plan to guide his actions when playing a particular 18-hole golf course, a less extensive plan, or strategy, for each of the 18 holes, and a specific tactic for executing each shot.

The program for executing a skill cannot be built into the human organism by an outsider. The teacher can, however, give the student a plan in the form of verbal instructions to follow or he can supply the student with a model to observe and imitate. The student, of course, must learn to carry out the plan through practice.

2. Differentiation of Cues

Imagine that you are walking from one place to another. As you walk, you see such things as the sidewalk, a brick wall, a sign, etc. Besides seeing things ahead and to the side, you hear sounds, particularly from behind you. These are the extrinsic visual and auditory cues that guide your walking. There also are continuous internal kinesthetic cues from the muscles and joints. These tell you that you are moving and in what direction.

In the early stages of skill development, the individual is learning which cues to respond to as well as to make responses he has not made before. The more obvious cues are noted and responded to first. Later, the less obvious cues that are needed for excellent performance are noted. Thus the beginning golfer, when putting, may notice only the distance from the ball to the cup, the slant of the green in an uphill or downhill direction, and his gripping of the putter. Later he will attend to many less obvious cues, including the length of the grass, the direction in which the grass has been mowed, the softness of the green, any slight indentations in the green, and also slight variations in the positions of his own hands, body, and feet.

The more skilled individual responds to more but less obvious cues; furthermore, he may also carry out a sequence of movements in the presence of *fewer* cues than does the beginner. For example, the piano student beginning to play a particular selection needs to look at the music constantly; after he has learned to play it well, he needs only an occasional glance at the music, and when he has mastered the piece completely — memorized it — he does not need the music at all.

3. Feedback and Correction

Receiving information after each consecutive response or movement is essential for carrying out a series of movements. Thus the typist makes a second movement only after having sensory information, or feedback, that the first one is adequate, accurate, or correct. The beginning typist may have to look at the paper or stop momentarily to think whether a certain letter or word has been completed properly, but the skilled typist realizes without visual input or any slowing down that the word is completed and that the next one is called for. Nevertheless, the skilled typist is dependent on feedback to guide consecutive responses. The same is true of driving a car, riding a bicycle, handwriting, and the many other skills that one performs.

In some skills, such as driving a car under normal conditions, the individual is able to secure relevant feedback directly through his own sense organs and can assess the adequacy of his own responses. In other skills, such as playing a musical instrument, the student cannot independently ascertain whether he has performed correctly. Here feedback from an external source is required.

The effects on learning of delay in feedback, which have been studied in laboratory settings, are summarized by Bilodeau (1966). In any skill where movements are continuous, such as in speaking, handwriting, and operating a device where the individual responds without interruption to a continuously changing set of events, any temporal lag in the response-feedback sequence disrupts behavior. Similarly, delay in terminal feedback that might be given after a series of movements, rather than immediately after each movement, also is disruptive.

The use of feedback from earlier actions is difficult to describe. For a concrete experience with feedback that will make its importance clear, take a soft pencil and a mirror, place the mirror slightly above the star in Fig. 13.2, and then, looking *only* at the mirror, trace the outside outline of the star with the pencil. Note how you have to stop, check the outline itself to see where you are, and then correct for errors or difficulties. You cannot proceed rapidly because the mirror image does not give you the accustomed feedback. (If a mirror is not readily available, place your pencil at a point of the star, then look away from it and try to follow the path from memory without any visual feedback.)

Fig. 13.2. Five-pointed star for use in experiencing feedback effect.

4. Coordinated Movement Patterns

The change from a low level of skill to highly skilled action is accompanied by a change from slow and inaccurate movements, or responses, to rapid and accurate ones. Furthermore, quick and accurate movements and other responses occur at precisely the right times in a skilled performance. In such an apparently simple task as writing a sentence legibly, there are many muscular movements and mental operations. The skilled writer does not hesitate about whether or not to capitalize words, how to punctuate, how to join letters within a word, or how to start and end words. As he writes, making rapid changes in vertical, horizontal, and circular movements, an observer sees only a continuous series of smooth and correct movements coming at exactly the right times, with no jerks or stops.

The skilled typist not only has integrated effector and feedback operations to reproduce individual words quickly, but he also perceives a relatively long series of words in one visual fixation on the page. One fixation on five or six words provides all the cues needed to reproduce the words. Furthermore, little or no conscious thought is given to such motor acts as striking the letter keys, the space bar, or the shift key. Similarly, as the expert typist types material heard through a tape recorder, the auditory cues available through listening, and the production of successive words and other symbols, provide the continuous, steady cues essential to rapid production of evenly typed copy with few or no errors.

5. Stability

Figure 13.3 shows continuing improvement in a relatively simple skill, cigar-making, over a period of years. This information obtained by Crossman (1959) on the same individual implies that the skill becomes increasingly stable and is performed well under a variety of changing circumstances. Stability also is observed in championship performances in individual athletic competition and in group sports, done before large audiences. On television and on stage, star actors and musicians, including teen-agers, perform superbly under potentially distracting circumstances, such as bright lights, noise, and unpredictable audience behaviors. In addition, they often perform at top level despite physical ailments and psychological problems that would tend to incapacitate the less skilled person.

Phases in Skill Learning

Fitts (1964, 1965) identified three phases in skill learning that may readily be related to the five characteristics of a skilled performance that have just been discussed.

(1) Skill learning begins with a *cognitive* phase, usually of relatively short duration, during which the student does not engage in much practice but does cognize the nature of the skill. Observing a model, cognizing instructions, describing the skill to himself, and learning to make the required responses are typical of this initial phase. Related to the characteristics of a skilled performance, the skill is under voluntary control, only the more obvious cues are differentiated, feedback is elementary and errors are many, speed and coordination are low, and the responses are not stable.

(2) During the intermediate, or *organizing*, phase, the receptor-effector-feedback operations gradually become more highly organized with practice until the skill is automatic. There is less emphasis on the cognitive aspect and more on the motor. Less attention is given to specific actions, cues that are less obvious are differentiated, feedback becomes instantaneous, speed and coordination improve, and the skill becomes relatively stable.

(3) In the last, or *perfecting*, phase, there is continuing improvement over a long period of time (as noted earlier in Fig. 13.3). Larger behavior units replace the single and intermediate units of the earlier phases.

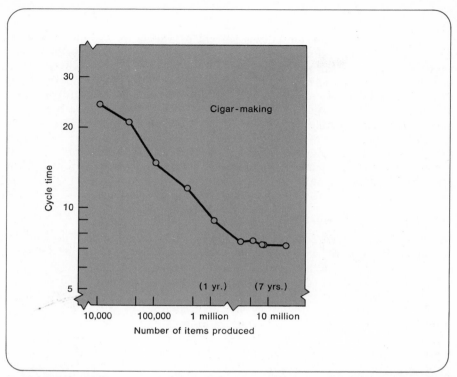

Fig. 13.3 Gradual improvement in the performance of an industrial task over several years of work. (After Crossman, 1959, p. 157)

Highly complex skills are performed at an automatic level. The precise combination of motor, cognitive, and affective characteristics that produces this stability and continued improvement is not well understood.

13.1. Briefly verbalize your plan for writing your name; studying a chapter of this book; parking a car parallel to the curb. Which of the three plans is the most difficult to verbalize?

13.2. Describe how feedback operates as you read a page of this book.

13.3. What is the relationship between the coordination of movements and a voluntary or involuntary plan for carrying out the movements?

13.4. Which of the following do you think you could perform least well under a variety of potentially distracting circumstances: copy a page from this book; take an examination; model a prosocial behavior for young children to imitate? Why?

13.5. Which skills have you personally developed to the intermediate phase? The final phase? Are there any—for example, handwriting—that have already begun to deteriorate? If so, why?

THE NATURE AND TYPES OF PSYCHOMOTOR ABILITIES

In Chapter 3 the distinction between abilities and skills was noted briefly. An ability was defined as a mediator inferred from the observed consistencies among separate performances. Five defining attributes of abilities were indicated, one of which was that abilities are more inclusive than skills. Thus the skills involved in a complex task such as flying an airplane may be described in terms of a smaller number of more basic and more inclusive abilities. In other words, some of the basic abilities involved in flying an airplane may be involved in operating other machines that require use of the hands and feet. The ability-skill distinction will become more clear through further study of abilities and the relationship between abilities and skills.

Physical Proficiency Abilities

In Chapter 3 a matrix of abilities in the psychomotor domain and related outcomes of learning were outlined. Also, the eight physical proficiency abilities that Fleishman (1964) found to underlie an entire battery of 60 physical fitness tests administered to boys and girls aged 14 through 18 were discussed. The eight abilities are: static strength, dynamic strength, trunk strength, extent flexibility, dynamic flexibility, gross body equilibrium, gross body coordination, and stamina. You may wish to return to Chapter 3 and review these abilities, because Fleishman (1964) considers them the main abilities involved in physical proficiency; further proof of their importance is that many current physical fitness programs are designed to strengthen these abilities.

Manipulative Abilities

Fleishman (1964) also reported on the perceptual motor abilities, or manipulative abilities, that he and others identified or validated from 1954 through 1964. In 1954, 40 different tests were given to 400 young men. The results were analyzed in order to validate all the psychomotor abilities previously identified. During the next years, more than 150 additional tests were conducted, using thousands of subjects, in a systematic attempt to identify all the abilities and to specify the best tests to measure each of the abilities identified. In addition to the identification of 11 manipulative abilities that will be discussed, the research resulted in one important overall conclusion: There is no general physical proficiency ability or general psychomotor ability; instead, there are a number of unitary abilities. This conclusion is in line with the view of many psychologists, such as Guilford (1967), that there is no such thing as a general intellectual ability.

The 11 manipulative abilities identified through these studies are now described briefly. They are abilities of the kind involved in operating machines and manipulating objects and tools and they are relatively independent of the physical proficiency abilities. Most of these abilities were derived from research using laboratory tasks that were carried out on special devices. Nine of these laboratory devices used to measure nine of the abilities are shown in Figs. 13.4-13.12. This series is the most complete representation of laboratory apparatus in this book; furthermore, the original research itself used one of the most extensive collections of devices ever designed for the systematic study of human abilities. A more complete description of the abilities and citations of further studies related to each ability may be found in Fleishman (1964).

1. Control Precision. This ability is common to tasks that require fine, highly controlled muscular adjustments with the hands or feet. It is especially important in the operation of machines where careful positioning of the hands or feet is required and where adjustment of the position must be rapid or precise. Figure 13.4 shows a rotary pursuit device used to measure this ability.

2. Multilimb Coordination. This is the ability to coordinate the movements of the two hands, the two feet, or the feet and hands. This ability also is involved in operating machines. It is measured best by devices incorporating multiple controls of the type shown in Fig. 13.5.

3. Response Orientation. This is the ability to make the correct movement in relation to the correct stimulus, especially under highly speeded-

Fig. 13.4. Rotary Pursuit Test. The subject tries to keep the stylus tip in contact with the target set near the edge of a revolving turntable. Score is the total time "on target" during the test period. Ability: *control precision.* (Fleishman, 1964, p. 17. © 1964. Reprinted by permission of Prentice-Hall, Inc.)

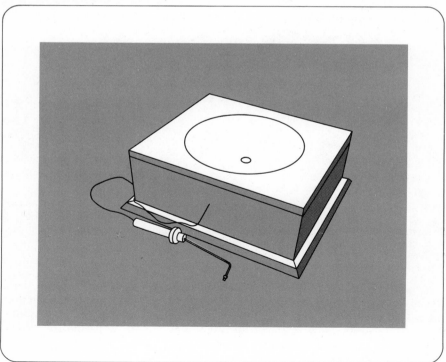

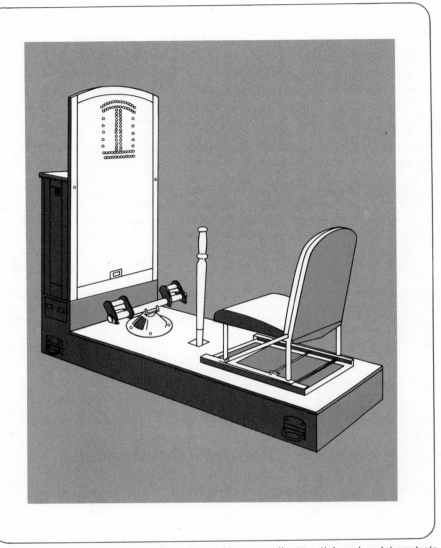

Fig. 13.5. Complex Coordination Test. The subject coordinates stick and pedal controls to match the indicated positions of stimulus light patterns. Score is the number of matches in the time period. Ability: *multilimb coordination.* (Fleishman, 1964, p. 17. © 1964. Reprinted by permission of Prentice-Hall, Inc.)

up conditions. This ability emphasizes the *selection* of the appropriate response to make, in contrast to control precision, which represents proficiency in *controlling* the movements, and multilimb coordination, which represents proficiency in *coordinating* the movements. Response orientation is measured by the laboratory apparatus shown in Fig. 13.6.

4. **Reaction Time.** This is the ability to respond quickly to a stimulus

Fig. 13.6 Discrimination Reaction Time Test. The subject throws one of four switches in response to rapidly changing light patterns. Score is the cumulative response time. Ability: *response orientation*. (Fleishman, 1964, p. 19. © 1964. Reprinted by permission of Prentice-Hall, Inc.)

when it appears. Reaction time is independent of the nature of the stimulus — auditory or visual — and of the type of response required. However, when either the stimulus situation or the response situation involves complicated choices, another ability is involved. Figure 13.7 shows a device for measuring reaction time.

5. Speed of Arm Movement. This is the ability to make rapid, gross, discrete arm movements where accuracy is not required. It is independent of reaction time. It is measured by tasks requiring rapid, alternative tapping of two metal plates, as shown in Fig. 13.8.

6. Rate Control. This is the ability to make continuous anticipatory motor adjustments relative to changes in the speed and direction of a continuously moving target. An element of pursuit or anticipation seems to be involved. Figure 13.9 shows a laboratory device used to measure rate control.

7. Manual Dexterity. This ability is involved in making skillful, well-directed arm-hand movements when manipulating fairly large objects under speed conditions. Tasks requiring tool manipulation, the assembly of large components, and the wrapping of packages appear to require manual dexterity. Figure 13.10 shows a laboratory device designed to measure manual dexterity.

8. Finger Dexterity. This is the ability to make skillful, controlled manipulations of tiny objects involving the use of the fingers. Finger dexterity has been identified as an important ability in wiring electrical cir-

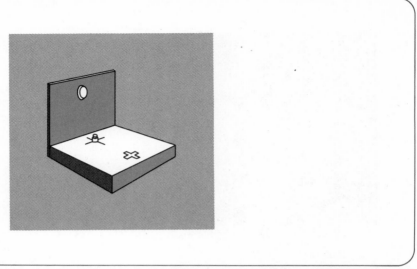

Fig. 13.7. Reaction Time Test. The subject presses the button as rapidly as possible when the light comes on. Score is the cumulated response times to the total series of signals. Ability: *reaction time.* (Fleishman, 1964, p. 21. © 1964. Reprinted by permission of Prentice-Hall, Inc.)

cuits, in assembling units with small parts, in watch-making, and in similar tasks requiring skillful finger manipulation. Finger dexterity is measured by the device shown in Fig. 13.11.

Fig. 13.8. Two-Plate Tapping Test. The subject strikes each metal plate with the stylus, alternately right to left and back as rapidly as possible. Score is the number of taps during the test period. Ability: *speed of arm movement.* (Fleishman, 1964, p. 21. © 1964. Reprinted by permission of Prentice-Hall, Inc.)

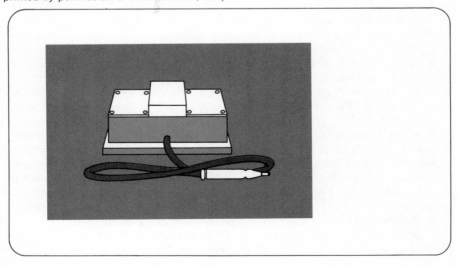

Fig. 13.9. Rate Control Test. The subject attempts to keep the hairline superimposed on the targetline as it deviates in unpredictable directions and rates. Score is time "on target." Ability: *rate control*. (Fleishman, 1964, p. 22. © 1964. Reprinted by permission of Prentice-Hall Inc.)

9. Arm-Hand Steadiness. This is the ability to make precise arm-hand positioning movements where strength and speed are minimized; steadiness of movements is the critical feature. Arm-hand steadiness extends to tasks involving needle-threading and rifle marksmanship. Figure 13.12 shows the laboratory apparatus used to measure this ability.

10. Wrist-Finger Speed. This is the ability to tap rapidly; pendular as well as rotary wrist movements are involved. Wrist-finger speed is restricted in scope and does not extend to many tasks. Printed tests requiring tapping are used to measure it.

11. Aiming. This ability involves controlling the hand when placing small dots in circles; it is referred to also as eye-hand coordination. Aiming is measured by printed tests.

Other abilities in addition to the 11 just described may be identified as research continues. These other abilities are thought to account for some of the differences among individuals in the skilled performance of many school, industrial, and military tasks—differences that are not completely accounted for by differences in the 11 manipulative abilities. In any case, the exact perceptual or manipulative abilities underlying many tasks in and out of school have not yet been charted precisely. Furthermore, there is still a tendency to study task requirements in relation to characteristics of individuals in *both* the cognitive and psychomotor domains, rather than to proceed separately from the psychomotor viewpoint.

It is obvious that much research is still needed. Think of the effects on the astronauts of their extended and intensive educational program—a

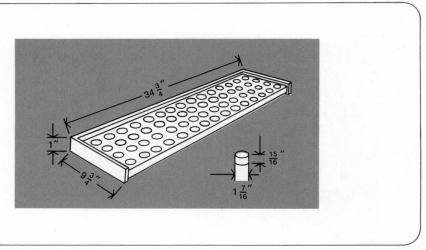

Fig. 13.10. Minnesota Rate of Manipulation Test. The subject fills the board with blocks, using one hand, as rapidly as possible; or he may be required to turn the blocks over in their holes as rapidly as possible. Score is the time to complete the task. Ability: *manual dexterity*. (Fleishman, 1964, p. 24. © 1964. Reprinted by permission of Prentice-Hall, Inc.)

Fig. 13.11. Purdue Pegboard Test. The subject is required to place pegs in holes or to complete as many peg-washer-collar-washer assemblies as possible in the time allowed. Score is the number of assemblies completed in the time period. Ability: *finger dexterity*. (Fleishman, 1964, p. 24. © 1964. Reprinted by permission of Prentice-Hall, Inc.)

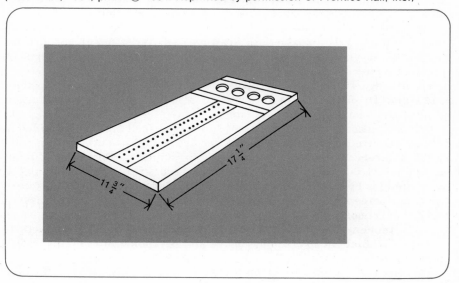

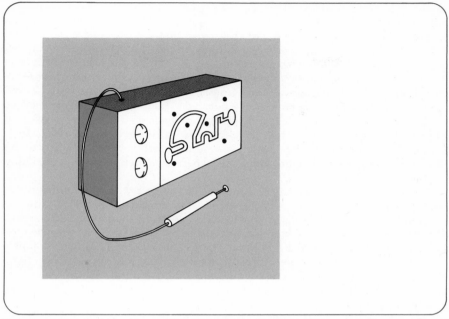

Fig. 13.12. Track Tracing Test. The subject inserts the stylus in the slot and then moves it slowly and steadily and at arm's length, trying not to hit the sides or back of the slot. Score is the number of errors (contacts) for the total trials. Ability: *arm-hand steadiness.* (Fleishman, 1964, p. 25. © 1964. Reprinted by permission of Prentice-Hall, Inc.)

program that focuses knowledge and practice from many fields. When we think of what has been achieved with the astronauts, even considering the limitations to our knowledge, we begin to feel the urge to seek further knowledge. We begin to feel the excitement that comes with a career in research, development, and education—a career dedicated to identifying and greatly extending the abilities of all human beings.

Changes in Abilities with Improved Performance

Woodrow (1938) reported the earliest systematic studies of changes in abilities with practice. He was particularly concerned with the relationship between various indices of learning and general intellectual ability. His subjects practiced about 10 minutes daily on each of seven tasks for 39 days. An initial score, a final score, and a gain score were obtained for each task, a total of 21 task scores. Two intelligence test scores and other test scores of more specific cognitive abilities were also obtained. The methods Woodrow used to analyze the data were not completely adequate to answer the questions concerning changes in abilities that occurred with improved performance. Anderson (1967) analyzed Woodrow's data with a more appropriate factor analytic method and arrived at two of the same main conclusions as Woodrow. First, the relative weight or importance of various abilities changed from initial to final performance; second, general intellectual ability was not highly associated with the change in performance on most of the seven tasks.

Fleishman and Hempel (1955) similarly noted that the relative importance of abilities varied with improvement in performance. The left part of Fig. 13.13 presents learning curves for two groups on a discrimination reaction time task; one group was high and the other was low on word knowledge. The difference in performance between the two groups decreased as proficiency on the task increased. The other part of the figure shows the learning curves on the same task for two other groups, one of which scored high and the other low on a visual reaction time test. Here the difference in performance between the two groups increased as proficiency on the task increased.

Figure 13.14 visualizes the change in the relative weight or importance of eight other abilities as proficiency in discrimination reaction time increased. One estimates, based on visual inspection, that about 20 percent of the variance in scores was accounted for by *specific discrimination reaction* time itself on trial 1 but about 35 percent on trial 15; about 30 percent of the variance was accounted for by *spatial relations* on the initial trial but only about 8 percent on the last trial. Changes in the degree of influence of the other abilities may be similarly estimated. Fleishman concludes as follows:

> These studies, using a great variety of practice tasks, show that (a) the particular combination of abilities contributing to performance changes as practice continues, (b) these changes are progressive and systematic and eventually become stabilized, (c) the contribution of "nonmotor" abilities (e.g., verbal, spatial), which may play a role early in learning, decreases systematically with

Fig. 13.13. Comparison of discrimination reaction time acquisition curves for groups stratified on different ability test variables, at different stages of practice. (After Fleishman & Hempel, 1955)

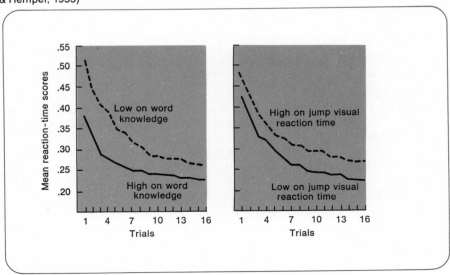

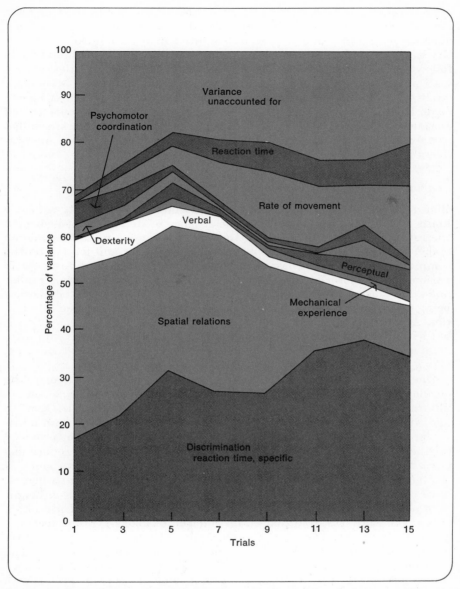

Fig. 13.14. Percentage of variance represented by each factor at different stages of practice on the Discrimination Reaction Time Task (percentage of variance is represented by the area shaded in for each factor). (After Fleishman & Hempel, 1955)

practice, relative to "motor abilities," and (d) there is also an increase in a factor specific to the task itself. (Fleishman, 1967, p. 179)

In applying this information to psychomotor learning in school situations, we properly infer that reliable prediction of a student's performance at the end of a semester or year of instruction cannot be made from performances during the first month. Also, if we measure the performances of beginning piano players, or beginners in any other skill, and identify the factors that comprise the beginners' abilities, we will have to do follow-up studies to ascertain the extent to which these abilities change with practice and improved performance. A second inference is that the quality of a skilled performance changes from a beginning to a higher level. In other words, a sequence of movements is not merely performed more rapidly or precisely; rather, all the characteristics of a more skilled performance previously discussed are brought together into a qualitatively *different* skill.

Conditions Affecting the Development of Abilities

Biological and physiological conditions associated with heredity set some limits on an individual's abilities. The absence of well-developed cones in the retina of the eye limits the visual discriminations an individual can make; the sensitivity of the sense organs in muscles and joints and the composition of muscular tissue are related to individual differences in various psychomotor abilities (Fleishman, 1964, p. 10). Simply being taller and more muscular is associated with greater physical strength, whereas being deficient in sight or hearing is associated with lower musical abilities. According to Fleishman (1964), genetic factors fix the upper limits, but within these upper limits, which are most difficult to ascertain for individuals, environmental conditions, including instruction and learning, play a major role.

The effects of instruction, including guided activity or practice, on the development of psychomotor abilities and skills are clear. People remain illiterate—they do not read or write—in an environment in which reading and writing are not taught to the children. Whole nations remain undeveloped, socially and economically, when good education is not provided for the children. The inner cities and rural areas of America produce disadvantaged children through environmental neglect and deprivation.

The effects of deprivation on physical characteristics, such as height, have been estimated (Bloom, 1964). Figure 13.15 shows growth in height of boys under three different environmental conditions. The Tuddenham and Snyder data (1954) are based on children of above-average socioeconomic status growing up in Oakland, California, according to measurements taken during the late 1920s, the 1930s, and the early 1940s. The Dreizen et al. (1953) children grew up in Alabama; the measures for both the experimental (nutritive failure group) and the control group were taken from 1941 on. The two sets of Alabama children had identical ethnic backgrounds and came from the same geographical area. The conclusion is inescapable that inadequate nutrition has a permanent stunting effect. Similar adverse effects of orphanage life on growth were established by Keys et al. (1950). The adverse effects of an impoverished environment are greatest during the early years of life when growth is most rapid (Bloom, 1964).

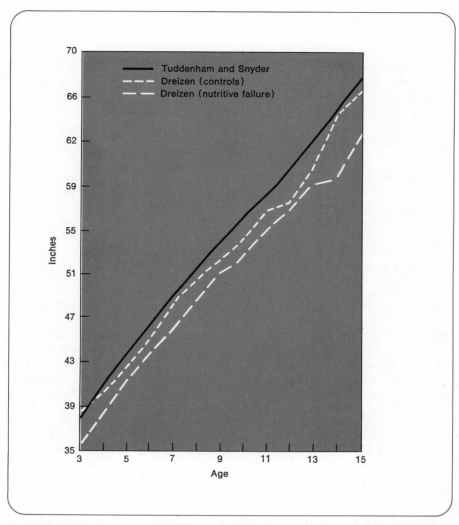

Fig. 13.15. Height growth for males under different environmental conditions. (Adapted from Bloom, 1964, p. 39)

13.6. It is possible that physical education classes stress activities that lead to the development of leg and lower body muscles but not to a concomitant development of arm and upper body muscles. If this is true, which abilities, as outlined by Fleishman, should receive more emphasis in a physical education program? What games, sports, and activities might be useful in developing these abilities?

13.7. Which of the following is (are) true of an ability, but not of a skill?

a. It is a product of both maturation and learning.

b. Once developed, it is stable during adulthood.

c. It transfers to a greater variety of other more specific performances.

d. It is more general and inclusive.

13.8. How do abilities change with practice or improved performance? What are the implications of these conclusions for predicting later success based on early measures of ability?

13.9. Based on your observations, do our inner cities appear to produce greater deficits in the gross body abilities or in the more complex perceptual motor abilities?

DEVELOPMENTAL TRENDS

The newborn infant shows no skilled performances, but he does as he grows older and his bodily structures change. For example, changes occur in height, weight, proportions, muscular tissue, bone texture, and the central nervous system. With these changes that come in connection with growth, and also with the practice or activity that is normal for growing children, the abilities dependent on the structures also change. As noted in Chapter 3, the course of psychomotor abilities has not been charted systematically with age; however, it is known that the various abilities develop at different rates within the same individual and also among individuals. Also, most abilities are fairly stable by age 21 or even earlier.

To appreciate the changes that occur in psychomotor performances and the differences among individuals of about the same age, try to observe four widely separated age groups within the same week or month. Go to a nursery room in a large hospital and notice the behaviors of newborn infants. Observe children of ages 6 to 9 in the gymnasium or on the playground of an elementary school. Visit a comprehensive high school to observe an advanced typing class, an instrumental or vocal music class, an art or industrial arts class, or an athletic team in practice. Finally, observe a skilled surgeon, dancer, musician, or athlete. Though you would see only a small sample of each age group, the vast changes in psychomotor performances from infancy to maturity would be more immediately apparent than they can ever be through reading about them. With these facts in mind, only a few descriptions of changes in abilities and skills with age are presented here.

Strength

Strength of grip of the hand, a measure of static strength, is correlated with vitality. Children of the same age who have a stronger grip are able to mobilize their strength more effectively than can those with a weaker grip. This difference seems to carry over to mental tasks: Mentally retarded children do not seem to be able to mobilize their energies for either physical or mental tasks as well as bright children can (Klausmeier et al., 1959). Strength of grip correlates higher with other indices of strength than does any other single measure; in addition, it is easily measured with a hand dynamometer. For these reasons, it holds more promise of providing useful information to the teacher than do measures of height and weight.

Figure 13.16 shows growth curves in strength of grip for boys and girls, ages 6 to 18. The dynamometer readings are in kilograms. A rather steady increase in strength occurs with age, with the rate of increase about the same for boys and girls until age 13. At that age the curve rises quite sharply for boys, and although it continues to rise for girls, it rises slowly and at a decelerating rate. These curves are based on averages for many individuals; each individual's curve is not so smooth. The same is true of other curves presented in this section.

The influence of cultural factors on this difference between the sexes in the age at which no further increase in strength occurs is not known. Boys, however, are encouraged to participate in more strenuous physical activities than are girls. Furthermore, strength is usually considered a prestige gainer for boys, whereas many girls during adolescence want to give the impression of being dainty and feminine rather than strong and masculine. Girls who star in athletics, such as swimming and gymnastics, do seem to increase in strength into their 20s.

Reaction Time

Reaction time is important in many activities. Emergency situations — braking an automobile, piloting an airplane under certain conditions, re-

Fig. 13.16. Growth curve for strength of grip. (Adapted from Jones, 1944, p. 103)

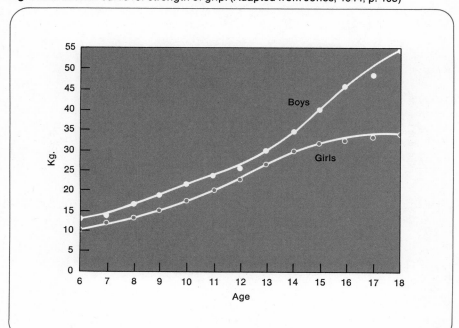

sponding to a starter's signal in an athletic contest—require a quick motor response. Other tasks demanding rapid reactions to successive stimuli include playing a musical instrument, typing, dancing, and the like.

Figure 13.17 shows different measures of reaction time according to age. All reactions of the subjects were elicited by an auditory stimulus. The measures are pursuit reaction using the hands, digital reaction using the forefinger, and foot reaction. The speed of pursuit movements increases regularly until about age 18 and holds a fairly steady level until about age 30; then decline starts, becoming quite rapid at about age 70. Although the curves are somewhat different, the general pattern of digital and foot reaction is a rise until the 20s, then a tendency to level off or decelerate until about age 60, when the deceleration becomes quite rapid. The figure shows that during the school years reaction time increases noticeably. How much of this rapid increase is related to instruction and how much simply to maturation is unknown. Athletic coaches and others apparently believe that reaction time can be improved, for they spend much practice time toward achieving that goal.

Fig. 13.17. Changes in reaction time with age. (Adapted from Miles, 1931, p. 631)

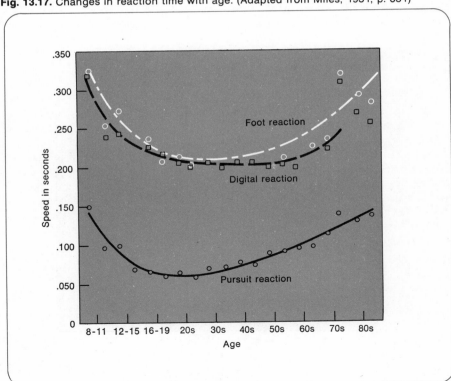

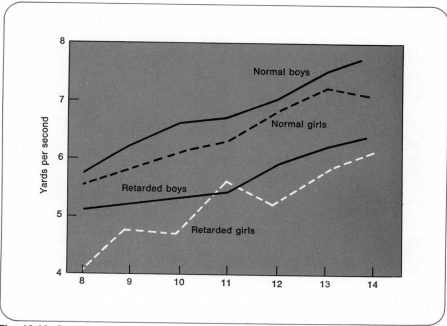

Fig. 13.18. Speed of running in normal and mentally retarded children. (Adapted from Francis & Rarick, 1959, p. 806. Copyright 1959, American Association on Mental Deficiency. Reprinted by permission from the *American Journal of Mental Deficiency*.)

Speed

Figure 13.18 shows speed in running the 35-yard dash for normally developing and mentally retarded children, aged 8 to 14. The curve for normal boys shows a rather continuous increase from age 8 to 14 and beyond. With normal girls speed starts to fall off at about age 13. (Here a cultural factor is almost certainly involved.) Notice that the mentally retarded boys were lower than the normal girls at all ages; however, the curve shows an increase with age for the retarded boys, and at age 14 they are closing the gap between themselves and the normal girls. The irregular curve for retarded girls results partly from the small sample used in the study. Whether the relatively better performances for the retarded girls at ages 13 to 14 might continue is not known.

Balance

We know that young children have difficulty maintaining their balance when learning to walk. What happens as they grow older? Table 13.1 shows a consistent rise in the mean or average balance scores for both boys and girls from age 4 to 6 until age 11 to 12. The gradual falling off from that age onward is somewhat more apparent for the girls than the boys. However, in this study girls at age 13 and above appeared more self-

Table 13.1 Balance Scores by Sex and Age

Age groups	n	Boys' scores							Aver-age	Girls' scores							Aver-age	Totals Aver-age
		0	1	2	3	4	5	6		0	1	2	3	4	5	6		
13-15	54	3	2	2	8	11	2	7	3.7	1	7	4	5	2	0	0	2.0	3.1
12-13	57	2	1	7	4	12	6	4	3.6	2	6	2	7	3	0	1	2.3	3.1
11-12	52	0	3	4	8	7	6	6	3.8	2	3	3	5	3	2	0	2.5	3.3
10-11	62	3	9	6	5	7	8	3	3.0	2	5	4	6	0	4	0	2.4	2.8
9-10	64	2	8	7	7	5	4	3	2.8	5	4	7	7	4	1	0	2.1	2.5
8- 9	80	7	11	8	9	11	2	2	2.5	7	6	6	5	4	2	0	2.0	2.3
7- 8	61	12	10	9	7	0	4	0	1.6	5	3	3	3	3	2	0	2.1	1.8
6- 7	48	17	11	7	1	0	1	0	0.9	3	2	3	2	1	0	0	1.6	1.1
4- 6	23	10	1	0	0	0	0	0	0.1	9	1	2	0	0	0	0	0.5	0.3

Source: Cron & Pronko, 1957, p. 35.

conscious than did younger girls or all boys while performing the required task. Therefore, the results for the older girls are questionable. It is interesting, too, that up through age 8 the girls had higher balance scores than the boys; thereafter, the boys scored consistently higher than the girls.

Flexibility

Extent flexibility is the ability to extend or stretch the whole body or parts of it as far as possible in various directions. Dynamic flexibility also involves the ability to extend and stretch; however, the criterion is not the extent or distance of maximum movement but the rapidity of repeated movements. Tests that measure the amount of abdominal and back stretching are used as indicators of extent flexibility; more rapid bending and twisting activities are used to arrive at "cycle" scores of dynamic flexibility. Figure 13.19 shows growth curves for boys and girls for the two abilities (Fleishman, 1964).

These curves are interesting. Extent flexibility in boys increases at a rapid rate from 12 to 15 and then at a decelerating rate from 15 to 18. An opposite pattern holds for girls, who show an actual decrease from 14 to 17. Dynamic flexibility shows a decrease for both boys and girls from age 14 or 15 to 18. Of some 25 abilities, dynamic flexibility is the only one that shows this pattern of decrease for boys before age 18. However, the performance of girls during the senior high school years deteriorates in a number of psychomotor abilities, probably from lack of use, or practice.

Writing Skill

Writing is one of the few activities highly dependent on motor abilities in which most children receive formal instruction. It therefore should be much more carefully investigated than it has been so far. Ames and Ilg (1951) reported the developmental trends in writing behavior of younger children. Some of them are as follows.

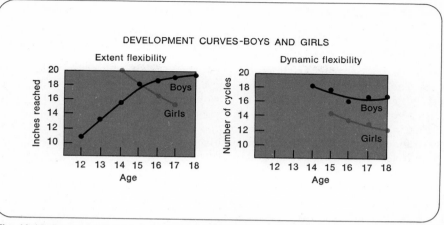

Fig. 13.19. Developmental curves for extent flexibility and dynamic flexibility in boys and girls. (Adapted from Fleishman, 1964, pp. 122, 124. © 1964. Reprinted by permission of Prentice-Hall, Inc.)

6 YEARS

Circle is now drawn counterclockwise, starting at the top.

Letters are printed, usually large and somewhat irregular.

Words are printed by some children at this age. Some reversals of single letters or order of letters in words may appear.

Name is printed in large letters.

Numbers from 1 to 20 or higher are written; some reversals of 3, 7, 9.

7 YEARS

Words: The majority can now write, although an appreciable number prefer to print. The printing is now smaller and more regular.

Name: The majority can now write their given names and surnames; most still print.

Numbers: The majority write 1 to 20, with the figures now written smaller and in rows.

8 YEARS

Words: The majority write single words, printing seldom being used. Important individual differences in writing skill are discernible. Reversals seldom appear.

Name: Nearly all write both their names, well spaced and small letters other than the initial letter of each word. Important variations in style of writing appear.

Numbers: Figures are much smaller and better spaced; few errors are made.

9 YEARS

Words: Writing is smaller, neater, lighter, more even and slanted, though some still write straight up and down and about one-third still have very irregular letters. Letters are now much better proportioned.

Name: Beginning of individual styles, with sex differences being observed. Letters are more evenly made and more correctly proportioned.

Numbers: Numbers are now small and well formed. (Ames & Ilg, 1951, pp. 32-34)

These gradients in writing, like the curves throughout this section that show the development of various psychomotor abilities, conceal individual differences among the children at various age levels and do not show the wide overlapping between best and poorest performers at various ages. Referring back to Table 13.1, for instance, you will see that scores of 0 to 6 were made by all the boys from 8 through 15 years of age (except that none in the 11 to 12 group scored 0).

13.10. On the average, high school boys, in comparison with high school girls, show a continuing rapid increase in strength of grip, running speed, and balance until about three years later than girls. This is typical of sex differences in physical measures. What do you think are two or three of the most important implications of this sex difference for educational programs designed to develop the psychomotor abilities of all students fully?

13.11. Table 13.1 shows that two boys age 8-9 made the highest possible balance score and seven boys age 13-15 did. Similar large differences are found among members of the same sex in all psychomotor skills and abilities. What do you think are two or three of the most important implications of these within-sex differences for educational programs?

13.12. Some critics say that it is more harmful than helpful for teachers to know the mean or typical performance of a group, such as boys' and girls' strength at age 13, and also the individual scores for each member of the class. Under what conditions might this information be used to the detriment of the student? Under what conditions might it prove helpful?

PRINCIPLES FOR IMPROVING SKILLS

Much skill learning is the learning of new responses or movements. In this connection, the learning of motor skills is much like the learning of language. Both first require making fairly specific responses that the individual has not made before, and then putting these separate responses together into some larger unit. Words are put into phrases and sentences and steps into walking and running. Practice with feedback is essential in learning both language and skills of all kinds.

At all school levels, students may learn to make motor responses, or movements, that they have not made before. The principles given here are stated in such a way as to help the student in learning skills; the parallel instructional guides outline the external conditions that facilitate skill learning. Before turning to the principles and guides, you may find that it is interesting to review the sequence in purposeful learning outlined in Chapter 3. You will observe high correspondence between the principles given here and that sequence. These principles for improving skills imply that learning is most effective when the student sets a realistic level to attain in a particular skill and then tries to attain it. The guides are now discussed in detail.

Principle	Instructional Guide
1. Attending to the characteristics of the skill and assessing one's own related abilities facilitates the learning of the skill.	1. Analyze the skill in terms of the learner's abilities and developmental level.
2. Observing and imitating a model facilitates initial learning of skilled movements.	2. Demonstrate the correct response.
3. Verbalizing a set of instructions, or a plan, for carrying out a sequence of actions enhances the early phase of skill learning.	3. Guide initial responses verbally and physically.
4. Practicing under desirable conditions facilitates the learning of skills through eliminating errors and strengthening and refining correct responses and form.	4. Arrange for appropriate practice.
5. Securing feedback facilitates skill learning through providing knowledge of results.	5. Provide informational feedback and correct inadequate responses.
6. Evaluating one's own performance makes possible the continued improvement of skills.	6. Encourage independent evaluation.

1. Analyze the Skill in Terms of the Learner's Abilities and Developmental Level

Teaching requires knowledge of skills to be learned, of the learner's abilities, and of principles of teaching. It also requires continuous feedback and correction while teaching. Teachers cannot measure all the abilities for the various skills taught in school, simply because no one has the necessary knowledge about abilities. Nevertheless, there is enough knowledge so that many gross violations of this guide can be eliminated, as illustrated in the following discussions of handwriting for left- and right-handed children and vocal music for boys whose voices are changing.

Handwriting. How is handwriting different for left-handed and right-handed children? In most situations, seats or desks are arranged so that the light comes from the left—proper for right-handers, but not for left-handers. Because one is taught to write from left to right on a page, the left-handed child is continuously covering what he has just written, whereas the right-hander can see immediately what he has written. Printed models of handwriting are for right-handed persons. The downward slant of letters is to the left; this is appropriate for right-handers, but left-handed children normally slant the letters straight down or toward the right so that they can see what has been written before it is covered by the left hand moving to the right across the page. Suppose, then, that a teacher has a left-handed child in class. What sort of an analysis of the skill in relation to left-handed children's ability to write should be made before instruction begins? Without careful analysis, it is possible that the teacher might insist that the left-handed children use precisely the same slant and spacing of letters as the right-handers and do nothing to make other needed arrangements for seating and lighting.

Vocal Music for Adolescent Boys. A recent survey of high school boys and girls participating in chorus groups showed the ratio to be approximately four girls to one boy (Swanson, 1959). A primary reason for this imbalance is that music teachers do not recognize the true nature of the singing task for boys going through the period of voice change. Music teachers in the junior high school generally pitch the music too high, select melodies that have far too broad a range for adolescent boys, and give instruction in songs that have little or no interest for boys of this age. Swanson, a successful music teacher who makes national tours with a male vocal junior high school group, found that a rating of the level of physical development was useful for identifying the stage of voice change in adolescent boys. After rating the boys on physical development, he regrouped junior high school classes for instruction in vocal music. When he arranged proper vocal exercises for the boys, selected interesting songs, rearranged many melodies, and proceeded to instruct them in groups brought together according to stage of voice change, they enjoyed the music activities as much as the girls did. When given the opportunity to volunteer to enroll in a vocal music class in the next grade, the boys did so.

We do not know how much direct damage to the singing voice is caused because teachers do not understand the singing ability of boys from about grades 5 to 9. The vocal-music teacher who insists that boys handle the same songs as girls is proceeding without accurate information and without using available feedback to improve the situation.

Implementation in Speech Correction. Through the rest of this chapter, implementation of each guide is described by a beginning speech therapist, working with a girl aged 10, whom we shall call Sarah. In the last section of the discussion of each guide, we quote the appropriate part of the account in the first person by the speech therapist (with only minor modifications to save space).

In connection with this illustration, we realize that it may not seem directly relevant to most future teachers, because instruction in speech therapy is done on a one-to-one basis (as is instruction in instrumental music and some other more specialized areas). Nevertheless, because the speech therapist was working with only one student, he was able to implement each guide to the fullest extent. The illustration, carried through all the guides, does, therefore, give a complete idea of what *can* be done to implement them. In any case, this one-to-one illustration is now more generally relevant than it may at first seem to be. It is true that typing instruction and physical education, for example, are often carried out in groups of 100 or more. Obviously, even though this large-group instruction is effective with many students, it is not with others. The reason is that the teacher simply cannot carry out many of the instructional guides with such large groups. Increasingly, therefore, aides and team teaching are being used with large groups in an effort to give more one-to-one instruction or at least small-group instruction. Under such arrangements it is possible, fortunately, to implement the guides very effectively.

The first part of the speech therapist's account is as follows:

> Before I met Sarah I had read about the correct means of producing the "s" sound, and I had identified the various auditory, visual, tactual, and kinesthetic aspects of the correct production of the sound. The objectives of my first meeting with Sarah were:
>
> 1. to discover how she produced the "s" sound;
> 2. to determine how her production of the sound differed from the correct production of the sound;
> 3. to determine the ways in which her means of production of the sound should be changed; and
> 4. to determine her abilities to correctly evaluate her production of the sound, to discriminate between correct and incorrect sounds and to identify the differences between them.
>
> To accomplish the first objective in my first session with her, I watched her, listened to her, asked her to describe the tactual and kinesthetic elements of the sounds she produced, and tried to duplicate her production of the sound. I then analyzed my duplication in an effort to discover how she made the sound.
>
> To accomplish the second and third objectives, I reviewed in my mind the correct means of producing the sound and compared her means of production to this mental model. I tried to determine which elements of her production were incorrect and the ways in which these elements were wrong. At this point I formed tentative judgments about how these incorrect elements should be changed.
>
> To accomplish the fourth objective I presented her with a variety of tasks. To begin with, I had to produce the sound and then ask her to tell whether or not she thought her own subsequent production was correct. I then presented her with a series of discrimination tasks. These required her to discriminate between correct and incorrect sounds when I made them, to point out differences between correct and incorrect sounds, to compare her production of the sound to my productions, and to try to point out differences between the productions made by her and by me. Among the various ways in which she performed these tasks were the following: with her unaided hearing alone, with an auditory training unit, with a tape recorder, with a mirror, with face-to-face contact, and with various combinations of these methods.
>
> My evaluation showed that she was substituting Θ, the voiceless "th" sound, for the "s" sound. Her tongue was protruding between her teeth. In order to produce the sound correctly she would have to learn to place her tongue in the proper position behind her teeth. Regarding her feelings toward her production of the sound and her ability to discriminate between correct and incorrect sounds, I discovered that she knew her production was incorrect and had already learned to recognize the auditory and visual differences between correct and incorrect sounds.
>
> She knew that she was not supposed to protrude her tongue, but she did not know the proper placement for it. When she tried to produce the sound with her tongue behind her teeth, she failed to groove it properly and she blocked the air stream from coming out of the center of her mouth.

As a result of my evaluation I formed the following plan of action:
1. to teach her to analyze more fully the various aspects of my correct and incorrect productions of the "s" sound;
2. to teach her to analyze more fully the various aspects of her production of the sound;
3. to teach her to compare the various aspects of her productions with those of my correct productions; and
4. to try to teach her to modify the incorrect aspects of her productions so she could learn to say the sound correctly.

Subsequent discussions of implementation of the guides deal only with the fourth part of this plan of action.

2. Demonstrate the Correct Response

As noted in Chapter 3, Bandura and Walters (1963) have shown that novel responses may be learned through observation and imitation of a model. A good demonstration by the teacher provides an overview of the skill to be acquired and a model to be imitated. If a demonstration is to be effective, the teacher must, of course, be able to perform the total skill and its various components well. On the other hand, it should not be assumed that a learner should follow the demonstration precisely, even if he can. For example, as already noted, the left-handed child cannot follow the right-handed teacher exactly. Accordingly, in demonstrations of physical movements, the teacher does not assume that any student will exactly duplicate the demonstration; rather, he assumes that each learner will make the needed adaptations in terms of his own characteristics. The teacher can use other ways to provide models, in addition to or instead of serving as one himself. Models can be presented in printed materials, sound films, video tapes, audio recordings, and the like. Older children, too, serve well as models.

In some situations it is appropriate to make clear to the students that an *example* is being modeled, rather than a final output. The teacher of creative dance and the teacher of creative writing demonstrate what creativity means to them. Such a demonstration simply illustrates to the students what creativity or appropriate expression is for the demonstrator. Similarly, in art instruction, to help the learners acquire certain technical skills, these skills may be demonstrated. When the student is to develop his own art product, however, the teacher should not try to demonstrate this final product. In other words, the art teacher helps the student with technical skills as necessary, but he leaves ideas, composition, and color to the student.

Implementation in Speech Correction. It was relatively easy for the beginning speech therapist to provide exemplary models and thus demonstrate correct responses. Notice how this was done:

After Sarah was able to analyze and compare the various aspects of her production of the "s" sound with my productions, it was time for her to learn to produce the sound correctly. As a first step in this process, I demonstrated the correct production for her.

As preparation for the demonstration, I verbally reviewed the various aspects of the sound and asked her to watch and listen for them as I said the sound. After I had made the sound three times I helped her to give a verbal review of what she had seen and heard. I then produced the sound three more times.

Although the formal demonstration was thus concluded, it was to be repeated many times, both partially and completely, before she finally learned to produce the sound. In addition, demonstrations also were given of various methods and techniques throughout the corrective process. These demonstrations served more than one function. They provided a model for imitation, they showed how the various aspects of the sound were combined to form the whole, and they were a means of frequent review of the correct production of the sound.

3. Guide Initial Responses Verbally and Physically

Information given verbally, as well as in a live demonstration, may be useful for describing the nature of the final performance desired, as indicated in the preceding discussion. Miller et al. (1960), as noted earlier in this chapter, have shown that verbal instructions can be used successfully to outline a strategy or method of attack for developing a skill. Parker and Fleishman (1961) found that giving students information both about the abilities that contribute to performance of a task and about the relation of specific components to the overall task proficiency contributed to improved performance. These kinds of helpful verbal guidance are given early in the instructional sequence before much practice is done.

In an interesting experiment, Davies (1945) showed the value of instruction to students learning archery. She divided her students—all women—into two groups: (1) The experimental group, called the *tuition* group, was given verbal instruction in shooting a bow and arrow throughout the course. In this instruction, the experimenter told the women what she thought necessary for them to understand the nature of the skill and to become proficient in it. (2) The *control* group of women was given only the necessary equipment and minimum safety instructions and then left to proceed on their own. Each group met for 18 class sessions during a three-month period. Differences favoring the tuition group became apparent early in the semester and increased as practice progressed. At the end of the semester, this group definitely performed better than the other one. The control group members tended to acquire inefficient methods and to stay with the methods during successive class periods, even though their progress was poor.

Davies concluded that the teacher, by verbal guidance, helps the learner to vary and improve his learning behavior in at least three ways: (1) by directing the learner's attention to more adequate techniques than those he has acquired and has been employing; (2) by promoting the growth of the learner's insight into the factors related to his success; (3) by giving the learner a feeling of security and confidence in relinquishing a familiar mode of behavior and seeking one that is better. Physically guiding the actions of students may also be helpful with some students who have exceptional difficulty in making the correct responses initially.

Verbal instructions for mental practice of a skill also are effective, as Waterland (1956) showed in teaching students to bowl. Under the old system, certain verbal and manual instructions were given. In this experiment, however, instructions to engage in mental practice of the task were given to three successive groups of students: (1) The first instructions incorporated a kind of mental practice, only in connection with the arm swing. Before each attempt, the student was instructed to think about such things as, "Let the arm go with the weight of the ball; resist the weight of the ball during the backswing by leaning forward from the ankle joint; follow through with the arm in the desired direction of the ball." This kind of mental practice did not lead to the desired smooth, continuous pattern of movements. (2) With the next group, the instructions were expanded by preceding the above suggestions with, "Imagine or concentrate on a continuous movement pattern." (3) With the third group, the same instructions for mental practice were given. In addition, however, the bowling pins were placed at the end of the alley during the second week of instruction (this had not been done with the first two groups). Placing the pins in the proper position seemed to have the important psychological effect of giving further purpose to the practice. Although no more time was spent in practice by the second and third groups, efficiency in bowling for both groups increased by about one-third over the group instructed by the original method.

Implementation in Speech Correction. We now continue with the beginning speech therapist. Before going on, think how you would verbally guide the responses of a beginner in some skill. Notice, too, the physical guidance provided for Sarah:

After the demonstration of the "s" sound was completed, I instructed Sarah to review verbally how to produce the sound and what she was to remember to do to change her present means of production. I then said the sound three times before she tried to say it. When she was still unable to produce the sound correctly, this entire process was repeated several times. Throughout the repetitions I gave verbal suggestions before, during, and after her attempts at production.

When it became evident that verbal guidance was not sufficient, other methods were utilized. Among these were the following:

1. Sarah was instructed to move her tongue about randomly in an effort to come closer to the correct production. Evaluations of progress were made with and without mechanical aids.
2. She was instructed to move her tongue in directed ways. Evaluations were again made with and without mechanical aids.
3. She was instructed to put a toothpick on a certain place on her tongue while she made the sound. This served to hold her tongue in place and to help to groove the tongue properly.
4. She was instructed to hold a straw at a certain place in front of her teeth as she made the sound. This helped to establish the correct position of the tongue, the proper grooving of the tongue, and the proper emission of the air stream.

It was with the help of the straw that Sarah learned to produce the "s" sound correctly. The removal of the straw was gradual, beginning with removing it while she was in the process of production. Finally she was able to produce the sound without the help of the straw and with only occasional verbal reminders of things she was doing wrong. Throughout this corrective process I also gave many demonstrations of various types.

4. Arrange for Appropriate Practice

Practice is, of course, essential to the improvement of skills. The practice must be carried out under desirable conditions, however. Whole-part arrangements, the context in which the skills are practiced, and the length and spacing of practice sessions are the more important conditions associated with effective practice. Feedback is important also, but it is discussed next as a separate guide.

1. Whole-Part Arrangements. One useful way of looking at the whole-part dimension of skills is from the standpoint of the organization of the skill itself. Some skills are closely knit; others are loosely organized. Diving is a closely knit skill that is practiced as a whole. Football and baseball are loosely organized skills that are aggregations of component skills. Each component skill must receive concentrated practice. The three examples now discussed indicate the best procedures for early practice.

(1) In juggling three balls, best results were obtained when the practice was done on the whole act, that is, juggling all three balls at once, rather than one, then two, and finally three (Knapp & Dixon, 1952). Practice on the whole activity cut about 20 percent off the time needed to attain the goal of 100 successive catches.

(2) In rifle firing, practice on the entire sequence of seven subtasks in order produced better results than practice first on one subtask, then the first and second combined, then the first, second, and third, and so on, in a progressive-part method (McGuigan & MacCaslin, 1955). It is interesting that though the whole method produced far better results for trainees with IQs of 100 and above, only a small difference was found between the two methods for trainees with IQs of 99 and lower.

(3) The results of experiments carried out from 1890 to 1952 in connection with learning to receive International Morse Code are unequivocal (Woodworth & Schlosberg, 1954). Among several features that were finally incorporated into the teaching procedures, four are appropriate to the present discussion of skill learning: the whole method of teaching, prompt reinforcement of the correct response, a standard-speed presentation of signals, and distributed practice. In the whole method, all 36 code symbols (26 letters and 10 digits) were introduced in the first practice session. This method contrasted sharply with previous ones that involved early instruction devoted to lengthy practice on separate symbols (similar to the progressive-part method in rifle firing). The application of the best information about skill learning led, in this case, to the following dramatic results:

> Students spent 8 weeks at code school. Normally, they practiced code for 7 hours a day for the first 5 weeks, and devoted the last 3 weeks to other topics. Keller thought such massed practice might be wasteful, so he tried spreading out the code instruction over the whole 8 weeks, devoting 4 hours daily to code,

and the rest to other topics. It turned out that the 4-hour group was as good as the usual 7-hour group at the end of 5 weeks, despite the shorter hours of practice. Of course they still had 3 more weeks to practice code, for they had been taking up their other topics along with the code; they ended up markedly superior to the massed group. (Woodworth & Schlosberg, 1954, p. 812)

Practice on the last two skills, which are complex aggregate ones, thus could be handled in single practice sessions. Complex skills of this type are acquired better when part or all of each practice session is devoted to practice on the whole skill or the entire sequence of skills. This in no way denies that highly skilled performers do not spend time profitably practicing the component skills. When a component is poorly executed, with unfavorable results on the total performance, one practices on the component to bring it under better control.

2. *The Context for Practice.* The more closely the conditions of practice approach the conditions under which the skill will actually be used, the more effective the practice is. This fact, implied in the discussion of learning Morse Code, is now made explicit in connection with typing. Other principles connected with instruction in typing are also presented, for the sake of continuity.

West (1969), summarizing the research of the past decade on typing and other business education subjects, arrived at certain conclusions, unequivocally stated, about the type of practice material, the acquisition of ordinary stroking skill in typing, and the application of stroking skill to realistic typing on the job. In connection with practice material, ordinary prose that is readable by the student works better than nonsense sequences ("jum," "frv," etc.) for keyboard learning at the outset of typing instruction. At later stages, ordinary unselected English prose produces better results than selected common words or specially contrived practice material. Thus the more nearly the practice material replicates material typed in everyday life, the better are the results.

Stress on speed results in greater proficiency than stress on accuracy. The correlation between speed in words per minute and errors made was only .14 for a group of students who ranged in typing speeds from 9 to 108 words per minute. In other words, fast typists make no more errors than do slow typists. West (1969) recommended emphasizing speed during most of the practice time but reducing the speed emphasis during shorter practice sessions when good overall performance with fewer errors is sought. In addition, errors should not be given great weight in evaluating ordinary typing skill.

West also stated that extensive research had shown that the following conventional procedures do *not* produce higher accuracy: retyping mistyped words, using particular drill material aimed at particular errors, attempting to secure perfect copy, rhythm drills, and typing to music. Accuracy does appear to depend primarily on stroking at the right speed *for the individual.* To develop accuracy, therefore, short practice sessions at a speed a little below normal speed for the individual are recommended.

Typing is not highly fatiguing, according to West. Continuous typing for 30 minutes by typists representing a range of 9 to 108 words per minute was accompanied by a slight increase in errors (four more errors in minutes 26-30 than in minutes 1-5), but by no decrease in speed. There-fore, the "snail's pace" conventional high school pattern of five minutes of active practice followed by rest should be permanently abandoned. West also pointed out that repetitive drill on the same material has no advan-tage over nonrepetitive practice on a larger body of varied material. Self-paced practice, with the individual setting consecutive goals only slightly higher than recent achievement levels, produces excellent results.

Finally, according to West (1967), in the acquisition of ordinary stroking skill, the conventional insistence on touch only (not permitting the student to see the placement of his hands and fingers or the copy that he produces) is wrong. Kinesthetic and muscular sensations were found to be unreli-able until a minimum speed of 30 words per minute was attained. Free visual access to the typewriter and typescript during the early weeks of instruction gives the student visual cues for making correct responses, reinforcing correct responses, and identifying incorrect responses.

In connection with on-the-job, or production typing, the main conclu-sion drawn from many studies is that direct practice on actual or simu-lated production tasks (performing typing that really needs to be done) pays high dividends. In one research study, Crawford (1956) reported that instruction totally directed toward production typing in the third se-mester of a school year resulted in much better performance than in-struction directed toward straight-copy skills. West summarized the large amount of research dealing with preparing for production typing thus:

> These various lines of evidence, experimental and correlational, point over-whelmingly to the disadvantage of the traditional focus on ordinary copying skills and on stroking errors in straight-copy work and to the merit of early and continuous attention thereafter to "problem" or production typing on realistic tasks done under realistic conditions. (West, 1969, p. 109)

Although this discussion of the context for practice has been based on typing instruction, it seems likely that the results of this research can be broadly generalized to many other fields. For example, it is becoming widely known that in teacher education programs it is essential to provide practice of teaching skills in real, or at least simulated, teaching contexts.

3. Length and Spacing of Practice Sessions. The dramatic results in learning Morse Code, achieved in part through distributed practice, have been discussed. West (1969) showed that 30 minutes of continuous typing practice worked well. Equally significant results for distributed practice have been obtained with other skills. For example, learning to juggle is more efficient when practiced for 5 minutes each day, rather than 15 min-utes on alternate days (Knapp & Dixon, 1950). In fact, the distributed practice was almost twice as effective. Similar results have been attained with high-speed perceptual motor tasks (Mackworth, 1964) and with simple skills (Ammons, 1950; Duncan, 1951).

Many other studies could be cited to show that superior performance results from the proper length and spacing of practice periods. Both the proper length and the proper interval of rest between active practice ses-sions depend on the nature of the skill and the characteristics of the stu-

dent. The conclusion is clear: distributed practice produces excellent results when the practice sessions are long enough to bring about
improvement and when the time between sessions is long enough to overcome fatigue but not so long that forgetting occurs. The most important
factor in being able to regain a skill from one session to the next, after a
reasonable length of time, is the level of proficiency achieved during earlier trials (Fleishman & Parker, 1962).

Implementation in Speech Correction. The beginning therapist designed
practice tasks for Sarah in making the "s" sound that were appropriate
on several counts. Primary among these was the child's level of skills at
any specific time. The nature of the tasks changed as her skills progressed:

> The first practice tasks were of a type that did not require her to actually
> produce the sound. The tasks then progressed to having her produce the sound
> in isolation, to having her produce the sound in the various positions of syllables
> and words, and finally to having her produce the sound in words and sentences.
> When she reached the stage of syllables, it was necessary to first give her tasks
> which allowed her to say the "s" sound separated from the other sounds of the
> unit. After she mastered this, tasks were devised to give her practice at uni-
> fying the sound combinations.
>
> The tasks were varied at each level and were performed with and without
> mechanical aids. At each level she was required to master tasks ranging in diffi-
> culty from simple to complex before she was allowed to progress to the next
> stage. Among the most difficult tasks at each level were those that required her
> to perform well at her present ability level in some situation other than the ac-
> tual speech class.
>
> Practice was distributed during the week rather than massed, since Sarah
> was seen each Monday, Wednesday, and Friday from 9:10 until 9:30 in the
> morning. When Sarah was learning to say the "s" sound, a typical session would
> begin with a quick review of the correct production of the sound. In this review
> I would make a series of correct and incorrect productions and she would tell me
> which were correct and incorrect and why. Then she would verbalize the things
> she had to remember in trying to make the sound and would try to produce the
> sound. She would usually produce the sound quite poorly on her first few at-
> tempts. With successive repetitions her productions would usually improve up to
> a point and then remain on a plateau. When this plateau was reached, or when
> it could be seen that she was not going to make any progress, a different method
> was used. If, for example, we had been working with only a mirror, some me-
> chanical aid such as a toothpick would be introduced. If we were working with a
> toothpick, a different aid such as a straw would be used. When it appeared that
> no further progress would be made immediately, even with a change in meth-
> ods, practice on the production of the sound was discontinued and discrimina-
> tion practice was given. After she had had a few minutes to rest from her at-
> tempts at production, these attempts were resumed.
>
> After she was able to produce the sound correctly, distribution was
> accomplished primarily through the varying of activities. Throughout the
> corrective process it was noted that most progress was made when the session
> moved at a fairly rapid tempo and when the types of activities were varied
> often. In addition to these means of distributing the practice, Sarah was given
> various out-of-class assignments. These included such tasks as listening to her-
> self and/or others, practicing with a straw, and doing exercises in her speech
> book.

5. Provide Informational Feedback and Correct Inadequate Responses

Knowledge of results is one of the most powerful variables in skill learning. There is no improvement without knowledge of results; there is progressive improvement with such knowledge; there is deterioration after its withdrawal (Bilodeau & Bilodeau, 1961). Obviously, feedback of information is required to give the student knowledge of results. In many skills, of course, the student himself can directly observe the results of his actions. In others, he cannot, and the teacher should provide information.

Progress in many skills is quite easily measured; furthermore, there are many ways the teacher can use to provide the learner with knowledge of his progress. Information can be given verbally in such simple statements as "correct" or "incorrect"; a verbal analysis can be given of anything the student has produced; and the results of performance tests of all sorts can be incorporated in charts or given to the student directly. Verbal presentations, however, do have limitations. In some skills the actions cannot be explained verbally, nor can the accuracy or speed always be measured. In this case the teacher may demonstrate and the student, by observing, can compare his performance with the teacher's. As was suggested in connection with several studies, the learner also can be encouraged to engage in mental practice of the task both before and after he has completed it. This mental practicing is sometimes useful in helping the learner to intellectualize his knowledge of results, both in ascertaining what he has done well and, possibly, where he has made an error.

Incorrect responses or poor movements should be corrected. A primary determiner of the efficiency with which pupils acquire any skill is the quality of the help given when *incorrect* movements or responses are made. When the individual performs a bodily movement incorrectly and receives no feedback to the contrary, he tends to repeat it. In some cases, individuals overcome their deficiencies independently. In many cases, however, learning progresses only when the inadequacy is identified and appropriate corrective methods are devised by the teacher.

Implementation in Speech Correction. How often should knowledge of results be made available to a child who cannot evaluate the adequacy of his own responses? When should errors be corrected? In a few concise statements, the beginning therapist answers these questions:

> This principle was implemented at all stages with Sarah in such a way as also to lay the basis for the next principle. In the early stages of therapy, I verbally evaluated each of her responses. Instead of merely labeling a response as correct or incorrect, I told her why it was right or wrong, gave her suggestions for the correction of inadequate responses, and informed her of progress toward or regression from the correct response. With the help of such mechanical aids as a mirror, an auditory training unit, and a tape recorder, I tried to help her to understand fully the basis of my evaluations.

6. Encourage Independent Evaluation

This guide applied to skill learning carries the same meaning that it does when applied to the other learning outcomes that have been treated in

514 III: ACHIEVING LEARNING OUTCOMES

Chapters 10, 11, and 12, and this chapter. Under the direction of the teacher, the learner has the opportunity to profit from the guidance provided. Most skills, however, eventually are performed independently; skills, therefore, are taught in school so that learners can use them independently and in many activities. In addition to guiding and monitoring active practice in school, the teacher should encourage discussion and analysis in which each learner acquires skill in evaluating and improving his performances independently. It is very likely, indeed, that no person will acquire a high degree of skill so long as he remains dependent on someone else for the guiding and monitoring of his activities.

Implementation in Speech Correction. When we work with 25 to 50 or more students in a class, it is difficult to help all students in evaluating their performances. In a one-to-one situation, however, as is the case in some speech therapy, it naturally is easier to help the child in self-evaluation. The beginning speech therapist used some ingenious procedures with Sarah:

> Throughout corrective therapy I tried to teach Sarah to evaluate her own responses. Although I assumed the initial responsibility for the evaluations, I did so in such a way as to prepare her for making her own evaluations.
>
> I helped her to analyze the various aspects of the correct production of the "s" sound and helped her to learn to compare her productions with this model. I introduced the use of the tape recorder to help her to hear her errors. When she was able to do well at discrimination tasks I helped her to evaluate her responses by asking questions in such a way that she would be able to arrive at the correct evaluations. When I felt that she was capable of evaluating her own responses, I let her try to do so. If she made errors in these evaluations, I helped her to correct those errors by again asking appropriate questions.
>
> Sarah eventually reached the point where she was able to correctly evaluate her own responses and to modify her incorrect productions of the sound without my help. She was then able to do much practicing of the sound outside of the actual speech class.

13.13. How should demonstrations and accompanying verbal instructions be carried out for each of the following?

a. A left-handed child learning to write.

b. A high school girl learning to cut out a dress pattern.

c. A college student learning to make pottery.

13.14. Recall in your own past the learning of a skill that was accomplished with some frustration, for example, playing golf, skiing, parking a car.

a. Identify the component or components that appeared to be exceptionally difficult to master.

b. What two principles, if applied properly, might have assisted most in overcoming the difficulty?

13.15. Implementation of each guide for improving skills was illustrated in speech correction. Two criteria of the usefulness of an illustration are: It clarifies the guide. It helps the reader to find other applications. Evaluate the illustrations in speech correction on these two criteria.

13.16. Two criteria for evaluating the validity of a principle are: It is based on clearly stated theory and research; from it a teaching guide can be inferred.

Evaluate the validity of the six principles for improving skills. Take into account relevant information presented preceding the principles in this chapter and in Chapter 3.

SUMMARY

Psychomotor abilities such as strength, speed, precision, coordination, and flexibility underlie skilled performances in typing, playing a musical instrument, drawing, and many other activities. The change from a lower to a higher level of skill is accompanied by voluntary to involuntary control of movements, better differentiation of cues, better feedback and correction, more rapid and accurate movements, and better coordination of movements and responses. Skills vary in the amount of motor and perceptual involvement. Walking, for example, is high in the motor and low in the perceptual component, whereas reading is high in the perceptual and low in the motor.

Psychological knowledge and theory permit the stating of instructional guides that are applicable to all skill learning: (1) analyze the skill in terms of the learner's abilities, (2) demonstrate the correct response, (3) guide initial responses verbally and physically, (4) arrange for appropriate practice, (5) provide knowledge of results and correct inadequate responses, and (6) encourage independent evaluation.

The development of high-level skills in all children is necessary in attaining adequate vocational opportunities, avocational opportunities, and physical fitness and health.

SUGGESTIONS FOR FURTHER READING

EBEL, R. L., ed. *Encyclopedia of educational research.* New York: Macmillan, 1969.

Titles of articles in the encyclopedia of high interest to persons responsible for instruction in various curriculum areas involving some skill learning are as follows: G. I. Swanson and E. Persons, "Agricultural Education," pages 66-76; E. E. Eisner, "Art Education," pages 76-86; L. J. West, "Business Education," pages 105-116; R. Braddock, "English Composition," pages 443-461; W. Otto, "Handwriting," pages 570-579; H. Y. Nelson, "Home Economics," pages 607-619; S. Duker, "Listening," pages 747-753; S. S. Willoughby, "Mathematics," pages 766-777; J. B. Carroll, "Modern Languages," pages 866-878; E. A. Fleishman, "Motor Abilities," pages 888-895; E. H. Schneider, "Music Education," pages 895-907; H. J. Montoye, "Physical Education," pages 963-973; T. L. Harris, "Reading," pages 1069-1104; H. F. Seabury, "Speech," pages 1263-1277; T. D. Horn, "Spelling," pages 1282-1299.

FLEISHMAN, E. A. *The structure and measurement of physical fitness.* Englewood Cliffs, N. J.: Prentice-Hall, 1964.

Chapter 2, "Abilities and Motor Skills," is of interest not only to majors in physical education but also to anyone interested in measuring and teaching skills.

FLEISHMAN, E. A. Individual differences and motor learning. In Gagné, R. M., ed., *Learning and individual differences.* Columbus, Ohio: Merrill, 1967, pages 165-191.

Fleishman, in a highly readable style, presents a taxonomy of motor abilities, relates abilities to skills, and summarizes many years of productive research.

KUHLEN, R. G., ed. *Studies in educational psychology*. Waltham, Mass.: Blaisdell, 1968.

Chapter 12, pages 383-419, has a short introduction and three articles dealing with skills: R. M. Gagné, "Skill Training and Principles of Learning"; P. M. Fitts, "Factors in Complex Skill Training"; E. J. Gibson, "Learning To Read."

NATIONAL SOCIETY FOR THE STUDY OF EDUCATION. *Learning and instruction*, 49th yearbook. Chicago: University of Chicago Press, part 1, 1950.

The conditions for encouraging motor learning were described well by C. E. Ragsdale two decades ago in Chapter 3, "How Children Learn the Motor Types of Activities," pages 69-91.

Chapter 14 Attitudes and Values

The Nature of Attitudes and Values

cognitive component
affective component
action-tendency component
primary groups
reference groups
imitation, conditioning, and attitude learning

Developmental Trends

social attitudes
adolescent idealism
traditional and emergent values
characteristics of student activists
rebellious independence

Instructional Guides

identify the attitudes to be taught
provide exemplary models
provide pleasant emotional experiences
extend informative experiences
use group techniques
arrange for appropriate practice
encourage independent attitude cultivation

t is generally recognized that the schools have a responsibility for guiding the development of prosocial attitudes and values in students. It is also recognized, however, that attitudes and values are changing as society changes. The important question, therefore, is: Which attitudes and values should children learn in school? Obviously, the answer to this question is not so clear as the answers are to similar questions about outcomes in the cognitive and psychomotor domains. For one thing, many people consider that the teaching of attitudes and values is more the responsibility of the home and the church than the school. Beyond the problem of differing opinions about *who* should do the teaching, there are differing opinions in many communities about *what* attitudes and values children and youth should acquire concerning race, religion, government, drugs, family planning, and other important aspects of modern life. For these reasons, therefore, it is difficult to get widespread agreement among school people and parents on specific attitudes and values to include in any school curriculum.

Despite these problems, the authors believe that attitudes and values are an important outcome of school learning and that it is possible to agree on many values that are essential to an urban industrialized society. Each teacher, however, must decide which attitudes and values to teach. To help the teacher make this decision and also to help the school in developing prosocial values in students, this chapter discusses: (1) the nature of attitudes and values, (2) developmental trends, and (3) principles and instructional guides pertaining to attitude learning.

THE NATURE OF ATTITUDES AND VALUES

Attitudes are learned, emotionally toned predispositions to react in a consistent way, favorable or unfavorable, toward persons, objects, situations, or ideas. An individual's attitudes are inferred from his behavior and cannot be measured as directly as skills, facts, and concepts. The main difference between concepts (as defined in Chapter 11) and attitudes is that attitudes influence the individual's acceptance or rejection of persons, objects, situations, and ideas, referred to as *attitude objects*. Attitudes do have meaning for the individual, as do concepts.

As Fig. 14.1 indicates, there is no sharp distinction between tastes, attitudes, and values on five important criteria. (1) From the standpoint of *stability*, tastes are most temporary and values most stable, with attitudes somewhere in between. Tastes may shift readily from day to day or week to week, attitudes change less frequently, and values are quite resistant to change. (2) In *scope*, tastes refer to something specific, such as the like or dislike of a particular animal or color; values are more general and encompass larger areas of experience. For example, we might think

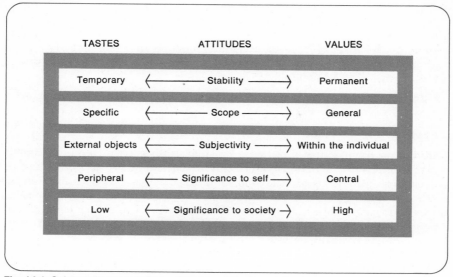

Fig. 14.1. Schematic organization of tastes, attitudes, and values.

of a taste as applying to a specific arrangement of a musical composition; an attitude as acceptance or rejection of certain categories of music such as classical or jazz; and a value as the entire scope of music in the life of the individual. (3) In connection with the *subjectivity* dimension, a taste is usually thought of as the individual's perception of the attractiveness or unattractiveness of an external object; an attitude is involved in the relationship between a person and the object; and a value is more intimately within the individual. (4) As applied to *significance to self*, an individual's tastes may change without much modification in his total personality or self-organization. Attitudes also can change, but when there are many changes of attitude, there also is an accompanying change in the self. When there are large and significant changes in the value system, there is also a basic change in personality. (5) On the last dimension—*significance to society*—tastes are not considered of high importance, being unique to individuals within the larger social group. Values, however, are of high importance to organized segments of society, such as the community, state, and nation. Large differences in values or in the means of achieving the same values among subgroups within the community or nation result in conflict and disorganization of the larger society.

These differentiations among tastes, attitudes, and values are important. In general usage, however, the terms often are interchanged. For example, some authors define attitudes as feelings or sets toward a specific object or idea and others refer to attitudes as enduring and stable values. Nevertheless, two important facts about attitudes are widely accepted: (1) the actions of the individual are governed to a large extent by his attitudes; (2) an attitude is a system of three interrelated components—a cognitive component, an affective component, and an action-tendency component (Krech, Crutchfield, & Ballachey, 1962). The cognitive component refers to the informational content, the affective component to the feelings, and the action-tendency component to the predisposition to take action with respect to the attitude object. It also is generally agreed that aspects of the individual and the group are important determinants of the acquisition and development of attitudes.

Components of Attitudes

Individuals have many attitudes; most attitudes are interconnected in clusters, but some are relatively isolated. Occasionally, attitudes are acquired through one traumatic emotional experience, but with little information about the attitude object. More often they are acquired through a series of lesser emotional experiences and with more information. Some are acquired with very little feeling or emotion and considerable information about the attitude object.

The most crucial *cognitive* component of attitudes is informational content—the factual information one has about, for example, the Protestant Reformation, John F. Kennedy, or Students for a Democratic Society. The *affective* component of an attitude refers to the emotions one associates with the attitude object. That is, the object is felt to be pleasing or displeasing; it is liked or disliked. Figure 14.2 shows relative weightings of

Fig. 14.2. Relative weighting of the affective and cognitive components of attitudes.

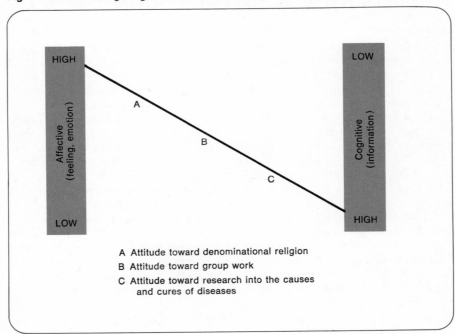

A Attitude toward denominational religion
B Attitude toward group work
C Attitude toward research into the causes
   and cures of diseases

the affective (feeling, emotional) and cognitive (informational) components in attitude acquisition. As the figure indicates, weighting may vary from very high to very low for both the affective and the cognitive components. Consider the three examples of attitude objects named in the figure. It is possible for the attitudes toward the objects (A, B, C) to be held by the same individual. (In this context, the attitudes may be either favorable or unfavorable.) Attitude A is based largely on emotional experiences and little on informational experiences with denominational religions. Attitude B is based about equally on informational and emotional experiences with group work. Attitude C is largely based on information experiences, with relatively little emotional experience.

In general, commercial advertising uses the A type of approach; schools use the C type of approach. The advertiser, of course, wants individuals to acquire a favorable attitude toward a product, so he presents it in a most pleasant emotional setting with a selectively favorable amount of information. On the other hand, when a teacher wants individuals to acquire an attitude without attempting to influence the accepting-rejecting, favorable-unfavorable dimension, all information is provided—favorable, unfavorable, and neutral.

No matter how an attitude is acquired, it guides behavior in a consistent way—the *action-tendency* component of the attitude. If an individual holds a favorable attitude toward a given attitude object, he will be disposed to behave consistently in a way that is supportive of the object; if he has an unfavorable attitude, he will be disposed to behave consistently in a way that is negative toward the object. For example, if the individual has a strong negative attitude toward religion, he probably will not attend church regularly nor, when he does attend, for the same purposes as church members with strong positive attitudes toward religion. If he has a strong positive attitude toward research into the causes and cures of diseases, he will probably contribute to various fund-raising campaigns to extend medical research.

It is possible, of course, to have attitudes that at times lead to contradictory actions and conflicts. A person may have a strong negative attitude toward the medical treatment of illness and a strong positive attitude toward the curative powers of faith. Nevertheless, if he has a ruptured appendix or a broken leg, he may secure medical treatment. Also, two or more individuals having a favorable attitude toward a given attitude object do not necessarily behave identically toward related attitude objects. For example, sharing a strong positive attitude toward the idea of freedom of the individual does not automatically lead to similar positive actions regarding labor unions or "wars of liberation."

Bases of Attitudes

An individual develops some attitudes in coping with the various problems he encounters in satisfying his own needs. Favorable attitudes are developed toward attitude objects that satisfy needs and unfavorable attitudes are developed toward those attitude objects that thwart or block individual need satisfaction. Just as an individual acquires his own facts and concepts, so he acquires his own attitudes.

The group affiliations of the individual, however, also play a vital role in the formation of his attitudes. Many of the attitudes of the individual have their source and support in the groups to which he gives his allegiance. Membership in groups exercises a more important influence on attitudes than on concepts and skills. Because an individual's attitudes tend to reflect the beliefs, values, and norms of his groups, the nature of his group memberships and identifications must be understood if we are to understand the development of his attitudes.

Every individual in society is a member of small, face-to-face, or *primary groups*. A primary group, such as the family, a religious group, or a friendship group, usually has a core of common attitudes that holds its members together. The members of these primary groups tend to have similar attitudes. Also, an individual's *reference groups* – groups with which he identifies, whether or not he is a member of them – importantly influence his attitude development. A reference group is one that the individual uses as a standard to judge the adequacy of his own behavior.

There are several reasons why members of primary groups tend to share a common core of similar attitudes: (1) conformity pressures within the group induce attitude homogeneity among individuals as a price of retaining group membership; (2) individuals tend to seek out groups to join in which prevailing attitudes are similar to theirs; (3) members of primary groups share the same environment and thus are exposed to the same information; (4) new members of a group assume the group attitudes as a means of obtaining group acceptance.

It is important to remember this: An individual's primary membership groups influence the development of his attitudes only to the extent that he uses them *as reference groups* – as groups he uses to judge the adequacy of his own behavior. As mentioned, nonmembership groups may also serve as reference groups for the individual and influence his attitude development. As we shall soon see, the nature of an individual's reference groups changes as the individual develops.

The explanations that have been given do not mean that diverse attitudes are never acquired by members of the same group. The influence of groups on an individual's attitudes is often subtle, indirect, and complex. Although a core of common attitudes serves to consolidate a small neighborhood friendship group, the various members may have markedly different attitudes toward areas of life outside the neighborhood group. Conflicting group affiliations and conflicting individual needs also serve to create diverse attitudes. Such factors as the purposes or functions of the group, the feelings among the members, the amount and closeness of associations among the members, the importance of group membership to the individual, and the type of group leadership affect the extent to which either common *or* diverse attitudes emerge.

For example, apply these group characteristics to a large college class. Frequently, in such a group students have a common but vague purpose — to learn certain subject matter. Strong likes or dislikes are not felt among members of the class, few close associations are made during regular class periods, the importance of the course varies from student to student, and the leadership is vested in one person — the teacher. In such a classroom a core of common attitudes cannot be expected. Instead, each individual has unique attitudes affecting most areas of life; the common attitudes that do exist affect only the small area of the particular classroom. Nevertheless, such a group can be organized and led so that attitudes are influenced. In an experiment with college students, (1) the attitudes of individuals shifted with their perceived estimates of how most of the members of their group reacted to the particular attitude object; (2) classes taught by a group-centered technique created more amiability among members than did leader-centered classes; (3) a group-decision method was more effective than a lecture in reaching a conclusion about an attitude object; (4) individuals within groups and the groups themselves did not change all attitudes in the same manner — certain attitudes apparently were more resistant to modification than others (McKeachie, 1954).

It is also true that if large classes are reorganized into small group sections and an attempt is made to personalize and humanize the classroom through small-group dynamics, the student's image of himself can substantially improve. For example, Trowbridge (1969), using a self-concept scale, found such improvement in attitudes toward self in students taught in small groups as compared with students taught in the traditional large sections.

Imitation and Conditioning in Attitude Learning

Earlier (in Chapter 2) we noted that much social learning occurs through imitation of models (Bandura & Walters, 1963). A brief review of the main concepts of imitation, with specific application to the learning of attitudes, will lay the basis for some of the principles and instructional guides that will be discussed later in this chapter.

Imitation works in three ways to increase the number, range, and intensity of the observer's matching responses. (1) Observing a model enables the observer to acquire new behavior that he has not previously shown. For example, a child observes a model and then exhibits new behavior similar to that of the model. (2) Observing a model may strengthen or weaken inhibitory responses of the observer. Here the observer already has the behavior in his repertoire, but it has been inhibited. Inhibited behavior seen in a model that is punished is inhibited further, or weakened; that seen in a model that is rewarded is disinhibited, or strengthened. (3) Observing a model may have the effect of eliciting previously learned behavior that has not been shown recently. The difference between the disinhibiting effects of imitation and the eliciting effects can be determined only by knowing the history of the observer. The amount of imitating done by an individual is influenced by the rewards and punishments received by the model. The observer will tend not to imitate if the model is punished for his behavior; however, if a certain behavior brings reward, the observer is more likely to imitate. Individual characteristics and circumstances also are influential. Imitation is more prevalent in the person who lacks self-esteem, lacks competence, or believes he is very similar to a model. One is also more likely to imitate if in the past he has been rewarded for copying someone else's behavior.

As you remember, a response made for the first time is strengthened through reinforcement. Except in the laboratory, the schedule of reinforcement is not well controlled and is intermittent, rather than systematic. Nonetheless, even if reinforcement by an authority figure such as a parent or teacher is intermittent, it has a strengthening effect. On the other hand, responses already in the learner's repertoire are inhibited by punishment and nonreward. When a child's responses are considered to be a threat to himself or to society, positive reinforcers are removed (a privilege is taken away) or an aversive stimulus such as punishment is used. Although these active techniques lead to inhibition of undesired responses, their effects may be only temporary—they may not result in permanent extinction. As noted in Chapter 2, classical conditioning procedures may be more effective than punishment and nonreward because they eliminate an undesirable response by displacing it with a desired one.

The effect of classical conditioning on attitude behavior was reported in a study by Early (1968). A classical conditioning situation was set up with fourth- and fifth-grade children. First, social isolates were identified through observation. The experimental treatment involved having their classmates learn paired words, one of which was the name of a social isolate and the other a positive evaluative meaning word (e.g., "fun," "neat"). A control group learned the isolate's name paired with a nonevaluative word (e.g., "table," "and"). Initial observations of the isolated children had revealed that they tended to be unresponsive to others. They did very little during free play at recess and only infrequently spoke to other children. During the period of treatment a noticeable change in the isolates' behavior with the experimental group was observed. They became more animated and participated in games with other children when they had not done so before. Their classmates responded to these behaviors in socially reinforcing ways. Because the isolates' classmates did reinforce their approach behavior, it was continued, although extinction might have occurred without reinforcement. None of these positive interactions occurred between the isolates and their classmates in the control group.

Considerable evidence for the learning of attitudes through imitation and through reinforcement of desired responses and punishment of undesired responses is found in studies of the attitudes and prejudices of young children. Radke, Trager, & Davis (1949) found that 250 kindergarten and first- and second-grade children demonstrated stereotyping and the rejecting of other groups of human beings, such as Negro, white,

Jewish, Catholic, and Protestant. We observe also that young children may acquire the religious beliefs of their parents through imitation, reinforcement, and punishment. It should not be inferred, however, that attitudes are learned only through imitation, followed by reinforcement or punishment. As noted in the previous discussion in this chapter, the development of attitudes is influenced by cognizing information about attitude objects as well as by interacting in groups.

14.1. What are the differences among tastes, attitudes, and values? Apply these to yourself by giving examples of each that characterize you at the present time.

14.2. Identify some of your own strongest attitudes and values. Can you separate their affective and cognitive components? How have the action-tendency components of your attitudes and values guided your own behavior?

14.3. Think of all the groups to which you belong. Which of them do you use as reference groups? Have your reference groups changed during your life so far? Do you anticipate further changes in the nature of your reference groups as you grow older? How has the history of your reference groups affected your own attitudes and values? How do you expect to change in your attitudes and values in terms of anticipated future reference groups?

14.4. Considering your personal experiences, how have imitation and conditioning played a role in the formation of your attitudes and values?

DEVELOPMENTAL TRENDS

Individuals acquire and change their attitudes from infancy into adult life. Some attitudes appear to be acquired in early childhood and remain fairly stable thereafter; others are not acquired until considerably later, in adolescence, and are readily subject to modification.

A developmental sequence in the learning of attitudes involves (1) being aware of and receiving stimuli, (2) responding to stimuli in ways ranging from mere acquiescence through obtaining satisfaction from the response, (3) forming values in a sequential pattern from first acceptance through commitment, (4) organizing values in a conceptual system, and (5) of building a philosophy of life that characterizes the individual as a unique personality. This developmental sequence is arranged schematically in Fig. 14.3.

Turning to specific developmental trends, we can begin by comparing the learning of attitudes with the learning of concepts. As was shown in the outline of a sequence in concept learning in Chapter 11, only the most elementary concepts are learned during the early years of life. Similarly, it seems likely that conceptualization of favorable or unfavorable attitudes does not occur, except at a most elementary level, before the school years. Nevertheless, emotionalized reactions—pleasant and unpleasant— are present as early as the second year of life (Bridges, 1932), and parents report that their children express favorable attitudes toward school be-

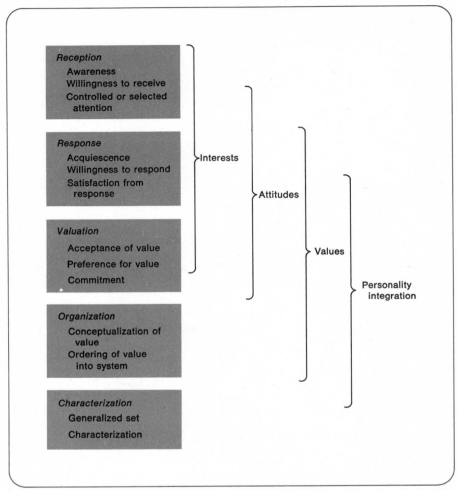

Fig. 14.3. A theoretical sequence in the development of attitudes. (Based on Krathwohl, Bloom, & Masia, 1964)

fore starting the first grade (Stendler, 1951). Apparently, young children are aware of and respond affectively to stimuli early in life, before school age, although valuing, organization, and characterization come later. More specific inferences about a developmental sequence and the learning of attitudes can be drawn from the following discussion of the elementary school years, the high school years, and the college years.

Elementary School Years

During the elementary school years, children's attitudes generally are close approximations of the attitudes held by the significant adults in their world—particularly their parents and family group and their teachers. Variations among children's attitudes are, thus, a function of variations among their adult reference groups. Children's attitudes are stable in some respects and change in others during the elementary school years. For example, social attitudes directed toward groups other than one's own social group are only beginning to form by the age of 5. Although they remain subject to modification by a variety of influences, by age 14 these attitudes have crystallized in the vast majority of children (Harding et al., 1954).

Noting the complexity of children's attitudes toward school, Jackson (1968) reviewed several studies that show a generally favorable attitude toward school among elementary grade children. Although the proportions differed for boys and girls—girls having more favorable attitudes—approximately 80 percent of the students indicated favorable attitudes toward school. As grade level increases, favorable attitudes toward school tend to decrease. These same progressively more negative attitudes toward school as children go up the grades were also found by Neale and Proshek (1967). Nevertheless, contrary to the results of previous research, these investigators found that disadvantaged elementary school children are *not* negative about school in the sense of devaluing school and school-related activities.

Two studies by Flanders, Morrison, and Brode (1968) showed significant changes in children's attitudes toward school over a four-month period (October-January). There was a significant reduction of positive pupil attitudes in four subscales: (1) teacher attractiveness, (2) fairness of rewards and punishments, (3) teacher competence, (4) interest in school work. The investigation yielded two factors related to the observed changes in attitude. Students who were identified as *external* (tended to believe that successes and failures are caused by forces beyond one's own control) had a greater negative shift in attitude than children identified as *internal* (tended to believe that successes and failures are self-determined and products of one's own behavior). Also, in classrooms of teachers who provided less praise and encouragement there was greater loss of positive attitudes than in classrooms of teachers who provided more praise and encouragement.

Estvan and Estvan (1959) conducted a study that further revealed stability in some respects and change in others toward a number of pervasive and significant attitude objects from first grade to sixth grade. For example, negative attitudes toward lower-status living were acquired before the children reached first grade and remained relatively unchanged through the sixth grade. The children acquired favorable attitudes toward upper-status living during the first six years of school. The sixth-graders showed many more positive and many fewer negative attitudes toward upper-status living than did the first-graders. Although boys and girls had similar attitudes about lower-status situations, the girls were more attracted to upper-status situations than were the boys. The Estvans interpreted this to mean that the girls were more socially responsive and had internalized attitudes at a younger age than the boys.

From these types of studies it can be concluded that some attitudes in elementary school children—for example, toward social status and social groups other than their own — are acquired quite early in life and become more fixed with further learning. Other attitudes — for example, those toward school — appear less stable and change direction. Generally, children's attitudes reflect the attitudes of their adult reference groups.

High School Years

Less than 10 years ago, adolescents were described by investigators as benign, uninvolved, and bland in their attitudes and values (Ginzberg, 1961; Remmers, 1963). They were thought to be occupied for the most part with their own concerns. They seemed to support "official" socially desirable attitudes and values. Their support, however, did not extend to a concerted urge to strike a blow for civil liberties or for individual freedom, even in the face of governmental pressure. As we all know, this is not the case in the 1970s. Student involvement in demonstrations for peace and against war, for civil liberties, for a greater role in student government, against pollution, against racial discrimination, and other causes has swung the pendulum. Many worried adults are now disturbed by what they see as the impetuous and irresponsible way in which young people align themselves with social issues.

During adolescence there is a growing shift of influence from the family to peers as a reference group. Personal and social factors become more important; indeed, they attain their maximum influence at the high school level. It is at this stage that young people in our society exhibit the greatest conflict as to who they are and where they belong in the world. Thus, adolescence is a critical period for the fate of attitude development. The adolescent is caught in a conflict between identification with the role of the child (from which he is emerging) and the role of the adult (which he is beginning to assume), a conflict he resolves by greater involvement in the peer group. The uncertainty and ambiguity he finds in adult behavior expectancies and the apparent clarity of peer-group norms and standards lead the adolescent to use the latter to judge the appropriateness of his behavior.

The differences between what the adolescent feels and what he thinks *adults* feel can be inferred from a study by Hess and Goldblatt (1957). Adolescents rated (1) the average teen-ager, (2) the average adult, (3) teen-agers from the viewpoint of an adult, and (4) adults from the viewpoint of an adult. Also, parents of these same adolescents rated (1) the average teen-ager, (2) the average adult, (3) teen-agers from the viewpoint of a teen-ager, and (4) adults from the viewpoint of a teen-ager. Thus, agreements and disagreements in how adolescents and parents view one another were revealed. Some of the conclusions follow.

1. Adolescents and parents agree in expressing mildly favorable opinions of teen-agers.
2. Adolescents tend to idealize adults — that is, they have much higher opinions of adults than parents have.
3. Adolescents see a relatively greater status difference between teen-agers and adults than the parents see.

4. Adolescents believe the average adult has a generalized tendency to depreciate teen-agers. They feel teen-agers have a uniformly low reputation among adults.

5. Parents expect teen-agers to have a selective tendency to undervalue adults. They predict that adults will get lower ratings than they deserve on aspects of interpersonal relationships, but that they will be accurately evaluated on noninterpersonal maturity aspects.

6. Adolescents believe the adults will evaluate themselves relatively accurately.

7. Parents believe teen-agers have unrealistically high opinions of themselves.

8. Both adolescents and parents believe the status difference between teen-agers and adults will be distorted to approximately the same extent by the other group.

Characteristic adolescent attitudes must be interpreted with caution. For one thing, individual differences in all aspects of development become pronounced during the high school years. In addition to these vast individual differences, even when individuals do share the same or similar attitudes, their opportunities and methods for expressing them may differ considerably. In other words, from the teacher's point of view, the broad picture of characteristic adolescent attitudes is probably less important than are the particular attitudes of any given adolescent and of his adjustment.

We have discussed the shift in influence on adolescents from adult groups to peer groups and the reservations with which characteristic adolescent attitudes must be assessed. It is important also to recognize the considerable influence that changing times have on the acceptability of various attitudes. From generation to generation, different attitudes become possible, acceptable, and perhaps even expected. And there is usually a lag from generation to generation. It is difficult for adolescents, involved as they are in the peer-group expectancies of their own generation, to appreciate the views of adults whose reference point is a previous generation. In this sense, indeed, the adolescent may be more in tune with his times than the adult. There are many examples, ranging from such things as the length of male hair, the acceptability of women smoking, dress fashions, and the use of cosmetics to attitudes toward cheating, war, government, and religion.

Other aspects of adolescent attitudes concern conformity and idealism. Society expects conformity of its members as a means of regulating stability and order. The adolescent peer group tends to be more intolerant of nonconformity than the adult group. That is, it is very difficult for the adolescent to deny the acceptability of attitudes held by his peer group. Obviously, when these attitudes conflict with those of significant adults, such as parents and teachers, the adolescent may have adjustment difficulties and confused attitudes. At the same time, the adolescent tends to be a highly idealistic person. He is likely to hold high ideals for himself and others, including his parents and teachers. It is not unusual to find that an adolescent is intolerant of those who do not conform to his ideal point of view.

In the context of all the foregoing considerations it can be said that during adolescence, as in the elementary school years, some attitudes become more stable and others change. Some representative investigations dealing with emerging values, prejudice, dogmatism in religion, and cheating give us more insight into adolescent attitudes. A contrast between traditional and emergent values was noted by Thompson (1965). Traditional values were seen as interest in successful work, plans for the future, independence from social pressures, and Puritan morality. Emergent values were defined as centering on the present rather than the future, social relations, conformity, and less rigid morality. The study extended from the freshman to the sophomore year in high school. There was little *change* in individual students during the year, but the following factors differentiated students holding these contrasting sets of values:

1. Girls had significantly higher scores than boys in morality and sociability but lower scores on the values of success, conformity, and concentration on the present.
2. Students who attended church, regardless of sex, showed higher value scores in morality and independence than students who did not attend church regularly. The value placed on the future was high among church-goers; the value placed on the present increased as students had less and less interest in church.
3. Students with high grades in high school tended to hold traditional values and to emphasize future success and independence.
4. Students in the college preparatory curriculum had traditional values.

A study reporting on ethnic attitudes during the high school years indicates developments from age 13-14 through 17-18 (Wilson, 1963). Table 14.1 shows the average level of attitudes for three age groups attending a suburban school near Boston. A low score indicates a *more* favorable attitude, a high score a *less* favorable attitude. Attitudes toward Jews and Negroes improved slightly with increasing age. Attitudes toward Southerners, however, deteriorated; this change apparently was associated

Table 14.1. Average Level of Attitude by Age for Five Scales

	Age		
Scales	**13-14** **($n = 317$[a])**	**15-16** **($n = 150$[a])**	**17-18** **($n = 150$[a])**
Opinion of Jews	31.4	31.7	29.9
Opinion of Negroes	32.7	32.5 .	31.7
Opinion of Southerners	31.7	33.4	33.7

[a]n's for the "Opinion of Negroes" scale were 288, 194, and 193. This scale was based on a questionaire administered on a different day from the one containing the other scales.
Source: Adapted from Wilson, 1963, p. 251. Copyright 1963 by The Society for Research in Child Development, Inc.

with events in the South during the early 1960s. The attitudes among the boys (not shown in the table) did not vary as widely at the oldest age as at the youngest age. The average scores made by all groups at all ages were neither highly favorable nor highly unfavorable toward the ethnic groups.

Hebron and Ridley (1965) contrasted the attitudes of boys of all ages who made high scores in tests of prejudice with those who made low scores. Two factors were found to be especially significant in distinguishing these two groups. The highly prejudiced boys revealed an exaggerated esteem for themselves, their friends, and their own social status. Their view of themselves was unrealistic, distorted, and not supported by objective facts. Also, they were extremely anxious and insecure. The boys with the least prejudice had a self-image that was in accord with their actual social position. They felt relatively secure and satisfied with life.

Religion continues to play a vital role in the life of the adolescent in formulating values and standards of conduct. An increased interest in religion, along with a revolt against traditional dogma, is an integral part of adolescence. For example, a study of dogmatism in religion and other fields (Anderson, 1962) in grades 8, 10, 11, and 12 revealed a decrease in the degree of dogmatic attitudes with increasing grade level. Further, there is evidence that a greater emphasis on personal rather than institutionalized religion is characteristic of today's adolescents (Shepherd, 1966).

Attitudes toward cheating in school work varied among students of high school age (Eames et al., 1965). The largest proportion (60 percent) condemned cheating, but 36 percent sanctioned cheating as a revenge for poor teaching, 33 percent thought cheating was all right if you did not get caught, and 33 percent thought marks were more important than honesty. It appears that although most of today's adolescents condemn cheating in school in principle, the guilt associated with cheating is diminishing. In a 1966 study of high school and college students, 96 percent admitted cheating on school tests (Shepherd, 1966).

College Years

As college enrollments have increased, it has become more important to recognize and take into account the way attitudes develop from the freshman through the senior years. The college years are similar in attitude development to the high school years, but the trends are intensified. Changes in college students' attitudes and values are still more a product of peer-reference group influences than of faculty and institutional influences. The student shows a greater concern with what he sees as important to his peers than with what he sees as important to the institution. Indeed, many student activists have directly attacked the institution by leading demonstrations, protests, building occupations, and other institutional disruptions aimed at enforcing their views on pollution, war, discipline, Black Studies programs, faculty appointments and dismissals, military recruiting, and general university governance. At considerable personal risk, these students seem determined to transform the institution into one that is more responsive to new and different attitudes and values. Student activists probably are quite representative of college students generally. Table 14.2 gives some figures that support this view (at least in connection with cognitive abilities).

Table 14.2. Distribution of Scholastic Aptitude Scores

Scores	Verbal		Quantitative	
	Activists	All	Activists	All
750–800	11%	13%	15%	13%
700–749	33	26	22	24
650–699	30	25	28	24
600–649	13	18	22	19
550–599	11	12	4	12
500–549	2	4.5	9	5
Below 500	0%	1.5%	0%	3%

Note: For the entire group (All), $n = 700$; for Activists, $n = 46$.
Source: Schwab, 1969, p. 32. Copyright ©1969 by The University of Chicago.

Keeping in mind that for college students, as for high school students, there are individual differences in conformity, idealism, and influence of peers as reference groups, let us look at some representative investigations of attitudes and values in college students.

Lehmann (1963) tested more than 1000 college students as freshmen and again as seniors in their ability to think critically, their tendency to be dogmatic, their acceptance of traditional moral values, and their religious, social, and political views. During the four-year period, both men and women improved significantly in their ability to think critically and in their willingness to accept new ideas. They became less dogmatic and less inclined to believe in stereotypes. They placed less value on traditional morality. The variation in attitudes was greater at the end of the last year than at the beginning of the first. It seems likely that this increased variation appeared because although many students rejected their earlier attitudes, others clung to theirs.

Huntley (1965) was also concerned with value changes during the four years of college; this study covered more than 1000 men students. Attitudes and interests were measured in general theoretical problems, economics, aesthetics, social relations, politics, and religion. Students majoring in the humanities scored above average as freshmen in values placed on theory, aesthetics, and religion and below average on economic, social, and political values. As seniors they scored as high as was possible in aesthetics and increased in politics. In the other areas their scores decreased, particularly in economics and religion. Majors in the social sciences changed in only two respects: They placed greater value on aesthetics and less on religion.

Students in college show less ethnocentric ideology — the tendency to exalt the superiority of the group to which one belongs — than high school students. During the four-year college period, males change less than females in this tendency. At the end of the first two years of college, females are less ethnocentric than males, and there is no difference between members of fraternities or sororities and nonmembers. Further, intelligence is not associated with change in ethnocentrism (Plant, 1958a,b).

In another study of changes in attitudes during the college years, attitudes of students toward religion as freshmen and again as seniors were measured (Hites, 1965). The changes showed mainly a trend from acceptance to less acceptance; for instance, the number responding "true" to such items as "A belief in God is necessary to give meaning to life" decreased. There was also a trend from a more to a less literal interpretation of religion to a recognition of the need for religion to change constantly if it is to try to help in solving the new problems of each generation. Finally, there was a change in the direction of a more naturalistic (and psychological) interpretation of the world and, although the idea of immortality was not completely rejected, belief in it decreased. Obviously, the changes were in the direction of liberalism.

This review of representative investigations shows quite conclusively that there are changes in attitudes during the college years. Generally, the changes are characterized by great variation in attitudes and movement toward more liberal attitudes.

14.5. Have some of your strongest attitudes and values changed since you were in junior high school? How did this happen? Which ones remain the same? Why?

14.6. Do you think high school students today have attitudes and values similar to those held by you and your classmates when you were in high school? If you think not, how and why are they different?

14.7. What does it mean to say that there is a "generation gap" in attitudes and values? Is the claim that there is a "generation gap" valid? In what sense? Can it be bridged? How?

14.8. Can you generalize about the attitudes and values of today's college students? If you can, how would you describe them? Do you fit this description?

14.9. In what ways have you become more like your classmates during your college years? In what ways have you become more different from them?

PRINCIPLES PERTAINING TO ATTITUDES

Seven principles and related instructional guides are now presented in the same manner as in the preceding five chapters. These principles and guides are applicable not only to the class of affective outcomes that we have discussed—tastes, attitudes, and values—but also to other outcomes that have a high affective component—interests and motives. We could substitute any of the four other terms for "attitudes."

The principles and instructional guides do not imply that a teacher should be highly directive and assume all responsibility for decision-making about the learning of attitudes. On the contrary, the teacher can be most effective if he serves as a guide and organizer. In many situations, starting as early as kindergarten, in fact, and extending through college, the students should, of course, participate in implementing the principles.

Careful study of the principles shows that the middle five follow a sequence of learning and instruction, from initial acquisition through use. The first principle is included because the schools have not done an adequate job of determining their role in the teaching of attitudes. Most schools have definite programs in mathematics, language arts, and other subject matter, but there are almost no similar programs dealing with attitude development. The last principle is included to help individuals in modifying their own attitudes. The guides are now discussed in detail.

Principle	Instructional Guide
1. Teaching and learning attitudes, as other outcomes, begins with clear objectives.	1. Identify the attitudes to be taught.
2. Incorporating a model's behavior into his own repertoire occurs in a receptive, responding observer through imitation.	2. Provide exemplary models.
3. Strengthening attitudes through positive reinforcers involves contiguity of response and reinforcement and the linking of pleasant experiences with the reinforced response.	3. Provide pleasant emotional experiences with attitude objects.
4. Cognizing information and thinking productively modify attitudes differentially, according to the strength of the attitude.	4. Extend informative experiences.
5. Interacting in groups provides for testing of and commitment to behavior in harmony with group standards.	5. Use group techniques to facilitate commitment.
6. Practicing an attitude in relevant situations provides for stable organization.	6. Arrange for appropriate practice.
7. Acquiring or modifying his own attitudes may be initiated by an individual through purposeful learning.	7. Encourage independent attitude cultivation.

1. Identify the Attitudes To Be Taught

There is great variety in attitudes and values at any given time in our society; furthermore, rapidly changing times are constantly causing attitudes and values that were unacceptable at other times to become generally acceptable. (Consider, for example, the changed attitudes toward women smoking in public or the feelings about Germany and Japan during World War II and then shortly after the war.) It is not surprising, therefore, that there is much confusion about *which* attitudes should be taught.

Another problem in identifying attitudes and values to be taught in schools is described succinctly thus:

> More difficult for people to understand and cope with is the value gap between school and pupil. This is partly because the values which the pupil should learn are not so clearly understood and stated in the school curriculum as are the knowledge and skills he should learn, and partly because there are subtle or not-so-subtle value differences between the parents and the schools. Where the parents and the schools differ in values there is a competition between parent and teacher that does not exist in the area of knowledge and skills. The poorly educated parent recognizes that the teacher is a better reader, speller, and master of arithmetic and history, and expects the teacher to help his child become superior to him. But he does not recognize so clearly that his child may become superior to him, in certain values, with the aid of the school. (Havighurst, 1966, p. 47)

Indeed, the schools often are criticized for promoting middle-class values at the expense of other value orientations. There is no general agreement on what middle-class values *are*, however. For instance, Havighurst (1966) asserts that certain values that the American schools must teach if they are to succeed with their pupils are *not* social class values, but values essential to the functioning of an urban, industrial, democratic society. These values (discussed in more detail in Chapter 6) are: punctuality, orderliness, conformity to group norms, desire for a work career based on skill and knowledge, desire for a stable family life, inhibition of aggressive impulses, rational approach to a problem situation, enjoyment of study, and desire for freedom of self and others.

The schools do not have a coherent and effective set of values and do not exert effective leadership in promoting desirable attitudes and values. Many would agree with Havighurst when he contends that if each school were to state explicitly a program for teaching some set of values and were to organize itself for the task, most people would support the school. Although identifying the attitudes to be taught is difficult, the task is not so difficult as to be "missionary work in a value-hostile territory." The task is, rather, to identify those attitudes and values that lead to competence in an urban, industrial, democratic society — values that are common to people at *all* socioeconomic levels. Although problems are involved, schools can be organized to teach these attitudes explicitly and positively, starting in the kindergartens and continuing through graduate levels of the universities.

Consider the values listed by Havighurst. If a group of teachers, administrators, and parents began discussing them in order to draw up a program for teaching them, questions of definition would immediately be raised. Even after the meanings were clarified, there would undoubtedly be considerable disagreement about *applying* the values to daily situations and further disagreement about behavioral criteria that could be used to evaluate the effectiveness of their attainment. Nevertheless, this kind of effort must be made if the school is to mount a coherent and organized program in the area of values.

Once values have been agreed on, how should they be taught? Havighurst, discussing this question, describes two cultures of the school. One is the *instrumental* culture—the activities that lead to the knowledges, skills, and values considered to be the objectives of education. The other is the *expressive* culture—the activities that students and teachers take part in for the sake of the activity itself, such as playing games at recess, eating lunch, and so forth. The expressive culture is seen as being particularly good for

> teaching values, since most pupils can succeed in the expressive culture and there is not such severe and explicit competition as there is in the instrumental culture. Thus a pupil can learn to like school, and to value punctuality and conforming behavior through successful participation in the expressive culture as well as in the instrumental culture. Also, the parents can generally be involved in the expressive culture and can thus learn some of the school's values. (Havighurst, 1966, p. 52)

To summarize, the task that faces schools and teachers is not to overcome a hostile set of values, but to identify those values that are desired and to help students whose values are confused and underdeveloped to clarify their own values and to work effectively toward the realization of the desired values. It is not negative combat that confronts schools and teachers; it is positive cooperation that challenges them. The next six principles and guides should be helpful in achieving these positive results.

2. Provide Exemplary Models

The psychological explanations of how an observer acquires prosocial and antisocial behaviors and attitudes through modeling were discussed in Chapter 2 in connection with the effects of imitation. It was pointed out that the real-life, symbolic, and representational models supplied (or not supplied) in schools have a marked effect on students.

The importance of model or exemplary identifying figures and their influence on behavior are well illustrated in modern advertising, especially television commercials. A favorite technique is to have the product endorsed by someone with wide-ranging, popular appeal as an identification figure. Similar techniques associate prestige with the product: "Scientists have found . . . ," "four out of five doctors recommend . . . ," "the thinking man . . . ." So personal is the appeal that it implies that the buyer will feel better if he buys the product, because he will be like whoever does the endorsing or recommending.

Before turning to implications for the schools, it is important to realize that the opposite of identification, *rejection*, also can happen. The model one identifies with must provide satisfaction, reward, good feelings, a better state of affairs for the observer or individual. For example, a child can reject a parent or teacher if he feels that the adult is not providing satisfaction, help in overcoming difficulties, and love and understanding.

In view of the discussion so far, it would seem rather obvious that the school should assess the effectiveness of two vital aspects of its program in providing exemplary models — the teachers themselves, of course, and the instructional materials. Unfortunately, the schools have not been notably successful in providing models in either of these ways.

Consider the teachers. All too often, they have not regarded themselves as possible identifying figures for their students. Particularly at the elementary school level (but also at junior and senior high school levels), teachers do have considerable identification potential. As a matter of fact, the teacher often is referred to as an authority in the home and quoted by the child in discussions with his parents. Boys, however, have particular difficulties in finding models in the elementary school because it is dominated by women teachers; about 85 percent of elementary school teachers are women (N.E.A., 1967). Fortunately, the teachers are more balanced in the secondary schools; at those levels about 54 percent of the teachers are men and 46 percent women (N.E.A., 1967). In addition to a more even sex balance, a wider range of teacher personalities representing different types of persons would increase the possibility of students finding some teachers with whom they can identify. Obviously, each teacher appeals to some students more than to others.

Sex of the teacher is an objective attribute that could easily be considered when selecting the staff of a school. There are other intangible attributes that are equally important, though more difficult to predict or assess. In Chapter 7 some of the terms used to describe the most admired and most successful teachers were listed. They include warm, enthusiastic, friendly, cheerful, sociable, interesting, knowledgeable, businesslike, and so forth. Recall the teachers you admired most. To what extent did you admire them because of the kinds of characteristics just mentioned? It is highly likely that teachers so characterized have more potential as identifying figures and thus are able to influence student attitudes in wholesome, desirable directions. It is also quite likely that a teacher who lacks such characteristics will be rejected by the student, who will thus reject not only the teacher, but also the attitudes and values associated with the teacher and the school.

Instructional materials used in the school also need careful examination. Just as an insufficiently wide range of teacher types or models is available for students to identify with, instructional materials also may not provide an adequate range of identifying models. The basic textbooks and library books, including fiction and biography, are often inadequate for many students because the possible identifying characters are too unrealistic to serve as exemplary models. Also, a disproportionate amount of school literature depicts the lives and circumstances of only a small segment of the total population. In other words, it is not representative of the family and home situations from which many children come or of the occupations and successes they will achieve as adults. Too frequently, overly dramatic achievement is stressed. In many books the hero is so magnificently successful and the circumstances are so different from usual life that many boys will not imitate him. Heroines are usually of two types — highly ambitious and eminently successful or excessively kind, timid, and lacking in ambition. Many girls will not imitate either type.

Reading material should be carefully examined to assess the attitudes and values presented. For example, how many stories or biographies are there of men who have become famous through victory in war, as compared with men who have worked industriously for peace? How many are there of men who have been leaders in labor organizations, teaching, and the ministry? How many are there of men who have achieved eminence who came from wealthy as compared with poor economic backgrounds? How many are there of women who have achieved prominence in the theater, literature, and music, as compared with successful careers in teaching, stenographic work, and homemaking?

3. Provide Pleasant Emotional Experiences with Attitude Objects

The pleasure principle carries strong weight in the learning of attitudes. If a teacher wishes to have children develop favorable attitudes toward school, he will make the classroom a pleasant, attractive, and comfortable place. Presenting a good personal appearance, showing warmth and enthusiasm toward students, demonstrating interest in the subject matter, and making it possible for each student to experience success with some school learning tasks — all contribute to making the school and the school day a pleasant emotional experience for students. Recall that in classrooms of teachers who provide less praise and encouragement, there is a greater loss of positive attitudes than in classrooms of teachers who provide more praise and encouragement (Flanders, Morrison, & Brode, 1968). Pupil attitudes toward the teacher and the learning activities are related to teacher behavior. The complexity of differential pupil reaction to teachers is probably caused by underlying attitudinal factors. That these attitudinal factors influence students' perceptions of teachers' behaviors and their consequent learning in school is pointed out by Goldberg (1968). In this study, students classified as "high compulsives" perceived teachers as significantly less authoritarian than did students classified as "low compulsives." The high-compulsive students did less work when the teacher was perceived as nonauthoritarian. The low-compulsive students did more work when the teacher was perceived as nonauthoritarian.

Because acquiring and changing attitudes involve changes in feelings also, teachers and others who wish to facilitate positive attitude development should make common-sense use of pleasant emotional appeals. Any emotional experience for an individual is likely to have effects on his attitudinal behavior. Emotional appeals through real-life situations, motion pictures, and reading materials generate the identifying responses in an observer that he would have if he were experiencing the emotion himself. For example, a person winces if he sees someone else stub his toe or cut himself.

A note of caution, however, is in order. Too strong an emotional appeal may lead to unanticipated and undesired effects — particularly if threats of fear or strong negative emotional appeals are made. For example, an attempt was made to influence high school students to practice good dental habits by emphasizing the ill effects of improper habits. Two comparison groups were given similar information but with graded decreases in the emotional fear-arousal appeal. Follow-up questioning of all these students about brushing their teeth indicated decreasingly good habits, ranging down from those to whom little emotional appeal was made to those with whom a strong negative emotional appeal was used (Janis & Feshback, 1953).

Apparently, too strong an emotional appeal causes the individual to reject the attempt to modify his attitudes. Factors associated with the characteristics of individuals who are more or less capable of accepting and adjusting to intense, sustained emotional appeals are not known. It does appear, however, that common sense use of mildly pleasant emotional experiences and appeals associated with attitude objects leads to desirable attitude acquisition and modification.

4. Extend Informative Experiences

Let us consider first the role of information in the initial acquisition of attitudes. The term *information* as used includes all sources of experience with an attitude object. There are many sources of information; they include direct experiences with persons, ideas, and objects, reading books and other printed material, listening to the radio, watching television, seeing films, and the like. Even though information is most effective in the initial acquisition of attitudes, it should be kept in mind that it is not completely determining. New attitudes based on information are usually formed in the context of other preexisting attitudes and are formed so as to be compatible with these related preexisting attitudes.

The effect of informative experiences on the development of attitudes depends on whether or not the individual already had an attitude toward the attitude object. Not surprisingly, informative experiences are most effective when the individual does not have a well-established attitude. In such a case an individual's attitude is shaped by the information to which he is exposed, and initial acquisition is facilitated. If the individual already has a firmly established attitude, the role of information on attitude modification is more complex. The influence of additional information on the direction and degree of attitude change is a function of situational factors and of the source, medium, and form and content of the information (Krech et al., 1962).

Arranging for direct experiences with attitude objects as an informational source is highly effective in initial attitude acquisition, as well as attitude modification. One possible difficulty in arranging such direct experiences is that unpleasant emotions may be produced and unfavorable information gathered. For example, more direct contacts between black people and white people may produce favorable attitudes or they may intensify prejudices. The public schools are in the midst of a vast social experiment based in part on the assumption that integration of black and white children in schools will result in more harmonious relations between these groups. Under various exchange programs between the

United States and other countries, high school and college students are studying in foreign countries on the assumption that these exchange programs will result in better understanding and more favorable attitudes. (The effectiveness of such programs is reflected in the increased frequency of junior-year-abroad options at the college level.)

Turning to the influence of additional information on preexisting attitudes, note that situational factors, source, medium, and form and content of the new information all affect the direction and degree of attitude change. Most *situational factors* relate to group, as opposed to individual, informational experiences. These factors will be discussed in the next section. It should be noted here, however, that one highly effective situational factor concerns commitment of attitude change. If a person makes a public commitment to a change in attitude, he will be less likely to revert to the attitude held before information exposure. In general, public commitment has been found to be an effective attitude change procedure. Making an attitude change decision that is not public, however, has been found to be ineffective (Hovland, Harvey, & Sherif, 1957).

As is the case in initial attitude acquisition, the *source* of the information is critical in determining its effectiveness in attitude change. Who says what is crucially important. Among the salient characteristics of an effective information source are the individual's perceptions of its attractiveness and credibility. If the information source is a person, his group affiliations are also important. An individual will have a greater tendency to modify his attitudes as a result of new information if he sees the information source as trustworthy or credible, if the source is attractive to the individual, if the source is in accord with the preexisting attitude, and if the group affiliations of the source are similar to those of the individual. For example, the presumed generation gap stressed by young people who assert that you cannot trust people who are more than 30 years old is based on the idea that people more than 30 are not credible or attractive and do not have group affiliations that are consistent with youth groups. Likewise, student demonstrators are more likely to be influenced by student leaders than institutional leaders.

The nature of the information *medium* is also an influential factor in effectiveness of attitude change. Radio, television, films, newspapers, magazines, personal word of mouth—all are communication media that carry information with attitude-modification potential for the information receiver. Indeed, the vastly increased means of rapid communication in recent years are seen by some to have caused a communication implosion (McLuhan, 1967). Nevertheless, despite the improvement in the range and instantaneous reporting qualities of mass communication media, there is almost universal agreement that personal influence and word-of-mouth communication are more effective in changing attitudes (Krech et al., 1962). Mass communication media can influence face-to-face, word-of-mouth communication, however, and through that route the media do have enormous potential for effecting change in individual attitudes. The wise teacher takes advantage of the effectiveness of mass communication media in graphic and dramatic information presentations. Television and radio are essential to the modern school, as a matter of fact. Furthermore, discussions led by teachers that are related to presentations on mass communication media outside of schools, but that also are pertinent to subject matter or other educational objectives, offer increased possibilities for effective change in student attitudes.

The *form and content* of information are important influences in attitude change. New information sometimes changes attitudes in the direction implied by the content, but not always. When the distance between an individual's preexisting attitude and the information content is small, he judges the information as fair and factual and tends to change his attitude in the direction of the content. However, with increasing distance between the individual's attitude and the information content, the favorable judgment is sharply reduced, the information is perceived as propagandistic and unfair, and the individual tends to entrench his former attitude (Hovland & Pritzker, 1957).

Implications for teachers in implementing the instructional guide "extend informative experiences" in school classrooms are numerous for both initial attitude acquisition and attitude modification. The reader can now make certain inferences about the source and nature of informative experiences. To round out the picture, however, a curriculum example is presented later in this chapter.

5. Use Group Techniques To Facilitate Commitment

Three group techniques for attitude modification that almost any teacher may use are: (1) receiving and discussing information in groups; (2) group decision-making; (3) role-playing.

Receiving and Discussing Information in Groups. Watching television, listening to the radio, or receiving information through a lecture are much more effective if done in group settings, rather than individually. Supporting evidence can be found in a study by Kelly and Woodruff (1956). An experimental group of college subjects who heard prestigious members of their college group support (through applause and other means of visible approval) a speech that opposed their preexisting values and attitudes changed more in the direction of the speech than did a control group that was told that the applauding audience was a group of townspeople. More informal evidence in the practices of public performers also supports this point. For example, producers of a performance often use paid "plants" who sit in the audience and show visible signs of appreciation to generate audience approval. To some extent, the use of "canned" laughter and applause is intended to fulfill the same purpose in radio and television.

On a more personal level, the experience of listening to the radio or watching television is different if done in groups than alone. Group listening is more effective than solitary listening, particularly if the majority of the group is favorable to what is being presented; it is less effective if a majority of the group is opposed to the content of the presentation. Some evidence from a study by Mitnick and McGinnies (1958) supports this assertion and also provides a bridge between individual and group *reception* of a communication and group decision-making resulting from *discussion*. These investigators assessed the effects on groups of high school students of a film on racial tolerance. Students who scored high, middle, and low in ethnocentrism were identified and were then assigned randomly to one of three groups. One group saw a film unfavorable to ethnocentrism but did not discuss it; another group saw and discussed the film; the control group neither saw nor discussed the film. The film significantly reduced prejudice in highly prejudiced students in the "film-alone" condition. In the "film-discussion" condition, the effects of the film on these students were much smaller. Apparently, the discussion tended to *counteract* the effect of the film on them. Examination of the transcripts of the discussions revealed that the highly prejudiced students spent most of the discussion time expressing their anti-Negro attitudes, thus reinforcing their attitudes and counteracting the film. The low-prejudiced groups, in contrast, tended to examine the general problem of group prejudice raised by the film, thus reinforcing their attitudes and, therefore, reinforcing the effects of the film on them. Two further findings are of interest. The stability of the attitude change one month later was greater for the film-discussion groups than for the film-alone groups. The latter had regressed significantly toward their original attitudes.

Group Decision-Making. When an individual shares in making a decision he will tend to behave in accordance with that decision to a greater extent than when he does not take an active part. Small groups permit relatively free discussion. It is possible for attitudes and behaviors to be changed by the give and take in discussion, by the reinforcing and negating of expressions by the members, and by the emotional commitment involved in decision-making. It is obvious that students want to be involved in group decision-making—their pleas for self-governance (particularly at the college level but also in high schools) are increasing in number and intensity. True self-governance could be beneficial to all. For example, it could be arranged in the schools at all levels that most of the students, organized into small groups, would agree themselves on certain behaviors implied by the attitudes they also agreed to be desirable. They might agree on such things as getting to class on time, keeping the school clean, and similar behaviors. The result of this group agreement would be group commitment, with the further result that there would be much less need for the policing and the strict rules now thought necessary in many schools. In schools, as well as in other aspects of community living, commitment to socially approved attitudes is sorely needed.

Role-Playing. The technique of role-playing, in which one publicly expresses attitudes opposed to one's private attitudes, is also a promising group method to foster desirable attitude change. Often the individual begins to adopt the attitudes he publicly espouses. As a matter of fact, in real life, people often find themselves in situations in which behavior norms require them to act toward members of a minority group or toward other attitude objects in ways that are opposed to their private attitudes. It seems that role-playing results in attitude change when social support is a reward for such change.

In school situations, various forms of role-playing are employed, but usually unrehearsed dramatizations dealing with a social or psychological problem are the method chosen. In most role-playing situations, students use only the information they already have, but sometimes information is given to the students. There is none of the rehearsing, memorizing of lines, or coaching that are essential to ordinary dramatic presentations. Role-playing in classroom settings is generally based on informal class discussions dealing with a wide variety of topics. Students informally dramatize such behavioral characteristics as shyness, aggressiveness, good manners, prejudice, courtesy, and dishonesty. They may also carry out roles drawn from novels, short stories, newspaper stories, and plays which the class has studied. As they portray roles, students express their feelings as well as present information, thus combining emotional and informational experiences related to the underlying attitudes.

Attitude changes resulting from role playing may come about because the role player is impressed by his own arguments and illustrations and the convincing appeals that he uses to stimulate others. Perhaps, also, the role-player interprets his performance as a rewarding experience that gives him emotional satisfaction. Another possible explanation for attitude change through role playing is related to Festinger's theory of *cognitive dissonance* (Festinger, 1957). Dissonance is defined as having contradictory cognitions—attitudes or opinions—at the same time. Such dissonance is thought to be psychologically uncomfortable and to motivate the individual to make an attempt to reduce it, to strive for consonance. Dissonance may occur within the individual who, in playing a role, must express an attitude different from his actual private attitude. One way to reduce the dissonance is to change the private attitude so that it is consonant with the attitude expressed in role-playing.

Whatever the explanation, the effects of role-playing on attitude change seem to be considerable on college subjects used in research. Its effects on children and high school students are not as clearly established. It seems likely, however, that role-playing is more effective in helping these younger students acquire new attitudes than in changing attitudes already firmly fixed. It can be hypothesized also that role-playing is more effective in general with school-age children than with adults.

There are some cautions connected with role-playing that should be remembered. A teacher should not put a student in a role-playing situation in which he would feel highly uncomfortable. For example, it would be most unfortunate to have a shy, withdrawn child try to play the role of either a shy, withdrawn child or a boisterous, aggressive child in front of his classmates. The best procedure for a teacher who knows the children well is to discuss the role-playing situation, including the range of characters or roles, with the whole class and then to ask for volunteers. (Needless to say, the teacher *should* know the children well before trying role-playing.)

6. Arrange for Appropriate Practice

This guide carries the same meaning here as in earlier chapters. Attitudes are not acquired through memorizing and talking about verbal statements. Rather, from many specific experiences the individual integrates the meaning and feeling components into increasingly larger and more stable behavior patterns. Gradually, with increasing age, attitudes and values are internalized, and the individual is characterized by behavior patterns that reflect these internalized attitudes and values.

The school that proposes to influence student attitudes must provide appropriate practice contexts within the classroom, the school building, and the school-community environs. If having students friendly with one another is desired, what kinds of practice opportunities might be arranged? First, the teacher, recognizing the possibility of being an exemplary model, makes certain that he manifests lively, favorable interest in the students. As the students show their liking for one another, the teacher confirms or reinforces these responses with verbal statements, positive remarks about the behavior of good friends, an approving nod, a smile, or other gestures. The teacher does not reject any child; nor does he condone rejection. Much teacher guidance is needed to prevent some children from rejecting others. The child who comes to school dirty is sent to the washroom to clean up when he first arrives at school; a suitable task is found for the slow-learning child; the highly aggressive child is given opportunity to express his aggressive feelings against indestructible objects or in other ways; the withdrawing child is helped to develop some skill or interest gradually, then is incorporated into smaller groups of two or three, and finally into the total classroom group.

Elementary school teachers are generally aware of the need to help most children make at least one or two good friends in the classroom group, and they often are effective in giving such help. High school and college teachers frequently do not accept the fact that having students friendly with one another is a worthwhile objective; thus they may be unconcerned or even unaware that some children are completely rejected by the rest of the class. There are boys and girls who, as they sit through five or six high school classes each day, cannot forget that among all the other adolescents in all these classes, there is not one whom they can call a friend.

Consider another positive value—to make a contribution to society. The child's society is his classroom when he is in school. Each student can be helped to identify something unique he can contribute within and for the classroom group. In the primary grades the "sharing" or "show-and-tell-time" periods serve this purpose. During these periods the children report out-of-school experiences and/or bring objects to school, and each has an opportunity to bring something of high interest to the classroom group. In the intermediate grades making a mural, decorating the room, making oral reports, and finding and bringing together various collections provide practice opportunities. In high school and college classes sharing activities do not usually take place in regular class settings. Students make their unique contributions to a group in special classes or extracurricular activities, such as the band, the school play, the school newspaper, athletic events, and the many club activities.

Another set of attitudes—respect for others, respect for property, and honesty—can be practiced effectively in schools if students are given opportunities. High school students can practice these attitudes through student council or student government activities. Another way to provide opportunities to practice and apply these attitudes is to follow a policy of leaving lockers unlocked. If students accept the attitudes, they will not steal property from the lockers of their schoolmates. If these kinds of attitudes cannot be practiced in school through opportunities provided by teachers and other school authorities, students cannot be expected to apply them in the larger community outside the school.

Most of the examples given of opportunities to practice behavior associated with attitudes have to do with nonsubject-matter areas. Teachers should also plan ways to arrange for appropriate practice opportunities within basically cognitive subject-matter areas through small-group work, role-playing, and the like. An example of such opportunities will be described and discussed after a brief consideration of the final instructional guide.

7. Encourage Independent Attitude Cultivation

The process of acquiring a new attitude is much the same as acquiring *any* new habitual way of behaving, for example, brushing one's teeth after eating, writing more legibly, or driving with more consideration for other motorists. One begins with intent and then practices. Carefully considering the importance of the attitude in one's life, deciding to carry out the behavior, and taking every opportunity to act on the new attitude lead to stability and eventual incorporation of the attitude without conscious effort. It is easier to read these words than to carry out what they imply. Anyone with a deeply ingrained habit of smoking cigarettes who has tried to stop will testify to the truth of that statement. Frequently, one needs social support for individual efforts.

Nevertheless, although a beginning must come from the individual's intent, teachers can help students to develop positive attitudes through encouraging independent attitude cultivation in a number of ways. For one thing, they can facilitate attitude self-improvement efforts by students through personal counseling. Successful attempts to change behavior in accord with favorable attitudes should be recognized and rewarded. Often, keeping a record or tally will help. Consider, for example, the student who always seems to be getting into trouble at recess or disrupting classroom activities through displays of overly energetic aggressive behaviors. It is quite proper for the teacher to offer praise after non-aggressive recess times or after prolonged periods of good behavior in the classroom. In this way an intent to persist in nondisruptive, nonaggressive behavior can be fostered.

A deeply ingrained habit, such as smoking or writing illegibly, is not easily broken. A firmly established attitude, such as prejudice in the area of religion, race, or politics, is perhaps equally difficult to change deliberately. The suggestions given here are thus more applicable to the acquisition and establishment of *new* attitudes than to the extinction of attitudes already firmly established. This statement has serious implications for teachers and teaching. If for any reason a prospective teacher does not seem to be able to acquire a liking for the subject matter, for teaching duties in general, and for the actual day-to-day living in a classroom with pupils, and if he cannot deliberately change his own attitudes, he should consider another career. A prospective teacher should realize, therefore, how vital his student teaching experiences are—not only in enabling him to learn how to apply actual techniques and methods, but also in enabling him to assess his own attitudes and feelings toward teaching.

A Curriculum Illustration

This description of a one-year course, "Man: A Course of Study," for upper elementary grades illustrates the application of some of the principles and instructional guides related to attitudes as they might interact with subject matter. (The course was developed by the Social Studies Curriculum Program of the Educational Development Center, Inc., in Cambridge, Massachusetts.) The general concerns of the course are defined by three questions:

> What is human about human beings?
> How did they get that way?
> How can they be made more so?

The content of the course is man: his nature as a species and the forces that shaped and continue to shape his humanity. Fundamental questions about the nature of man are introduced by way of animal contrasts. In sequence, students study the life cycle of the salmon, the behavior patterns of herring gulls, the social behavior of baboons, and the concept of culture through the Netsilik Eskimos. Attention is focused on the interaction of five humanizing forces or themes: (1) tool-making, (2) language, (3) social interaction, (4) child-rearing patterns and the management of man's prolonged childhood, and (5) cosmology—world view or man's urge to explain.

The objectives of "Man: A Course of Study" are summarized in a nontechnical manner as follows:

1. To give students confidence in the power of their own minds.
2. To give them respect for the powers of thought concerning the human condition—man's plight and man's potential.
3. To provide them with a set of workable models for analyzing the nature of the social world in which they live, the condition in which man finds himself.
4. To impart an understanding of the capacities of man as a species in contrast to other animals.
5. To instill concern for the human condition in all its forms, whatever the race or the culture.

The course is abundantly rich in learning materials in a broad range of media, styles, and complexity. The primary source of data is ethnographic film in color with natural sound and a minimum of commentary. Children gather information and form questions on the basis of repeated film viewings in small and large groups. Some 23 booklets accompanying the course are another important source of data. Some of these are data booklets; others are concept booklets. In addition, some booklets are devoted to field notes, journals, poems, songs, and stories. Other learning activities that permit children to work with a minimum of teacher direction in small groups and individually are games, construction exercises, and observation projects. Tapes, film strips, maps, posters, and photomurals round out the course materials.

The materials were developed and chosen not only for their cognitive aspects, but also with consideration for the *affective* characteristics of learners—the emotions, attitudes, and values of the child. For example, stories and poems were selected with drama, pathos, and humor in mind. Through the films, booklets, and other course materials and activities, an atmosphere is established that encourages children to express their feelings openly and to create other materials that reflect their *own* thoughts, interests, and attitudes.

The course was constructed to be taught in a student-centered, open-ended, inquiry-discovery fashion. A teacher in-service workshop program for use with the course includes readings, tapes, and other materials to acquaint teachers with the underlying pedagogy. Teachers are encouraged to work with materials that honestly and in a personal way raise questions with no clear-cut answers. Controversial issues such as reproduction, aggression, killing, religion, life, and death are traditionally taboo areas in schools, but students quite naturally are much interested in them. Because this stage of development in the student is crucial for the acquisition of attitudes about these issues, teachers are encouraged not to avoid them, but to promote positive attitude acquisition about them and encourage independent attitude cultivation by the children.

A curriculum such as "Man: A Course of Study" is profuse with opportunities to apply the principles and instructional guides discussed in this chapter. Because the content of the course *is* man, salient characteristics of important attitude objects constantly come up; furthermore, the course provides an excellent forum for identifying the attitudes to be taught in such areas as aggression, intergroup relations, parenthood and family living, the cooperative activities of a society, and the like. Also, exemplary models are provided in abundance in the materials, as well as in teacher behaviors. Students can compare episodes involving the behavior and feelings of characters in the films with their own behaviors and feelings. The Netsilik films, particularly, enable the students to make comparisons with their own behaviors and feelings in the context of pleasant emotional experiences. Note, for example, one student's reaction:

> In the films, I liked the Eskimos best because when they showed a film, they seemed more like us. They sort of gave me a picture of my family if I were out there. Like the time they were crossing the river. If my father were there, I guess he would cross it first, just to see how deep it was, and then he would carry my mother across. And I'm just as tall as he is, so I could walk across, but my sister would have to be carried. And my mother would help carry something on her head as we walked across. I could, so could my father. That's one thing in the picture I saw. And my mother always combs her hair and makes my father

happy. And we are always together, and they looked sort of happy together. When you're young, whatever they do and your mother is happy, that makes you more happy. (E.D.C., 1969, p. 5)

Extending informative experiences is implicit in the content and materials of the course. In this connection, the credibility of the information sources is increased because the course materials are prepared by anthropologists and ethnologists and often presented in the form of film, tape, and data books produced during actual ethnographic field studies and field research. Group techniques are employed frequently as the teacher becomes less the focus of the classroom and students grow in their ability to express ideas and discuss ideas with one another. That students recognize the value of small-group work can be seen in another quotation from the course evaluation. One student reported in an interview:

In a small group you can talk about one thing and everybody can talk. In big groups you have to wait and then you have to listen and everybody's going to talk and it gets confusing. If we worked in a big group . . . we couldn't say whatever we wanted to say. But in the small ones we could say, and then we could build onto it, and then we could tell it to everyone. (E.D.C., 1969, p. 7)

Many opportunities for group activities, group decision-making, role-playing, and other group techniques can be employed within the course format to achieve the feelings of group solidarity and group goals that in turn facilitate attitude commitment. For example, studying the social organization of baboons leads to children working together in groups to re-create the environment and its inhabitants.

Opportunities to arrange for appropriate practice also are plentiful. Because the course is dependent on the *sharing* of learning among students, children who do not read or write easily can still view or listen and can effectively express their thoughts in discussion. For example, in an initial activity, the teacher might start a discussion of what makes man human—what differentiates man from lower animals. Invariably, man's emotions will be identified as one differentiating characteristic. This can lead to examination of emotional expressions shown in the human beings who appear in the photographic *Family of Man*. The teacher can then introduce the idea that each student can create his own montage box: Each student identifies an emotion he is interested in, searches for examples of manifestations in human figures in magazines, clips these out, and pastes them in unique ways on a box. On completion each presents his montage box to the classroom group and has classmates guess the emotion being represented; then all discuss aspects of the emotion from their own points of view. In this way, students of all ability levels can make unique contributions, discuss their attitudes, and practice them in relevant situations.

14.10. What does it mean to say that education should clarify the meanings of attitudes and provide informative experiences about them, rather than indoctrinate? Can you identify teachers of yours who did indoctrinate? How do you intend to behave as a teacher in this aspect of teaching?

14.11. Who should identify the attitudes to be taught in schools? Which attitudes do you think the schools should teach?

14.12. With whom do you identify? Have these figures affected your attitudes? How? Do you consider yourself a good identifying figure for students you might teach? Why?

14.13. Why are pleasant emotional experiences especially important in the modification of attitudes?

14.14. What factors should be considered in connection with attitudes in extending informative experiences in school settings?

14.15. How can role-playing, group decision-making, and receiving and discussing information in groups be used in school situations to influence student attitudes? Under what conditions might each of these techniques produce attitudes opposite to those intended?

14.16. Select any specific attitude. How might a teacher arrange appropriate practice opportunities to exercise the attitude?

14.17. Do you think you can deliberately cultivate and/or change your own attitudes? How would you go about it? Try it.

14.18. Think of the attitudes you consider desirable that are associated with the subject matter you intend to teach. How can you organize the subject matter so that in teaching it, you will increase the probability that your students will adopt the attitudes?

SUMMARY

Attitudes and values are among the most vital outcomes learned in school, for they are important in determining how the individual reacts to situations and also what he seeks in life. Thus attitudes and values serve both as mediators of responses and as motivational forces. An attitude is a system of three interrelated components — a cognitive component (information), an affective component (feelings), and an action-tendency component (behavior predisposition). The main difference between an attitude and a concept is that the former directly influences the individual's acceptance or rejection of attitude objects — ideas, persons, things, situations. Attitudes, to a greater extent than concepts and psychomotor abilities, are acquired through imitation and conditioning. Attributes of individuals and of the groups they belong to are important determiners of attitude acquisition and development. Particularly important are primary groups and reference groups — groups the individual uses as a standard against which he compares the adequacy of his behavior.

Some attitudes are learned early and become more firmly established with increasing experience; others undergo change. Attitude learning and modification have been demonstrated at all school levels. Pleasant feelings, success, and rewards produce favorable and lasting attitudes; unpleasant feelings, failure, and punishments lead to unfavorable attitudes and also, in some cases, to the extinction of previously favorable attitudes.

When the attitudes children and youth *should* learn in school have been identified and agreed on, a program of instruction can be organized that will result in the efficient learning of these attitudes. The learning of attitudes is facilitated through (1) providing exemplary models, (2) providing pleasant emotional experiences, (3) extending informative experiences, (4) using group techniques, (5) arranging for appropriate practice, and (6) encouraging independent attitude cultivation. These principles and guides, as the discussions throughout the chapter imply, are applicable to all outcomes in the affective domain—tastes, attitudes, preferences, values, interests, and motives.

SUGGESTIONS FOR FURTHER READING

BORGATTA, E. F., ed. *Social psychology: Readings and perspective*. Chicago: Rand McNally, 1969.

W. H. Sewell, "Some Recent Developments in Socialization Theory and Research," pages 213-222, points out how the study of roles, social class, and social structure is contributing to a better understanding of socialization—the processes by which individuals selectively acquire the skills, knowledge, attitudes, values, and motives of the groups of which they are or will become members. M. Rokeach, "Definition of Attitude," pages 404-410, discusses an attitude as an enduring, persistent organization of predispositions.

ERON, L. D. Relationship of TV viewing habits and aggressive behavior in children. In Sarason, I. G., ed., *Contemporary research in personality*. Princeton, N. J.: Van Nostrand, 1969, pp. 189-192.

About 700 children participated in this study which showed a positive correlation between the aggressive behaviors in boys and the extent of violence portrayed in their favorite television programs.

HAMACHECK, D. E., ed. *Human dynamics in psychology and education: Selected readings*. Boston: Allyn and Bacon, 1968.

Three of five essays are helpful in understanding the attitudes of children, youth, and teachers: F. Redl, "Our Troubles with Defiant Youth," pages 451-458; M. L. Haimowitz, "Criminals Are Made, Not Born," pages 459-476; H. Beilin, "Teachers' and Clinicians' Attitudes Toward the Behavior Problems of Children: A Reappraisal," pages 477-490.

KUHLEN, R. G., & HOULIHAN, N. Adolescent heterosexual interest in 1942 and 1963. In Grinder, R. E., ed., *Studies in adolescence: A book of readings in adolescent development*. New York: Macmillan, 1969, pp. 184-187.

Heterosexual interest is greater among adolescents, but it does not necessarily start at an earlier age. (Most other readings in this book are concerned with socialization and provide useful insights into understanding adolescent behavior.)

MUSSEN, P. H., CONGER, J. J., & KAGAN, J. *Child development and personality*. New York: Harper & Row, 3rd ed., 1969.

This is the most complete, readable, integrated information on attitude and personality development. Teachers at different school levels will profit from studying the appropriate part: the preschool years, pages 281-423; middle childhood, pages 427-601; adolescence, pages 605-759.

NEALE, D. C., & PROSHEK, J. M. School related attitudes of culturally disadvantaged elementary school children. In Ripple, R. E., ed., *Readings in learning and human abilities*. New York: Harper & Row, 2nd ed., 1971.

The school-related attitudes of disadvantaged children are identified and discussed.

Chapter 15 Personality Integration and Discipline

The Nature of Personality Integration

personality
model of integrative adjustment

The Bases of Personality Integration

health and psychomotor skills
cognitive abilities
adequate means of adjustment
adequate self concept

Developmental Trends

presocial stage
symbiotic stage
impulsive stage
self-protective stage
conformist stage
conscientious stage
autonomous stage
integrated stage

Instructional Guides for Encouraging Personality Integration

develop an emotionally secure environment
encourage self-understanding and self-acceptance
help students to attain realistic goals
provide practice in meeting conflict situations

Personality Integration and Discipline

orderly classrooms to attain instructional objectives
classifications of behavior problems
causes of behavior problems
disciplinary practices
practical suggestions

many youth of today feel alienated from adult society, including their parents and their teachers. They feel they are not understood. Many also do not identify with the value systems of their parents or teachers. For example, they cannot see how adults can support mass murder by their sons in Vietnam and yet oppose peaceful demonstration by their children at home or how their parents can strive for even more of the good things of life for themselves and yet let the poor children of our inner cities and rural areas go hungry, cold, dirty, and neglected. Not finding satisfaction with the world as it is and becoming disillusioned about being able to change it for the better, many youth are turning to drugs, open rebellion against adults, and rejection of much of the curriculum content and code of conduct of the schools.

The dissatisfaction and disillusionment felt by many youths of today may make the teacher's task somewhat more difficult. But they also present the teacher with a challenge that is well worth meeting. In other words, despite the rebellion and rejection shown by many young people, it is still true that a skillful and understanding teacher can be helpful to almost every boy and girl in meeting and solving his daily problems of living with himself and others, in eventually becoming a well-integrated person. It hardly needs saying that the school and the classroom teacher *should* be concerned with the personality integration of students. Each individual strives toward integration, and the school should help the students in their search for human wholeness and integrity of personal development.

In this chapter, the role of the school and of the classroom teacher in furthering personality integration is examined by considering (1) the nature of personality integration, (2) the bases of personality integration, (3) developmental trends, (4) principles and instructional guides for encouraging personality integration, and (5) personality integration and discipline.

THE NATURE OF PERSONALITY INTEGRATION

There are many different organized theories about the nature, structure, and development of personality. These different views have evolved because they are based on a variety of ideas, methods, and assumptions. Our main guiding principle here, however, is this basic fact: Every individual is a unique person, not quite like anyone else. *Personality* is the concept or construct that describes this uniqueness and totality of an individual as a social being. It is interesting to note that the word "personality" is derived from the Latin word *persona*, which in ancient Rome referred to a mask worn by an actor or to the character being acted. From this comes the idea of the individual as a socially *perceived* entity (Horrocks, 1969).

Consider a definition of personality by a leading theorist, Gordon Allport. He defines personality as "the dynamic organization within the individual of those psycho-physical systems that determine his unique adjustment to his environment" (Allport, 1955, p. 48). A somewhat different definition is offered by Johnson and Medinus (1965, p. 444), who define personality as "the distinct and unique organization of traits in an individual as reflected in how he reacts to himself and others and in how they react to him, and also in how he meets frustrations and conflicts—that is, how he adjusts to his environments." Close study of these two definitions leads to the conclusion that personality has more than one attribute. The principal attribute of personality is the organization of the psychophysical systems within the individual. These systems include the knowledge and skills of the individual, his values, and his motives. Other corollary attributes include the individual's reactions to others, others' reactions to him, and his methods of adjusting to his environment. It follows that if the school is to help an individual reach human fulfillment and self-realization, it must seek to facilitate the development of an individual whose knowledge, skills, value system, and motives comprise an integrated whole.

One model of such an integrative adjustment has been summarized thus:

> This model of integrative adjustment as characterized by self-control, personal responsibility, social responsibility, democratic social interest, and ideals must be regarded only in the most tentative fashion. Nevertheless, it does seem to take into account some realistic considerations. It avoids the impossible conception of the normal person as one who is always happy, free from conflict, and without problems. Rather, it suggests that he may often fall short of his ideals; and because of ignorance, the limitations under which an individual lives in a complex world, or the strength of immediate pressures, he may sometimes behave in ways that prove to be shortsighted or self-defeating. Consequently, he knows something of the experience of guilt at times, and because he tries to be fully aware of the risks he takes, he can hardly be entirely free from fear and worry. On the other hand, a person who is congruent to the model is likely to be one who enjoys a relatively consistent and high degree of self-respect and who elicits a predominately positive and warm reaction from others. Moreover, it is such a person who seems to learn wisdom rather than hostile bitterness or pathologically frightened withdrawal from whatever disappointments or suffering may be his lot. . . . (Shoben, 1957, pp. 188-189)

Note that in evaluating adjustment one must make judgments about self-control, personal responsibility, social responsibility, democratic social interest, and ideals. This means, for example, that the thief or the delinquent cannot be considered well-adjusted personalities, no matter how well they may satisfy their own needs and no matter how rational their behavior may appear to themselves. Ethical values, including what is generally considered to be character, cannot be reasonably treated as separate from personality integration or integrative adjustment.

Character development usually refers to the internalization of ethical values. Separating character development from personality integration is impractical in education at home or in school. Teaching ethics unrelated to the emergent personality of the student is similar to being concerned with the student's actions but not his motives and goals. Encouraging student acceptance of ethical values is an entirely justifiable objective of education. It is part of the broader objective of influencing his personality.

THE BASES OF PERSONALITY INTEGRATION

The educational objective in connection with personality integration is to help develop students who can live comfortably with themselves and who accept a reasonable amount of responsibility for the welfare of others. Achieving this objective would result in buoyant, productive individuals with much zest for life and learning—fully functioning, self-actualizing persons who realize the richness of human fulfillment (Maslow, 1968; A.S.C.D., 1962).

Before treating conditions within the individual and the environment that are bases of personality integration, a brief discussion of the ethos of "modern" youth may reveal directions in which efforts are needed to help achieve the objective of personality integration. Many worried adults in the middle of the second half of the twentieth century point an accusing finger at the disorganization, lack of responsibility, absence of self-control, and so forth that they see in young people. Consider the following two quotations:

> Our youths now love luxury. They have bad manners, contempt for authority, disrespect for older people. Children nowadays are tyrants. They no longer rise when their elders enter the room. They contradict their parents, chatter before company, gobble their food, and tyrannize their teachers.

> Our young men have grown slothful. Their talents are left idle, and there is not a single honorable occupation for which they will toil day and night. Slumber and languor, and an interest in evil which is worse than slumber and languor, have entered into men's hearts. They sing and dance and grow effeminate, and curl their hair, and learn womanish tricks of speech; they are as languid as women, and deck themselves out with unbecoming ornaments. Without strength, without energy, they add nothing during life to the gifts with which they were born, and then they complain of their lot.

Concern about youth certainly is not unique to this adult generation. The first quotation is attributed to Socrates in about 399 B.C.; the second quotation is from the writings of Seneca in the first century A.D. (Cole & Hall, 1970).

Nevertheless, there are some scholars who deny that the current scene is simply an intensification or revisitation of the past. Mead (1970), for example, contends that we are in fact entering a totally new phase of cultural evolution. Her belief that we are on the verge of developing a new kind of culture rests on such analyses as the following:

> Today, nowhere in the world are there elders who know what the children know, no matter how remote and simple the societies are in which the children live. In the past there were always some elders who knew more than any children in terms of their experience of having grown up within a cultural system. Today there are none. It is not only that parents are no longer guides, but that there are no guides, whether one seeks them in one's own country or abroad.

There are no elders who know what those who have been reared within the last twenty years know about the world into which they were born. (Mead, 1970, p. 25)

There is little question that today's students know more and are more socially aware than any previous generation. Often their idealism takes the form of contempt for the older generation's hypocrisy, its failure to break out of institutional restraints and to act on its professed ideals in personal life. The resulting reactions are numerous — signs of disruption and discontent are apparent on many fronts.

Student activism at the college level in connection with civil rights, school governance, the Vietnam War, pollution, the draft, R.O.T.C. programs, racial prejudice, and other explosive issues is a manifestation of social and personal idealism. Many see society as absurd and the "establishment" as the enemy. They are concerned about the lack of relevance in institutions, and particularly in education. There are signs of a humanistic revolt favoring altruistic notions of service and a return to simplistic forms of life; as might be expected, those who hold these beliefs are opposed to technology, scientism, and depersonalization. And students are not passive about any of these issues. Social and political activism by groups such as the Students for a Democratic Society, the Black Panthers, the Weathermen, and many other organized and unorganized groups takes the form of mass demonstrations, building occupations, and other activities deliberately intended to disrupt. These behaviors and reactions are not restricted to college students of radical or revolutionary bent. There are signs of tension and unrest among some of the more conservative college students and among high school students as well. One report indicates that the "wave of student activism that engulfed college campuses in the late '60s is now beginning to hit high schools in full force. . . ."[1] This recalls the example of "protest" at the elementary school level quoted in Chapter 1.

Another identifiable reaction of the youth culture, a nonactivist reaction, is hardly more encouraging:

> Few of these young men and women have any doubt that they will one day be part of our society. They do not actively or enthusiastically *choose* to be part; rather they unreflectively assume that they *will* be part; and problems of "choosing" conventional adulthood . . . rarely even occur to them as such. They wonder about where they will fit, but not about whether. They take it for granted that they will one day "settle down"; and if it troubles them, they push it out of their minds or consider it a problem to be solved by finding a suitable wife and career. By and large they "approve" of American society if asked, though normally they do not think in these terms. Society is simply there.
>
> But at the same time, these young men and women often show a lack of deep commitment to adult values and roles. They are not alienated as are beatniks, delinquents. . . . Rather, they view the adult world they expect to enter with a subtle distrust, a lack of high expectations, hopes, or dreams, and an often unstated feeling that they will have to "settle" for less than they would hope for if they let themselves hope . . . the point is that they expect little in the way of personal fulfillment, growth, or creativity from their future roles in the public

---

[1]*Newsweek*, February 16, 1970, p. 65.

world. Essentially, they recognize that adulthood is a relatively cold, demanding, specialized, and abstracted world where "meaningful" work is so scarce they do not even ask for it. Thus, the majority stay "cool" when it comes to the "real world"; and "coolness" means above all detachment, lack of emotion, absence of deep commitment, not being either enthusiastic *or* rejecting of adulthood. (Keniston, 1965, pp. 396-397)

Other aspects of the youth culture that concern adults range from the increasing rate of delinquent behavior to long hair in boys, miniskirts in girls, the "hippie" cult, and the use of drugs. Drugs, in fact, have been elevated to the dimension of a severe legal and social problem in the last few years. An estimated 30 to 50 percent of all American secondary school students (approximately 14.5 million total) have tried a variety of drugs, particularly marijuana.[2]

Not all young people, of course, perhaps not even the majority of them, fit the descriptions we have given. However, the number who can be thus characterized is sufficiently great to demonstrate a need for the school as one agency of the community to intensify efforts to promote personality integration among students. With this consideration of youth today as a context, then, we turn our attention to the five conditions within the individual and the environment that are bases of personality integration, as illustrated in Fig. 15.1.

[2]*Newsweek*, February 16, 1970, p. 66.

Fig. 15.1. The building blocks of personality integration.

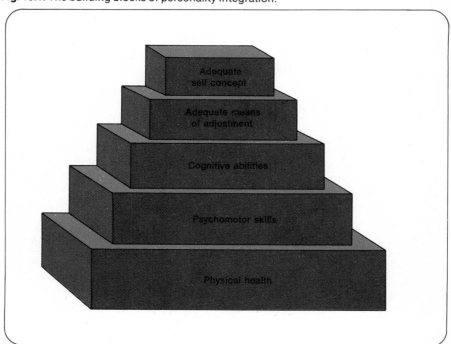

Health and Psychomotor Skills

Being extremely deficient in one or more of the psychomotor skills that are common to other children of about the same age may constitute a serious block to personality integration. Not being able to perform prestige-giving physical skills may lead the child to perceive himself in an unfavorable way, and he may later show withdrawing or aggressive behavior. Similarly, it may prevent his experiencing the usual give-and-take social relationships in play and recreational activities that other children normally enjoy. Just as the handicapped child can learn to adjust to a variety of home and school situations, so also the child much less proficient than others in such tasks as writing, singing, and football or basketball can learn to adjust, but to do so he needs much help from the teacher.

Chronic poor health or a physical handicap may color the individual's entire perceptions of himself and the world about him unfavorably. In so doing it may prevent him from acquiring adequate means of adjustment. It may interfere with, or at least limit, his acquisition or use of psychomotor and cognitive abilities. Not everyone with a chronic illness or physical handicap is maladjusted, of course. Some people with severe handicaps, such as being blind or deaf, being crippled, or being shut in for long periods of time, have made excellent adjustments. These people have themselves found adequate means of adjusting, despite their handicap or illness. In general, however, the school and the home justifiably attempt to promote good physical health in children and give considerable attention to such matters as adequate nutrition, adequate facilities for rest and relaxation, protection from disease and physical injuries, and cure or correction of a variety of illnesses and other physical impairments. For example, the statistics on drug use in high schools indicate that the school has both an *information* and a regulatory responsibility.

Cognitive Abilities

As health and psychomotor skills affect personality integration, so do intelligence and cognitive abilities. Children and youth of low intelligence and academic achievement are often less well accepted in the classroom than are those of low psychomotor abilities. Because of unfavorable reactions from others and less ability to deal with symbolic learning, the child of low intelligence may experience relatively severe adjustment problems. He may have difficulty in accepting himself, especially if he feels that his teacher and classmates do not accept him. It is not surprising, therefore, that anxiety and emotional disturbance are higher in children of low and average abilities than in children of high abilities (Feldhusen & Klausmeier, 1962). Appropriate individualization of instruction by the teacher, fitting what a student is asked to learn as closely as possible to what he is able to learn, can minimize negative personality effects.

Adequate Means of Adjustment

Living involves a continuous series of adjustments between satisfaction of individual needs and the demands of the environment, including the demands of other people in groups and society. To adjust means to change

in some way appropriate to certain requirements. It should be emphasized that psychological adjustment is *not* simply accepting the status
quo or conforming to present conditions and group demands with no attempt to alter circumstances. Maslow states it well:

> Adjust to what? To a bad culture? To a dominating parent? What shall we
> think of a well-adjusted slave? ... It seems quite clear that personality prob-
> lems may sometimes be loud protests against the crushing of one's psychological
> bones, of one's true inner nature. What is sick then is *not* to protest while this
> crime is being committed. (Maslow, 1968, p. 8)

With this emphasis in mind, the study of adjustment has to do with how
we make accommodations to fit the demands of our environment. Adjustment consists of the *processes* we use to manage these demands. As we
shall be concerned with it here, learning adequate means of psychological
adjustment refers more specifically to intrapersonal and interpersonal
relationships, particularly in frustrating situations where there is a conflict between demands.

A person's adjustment depends on his success in resolving conflicts.
Adequacy or inadequacy of adjustment may be less a matter of the
amount of conflict to which a person is exposed than of the extent to
which he has adequate means or techniques that permit satisfactory *solutions* to conflict. The crucial factor is the availability of some response
that meets the conflict successfully.

Lazarus (1963) has conceptualized two fundamental solutions in conflict situations—assimilation and accommodation. *Assimilation* involves
mastering or eliminating or rejecting one of the conflicting demands.
Goal-directed effort at mastering a demand, for example, involves al-
tering and improving a response. This, in turn, usually involves additional information or further practice of some skill. At this point the
problem-solving approach to social and emotional problems can be as productive as it is when applied to more purely intellectual problems, such as
those encountered in science, mathematics, and other subject-matter
fields. Once the new information or the higher-level skills are acquired, a
situation that was conflicting can, when encountered again, be a source of
satisfaction. Resolute trying is to be encouraged. Goal-oriented effort toward achievable goals resolving conflict, if developed in younger children,
should prove useful throughout life.

One difficulty in applying problem-solving techniques to frustrating
interpersonal problems is that self-esteem cannot easily be maintained
while the individual is securing information or developing the higher-
level skill. The adolescent who is fearful of having to be the announcer of
an assembly program hesitates to ask for help from his teacher or classmates, feeling that this would lower his status in the eyes of those who
selected him. Starting in the elementary grades, many children will not
attempt a new activity in a group situation for fear of presenting an unfavorable performance or appearance in the presence of others. In many
situations like these, one means of adjustment is through helping students to a better understanding of themselves and of the situation. If the
classroom is the nurturing environment that it should be, the students
will recognize that the teacher and classmates are helpful people. The

teacher can do much to create this type of environment and to facilitate better understanding.

Accommodation, the other fundamental solution to conflict situations, involves subordinating one of the conflicting demands and gratifying the other. For example, some students who try out for the athletic team, the school play, the music festival, or the art exhibit may not be accepted. Conflict can be quite intense for those who highly desire to be accepted but are rejected. If one goal is unattainable, however, an attainable goal can be substituted. In helping students find appropriate substitute goals, teachers should try to lead each student not to give up his original goal if he has a reasonable possibility of success. If a substitute goal seems advisable, it should be one that helps the student satisfy the same needs as the original goal as nearly as possible. For example, the high school student who wants to be a scientist but who is having difficulty in chemistry should not be encouraged to accept a substitute goal if there is reason to believe that he may do better in this and other science courses with improved or more persistent efforts. If this student has, with great effort, performed at only a mediocre level in previous science and mathematics courses, perhaps his interest in science could be related to mechanical drawing, advertising, or the like.

Several types of unconscious efforts to resolve conflict are classified under accommodation. These are basically ego-defense mechanisms whereby individuals deny or deceive themselves about actual circumstances to a greater or lesser degree without being aware of doing so. There is no universally agreed on list of ego defenses, but a summary table of ego-defense mechanisms, such as Table 15.1, is useful (this one was prepared for a text in abnormal psychology). The defenses described in the table, like other adjustment techniques, are neither desirable nor undesirable in themselves. Nevertheless, if they are used in meeting a large number of situations for long periods of time, the effects are damaging to mental health.

Adequate Self Concept

There are many definitions of self in the psychological literature (Patterson, 1966). The self is the person as he is known to that person. It is his private conception of his own personality. *Self concept* is what the individual refers to as I or me; it is the totality of meanings, attitudes, and feelings that the individual has about himself—the most complete description an individual could give of his present self. The self concept develops as the infant gradually becomes able to recognize the existence of a world separate from himself. As the individual grows and learns, his awareness of self intensifies and broadens to include more complete interpretations, in part through conditioning, identification, and imitation. Continually changing in its development, the self is highly flexible and responsive to environmental conditions. In this flexible sense, a person's self concept moves toward stability with increasing age; the individual does not markedly change his attitudes, feelings, and ideas about himself as time goes on.

Table 15.1 A Typical List of Ego-Defense Mechanisms

Mechanism	Function
Denial of reality	Protecting self from unpleasant reality by refusal to perceive it.
Fantasy	Gratifying frustrated desires in imaginary achievements.
Compensation	Covering up weaknesses by emphasizing desirable trait or making up for frustration in one area by overgratification in another.
Identification	Increasing feelings of worth by identifying with person or institution of illustrious standing.
Introjection	Incorporating external values and standards into ego structure so individual is not at their mercy as external threats.
Projection	Placing blame for difficulties on others or attributing one's own unethical desires to others.
Rationalization	Attempting to prove that one's behavior is "rational" and justifiable and thus worthy of self and social approval.
Repression	Preventing painful or dangerous thoughts from entering consciousness.
Reaction formation	Preventing dangerous desires from being expressed by exaggerating opposed attitudes and types of behavior and using them as "barriers."
Displacement	Discharging pent-up feelings, usually of hostility, on objects less dangerous than those that initially aroused the emotions.
Emotional insulation	Withdrawing into passivity to protect self from hurt.
Isolation	Cutting off affective charge from hurtful situations or separating incompatible attitudes by logic-tight compartments.
Regression	Retreating to earlier developmental level involving less mature responses and usually a lower level of aspiration.
Sublimation	Gratifying frustrated sexual desires in substitute nonsexual activities.
Undoing	Atoning for and thus counteracting immoral desires and acts.

Source: Coleman, 1950, p. 95. Copyright 1950 by Scott, Foresman and Company.

Even during the turbulent period of adolescence, an individual's self concept is relatively stable. For example, an investigation by Engel (1959) reported changes in self concept over a two-year period for students who were in the eighth and tenth grades. The relative stability of the self concept was demonstrated by an overall correlation of .53 between the tests given two years apart. Increased stability and movement toward a positive self concept with age was indicated by comparisons between the grade 8-10 group and the grade 10-12 group. Also, students whose self concept was negative at the first testing were significantly less stable in their self concepts than students whose self concept was positive initially.

It seems that a positive and stable self concept is likely to become more positive and more stable with age. Persons with stable and positive self concepts are characterized by certain approaches to perceiving themselves, responding emotionally to themselves and others, and to thinking about themselves and the events they experience. For example, a prospective teacher with a stable, positive self concept feels that he is attractive as a person, has acceptable social attitudes and goals, and is congenial but has enough independence to maintain his self-esteem and individuality in thought and action. He sees himself as a wholesome person, a desirable human being whose self concept is not far removed from his ideal self.

The *ideal self* is the desired self—the image the person has of what he wishes to be, what the person wishes most to be like. In persons with a positive, stable self concept there is enough difference between the real self and the ideal self to serve as a motive for self-improvement; yet at the same time the person feels that he is a desirable human being. An increasing discrepancy between the real and ideal selves brings maladjustment. Social adjustment, a sense of personal worth, and feelings of belonging are all correlated with proximity of the real and ideal selves or self-satisfaction. This assertion has been corroborated by several investigations. Mitchell (1959), for example, reports a study that shows that adolescents with a low degree of self-satisfaction (high discrepancy between real and ideal selves) felt themselves unable to meet parental expectations. They were tense, distractible, anxious, restless, unhappy, and oversensitive. Regardless of age, having a reasonably well-integrated personality involves acceptance of the present self, comfortable feelings in a variety of situations, and self-perceptions that are stable enough so that most situations encountered do not threaten one's feelings as a worthwhile individual.

The acceptance of one's self is positively associated with tolerance and willingness to accept others. For example, positive correlations ranging from .36 to .70 were found between scores of self-acceptance and acceptance of others (Berger, 1952). Also, Fey (1957) found different combinations of self-acceptance and acceptance of others to be related to personality integration as follows:

1. Students high in self-acceptance, but low in acceptance of others, overestimated their personal acceptability to others while ascribing degraded motives to others about them.

2. Those high in self-acceptance and in acceptance of others were healthiest in their positive confidence in self and others and asserted considerable self-determination and acceptance of personal responsibility for conduct and actions.

3. Those low in acceptance of self and high in acceptance of others shunned leadership almost completely.

4. Those low in acceptance of self and in acceptance of others exhibited high anxiety, impulsivity, low morale, overdependence, and a marked tendency to accommodate others.

15.1. What is the school's role in connection with personality integration?

15.2. What are the arguments for and against the uniqueness of "modern" youth? Which arguments are more convincing to you?

15.3. How can the use of problem-solving techniques contribute to personality integration? What are their limitations?

15.4. Can you provide examples of assimilation and accommodation (as used in the text) in your own efforts to meet conflict situations? How do you typically meet conflict situations?

15.5. Identify the bases of personality integration and relate them to your own life. In connection with school situations, which of them are less relevant to a teacher than to a student? Why?

DEVELOPMENTAL TRENDS

A general trend in personality development has already been indicated in Fig. 14.3. In this section the general trend will be treated more specifically by quoting from two case histories evolved in a longitudinal study of psychological development and by presenting a developmental conception of ego as one fundamental concept of personality.

Changes in Personality Variables with Age

Figure 15.2 shows correlations between the ratings of a number of personality variables at various points in the lives of children and young adults. The behavior of the children was actually rated as early as the first three years of life, but it is at the ages given in the figure that there is considerable stability with similar behavior in young adulthood. The following indication of what the terms imply may be helpful in interpreting the results:

Passivity refers to acquiescing or withdrawing in the face of attack or frustrating situations. *Affectional dependence* involves seeking affection, acceptance, and emotional reassurance from adults. *Behavior disorganization* implies uncontrolled behavior, such as violent crying and tantrums during the early years and destructive activity, rages, and tantrums during the school years. *Heterosexuality* during ages 10 to 14 involves interactions with members of the opposite sex, with special attention given to dating behavior. *Intellectual achievement* designates mastery over school tasks, including involvement in knowledge acquisition, amount of time spent in reading, and interest in scientific projects. *Sex-typed activity* is activity during childhood in line with the role of the particular sex. *Spontaneity* is the opposite of inhibition and apprehension with peers; one who is spontaneous interacts freely with his peers, without tension and discomfort in social situations.

A brief examination of Fig. 15.2 shows that there are sharp sex differences on many variables, especially dependence, behavior disorganization, and heterosexuality. Therefore, one should not generalize about either sex. For example, on the basis of heterosexual activity at age 10 to 14 one can predict sexual behavior in adult males with a fair degree of reliability; however, with females the prediction would not be better than chance. On the other hand, intellectual achievement and spontaneity

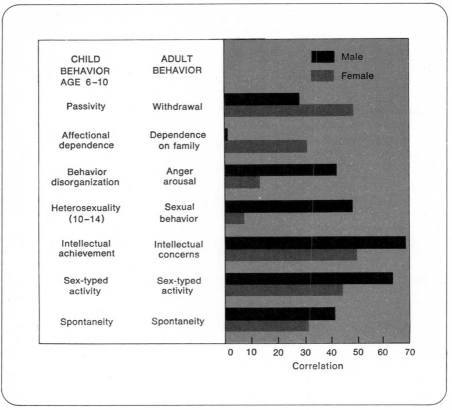

Fig. 15.2. Correlations between selected child behaviors (6 to 10 years of age) and phenotypically similar adult behaviors. (Kagan & Moss, 1962, p. 267)

show about the same correlations for both sexes from childhood to young adulthood. Inasmuch as the correlations between younger ages and young adulthood were even lower than those given in Fig. 15.2, the safest conclusion that one can draw from all this information is that it is unwise to attempt predictions about the personality of high school students, based on reliable information about them during infancy and early childhood.

An example of the change between early childhood and young adulthood in one personality characteristic, *aggressive behavior*, is shown in the following excerpts drawn from one of the case histories that show the richness and variety of personality development. You will note that this girl was aggressive and destructive as a child, but that as adolescence approached, she did not display her hostile feelings and was not aggressive because this would have violated the standards that she had set for herself to achieve as a young woman.

At 2 years of age S's nursery-school behavior was often punctuated with aggressive outbursts.

"S seldom talks or shows any outward sign of emotion. She is by far the most physically bold child, doing much jumping and climbing. She often reacts to other children destructively, pushing them down, pulling out hair, and absconding with toys. . . ."

Two years later, at 4 years of age, S's nursery-school behavior was clearly competitive and aggressive.

"S was habitually aggressive, but she was not a successful leader. She was very competitive and seized every opportunity to equal or excel the feats of the other children. She liked to tease, and she had great sport with Mary and Peter, both of whom would yell or whine when she plagued them. Occasionally she played cooperatively with others, but more often she put herself in the role of a rival. S complied with adult requests at times, but at other times resisted with all her might. She needed to be reminded to take turns and to respect property rights. It was not because she did not know about these nursery-school principles, but rather because she could get such a rise out of other children by pushing in front of them or by snatching at their toys."

When S visited day camp at 6½, the predisposition toward unprovoked aggression was still clearly present.

"S was somewhat shy and wary in social situations and made few social advances. She was almost eager in her response when others made advances to her. She seemed to expect that she might not be accepted and was surprised and pleased when other children were nice to her. S was very easy to have around when she was busy. Sometimes in free moments she went a little wild. The other children complained that she pushed them, knocked their sand constructions down, or poked her finger in their clay work. These outbursts were over in a flash. She needed no provocation other than idleness to start her off. She never made excuses for her behavior or even admitted anything about it. S was out for her own advancement and was sort of a lone wolf. She seemed to feel no deep identification with the group or with any of its members."

During the early school years S was independent, and verbally rebellious and attacking. She was competitive with peers and began to gain some peer respect because of her daring, verbal skills and athletic prowess. By age 10 a dramatic shift occurred in her behavior. She became interested in her attractiveness to boys, and this new motive was accompanied by a sharp decrease in overt aggression. At age 10 the day-camp observer wrote:

"There has been a good deal of change in S's appearance: straightened posture, hair washed clean with French braids, and frilly, nice clothes. The big thing seems to be the big shift in S herself. She no longer needs to express her hostility and alienation toward the world. She has the possibilities of becoming a very attractive little girl. Socially S has loosened up a great deal. Though no one in this group was congenial with her, she was much more outgoing than in previous years. At the races she got to the tomboy state, loudly boasting and jeering at one girl for being so awkward. *Most of the time she had a quiet, almost demure, air about her, listening to what others had to say and smiling in a friendly fashion. . . .*"

By 12½ years this girl had adopted more completely the traditional feminine-role behaviors. The home visitor wrote:

"S has passed conspicuously into adolescence. Since the last time I saw her, her breasts have developed noticeably, and she has a very pretty figure and is becoming quite attractive. The mother told me privately that S had bought a new bathing suit, a one-piece affair, and when she tried it on for the family, her older brother gave a long, low whistle, which embarrassed her terribly. Mother shows considerable interest in S's appearance and in helping her to become attractive. She mentioned today that before school starts, she plans to take S to a hair stylist for a special cut. She also remarked that S says she wants to grow up and marry and have children, 'so that's what we're getting ready for.'"

S did very well academically in high school and college and decided to go to graduate school. On first impression S appeared quiet, reserved, and neither competitive nor aggressive. She became conflicted over an intellectual career because the required competition in graduate school threatened the self-image she was trying so hard to retain. She was sufficiently insecure about her conception of herself as a woman that intense involvement in an intellectually aggressive atmosphere made her uncomfortable. During the adult interview she tried to explain why she withdrew from graduate school. (Kagan & Moss, 1962, pp. 112-115)

In this case, a marked change in aggressive behavior is seen from early childhood to adolescence. However, from adolescence into young adulthood, the pattern is quite stable.

In connection with *achievement*, which shows a higher correlation between childhood and adulthood than aggression, there nevertheless often is discontinuity from early life into adulthood, as shown in these excerpts from the case history of a boy:

S was a highly motivated and excellent student in elementary and high school. He received a scholarship to college, graduated valedictorian of his college class, and won a competitive fellowship to graduate school. When interviewed as an adult, he expressed a strong motivation for achievement and recognition, and he looked forward with confidence to an intellectually creative career.

However, at age 2½ S was distractible and gave no clue to his future achievements.

"S spent an unhappy first week at nursery school. He cried a great deal and looked ready to cry even when he was not actually doing it. He drew away when other children approached him as if he were afraid of them. He required much adult attention to get him to do anything. He stood around, did nothing, and looked rather lost. After the first week, he became happier and played primitively in the sand out-of-doors. He did some climbing on ladders and slid alone. In the room, his activity was not constructive. He did a lot of wandering from room to room, and he liked to throw things: balls, colored cubes, or tin dishes. He watched the other children a great deal, identifying himself with the play of others by laughing when they did. Despite S's lively coloring he was not a lively, dramatic child. In fact, the teachers remarked that when they were tallying up the children to see who was there, they were always most likely to forget S's presence."

Let us contrast this summary at 2½ with a nursery-school report three years later, at 5½ years of age.

"S was one of the most adult-centered children in the group. The particular quality of his relationship is hard to describe. It was on a very verbal level. He came to tell you things, show you things, act things out, and explain things. S has a very active play life. There was a constant stream of verbal descriptions, and an observer would know every minute of the time what S was doing, what technique he was using, and why he was doing it. *S seemed to have a very strong calvinist sense of needing to get things done and not wasting time.* He would say, 'In a few minutes I will be through with this.' Although he was still ineffectual in holding on to things, he had really become more skilled.

"By choosing the less coveted objects and getting into an obscure corner in which to work, he had a chance of carrying his projects through. *S seemed really* *happy just to be making things.* There was a great emphasis on the detail without an over-all pattern. The Christmas tree gave him a very good goal to work toward, and he did more than his share of hanging materials. At the end of the session S was one of the most jubilant in wrapping up his booty to take home.

"In his scrutiny of the books and the retelling of the stories there was an emphasis on every tiny detail; every part coming in its sequence. S often asked questions to find out where parts fit in; how this different world of nursery school was supposed to run; what peoples' ideas about things were. Once told, he would store the knowledge away for the future. S was a great storyteller; long lectures on how things worked and on events at home. S's exceedingly high standards and an inability to relate to the world are his most salient features."

At 16½ years of age he was interviewed at the Institute.

E: "Would you tell me some of the things you are interested in?"

S: "Oh—my grade standards, various forms of amateur scientific research—I like to play around with. Like down at school, every once in a while I read about something interesting that someone has done, and if facilities permit, I like to try it out."

E: "Anything else you are interested in?"

S: "Well—I read a good bit—my main format of reading is in the science fiction class. I kind of enjoy learning. Of course, I may be rather conceited, but I don't think, except in a few classes, I actually learn anything. However, it excites my interest toward discovering things for myself."

E: "Are your grades important to you?"

S: "Oh, I like to have them—I figure I should get along with a B just as well as an A, but then I don't have to work much harder to get an A, so I might as well have it." (Kagan & Moss, 1962, pp. 126-127)

Obviously, one cannot make predictions from two cases. One does, however, get the clear impression that marked changes occur as late as adolescence in important personality variables. From other information, we also know that some personality change occurs in adults (Mischel, 1969). The teacher thus should operate on the assumption that changes in desirable directions are possible.

Ego Development

Loevinger and Wessler (1970) present a developmental conception of ego, summarized in Table 15.2, as one fundamental concept of personality. The table does not list age levels because the scheme seeks only to reflect what is common to a certain developmental *sequence* and to avoid the assumption that everyone of the same age is at the same ego level. The table is, however, a hierarchical model based on an ordinal sequence. That is, each stage builds on and sometimes incorporates the previous one. (The question of a transition across the stages at typical ages is not included in the data in the table.) A discussion of the successive stages shown in Table 15.2 will clarify their developmental nature.

1. The first stage is divided into *presocial* and *symbiotic* stages. Animate and inanimate parts of the environment are not distinguished in the presocial stage, but in the symbiotic stage the child is able to distinguish

Table 15.2. Some Milestones of Ego Development

Stage	Impulse control, character development	Interpersonal style	Conscious preoccupations
Presocial Symbiotic		Autistic Symbiotic	Self vs. nonself
Impulsive	Impulsive, fear of retaliation	Receiving, dependent, exploitive	Bodily feelings, especially sexual and aggressive
Self-protective	Fear of being caught, externalizing blame, opportunistic	Wary, manipulative, exploitive	Self-protection, wishes, things, advantage, control
Conformist	Conformity to external rules, shame, guilt for breaking rules	Belonging, helping, superficial niceness	Appearance, social acceptability, banal feelings, behavior
Conscientious	Self-evaluated standards, self-criticism, guilt for consequences, long-term goals and ideals	Intensive, responsible, mutual, concern for communication	Differentiated feelings, motives for behavior, self-respect, achievements, traits, expression
Autonomous	Add: Coping with conflicting inner needs, toleration	Add: Respect for autonomy	Vividly conveyed feelings, integration of physiological and psychological, psychological causation of behavior, development, role conception, self-fulfillment, self in social context
Integrated	Add: Reconciling inner conflicts, renunciation of unattainable	Add: Cherishing of individuality	Add: Identity

Note: "Add" means in addition to the description applying to the previous level.
Source: Adapted from Loevinger & Wessler, 1970, pp. 10–11.

"mother" from the environment. The problem in this first stage is to distinguish self from nonself and to construct a stable world of objects. Before the end of this stage, the ego can hardly be said to exist at all. In any case, it is inaccessible to study by means of verbal tests. The period comes to an end with the emergence of language.

2. The next stage is described as *impulsive*. The child has confirmed his existence separate from the mother, but control of impulse is lacking, and rules as such are not recognized. Actions are considered to be bad only if they are punished. Although people are seen as sources of supply, the dependence is not recognized as such. Conscious preoccupation is with aggressive and sexual drives. Some behavioral manifestations of this stage, such as temper tantrums, are not specific to the age (that is, they remain constant throughout the life span); others, such as preoccupation with body functions, take different forms at different ages.

3. In the next stage the morality is strictly expedient; rules are acknowledged, but are followed only if doing so gives one an advantage. The stage thus is called *self-protective*. Behavior is still not considered bad unless one is caught. Despite a shift away from dependence, interpersonal relations are characterized as manipulative and exploitive. As the character in the television commercial says, "I'd rather do it myself," the adolescent at this stage asks bitterly, "Who needs them?" Life is considered as a zero-sum game in the sense that "What you win, I lose." Conscious preoccupation is with gaining control and advantage over things and people; for example, getting the better of someone else.

4. At the *conformist* stage, rules are partially internalized and followed just because they are rules. Shame is the penalty experienced for nonconformity; although there is stereotyped prejudice against outgroups, the golden rule is observed for ingroups. Interpersonal style is characterized by the individual in terms of actions, rather than feelings or motives. Conscious preoccupation is with reputation, the superficial appearance of things, and with material things. References to inner feelings are stereotypically bland and often moralistic.

5. During the *conscientious* stage, morality is internalized; that is, inner moral imperatives replace group-sanctioned rules as the bases for behavior, and guilt replaces shame as the feeling reaction to violation of such internalized rules. Interpersonal relations become more intensive and meaningful, and they are viewed in terms of feelings rather than actions. Inner feelings are differentiated and serve as standards for meeting obligations, measuring up to ideals, and making contributions and achievements. This stage is characterized by the capacity for self-criticism, which is a major trait differentiating it from the conformist stage.

6. The next stage is called *autonomous*. Impulse control gives way as a problem to coping with conflict—inner conflict, conflicting needs and duties. These conflicts are met squarely through coping behavior. Although the conscientious and conformist stages are characterized by moral condemnation of persons who propose conflict resolutions other than one's own, the autonomous stage is marked by greater tolerance. Interpersonal relations involve the recognition of the autonomy of other people, in addition to mutual interdependence. Loevinger gives these examples: a typical conscientious mother feels obliged to prevent her children from making mistakes; a typical autonomous mother emphasizes the need for her children to learn from their own mistakes. Conscious preoccupations are with a conceptualization of role differentiation, individual development, and self-fulfillment.

7. The final and highest stage is the *integrated* stage. The person transcends coping with conflict and achieves reconciliation of conflicting demands. This might involve renunciation of unattainable goals. Individual differences are valued, not merely tolerated. Role differentiation is succeeded by a sense of integrated identity. Persons who attain this stage, called self-actualizing people by Maslow (1968), represent the highest levels of maturity of integration.

Loevinger points out that each stage has a potential for both maladjustment and growth. The descriptive scheme (mode of impulse control, interpersonal style, and conscious preoccupation) is not age-related. Nevertheless, it does represent a hierarchical model. In other words, the stages are in invariable ordinal sequence, and no stage can be skipped. Each stage is based on the preceding one, is more complex than the preceding one, and prepares for the succeeding one. Although there is one characteristic level for each person, the person can and does function on several levels over brief periods of time.

Teachers will find it very valuable to think about developmental trends in personality in terms of some kind of coherent model such as the one given in Table 15.2. In addition to providing a framework or structure that can be used to interpret individual and interpersonal behavior in the classroom, organizing one's thoughts in terms of such a model increases introspective personal insights into one's own behavior. Furthermore, a better perspective may be gained into the collective behavior of modern youth developing in a society that itself is in a period of rapid change.

15.6. What general statements can you make about the stability of personality? What are the implications of these statements for education?

15.7. Is age a good indicator of ego-development level? Why or why not? In what sense is the Loevinger conception of ego development a hierarchical model?

15.8. How would you characterize your own level of ego development? —

15.9. What does it mean to say that each stage has a potential for both maladjustment and growth?

15.10. How can thinking in terms of developmental trends in personality help the teacher in working with students?

PRINCIPLES FOR ENCOURAGING PERSONALITY INTEGRATION

The principles and related instructional guides discussed in Chapter 14 in connection with attitudes and values are relevant also to personality integration. Providing exemplary models for students, providing pleasant emotional experiences, extending informative experiences about attitudes and values, using group techniques to facilitate commitment to socially approved attitudes and values, arranging appropriate practice opportunities to implement more stable organization of the value system, and encouraging independent and deliberate cultivation of attitudes and values apply to personality integration as well.

Four additional principles and related instructional guides for encouraging personality integration are presented here. These principles and guides should be considered as useful hypotheses to guide behavior in teaching and other situations, rather than as established laws. It should be pointed out that persons with different conceptions of personality, analyzing the same large body of research and expert opinion, might use different terminology. The guides are now discussed in detail.

Principle	Instructional Guide
1. Developing a stable personality organization is facilitated by a secure emotional environment. (High stress and chronic anxiety produce inefficient learning and eventual personality disorganization.)	1. Develop an emotionally secure environment.
2. Accepting oneself (adequate self concept) and others and being accepted by others are interdependent and are necessary for personality integration.	2. Encourage self-understanding and self-acceptance.
3. Attaining independence and a sense of achievement are essential to personality integration.	3. Help students to attain realistic goals.
4. Acquiring rational methods of adjustment to frustrating situations through learning may reduce excessive use of defense mechanisms.	4. Provide practice in meeting conflict situations.

1. Develop an Emotionally Secure Environment

Feelings of acceptance and belonging are important in achieving an emotionally secure classroom. Responding to the student in a positive manner and making sure that each child in the room has several friends will increase such feelings. A review of research suggests that emotionally secure classrooms will be more likely when the affective qualities of teachers and classrooms are characterized by: a feeling of general warmth; encouraging moderate expressions of emotion and feeling by students; democratic group decision-making leading to stimulating activities; the use of nonpunitive control techniques high in clarity and firmness; reduced frustration and anxiety in learning situations; and shifting states of order (much talking, then complete quiet, etc.) based on organizing emotions toward the achievement of goals (Ripple, 1965).

The role of anxiety in learning situations is exceedingly complex; indeed, a *mild* degree of anxiety appears to facilitate learning. Nevertheless, teachers should not deliberately arouse feelings of insecurity and anxiety in students. Most learning situations in school are sufficiently anxiety-producing in themselves, and the better approach is to attempt to reduce anxiety. This recommendation is in accord with the conclusions of Sarason and his associates; on the basis of several years of research on anxiety in elementary school children, they wrote:

> From our observations we have concluded that one of the most important dimensions on which teachers vary is the degree to which they establish an atmosphere in which the child's sense of security and level of self-esteem are very much determined by the adequacy of his performance. . . . In the case of

the anxious child, we feel that the teacher's response to an inadequate performance must avoid reinforcing the attitude that failure and being personally liked
and accepted are in any way related. (Sarason et al., 1960, p. 273)

Students feel quite secure emotionally if standards of conduct are
made known and are consistent. They do not resent reasonable rules and
regulations; on the contrary, they prefer to know the kind of behavior
that the teacher consistently will approve or disapprove. Often the new
teacher is tested to find out what his limits are. Particularly in the upper
grades and in high school, an effective way to get behavioral standards
clarified and accepted by the students is to have them participate in their
formulation.

Pleasant emotions are too infrequently expressed in many classroom
situations by either the teacher or the students, and there is probably too
much suppression of feelings generally (Jones, 1968). In the kindergarten
and primary grades, the teacher does usually tend to express his or her
own pleasant feelings quite freely and to encourage pleasant emotional
expressions in students. This is relatively easy because young children
raise all sorts of questions about themselves and their environment. They
are curious and want to learn. For many children, however, this free emotional expression and this zest for learning become blunted during the
later elementary years and the secondary school years. As the demand to
learn more organized subject matter increases and also as restrictions
arising in the home, the neighborhood, and the school increase, pleasant
emotional expressions in the classroom decrease. The urge for activity
leading to new discovery is thwarted by the pressure to conform. Answers
the child needs to solve a problem that is important to him are deferred
because a problem the teacher wants solved takes precedence.

Eventually, the student no longer experiences pleasant emotions or
challenges in the classroom learning situation. His earlier eager
searching for solutions becomes passive tolerance or even open resistance. When this happens, undesirable means of adjusting (such as the
defense mechanisms listed in Table 15.1) become prevalent. The emotional atmosphere of most classrooms would be improved if the instructional program elicited more pleasant emotional reactions and if time
were spent helping students deal more effectively with their emotions
(Mager, 1968). Such an improved feeling or emotional tone of the classroom would, in turn, contribute both to the more efficient attainment of
cognitive goals and to the fostering of personality integration.

2. Encourage Self-Understanding and Self-Acceptance

By the time the student finishes high school, he should have a fairly realistic appraisal of himself, his motor skills, his knowledge and intellectual
abilities, his interests, and his emotional makeup. One of the weaknesses
of our total educational program, including the college level, is that we do
not give enough help to students in understanding their strengths and
weaknesses. Often a counselor makes a fairly adequate appraisal of the
student's assets and limitations and uses this for placing him in various

curricula and classes. However, the information on which the appraisal is based is not interpreted *to* the student, so that he himself can understand the strengths that he may capitalize on, weaknesses that he may over- come through persistent effort, and possible limitations that he cannot overcome but must accept.

Besides some inadequacies in encouraging self-understanding, there is even less deliberate attempt to encourage self-acceptance. Rather than helping students accept and appreciate their special individual selves, we encourage unrealistic striving: "Anyone can become president of the United States." "Everyone should make a perfect score on this test." "Ev- eryone should finish in 10 minutes." Similarly, grading systems tend to encourage a lack of self-acceptance except in those who receive high marks. Though giving students low or failing marks may encourage realism, it does not lead to self-acceptance, especially if the idea is also expressed that one should not be satisfied with low marks even though he has done his best.

Deliberate attempts to teach for improvement in the self concept, both within the regular classroom and outside the classroom but within the school, have produced favorable results (Staines, 1958). Also, Bruce (1958) reported on instruction during grades 6 and 8 that was designed to help children acquire a more understanding and analytical approach to their own and others' behavior; the instruction resulted in higher self- acceptance and lower feelings of anxiety and insecurity in the children. An example of an attempt at improving self concept in junior high school out- side of the regular classroom setting is reported by Caplan (1957). Boys ex- periencing behavior problems in school met in small groups for 10 50-min- ute counseling interviews with their regular high school counselors. In early meetings, held in a fairly permissive environment, the boys spent a considerable amount of the time relating lurid stories of their real and fan- cied misdeeds. Once the boys were satisfied that the counselor could be trusted, they released many violent and aggressive feelings, some against the school, some against teachers, and some against parents. In the later sessions, they discussed freely with the counselor their in-school behav- ior, rules and regulations set up by the school, and other requirements that had been placed on them. The boys' concepts of themselves as worth- while individuals improved from the beginning to the end of the group counseling. Desirable change in behavior and attitudes toward self oc- curred first, followed by an attitude change toward others.

Self-acceptance is the primary requisite for an adequate self concept. Further, acceptance by others and acceptance of others is positively re- lated to acceptance of self. One cannot determine which is cause and ef- fect. Since this is the case, it is well to work on all of them simultaneously. The teacher's rejecting a child or condoning classmates' rejection of him will not encourage self-acceptance. Similarly, permitting a child to gain a better perception of self through bullying others and treating them as inferior will not encourage a healthy self concept.

The following point of view about the members of a family applies equally well to the school.

We might set down here three insights that have become so well established that we can call them psychological axioms. One is that no human being can be his best self if he is always trying to be someone else instead of himself. The second is that he cannot be his best self unless he enjoys a reasonable self-respect and sense of worth. The third is that—particularly in childhood, but in some measure throughout life—his estimate of himself reflects the treatment he receives from the key figures in his environment; it is not something he makes out of nothing, but something he makes of other people's responses to him. As others see him, so he gradually tends to see himself. (Overstreet, 1955, p. 81)

3. Help Students To Attain Realistic Goals

Some adults still believe that the student ought to experience failure in school in preparation for meeting failure in adult life. However, the evidence is clear that highly productive, happy adults have a backlog of earlier successes starting in childhood and that repeated successes do not necessarily lead to an inflated opinion of self nor to undue self-centeredness. Our psychiatric wards and penal institutions are occupied primarily by persons who have experienced failure repeatedly.

As discussed in the preceding section, it is important that pupils not only learn to understand themselves but also that they have experience in setting and reaching realistic goals. Many pupils set their sights too high in learning tasks such as spelling, mathematics, science, or other fields. With the emphasis on science and mathematics as preparation for careers in engineering or science, high school students of relatively low ability are taking more of the advanced science and mathematics classes. Large numbers of them, however, are experiencing failure rather than success. And many high school graduates of lower abstract abilities who enter college are disappointed and at times become seriously disturbed when they are dropped for academic failure.

4. Provide Practice in Meeting Conflict Situations

Conflict situations inevitably arise in the classroom. The first response to such situations often is emotional. We expect younger children to respond with rather free expression of emotions in conflict situations. Although this free emotional expression tends to relieve tension, it does not resolve the conflict. If we are to make progress in human affairs, more conflict situations, such as those between minority and majority groups, labor and management, older generation and youth, nation and nation, will have to be solved in a manner that is more rational and less emotional. Youth in school today need practice in rational and intelligent methods for meeting the various conflict situations they encounter.

Conflict situations in school may provide the basis for fruitful learning experiences that promote personality integration. As was suggested in the last chapter, role playing, group discussions, and group decision-making promote better understanding of social and ethical values and acceptance of such values. Disagreements among students about such matters as responsibility for performing various tasks, appropriate conduct, and the cause of conflict can initiate a role-playing situation or a group discussion in which the emphasis is on rational means of solution, rather than on fighting, arguing, blaming, and punishing.

15.11. How were the principles for encouraging personality integration implemented in your own school experience? Do you think the implementation of these principles is different in different subject-matter areas? Why or why not?

15.12. What is the role of anxiety in learning situations? Can you think of any situation in which it might be useful for a teacher deliberately to promote anxiety in students?

15.13. Can you devise a grading system that would encourage self-understanding and self-acceptance? What would such a system be like?

15.14. Why should the teacher provide practice in meeting conflict situations?

PERSONALITY INTEGRATION AND DISCIPLINE

In Chapter 9 we pointed out that motivation and discipline are integrally related and cited four principles of democratic discipline, as identified by Sheviakov and Redl (1944). It was further indicated that classroom discipline cannot be separated from the motivational procedures employed or from the rest of the school curriculum. Because many prospective teachers, as well as teachers in service, express a need for help and advice on matters of discipline, this section includes an additional discussion of discipline. This discussion, as others throughout this book, should be interpreted as a guiding framework—not as prescriptive advice.

In a general sense, discipline refers to the acceptance of certain goals and to the order necessary to achieve them. It is a part of life outside of schools as well as within schools. Every social system, including the school and classroom system, requires some regulation of its members to enable it to function effectively. In classrooms, discipline refers to the control of classroom procedures in order to facilitate the attainment of educational objectives. For the most part, classroom teachers assume the responsibility for maintaining such control and for dealing with the various forms of disorder that may occur in school.

With some notable exceptions, characteristic discipline procedures in the schools historically have moved from the use of force to attempts to use persuasion to the current focus on self-discipline. Formerly, order was obtained by coercion devices—rules were established that were enforced by penalties such as detention, corporal punishment, and expulsion, depending on the severity of the transgression. Such procedures are far less frequently used in the modern school. Current conceptions of discipline as self-control imply learning a sense of responsibility to self, other classmates, and the school. When a program aimed at guiding the development of self-control is successful, the organization and operation of the school and classroom can proceed in such a way that situations leading to disorder are largely avoided.

As the discussion proceeds, recall the portion of the model on ego development (Table 15.2) devoted to impulse control and its developmental nature. Recall, also, the discussion earlier in this chapter of the rapidly changing social world and accompanying changes in the behavior of modern youth in the current scene. Particularly relevant here are the problems of use of drugs, dress codes, length of hair, and student unrest, all in the context of less certainty among adults and youth of what is right and what is wrong—remember: "It is not only that parents are no longer guides, but that there are no guides . . ." (Mead, 1970).

Some of the unrest at the high school level is reflected in the following news report:

PROTESTS FOUND IN 18% OF SCHOOLS

Eighteen percent of the country's high school principals who responded to a Congressional questionnaire reported that their schools experienced "some form of student protest" in the 1968-69 school year. Only 1 percent of the principals categorized their disturbances as "riots."

Fourteen percent of the principals who answered the questionnaire said they expected protests in 1969-70. The list of 23 questions was sent to all 29,000 public and private high school principals in the country.

The survey was released last week by Representative Roman C. Pucinski, Democrat of Illinois, the chairman of the House General Subcommittee on Education, and Representative Alphonzo Bell of California, the ranking Republican on the subcommittee.

Mr. Pucinski said he did not expect legislation to result immediately from the survey, but he said a determination of the extent of student unrest was necessary to measure the educational needs of the 1970's.

Among the highlights of the survey were the following:

¶Twenty percent of the principals reported that their schools had a significant increase in "ethnic enrollment" in the last five years. More than 80 per cent of these schools were in cities or rural areas, and only 17 percent were in the suburbs.

¶Schools with such an increase in ethnic enrollment were slightly more likely to have protests than schools where the racial composition did not change.

¶The major issues resulting in demonstrations were "general disciplinary rules" and "dress codes."

¶Racial issues were involved in about a third of the protests. In big-city public schools, 59 percent of the protests concerned race.

¶Forty percent of the schools where there were protests altered school rules as a result of the demonstrations.

¶In more than 90 percent of the protests, no one was injured and there was less than $100 damage to property.

Mr. Pucinski said he was impressed with the indications that, while there were numerous protest activities, "young people generally do not turn to violence."[3]

In an attempt to change in ways appropriate to new social conditions and characteristics of modern youth, many high schools have modified their organization and operations dramatically. Not all are successful in maintaining such changes. For example, Nova High School in Fort Lau-

[3]David E. Rosenbaum in *The New York Times*, February 24, 1970. Copyright© 1970 by The New York Times Company. Reprinted by permission.

derdale, Florida, was one of the most experimental high schools in the country when it opened in 1963. It pioneered in the use of educational technology, and students were given an exceptional amount of freedom to pick and choose, come and go as they pleased. A journalist's report implies that there had been changes by 1970:

> Today's rules and regulations have replaced Nova's initial freedom and individuality. A yellow poster on the door of an art room asks, "Dear God—how come you only have ten rules but Nova has a million?" Last month half a dozen students were suspended for five days and their grades lowered one point—because they parked their cars in the faculty parking lot; they said the student parking lot was filled with broken glass.[4]

Another innovative attempt at reorganizing the high school to accommodate modern students is described as follows:

ADAMS HIGH: "BEST AROUND"

> John Adams High School in Portland, Ore., is perhaps the most interesting public school in the U.S. today. "Adams," says graphics teacher Dick Johnson, "has thrown everything I learned in the last twenty years of teaching into a cocked hat. But I think it is the way schools should be for the next twenty years."
>
> Adams was the brainchild of seven young Ph.D. candidates at the Harvard Graduate School of Education. Three years ago, they decided to set up an experimental high school combining a new curriculum with teacher training and research and sent a long proposal to dozens of school systems across the country. Portland, which already had started construction on Adams, bought it. Four of the Harvard group went to Oregon and, after a year of planning, Adams opened last September with 1,300 students in grades nine through eleven, most of them from middle-class families and about 25 percent black.
>
> At the start of the year, to break down the school's size and to give students an identity in small groups, both students and teachers were assigned at random to one of four "houses" in the school's single building. Within limits, students are allowed to pick from several "general education" courses offered by their houses, and they spend half their day in interdisciplinary courses in English, social studies, math and science. "These are problem-centered courses," explains Robert B. Schwartz, Adams's 31-year-old principal and one of the Harvard four. "We want students to do things rather than just read about them." One of the 23 courses given by Shabazz house is described as: "What's going on? What can be done to change it? You pick the time and the area. But think in terms of social problems."
>
> The other half of the day, students are totally free to fill "option periods" as they wish. They can go to "resource centers" scattered around the building where teachers are posted to assist them; they can study on their own, or they can sign up for dozens of six-week mini-courses, including "bachelor cooking" and "ecological action planning." In fact, the option system allows scores of students to wander around the hallways, smooch in the school boiler room or trade drugs in a nearby park.
>
> **Express:** Such freedom at first upset parents who expected their children to attend regular classes, perform regular assignments and be rewarded with regular grades. But now most parents seem to support the school. "Some kids and even some teachers," Schwartz told *Newsweek's* Peter Janssen, "had the atti-

[4]*Newsweek*, February 16, 1970, p. 68. Copyright by Newsweek, Inc., 1970.

tude of telling parents to get out of the road — the express train is coming through. But it's difficult for parents to keep up criticism if the kids are happy."

Almost all of Adams's students are indeed happy — and with good reason. The school has few rules and no dress codes. Classes are informal, students call teachers by their first names, paint flowers and animals on classroom windows and even sit on the three-man committee that interviews future teaching prospects. "The sense of community here is unbelievable," says Peter Handel, a 17-year-old junior. "Nobody orders anybody around or says 'no.' The atmosphere is free — so we want to do things."

It is far too early to tell whether Portland's experiment in freewheeling, nonauthoritarian education will turn out graduates any better prepared for future intellectual challenges than the products of standard U.S. high schools. For the moment, what concerns Adams teachers most is not that their innovations go too far, but that they start too late. By the time a student enters high school, he has already been conditioned by nine years of following orders and letting others make decisions. "If you lock a kid in a room and tell him that playing means he should draw circles, he will draw circles and be happy," says Trudy Johnson, an Adams teacher. "But if you then tell him to go out and play, he won't know how. He'll keep looking for the circles. That's where Adams is at now. It's the best school around, but it may be too late."[5]

It is quite obvious that conceptions of discipline are changing — both in schools such as the two just described and in a society outside the schools which is characterized by rapid change and considerable diversity and many inconsistencies in goals and values. Factors such as these should be kept in mind as we now consider (1) classifications of disorder and behavior problems, (2) causes of disorders and behavior problems, (3) disciplinary practices, and (4) some practical suggestions.

Classifications of Disorder and Behavior Problems

Most attempts to classify behavior problems and disorder in classrooms have resulted in descriptive categories based on seriousness and frequency of occurrence (Smith, 1969). For example, research by Kooi and Schutz (1965) suggested a scheme of 18 separate types of classroom disturbances; these were then consolidated in the following five categories: *physical aggression* (the pugilist, e.g., hitting, pushing, bullying); *peer affinity* (the socializer, e.g., whispering, moving without permission); *attention-seeking* (the attention-seeker, e.g., passing notes, making wisecracks); *challenge of authority* (the rebel, e.g., disobeying authority, protesting amount of work); and *critical dissension* (the complainer, e.g., making criticisms that are not constructive, laughing so as to disturb others).

In high school, the most frequent reasons for penalizing students until recently were: talking when silence is expected for girls and inattention and class disturbance for boys (N.E.A., 1957). Certainly serious behavior problems among high school students now include various forms of unrest and the use of drugs, as can be inferred from earlier discussions in this chapter.

[5]*Newsweek*, February 16, 1970, pp. 68-69. Copyright by Newsweek, Inc., 1970.

Among college students, offenses include such things as theft, gambling, violations of housing regulations, academic offenses, auto cases, and disorderly conduct (Prusok, 1961). Again, the mass protest demonstrations and other manifestations of student unrest of recent years must be added. Although classroom disturbances have not been considered an important problem among college students, there are indications that recent trends may be to the contrary, as shown in this news report:

PROTESTERS NOT IN CLASS WITH PROFESSOR

SEATTLE, Wash. (UPI) — Diminutive economics professor Henry T. Buechel was flabbergasted yesterday by the public acclaim for his threat to fight five demonstrators who interrupted a classroom lecture.

"I'm utterly amazed that when a professor protects his own rights in a classroom, it's news all over the United States," the 62-year-old teacher said during an interview at his paperstrewn University of Washington office.

"I would think the question would be what the hell else would I do," he said. "I think the good student majority should organize against these slobs."

The 150-pound professor took off his coat and glasses and threatened to take on five demonstrators last Wednesday when they invaded his Economics 200 class and demanded to discuss the Vietnam War and the Chicago conspiracy trials.

"How many men are willing to help me throw them out?" Buechel asked his 350 students. Several volunteered and the protesters left, shouting obscenities.

Since then, Buechel, who describes himself as a "square" who believes Hubert Humphrey is "our greatest living American," has spent a lot of time answering the telephone.

He received calls from persons throughout the nation who said, "God bless you" and "This is the best news I've read in three years." He reported no crank calls.

Many faculty members and students have also stopped at his office to congratulate him for his stand, Buechel said. But others voiced concern about the possibility of physical strife between professors and young toughs.[6]

In addition to drawing up their own classifications of behavior problems, researchers have studied *teachers'* perceptions of the seriousness of various types of misbehavior. In a classic investigation that is still relevant and important, Wickman (1928) had teachers and clinical psychologists rank 51 different forms of behaviors and personal traits that disrupt orderly procedures in the classroom. The correlation between the rankings by the two groups was —.05. Most serious according to the teacher rankings were traits such as immorality, dishonesty, impertinence, and rudeness. For the clinical psychologists, some of the more serious characteristics were shyness, suspicion, oversensitiveness, and daydreaming. The teachers were concerned basically with aggressive behaviors; the clinical psychologists were concerned basically with withdrawing behaviors. In other words, the teachers seemed to be concerned with traits and reactions that bothered *them*, whereas the psychologists were concerned with the *pupils'* personality integration and development. When Tolor,

[6]Paul Bridge in the Rochester, New York, *Democrat-Chronicle*, February, 1970. Reprinted by permission of United Press International.

Scarpetti, and Lane (1967) followed up on the Wickman study almost 40 years later, again reporting differences between teachers and clinicians in rankings of categories of aggressive behavior, regressive behavior, and emotional expression, the teachers viewed all these more or less rebellious types of behavior as more abnormal than the clinicians did. The amount of experience of a teacher was found to be a significant variable, with inexperienced teachers differing more from the clinicians, ascribing more pathology to a variety of child behaviors than experienced teachers. There is some suggestion that in recent years teachers have become less interested in maintaining order and more interested in developing personality integration among their students.

Causes of Disorders and Behavior Problems

Student behavior problems and disorders formerly were attributed to students' deliberately evil intentions. As might be inferred from the preceding discussion, however, theories about the causes of student disorders and behavior problems are currently being cast in psychological and mental health terms—personal maladjustment, home background, tension and anxiety, frustration and inhibition, academic failure, and so forth. For example, Sheviakov and Redl (1944) attribute student misconduct to six factors: dissatisfaction in schoolwork, emotional unrest in relationship to others, disturbances in the classroom climate, lack of harmony between classroom control and the need of each student for emancipation, emotional strains that accompany sudden changes from one activity to another, and composition of the classroom group.

Barnes (1963) reports some of the causes of student misconduct most frequently mentioned *by elementary school teachers* as follows: incompetence of teachers, differences in pupil interests, desire for attention by pupils, differences in family values, insufficient parental interest, limited intelligence, and home background. Again, there is a social-mental hygiene flavor to the categories. A study by Williamson (1956) lists conditions associated with college disciplinary cases, such as repressive rules and mores of institutions, lack of proper institutional climate, transfer from parental restrictions to campus freedom, struggle for independence from parents transferred to college authorities, pathological character, and natural prankishness. This list must now, of course, also include intergroup relations (particularly a perceived discriminatory racism) and the recent emergence of militant ideologies. In addition, perhaps the psychology of helplessness leading to alienation (discussed earlier in the chapter) should be included.

Disciplinary Practices

As noted earlier, the teacher's best efforts are directed toward creating a classroom environment supportive of healthy personality integration and rich with learning experiences that capitalize on the enthusiasm of youth. The good modern classroom is not especially quiet—certainly not the "you can hear a pin drop" kind of quiet. It is often a beehive of activity in which most students are actively engaged in constructive learning situations. In this way situations that require disciplinary attention are avoided and minimized — a kind of preventive discipline. With the development of guidance and counseling facilities in schools and greater knowledge among teachers about the causes of misbehavior in terms of personality maladjustment, referring some problems to school psychologists and counselors has become an increasingly used procedure.

Surveys of disciplinary practices at the elementary school, high school, and college level are available. Barnes (1963), for example, reports four types of techniques at the elementary school level: ignoring the misbehavior, providing enrichment activities and specialized assistance, reasoning with children, and individualizing school work. At the high school level, methods of disciplinary control most frequently employed are: reprimand in front of the class followed by reprimand in private, detention, assignment to special tasks, sending the student from the room, giving him a special seat, sending him to the principal, and reducing his grades (Garrison, 1959). At the college level, handling disciplinary cases is more complex. Many colleges and universities have set up disciplinary committees composed of students and faculty members to adjudicate difficult cases of student misconduct. Those who perform counseling functions in the offices of the deans of men and women are usually separated from these disciplinary committees and act in an advisory role to them.

Reduction in the use of corporal punishment as a disciplinary technique has accompanied the general movement from coercive to self-control forms of discipline. Although corporal punishment has not been completely abandoned (e.g., Kozol, 1967), it is prohibited by law in some states. In most states cruel treatment of children in general is prohibited by law and thus in cases where corporal punishment is excessive, the teacher is subject to arrest also in those states.

Dimensions of disciplinary behavior have been uncovered through research conducted in classroom settings. For example, the effects of disciplinary control techniques on students other than the one they are directed to have been studied by Kounin and Gump (1958). The effects of such techniques have been found to spread beyond the target of disciplinary actions to those who are watching the situation. Such effects are likened to the ripples caused by throwing a stone into a pool of water. The degree of orientation toward the disapproved behavior by other students, as well as the clarity, firmness, and roughness of the control techniques used, are factors governing the reactions of other students. The observing students are less apt to misbehave if the teacher's control technique is clear in the sense of identifying the target pupil and his misbehavior and if the control technique is nonthreatening and constructive. Also, observers of the control technique used by the teacher are more apt to respond favorably if the technique is not overly rough. Roughness tends to increase anxieties in other students, with, as might be expected, ill effects. Generally, teacher behavior that is clear and firm has positive effects on other students' behaviors; teacher behavior that is rough and threatening leads to disruptive conduct by other students.

In addition to the factors mentioned that are dimensions of teacher behavior related to student classroom conduct, there is another factor Kounin, Friesen, and Norton (1966) call "with-it-ness." With-it-ness refers to the students' perception of whether or not the teacher is aware of what is going on. For example, a teacher who is not "with it" responds to a minor deviancy while a major one is actually going on (e.g., paying attention to two children who are whispering while two others are chasing each other) or reacts to misconduct too late (e.g., after it has increased in seriousness or spread to other children). The higher the degree of with-it-ness in teacher behavior, the greater the involvement of pupils in their school work and the lower the amount of misconduct.

Some Practical Suggestions

The use of rewards and punishments has already been discussed in Chapter 9. The negative effects of punitive measures were discussed there, as well as in the section immediately above. Furthermore, it has been pointed out that through motivational procedures and a rich in-structional program, situations requiring disciplinary attention are avoided and minimized. This kind of preventive discipline is the most effective procedure.

Nevertheless, in the normal course of events in a school classroom, there are times when the exercise and establishment of control tech-niques are necessary. One such occasion is when the class meets a new teacher for the first time. Stenhouse describes the circumstances well:

> The class explores the situation by a process which might be called "testing the limits." There are inevitably areas of uncertainty in their relationships with a new teacher, areas in which the practice of teachers diverges. The class sets about clearing up these uncertainties by confronting the teacher with test cases. One might say that the class experiments with the teacher. It may not do this consciously and in planned fashion, but every experienced teacher will rec-ognize the process we have in mind. It is almost as if the teacher were the sub-ject of an experiment in social psychology in which the class plays the role of the experimenter, seeking to discover the laws which will help them to predict, and perhaps even to control, their teacher's behavior. Only in the light of these laws can they shape their own reaction. Thus the class seeks to discover for example under what circumstances the teacher is prepared to allow them to talk to one another, to walk about the room or to read their own books. It may also try to find out whether it can seduce him from his purpose by introducing red herrings, whether it can embarrass him by introducing sexually loaded ques-tions or whether it can make him lose the thread of a mathematical explanation by interrupting him with questions.
>
> By its very nature this experiment turns into an attempt to discover the limits to which the class can go: the lowest standards of work the teacher will accept, the extremes of disorder which he will tolerate. The class "tries to get away with things," because this is the only way in which it is possible to trace the boundary line between what is acceptable and what is unacceptable. (Sten-house, 1967, p. 52)

In such a situation and in other situations where the establishment of standards for order or the exercise of disciplinary techniques is required, the teacher should be guided by a procedural basis implied in some of the research and discussions offered earlier in this section and other portions of this book. Good discipline is characterized by the following: it is related to the misbehavior; it is consistent; it is clear, firm, and devoid of threats or roughness; it is constructive, leading to self-control; it is perceived as fair by the misbehaver and the rest of the class. Disciplinary techniques should not involve the assignment of extra loads of school work. The teacher who requires a misbehaving student to do 10 more arithmetic problems or translate 30 extra lines of Spanish because he misbehaved in class is inviting a disrespect and disinterest in school work as an exciting and stimulating activity. A teacher cannot present school work as attractive on one day and use it as a punitive threat on another day without affecting students' attitudes toward school unfavorably.

The educational literature includes many suggestions for specific behaviors appropriate to emergency discipline situations—first-aid techniques, what to do at the first class meeting, and the like. It should be recognized that such techniques do not strike at the fundamentals involved in disciplinary situations. Often, suggestions about what *not* to do are as helpful as what to do.

Some typical practices to avoid are listed as the following *don'ts*:

- use sarcasm
- play favorites
- insist on apologies
- make threats
- give overly difficult assignments
- punish the entire class for the misbehavior of one or a few
- appeal to fear
- sit at the desk all the time
- get sidetracked by irrelevant questions
- tie yourself to the textbook
- use a vocabulary over the students' heads
- talk too rapidly or nervously
- neglect the physical comfort of students in the room
- express anger in front of the class

Some typical suggestions that are helpful include:

- know all the students' names
- have the lessons well prepared
- call on students whose attention is wavering
- be businesslike
- use the standards of the group to establish rules
- stop the little disturbances before they become serious
- use your voice effectively
- display promptness, vitality, and enthusiasm
- show a sense of humor

Actually, the list of helpful suggestions could go on almost endlessly. The basic tenet is that good discipline is a function of good teaching. Implementing some of the procedures listed above is really a question of the intelligent recognition of the interaction between situational requirements and a teacher's personal style.

15.15. What is the relationship between classroom discipline and motivational procedures?

15.16. What are the advantages and disadvantages of conceiving of discipline as self-control? Is the use of coercive disciplinary devices ever justified in the classroom? When?

15.17. What disciplinary role should the school play in connection with drugs? Dress codes? Length of hair? Student protests?

15.18. What do you think of the "Adams High" type of school in connection with discipline? Would you like to be a student in a school such as Adams High? A teacher? Why or why not?

15.19. What kinds of student misbehavior would you consider to be serious? Not serious? Why?

15.20. As a teacher, what types of disciplinary practices will you use? How do they relate to your idea of what constitutes good discipline?

SUMMARY

As they develop, individuals strive toward personal integration. The schools have a responsibility to facilitate personality integration in students and to help them to realize the richness of personal, human fulfillment. Although there are many definitions of personality, fundamentally it is the concept or construct that refers to the uniqueness and totality of an individual as a social being. A model of integrative adjustment includes self-control, personal responsibility, social responsibility, democratic social interest, and ideals. Character development, including the internalization of ethical values, is part of the broader conception of personality integration.

Some writers contend that rapid changes in society's attitudes and values and in the behavior of modern youth reflect our entering a totally new phase of cultural evolution. This new kind of culture is based on an absence of guides among adults. Whether or not we are on the threshold of a new cultural evolution, student unrest (born, in many instances, of personal and social idealism), activism, alienation, and other aspects of the modern youth scene (including dress codes, personal grooming, drug usage, etc.) are clearly evident. The school's responsibility for helping youth in their quest for personal integration based on health, psychomotor skills, cognitive abilities, adequate means of adjustment, and adequate self concept is intensified under such rapidly changing conditions. Although the school may not explicitly try to shape personality through an organized program of instruction, children and youth in school can learn knowledge, abilities, skills, attitudes, values, motives, and interests which are at the very heart of personality.

Sharp changes in many behaviors occur between early childhood and young adulthood. Although this rules out confident predictions about personality, it leads to the concurrent conclusion that changes in desirable directions are possible at various developmental levels. Stages in developing the self concept are identifiable and can be conceptualized to provide for continuity in interpretation. Ego development, a fundamental concept in personality, is described in terms of impulse control, interpersonal style, and conscious preoccupation. Such a hierarchical model provides a framework to interpret individual and interpersonal behavior and obtain a better perspective on the collective behavior of modern youth.

Inasmuch as attitudes and values are integral components of personality, the instructional guides for facilitating the learning of attitudes and values presented in Chapter 14 are also applicable to personality. Four additional guides invite thoughtful examination in connection with the teacher's role in personality development: (1) Develop an emotionally secure environment. (2) Encourage self-understanding and self-acceptance. (3) Help students to attain realistic goals. (4) Provide practice in meeting conflict situations.

Motivation, discipline, and personality integration are integrally related. Every social system, including the school and classroom as a system, requires some regulation of its members to enable it to function effectively. In school settings, discipline refers to control of procedures in order to facilitate the attainment of educational objectives. Discipline procedures in the schools historically have moved from the use of force to self-discipline. Current conceptions of discipline as self-control imply learning a sense of responsibility to self, other classmates, and the school. Attempts to implement such a conception require reorganization of schools and classrooms.

Classifications of disorder and behavior problems reflect descriptive categories that are traditional and also those of a society characterized by rapid change, considerable diversity, and many inconsistencies in goals and values. Causes of such disorders and behavior problems are currently conceived in psychological and mental health terms. Good discipline is a function of good teaching. The teacher's best efforts are directed at creating a classroom environment supportive of healthy personality integration and rich with learning experiences that capitalize on the enthusiasm of youth. With such preventive discipline approaches, situations that require disciplinary attention are avoided and minimized. Surveys of disciplinary techniques employed at the elementary, secondary, and college levels show that they have moved away from severe punitive measures to self-control forms of discipline.

SUGGESTIONS FOR FURTHER READING

BUGENTAL, J. F. T. *Challenges of humanistic psychology.* New York: McGraw-Hill, 1967.

The 34 readings in this paperback are representative of the modern protest against a narrowly conceived behavioristic psychology that gives insufficient attention to the individual as a total person.

FLAVELL, J. H. Piaget's theory of moral judgment. In Wrightsman, L. S., ed., *Contemporary issues in social psychology.* Belmont, Calif.: Wadsworth, 1968, 23–27.

Piaget's ideas about developmental stages in the moral development of children are outlined.

HAVIGHURST, R. J. Overcoming value differences. In Strom, R. D., ed., *The inner-city classroom: Teacher behaviors.* Columbus, Ohio: Merrill, 1966, pp. 41–56.

This essay is especially helpful in clarifying the values essential for civilized life in an urban, industrialized society.

HOBBS, N. Helping disturbed children: Psychological and ecological strategies. In Sarason, I. G., ed., *Contemporary research in personality.* Princeton, N.J.: Van Nostrand, 1969, pp. 352-362.

The development of residential schools and procedures for reeducating emotionally disturbed children are described.

HOFFMAN, M. L., & SALTZSTEIN, H. D. Parent discipline and the child's moral development. In Parke, R. D., ed., *Readings in social development.* New York: Holt, Rinehart and Winston, 1969, pp. 541-561.

Frequent use of power by the parent and withdrawal of love were not associated with the moral development of seventh-grade students; however, the frequent use of induction—focusing on the effects of the child's actions on others—was.

MOSKOWITZ, R. Leaving the drug world behind. *American education,* 1970, 6, pp. 3-6.

An education reporter for the *San Francisco Chronicle* describes the education of young former drug addicts and their roles in "awareness" houses. Awareness houses are being developed as places where adolescent drug-users who want to quit can come to meet with ex-addicts and others.

RINGNESS, T. R. *Mental health in the schools.* New York: Random House, 1968.

Chapters of particular interest, in part because of anecdotal material, are "Common Sources of Stress in Schools," pages 252-284; "Working with Individual Pupils —Learning Principles," pages 317-341; and "Working with Individual Pupils—the Self," pages 342-371.

SMITH, M. B. Explorations in competence: A study of Peace Corps teachers in Ghana. In Sarason, I. G., ed., *Contemporary research in personality.* Princeton, N.J.: Van Nostrand, 1969, pp. 21-30.

The characteristics of peace corps teachers, and also the methods used to identify the characteristics, are given. Commitment to and competence in teaching rated at the top.

WATTENBERG, W. W. *Social deviancy among youth,* National Society for the Study of Education, 65th yearbook. Chicago: University of Chicago Press, part 1, 1966.

Delinquency, teen-age pregnancy, emotional disturbance and other forms of undesired deviancy are described. Educational provisions are outlined briefly.

Chapter 16 Retention and Transfer

Retention and Forgetting

disuse
interference
reorganization
obliterative subsumption
motivated forgetting
attributes of memory

Transfer

positive and negative transfer
vertical and lateral transfer
formal-discipline theory
identical-elements theory
generalization theory
transposition theory
abilities theory

Instructional Guides

foster intent to learn and remember
help the learner to identify meaningful relationships
provide satisfying consequences of correct responses
emphasize concepts and abilities
provide opportunities for application
provide for sequential, cumulative learning

earning as usually defined implies a *relatively permanent change* in behavior that results from practice or activity and thus involves a three-step sequence of initial acquisition, retention, and use. When the child, for example, correctly spells a word or solves a problem for the first time, we say that he has then *acquired* the particular behavior. If the same child correctly repeats the performance later, we say that he has remembered, or *retained*, what he acquired earlier. *Transfer* occurs when whatever is learned in one situation is used in a new or different situation.

The effective teacher is concerned about the extent to which material learned during a day, week, or month will be remembered later. He also is concerned about whether what is learned and remembered will help in meeting new or different situations. In point of fact, formal education is based on the assumption that human beings *can* transfer what they have learned in one situation to another, either in school or outside the school setting. The conditions of and relationships among initial learning, remembering, and transfer of learning are treated in the following discussion of retention and forgetting, transfer, and principles and instructional guides for encouraging retention and transfer.

RETENTION AND FORGETTING

Memory was one of the first phenomena to be studied in a psychological laboratory (Ebbinghaus, 1964). For several decades, much attention was then given to memory, and various explanations of forgetting were formulated. The study of memory then lapsed, but it has been renewed during the last decade. In this section, earlier theories of forgetting are treated. These are followed by brief outlines of some of the results of two recent, important, and related lines of study of short-term memory and the attributes of memory. Then some findings about the retention of specific school subject matter are presented.

Explanations of Forgetting

Try to remember everything that happened during the third, sixth, or tenth year of your life. You certainly cannot recall everything, but why have you forgotten so much? There are five explanations, none of which is completely satisfactory in itself.

1. **Disuse.** When something is learned and used repeatedly, it is remembered, but when it is not used, it is forgotten. This explanation in terms of disuse suggests deterioration or decay of the connections in the brain as the reason for forgetting. Disuse is not satisfactory as the sole explanation, for we do not seem to forget while we are asleep, and while we are awake there is a constant stream of new experiences that would seem to produce interference that results in forgetting, just as disuse seems to.

2. **Interference.** Interference of present learning with what has been previously learned leads to forgetting. For example, you read and studied

the last chapter and remembered much of what you studied. Now you are into this chapter; possibly your reading here will interfere with your remembering the earlier material. This phenomenon is called *retroactive inhibition.* Another kind of interference works in the opposite direction. In what is called *proactive inhibition,* initial learning interferes with subsequent learning. Thus the study of English history during the first period may interfere with the learning of American history in the second period or learning to spell "believe" may interfere with learning to spell "receive." The main difference between the two is in sequence: in proactive inhibition, the interfering material is encountered first; in retroactive inhibition, it is encountered last.

3. Reorganization. An individual learns certain material or a skill, but does not learn it well and does not use it for some time. He then needs to use it, and, in the process of recall, reorganizes what he had previously acquired into some new patterns that make sense to him now. For example, a child learned to spell "believe" correctly as part of the organized program of spelling instruction, but did not write it again for several weeks. Now he needs the word in a story. His best present version is "beleve"; in the active reorganizing process to meet the present situation, an incorrect spelling is accepted.

4. Obliterative Subsumption. A slightly different viewpoint about forgetting is that embodied in the *subsumption* theory discussed in Chapter 2 (Ausubel, 1963). You may recall that in this theory forgetting occurs as once dissociable items become subsumed into more inclusive concepts or principles and thereby lose their identity. For example, a person now has learned the concept *red circle.* Although he remembers the attributes of red circle so that he will correctly label any such object encountered, he probably has forgotten the many events that in early childhood led to his forming the concepts of *red* and *circle.* The earlier events that were eventually subsumed under the concepts *red* and *circle* have lost their dissociability and have, therefore, been forgotten. They are no longer discriminable and hence are not remembered because they have been incorporated into the more general and inclusive concept *red circle.*

5. Motivated Forgetting. Apparently, as we study we constantly decide what we will try and will not try to remember; part of this deciding not to remember could represent motivated forgetting. Furthermore, most human beings try to forget unpleasant experiences but are not completely successful; others sometimes forget so completely as to experience *amnesia* — the inability, not associated with known damage to the brain or central nervous system, to recall past experiences. In some cases, the individual can recall nothing of his previous experiences; in other cases, there is recall of events only up to a certain period. Because most amnesia victims are helped by various therapeutic processes to recall the experiences they previously could not, it is assumed that they wanted to forget but now no longer do. Amnesia victims usually have experienced exceedingly unpleasant events before the onset of the condition.

In daily affairs, there also is some suggestion of motivated forgetting. Some adults forget appointments they expect will be unpleasant. Also, the boy who is ordered to see the principal immediately after school may honestly forget that he is to do so, even though he remembers that his gang is to meet a week hence for a football game. Although the bases of motivated forgetting are not fully understood, the teacher or parents should not immediately conclude that a child is deliberately lying when he says he forgot an appointment or forgot to carry out some activity he perceived as being rather unpleasant. We do not treat the adult amnesia victim as a deliberate liar and should not so treat the child.

Motivated forgetting may also occur in relation to classroom learning if the events surrounding the learning experience are unpleasant for the student. Thus if a student is embarrassed while discussing the content or mood of a Longfellow poem, he may actively, but not consciously, attempt to forget the material while attempting to forget the unpleasantness of the situation.

Short-Term Memory

Try to recall the words and sentences of the last paragraph. Ability to recall them is indicative of short-term memory. Most experiments on short-term memory do not use sentences; rather, unrelated words, numerals, and other symbols are used (Postman, 1964). Figure 16.1 shows theoretical curves for the short-term memory of consonants that were presented visually. The curves show that, as might be expected, short-term retention decreases (forgetting increases) as the amount of material increases.

Fig. 16.1. Theoretical retention curves for different numbers of items in short-term memory. (Melton, 1963, p. 12)

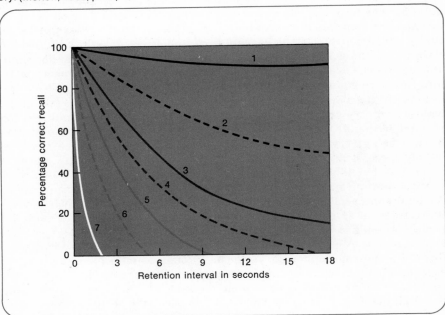

One clear implication of short-term memory for instruction is that large amounts of information should not be presented in a short period of time if the intention is to have it learned and recalled. For example, adults on the average can recall only seven digits when presented in a random sequence. Similarly, the reader is not expected to recall sentences in the last paragraph verbatim. He might, however, recall the words "short-term memory" and the relationship between the amount of material presented and the amount of forgetting.

In school situations, the recall of specific information is often desired, such as the correct spelling of words, the vocabulary of a second language, the symbols that stand for the various chemical elements, and other factual information of low meaningfulness. Here a review of research on short-term memory (Postman, 1964) demonstrates clearly that the teacher must not present more items than the student can incorporate in his short-term memory. This relatively small number of items then requires practice or review until it is mastered and can be recalled for long periods of time.

Only a few of the many strategies that human beings employ, other than review and practice, to organize material to facilitate retention have been identified. Some of these have been clarified through research on short-term memory. In one experiment, a situation was arranged so that college students were to learn a list of 22 nouns, each starting with a different letter of the alphabet (Tulving, 1968). Before the list of words was first presented on a screen, all the students were given the same standard printed instructions intended to get them to learn and remember the words; these read: "Do your best on each recall trial and put down as many words from the list as you can." Before the fourth trial, these instructions were again given to half the students. New instructions, however, were given to the other half, which read: "Try to organize your recalled words alphabetically. When you look at the words on the screen, note their first letters, and make an attempt to associate the words with the letters. When you write the words down, go through the letters of the alphabet one at a time and try to remember the word that goes with each letter."

Figure 16.2 shows the learning curves for the two groups. For the first three trials the curves are almost indistinguishable. From trial 4 on, however, the curves are greatly different, favoring the group that received the instruction to use the alphabetical association strategy. Tulving interpreted this result to mean that the method of organization is very important for initial learning. The students who got them obviously were helped by the instructions in how to organize the material. The students did associate the first letter with each word during initial learning and used this and their previously acquired knowledge of the alphabet to facilitate recall. Those who did not get these instructions did not employ this effective strategy.

Tulving (1968) also demonstrated another procedure that dramatically improved short-term recall of words. In an experiment, high school students were treated identically until the beginning of the recall test; that is, they were told to learn and remember words presented in lists. The

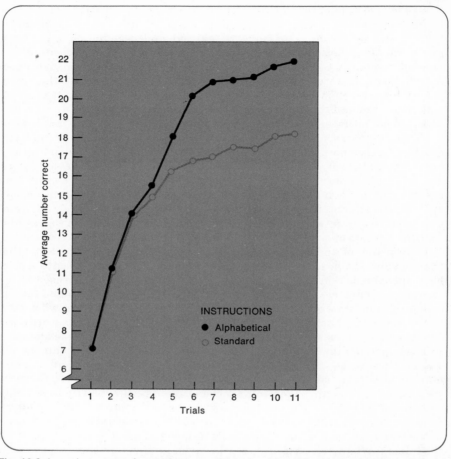

Fig. 16.2. Learning curves for students taught and not taught a strategy for learning and remembering. (Tulving, 1968, p. 6)

lists of words varied in length – 12, 24, and 48 words. Also, the words representing things belonging in the same category varied in number – 1, 2, and 4. Things belonging in the same category were of this kind: things found on the farm – wheat, tractor; substances for flavoring food – sugar, cloves; musical instruments – drum, flute. Half the students, after being presented with the list, were simply asked to recall all the words they remembered. The other half were presented with the category names as *retrieval cues* and were asked to write down all the words belonging to each category that they remembered from the list. Table 16.1 shows that the effectiveness of cueing in facilitating recall increased as the length of the lists increased – 12, 24, 48, but usually decreased as the number of words per category increased – 1, 2, 4. Thus giving the category name to cue the recall of words was more effective when there were only one or two words to recall in a category than when there were four. Also,

Table 16.1. Average Number of Words Recalled for the 18 Experimental Conditions

List length	Recall conditions	Number of Words per Category		
		1	2	4
12	Cued	10.70	10.94	9.98
	Noncued	7.70	8.13	9.31
24	Cued	21.70	19.31	15.11
	Noncued	11.18	11.82	13.38
48	Cued	35.35	35.76	29.60
	Noncued	15.57	18.79	19.33

Source: Adapted from Tulving, 1968, p. 10.

cueing with the category word was much more effective with 48 words in comparison with 24 and with 24 in comparison with 12. Apparently, the 12-word tasks were easy enough so that cueing did not make much difference. Again, these students did not use this effective strategy associated with category names without being instructed to do so.

Tulving indicated that he thought it was more important for the teacher to help the student in organizing material than to organize it for him. Tulving agreed that much could be done through organizing learning activities to facilitate students' initial learning and retention; however, each student should also learn to do this himself, so that he would be able to learn well without the teacher's assistance. In other words, Tulving advocated giving considerable attention to teaching students strategies such as those used in the two experiments. If a teacher is to do this, he must analyze the particular subject matter critically and be creative in formulating possible strategies that students may adopt. In the later discussion of the attributes of memory, other aspects of memory that may be associated with recall are described.

Attributes of Memory

Underwood (1969) analyzed the attributes of memory, that is, what gets associated with what during initial learning that is remembered and permits subsequent recall. He defined a memory as an organism's record of an event. The memory, or record, is established initially as the individual encodes encountered material. For example, when a student first sees the words "conservatives support tax reduction," he translates this set of words to their meanings and later recalls the meanings, not just the words or symbols. The attributes that are stored permit the recall of the event or material. One or more attributes comprise the memory, or record. This record is inferred when the individual responds in a way in which he would not have responded if the earlier event had not been experienced.

Underwood's analysis is one of the most comprehensive and stimulating approaches to the study of memory in decades. The analysis is, potentially, among the most influential that have been done in psychological research. A major reason for this is that the analysis promises to make possible the isolation of conditions that, in turn, may be found applicable to the actual designing of instructional materials and the developing of instructional methods. This means that a teacher might identify one or more specific attributes that could be dealt with more effectively when students in his class repeatedly or persistently were unable to recall desired verbal information. It means also that the teacher could be provided with specific guides for dealing with such recall difficulties.

Figure 16.3 shows how Underwood has classified the attributes of a memory; each of these is now discussed. The examples and the information or questions that appear in parentheses are intended to help the reader understand each attribute.

Attributes Independent of the Task

Temporal Attribute

Examples: Recalling the day of high school graduation.

Remembering that a French class was taken the semester earlier, or later, than one in geometry.

Perception of an event occurs at a given point in time; yet a given point in time can have no representation in memory except in terms of the events that occurred at the time. Therefore, the temporal attribute of a memory must consist of a contiguous event associated with a point in time or a time range. The contiguous events associated with the point in time may be the words used to identify points of the time dimension, e.g., yesterday, last year, this morning. Also, the temporal attribute may identify a memory in relation to another event as before or after. (Events carrying distinct time tags are presumed to be less susceptible to interference from memories of other events. Temporal separation of certain learning tasks may be important in school. Does recalling the time sequence in which things were carried out help to recall where one has misplaced glasses, car keys, etc.?)

Spatial Attribute

Examples: Recalling the content of a figure according to where it appeared on a page.

Remembering a word or words according to their position on a page.

Yates (1966) pointed out that some public figures who deliver long speeches without notes use memory systems that include a spatial dimension. Various positions in a building—a column, a corner, a vase, a statue, and so on—are associated with the focal points of the speech. Later, when actually delivering the speech, the speaker goes through the room or building in his mind's eye, calling up each successive point. Slamecka

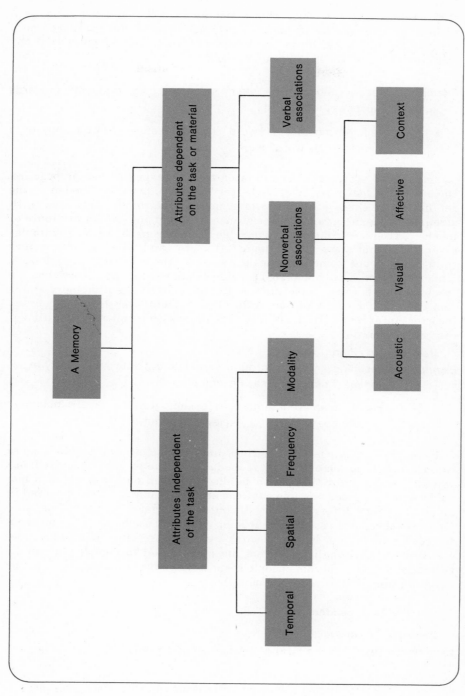

Fig. 16.3. The attributes of a memory. (Adapted from Underwood, 1969)

(1967) tentatively confirmed this attribute in a verbal learning experiment. (Can one specifically note exactly where something is placed on a printed page or place things in such a way when writing notes that the content will later be better remembered?)

Frequency Attribute

Examples: Recognizing that the letter "s" occurs more frequently in words than does the letter "q."

Recognizing that the word "the" appears more frequently on a page than the word "page."

Underwood states that the greater the frequency of use or practice, the better the learning. Also, the better the initial learning, the better the retention. In these statements, frequency is directly associated with strength of learning, or with resistance to forgetting. As an attribute of memory, frequency must be separable from strength. In the examples given, "s" is not a stronger response than "q" and "the" is not stronger than "page," but somehow one is aware of their relative frequencies. Underwood and Ekstrand (1968) provided evidence for the theory that the frequency with which something occurs is an attribute of memory and is relatively independent of strength. (The student may often encounter incorrect information that will interfere later with recall or recognition of correct information.)

Modality Attribute

Examples: Recalling an event through associating it with an auditory experience: "I heard him say he would go."

Recalling an event through associating it with a visual experience: "I remember seeing it in a television commercial."

Here the concern is not whether material is initially acquired more rapidly as a function of the input modality or the way it is acquired, but whether memory for things can be discriminated on the basis of a modality attribute. It is possible that the storing of material encountered in an auditory way differs from the storing of material encountered visually. Underwood reports research that supports this possibility. (Do you seem to recall information better through hearing or seeing something associated with it? Though this is not directly related to modality as an attribute of memory, do some people seem to learn better through seeing, or manipulating, than through hearing?)

Attributes Dependent on the Task

Acoustic Attribute

Examples: Recalling the form of a letter, word, or phrase on the basis of its sound.

Remembering a word when a rhyming word is associated with it.

This is the first of the nonverbal, associative task, or material, attributes. These four attributes are nonverbal, but the tasks in the learning experiments from which they have been inferred are verbal—they involve words. Each word in turn is comprised of letters that have sounds. The acoustic attribute, that is, hearing a sound for a letter or word when it is presented orally or saying the letter or word sound to oneself when it is presented visually, cannot be completely separated from other attributes to be discussed, because it is always present in hearing subjects. The point here, however, is whether or not the acoustic attribute plays a discriminative role in memory. The evidence indicates that it does, at least under certain circumstances. For example, Underwood and Freund (1968) found that the acoustic attribute plays a more prominent role in the recall of material of low meaningfulness. With material of high meaningfulness, the verbal attributes to be discussed later are more prominent. (In which set does the sound of the last item facilitate recall of the first: glux, brux, nux, wux—terrier, cow, chicken, mollusk? According to the theory, one rhyming word facilitates the subsequent recall of another rhyming word, whereas an unrelated sound does not facilitate memory and recall.)

Visual Attribute

Examples: Recalling the form or sound of a letter, word, or phrase on the basis of its appearance.

Recalling a word or phrase on the basis of the image of the thing represented by the word or phrase.

One may look at a word, close his eyes, and see the word in his mind's eye. A word may also represent something, and the object or event represented by the word may take the form of an internal image. Visual images accompanying initial learning become an attribute of memory. As there are differences among individuals in visual imagery during learning, so also there may be differences in the extent to which this attribute functions in storage and recall as an attribute of memory. That is, one person may have more mental images than another that "call up" a word, phrase, or sentence. (Might telling students to stop, close their eyes, and "see the correct spelling of 'weird'" facilitate later recall? Does trying to create an image of a table or figure in this book help you to recall its content later?)

Affective Attribute

Example: Recalling the pleasant-unpleasant feelings associated with words, even though the words themselves may not be recalled.

This is the third nonverbal associative attribute. It is known that events and words that represent events may be associated with feelings on a pleasant-unpleasant dimension. Feelings, in turn, may be represented, or described, by words. The focus here, however, is directly on the feelings, not on the words that describe them. Memories for events may be discriminated on the basis of the feelings associated with them during the initial learning. This attribute is, of course, closely related to motivated forgetting, which was discussed earlier. The affective attribute of memory, like other attributes, may facilitate *or* interfere with recall. We have discussed only the facilitating effects of the attributes on subsequent memory throughout this section. (Do advertisers present only pleasant scenes to encourage viewers to recall brand names? Might the same strategy work in school?)

Context Attribute

Example: Recalling the context in which "their," "there" were initially learned facilitates recall of the correct spelling of each of them.

Underwood points out that the number of ways in which the context may be varied in experiments is enormous and that no general principles have yet been formulated that might indicate when the context attribute influences memory for an event. (Are children more able to recall the correct pronunciation of a word when it is encountered in the same paragraph in which it was initially learned or when it is presented by itself on a flash card?)

Verbal Attribute

Examples: "Strong," associated with the word "powerful" during initial learning, becomes a memory attribute for the recall of "powerful."

"Number," the word associated with a series of numerals initially learned, facilitates the recall of numerals only, rather than nonnumerical words.

In laboratory experiments, a subject is often asked to learn lists of words. He may respond to the words in a list with implicit verbal responses (saying words to himself) which are associates, such as antonyms or synonyms, of the words to be learned. These implicit verbal responses become attributes of the words in the list to be learned and may facilitate subsequent recall of the list. Similarly, the words to be learned might elicit a category or concept name. When several words elicit the same category name, recall of the list is facilitated. Moreover, the subject organizes his recall in terms of the concepts represented in the list. Verbal attributes can also cause interference. When a subject is asked to recall a word, he may not be able to distinguish between the word he actually learned and the implicit verbal response he made to the word during learning. (Compare the ideas here with the theoretical curves for forgetting discussed earlier in this chapter and with the information presented about short-term memory.)

The preceding discussion deals with the specific attributes of memory. Three brief quotations indicate how Underwood thinks of memory in a larger context:

> A memory is conceptualized as a collection of attributes which serve to discriminate one memory from another and to act as retrieval mechanisms for a target memory. . . .
> It is quite common to speak of the *encoding* of material by the subject (*S*) as

it is presented for learning. In the context of the present discussion, encoding represents the process by which the attributes of a memory are established, although no assumption is made about the necessary intentionality on the part of S in these processes. When a memory is conceptualized as consisting of an ensemble of attributes, memory for an event per se has no psychological meaning because a memory without attributes is incapable of being remembered (retrieved). There is no "corpus" which can be recalled directly. Furthermore, differences in the attributes for different memories are fundamental for discriminating or differentiating memories, hence are fundamental for understanding the failure of S to perform perfectly on a retention test, that is, for understanding forgetting. . . .

Whenever one or more attributes overlap for two or more different memories, interference may occur in recall attempts. The greater the number of attributes associated with a memory, and the less the attributes are associated with other memories, the less the interference, hence the less forgetting. . . . (Underwood, 1969, pp. 559, 571)

Type of Material and Retention

The theories that have just been outlined are, of course, based on many experiments. During these and other experiments, much has also been learned about exactly which types of learning outcomes are remembered most easily and for the longest times. Figure 16.4, summarizing the results of extensive investigation, shows theoretical curves of retention for three kinds of outcomes. Ideas, corresponding to concepts and principles, are remembered for long periods of time. Many concepts, such as of time and life, which are acquired at a low level of mastery in early childhood, become stronger and remain strong. On the other hand, factual informa-

Fig. 16.4. Traditional hypothetical retention curves for different classes of material. (Deese & Hulse, 1967, p. 383)

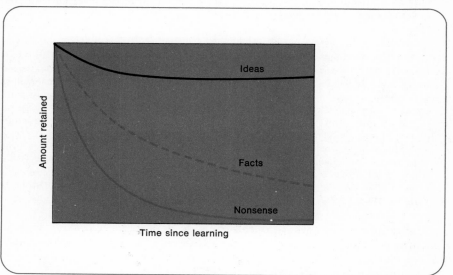

tion is forgotten quite rapidly, and the less meaningful it is, the more rapidly it is forgotten. Nonsense syllables, such as "nvx," "bzy," "gln," "pbf," "rcn," are forgotten very rapidly. This is a good place to point out that the materials a child encounters in school sometimes have as little meaning for him as nonsense syllables have for you.

These varying degrees of retention are reflected in actual school learning, of course. For example, an extensive review of studies dealing with retention of subject matter by elementary, high school, and college students points to differential retention of various outcomes:

1. Elementary School Subjects

Studies in elementary school subjects indicate that reading ability tends to increase during summer vacation. Studies of history show a difference in the rate of forgetting types of historical material—a gain in the second test in the case of easy material but a loss for more difficult material. Arithmetic studies tend to show that advanced material is more easily lost than fundamentals. The degree of difficulty of the material studied appears to affect the rate and amount of loss.

2. Secondary School Subjects

Studies conducted in mathematics in secondary schools showed a definite loss varying from 10 percent during the summer vacation to as much as 33 1/3 percent during a year interval. In a standardized algebra test some items were retained by 100 percent of the class, whereas other items showed a 100 percent loss. In some of these studies there would appear to be little relation between amount of initial acquisition and the amount retained. Studies in science show a definite loss varying with different types of material. Retention appears higher in the area of general information and application of facts and lower in ability to recall chemical terms and to write equations. In a study of high school and college chemistry, high school seniors showed a 42 percent loss of informational material after a period of three months. After a five-year period college students were able to recall approximately 19 percent of the informational material studied in high school chemistry.

3. College Subjects

Studies in college science courses show a definite loss over the time intervals measured. The amount of loss varies from 50 percent over a four-month period to as high as 94 percent loss of initial gain after one year. The greatest loss appears to be in technical information, with little loss in ability to apply principles to new situations. Retention in general subject-matter areas after an interval of four years or more indicated highest retention in U.S. history, ancient history, and geometry, whereas the lowest retention was in physics, chemistry, and Latin. In a world history test given to college freshmen, retention scores appeared to be closely related to grades received in high school courses. In an American history test based on factual information, a group of college girls showed a loss of 40 percent of the initial acquisition after one year. (Sterrett & Davis, 1954, pp. 455-456)

This summary shows that retention is related to varying types of learning outcomes and to their difficulty. In general, factual and technical information is forgotten rapidly; more general information, application of facts, and principles are retained better.

16.1. Five explanations, or conditions, of forgetting are discussed briefly. Which one, or combination of them, seems to best account for the forgetting of subject matter learned in school?

16.2. Which of the possible conditions of forgetting does a person appear to have most control over? Which condition might be most critical in connection with remembering a foreign language? A poem? A speech? A problem-solving method?

16.3. Which of the following lists is easier for you to memorize in exact sequence?

    a. Word, sentence, paragraph, page, book, library.

    b. Light, teacher, dandelion, town, circus, steal.

Why is one more difficult to learn than another? Devise a few words that, when given to a person, would help him to retrieve or recall each list at some later time. Which words are most difficult to devise? Why?

16.4. Which of the attributes of memory described by Underwood do you think you might use to remember the names of the attributes? Which of the attributes are incorporated in the design of this book in presenting the names of the attributes and discussing them? Can you identify any new strategies based on Underwood's list that might be used to remember the list or some other list?

TRANSFER

Transfer may be positive or negative. *Negative transfer* occurs when performing one task interferes with learning a second one. As discussed in connection with problem-solving, when an individual learns to use some instrument or method of approach in a particular way to solve a problem successfully, he tends not to use that instrument or method to solve a new problem (Birch & Rabinowitz, 1951). *Positive transfer* occurs when an outcome learned in one situation is remembered and is applied to a new situation. Neither negative *nor* positive transfer occurs when the learning in one situation is not perceived by the individual as related to a new situation.

Transfer may be lateral or vertical (Gagné, 1965). In *lateral transfer* the individual is able to perform a different but similar task of about the same level of complexity as that which he has learned. For example, a child has learned at school to recognize new words. He then recognizes in a newspaper article words of about the same difficulty as those read in school. In *vertical transfer* a person is also able to learn similar but more advanced or more complex outcomes. Here information and abilities acquired in one situation transfer to a more complex one, usually in the same subject field. For example, information learned about square permits one to develop a more complete concept of square; having the concepts of square, rhombus, and quadrilateral enables one to form the principle that quadrilaterals vary according to equality of length of sides and parallelness of sides; and knowledge of the principle facilitates solving problems (finding perimeter or computing areas) where squares and rhombuses are involved. Abilities to be discussed later are also involved in lateral and vertical transfer.

The teacher, as well as others who decide what to teach, is concerned with securing positive transfer, both lateral and vertical, to situations both inside and outside the school setting. Also, the teacher explicitly or implicitly acts on a theory or combination of theories of transfer in making his decisions. Understanding the theories, however, will make the decisions more rational. Five theories, in order of their historical origin, are: formal discipline, identical elements, generalization, transposition, and abilities (Klausmeier & Davis, 1969).

1. Formal-Discipline Theory

The formal-discipline theory of transfer was prevalent during the nineteenth century and earlier when it was assumed that the mind was composed of many separate faculties, such as memory, reason, attention, will, and imagination. According to the theory, these faculties should be strengthened through practice much as muscles are strengthened; systematic drill in certain subject fields was thought to have the same effect on the mind as physical exercise on the body. Because during the late 1800s Latin, Greek, and mathematics were thought to be the most difficult subjects, they were considered the most useful for strengthening these faculties and for improving the mind generally and thus were thought to be the most desirable subjects. In accordance with the theory, memory drills (it made little difference what was memorized) were employed to develop the memory faculties. Long and difficult assignments were made because they were supposed to develop the faculties of will power and attention. Furthermore, such subjects as Latin, Greek, and mathematics were thought to have inherent qualities that facilitated the simultaneous development of many other faculties. In turn, as these faculties were well developed through education in the school, the results would automatically transfer to out-of-school situations, including the practical daily affairs of life.

Edward L. Thorndike, after studying the effects of different subjects taken in high school on increases in students' ability to reason, concluded that one subject was no better than another for improving reasoning ability (Thorndike, 1924). As the courses were taught during the 1920s, physics, trigonometry, Greek, and Latin produced no better reasoners than did physical education and dramatic arts; however, students who were enrolled in the more difficult courses did make higher scores initially than those in the more practical courses. Humphreys (1951) came to similar conclusions: (1) Taking a course in English literature does not automatically result in the students' showing greater appreciation of literature outside the course; (2) teaching moral or ethical values in Sunday school does not necessarily have any effect on moral behavior outside the class; (3) a foreign-language course does not sharpen the intellect of those who take the course; (4) a laboratory course in physical science does not necessarily result in a carry-over of scientific methods to social sciences or biological sciences; (5) a traditional geometry course does not necessarily result in an increase in ability to solve problems, except in geometry. Humphreys asserted that it is a mistake to assume that there is automatic transfer from any subject field to any other subject field or to situations outside the school.

Nevertheless, some teachers still justify certain subject matter and instructional procedures on such vague grounds as "it is good for the mind" or "it disciplines the student." We should not summarily dismiss such teachers as hopelessly old fashioned, however. As was shown in earlier chapters, it is true that concepts, principles, and abilities that students acquire through study in some subject fields may transfer to other subjects or situations where the same or similar outcomes are encountered. Mathematical concepts, for example, may transfer to those subjects where information is presented in mathematical terms, and the ability to read well is essential for achieving well in the many subject fields that require the learner to read to secure information. In other words, it is possible that some teachers who use such terms as *intellectual discipline* and *mental discipline* are referring, at least implicitly, to the transfer of these more pervasive concepts and abilities.

2. Identical-Elements Theory

The identical-elements theory of transfer, which was formulated by Thorndike (1913), assumes that elements present in the initial learning situation must also be present in the new situation for transfer to occur. The identical elements were presumed to be specific facts and skills. Thus, after the student has mastered the facts of addition, e.g., $7 + 3$, he can use them in solving new problems in which the same facts appear. After he has mastered skill in using an index in one book, the skill transfers to other indexes organized in a similar way. This theory as set forth by Thorndike provided a more reliable basis for considering transfer than the formal-discipline theory. The theory also pointed to a practical way to help students learn certain subject matters and skills that would be essential or helpful to them in later life, that is, simply to teach those subjects and skills. Then students would be equipped with identical elements that would transfer when needed. Accordingly, the application of Thorndike's theory to education by his followers did result in more relevant curricula in many cases, although it also may have produced an unwarranted emphasis on specifics and on memorizing rather than understanding.

Nevertheless, the results of Thorndike's theory in the introduction of more useful subjects were profound. The natural sciences were brought into the high school curriculum in the present century. Modern foreign languages came in on a widespread basis after World War II. Typing, shorthand, bookkeeping, and English composition are now offered in business education in the high schools. Courses in welding, machine operation, woodworking, auto mechanics, blueprinting, and the like are offered to help boys get jobs in factories. In rural areas, boys are given instruction in animal husbandry, soil conservation, and allied subjects in order to help them assume their roles as farmers. Distributive education, in which the student works half time and goes to school half time, is available for students who are more interested in doing things than in studying, particularly if they need the income. The high school student intending to enter a profession via higher education concentrates his work in English, mathematics, science, social studies, foreign languages, and the fine arts—not to train his mind or to become disciplined but to acquire the outcomes and abilities that will transfer to higher education and an eventual career.

In elementary education, the idea of identical elements led to identifying the vocabulary and arithmetic facts most widely used by adults. For example, letters written by adults were examined, and the frequency with which various words appeared was noted. The most frequently used words were given the highest priority in reading and other elementary school textbooks. Much emphasis was also given to the specific facts and specific skills in arithmetic that adults used frequently. Along with the emphasis on specifics, drill to achieve a high level of mastery was encouraged. It is not surprising that all this emphasis on facts and drill virtually shunted concepts, principles, and relationships aside, with the result that they were not given enough attention. Although these events occurred during the present century and are in harmony with the theory of identical elements, not all of them can be ascribed solely to the theory. However, not until after World War II was a serious attempt made, nationwide, to change this pattern of content and method of learning.

3. Generalization Theory

The generalization theory holds that generalizations, or principles, are learned from a variety of experiences and that these generalizations transfer to and guide behavior in new situations. In an interesting early experiment dealing with generalization (Judd, 1908), two groups of boys threw a small dart at a target placed under water. Refraction was explained to one group before starting, but the other group was given no explanation of the principle. Both groups began their practice with the target placed under 12 inches of water; the same amount of practice was required for both groups to reach the same results. At this point, knowledge of the principle appeared to be of no value. Then the task was changed, but only by reducing the depth of the water. The difference between the performances of the two groups was striking in that the boys who understood the principle now performed the task much more efficiently than those who did not. It was not the identical elements in the two situations that was transferred, but the understanding of the principle of refraction.

This experiment by Judd was replicated as nearly as possible much later. (These experimenters could not be sure of an exact replication because Judd did not describe his procedures in detail.) The results of the second experiment were as follows: (1) understanding the principle facilitated positive transfer; (2) understanding the principle also facilitated the original learning; (3) the completeness of the theoretical information had a direct effect on both initial learning and transfer—the more complete the information, the better the results (Hendrickson & Schroeder, 1941). The examples just given deal with skill learning. It has been shown that understanding a principle also facilitates the learning of outcomes in the cognitive domain (Klausmeier, Harris, & Wiersma, 1964; Wittrock, 1963a).

Transfer by generalization is an extension of transfer by identical elements. Unless the new situation has enough in common with the previous one for the learner to perceive applications, no transfer occurs. Generalization provides a more mature, broader viewpoint for effective curriculum and teaching practices. When the teacher is freed from attempting to teach a large number of specific facts and skills in many different subjects, more interesting and meaningful concepts and principles can be taught. More long-term projects and assignments, problem-solving activities, class discussions, and units of work that stress generalizations can be used rather than short daily lessons with drill on many specific facts, skills, and attitudes.

4. Transposition Theory

The theory of transposition goes further than that of generalization in that the entire pattern of means-ends relationships is proposed as the basis of transfer. For example, after an individual recognizes the "Star-Spangled Banner" in the key of F, he readily recognizes it when it is transposed into the key of G, although no individual note is the same at the same point in the tune in the two keys. Applied to Judd's dart-throwing experiment, the transposition theory would suggest that it is not only the principle but the individual's entire perceptions of the relationships among the principle, the use of the dart, the depth of the water, and the placement of the target that were transferred. Transposition applied to arithmetic means that the specific facts and skills of addition, even the principle underlying addition, are not the basis of transfer from in-school to out-of-school situations; instead, it is the understanding of the _relationships_ among the facts, processes, and principles. The more extensive the knowledge of relationships gained during initial learning, the greater the transfer (Johnson & Zara, 1960).

5. Abilities Theory

Ability in this book has been defined as the union of a process, or operation, and a content or contents. An ability theory of transfer suggests that improved performance on a second task depends on (1) the extent to which the individual has acquired and later recalls the necessary content—factual information, concept, principle—from study or practice of the first task, and (2) the extent to which the individual has developed a specific ability or abilities from study or practice of the first task. Furthermore, there may be a more general ability common to the initial and the second task that is developed to a higher level through practice of the first task or tasks; also, although the second task may require the recall of information other than that learned in the first task, this information can be recalled. Figure 16.5 diagrams this basis of transfer.

For example, a child has completed his first subtraction exercise that involves borrowing: $22 - 6 =$ and then encounters a second exercise: $23 - 8 =$. Obviously, the second exercise requires the use of *information* not contained in the first, namely that $13 - 8 = 5$. Without breaking down the first task into all the possible distinct abilities, we see that it involves (1) recognizing the principle that 6 cannot be subtracted from 2 but that 10 can be taken from 20 and added to the 2 to make 12, (2) applying this principle, and then (3) performing the operations: $12 - 6, 1 - 0$. This *ability*, acquired in performing the first task, will lead to a quick performance of the second task if the learner sees the similarity between the two tasks, has the information, $13 - 8$, and has acquired the specific ability in the first situation. It is apparent also that if the specific ability, or skill, involved in the two exercises is mastered, transfer is possible to many other exercises of the same class. In other words, a more general ability, arithmetic computation, may be strengthened by completing the first exercise.

In comparing the role of abilities and information as related to transfer, Gagné (1968) took the following example from Guilford (1967, p 42): "Which of these letter combinations does not belong with the rest?"

PXNO   VRIM   AQES   GUVC
  1   2   3   4

Fig. 16.5. Information and ability bases of transfer.

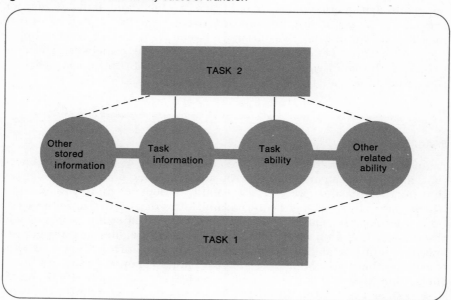

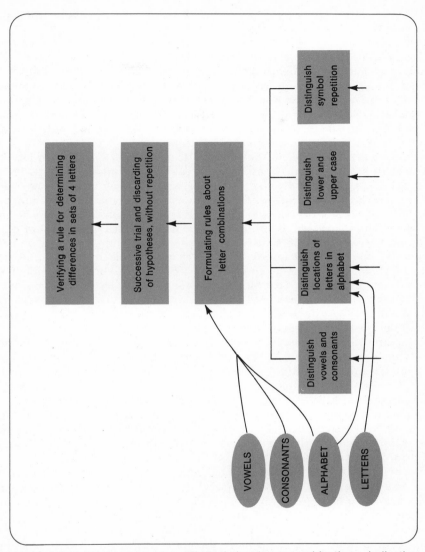

Fig. 16.6. A learning hierarchy for differentiating letter combinations, indicating the contribution of intellectual skills (boxes) and verbal information (circles). (Adapted from Gagné, 1968, p. 5)

(The answer is combination 3, because it has two vowels.) Gagne then ana-lyzed the task into its component intellectual skills—referred to by the present authors as specific abilities—and its knowledge components, as shown in Fig. 16.6. The intellectual skills include distinguishing vowels and consonants, distinguishing locations of letters in the alphabet, formu-lating rules about letter combinations, trying out and discarding hypothe-ses, and eventually verifying a rule for determining the differences in sets of four letters. Some factual information about the alphabet, letters, consonants, and vowels is also needed in this task, and it must be recalled in order to get the correct answer.

Gagné indicated that the abilities have an ordered relation to one another, each succeeding one built on the one preceding it. This is another way of saying that there is vertical transfer from subordinate to superordinate abilities. Gagné also pointed out that the more important things learned in school are the specific abilities, rather than the factual information. The factual information can be located when needed, but the abilities must be developed over time and with practice.

Abilities are involved not only in vertical transfer but also in lateral transfer in both the verbal and motor areas (Fleishman & Bartlett, 1969). In some cases, the terms *skills*, *strategies*, and *learning to learn* are used, rather than abilities. Thus when Harlow (1949) demonstrated a nonspecific basis of horizontal transfer, he called it learning to learn. In a series of experiments, successive different tasks of about the same level of difficulty were given to subjects. At first there was little improvement in performance, but suddenly improvement was very rapid in terms of fewer errors or less time. The term *learning to learn* was given to this phenomenon: practice on tasks of the same type was followed by greatly improved performance on other tasks of the same type. It is quite clear that some kind of ability was developed to a higher level during the practice that accounted for the learning to learn.

Learning to learn has been demonstrated in many other experiments involving a variety of tasks. For example, in numerous experiments on concept attainment in different subject fields, we observe improvement in performance across trials. Similarly, in school settings, the 7-year-old shows improvement in successive reading tasks, the 12-year-old in successive instrumental music performances, and the high school student in acquiring successive principles in physics. Although these improvements can be called learning to learn, more specific abilities underlie each kind of improvement.

Bruner, et al. (1956) indicated that successive concepts were learned with less difficulty as the individual acquired a strategy. Both strategy and learning to learn refer to the same phenomenon: the individual practices or works at something, develops some ability or skill related to the specific task content, and with higher development of the ability performs tasks of a similar kind much more effectively. The improvement sometimes is sudden; at other times it is more gradual. A key to successful classroom teaching is to analyze tasks carefully and teach the specific *abilities* involved. Examples of these tasks are learning to read or spell at successively higher levels, to form concepts and principles in the various subject fields, and to solve problems.

Agreements About Transfer

The transfer theories (except the formal-discipline theory) are based on reliable evidence that transfer *does* occur, but they do not agree on exactly what it is that transfers. In the identical-elements theory it is the more specific facts, skills, or attitudes; in the generalization theory it is the principles; and in the transposition theory it is the broader patterns of means-ends relationships. The abilities theory proposes a basis of knowledge—it may be specific information, a principle, a relationship, or all three—and also a basis of abilities. Thus, although the theories of transfer do not agree on their bases, they are successively more inclusive, and in that sense they are in agreement.

16.5. Does any one theory of transfer seem to apply more directly than another to the learning of facts? Concepts? Attitudes? Motor skills?

16.6. What are the possibilities for positive transfer between what you learn in this course and your teaching later? Related to this course, can you give an example of positive lateral transfer and of positive vertical transfer? What might be done to increase the amount of positive transfer?

16.7. If the elements in the identical elements theory of transfer are interpreted to be not only facts and skills but also generalizations and abilities, does this theory become inclusive? What besides such identical elements might be transferred across situations? Do the theories presented seem to explain both negative and positive transfer equally well? Lateral and vertical transfer?

PRINCIPLES OF RETENTION AND TRANSFER

Two important facts may be inferred from the discussion thus far: (1) Retention can occur only if something has been acquired initially; (2) transfer of an acquired outcome to a new situation can occur only if the outcome has been retained. Motivation is essential for both initial learning and retention. Motivation and initial learning, the keys to retention and transfer, are therefore related to them in the principles and instructional guides for encouraging retention and transfer and in the following detailed discussion of the guides.

Principle	Instructional Guide
1. Setting and starting to attain a goal initiates and focuses activities.	1. Foster intent to learn and remember.
2. Perceiving the relatedness of components of a task facilitates the initial learning and retention of all types of learning outcomes.	2. Help the learner to identify meaningful relationships.
3. Experiencing feelings of success in connection with initial learning promotes retention.	3. Provide satisfying consequences of correct responses.
4. Attaining concepts and principles and developing abilities facilitate vertical and lateral transfer.	4. Emphasize concepts and abilities.

Principle	Instructional Guide
continued	*continued*
5. Applying newly acquired concepts, principles, and abilities increases their permanence.	5. Provide opportunities for application.
6. Learning over a period of time is essential for developing stable abilities and comprehensive knowledge.	6. Provide for sequential, cumulative learning.

1. Foster Intent To Learn and Remember

An intention to achieve or complete something energizes and directs immediate action in getting started (Miller, Galanter, & Pribram, 1960). The individual who intends to achieve something also continues his efforts, coming back to the task after other events have intervened. As discussed earlier in connection with motivation, goal-setting implies intending to attain a goal and keeps effort directed toward goal attainment. An intention to learn well and to remember also has a beneficial effect on retention. For example, undergraduates in an educational psychology course were given a passage of about 1400 words on the history of drug addiction (Ausubel, Schpoont, & Cukier, 1957). They were divided into two groups: (1) The control group was instructed to read the passage at normal speed, to use the rest of the period to study the facts and ideas, and to be prepared for a test that would immediately follow their reading and study. Fourteen days later they were given a second similar test of retention, not announced in advance. (2) The same procedure was used with the experimental group, except that immediately after completing the first test this group was told that another test on similar material would be given in 14 days. The scores of the two groups were about the same on the first test. The experimental group, however, the group told at the end of the first test that it would be retested in 14 days, scored *lower* than the control group on the retention test. These results led to the conclusion that intent to learn facilitated retention but that intent to remember when introduced *after* learning had little effect on retention.

The implication for classroom teaching situations is that intent both to learn and to remember should be encouraged before the pupils start the learning task, rather than after the teaching is completed. The best way to accomplish this is to work with students in setting realistic goals in connection with school learning tasks. When this is done the students will attempt to recall during each successive practice or study session what has been learned previously in order to progress toward their goals.

2. Help the Learner To Identify Meaningful Relationships

Understanding a principle or the meaningful relationship among parts leads to better retention and transfer than memorizing and reviewing less meaningful information. For example, children of similar characteristics were taught subtraction by a meaningful (rational) method or by a mechanical (rote) method (Brownell & Moser, 1949). Those taught by the meaningful method were given a variety of suggestions to help them understand the process of borrowing in subtraction. The other group was taught one mechanical method and then drilled, using exercises that required borrowing. Those taught by the mechanical method made more rapid progress in the first few days because the meaningful method required more time to learn. At the end of 15 days, however, they were already dropping behind those taught by the meaningful method. More important, when a transfer situation was arranged, those who had been taught *understanding* of subtraction performed far better than those who had not.

An example clarifies the basis on which these and similar results are obtained. Assume that a child understands that adding is counting upward and is taught, when he first is confronted by 3 + 3, to count 3 somethings (dots) and 3 more somethings (dots) to get 6. When this child later meets a new fact, such as 6 + 4, he can independently get the correct answer by counting 6 dots and 4 dots to get 10. On the other hand, if the child is taught the addition facts by rote, that is, if he is given the facts to memorize but does not understand that adding is counting upward, when he meets the transfer situation, 6 + 4, he will not know what to do. Some children, of course, arrive at the generalization of counting upward independently. Nevertheless, in the study of subtraction, even bright children did not understand the process of borrowing when taught by rote methods and therefore were unable to transfer.

In another situation, problem-solving tasks were presented to 60 students, with one group being taught the solution by memorizing and the other by understanding (Hilgard, Irvine, & Whipple, 1953). In this case, (1) more time was required to teach the problem initially to the understanding group than to the memorizing group, (2) overnight retention was equal for the two groups, and (3) the understanding group did significantly better than the memorizing group on all three problems used in measuring transfer. (The "new math," of course, emphasizes meaningfulness and deemphasizes rote memory.)

Thorough initial learning also facilitates recall in children of varying IQ levels. When a heterogeneous group of children is given the same material to learn, it is invariably too difficult for the low-IQ children in the group. They therefore do not fully understand it and do not acquire it so well initially. The rather natural result is that the low-IQ pupils forget more than the high-IQ ones. But when the material is appropriate to each child's achievement level, there is no difference in retention among children of low, average, and high IQ (Feldhusen, Check, & Klausmeier, 1961; Klausmeier & Feldhusen, 1959). In one study that led to the conclusions just summarized, each child was pretested and then taught a series of 10 subtraction items above the level of difficulty at which he had performed correctly in the pretest. Each child was taught each item in the series as meaningfully as possible and then given an acquisition test. A five-minute interpolated activity followed the acquisition test; this activity, intentionally exciting and attention-holding, involved the children in listening to a

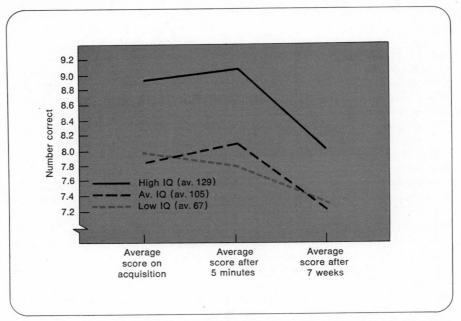

Fig. 16.7. Retention in subtraction problems by children of low, average, and high intelligence. (Based on Klausmeier, Feldhusen, & Check, 1959, p. 69)

tape-recorded selection of music and stories. As Fig. 16.7 shows, the retention scores after this interpolated activity went up slightly for two groups. The significant result, also shown in the figure, is that when the same test was repeated seven weeks later, the amount of retention was much the same for the *three* groups — slightly above 90 percent of what each group had retained earlier. Similar results were obtained with the same children in counting and addition (Feldhusen & Klausmeier, 1959; Klausmeier & Check, 1962).

In addition to helping students to find the relationships among different areas of study, the school can try to avoid the undesirable effects of interference. Table 16.2 shows applications of the effects of interference (interpolated activities) on remembering. Suppose that students take beginning conversational Spanish during the first period. This class period might be followed by Spanish history, mathematics, or beginning conversational French. Spanish history immediately following conversational Spanish has a positive effect on remembering conversational Spanish, because the two are complementary and do not interfere with each other. A mathematics class has little effect on subsequent recall of conversational Spanish, because it neither complements nor interferes with it. French immediately following Spanish has a large and undesired negative effect on remembering the Spanish. French, though similar to Spanish, does not complement but interferes with the Spanish; the same English words call for different responses in Spanish and in French, and this is the source of interference and confusion.

Table 16.2. Effects of Interpolated Activities on Remembering

I. Learning activity, first class period	II. Interpolated learning activity, second class period	Effect of II on remembering I
Beginning Spanish	Spanish history	Positive and small
Beginning Spanish	Mathematics	Small and possibly negative
Beginning Spanish	Beginning French	Negative and large

It is possible that the French might be taught in such a way as not to interfere with beginning Spanish. Nevertheless, if the emphasis is on acquiring vocabulary and if the same words in English are used in both beginning Spanish and French, two undesirable effects are very likely: the French decidedly interferes with remembering the Spanish, and the initial Spanish instruction markedly interferes with acquiring beginning French. As stated near the beginning of this chapter, the terms used for these phenomena are *retroactive inhibition* and *proactive inhibition.*

Meaningful material is not subject to interference to the same degree as material of low meaningfulness, as shown in Table 16.3. Three groups received meaningful learning. The control group was then allowed to rest;

Table 16.3. Number of Completion Items Correctly Recalled

Group	Kind of interpolated material	N	Immediate	After 45 min.		After 21 days	
			Average	Average	Percent recalled	Average	Percent recalled
Control	Rest	14	23.36	23.14	99.1	18.93	81.0
Exp. 1	Dissimilar material	15	23.20	23.53	101.4	19.33	83.3
Exp. 2	Similar material	16	23.31	22.94	98.4	18.81	80.7

Source: Hall, 1955, p. 50.

experimental group 1 received interpolated dissimilar material that supposedly would not produce interference; experimental group 2 received interpolated similar material that supposedly would produce interference. Immediately after these interpolated activities, there was practically no difference in recall of the original learning by the three groups. After 45 minutes and again after 21 days, the amount recalled was still much the same for the three groups. Thus, interpolated material similar to the original meaningful learning did *not* produce interference and forgetting. It is interesting, too, that after 45 minutes, experimental group 1, which had received dissimilar interpolated material, actually showed some reminiscence. That is, they showed some improvement over initial learning, as indicated by the higher average score.

3. Provide Satisfying Consequences of Correct Responses

As was shown in previous chapters, the pleasant effects of success and reward facilitate learning, whereas the unpleasant effects of failure and punishment retard it. In about the same way, feelings of success and satisfaction and of failure and dissatisfaction are related to recall. Experimentally induced threat to the individual results in poorer recall of material than no threat, and subsequent alleviation of threat results in better recall (Aborn, 1953). A more pleasant, cooperative atmosphere under a democratic leader facilitates the recall of factual information more than a competitive atmosphere under an authoritarian leader (Yuker, 1955).

Consequently, deliberate attempts to produce unpleasant feelings in connection with learning activities should be avoided. The aim should be positive, for when initial learning activities are managed so that satisfying consequences are experienced, the initial behavior is confirmed and can be recalled and used in subsequent situations. Difficult tasks that challenge the learner but that he can master are recalled well and are not inherently unpleasant. They may become so, however, if the learner is punished or reproved for not doing well, rather than being praised for consistent trying.

4. Emphasize Concepts and Abilities

The high transfer value of concepts and principles has a long history in research. McDougall (1958) demonstrated that concepts based on a relatively large number of facts were retained better than the facts per se and showed greater possibility of transfer. More recently, Wittrock (1963b) and Klausmeier, Harris, and Wiersma (1964) showed that the rules or principles taught to subjects facilitated the attainment of successive concepts of the same class. Concepts and principles show higher positive transfer than factual information for these reasons: (1) there is more likelihood of similarity between the general components of two tasks than between the specific factual components and therefore more transfer; (2) concepts facilitate the recall and retrieval of more specific information when it is needed.

Modern curriculum improvement programs are specifically aimed at having students better understand the organization of subject matter, acquire the major concepts and the principles that express relationships among concepts, and develop abilities. An example of these programs is a curriculum for instruction in science that was prepared in brief outline form for use in the early grades (Commission on Science Education, 1963). A primary objective of this program is to teach general abilities that will be needed later to develop more specialized abilities. The abilities emphasized are: observing and classifying, describing, recognizing and using numbers and number relations, recognizing and using space and time relations, measuring, inferring, and predicting. The conceptual knowledge to be developed simultaneously is implied by the vocabulary of the first three proposed exercises: "liquid," "solid state," "solution," "gas," "gaseous state," "carbon dioxide," "oxygen." The relationships that the children are to identify among concepts are represented in desired outcomes, such as classifying matter in any of three states—solid, liquid, and gas— and inferring that air makes water disappear. These abilities and concepts are to be learned through an instructional program in which the teacher provides experimental materials and asks questions while the children manipulate, raise their own questions, respond to the teacher's questions, observe, describe, etc.

Work-study skills related to almost all subject fields at all school levels can be taught and learned. Leggitt (1934) instructed ninth-grade students in the use of reference books, interpretation of charts, and construction of outlines and summaries. Positive transfer occurred from the initial tasks to later tasks in the same course. Howell (1950) noted steadily improving work-study skills in grades 4 through 8 and better performance in various school subjects that he judged were related to the work-study skills. Work-study skills thus were investigated some years ago, but little attention was given them after that until recently.

Holtzman and Brown (1968) developed and standardized a 100-item inventory of study habits and attitudes. Students in grades 7 through 12 were used in the standardization. It was found that correlations between inventory scores and grade-point averages were about as high as between IQ scores and grade-point averages. However, low correlations were found between the inventory scores and IQ scores. Holtzman and Brown therefore concluded that study habits and attitudes are related to school achievement but cannot be related to IQ. Furthermore, Haslam and Brown (1968) showed that instruction in study skills produced substantial improvement in scores on the inventory and in academic grades.

In this connection, it is interesting and useful to consider what is emphasized in a popular paperback book, *How To Study* (Morgan & Deese, 1969). The book, intended for high school graduates who have embarked on any form of higher education, has 11 chapters, with these titles: "Efficient Learning," "Organizing Time," "Classroom Learning," "Reading Better and Faster," "Studying Textbooks," "Taking Examinations," "Writing Papers," "Studying a Foreign Language," "Studying Mathematics and the Sciences," "Getting Help and Being Helpful," "Living College Life." The prospective teacher will find the book interesting both for reviewing his own practices that may promote or hinder the development of study skills and for identifying ideas that may be used in high school classes to teach students more effective study skills.

5. Provide Opportunities for Application

Students may study and enjoy Shakespearean plays for the inherent satisfaction they receive. If, however, the purpose of such study is to help in interpreting English history or the present scene in England or America, most students need guidance in applying the pertinent ideas from the plays. The applications might take the form of comparing Shakespeare's account of a battle with an account by a modern historian, his style of writing with modern writing, the characters in his plays with those in modern plays or in life generally, the themes of his plays with themes of modern living, and so on.

Suppose that a teacher intends to secure lateral transfer from one problem to similar problems. Practice on a variety of problems like the initial one, rather than on problems of exactly the same type, facilitates transfer (Lloyd, 1960; Morrisett & Hovland, 1959). Does the same conclusion hold when the attempt is made to secure transfer from one class to other classes of problems or knowledge? Here, also, practice on several classes of problems in the initial situation produces more transfer than does practice on problems of the same class (Wittrock & Twelker, 1964). Teachers who know both the subject matter and its applications well can be more effective in securing transfer than those who know the subject matter but are weak on its applications.

6. Provide for Sequential, Cumulative Learning

Most skills, concepts, attitudes, and abilities are not fully acquired in one day, week, or year but cumulatively, through distributed practice and study over a period of time. To become even moderately literate in the various disciplines, one must study for many years. Accordingly, those who outline a general sequence of instruction from kindergarten through grade 12 must give careful consideration to encouraging continuity in learning. At the same time, the teacher is faced daily with the problem of deciding how large or comprehensive a unit of learning he can attempt and still be sure that each student will acquire something that can be carried through to the next day or week.

Obviously, if nothing is learned today, it cannot be retained or used tomorrow. In spelling, for example, it is better to learn three words well each day of the week than to be given 15 words at one time and come to the end of the week not knowing any of them. In foreign language instruction, it also is better to emphasize a shorter dialogue than to assign a long one and, in the process, produce so much reorganization that nothing is recalled. In science, the situation is much the same. To attempt to make physicists out of tenth- or eleventh-grade pupils is unrealistic. Instead, the study of physics in high school must be organized into appropriate segments that the student can learn well; his knowledge, skills, interests, and abilities will in turn enable him to go on to advanced study of physics in college. Only then will he become a physicist.

Retention of many important outcomes improves significantly with systematic review. To illustrate, in one study, review tests were given to groups of children at intervals after initial instruction of 1 day, 14 days, 28 days, and 63 days (Tiedeman, 1948). Best results were found when the review tests were administered only one day after the initial instruction, rather than later. The amount of review needed in various classroom situations cannot be prescribed, but we are certain that factual information must be overlearned immediately and must be reviewed more often afterwards than concepts and principles. Also, if factual information, concepts, and principles were acquired more completely and also used in later ongoing learning activities, there would be less need for review or re-learning later. For example, if junior high school students learned history more completely and used what they learned later, less review of the same material would be needed in the senior high school.

Recent revisions of school curricula have followed theoretical proposi-tions advanced by Bruner (1960). In particular, Bruner proposed the *spiral curriculum*, which essentially consists of two ideas: (1) Basic con-cepts or principles of a discipline, such as physics, chemistry, or mathe-matics, are identified. There usually are a few powerful and pervasive concepts and principles. (2) These concepts or principles are taught at recurring times at increasing levels of difficulty to assure ultimate deep understanding. The emphasis in this approach to instruction is both se-quential and cumulative.

16.8. Most students read and study with the intention of learning and re-membering. What more specific things might be done in your own field of in-terest to facilitate retention by students? What procedures might you use right now to help you remember the concepts and principles dealt with in this chapter?

16.9. Analyze the relationship between retention and transfer. Are some of the guides more relevant to retention than to transfer?

16.10. Some students do not find their study of history, English, or some other subject worthwhile. Which of these conditions might be primary con-tributors?

a. The student does not have enough direct experience with the concepts and principles and therefore does not understand them.

b. The student does not have enough opportunity to apply, or test, the con-cepts and principles outside the actual classroom settings.

c. The real world does not permit application of the concepts and princi-ples.

d. The student is not committed to learning and has not set realistic goals in connection with the course.

e. The student forgets most of what he learns within a few weeks after the end of the school year.

Which of these conditions could an instructor try to deal with constructively? What specific suggestions do you have for dealing with each of them?

SUMMARY

Forgetting is explained by different theorists as resulting from disuse, interference, reorganization, obliterative subsumption, and motivated forgetting. The evidence is now clear that (1) meaningful material is re-tained better than meaningless material, (2) material acquired with pur-pose is retained better than material learned incidentally, and (3) having knowledge enables one both to acquire and retain new knowledge better.

Four generally accepted theories of transfer are: identical elements, generalization, transposition, and abilities. All incorporate the idea of positive transfer but disagree on precisely what it is that transfers. According to any theory, however, the individual must perceive the new situation as being similar to that in which the initial learning occurred. Also, general information transfers more readily to new situations than specific information. Abilities, including strategies or methods of learning developed over a period of time, transfer from one class of events and situations to many others.

Retention is related to initial learning in that something must be learned in order to be remembered. Retention and transfer are closely related—if something is not remembered, obviously it cannot be transferred later when a new situation is encountered. For facilitating retention and transfer, then, the teacher (1) fosters intent to learn well and remember, (2) makes the initial learning meaningful, (3) provides for satisfying consequences of correct responses, (4) emphasizes general concepts and abilities, (5) provides for application, and (6) provides for sequential, cumulative learning.

SUGGESTIONS FOR FURTHER READING

ELLIS, H. C. *The transfer of learning.* New York: Macmillan, 1965.

This short paperback (200 pages) deals with both theory and educational applications.

KLAUSMEIER, H. J., & DAVIS, J. K. Transfer of learning. In Ebel, R. L., ed., *Encyclopedia of educational research.* New York: Macmillan, 1969, pp. 1483-1493.

Research and theory on transfer are summarized and means for securing positive transfer are outlined.

KLAUSMEIER, H. J., WIERSMA, W. W., & HARRIS, C. W. Efficiency of initial learning and transfer by individuals, pairs, and quads. In Ripple, R. E., ed., *Readings in learning and human abilities.* New York: Harper & Row, 2nd ed., 1971.

The effects of working as an individual, in pairs, and in groups of four on initial learning and later on learning when working alone are described.

KUHLEN, R. G., ed., *Studies in educational psychology.* Waltham, Mass.: Blaisdell, 1968.

Chapter 13, pages 420-447, contains an excellent introduction and four short articles dealing with forgetting: P. Fitzgerald and D. P. Ausubel, "Cognitive vs. Affective Factors in the Retention of Controversial Material"; N. J. Slamecka, "Studies of Retention of Connected Discourse"; E. B. Coleman, "Sequential Interferences in Serial Reconstructions"; J. H. Reynolds and R. Glaser, "Effects of Repetition and Spaced Review on Retention." Chapter 14, pages 448-475, also has a good introduction and four articles dealing with transfer: H. F. Harlow, "The Formation of Learning Sets"; M. F. Dorsey and L. T. Hopkins, "The Influence of Instruction upon Transfer"; E. P. Torrance and J. A. Harmon, "Effects of Memory, Evaluative, and Creative Reading Sets"; R. L. R. Overing and R. M. W. Travers, "Effects upon Transfer of Variations in Training Conditions."

TULVING, E. Organized retention and cued recall. In Klausmeier, H. J., & O'Hearn, G. T., eds., *Research and development toward the improvement of education.* Madison, Wisc.: Dembar Educational Research Services, 1968, pp. 3-13.

This scholarly article points out the limitations of laboratory experiments on retention and forgetting and stresses the importance of the learner in organizing information for later recall.

Part IV Measurement, Evaluation, Statistics, and Research Design

measuring and assessing students' abilities, characteristics, and progress in learning are essential components of an excellent instructional program. Tests and other devices and procedures may be developed that are valid, reliable, and usable. In general, objective measurement procedures are better than subjective ones. Standardized published tests and a variety of teacher-developed tests and procedures are useful in measuring and assessing in the cognitive, psychomotor, and affective domains. The principal reasons for inferior measurement and assessment are: insufficient teacher time and expertise, an insufficient number of content-valid published tests, and too much attention to grading and too little assessment by school personnel.

Evaluation goes beyond measuring. In evaluation, criteria are developed to which measurements subsequently obtained can be related. Both a student's progress in learning and instructional program are evaluated against one or more criteria. The more recent instructional programs, including complete curriculum packages, state criteria in terms of the level of achievement a student must attain before he can move on to the next unit or set of activities. These instructional programs also are tested against clearly stated criteria. The national assessment of education, now underway, is a massive evaluation effort designed to secure information about samples of students and schools that will enable the quality of public education to be assessed throughout the nation.

The reliability and predictive validity of tests can be inferred only through applying statistical procedures to information collected on students who take the tests. This process requires understanding some elementary statistical terms. Similarly, a knowledge of statistics is helpful in interpreting data collected on one's own students and in evaluating research reports and using their findings. Statistics are also used in the development and evaluation of educational programs, in research designed to help improve educational practices, and in basic research designed to increase knowledge about learning, human abilities, and instruction.

Chapter 17 Measurement Tools and Procedures

Types and Characteristics of Measurement Procedures

paper-and-pencil tests
work samples
observation of behavior
performance tests
objectivity
validity
reliability
usability

Measurement in the Cognitive Domain

published tests
individual intelligence tests
group tests of general intellectual ability
tests of educational achievement
diagnostic tests
criterion-referenced tests
tests of creativity
teacher-devised assessment procedures

Measurement in the Psychomotor Domain

Measurement in the Affective Domain

personality and attitude inventories
interest inventories
projective tests of personality
teacher-made inventories and checklists
observation

good instruction requires measurement, assessment, and evaluation. (1) *Measurement* is defined as directly observing or testing behaviors or characteristics of an individual and assigning a numerical score or a rating to whatever is measured. (2) *Assessment* involves securing two or more measurements of the same individual, for example, his level of achievement in reading, mathematics, social studies, and science or his height, weight, strength of grip, and running speed, in order to get a better understanding of the individual. Neither measurement nor assessment involves the use of any criteria—explicit or implicit—that indicate what a single measurement or a set of measurements for an individual *should* be. Some writers, in fact, use measurement and assessment interchangeably. (3) *Evaluation*, which is discussed in detail in Chapter 18, includes measuring, identifying criteria, and relating the obtained measurement to the criteria. Thus evaluation implies what should be in terms of criteria. For example, a man aged 50 who is 5 feet 8 inches and weighs 200 pounds is judged to be 20 pounds overweight if a criterion of 140 to 180 pounds has been established for males of this age and height. Or it is judged that a child who spells 5 of 10 words correctly needs to learn the other 5 words if a criterion of 10 of 10 words spelled correctly has been set for proceeding further in a spelling program. In dealing with these situations, decisions might be made to put the man on a diet and to tutor the child in the five words. These decisions on courses of action are not considered to be part of the evaluation process.

In this chapter, measuring instruments, mostly tests, will be described and discussed. A comprehensive survey of this field is, of course, beyond the scope of this book. Our intention here is to familiarize the reader with the kinds of tests and other measuring procedures most often used in schools; specific examples are included for illustrative purposes. The ways in which the various tests and other tools of measurement are used in assessing students' characteristics and evaluating instruction are discussed in the next chapter.

This chapter opens with a scheme for classifying measuring procedures and a discussion of some desirable characteristics of published and teacher-made tests: objectivity, validity, reliability, and usability. Tests and other data-gathering instruments used to assess performance in the cognitive domain are then described. Measurement procedures in the psychomotor and affective domains are presented last. In each domain, published tests are considered first, followed by types of teacher-developed measurement procedures. Because most teachers are primarily concerned with their pupils' attaining objectives in the cognitive domain, the section on instruments and procedures associated with this area is longer than the sections on the psychomotor and affective domains.

TYPES AND CHARACTERISTICS OF MEASUREMENT PROCEDURES

There are many ways in which tests and other procedures for measuring

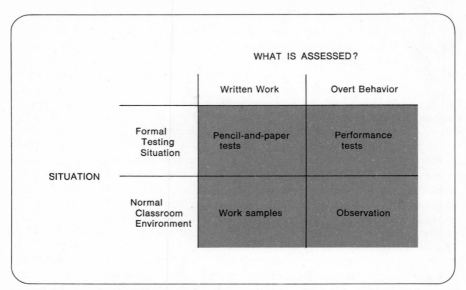

Fig. 17.1. Four classes of measurement procedures.

behavior may be categorized. Figure 17.1 shows one way to classify measurement procedures used in schools by teachers and psychologists.

In two of the four situations students know they are being tested and may thus be expected to exhibit a maximum level of performance. Pencil-and-paper tests, published or not, are usually given in a teacher-monitored setting, with rules about talking and other forms of interaction imposed. When standardized tests are administered, the procedures for testing, provided in a manual by the test-developer, are almost completely specified. In the case of performance tests, which are often individually administered, the rapport established by the examiner with the examinee may suggest less formality than in the group-testing situation. Nevertheless, the setting is atypical because it is contrived specifically to measure behavior, and the task presented to the examinee is prescribed by the teacher or examiner.

Only a small portion of school time is used for formal testing. The rest of a pupil's school activities may be monitored to provide information about his usual performance in written assignments or his usual overt behavior. In either case, measurement procedures are applied to only a sample of the written work or overt behavior.

How are the four classes of measurement procedures used in the various domains of behavior? To assess *cognitive* abilities, including what has been learned in subject-matter areas, teachers generally use published and teacher-prepared pencil-and-paper tests and samples of written work. Performance tests and observation are useful as well, but are more time-consuming, because they require the teacher to attend to a single student at a time. By their nature, *psychomotor* skills must be measured primarily by performance tests and observation. *Affective* characteristics often are measured by pencil-and-paper instruments and observation, but each type has serious limitations. In the affective domain, standardized procedures offer objectivity, but what is measured may not represent the pupil's typical behavior. On the other hand, observations are subjective. In measuring attitudes, interests, and other affective outcomes, therefore, instructional personnel should use several procedures, including the judgment or observations of more than one person whenever possible.

As mentioned, four desirable characteristics of measuring procedures used in schools, whether standardized or not, are: (1) objectivity, (2) validity, (3) reliability, and (4) usability. These attributes are now discussed.

1. Objectivity

Measurement involves using an instrument or other measuring procedure to assign a number or other specific classification (such as a letter grade) to the person whose behavior, often achievement in a curriculum area, is measured. A desirable feature of any measurement procedure is *objectivity*. An objective test is one in which the same score is assigned, no matter who scores the test. Multiple-choice tests are objective, but essay tests are not. In a multiple-choice test a single scoring key completely specifies the score a pupil attains; in an essay test one reader's judgment may lead to a different score than another reader would assign. When overt behavior is rated, two independent observers do not always agree on the measurement associated with the observed performance. Accordingly, measurements such as essay scores and behavior ratings are called *subjective*.

Scoring is objective when an item can be scored right or wrong. In other cases judgments have to be made, and careful instructions are required to ensure similarity in the scores or ratings assigned by different judges. For instance, the *Handbook for Essay Tests, Level 1, College, Sequential Tests of Educational Progress*, suggests that students' essays be rated from 1 to 7, 7 being the highest rating (Sequential Tests of Educational Progress, 1957). Norms were based on an earlier scoring of essays in which readers scored on the basis of three factors: quality of thought, 50 percent; style, 30 percent; and conventions, 20 percent. The factors were defined as follows:

Quality of thought: "the selection and the adequacy of ideas and supplementary details, and the manner of their organization (i.e., the way in which their connections are derived from the arrangement of parts)."

Style: "clearness, effectiveness, and appropriateness, including matters of structure and diction, emphasis, the *means* of transition between ideas, and the finer points of simplicity, economy, variety, and exactness of expression."

Conventions: "the properties of mechanical form, including grammar and usage, capitalization, punctuation, and the mechanical aspects of the structure of sentences." A number of essays are then presented in the handbook with ratings and comments to guide the rater in making his judgments.

The term *norm* will be used frequently from now on. It is important to note that a norm is not a score to be reached, but a range of values or scores consisting of the performances or scores made by the group on which the test in question was standardized. Always, 50 percent of the scores fall at or above the median score and 50 percent below the median score of the standardization population. One can compare a score made by his student with the scores made by the standardization population and thus ascertain where the student's score places him in relation to the median, or some other point, of the standardization population.

2. Validity

In this chapter we focus on measurement in the school setting that is related to the instructional program in one of two ways: (1) Students are assessed to determine the degree to which they have attained the objectives of instruction; (2) students are assessed so that they can be selected for some instructional program. In either case, the purpose of testing is clear. A sound judgment, however, depends partly on selecting an appropriate instrument for the particular purpose.

Validity is a concept that relates a measurement instrument to the *purpose* of testing. A test may be valid in one situation but not in another. In essence, therefore, validity involves this question: Does the test measure what we want to measure? Validity, then, is discussed in the context of the purposes of testing. Because only the test-user knows exactly what his purposes are, the burden of deciding whether or not a test is valid in a given situation ultimately rests with him. Through research, publishers of tests identify the purposes for which a test is valid, but the user must then decide how closely *his* objectives match those for which the test has been validated.

Let us further consider the two purposes of tests and relate to them the two types of validity with which teachers are principally concerned.

Content Validity. As the term suggests, content validity is concerned with the representativeness of the content of the test. An instructional objective specifies the content of interest—subtraction of whole numbers involving regrouping, for instance. Often further analysis of the content is required, so that the major categories of the content can be identified. For the instructional objective in subtraction, analysis of representative textbooks suggests that examples with the following characteristics should be included in a test: regrouping once from tens to units, regrouping once from hundreds to tens, regrouping twice, and each of the preceding with zeros in the ones and tens positions and in both positions.

A content-valid test for a stated objective contains some items that measure each of the enumerated categories of the content. The relative proportion of each item type may be specified in addition, according to the relative emphasis given each in the instructional program or according to some other rule. The essential point is that the teacher wants to be sure that an educational achievement test used in his class measures what has been taught. The teacher also wants to make sure that the tests and procedures developed by him sample all the content and objectives, not just some of them.

Another example illustrates the logical way one proceeds in constructing a content-valid test. To measure knowledge about the concepts and information presented in this book, a subtopic within each chapter might be sampled and an appropriate question developed. On the other hand, if the instructor using this text in an educational psychology class emphasized Part II, deemphasized Part III, and wholly omitted Part IV, questions in a final examination might well reflect the proportion of course time devoted to various sections. Attempting to assure content validity, then, is a logical operation in which test questions are matched to course content or curriculum objectives and a subjective judgment about the "fit" is made.

In addition to constructing content-valid tests, professional educators must select published tests that are valid for the curriculum of the particular system. Test publishers try to construct tests that are valid measures of the content of a variety of widely used curriculums. The following description of content selection for the Stanford Achievement Test, a battery for elementary school children measuring various subject matters, including reading, language, and arithmetic, is taken from the test administrator's manual:

> The validity of *Stanford Achievement Test* is best thought of as the extent to which the content of the test constitutes a representative sample of the skills and knowledges which are the goals of instruction. This *content*, or *curricular*, validity must be assessed through a careful analysis of the actual content of each subtest in relation to the objectives of instruction in the various fields. . . .
>
> In preparing this latest edition of *Stanford Achievement Test*, a major goal was to make sure that the content of the test would be in harmony with present objectives and measure what is actually being taught in today's schools. To make certain that the test content would be valid in this sense, the construction of the new edition (as of each earlier edition) was preceded by a thorough analysis of the most widely used series of elementary textbooks in the various subjects, of a wide variety of courses of study, and of the research literature pertaining to children's concepts, experiences, and vocabulary at successive ages or grades. On the basis of this analysis, the authors prepared detailed outlines of the content to be covered by all tests at all grade levels. These outlines specified the relative proportion of content to be devoted to the various skills, knowledges, and understandings within each area and served as blueprints for the tests that were ultimately to emerge. At this stage, as well as throughout the whole developmental process, reliance was placed on the judgment of subject-matter specialists in the several areas. (Kelley, Madden, Gardner, & Rudman, 1964a, pp. 30–31)

Despite the care taken by test publishers to prepare tests that are content-valid for typical curriculums, the validity of a test for a particular curriculum in a local school district or area within the district (such as a central-city area) can best be determined locally. In general, if changes are made in the scope and sequence of the curriculum or if new texts are adopted, the question of content validity of standardized achievement tests should be raised. Curriculum innovations, such as the new math, often precede related standardized test development by several years, with the result that existing tests are not content-valid for the new curriculum for some time.

Predictive Validity.[1] Performance in an educational or employment situation is a criterion of interest to educational workers. Because poor performance is undesirable and because there are limited openings in courses or employment positions, individuals are selected for the openings at least partially on the basis of their likelihood to succeed. Tests that are valid for predicting actual later performance in a particular situation are used to improve the rate of success in selection.

High school counselors, for instance, frequently use test scores to predict how well a student will perform if placed in a course, e.g., shorthand, honors English, general mathematics, and counsel him accordingly. College admissions officers consider test scores in deciding which students to admit to college. Justification for using a test to select individuals for a course, college, or job is provided by strong evidence of the predictive validity of the test. An example of such evidence is data collected over the years on the same individuals — first their scores on the test itself and then their later performance in the course, college program, or job. If the test scores and performances are highly correlated, then one is warranted in making predictions or decisions for others on the basis of scores on the test. Obviously, this form of validity is determined by statistical procedures.

Again it is important to note that validity of a test is specific to the use that is to be made of it. A college entrance examination may be a good predictor of performance in one university but not in another. Similarly, a mechanical aptitude test may be highly related to performance in one factory job but not another. It is the responsibility of the test-user to demonstrate the predictive validity of an instrument he uses in prediction or selection. In fact, persons in counseling and in admissions or personnel offices are sometimes trained to undertake institutional validity studies.

3. Reliability

Just as bathroom scales sometimes are inaccurate and therefore cannot be relied on, so are measurements taken in the school setting subject to error. *Reliability* refers to the accuracy of a measurement. Underlying the idea of reliability is that of error of measurement: if a person is measured on some test a large number of times, his scores will vary somewhat because of such factors as fatigue, a good guess, health, attitude, carelessness in marking answers, and many others. Assuming he does not learn from the testing experience itself, his scores will vary somewhat from his average score in a predictable fashion: the scores will be normally distributed about an average and a statistic known as the *standard error of measurement* (SE_m) will express the degree of variation in his scores.

It is useful to think of an observed test score as a composite of the person's true score and the error, which may be positive or negative. If there were no error, there would be no variation in the observed score if an-

---

[1]Predictive validity is also known as a kind of criterion-related validity. The first term is used here to avoid confusion with criterion-referenced tests, discussed later in the chapter.

other measure were taken, and the test would be perfectly reliable. Perfect reliability is indicated by a reliability coefficient of 1.00. For all practical purposes, however, a reliability coefficient of 1.00 must be considered hypothetical; even in the exact sciences, measurement using precision tools is subject to slight error. Reliability coefficients in the .85 to .95 range are typical for subtests in batteries such as the Stanford Achievement tests (Kelley, Madden, Gardner, & Rudman, 1964a). Somewhat lower reliabilities are obtained for performance tests and ratings in which subjective judgments are required. In any case, test-users should be cautioned about making decisions concerning individuals when the test reliability is lower than .80.

Why are accurate, consistent measures needed? Why are the teacher and the commercial developer so concerned about reliability? The test-maker wants to produce accurate measuring instruments for the same reason that manufacturers want precise tools for linear measurement. If a measuring instrument has low reliability, it also has low predictive validity. For example, an unreliable reading readiness test administered early in the first grade is of little value in ascertaining children's present reading achievements or in predicting later achievements.

What conditions may result in the low reliability of a test? The five most important are as follows:

1. A test may be unreliable because of poorly constructed items that do not discriminate between students who possess the knowledge, skill, or other attributes being tested and those who do not. An exceptionally well-read student may think of an exception to the "correct" answer in a multiple-choice test and choose an "incorrect" alternative.

2. Even well-constructed items may not discriminate between students. This happens when the items are so easy that most students get all of them correct or so difficult that most students cannot answer them. Items too easy or too difficult do not spread the scores of the students. Thus, a test may be reliable for 9-year-olds in the average achievement range but unreliable for 7- and 11-year-olds; it may be reliable for 9-year-olds in the average achievement range but unreliable for those of exceptionally high or low achievement. Also, a test that has high reliability after a year of instruction may show low reliability if administered at the beginning of the year.

3. The length of a test also can be responsible for low reliability. A single spelling word or science concept is a poor and inadequate sample of a student's performance. If only 10 items are given, one student may merely guess three or four correctly. In that case, chance would be an important determiner of the score obtained. In a longer test of perhaps 50 items, we get more dependable scores—there is a better possibility that variations accounted for by guessing will cancel out. A test can, however, be made so long that students become tired or bored and respond unreliably.

4. Subjective scoring methods, too, may produce low reliability. This is one of the principal weaknesses of essay tests and rating scales, as we shall see later in the chapter.

5. Inadequate time to complete a test lowers reliability in any test

where time is not a criterion of performance. This is a difficult problem to overcome, for the rate at which students respond to a test varies markedly. If time is called when half of a group has finished, one cannot be certain how the other half would have scored if they had had time to finish.

The teacher who constructs tests should keep these five considerations in mind. Specific suggestions for improving the reliability of particular types of tests and other measurement procedures are discussed in the later sections dealing with teacher-developed procedures in each domain.

4. Usability

In addition to the more theoretical considerations of validity and reliability, a number of practical considerations must be taken into account. These are designated by the term *usability*—the extent to which a test can be used. The teacher must consider these factors: (1) the amount of time required to administer the test; (2) the amount of preparation or education required to administer, score, and interpret the test; (3) the amount of time required to score the test; (4) the ease of interpreting the test results after the scores are obtained; (5) the cost; (6) the mechanical makeup of the test. Because these considerations are important, published tests usually provide such information in the test manual, along with data on the reliability and validity of the test.

The best source for much of this information is the *Mental Measurements Yearbook* series that has been published periodically since 1938, continuing through 1965 (Buros, 1965). Often used in conjunction with *Tests in Print* (Buros, 1961) and *Personality Tests and Reviews* (Buros, 1970), the six yearbooks include not only descriptive information about many published tests, but also critical reviews of the various tests and a bibliography of articles and books about each test. Most of the evaluative comments about the well-known tests described in the later sections of this chapter are based on the authors' study of each test and its manual and the critical review of the test in one of the Buros books.

17.1. From the standpoint of measurement, why is it desirable to be able to score a student's response as right or wrong? What knowledge and skill have you yourself developed that cannot be categorized as right or wrong?

17.2. In your case, is there a close relationship between your grade-point averages in high school and in college? What might contribute to the moderately high predictive validity of high school grade-point average for college grade-point average?

17.3. Why might teachers generally be more concerned with the content validity of their tests than the predictive validity? What may a teacher do to assure content-valid measures of his students' achievements?

17.4. What may the teacher do to secure reasonably reliable measurements of students' achievements in his classes?

17.5. Objectivity, predictive validity, and reliability are consciously built into many standardized educational achievement tests. Indicate a practice or two related to each of the three that might make a test ineffective.

MEASUREMENT IN THE COGNITIVE DOMAIN

The vast majority of published tests given in schools measure either educational achievement or intellectual abilities. Increasingly, published diagnostic and criterion-referenced tests are becoming available; these also are forms of achievement tests, but they have a restricted scope of content and specialized uses. (They will be defined and illustrated later in the chapter.) Most published tests have standardized administration procedures. Ability and achievement tests, however, include norms to use in interpreting the scores; diagnostic and criterion-referenced tests may or may not have norms.

A variety of procedures are devised by teachers to assess educational outcomes in the cognitive domain. Most frequently used are pencil-and-paper tests; they differ from published achievement tests in several ways, including format, purpose, and scope of content. Furthermore, the teacher measures pupil performance by using many types of question forms, including completion and free response, and by using such techniques as observation and work sampling.

Published Tests

The testing movement during the first half of the twentieth century resulted in the development of ability and achievement tests intended to discriminate among individuals. Still widely used, these norm-referenced tests are interpreted by relating an individual's score to other scores of a standardization group. To facilitate the interpretation of scores on norm-referenced tests, tables of norms are included in test administrators' manuals. You remember that a norm is not a standard to be reached, but a *range* of values or scores—the performances or scores made by the group on which the test was standardized. Obviously, in any range of values, there is an average value, which is often the same as the median score. In any group of students, an equal proportion is above and below the median. In other words, the average score for a standardized test may be higher or lower than the average score that is made by a particular group of students. Thus the user has the responsibility to use the norm appropriate for his students; in many cases, the development of local norms is desirable.

In the Comprehensive Tests of Basic Skills *Bulletin of Technical Data* (1968), we find that a total of 212,509 pupils from 152 school systems in 50 states were included in the standardization of these tests. This total was distributed among the grades for which the tests are intended—grades 2 through 12. The bulletin also gives the proportions of the normative sample in the various geographical regions of the United States and in various kinds of districts, including parochial and private. Using this sample as a base, tables were developed whereby the actual scores made by any pupil who takes one of the tests can be interpreted in grade equivalents, percentile ranks, or stanines under three time conditions: tests administered at the beginning, at the middle, and at the end of the school year. The percentile ranks are available for a total battery score as well as for three main tests—reading, language, and arithmetic. Grade equivalent, percentile rank, stanine, and other terms for derived scores are defined and discussed in detail in Chapter 19. Two that we should define briefly here, however, are *percentile rank* and *grade equivalent*. A student's percentile rank indicates the percentage of students in the student norm group who scored *lower* than he. Thus if a student is at a percentile rank of 62, 62 percent of the student group performed less well than he did. Grade equivalents for raw scores are derived by test developers by keeping track of the scores made on the same test by students at different grade levels and then transforming the scores to grade equivalents.

Figure 17.2 shows one child's percentile ranks in profile form as measured by the Level 1 Comprehensive Tests of Basic Skills. Frank Smith is a hypothetical but quite typical second-grader.

Teachers should realize that pupils are not expected to perform close to perfection on norm-referenced tests. Many such tests, in fact, are constructed in such a way that pupils who answer only about half the items correctly will be judged to be average in performance in terms of the norms. This can be surprising for pupils and teachers used to classroom tests where scores in the 70 to 100 percent range are most common. If

Fig. 17.2. Profile of performance of Frank Smith as a second-grader on the Comprehensive Tests of Basic Skills (1968)

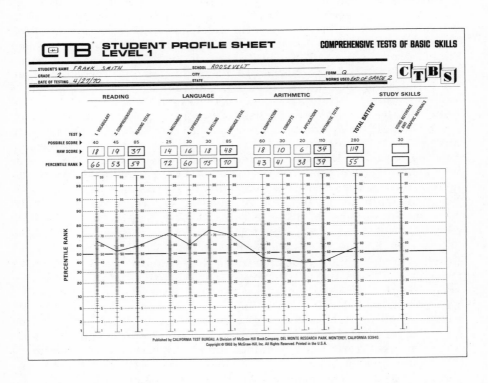

published achievement tests were constructed so that the average scores were higher, a greater number of items and thus longer times for administration would be required for a reliable test. The teacher should bear these facts in mind before making a hasty judgment that a particular test is too difficult for his pupils. Also, the teacher may use this same information about the difficulty of test items in norm-referenced tests in allaying pupils' worries following testing.

1. Individual Tests of Intelligence. The three individual intelligence tests most widely used today are the Revised Stanford-Binet Intelligence Scale (Terman & Merrill, 1960), the Wechsler Intelligence Scale for Children (Wechsler, 1949), and the Wechsler Adult Intelligence Scale (Wechsler, 1955). The Wechsler Preschool and Primary Scale of Intelligence (Wechsler, 1963), published more recently, is coming into widespread use. Each of these tests is administered to an individual by a skilled examiner. The tests are more reliable and valid measures of general intellectual ability than printed tests administered to groups. However, as has been pointed out previously, general intellectual ability changes to some extent with age and is subject to environmental influences. Also, we accept the idea of group abilities and of specific intellectual abilities, as well as general intellectual ability, although tests of specific abilities have not been used widely except in research. Thus, when describing the first two of these individual intelligence tests, we are not implying that intelligence is a unitary, fixed, or unchangeable characteristic. The limitations of the concept of general intellectual ability that we spoke of in earlier chapters apply both to these individual tests and to the group tests of intelligence to be mentioned later in this chapter.

Revised Stanford-Binet Intelligence Scale. The new 1960 Form L-M tests levels of mental development from age 2 to superior adult III, much as did the 1937 Forms L and M. However, Form L-M consists of the best items from the two previous forms. From ages 2 to 5, there are six tests at each half year of chronological age. Thereafter, to age 14, there are six tests for each year of chronological age. After age 14, the levels are average adult and superior adult I, II, and III, as shown in Fig. 17.3.

The examiner administers the scale, starting at the age level at which the subject passes all six subtests, and continues upward to the level at which no test is passed. For example, if an 8-year-old passes all tests for age 8, his mental age is judged to be 96 months; for each of the six subtests at each age level passed thereafter, he receives an additional 2 months. From this, his total mental age is computed (this is his raw score); the obtained MA is divided by his actual chronological age (CA) and multiplied by 100; the resulting score is his IQ. The 8-year-old with an MA of 120 months has an IQ of 125 ($120/96 \times 100$).

The older forms were based on the assumption that mental growth starts slowing down at age 13 and reaches its maximum at age 16. The new Form L-M is not based on this assumption and, although the idea of mental age is not abandoned, the IQ may now be converted into a *deviation IQ.* (For a more complete consideration of how scores are changed into deviation scores, see Chapter 19.) The principal advantage of the deviation IQ over the older ratio IQ (MA/CA $\times$ 100) is that with the earlier

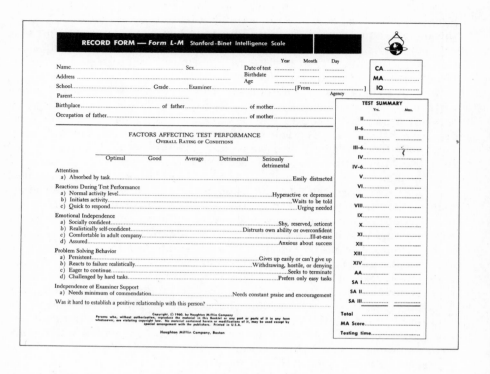

Fig. 17.3. Record Booklet—Form L-M, Stanford-Binet Intelligence Scale. (Terman & Merrill, 1960)

forms, changes in ratio IQ occurred in the same children at different ages, simply because the test was inadequately scored. A child at age 16 years 6 months might have received an IQ of 138 by having passed certain tests in the older forms; in the new form, his deviation IQ is 132 for passing the same tests. Besides getting a reliable estimate of IQ, the examiner observes and rates characteristics of the child affecting test performance: attention, reactions during test performance, emotional independence, problem-solving behavior, and independence of examiner support, as shown in Fig. 17.3.

Form L-M, like the 1937 forms, is based on the assumption that intelligence is an overall or general intellectual ability which is reflected in almost any activity undertaken. The items in the test, therefore, sample a wide variety of cognitive processes and, to a more limited extent, motor abilities. Memory, verbal reasoning, mathematical reasoning, vocabulary, drawing, and motor manipulation are required to pass certain items. The earlier forms showed quite high predictive validity, and it is possible that Form L-M will yield even higher correlations with achievements in mathematics, science, language arts, and social studies.

No test is perfect. The Stanford-Binet is heavily weighted with items calling for verbal abilities; furthermore, although the correlations in the older forms between the IQs of children at age 4 and of the same children at later ages have been significant and positive, they also have been of modest size, indicating that, whatever the general ability is as measured in preschool children, it is not exactly the same during school years.

Wechsler Intelligence Scale for Children (WISC). The three Wechsler tests now in common use include the Wechsler Adult Intelligence Scale for persons age 16 and over, the Wechsler Intelligence Scale for Children (WISC), appropriate for those of ages 5 to 15, and the more recent Wechsler Preschool and Primary Scale of Intelligence designed for ages 4 to 6½. These tests differ significantly from the Stanford-Binet because they are not based on the idea of mental age as an acceptable measure of intelligence. Rather, deviation IQ scores express the degree to which a child's score differs from the average of his age group. The WISC, because it is the most often used of the three tests in schools, is described here. (The adult and preschool scales have similar content.)

The WISC consists of 12 main tests divided into two subgroups called "Verbal" and "Performance." The six Verbal tests are: information, comprehension, arithmetic, similarities, vocabulary, digit span; the six Performance tests are: picture completion, picture arrangement, block design, object assembly, coding, mazes. The digit span and maze tests are supplementary—they are not used with normal subjects. Wechsler says:

> Most of the verbal tests correlate better with each other than with tests of the performance group, and vice versa. But, while the tests identified as verbal and performance differ as the labels indicate, they each tap other factors, among them non-intellective ones, which cut across the groups to produce other classifications or categories that are equally important to consider in evaluating the individual's performance. (Wechsler, 1949, p. 5)

The skilled examiner administers the test to the individual child according to standardized instructions and scores according to standardized procedures. The raw scores in each subtest are changed to scaled scores, using appropriate tables for children of various chronological ages, starting at 5 years and proceeding in three-month steps to 15 years 11 months. The Verbal score is secured by adding the five scaled scores of the verbal tests; the Performance score is the sum of the five performance tests; and the full-scale score is the sum of the Verbal score and the Performance score. The examiner then uses appropriate tables to ascertain the Verbal IQ, Performance IQ, and full-scale IQ. Figure 17.4 is the WISC Record Form for entering results of the test.

The WISC is easier to administer than the Stanford-Binet, but its scoring requires more sensitive judgments. The Verbal IQ correlates more highly with school achievements than the Performance IQ, but considerable research is still needed to interpret and explain the large differences found occasionally in some children between Verbal IQ and Performance IQ. It has been suggested that a pupil who scores markedly higher on the Performance IQ may have a language problem and that a markedly higher Verbal IQ score may indicate emotional blocking (Cronbach, 1960).

Fig. 17.4. WISC Record Form. (From D. Wechsler, *Wechsler Intelligence Scale for Children.* Reproduced by permission. Copyright 1949 by The Psychological Corporation, New York, N.Y. All rights reserved.)

One can plot a profile of the 10 subtest scores. Some clinicians find such a profile useful in diagnosing brain injury, personality disorders, and the like; for this reason, the WISC is widely used in clinical settings. The WISC represents an important contribution in the field of individual testing and appraisal, meriting at least equal consideration with the Stanford-Binet for use with school-age children.

To what extent are IQs derived from different tests comparable? IQ tests are constructed so that the average score in the standardization group is 100. The standard deviation of intelligence tests varies, however; the Stanford-Binet has a standard deviation of 16 and the WISC of 15. The effect of differences in standard deviations is most notable at the scoring extremes. A very bright child, for instance, usually shows a higher IQ on the Stanford-Binet than he would on the WISC. IQ scores may be converted to standard scores, stanines, mental age, and percentiles. As mentioned, some of the derived scores are discussed in Chapter 19.

2. Group Tests of General Intellectual Ability. Group tests of general intellectual ability, sometimes called "scholastic aptitude" and "mental ability," are used far more extensively in schools after grade 1 than individual tests. The group tests do not require specially trained examiners. Furthermore, many group tests have predictive validity for certain school objectives that is just as high as those of the Stanford-Binet and Wechsler tests. The reliability of group tests, however, ordinarily is somewhat lower than that of individual tests.

The administration of any group test requires each student taking it to understand the directions, want to do his best, and be physically and emotionally in good condition. In small classroom groups, the test administrator, usually the teacher, can observe each student fairly well to see that these conditions are met. When they are not met, the teacher may ask that one or two individuals be retested with an individual test. When tests are administered to large groups, it is, of course, more difficult to be sure that the three conditions are met. In any case, individual intelligence tests are superior to a group test when a primary purpose of testing is to secure a more thorough understanding of certain students. Also, it is obvious that group verbal tests are not so useful as individual tests with younger children who cannot read, children with any sort of severe handicap, and any person who has not had the opportunity to learn to use the English language.

Group tests of intellectual ability for use in school situations have been developed primarily to help make two types of decisions: what the student is ready to learn now and how well he will achieve in the future, in school or in an occupation. In many cases, educational achievement tests (discussed in the next section) give more direct answers to these questions; in other words, often group intellectual ability tests should be used as supplements to achievement testing.

Items used in group tests of intellectual ability vary widely. Some are purely measures of educational outcomes which supposedly all pupils have had equal opportunity to learn; other items are intended to be novel, met for the first time in the test. The three sample items in Fig. 17.5, taken from the Lorge-Thorndike Intelligence Test, Form 1, Levels A-H, give an idea of the type of item used in verbal group tests of intelligence for elementary school pupils.

There are several other notable group tests of general intellectual ability. Among them are the College Qualifications Test (CQT), the Cooperative School and College Ability Tests (SCAT), the Henmon-Nelson Tests of Mental Ability, the Kuhlmann-Anderson Intelligence Tests, the

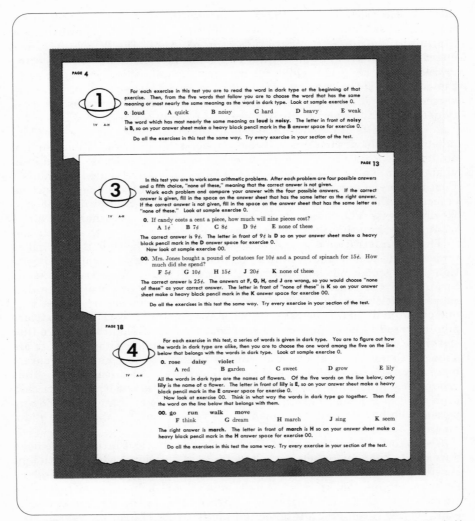

Fig. 17.5. Sample questions from the Lorge-Thorndike Intelligence Tests, Levels A-H, Form 1. (Lorge, Thorndike, & Hagen, 1964)

Miller Analogies Test, and the SRA Tests of Educational Ability. Although certain tests yield separate subtest scores, any test that combines all its subtest scores by any method is put in this general category, for the total is a summary measure of general intellectual ability.

Other Aptitude Tests. Test-makers and others have concentrated for years on trying to devise tests that will be better than the general intellectual ability tests in predicting success in the separate subjects, vocations, and the fine arts.

Most notable are the Differential Aptitude Tests (Bennett, Seashore, & Wesman, 1959) and the General Aptitude Test Battery (1959); the latter is used by the U. S. Employment Service and many state employment services. The DAT provides scores for eight *factors*: verbal reasoning, numerical ability, abstract reasoning, space relations, mechanical speed, clerical speed and accuracy, and two vocabulary scores (spelling and sentences). The GATB, on the other hand, provides measurements for nine *abilities*: general reasoning ability, vocabulary, numerical aptitude, spatial aptitude, form perception, clerical perception, motor coordination, finger dexterity, and manual dexterity. Other tests in this category are the Meier Art Judgment Test, the Employer Aptitude Survey, the Flanagan Aptitude Classification Tests, the Holzinger-Crowder Unifactor Tests, the Multiple Aptitude Tests, and the SRA Primary Mental Abilities Test.

3. Tests of Educational Achievement. Educational achievement tests are designed to measure the extent to which pupils have acquired various objectives of instruction. Of all types of published group tests, achievement tests are the most widely used. Furthermore, printed tests are among the better sources to which a teacher can turn to find models of well-constructed achievement test items. Consider for example, the items in Fig. 17.6 taken from the Word Meaning, Arithmetic Applications, Social Studies (Part B: Study Skills), and Science tests of the Stanford Achievement Test.

Other widely used achievement batteries are the Comprehensive Tests of Basic Skills (Fig. 17.2), the Iowa Tests of Basic Skills, the Metropolitan Achievement Tests, the SRA Achievement Series, and the Sequential Tests of Educational Progress (STEP). The subtests in most achievement batteries are also available as separate tests or can be administered separately from a complete booklet. A large number and wide variety of tests in the usual junior and senior high school subjects are published as separate tests.

A teacher or any other person selecting a test of educational achievement should make certain that the test measures what he wants to measure. If, for example, a teacher wishes to find out which specific concepts and processes in arithmetic are causing a child to have difficulty in arithmetic, he uses a specially designed diagnostic test, not an achievement test. Similarly, if a teacher wishes to find out how well problem-solving abilities and concepts are being acquired in mathematics, he does not use a test that includes only computational exercises.

As suggested in Chapters 10, 11, and 12, many of the outcomes in any subject field at any school level can be stated as factual information and verbal knowledge, concepts and principles, problem-solving abilities, and creativity. The early educational achievement tests primarily measured factual information, verbal knowledge, and routine skills closely related to specific subject fields; they gave little attention to such outcomes as understanding and application of principles, problem-solving abilities, or evaluation of facts. More recent tests, however, do attempt to measure the latter type of outcomes.

With this in mind we turn now to sample items intended to measure the ability to *apply* information, the ability to *analyze* information, and the ability to *evaluate* information. These examples and the related dis-

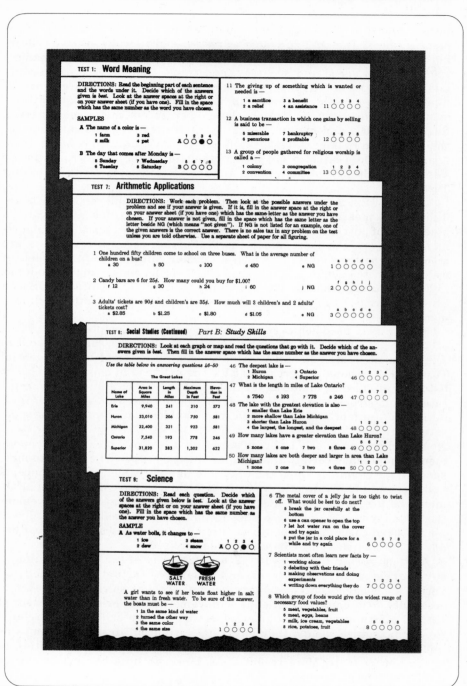

Fig. 17.6. Sample questions from the Stanford Achievement Test, Form W. Intermediate I. (Kelley, Madden, Gardner, & Rudman, 1964b)

cussion are drawn from Bloom (1956), who in turn selected the items from the *Yearbook of the National Society for the Study of Education* (Henry, 1946):

APPLICATION:

The italicized statement at the end of the problem is assumed to be a correct answer. You are to explain the italicized conclusion by selecting statements from the list following the problem. (The student checks the explanations.)

If a person is planning to bathe in the sun, at what time of day is he most likely to receive a severe sunburn? *He is most likely to receive a severe sunburn in the middle of the day (11 a.m. to 1 p.m.) because:*

____We are slightly closer to the sun at noon than in the morning or afternoon.

____The noon sun will produce more "burn" than the morning or afternoon sun.

____When the sun's rays fall directly (straight down) on a surface, more energy is received by that surface than when the rays fall obliquely on the surface.

____When the sun's rays fall directly (straight down) on a surface, more energy is reflected from the surface than when the sun's rays fall obliquely on that surface.

____When the sun is directly overhead the sun's rays pass through less absorbing atmosphere than when the sun is lower in the sky.

____Just as a bullet shot straight into a block of wood penetrates farther into the wood, so will the direct rays at noon penetrate more deeply into the skin.

____The air is usually warmer at noon than at other times of the day.

____The ultraviolet of the sunlight is mainly responsible for sunburn.

It is assumed that this is a new problem for the student and that the task is one of selecting the correct explanatory principle. Some of the alternatives offered are factually correct while others are incorrect. Some are relevant, others are irrelevant. Some merely repeat the conclusion, while others state the generalizations or principles which have explanatory value. Selecting the appropriate explanatory generalizations requires that the student be able to relate the appropriate generalizations to the situation. (Bloom, 1956, pp. 52-53)

ANALYSIS:

Statement of facts: The following table represents the relationship between the yearly income of certain families and the medical attention they receive.

Family Income	Percent of Family Members Who Received No Medical Attention During the Year
Under $1200	47
$1200 to $3000	40
$3000 to $5000	33
$5000 to $10,000	24
Over $10,000	14

Conclusion: Members of families with small incomes are healthier than members of families with large incomes.

Assumption (Select one):

1. Wealthy families had more money to spend for medical care.
2. All members of families who needed medical attention received it.

3. Many members of families with low incomes were not able to pay their doctor bills.
4. Members of families with low incomes did not receive medical attention. [Henry, 1946, p. 127]

If it is assumed that the data and the problem are essentially new to the student, it requires that the student be able to identify the assumption which must be made to support the conclusion in relation to the data. (Bloom, 1956, p. 53)

EVALUATION:

A 6A class was studying the geography of Europe and the land of the Dutch people. Someone in the class said that the homes of the Dutch people who live in America are always neat and clean. The teacher asked this question, "What reasons can you give for thinking that they are always neat and clean?"

Here are some of the reasons the children gave. Read them carefully and decide which are the best and which are the poorest.

____I heard someone say that they were neat and clean.
____I was in one Dutch home and it was clean.
____Our geography book said they were clean.
____I have been in many Dutch homes and all of them were neat and clean.
____I read in the story book that these houses were always neat and clean.

Here the student is expected to judge the value of reasons in relation to a new question which is posed in the problem. (Bloom, 1956, pp. 53-54)

Many teachers use such measurements of learning outcomes in daily instruction, rather than in written tests. Test-makers, however, are increasingly including such items in written tests, as they intensify their attempts to measure abilities.

4. Diagnostic Tests. The published diagnostic tests are less widely used than general achievement tests. Although the diagnostic tests do, in fact, measure achievement, there are significant differences between them and the typical achievement test:

First, an achievement test attempts to cover a broader range of areas within a given period of testing time than does a diagnostic test. The diagnostic-type test, on the other hand, provides more detailed measurement within a specific area, thus emphasizing the identification of strengths and weaknesses within this area. This difference could be summarized by stating that the general achievement test is concerned mainly with comprehensiveness of coverage across curricular areas while a diagnostic test is primarily concerned with intensiveness of coverage within a single curricular area.

A second important difference between these two types of tests relates to their difficulty level. In general, subtests within an achievement test are designed to have an average item difficulty in the 45-65 percent range, with about as many very difficult items as very easy items; and an achievement test attempts to cover, insofar as possible, the entire range of ability or performance for specified grades or age groups. A diagnostic test, however, should have a larger percentage of easy material, since it is developed primarily to assess below-average performance. The fact that the diagnostic test is relatively easy means that pupils who may be frustrated by even a well-developed achievement test should experience a good deal of success on the diagnostic test. Furthermore, more accurate, reliable measurement of below-average performance is afforded by the less difficult nature of a diagnostic test. In order to increase the reliability of measurement in identifying weaknesses of pupils and still keep the test administration time within reasonable limits, precision of measurement for the upper levels of performance is sacrificed in a substantial number of subtests. A high level of performance on a diagnostic subtest indicates that a certain area is not a weakness for a pupil or group, although it may *not* indicate exactly how strong the pupil or group is in that area. (Beatty, Madden, & Gardner, 1966, p. 3)

5. Criterion-Referenced Tests. Modern instructional programs are based on sets of explicitly stated objectives. Instruction is directed to helping the student achieve mastery of the objectives, one by one. How is mastery ascertained? Most frequently, the assessment tool is the criterion-referenced test. Such a test usually is brief, because it measures a single objective. Furthermore, the level of performance for mastery is usually specified. This criterion level is high—perhaps 90 percent. Because the criterion-referenced test is most often given after instruction directly related to the objective, it is not surprising that a high level of performance is demonstrated by most pupils.

An example illustrates the nature of a criterion-referenced test. One objective of the Wisconsin Design for Reading Skill Development makes explicit what the child can do if he has mastered the skill "listens for rhyming elements in words": "The child is able to tell when (a) two words pronounced by the teacher (man-pan, call-bell, when-pen) and/or (b) the names of two objects, do and do not rhyme (i.e., 'sound alike')" (Otto & Peterson, 1969, p. 25).

Construction of a criterion-referenced test involves identifying representative samples of the specified behavior. Some items related to the objective just described are shown in Fig. 17.7. It is obvious that the clear statement of the behavioral objective led directly to items of this type. An 80 percent criterion for mastery is recommended by the designers of the instructional program of which the tests are a part.

What are the essential differences between criterion-referenced tests, diagnostic tests, and published achievement tests? The chief difference between criterion-referenced and diagnostic tests is in their use. Diagnostic tests are most frequently used with students experiencing difficulty, in preparation for remedial instruction, whereas criterion-referenced tests more frequently follow instruction. However, it is possible to use a battery of criterion-referenced tests, such as the Wisconsin Tests of Reading Skill Development, before instruction to determine which students have not yet mastered which specific objectives. Such preassessment is often basic to an individualized, objective-based program.

Criterion-referenced tests are quite different from published achievement tests in the scope of their content, in the level of typical performance, and in the referent for an individual's score. Whereas the published norm or the class average is the referent for an achievement test, the criterion established for mastery is the referent on a criterion-referenced test. Embedded in a teach-assess-reteach cycle, criterion-referenced tests are an integral part of the instructional program, whereas achievement tests are more tangentially related to the school program.

Fig. 17.7. Items from "Rhyming Words" subtest of the Wisconsin Tests of Reading Skill Development. The child finds the picture of a word that rhymes with the word associated with the large picture to the left of the vertical line. The smallest pictures appearing at the beginning of each row are used instead of numbers to help young children keep their places. (Otto, Kamm, Peterson, Harris, & Miles, 1970, p. 2)

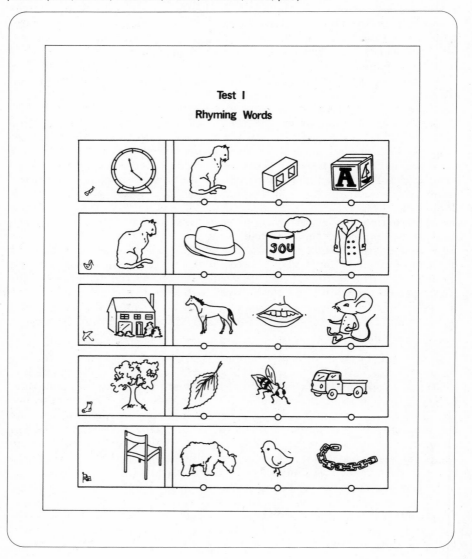

6. Tests of Creativity. In recent years a large number of tests that purport to measure creative abilities have been developed. One illustration is given, and the characteristics of creativity tests in general are discussed. Still among the most widely used tests of creativity are the Guilford tests of divergent production described in earlier chapters. Other more recent tests are mainly adaptations of them. For example, the Torrance Tests of Creative Thinking (Torrance, 1966), intended for use from kindergarten through graduate school, are tests of divergent thinking that include verbal and figural activities. Activities are scored for fluency, flexibility, originality, and elaboration, although the last score is more meaningful for verbal activities. National norms are not yet available against which to compare data; some data from limited samples have been reported, however.

These are some of the tasks in the Torrance tests:

1. Ask-and-Guess. Given a sketch, the pupil is told to (1) ask all the questions he needs to ask to know exactly what is happening in the drawing, (2) to guess as many causes as possible for the action in the picture, and also (3) to guess possible consequences of what is taking place in the picture.

2. Product Improvement. This task presents a picture of a stuffed animal and allows the pupil 10 minutes to list "the cleverest, most interesting and unusual ways" he can think of for changing the toy to make it more fun to play with as a toy, regardless of cost.

3. Unusual Uses. The respondent is given 10 minutes to list "interesting and unusual uses" for a common object, such as a tin can or a cardboard box.

4. Just Suppose. Here the respondent is asked to guess what would happen if a certain situation occurred. This is an example: "Just suppose clouds had strings attached to them which hang to earth. What would happen?" Five minutes are allowed for the test.

5. Picture Construction. Here the respondent uses a shaped piece of colored paper as the nucleus for a drawing. He has 10 minutes to draw a picture or object "that no one else will think of," incorporating the piece of colored paper, and to title his drawing.

6. Incomplete Figures. Ten incomplete figures are completed by the subject, and each is given a title.

7. Repeated Figures. The subject is given 30 parallel lines or 40 circles and instructed to draw a picture, using the given elements as the main part of the picture.

Although these tests are readily available from a commercial publisher, the fact that they are still considered to be a research edition should serve as a caution to the potential user. One reviewer criticized the tests on the basis that "no convincing empirical separability from intelligence has yet been demonstrated . . . it is not evident that one will obtain results that differ clearly from what can be obtained by spending an equivalent amount of time with additional assessors of general intelligence" (Wallach, 1968, p. 279). From these comments it is evident one should study any test author's definition of creativity before deciding to use his test.

In fact, the major problem facing developers of creativity tests is demonstrating that the test measures creativity that is explicitly described and can be observed. For adult subjects in industry or the arts, there are apparent criteria, such as number of patents and number of books published; in the case of children, however, criteria of creativity are not agreed on by behavioral scientists and educators. For instance, MacKinnon's concept of creativity has forced him "to reject as indicators or criteria of creativeness the performance of individuals on so-called tests of creativity" because "they fail to reveal the extent to which the subject faced with real-life problems is likely to come up with solutions that are novel and adaptive and that he will be motivated to apply in all of their ramifications" (MacKinnon, 1962, p. 485).

Another weakness of tests of creativity is their usually low reliability compared with that of educational achievement tests. Because multiple responses are given in many instances and because judgments of quality of response must be made, scorer reliability (the correlation between scores assigned to the same test by two judges) may also be lower than desirable.

Despite their weaknesses, we do not feel that modern tests of creativity should be discarded; nevertheless, they should be used experimentally, not to make decisions affecting students' schooling. As a matter of fact, the testing of creativity today is in many ways in the same stage the testing of educational achievement was in a half century ago. Now, as then, attempts are being made to measure something that is not clearly defined. The reliability and validity of tests of creativity are particularly in question. Until tests are more reliable and validly do measure actual creativity, their interpretation will be open to doubt.

Teacher-Devised Assessment Procedures

Measurement of the achievements and other characteristics of students is not accomplished solely, or even primarily, through the use of published tests. Rather, teachers continually assess pupil performance through a variety of measurement techniques, including pencil-and-paper tests, performance tests, observation, and work sampling. The techniques used to measure specific cognitive behaviors are discussed in this section. Interpretations of performance and other behaviors, as when determining report card grades, will be discussed in the next chapter.

1. **Teacher-Made Objective Achievement Tests.** In the intermediate grades, secondary school, and college, most tests are of the written type, comprised of objective items. As might be expected, the teacher-made test often has higher content validity for the classes of that particular teacher than a standardized educational achievement test. The reason for this is obvious: The teacher designs the test to measure the instructional objectives for a particular class, whereas the standardized test is intended to measure outcomes in a large number of school situations.

The following discussion of types of objective test items and guides for constructing objective tests is intended to lead to better understanding of various types of items and more skill in writing them.

Types of Objective Test Items. The principal types of objective test items are: alternate-choice, multiple-choice, matching, and completion.

1. Some strengths of *alternate-choice* tests are: they may be adapted to testing in many classes; a great deal of material may be tested in a short time; and they are easily scored. In testing achievement, the weaknesses of these tests are apparent: guessing is encouraged, so that the pupil may by chance get a score close to 50 percent; the learner is presented with a wrong as well as a right response, and it is extremely difficult to construct alternate-choice items in which either choice is always correct or always incorrect. When part of the items in the test are usually true and others are always true, the student is faced with the problem of deciding whether a usually true item should be marked "true" or "false."

2. The sample items from a standardized educational achievement battery presented earlier in this chapter are *multiple-choice* items in which the student selects one of three, four, or five choices as correct or better than the others. The multiple-choice item is used widely in standardized educational achievement tests because it is adaptable to measuring such outcomes as facts, understanding of concepts, the ability to apply information, and the ability to evaluate. Multiple-choice items are more difficult to construct than alternate-choice ones, but they are more adaptable to all outcomes of learning.

3. Sets of *matching* items call for pairing an item in the first column with a word or phrase in the second column. There are some kinds of learning outcomes that involve association of two things. Generally, matching items measure only whether the association has been made and whether the student recognizes it; matching items do not usually measure the extent to which meaning has been established. In constructing matching items the materials within each group of items to be matched should be related. For example, if you wish to test association of synonyms and association of men and events, use two sets of items—the first deal with synonyms and the second with men and events.

4. *Completion* tests are those in which words or phrases have been omitted in sentences; the student is to fill in the omitted words or phrases. This kind of test may measure either ability to recall or to perceive relationships. To facilitate scoring of completion tests, consecutive numbers may be placed in the blanks, with instructions that the answers corresponding to the numbers be placed in the left margin.

Guides for Constructing Objective Tests. It will be helpful to consider guides for constructing objective tests and also ways to evaluate the quality of the items.

A. Planning the Test
    1. Delimit the content to be covered in the test. This may be done in terms of behavioral objectives to be assessed or some other means of identifying the important outcomes of instruction. . . .
    2. Decide the proportion of the test that will be devoted to each objective. . . .
B. Preparing the Test
    1. Decide upon the item types to be included. The test may include more than one

type of item. . . .

2. Write more items for the first draft of the test than you anticipate using in the final form. . . .
3. After all items have been written, critically review them for ambiguities and select an appropriate proportion assessing the various objectives. . . .
4. Place items of a particular type together in the test. . . .
5. Arrange items of a particular type in ascending order of difficulty. . . .
6. Avoid a regular sequence in the pattern of correct responses. . . .
7. Write clear, complete, concise directions. . . .
8. Have some person reasonably knowledgeable about the topic take the test and offer critical comments on the items. . . .
9. Revise the test if necessary. . . .

C. Using the Test

1. Arrange for excellent testing conditions, including proper seating, lighting, ventilation, and quiet. . . .
2. Allow ample time for the test. For multiple-choice tests, one minute per item is generally sufficient for most students to complete the test. . . .
3. Before scoring begins, prepare answer keys and scoring rules. (Stanley, 1964, pp. 171-198).[2]

After the test has been scored the teacher is interested in evaluating both pupil performance and the test as a measuring instrument. Analysis of the data for each item is a sensible way of getting information that will help the teacher decide (1) whether the objective measured by that item has been attained by most students or whether reteaching is necessary and (2) whether the item has desirable characteristics that warrant saving it for later use. A *tally sheet* on which the responses to each alternative are indicated provides both kinds of information. When items that measure the same objective are grouped on the tally sheet, it will indicate on which concepts a large number of the class demonstrated mastery and on which there was confusion. If the teacher uses different tally codes for the students in the top quarter of the test scores and the students in the lowest quarter of the scores, he can determine which items were not good for discriminating between high and low scorers.

Such a coding sheet for 20 students who took a 10-item test measuring attainment of two objectives is shown in Fig. 17.8. The sheet gives much information: By counting the tallies within the boxes, one observes that the 20 students performed better on the first objective than the second — far fewer errors were made. Also note that, as one would expect, more of the five students with the five highest scores (⊘) got each item right than did those with the five lowest scores (△). An exception to this pattern, Item 8, indicates a poor item. Item 1 and most of the other items have the desirable characteristic that in those cases each of the incorrect alternative distracted some students. The third alternatives to Items 2 and 4 might be changed to make them better distractors. Item 4 may be too easy. Item 8 is not a good item for another reason: The responses of both high and low scorers are scattered randomly over all alternatives. Four of the top students got Item 1 right, but only one low scorer did — another

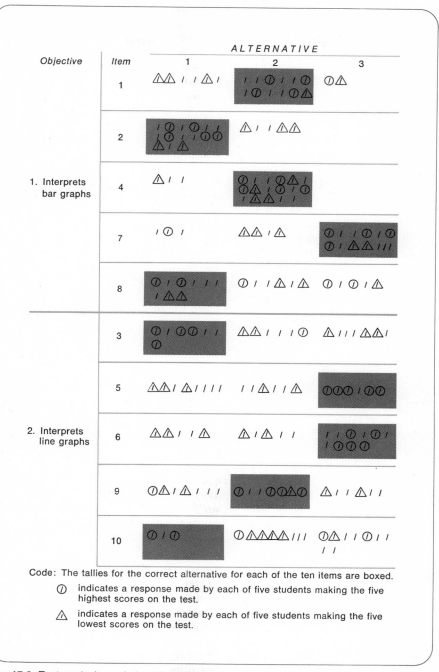

Fig. 17.8. Test analysis worksheet for a teacher-constructed 10-item objective test.

reason why this item is a good one. The second set of items is more difficult than the first, but these items seem to discriminate between the higher and lower scoring students. The last item is very difficult—only three of the 20 students answered it correctly.

Calculating the reliability of a teacher-constructed test is somewhat time-consuming without access to a computer. The *split-half method,* however, is a procedure that is widely used. Without computing a reliability coefficient, one can get a rough estimate of reliability by the procedure, which goes as follows: (1) Construct the best test possible and administer it. (2) Score the odd-numbered items first and then the even-numbered items. (3) Record the score on the odd-numbered items and then on the even-numbered items for each student. If the two scores for each individual are exactly the same, your test is 100 percent reliable—it has a reliability coefficient of 1.00. Suppose it is a 100-item test and many individuals have differences in scores of four or more on the two parts, some scoring higher and some lower on even-numbered items as compared with their odd-numbered scores. Your test in that case is not highly reliable. Suppose a student made a score of 38 on the 50 odd-numbered items and a score of 33 on the 50 even-numbered items. The percentage correct for each part of the test is 76 and 66, respectively. Suppose 70 percent is a passing mark. Which of the two scores should be used to decide whether or not the student passed? Your marking system should not have finer limits than the reliability limits of the tests used in arriving at the scores.

Teachers with access to a teletype or other input to an electronic computer might investigate the possibilities for computer analyzing of multiple-choice tests. The service is usually very inexpensive. Larger school systems are likely to have their own computer facilities that can be used. A Fortran Test Analysis Program for the 1108 Univac Computer is useful for test analysis (Baker, 1969). The main information secured from computer analysis is:

1. Each individual's test score.
2. The frequency distribution of the test scores, the number of pupils taking the test, the average pupil score, and the test's standard deviation.
3. The reliability coefficient based on the test's internal consistency.
4. Item statistics that express the difficulty of each item and indicate whether or not the item is a "good" item; that is, did pupils who scored high on the test as a whole tend to get the item correct, while others did not?

In other words, one not only gets information about the student's performance, but also about test and item characteristics. The teacher may use the latter information to improve later tests by building a large pool of good items. Item data may also reveal specific areas in which misunderstanding is widespread, so that corrective instruction can be provided.

2. Essay Tests. An essay test item may be responded to in a few minutes, during a class period, or during a longer period of time. If responded to in a few minutes, it is designated "short answer"; if during a class period, an "essay test"; and if during a time longer than a regular class period, an "essay examination." These are arbitrary designations, of course;

obviously, they do not apply in the same way to third-grade children and high school seniors.

Essay tests are sometimes preferred to objective tests because they are less time-consuming to construct. Nevertheless, as might be expected, they require considerably more time to grade. Another advantage cited is that essay tests motivate the student to study material for concepts, principles and generalizations, rather than merely facts. Most important, however, essay tests are often considered more useful than objective tests because they enable the teacher to appraise the student's ability to express himself clearly in writing, his ability to recall and organize relatively large amounts of material, and his ability to evaluate.

Essay tests, although widely used, do have some less desirable characteristics than objective tests in the measurement area. One problem of essay tests is that content validity may be low if not enough questions are included. In general, in a test of a given length, more short essay questions rather than fewer long ones should be used.

An even more critical problem is that of reliability. The subjective nature of the evaluation leads to a lower than desirable correlation between the grades one reader assigns and those another reader assigns. Two major approaches have been taken in attempts to minimize this problem. One, which is intuitively appealing, is to grade each essay on a number of separate factors, such as "writing style," "mechanics," "organization," and "ideas." A constellation of grades is then obtained for each student. However, studies comparing the reliability obtained by such an analytic approach to scoring with the reliability on holistically scored essays cast doubt on the approach.

In a landmark study undertaken by the College Entrance Examination Board, an alternate approach to increasing reliability was investigated. Specifically, five essays—three shorter and two longer—were scored independently by five different readers who were asked to make overall or holistic judgments of each essay. It should be noted that the measurement of writing ability, not knowledge of subject matter, was of concern to the authors. The authors conclude:

> *The reliability of essay scores is primarily a function of the number of different essays and the number of different readings included.* If one can include as many as five different topics and have each topic read by five different readers, the reading reliability of the total score may be approximately .92 and the score reliability approximately .84 for the sample. (Godshalk, Swineford, & Coffman, 1966, pp. 39–40)

How may the classroom teacher measure accurately and validly with essay tests? The research cited above suggests the following guidelines:

1. To improve the validity, use several short essay questions in preference to a longer question. To improve the reliability, grade each essay question as a whole, assigning it to one of three to five categories.

2. If possible, share the grading responsibilities with other teachers who know the subject matter well. (This is most feasible if a team-teaching approach is used.) Each reader might score a single question on each pupil's paper.

3. Have each question graded more than once by a different reader, if possible.

In grading essay tests the teacher might also do the following to ensure that judgments on one essay question are relatively independent of those made on another:

1. Place the grade for each essay answer on a separate sheet.
2. Make judgments on a single question on all papers before scoring a second question on each paper.

Finally, in making decisions about the kind of test to use, one might best decide to achieve a balance in the testing program by relying on several of the objective test forms, as well as the essay test.

3. Work Samples. In the course of daily assignments, the teacher has many opportunities to assess students' performance in connection with specific objectives. For instance, it may be unnecessary to design a test to measure a pupil's ability to solve simultaneous equations with two unknowns; a work sample consisting of a practice page or portion of a page done under controlled conditions may substitute for the test. Likewise, the elementary teacher may assess the child's skill in expressing thoughts in complete sentences by selecting a written social studies report and judging sentence structure.

A principal difference between work samples and formal tests is that the former measure *typical* performance whereas the latter usually measure *optimum* performance. The directions for most formal pencil-and-paper tests clearly call for the student to do his best—optimum performance. But in judging work samples we want to find out a student's typical level of performance. In the example concerning sentence structure, for instance, the child may be unaware that he will be assessed on this aspect of his social studies report. Because instruction aims to affect the typical performance of school children, work samples should probably receive more attention than they usually do. Although elementary school teachers frequently collect and file work samples, teachers of older students tend to rely on results of formal tests in making judgments. A discrepancy between optimum and typical performance in skills such as handwriting, spelling, computation, oral language, and typing is undesirable, of course; it may be decreased by more frequent assessment of objectives through work sampling.

In sampling daily work, either whole assignments or portions of one or more assignments may be selected for measurement purposes. Identification of specific instructional objectives of the kind discussed in Chapter 4 facilitates the selection of appropriate material from a student's work.

4. Performance Tests. In the category of performance tests are formal tests using a standard set of procedures and specified stimuli other than pencil-and-paper tests. As is not the case with work samples or observation, a testing situation is established, and behavior is elicited rather than being emitted in the course of normal daily activity. Because the student is aware of the contrived situation and because the directions ask the student to do his best, optimum rather than typical performance is assessed. For instance, the student in a typing class may type more words per minute in a testing situation than normally.

Teacher-developed performance tests are particularly appropriate in assessing skill development. Skill in laboratory procedures, in equipment utilization, or in sight-reading music can be assessed through performance tests. The elementary school child may be able to demonstrate complex relationships, such as those causing phases of the moon, through manipulation of objects before he can give adequate written explanations.

To ensure the validity, reliability, and usability of a performance test, the following points should be taken into consideration:

1. The behavioral objective associated with the testing should be identified.

2. Several instances of the behavior should be observed, rather than one.

3. Explicit written directions should be developed so that the administration of the test is uniform and so that the test can be given in the same form by more than one examiner.

4. The standards for judging performance should be explicit enough that all examiners would come to the same conclusion about a given performance.

5. The materials needed for the test should be gathered together before the testing is scheduled, and a suitable testing site should be selected with care.

The following directions make explicit the procedures to be used in assessing an oral reading skill objective for beginning readers: "reads in meaningful phrases."

1. To assess this skill, a selection written at the child's independent reading level is used, i.e., the level at which he makes fewer than five oral reading errors for each 100 words read.

2. Avoid using a selection written at either the child's instructional or frustration level. The child's instructional level is the level at which he makes approximately five oral reading errors for each 100 words read and needs teacher assistance to gain full meaning from the material. The child's frustration level is the level at which he makes more than five oral reading errors for each 100 words read.

3. Have at hand, with three pages marked in each, the basal readers for the following grade levels: primer; second grade, first semester; second grade, second semester; third grade, first semester. In teachers' editions, the logical phrasing units can be demarcated with vertical slash marks.

4. Choose the book you believe corresponds with the given child's inde-

pendent reading level. Ask him to read the first marked page in his copy silently and ask for help with any words he does not know. Then ask him to read the page aloud. (If during the silent or oral reading more than five words per 100 are missed, begin testing again with an easier selection.) As the child reads orally, notice whether his phrases correspond with those marked in your book. Count the instances where he does not phrase but should, as at the end of a sentence, or where he pauses inappropriately between words in a logical grouping, that is, a noun and its modifiers, a verb and its helping verbs, prepositional phrases.

5. Repeat the procedure with the second and third marked pages.

6. Compare the child's phrasing errors with a previously set standard, e.g., errors at 10 percent of the inserted slashes or two errors per page. A pass-fail decision may then be made.

Performance tests are most often individually given and therefore are time-consuming to administer. Nevertheless, the opportunity to spend a few minutes individually with a student can be used to good advantage in providing feedback, offering encouragement, and setting goals. Performance testing also may be desirable for use with young children or those with reading difficulties. Although performance tests are frequently devised for objectives that cannot easily be measured by other formal means, their use need not be limited to these situations.

17.6. In what ways, or attributes, are group and individual IQ tests alike and different? Why do schools use individual IQ tests so infrequently?

17.7. In what ways are items designed to measure creative abilities and those designed to measure general intelligence alike and different?

17.8. Would you use a group test of general intellectual ability or an educational achievement test in mathematics to predict mathematics achievements of students a year from now? Why?

17.9. What does the existence of several subtests in individual and group intelligence tests imply about the concept of intelligence adopted by the authors of the tests?

17.10. Get copies of some items from an achievement test or use the samples provided in Fig. 17.6. Decide whether each item calls for analysis, synthesis, evaluation, memory, or comprehension.

17.11. Consider the questions drawn from Bloom that measure a student's skills in application, analysis, and evaluation. Select the best answer or answers for each one. Defend your answers by showing why each is best and why other answers reflect errors or incompleteness in the execution of the skill being tested.

17.12. Prepare an objective test item, an essay question, or an assignment designed to measure memory, comprehension, analysis, synthesis, or evaluation of information contained in this chapter.

17.13. State three explicit instructional objectives and prepare objective test items, essay questions, or assignments that would yield work samples to measure mastery or attainment of each objective. (You may find it helpful to refer back to Chapter 4.)

MEASUREMENT IN THE PSYCHOMOTOR DOMAIN

Psychomotor tests are used in several areas of the curriculum in elementary and secondary schools. Physical education must be assessed, of course, but handwriting and typing are examples of other performances that must be judged. In some instances, classroom teachers and specialists are interested in diagnosing the perceptual-motor deficiencies often associated with low performance in reading by young children.

Performance tests are the principal means of gathering data on abilities in the psychomotor domain. Variables of interest include speed, accuracy, strength, endurance, distance, and form. In many cases these variables can be directly measured, whereas in other cases the quality of performance can be judged. (1) Speed may be measured in terms of the amount accomplished during a fixed time period, such as the number of words typed per minute, or in terms of time to completion of a task, such as a 100-yard dash. (2) Accuracy may be a simple count of errors or distance off target. (3) Degree of strength is inferred from the lifting of weights or pressure applied to a scale. (4) Endurance is inferred by performance in an unusually long or arduous task, such as a marathon or the decathlon. (5) Distance may be directly measured in the appropriate unit. (6) Form is rated by one or more judges.

Published Tests of Psychomotor Skills

Aptitude tests discussed in the last section frequently include performance tests that measure psychomotor skills. The General Aptitude Test Battery (1959), for instance, tests finger dexterity and manual dexterity through tests known as "Assemble and Disassemble" and "Place and Turn." In the first, rivets and washers are fitted into holes on a board, then the board is disassembled and the rivets are replaced in the bin and the washers on the rod where they are stored. In the Place and Turn test, pegs are transferred from one board to another as quickly as possible; in one form of the test, they are inverted as they are transferred.

One of the most widely used tests in schools today is the Youth Fitness Test (1965). Because elementary school teachers are frequently required to participate in its administration, this test is now discussed in detail. Developed and normed by the American Association for Health, Physical Education, and Recreation, the Youth Fitness Test is a direct result of a conference on fitness called in 1956 by President Eisenhower. It also is the first test of physical fitness for which national norms have been secured.

Appropriate for pupils in grade 5 through college, the battery includes subtests that measure different aspects of fitness. The tests and the factors measured are as follows:

[TEST]	[FACTOR]
Pull-up (flexed arm hang for girls)	arm and shoulder girdle strength
Shuttle run	speed and change of direction

| [**TEST**] | [**FACTOR**] |
continued	*continued*
Sit-up	abdominal and hip flexor muscles
Standing broad jump	explosive muscle power
50-yard dash	speed of leg extensors
Softball throw for distance	skill and coordination
600-yard run-walk	cardiovascular efficiency

Explicit directions are provided for administration of the tests. For example, see the instructions for the shuttle run, shown in Fig. 17.9.

The low correlations that have been found among the tests support the claim that different components of fitness are in fact measured. Criteria for selection of the tests, other than representation of a variety of factors, included familiarity of the task, suitability for both sexes and the age range, and no need for special equipment. (Aquatic tests initially identified were omitted from the battery for the last reason.)

Revised norms based on the performance of 9200 pupils are expressed in percentiles both for each age level and for various scale points on a classification index that takes into account height and weight as well as age. Modifications of the tests have been made and norms developed for educable mentally retarded pupils as well as normal children.

Teacher-Devised Measurements of Psychomotor Performance

The best procedure for a teacher who wishes to measure psychomotor skill in a curriculum area is probably to take a direct measure of the variable of interest. First, however, the teacher must decide whether typical or maximal performance is to be measured. If typical, the testing situation is, of course, not announced to the pupils; if maximal, it is. The principles for performance testing and work sampling that are outlined in the section on measuring cognitive abilities apply to the testing of psychomotor skills as well.

17.14. Estimate which one or two of the factors in the Youth Fitness Test would be most critical to successful performances by each of the following: quarterback, lineman, outfielder, catcher, boxer, ballerina, swimmer, tennis player. How might you obtain evidence that you were correct or incorrect in your selection of factors?

17.15. Imagine that you have ample funds to secure instructional personnel and audiovisual and other equipment as needed. State one or two instructional objectives and then describe excellent measurement procedures to be used in any one of these skill areas that particularly interests you: swimming, typing, instrumental music, speech correction, learning to speak a second language. (You may wish to observe a coach's analysis of a football movie or a speech clinician's analysis of a tape recording.)

EQUIPMENT

Two blocks of wood, 2 inches x 2 inches x 4 inches, and stopwatch. Pupils should wear sneakers or run barefooted.

DESCRIPTION

Two parallel lines are marked on the floor 30 feet apart. The width of a regulation volleyball court serves as a suitable area. Place the blocks of wood behind one of the lines as indicated in FIGURE 7. The pupil starts from behind the other line. On the signal "Ready? Go!" the pupil runs to the blocks, picks one up, runs back to the starting line, and *places* the block behind the line; he then runs back and picks up the second block, which he carries back across the starting line. If the scorer has two stopwatches or one with a split-second timer, it is preferable to have two pupils running at the same time. To eliminate the necessity of returning the blocks after each race, start the races alternately, first from behind one line and then from behind the other.

RULES

Allow two trials with some rest between.

SCORING

Record the time of the better of the two trials to the nearest tenth of a second.

shuttle run

BOYS AND GIRLS

3

—30ft—

Fig. 17.9. Example of a psychomotor test. (American Association for Health, Physical Education and Recreation, 1965, p. 19)

MEASUREMENT IN THE AFFECTIVE DOMAIN

We should emphasize at the outset that the teacher or counselor should use personality tests only with extreme care. In other words, he should put just as much planning and thought into using them as he puts into using cognitive and psychomotor tests—perhaps even more, for attempting to assess personality is attempting, in a way, to assess the motives, emotions, and problems of a person. These thoughts apply also to the judgments professional educators constantly make during school situations about how well students are attaining affective instructional objectives. In the affective domain, far more than in the other two domains, many judgments must be subjective. We have already pointed out that subjective judgments present special problems.

In spite of the formidable difficulties implied by the last paragraph, experts have evolved a number of published tests in the affective domain, as there is a definite need for them. In this section, the characteristics of these published tests are discussed. We also discuss procedures that teachers and other staff members may use to measure student growth toward objectives in the affective domain.

As might be expected, personality tests have definite limitations. Measurement of personality and attitudes obviously is less straightforward than measurement of cognitive and psychomotor performance. Indeed, the first problem encountered by the would-be examiner involves basic procedures. It is very difficult to find a valid way to measure a trait or characteristic. For example, in pencil-and-paper tests the respondent may choose answers he thinks the examiner will approve, rather than the ones that would reveal his true attitudes or traits. In other cases of observation and rating of personality, the mere presence of an observer or television camera may change the behavior being measured.

In addition to problems of validity, measurement in this area is generally less accurate than in the cognitive and psychomotor domains. For this reason, the use of testing instruments in making decisions that affect the lives of individuals can be challenged. These problems, as well as the ethical question of invasion of privacy, prompted the United States Congress to investigate the use of such tests—personality tests, in particular (Amrine, 1965). As a result of the investigation, the number and kinds of instruments used in government personnel work or government-sponsored research were curtailed. Some guidelines for other users are provided by Cronbach:

> There remains the question of using personality tests when the tester has authority over the person tested. The psychologist diagnosing mental patients, the military psychologist, or the school teacher can enforce tests on his charges. The standards with regard to such practice probably should vary from institution to institution. In general, it seems that subtle tests may properly be used if they are valid and relevant in making decisions which would otherwise rest on less valid information. The tester should avoid misrepresentation in giving the tests. For example, it is quite improper to study an individual's beliefs under the guise of an opinion poll. Test records made for employee counseling should never be made available to the employee's superior. (Cronbach, 1960, p. 462)

The attempts to construct and invent valid and reliable measurement procedures for the affective domain have resulted in a great variety of techniques. In adapting the fourfold table originally presented in Fig. 17.1 to the affective domain in Fig. 17.10, examples in each category are given.

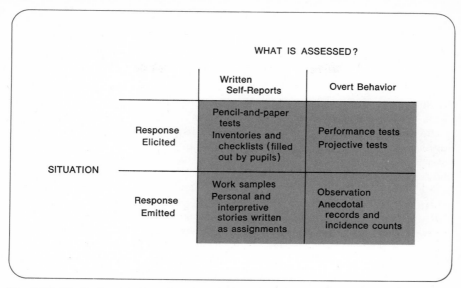

Fig. 17.10. Kinds of procedures for assessing pupils' affective characteristics.

Note that it is conventional in the field of measurement to refer to pencil-and-paper personality tests as *inventories* and *check lists*. Published tests, discussed next, measure elicited behavior. Teacher-devised procedures are used in systematically assessing both elicited and emitted responses.

Published Personality and Attitude Instruments

Despite the limitations of personality and attitude measurement, there are a number of notable published instruments. Some of them are discussed here to give an idea of the sweep of the movement at all age levels. One personality instrument of particular interest to teachers is the Minnesota Teacher Attitude Inventory (Cook, Leeds, & Callis, 1951). In forced-choice response and type of items this instrument is similar to other personality inventories. The MTAI consists of 150 statements designed to sample opinions of prospective teachers and other school personnel about teacher-pupil relations. It is given in about 30 minutes, and the scoring is simple. To each statement the person responds with: strongly agree, agree, undecided or uncertain, disagree, or strongly disagree. Four items are:

    1. Most children are obedient.
    2. Pupils who "act smart" probably have too high an opinion of themselves.
    5. Teaching never gets monotonous.
    14. Young people are difficult to understand these days.

This inventory is one of the few instruments designed to measure attitudes in relation to vocational success. The scoring is specified and, on the basis of the scores obtained, one uses tables to convert raw scores to percentile ranks for such groups as beginning education majors, graduating education seniors, experienced elementary teachers, and experienced secondary teachers. The scoring procedures are based on responses of experienced teachers who were judged to show varying degrees of excellence in the management of teacher-pupil relations. Although this is the case, there are many disagreements about desirable attitudes toward various teacher-pupil relations. The school administrator or other person who might use the test in selecting teachers should first take it himself, learn how he scores, and then decide whether or not he wishes his candidates for teaching positions to respond as he does.

A check list of personal problems completed by each student is often useful in facilitating counseling interviews, in making group surveys leading to plans for individualized action with a student, as a basis for guidance programs of the homeroom and orientation type, as a means of increasing teacher understanding of students in regular classroom situations, and in conducting research on the problems of youth. When students know that their responses will be kept confidential and that they will be given assistance with the problems that they have checked as troublesome, they tend to respond freely and frankly. Not intended as a refined measure of any aspect of personality, the check list can be used by teaching staff and counselors to good advantage as long as they know how to use it and are able to help the student with the problems he reveals. The Mooney Problem Check List (Mooney & Gordon, 1950) and the SRA Youth Inventory (Remmers, Shemberg, & Drucker, 1953) are two of the better-known check lists available.

Interest Inventories. Interests tend to become stable during later adolescence. Also, interest in an immediate activity in the classroom provides a favorable motivational set toward the activity. Although a teacher can readily ascertain the interests of students in connection with immediate classroom activities, helping the student decide which of many possible courses of study and occupations will be of interest over a period of time is a more difficult task. Interest inventories have been developed mainly to facilitate this type of educational and vocational decision-making.

In an interest inventory of many items, the respondent in a short time period checks his preferences for a large number of activities. Thus the preferences of the respondent for many activities can be compared with those of other individuals in the standardization populations. The *administration* of interest inventories is fully as standardized as the administration of educational achievement tests. However, the *interpretation of* interest inventories is not standardized, especially for junior and senior high school students who are not yet in adult occupations and whose interests are still in the formative stage. This will become more apparent in the following discussion of the Kuder Preference Record.

The Kuder Preference Record, Vocational, Form CH (Kuder, 1948), is intended for use in grades 9 through 16 and with adults. Form CH yields scores related to 10 clusters of occupational interests: outdoor, mechanical, computational, scientific, persuasive, artistic, literary, musical, social service, and clerical. The eleventh scale is masculinity-femininity. The items are arranged so that the respondent indicates which activity in a group of three he likes most and which he likes least—see Fig. 17.11.

The best use of the Kuder scores and profiles is to treat them as *one* source of information for helping the student to understand himself better in planning a high school and perhaps a posthigh school program of study

Fig. 17.11. The Kuder Preference Record: Vocational. Note the range of activities covered as illustrated in the practice examples. (Kuder, 1948. Copyright 1948, by G. Frederic Kuder. Reprinted by permission of the publisher, Science Research Associates, Inc.)

The *Kuder General Interest Survey* is exactly what its title suggests: a survey of your interests in a wide range of activities. It is not a test. There are no answers that are right or wrong for everyone. An answer is right if it is true for you.

At the back of this booklet, just before the corrugated paper, you will find an answer pad inserted. Check to be sure that it is there.

On each page of this booklet you will see a list of things to do, in groups of three. First read the list of all three activities in a group. Decide which of the three you like *most*. On the answer pad there are two circles on the same line as this activity—one in the column headed "Most" and one in the column headed "Least." Using the pin found on the cover of this booklet, punch a hole through the left-hand circle following this activity. (Hold the pin straight up and down when you punch your answers.) Then decide which activity you like *least*, and punch a hole through the right-hand circle of the two circles following this activity.

In the examples below, the person answering has indicated for the first group of three activities that he prefers the activity "visit a museum" *most*, and the activity "browse in a library" *least*. For the second group of three activities he has indicated he prefers the activity "collect signatures of famous people" *most*, and the activity "collect butterflies" *least*.

EXAMPLES

Put your answers to these questions in column O.

		O
P. Visit an art gallery		● P ●
Q. Browse in a library		● Q ○ ←LEAST
R. Visit a museum	MOST→	○ R ●
S. Collect signatures of famous people	MOST→	○ S ●
T. Collect coins		● T ●
U. Collect butterflies		● U ○ ←LEAST

Please pretend that you can do *all* of the things listed, even those that require special training. Make your choices as if you were equally familiar with *all* of the activities. Do not choose an activity just because it is new or different, or because you think others might consider it a good choice.

You may like all three activities in a group, or you may dislike all three. In either case, show what your choices would be if you *had* to choose. *It is important that you answer all questions.* For each group of activities, it is essential that you choose the activity *most* preferred and the activity *least* preferred.

Do not spend a great deal of time on any one group. Do not talk over the questions with anyone. Unless an answer represents what *you* think, it will not contribute to a helpful picture of your interests.

If you want to change an answer, punch two more holes close to the answer you wish to change; then punch the new answer in the usual way.

Start now and continue working until you have answered the questions on all pages, columns 1 through 12.

Be sure to put your name, sex (F for female and M for male), age at your last birthday, grade, and today's date— month, day, and year—on your answer pad.

or work. At present, school people properly give much more weight to results from achievement and intellectual ability tests than to results from
interest inventories in planning high school courses with students.

Two other inventories in this category are most often used for college
students: the Study of Values (Allport, Vernon, & Lindzey, 1960) and the
Survey of Study Habits and Attitudes (Brown & Holtzman, 1953). The
Study of Values aims to measure the relative prominence of six basic interests or motives in personality: theoretical, economic, aesthetic, social,
political, and religious. The test scoring procedure is ipsative; that is, a
high score on one scale can be obtained only at the expense of other
scales. A profile can be constructed on the basis of the responses made.
Figure 17.12 shows the profiles of values for average males and average
females and indicates the regions of average, high, and low scores. The
Study of Values is widely used in psychological and educational research
and in counseling and interview sessions with individuals. The purpose of
the Survey of Study Habits and Attitudes is to promote self-understanding in the student taking it and to provide information that can be
used in counseling the student.

Projective Tests of Personality. A projective test is a kind of performance test. A person is asked to respond — with as few restrictions as possible on the mode or content of response — to a relatively unstructured,
yet *standard*, situation. The purpose of a projective test is to ascertain the
respondent's characteristic mode of behavior, including attitudes, motivations, and dynamic personality traits, by observing his behavior elicited
by some standard stimulus. Although teachers and others at times use
simple projective devices, such as acting out a solution to some problem or

Fig. 17.12. Profile of values (averages) for males and females. (Adapted from Allport,
Vernon, & Lindzey, 1960, p. 12)

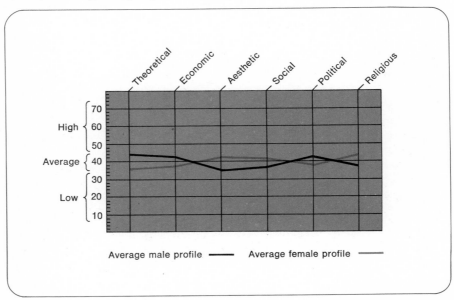

conflict, to elicit pupil responses, the three principal projective tests—the Thematic Apperception Test, the Children's Apperception Test, and the Rorschach Technique—are administered only by psychologists or psychiatrists. Interpretation of the responses is highly dependent on the experience of the examiner. Although these projective tests are used widely in clinical situations, their status is in fact more dubious at present than it was some 20 to 25 years ago.

The Rorschach Technique is a projective test for use with individuals age 3 and over (Rorschach, 1960). The original test consists of 10 inkblots of varying colors and irregular forms (there are many adaptations and revisions). The subject is shown each inkblot and asked to tell what he sees in the blot. The trained clinician asks questions and encourages the subject to respond.

Having noted the responses according to several standard categories, the clinician follows one or another fairly objective procedure for deriving scores from them. Generally, the scores fall into three major categories: location, determinants, and content. Location refers to whether the whole blot, subdivisions, or unusual details of it were responded to. Determinants take into account the shape, color, and shading of the blot to which the subject responded. Content refers to whether the subject saw in the blot a person or persons, parts of persons, clothing, an inanimate object, and the like. On the basis of these responses, the clinician infers the total personality organization of the individual and some of the possible perceptions of the individual of self and of others that may be related to one or more facets of his personality organization.

In a hospital or other diagnostic and treatment center, the psychologist, psychiatrist, social worker, and others use all the information each has collected, confer about the individual, and arrive at decisions as to the present status of the individual's psychological health, the need for further diagnosis, possible forms and duration of treatment, possible release date, and the like. Many institutions rely quite heavily on Rorschach data in diagnosing personality disorders, even though attempts to score and interpret the Rorschach responses objectively have not proven completely successful.

A number of reviewers of the Rorschach test, expressing skepticism about continued heavy reliance on the test by clinicians, have urged that more refined measures of personality organization and dynamics be developed. One of these reviewers, L. F. Shaffer, also indicates why the Rorschach may nevertheless continue in widespread use:

> In view of the relatively unfavorable evidence, why is the Rorschach held in such high esteem? Without attempting to be comprehensive, three reasons may be suggested. First, we have an intense need for a subtle and comprehensive instrument to assess personality. As recent research in social psychology shows, motivation and belief are highly related. When one has a strong need, evidence of little objective merit may be perceived as conclusive. Second, the Rorschach is projective for the examiner as well as for the examinee. One readily "reads into" the vague verbalizations of the Rorschach protocol all that one already knows and believes about the examinee. For each individual examiner, therefore, the Rorschach seems to confirm his other knowledge and he has an intui-

tive and personal sense of the validity of the instrument. Third, the Rorschach is not wholly without validity—it is sometimes "right." (Buros, 1959, p. 288)

Teacher-Developed Assessment Procedures

Some of the goals of instruction, of course, involve attitudes, and when the teacher wishes to assess attainment of specific affective objectives, he needs to develop procedures to obtain the information. Take, as an example, a goal related to the enjoyment of reading. The teacher who develops instructional objectives may have identified several behaviors which he believes are related to reading enjoyment and which are directly observable or measureable. For instance, a behavioral objective may specify that the child sometimes chooses reading from a number of possible spare-time activities. The teacher most often gathers evidence related to such an objective either through self-report, in the form of an inventory or check list, or through observation.

In gathering information about a child's choice of activities in his spare time, asking the question "How often do you read in your spare time?" may elicit a less than honest answer. The child may respond "often," rather than "seldom," simply because he believes the teacher will look favorably on the response. Nevertheless, an attractive feature of self-report information gathered from inventories or check lists is its efficiency in terms of data collection.

Observation is less efficient, but it does have the advantage of being unobtrusive—the pupil may not know he is being assessed for a particular purpose. In this section, both pencil-and-paper data collection and observation are discussed, as they are the most frequently used procedures for assessing affect. (Additional suggestions for classroom assessment of affect may be found in a book written for teachers, *Developing Attitude Toward Instruction*, Mager, 1968.)

1. Inventories and Check Lists. Pencil-and-paper devices to be used by children include inventories, check lists, and rating scales. Items such as those used in the published instruments already discussed can be devised by teachers. These include questions where a yes-no choice is made and questions requiring discrimination among categories arranged along a continuum. The most frequently used number of categories is five; each category may have a descriptive label or only the two extreme categories may be labeled. Another type of item that is sometimes used in the forced-choice question. In a teacher-developed instrument to assess attitude toward home reading, for instance, young children were presented with pairs of pictures depicting pleasant activities such as watching television, playing baseball, and reading a picture book. The child was asked to mark the picture in each pair that showed his preferred activity; his attitude score was simply the number of times reading was chosen over other activities.

An example of another teacher-developed behavior rating scale is shown in Fig. 9.9. This check list was constructed by the instructional staff of an elementary school in a low socioeconomic area as a way to measure change during a study of the effects of individual and small-group conferences in improving prosocial behavior. Chapter 9 contains a detailed description of this research and development activity. Briefly, however, one important point to note about the check list in the context of this chapter is that each child rated *himself* on the 20 behaviors before and then again after the experiment. Another important point is that, although the check list is generalized, rather than highly specific, it did help the children understand and focus on the instructional objectives, and it served as a basis for discussion and goal-setting in the conference situations.

2. Observation. Teachers quite naturally have almost unlimited opportunities to observe the children they teach. Furthermore, observations by a person who is both known to the children and who is performing in his usual role are relatively unobtrusive measures of behavior.

The fact that the teacher has so many opportunities for observing manifestations of pupils' attitudes certainly does not mean that his judgments will automatically be objective and informed. If the assessment is to be thorough and truly useful, the teacher should systematically plan both data collection and procedures for recording the information. If the teacher does not consciously identify the behaviors to be observed and take time to gather and record information, his impressions are apt to be formed on the basis of extreme incidents and behavior patterns, rather than by a less biased sample of behaviors of interest. For instance, the kindergarten teacher who takes five minutes a day to observe children and record the information accumulates a large amount of data on each child's usual activity choices, social behavior, and other variables of interest. Furthermore, systematic procedures for recording information serve the function of standardizing the data collected on each child. One of these procedures involves waiting for behaviors to be emitted and noting them on a check list or anecdotal record. In any case, having identified and recorded behaviors, the teacher may proceed to make overall judgments about behavior observed over a period of time.

1. The techniques for developing *rating scales* to be used by teachers are not greatly different from those discussed in connection with inventories and check lists to be used by pupils. Subjectivity, however, although unavoidable in a child rating himself, should be avoided as far as possible when teachers rate children. One way to compensate for the subjectivity that is inevitably associated with any observation of a person's behavior is to have several judges rate each student and then average their ratings. In a team-teaching situation, for instance, each team member may rate each pupil; thus a more reliable judgment is obtained than if a single teacher rated each particular student. (An efficient way to handle a large number of ratings is to have the team sit together and simultaneously hold up cards showing ratings, as judges in athletic competitions do; the median rating is then recorded for each child.)

2. When observations are recorded as the behavior occurs, techniques in addition to rating scales are used. The *incidence count* is an efficient system that involves simply tallying the behaviors of interest as they occur throughout the school day. For example, the number of times a kindergarten child chooses the book corner during playtime indicates his at-

titude toward reading. When collected over a period of time, incidence counts can provide information about changes in behavior. For instance, if a behavior modification program is undertaken for a problem pupil, weekly counts will build up a picture that will indicate whether or not there is improvement, even slight, over time. Other manifestations of school work habits that lend themselves to incidence or frequency counts include number of times late to class and number of incomplete assignments. A frequency count is by its very nature a more objective type of observation than the rating scales already discussed.

3. Sometimes more detailed reports of behavior in the form of *anecdotal records* are kept to gain insight into the reasons for certain behavior patterns. Relatively objective records of behavior in different situations give important clues to understanding a child and identifying the characteristics that make him unique.

The following procedures are helpful in making anecdotal records of behavior: (1) Briefly, but in enough detail to reveal important aspects, describe the situation in which the behavior occurs. (2) Record the pupil's behavior exactly as it occurs, including specific details. (3) Check what has been recorded to be sure that it contains no subjective elements—adjectives such as "good" or "bad," "bright" or "dull," "lazy" or "industrious." (4) Interpret the behavior if there is enough information to reveal a patter; indicate clearly that such judgments are your interpretation, and keep that portion of the record separate from the objective portion.

Studying children in different situations and recording observations enables one to learn much about behavior in general and to gain insight into the various methods for best coping with certain behavior. Anecdotal records are especially valuable for gaining better understanding of a child whom teachers do not understand well or who is not making good progress when the records are contributed by several teachers who have the child in their classes. Sometimes a useful overall pattern emerges in such a collection of records that does not show up in the observations of only one teacher.

17.16. Discuss the following statements and questions connected with interest inventories:

a. Can one dislike or like an activity before he has any real sense of what it involves?

b. If a person intends to become a historian, he will "like" books, reading, meeting scholars, etc. If he then finds out that it takes years of schooling to become a historian, he may decide to continue practicing his guitar. As a promising musician he will then "like" sheet music, solos, meeting musicians, etc.

c. Interests are learned.

17.17. Why might personality tests have lower predictive validity and reliability than achievement tests?

17.18. Describe how check lists and inventories can be used as instructional devices for students, in addition to being measurement tools.

17.19. "John acted very badly during the art period. Although he is usually somewhat argumentative, he was hostile today, and I had to ask him to leave the room." Criticize this as an entry in an anecdotal record. Rewrite the entry, imagining the specific situation, so that it reflects good assessment procedure.

SUMMARY

Measurement can be done either by formal testing during which students supposedly perform at an optimum level or by observing and scaling students' typical classroom behaviors. Pencil-and-paper tests should be supplemented by teacher observation and the collection of work samples, so that both the optimum and typical achievements and other characteristics of a student are sampled. Test-makers, including teachers, strive for (1) objectivity, to reduce measurement errors caused by scoring and scorer subjectivity; (2) validity, to assure that either the test items represent the actual content being measured or that the test score is useful in predicting behavior; (3) reliability, to reduce errors intrinsic to the test itself; and (4) usability, to assure that time, money, and effort are most efficiently spent.

Many individual and group tests have been prepared and standardized in such a way that any individual's score may be compared with the scores made by the standardization sample of students. These tests, which thus are norm-referenced, are available to test abilities, achievements, and other characteristics of students in the cognitive domain. For example, the Wechsler scales and the Revised Stanford-Binet Scale are intelligence tests used to test one individual at a time. Other intelligence tests commonly used in the schools are administered simultaneously to classroom-size or larger groups. Norm-referenced, group achievement tests measure the acquisition of outcomes in broad areas of instruction, such as reading, mathematics, or science. Diagnostic tests are designed explicitly to identify strengths and weaknesses within specific selected areas, such as word recognition in reading. Criterion-referenced tests and tests of creativity represent new emphases in measurement.

Objective teacher-made tests, as other measuring devices, should have high reliability and content validity. The preparation of good multiple-choice items requires careful thought in phrasing the item stem, selecting distractors, and avoiding incidental clues to the answer. Essay tests are easier to construct than objective tests but often lack objectivity, validity, and reliability, and, in addition, scoring the responses may be very time-consuming.

Psychomotor abilities are usually measured by tests of physical performances, as in the Youth Fitness Test, which assesses several indexes of speed and strength.

Published tests designed to measure affective characteristics have encountered difficulties in terms of both reliability and validity. Furthermore, the right of privacy of the individual has become of increasing concern as test results and other information are stored and rapidly retrieved by computer and may possibly become public information. Nevertheless, attitude scales, interest inventories, and projective tests of personality offer some information that a teacher can supplement with systematic observation and the use of informal questions and check lists.

SUGGESTIONS FOR FURTHER READING

BEATTY, W. H. *Improving educational assessment and an inventory of measures of affective behavior.* Washington, D.C.: Association for Supervision and Curriculum Development, 1969.

In addition to several highly readable articles on assessment and evaluation by the leaders in these fields, more than 100 inventories to measure affective behaviors of pupil and teachers are described and their sources listed.

CRONBACH, L. J. *Essentials of psychological testing.* New York: Harper & Row, 1970.

This edition of a classic in the measurement field focuses on assessment of ability, interests, and personality.

HEREFORD, C. F., NATALICIO, L., & McFARLAND, S. J., eds. *Statistics and measurement in the classroom.* Dubuque, Ia.: Kendall/Hunt, 1969.

There are four readings that deal with classroom testing and eight that deal with standardized tests. All are of an introductory type.

LINDVALL, C. M. *Measuring pupil achievement and aptitude.* New York: Harcourt, Brace & World, 1967.

Written for the teacher, this book has useful sections on principles of test construction, using tests to measure varied types of ability, using statistics to appraise a test, standardized achievement and aptitude tests.

WOMER, F. B. Testing programs—Misconceptions, misuse, overuse. In Ripple, R. E., ed., *Readings in learning and human abilities.* New York: Harper & Row, 2nd ed., 1971.

Here possible misuses of standardized test results are identified and discussed.

Chapter 18 Evaluating Student Progress and Instructional Programs

Evaluating Student Progress

matching the student and his instructional program
facilitating student progress
reporting student progress
reporting related to instructional objectives
report cards and grades
conferences

Evaluating Materials and Instructional Programs

formative evaluation
development of products
iterative cycle of development and evaluation
summative evaluation
user evaluation
comparison of programs
guidelines for introducing new curricula

National Assessment of Education

purpose of a national assessment
strategy of national assessment
control of national assessment

n the last chapter, testing and other means of gathering information about the student were discussed. That chapter is intended to familiarize teachers and other educational workers with published tests and also with teacher-developed measuring instruments and procedures. In this chapter, the process of evaluation, one element of which is measurement, is the topic.

Evaluation has been defined in a number of ways. The definition accepted here is taken from the first draft of a report issued by the Phi Delta Kappa National Study Commission on Evaluation (1969, p. 57): "the process of delineating, obtaining, and providing useful information for judging decision alternatives." A feature of this definition is that it stops short of the actual making of decisions. In other words, it emphasizes the continuing nature of evaluation. It implies that the evaluator must identify the alternatives about which decisions are to be made, specify the criteria or values by which the alternatives may be judged, and identify and collect the particular information needed to arrive at a decision. These are the continuing phases of evaluation, for, once a decision has been made, a new sequence of evaluation starts. In practice, of course, evaluators — including teachers — often make the decisions themselves.

It is obvious that all aspects of the educational system can be — and should be — evaluated; these aspects include administration, school-community relationships, teacher education, space planning and use, and the like. In this chapter, however, the discussion is limited to evaluating student progress and instructional programs and materials.

In the first section, on student progress, the disparities between traditional and more recent means of evaluation are considered. Report cards using letter grades and parent conferences, still the two most commonly used means of reporting student progress, are discussed.

The methods developers use to evaluate their products, mainly instructional materials, are described in the next section. Suggestions are made for adapting their large-scale evaluation procedures to local development activities. Finally, a program for assessing the quality of public education throughout the country is described.

EVALUATING STUDENT PROGRESS

Evaluation is an ongoing process. It is aimed particularly at providing information at three points in time for three related purposes: (1) Information on the student's characteristics and achievements is needed at the beginning of a school year, semester, or unit of instruction in order to set objectives and arrange an instructional program appropriate for the student. (2) Reliable information is needed throughout the instructional program, often on a daily basis, to provide feedback so that the student and the teacher may decide how well they have done and how to proceed. (3) Summary information is required at the end of a school year, semester, or unit so that a final indication of the student's progress may be made available to the student, teacher, parents, and possibly others who may make decisions based on how well the student has progressed.

Decisions are made by teachers and other educational personnel at the times indicated about individual students. These decisions affect the student's life for short or longer periods of time. For instance, a student may be placed in an ad hoc instructional group for a week or two and then reassigned on the basis of an evaluation of his progress. On the other hand, he may be accepted for an accelerated instructional program, or a decision may be made to retain him within a particular grade for a second year, based on a yearly evaluation. Judgments must also be made about the student's progress which in turn are reported to school officials, parents, and others periodically. How well this reporting is done vitally affects the student and also the attitudes of the parents and the public in general toward education. In this connection, students should participate in all phases of the evaluation of their progress in order to become more independent and self-directive through self-evaluation. Wilhelms puts it this way:

> The most fundamentally important outcome of evaluation is what happens within the learner himself. In the narrower terms of subject matter he needs to understand with some precision what is to be learned and "what it is all about" (i.e., why it is important, how it relates to other subject matter and to himself). To whatever extent he has succeeded, he needs to know about it, for a sense of success contributes energy for the next task; to whatever extent he has not yet achieved mastery, he needs to know what the gaps are, so that he can figure out what to do about them. In some degree he has to be equipped to be his own diagnostician, because in the final analysis he will be his own diagnostician anyway—he is the person who is in control of his learning energies—and it is better that he do the job well.
>
> In the broader terms of the learner's development as a person, it is essential that evaluation help him steadily toward a valid and healthy image of himself. It is especially important for him to learn about his strengths and resources, in a way that genuinely leads him to incorporate these into his self-concept. It is also essential that evaluation should enrich his conception of the life-space he has to operate in, by expanding his vision of the opportunities and the choices that can be open to him and by enriching his background perceptions of purposes and values to judge by. (Wilhelms, 1967, pp. 4-5)

In this section, the role of evaluation in matching the student and his instructional program, facilitating student progress through feedback, and reporting to parents is discussed. Current practices are described, and recommendations for improvement are made.

Matching the Student and His Instructional Program

A common instructional practice today is to place about 30 students together at the beginning of the school year in the same course or instructional program, or in two or three variations of the same program. For example, 90 students are placed in three sections of ninth-grade English for high achievers; 270 are placed in nine sections for average achievers; and another 90 are placed in three sections for low achievers. The placements may be based on the results of one group intelligence test given early in the ninth grade or on the grades made in English during the eighth grade. These are grossly inadequate bases for placing students. But — and this is even more deplorable — each English class is conducted in the same way for all the students in any one section. In other words, all 30 students supposedly will reach the same level of achievement at the same rate through the same instructional activities.

Teachers and administrators may feel compelled to continue these outmoded practices because they do not have the necessary instructional materials, space, and time to do any better. These, however, are the practices that should be followed: Each student's level of achievement in English should be assessed early in the school year by using both standardized tests and teacher-made tests and observations. Also, information about the student's earlier achievement in English and his other characteristics should be readily available from the preceding school years. Additional essential information is gathered when the teacher talks with each student to learn about his plans, interests, problems, and the like. An instructional program based on this more complete information and on knowledge of the program of English in the school is then arranged for each student. These programs provide for differences among the students in the rate at which they learn the same or similar material and also for differences among the students in styles of learning; for example, some learn better mainly by independent study, with little group discussion; others do better mainly by group discussion, with little independent work. The more precise the information that is available about a student, the more carefully must the teacher evaluate its importance in relation to a possible instructional program for the student.

Most schools do not yet devise a separate instructional program for each student. Nevertheless, some do have team-teaching or other arrangements in which students who have similar achievement levels and interests are grouped together for short periods of time and then regrouped at the end of a specified time interval or unit of instruction. In these situations, there is at least a tendency for more information about each student to be gathered and used. Also, there is the advantage that more than one teacher decides what might be best for each student.

There is another development that is encouraging, even though it also is something of a compromise between what should be done and what can be done under existing conditions. In this plan, which is being used in an increasing number of schools, instructional objectives are formulated in a curriculum area, and then a specific instructional program is outlined. (Sometimes one or two alternative programs are also outlined, to provide more flexibility — a desirable feature, of course.) All students follow the outlined program, but with as many planned individual variations as the time of the teacher and the adequacy of instructional materials may permit.

In this kind of situation teachers and others must decide early in the school year where each student should be placed in the preplanned instructional program. Each student is assessed early in the year on a number of specific behaviors directly related to the program. The placement test, or battery of tests and observations, may consist of a number of items keyed to the behaviors that are also the objectives of the program. (For example, a student may be required to spell 18 of 20 words correctly in order to start a particular instructional unit in English.) As the school year proceeds, the individual's instructional program is arranged to take him on from the level of skill or concept mastery at which he started and to help him acquire the additional skills or concepts incorporated in both the objectives and the instructional program. The instructional program may be either semiprogramed, in which case the student works primarily with materials, or it may involve his participating as a member of a series of small ad hoc instructional groups and using materials to a lesser extent. In either case, the student's level of achievement at the end of each set of instructional activities is measured and related to a criterion (e.g., 90 percent of the items correct). According to how well he has achieved, the teacher, or the teacher and the student, decide what he will do next.

In this connection, in individually prescribed instruction (IPI) in mathematics and in other curriculum areas as described for Project Plan (Chapter 6), short achievement tests are given early in the year to place students in the proper unit of a sequential series of units. When the student completes the first unit, that is, a set of instructional materials and related activities designed to attain certain objectives, he takes a criterion-referenced test. He must get a specified percentage correct in order to proceed to the next unit in IPI mathematics or to choose from among several units that have been developed in various curriculum areas worked out in Project Plan. Increasingly, instructional programs in these curriculum areas, consisting of printed text-workbooks, related audiovisual materials, related diagnostic and criterion-referenced tests, and suggested teacher and student activities, are being developed and marketed. They are still expensive, however, and the differences that they provide for are primarily limited to rate of learning.

What evaluation procedures are common for placing students in the instructional programs just described? (1) First, the purpose for assessing each student's present level of achievement and other characteristics is identified. That is, before any testing, observing, or sampling of work performed is done, the teacher and the student know why it is being done. (2) Criteria are set. That is, what the student must be able to do in order to start a particular group of assignments or activities is made explicit. This also implies that the nature of the assignments or activities is understood, so that the student's achievements and characteristics can be related directly to the instructional program. (3) The data, including standardized and teacher-constructed tests and teacher comments based on work samples and observation, are secured and taken into account. If there is only one source of information to consider for each student, the evaluation of the data is straightforward. When there are multiple data of unequal weight or when there are inconsistencies among them, the judgment of the decision-maker is required. For example, a child may achieve high in class in a particular curriculum area, but score at an average level or below on a standardized test. Which result is to be given more weight? (4) After the data are sorted, more subjective judgments are often made, based on accumulated observation. For instance, it may be considered undesirable to place two disruptive students in the same instructional group.

Thus we see that arranging an instructional program for a particular student, or placing him in an already developed instructional program, requires more than measuring his skills or knowledge. The process of evaluation takes into account the student's characteristics, the nature and requirements of an instructional program, and the evaluator's own system of values, particularly with respect to selecting and weighing the criteria on which the individual is evaluated.

Facilitating Student Progress

Assessing the student's progress means identifying what he has achieved and what he has not achieved and diagnosing any problems that may need to be overcome by the student, the teacher, or both so that the student may continue to progress. Most students secure some of this information themselves; the skillful teacher assists them, particularly in identifying and overcoming problems. Knowledge about the adequacy of one's responses, or performances, provides the feedback essential for correcting one's actions. Wilhelms described the importance of feedback through evaluation in this way:

> Instructional diagnosis lies at the very heart of good teaching. After each bit of evaluative data comes in, the teacher should be a little surer of how to proceed next. The all-too-common confusion of evaluation with grading tends to produce an image of evaluation as a terminal thing. But its far more significant function is a constant probing for the best way to move forward.
>
> It is not the teacher alone who needs the diagnosis. After each bit of evaluation, the student, too, should know better where he stands and how to move ahead. And this purpose of diagnosis should be so apparent in the evaluative devices used that the student will see diagnosis as an aid, not as a trap set to catch him in failure. (Wilhelms, 1967, p. 6)

Systematic monitoring of the student's progress is required in order to secure the essential information on which feedback is based. For example, an error in the early placement decision may have been made; the error should be detected and corrected early. Or a student may be correctly placed but after initial success he may experience difficulty with the pacing of the instruction. The proper pacing of instruction requires assessing the student's acquisition of the content or skills and his motivation. Evaluation so integrated within the instructional program provides corrective feedback. This kind of continuous monitoring and correcting does not occur accidentally. The teacher and other educational personnel must identify such evaluation needs, plan the collection of relevant information, and establish criteria against which the information will be judged.

A satisfactory technique for monitoring student progress in the instructional program is by use of work samples. Suppose a student has been placed in an instructional group to learn how to add and subtract fractions. He has demonstrated mastery in adding and subtracting like fractions, in writing equivalent fractions ($1/2 = 3/6$), and in expressing mixed fractions ($1\ 2/3 = 5/3$). A sample of daily work, after group instruction in adding unlike mixed fractions, shows that he has made many errors. The teacher *who is aware at this point* of the student's problems has several alternatives among which to choose based on the information at hand. If other pupils are having similar difficulties, group instruction with different procedures or materials may be planned. If some but not all pupils in the group are having trouble, those not experiencing difficulty may be assigned independent practice on more difficult exercises, and a smaller group comprised of those needing further instruction is formed. If a single pupil is experiencing difficulty, the teacher, an instructional aide, or another student may work with the pupil, using manipulative materials, until he demonstrates his understanding of the algorithm.

Teachers have other ways to monitor pupil progress. Sensitive teachers respond to puzzled facial expressions, for instance. Also, short, frequent quizzes may provide feedback to the teacher and the student. You may think of other ways in which you will become aware of how students are progressing on a day-to-day basis. The important point is that if monitoring of pupil progress is to lead to improved instruction, the evaluation act has to be brought to a conscious level and planned. This means that (1) the questions to be answered by the evaluation are identified, (2) the information that will answer those questions is specified, (3) criteria for evaluating that information are established, (4) the information is collected, and (5) the information is judged against the criteria. Finally, decisions among alternatives are made based on the evaluation.

Recording and Reporting Student Progress

Although monitoring of day-to-day progress in the instructional program is of great importance for making instruction beneficial for each student, it is also necessary to summarize the progress a student has made over longer periods of time. Progress reports must be prepared for school officials and parents periodically, and decisions about promotion must be made annually. More important, however, is the fact that the student's progress toward realizing broad educational objectives such as independence in word recognition and enjoyment of literature cannot be assessed merely through the kinds of daily monitoring of performance discussed thus far.

Reporting Progress According to Objectives. In an instructional program keyed to behavioral objectives, how is summary evaluation done? What are the implications for reporting? Let us assume that a definite number of behaviors are subsumed by a particular educational objective that has been set for all children in the school. For example, assume that mastery of 39 specified behaviors connected with word-attack skills will lead to attainment of the educational objective "recognizes 95 percent of the words encountered in fifth-grade textbooks independently." Thirty-nine units of instruction may be provided during the child's elementary school experience so that he may achieve this educational objective. It is evident that one way of looking at an individual's cumulative progress is to consider the number of behaviors he has acquired at a given point in time and to make a value judgment based on this and other information. For example, a child's having acquired six skills by the end of kindergarten will surely be judged differently than his having acquired six by the end of the third year in school. Likewise, if the child acquires no new skills during a six-week interval, this information is of interest. Also, the teacher may judge that two children who have mastered six and 15 behaviors, respectively, at the end of the first year are achieving as well as expected because of differences between them in level of mental development and use of language in oral and written form.

If this kind of summary evaluation is projected to all subject-matter areas and age levels, one sees the form that reporting would take—the number and description of the units mastered would be reported for each curriculum area. The numbers and descriptions reported for students who proceed rapidly would differ from those for students proceeding at an average pace. In secretarial skills, for instance, the report at the end of the last year would describe the level of proficiency attained as represented in various units completed by each student. By referring to a master list of unit objectives, a potential employer could determine the degree of expertise a student had acquired in shorthand. Increasingly, a larger segment of the public, and some government officials, are demanding that schools should clearly specify what students of specified characteristics should learn and then be held accountable for their learning it.

Report cards are presently not of the form described above for at least two reasons: (1) The majority of educational objectives related to the main curriculum areas are not broken down into distinct behavioral objectives, instructional units, or other communicable forms and (2) not enough people understand such a system to make it an informative way of communicating with students, parents, or others.

What are alternative ways of communicating progress in objective-based programs to parents? One alternative is to report to parents verbally exactly what the pupil has mastered. This may be done in written or oral form. For example, a skill folder, such as that used in the Racine, Wisconsin, Unified School District, part of which is shown in Fig. 18.1, may be shared with the parents in a parent-teacher or student-parent-teacher conference. Using a folder like this, it is possible to report precisely where the child is during a conference.

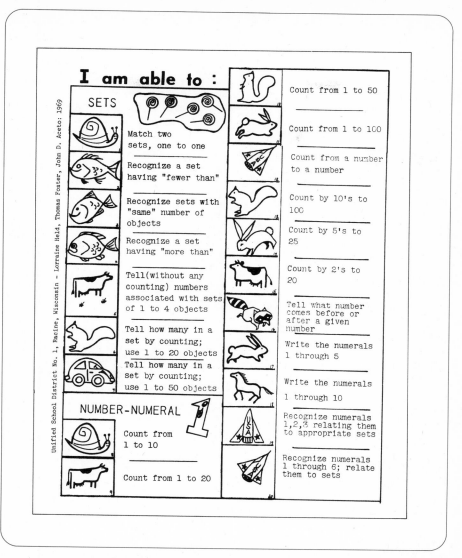

Fig. 18.1. First page of skill folder in elementary mathematics used in Racine Unified School District No. 1, Racine, Wisconsin.

Most school systems using objective-based instructional programs in some curriculum areas have not reconciled their system of reporting with the means of evaluating progress inherent in the instructional program. Furthermore, there is often strong pressure from parent groups to retain traditional forms of grading according to a scale of letters or numbers, or at least to give some information on the achievement of a pupil in relation to other pupils. At present, therefore, all we can do is point to the inconsistency shown when achievements are *reported* according to norms, or comparisons among students, while, at the same time, performance in the instructional program is *judged* according to behavioral criteria that students meet at varying individual rates. It is obvious that completely satisfactory solutions to reporting pupil progress in individualized objective-based instructional programs have not yet been worked out.

Present Patterns of Reporting to Parents. The results of a survey on methods of reporting pupil progress to parents are presented in Table 18.1. The widespread use of letter grades, particularly at the secondary

Table 18.1. Responses to the Question "What Method Do You Use To Report Pupil Progress to Parents?" in Terms of Percentage of Teachers Checking Each Category

	Elementary	Secondary	Total
A report card with a classified scale of letters	71.6	83.1	77.3
A scheduled conference with the parents	59.9	20.0	40.2
A written description of the pupil's performance	24.3	10.4	17.4
A report card with a classified scale of numbers	10.0	8.8	9.4
A report card showing percentage grades	2.4	10.0	6.2
A report card with either pass or fail	8.2	2.6	5.4

Source: Adapted from National Education Association, 1969a, pp. 75–76.

level, is shown in the results. (The fact that each column in the table adds to more than 100 percent reflects the fact that in many schools more than one method of reporting to parents is used.) Note also, however, how often parent-teacher conferences are used in elementary schools. In an earlier study, practices in cities with populations greater then 2500 were surveyed, and the six most frequent combinations of methods of reporting pupil progress were tabulated—see Table 18.2. Because letter grades and

Table 18.2. The Six Most Commonly Employed Methods of Reporting Pupil Progress in the Public Elementary Schools in Urban Places in the United States with Populations above 2500, by Percentage of Use

Exclusively by letter scale	30.7
By a letter scale and personal conferences	22.4
By a letter scale, informal written notes, and personal conferences	16.2
By a letter scale and informal written notes	8.2
By a word scale and personal conferences	4.3
Exclusively by a word scale	3.8
Total	85.6
Other methods	14.4
	100.0

Source: Dean, 1960, p. 64.

parent conferences are used so predominantly, they are now discussed in detail.

Use of Letter Grades. The assigning of letter grades on report cards is discussed here as an outcome of evaluation; that is, these grades involve more than measurement because of the multiple types of information used and the value judgments made in transforming that information into letter grades. Although it is true that (at the secondary and college levels especially) teachers may simply average scores attained in tests and assignments, rank-order them, and assign a letter grade, it is likely that subjective judgments also enter into the grading process. For example, the place at which to draw the line between a B and a C must be identified; also, the student who has persevered despite an illness may be given credit for his perseverance. Other factors, in addition to specific test scores, that are taken into account in grading include participation in discussion, noncredit outside work, regularity in completing daily assignments, the curriculum or track being pursued, and achievement in relation to the teacher's perception of the student's abilities and other characteristics.

Letter grades may be formulated in terms of either absolute or relative standards. In systems where an A is defined to mean 95-100 percent, the standard is *absolute*—a student is graded according to how close to perfect his work is. It is difficult to imagine how such a definition of a letter grade can allow factors other than scores on tests and assignments to be taken into account. More frequently, *relative* standards are used—A is defined to be outstanding or excellent work, B above average, and so on. (In some advanced college and high school courses only A's and B's are given.) Letter grades are sometimes related to the normal curve, especially at the college level in required freshman and sophomore courses, with C the most frequent grade, B and D the next most frequent, and A and F the least frequent.

It should be clear that the amount of progress that students make cannot be summarized well in a single letter grade. All of us can devise more faithful means of summarizing progress and reporting it than by means of such single letter grades. Furthermore, the undesirable effects of low grades on many hard-working children and youth are disastrous to their personal and educational development. In our country there are many penal and mental institutions populated mostly by persons who were failed by the schools and quit before high school graduation. Simply because single letter grades have been used for centuries and are still widely used does not mean that they are good or that they should be continued. Rape, murder, war, racism, and pollution of the air and water are also practices of mankind that have existed for centuries.

Conducting Parent Conferences. The limitations of letter-grade marking, particularly of younger children, are apparent to most teachers. The trend toward supplementing or replacing the report card letter grade by verbal and written statements is an encouraging one. The suggestions on conducting a parent conference that follow apply specifically to the face-to-face meeting, but many of the points are equally valuable for written comments or notes or for telephone conversations.

What is discussed with the parent in a conference? The answer depends on the purpose of the conference. If it is routinely scheduled to report student progress, the emphasis is somewhat different than if it is specially scheduled to resolve a learning or adjustment problem. The topics about which the teacher should be prepared to make evaluative comments are the following.

- The child's progress in his classroom work
- Work habits at school
- Social adjustment — relationships with other children in the classroom, on the playground, and in other groups
- Interests, aptitudes, and abilities
- Relationships with teachers and other staff members
- Health or emotional problems

From the parents the teacher may elicit information about the child's reaction to school, his personal relationships with members of the family and neighborhood friends, his interests, home responsibilities, health, and any particular problems.

The success of a parent-teacher conference is at least partially dependent on the teacher's preparation for it. A teacher should make notes on information he wishes to share with the parent and collect work samples or anecdotal records (see Chapter 17) to present in support of particular points he wishes to make.

The following tips for conducting a successful conference are drawn from several publications of the National Education Association (1969a):

- Accept the parent's feelings and attitudes. This does not mean that you approve or disapprove of them; you merely accept the fact that they are there.
- Develop real interaction. To obtain helpful information about the child, ask leading questions rather than those which may be answered with "yes" or "no." It is better to ask "How does Johnny feel about school?" rather than "Does Johnny like school?"
- Talk parent-talk, not pedagese. Don't say "peer group," say "children his own age." Don't drop a word curtain between you and the parent.
- Remember what you can and can't say. Find out beforehand what information you're not supposed to give to parents. In some districts, for example, a child's IQ is not revealed.
- Don't be tempted into unethical conduct. No matter how you feel about the teacher Johnny had last year, don't join in when parents criticize him. Keep them to the subject, which is: How can we help Johnny *now*?
- Avoid direct comparisons of the child with other children; encourage the parent not to compare one child with another, especially a brother or sister.
- Avoid open or implied criticism of the parent.
- Listen thoughtfully to criticisms of the school and plan later visits for parents who are critical of the school program.
- Be honest. Low test scores should be honestly, but tactfully, explained.
- Avoid the expression of judgments or opinions unless asked for.
- Suggest several possible remedies for problems, and let the parent choose which he will try. Encourage the parent to suggest his own

remedies for any problem that has appeared. If the problem is too complex for the school, be ready to suggest other sources of help.

Special thought should be given to how test information will be reported to parents. Parents are probably interested in the achievements and abilities of their child in comparison with others attending the same school and will ask questions about this if you do not provide such information. Chapter 19 includes suggestions for interpreting test scores.

Remember that in a conference situation you have a partner in evaluation. It is often desirable for the teacher to present information and let the parent make value judgments based on this information. The teacher, in summarizing the conference, can concur with parental judgments or add independent evaluations.

Report Cards. Two report forms are now presented and discussed to illustrate the variety of evaluative information the teacher is expected to provide.

Figure 18.2 shows the front of the comprehensive report form of a high school. The parents receive one of these reports each quarter for each subject in which the student is enrolled in school. A letter grade of A to D or F is given in each of the three main areas: "individual performance," "school citizenship," and "knowledge and skills in subject." These three areas are accorded equal weight in assigning the letter grade for "total growth and performance." The various marks—plus, no mark, and minus—are entered as appropriate for the 13 subareas: "works up to ability," "has a positive attitude," "shows self-direction," etc. (Space is provided on the back of the report form for parent and teacher comments, and the parent is asked to telephone the school if a conference is desired.)

Note that each teacher who has the student in his class must observe and rate behavior in connection with the three main objectives of the high school: to encourage desirable individual growth in each student, to encourage desirable citizenship behavior, and to encourage optimum development of knowledge and skills in the subject.

At this high school, individual performance is appraised as a valuable indication of the present and future success of the student in any type of work or play; the ability to plan, organize, and follow through on the plan; the skills developed in supervised study, in solving problems, in group research, in group discussion, and in individual research. All such habits and skills are part of the total growth of the students. Evaluation in this area is in relation to the student's own ability.

School citizenship represents the observed performance and growth toward the qualities of a competent, cooperative, participating school citizen. Such factors as care of personal and school property, the ability either to lead in worthwhile activities or to take an active part in carrying them out, and effective cooperation in group projects are important. Citizenship includes contributing something to the good of the school. A student who causes no trouble in school is not necessarily a good citizen; good citizenship involves active contribution to the welfare of others.

Knowledge and skills in the subject include the appraisal of strictly

REPORT TO STUDENTS AND PARENTS

MONONA GROVE HIGH SCHOOL — MADISON, WIS.

Fr. ☐   Jr. ☐

Name _____   So. ☐   Sr. ☐

Mr.
Subject _____ Teacher Mrs. _____
Miss

_____
Home Room Teacher
Term beginning September 3, 1968 -- ending June 6, 1969

A+ = 4.3	C+ = 2.3	F+ = .3
A = 4.0	C = 2.0	F = .0
A— = 3.7	C— = 1.7	
B+ = 3.3	D+ = 1.3	
B = 3.0	D = 1.0	
B— = 2.7	D— = .7	

GRADING SYSTEM

+ Mark indicates superior achievement
No Mark indicates average achievement
— Mark indicates need for improvement

	First Quarter	Second Quarter	Third Quarter	Fourth Quarter	Final Grades
INDIVIDUAL PERFORMANCE					
Works up to ability					
Has a positive attitude					
Shows self-direction					
Plans work wisely					KNOWLEDGE AND SKILLS AVERAGE
SCHOOL CITIZENSHIP					
Is courteous and considerate of others					
Is responsible					
Contributes his share					
Is a good leader or follower					
Takes care of school, personal property					
KNOWLEDGE & SKILLS IN SUBJECT					
Develops skills					
Indicates knowledge by assignments					FINAL EVALUATION / TOTAL GROWTH & PERFORMANCE AVERAGE
Recites effectively					
Scores satisfactorily on examinations					
TOTAL GROWTH & PERFORMANCE					
Days Absent					
Times Tardy					(over)

CEDERGREN PUBL. & PTG. CO.   McFARLAND, WISC.

Fig. 18.2. Form for reporting to students and parents. (Courtesy Monona Grove High School, Madison, Wisconsin)

academic achievement through tests, reports, notebooks, projects, discussions, demonstrations, and the like. Subject knowledge and skills are more than memorization of facts and acquisition of skills, but less than total growth and performance related to all the educational objectives.

Figure 18.3 indicates the wide range of objectives of instruction for the elementary schools in one system. Note the number of student performances and other behaviors that the teacher would be likely to rate by observation, rather than by using any form of published or teacher-made tests. (In both the primary and intermediate grades, there are, of course, additional performances and behaviors that might also be rated by observation rather than tests.) Note also that the behaviors associated with citizenship are quite specific. In the case of both the citizenship and work habits check lists, the teacher simply checks the behaviors the child has *not* acquired or does *not* consistently exhibit. Such check lists are helpful to teachers preparing the report card, both in guiding them as they for-

Fig. 18.3. Report card used by the elementary schools of Madison, Wisconsin. (Courtesy Madison Public Schools, Madison, Wisconsin)

Report of.. **Grade**............

Good citizenship and good work habits are necessary for satisfactory school progress.
The items checked suggest ways in which your child can and should improve:

CITIZENSHIP	Report Periods 1	2	3	4
Being self reliant				
Working well with others				
Playing well with others				
Observing rules of safety				
Practicing good health habits				
Showing regard for property				
Respecting rightful authority				
Showing courtesy to others				

WORK HABITS	Report Periods 1	2	3	4
Working carefully and accurately				
Getting to work promptly				
Completing work promptly				
Using spare time to advantage				
Listening to and following directions				
Sharing in group planning				
A conference with parent is desired (Call school for an appointment)				

SCHOOL SUBJECTS

✓—Indicates how your child compares with other children of this grade level. X—Losing position (little or no progress)
Effort: S—Satisfactory; U—Unsatisfactory; I—Improving

	1st Report Period						2nd Report Period						3rd Report Period						4th Report Period					
	Above Grade Level	At Grade Level	Below Grade Level	Effort S	I	U	Above Level Grade	At Grade Level	Below Grade Level	Effort S	I	U	Above Grade Level	At Grade Level	Below Grade Level	Effort S	I	U	Above Grade Level	At Grade Level	Below Grade Level	Effort S	I	U
Reading																								
Language																								
Spelling																								
Writing																								
Social Studies																								
Science																								
Arithmetic																								
Music																								
Art																								
Physical Education																								

Attendance	Days Present	Days Absent	Times Tardy	Days Present	Days Absent	Times Tardy	Days Present	Days Absent	Times Tardy	Days Present	Days Absent	Times Tardy
										TOTALS FOR THE YEAR		
Parent's Signature												

EXPLANATION OF REPORT CARD

1. **Grade Level:**

   A check in the "At Grade Level" column indicates achievement about equal to the average for that grade. "Above Grade Level" indicates achievement above the average for that grade; while a check in the "Below Grade Level" column indicates achievement below the average for that grade. An "X" indicates grade level and also that the child is not progressing as well as we think he should in that particular subject. Note that grade level is not a stationary position. A child who is checked "At grade level" each report period is making normal growth for the year.

2. **Effort:**

   Some of the children who find school subjects difficult are among the best of workers, and deserve credit for their efforts. On the other hand, some children with much ability do not apply themselves and never reach their best potential. Such a pupil might be checked "Above Grade Level" but "Unsatisfactory" for effort. This would mean that he is capable of doing much better and should be urged to do so.

3. **A Confidential Report:**

   Children often compare marks and, unfortunately, parents sometimes do also. This is very unfair for the children. It often inflates the ego of some and causes resentment and discouragement among others.
   You should receive the card in a sealed envelope. It should be discussed privately with your child, signed, and sealed in the enclosed envelope before returning.

4. **Citizenship:**

   One of the most important phases of a child's growth. (See reverse side for items included in citizenship.)

5. **Work Habits:**

   Good work habits are a necessity for good progress.

6. **A Conference With Parent is Desired:**

   If you find a check here, arrange a conference with the teacher as soon as possible. Many problems are prevented or corrected by close parent-teacher cooperation.

If you have questions about the report card, please feel free to call the teacher or principal.

Fig. 18.3 *continued*

CITIZENSHIP

This outline is included with your child's report to better enable you to interpret citizenship marks on the report card. Please keep it for future reference.

1. **BEING SELF RELIANT**—refers to the pupil's habit of depending on himself rather than on others.
   a. Has confidence in himself.
   b. Works independently.
   c. Assumes responsibility for doing things without being reminded.
   d. Can be trusted to do special tasks alone or with a group without constant supervision.
   e. Does not ask for unnecessary assistance.
   f. Can go ahead without constant prodding or praise from the teacher.

2. **WORKING WELL WITH OTHERS**—refers to the pupil's ability and willingness to cooperate with others, to act in desirable ways in work situations involving himself and others.
   a. Contributes something to the group.
   b. Can accept leadership.
   c. Can follow well.
   d. Has a "give and take" attitude.
   e. Does not interfere with the work of others.
   f. Accepts criticism and suggestions from the group graciously.

3. **PLAYING WELL WITH OTHERS**—refers to the pupil's ability and willingness to cooperate with others, to act in desirable ways in play situations involving himself and others.
   a. Works for his team rather than for himself.
   b. Follows the rules of the game.
   c. Gives others their turn.
   d. Does not isolate himself from the group.
   e. Is willing to share with others.
   f. Can control his temper.
   g. Is good natured.

4. **OBSERVING RULES OF SAFETY**—refers to the behavior of the pupil in relation to such basic safety practices as obedience to safety rules; also, in being mindful of the consequences of his acts which might possibly be injurious to others.
   a. Obeys traffic laws, including city bicycle ordinance.
   b. Uses care in handling tools and materials.
   c. Conducts himself properly during fire drill.
   d. Is careful at drinking fountains, on stairs, in halls, etc.
   e. Cooperates with boy patrols and traffic officers.
   f. Keeps away from railroad tracks and other dangerous places in going to and from school.
   g. Does not play with sticks, guns or dangerous toys.

5. **PRACTICING GOOD HEALTH HABITS**—refers to the behavior of the pupil in relation to those basic health practices designed to promote his own well-being and to protect the health of others.
   a. Is clean in dress, habits, and person.
   b. Stays home when there is evidence of a cold.
   c. Puts on wraps according to the weather.
   d. Sits and stands correctly.

6. **SHOWING REGARD FOR PROPERTY**—refers to the pupil's attitude toward the best possible care of all property whether it belongs to him or not.
   a. Handles school materials carefully and economically.
   b. Does not deface desks, walls, or materials.
   c. Does not trespass on lawns or disturb the peace or property of others.
   d. Is careful of and responsible for playground equipment.
   e. Takes good care of personal belongings, such as clothing, books, and supplies.

7. **RESPECTING RIGHTFUL AUTHORITY**—For every freedom that we have in our democracy we have a corresponding obligation. Freedom of speech, press, etc., is acceptable only as far as it is good for all. Recognition and acceptance of social discipline and lawful authority is of prime importance in good citizenship.
   a. Cooperates with boy or girl patrols and crossing guards.
   b. Responds promptly and cheerfully to teachers' directions.
   c. Accepts and gives constructive criticism.
   d. Shows growth in the use of the democratic process as it applies to the organization of room, clubs, committees, etc.

8. **SHOWING COURTESY TO OTHERS**—refers to the pupil's attitude and his willingness to act with consideration, tolerance, and respect in situations involving others.
   a. Helps others when there is need.
   b. Is considerate of a newcomer in the group.
   c. Does not tease others in embarrassing situations.
   d. Refrains from making unkind remarks.
   e. Shows racial and social tolerance.
   f. Is thoughtful of giving pleasure or comfort to others.
   g. Listens to what others have to say.
   h. Does not interrupt.

Fig. 18.3 *continued*

mulate their own judgments about each child and in explaining ratings in school subjects to parents. In Fig. 18.3 the two pages of explanation for parents are also shown; note that a detailed breakdown of the citizenship behaviors is included.

The fact that in both the high school and elementary school report forms the teacher is required to make certain ratings on the basis of the student's *ability* is important. Standardized tests like those discussed in Chapter 17 and written tests constructed by the teacher are often used in estimating the abilities of individual pupils. This is true even when objective-based instructional programs are used.

18.1. Assume that you have a heterogeneous group of students in your class in the subject matter and at the age-grade level you teach or intend to teach. For some unit of instruction do the following:

a. List specific behavioral objectives.

b. Tell how you would place students in the program.

c. Devise means of monitoring pupil progress with respect to each objective.

d. Determine how you would like to report progress with respect to the unit at the next reporting period.

18.2. When does a letter grade represent a measurement? When does it represent an evaluation?

18.3. In evaluating pupils, a number of criteria may be taken into account including performance on tests and daily assignments, class contribution, participation, leadership, and other factors.

a. List additional factors you would take into account in giving an overall letter grade to an individual.

b. Rank-order the list of criteria given and your additions according to your system of values.

18.4. Under what conditions would you prefer to use a student-parent-teacher conference rather than a parent-teacher conference? How would the content you reported differ in the two conferences?

EVALUATING MATERIALS AND INSTRUCTIONAL PROGRAMS

New materials and instructional programs are continually marketed. School systems set aside a portion of their budgets annually to buy these materials, often rotating the major expenditures among particular subject-matter areas. The adoption of a new program or new set of materials frequently is recommended by a curriculum committee on which teachers, as well as subject-matter specialists, serve. It is important, therefore, that teachers and other educational personnel be acquainted with the procedures used to evaluate educational materials at these three stages: (1) formative evaluation—during development by the developers, (2) summative evaluation—during testing in naturalistic situations before being marketed, and (3) user evaluation—during assessment by a local school system before possible adoption. These three stages are discussed in detail in this section.

It is unfortunate but true that not all developers proceed systematically in evaluating their product during or after development. Similarly, not all school systems use a sophisticated approach to selecting new materials. Teachers who are given the opportunity to order new materials for their classrooms frequently judge the product on its aesthetic appeal without considering other factors that might lead to a different choice.

Deficiencies in evaluation are serious, for it is clear that one way the educational attainment of children might be increased is by the selection of materials that have been rigorously evaluated by the developer and demonstrated to *work* as advertised. The research and development movement given impetus by the establishment during the 1960s of Research and Development Centers and Regional Educational Laboratories has emphasized the need for thorough product evaluation. Products of these centers and laboratories are not released for general use until they have been subjected to stringent testing. Fortunately, some publishers now ask the centers and laboratories to run quality verification tests on their products; in such cases, the result is high-quality materials. Other publishers, however, do not do this.

What are the quality verification procedures developers now use? Can the teacher who develops his own unit of instruction or materials adapt any of the procedures to his own needs? How might a school system proceed in evaluating alternative instructional programs before adopting one? Some answers to these questions are discussed in this section. We should add a caution, however: The field of evaluation methodology is presently in ferment; there is no universal agreement on any particular set of procedures. Nevertheless, it *is* generally agreed that the new procedures are not only better than none but also better than the haphazard ones they replace.

To see the points at which evaluation enters the development process, refer to Fig. 18.4, which is part of a flow chart associated with the development of programed instructional materials (the entire chart was shown in Fig. 5.2). Note when the product is tested. Note also the points at which the judgment of subject-matter experts might provide helpful feedback to the developers, that is, Steps A, B-1, D, F-2, G-2, and G-3. The quality of a product is best assured by subjecting the plans and specifications to expert review and the product itself to empirical testing. The following sections emphasize primarily the evaluation associated with these empirical tests.

1. Formative Evaluation

As the term implies, formative evaluation is concerned with judging a product as it is being formed or developed. This formative evaluation is

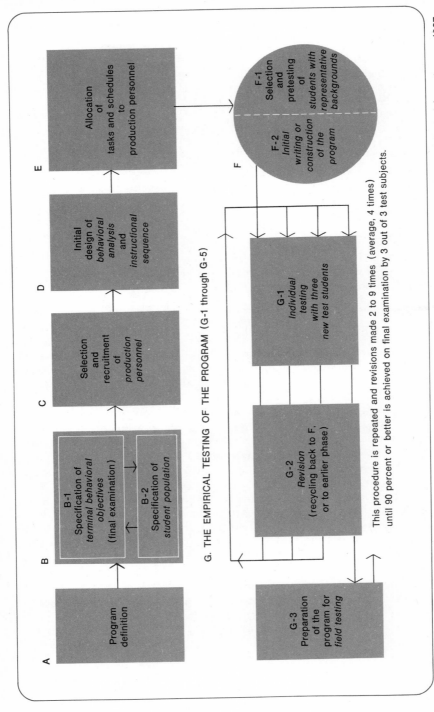

Fig. 18.4 Part of a generalized flow chart of program development, showing steps in formative evaluation. (Adapted from Lange, 1967, p. 58)

an integral part of the development process. In Fig. 18.4, the evaluation associated with Step G-1, "individual testing with three new test students," is formative because revisions are based on the outcome. Step G-1 is also known as a *pilot test* — its principal characteristic is that it is a preliminary tryout with a small number of persons representative of the *target population*, that is, those for whom the materials are intended. Note the iterative or recycling nature of the phase of the development effort in which formative evaluation is embedded. The development program does not proceed to larger scale testing and validation until the criterion set for performance in Step G-1 — 90 percent or better on the final examination by three out of three test subjects — is reached. Although the criterion set for judging the outcome of the formative evaluation is explicit in this case, the formative evaluation process frequently covers a broader field. The student's interest in the material and errors made on particular "frames" in the programed text are also of concern to the developer. Furthermore, if the criterion established is not met, it is helpful to have information that explains why. Was the reading level of the material too difficult? Were the directions and explanations not clear enough? The pilot testing of materials is a closely monitored process during which answers to these and other questions are sought.

Some adaptations of the model shown in Fig. 18.4 are made for materials other than programed instruction. For instance, the target population may be teachers instead of students. Perhaps the product consists of an outline of a procedure that teachers are to use with students — a small-group conference, for instance. It is then very likely to be appropriate in the formative phase of development to have three to five teachers study the proposed outline and demonstrate their understanding by enacting the procedure with a small group of their actual students or by simulating the procedure in some way. Performance criteria are set in advance. For example, the teacher is expected to utilize at least three of the following motivational principles: goal-setting, positive reinforcement, provision of feedback, and modeling. Furthermore, in a replay of the conference tape the teacher is to identify his use of these principles by name.

In the process of conducting a pilot study, the developers may become conscious of an unanticipated problem not related to the previously set criteria. In the case of the group conference, perhaps praise of the lowest performing student seems artificial to group members and observers, and more subtle reinforcement procedures are thought necessary. The identification of an omission in either material or criteria is also a result of the evaluation process associated with a pilot test. In fact, a principal outcome of the pilot test is the identification of weaknesses in the program itself, in the environment in which it is to be used, or both. These problems can then be taken into account in the further development and redesign of the materials before they are used on a wider scale. (In our example, the addition to the existing material of information on subtle reinforcement procedures may correct the deficiency identified.) The information gathered during a pilot test may also lead to the crucial decision to discard the product or to modify it greatly or slightly or to move on to the larger field test.

How can the teacher developing a unit of instruction in the local community adapt some of the formative evaluation procedures outlined above? Surely he can seek professional opinions from his colleagues and from curriculum specialists, especially in connection with the instructional objectives and outline of content. Most often such a review is helpful in suggesting additional or alternative objectives and concepts. The teacher might then use the unit with a single group of pupils, making clear and detailed notes on necessary modifications. When the modifications have been made, the unit can then be used with another group or groups of children.

Many excellent teachers, of course, do proceed in just this way as they continually improve the units and materials they develop. In a team-teaching situation, however, such a development effort can be even more rewarding for teachers and students. For one thing, a team has many more students than a single teacher. Thus development of a new unit of instruction can be accomplished much more quickly, and the tested unit can be made available sooner to other teachers in the building or system. This development can be done by a team in the following way, which has particular advantages: Each teacher on the team develops a facet of the new unit, solicits the opinions of his fellow team members, and then pilots the program with a small group of students, each teacher with a different group. Later, revisions are made, and a refined unit is presented to the rest of the students. Thus the students served by the team receive most of their instruction in sections of the unit that have already been pilot-tested. The potential of the procedure for improving instruction is obvious.

2. Summative Evaluation

Once a product or program has been developed and formatively evaluated, it is ready for a final evaluation. Although there is no widespread agreement on the nature of a summative evaluation, the practices described here are among those that are currently used.

Summative evaluation often is comparative. An advocate of the comparative procedure puts it this way: "When we come to *evaluate* the curriculum as opposed to merely describing its performance, then we inevitably confront the question of its superiority or inferiority to the competition. To say it's a 'valuable contribution,' a 'desirable' or 'useful' course, even to say—in the usual context—that it's very good, is to imply relative merit" (Scriven, 1967, p. 64). In practice, comparative evaluations are most often undertaken with experimental students using the new program and control students following some different program.

Summative evaluations rely on a number of criteria, including tests designed specifically to measure the content of the program, more general standardized tests through which norms can be referred to, attitude questionnaires, and factors connected with program implementation, such as teacher preparation time. (The last category is assessed through self-reports and observation schedules.) It is evident that the results for a particular program may show that it is superior to other programs in some criteria and inferior in others. Obviously, although the results of summative evaluation may have been satisfying to the developers, the program may or may not prove to be satisfying to potential consumers.

To illustrate the application of these practices, we now consider the summative evaluation of Project Physics, a new high school course developed at Harvard. A brief description of the course gives the background:

> Concerned about the steadily declining enrollments in physics (from 26 to 20 percent of high school students during the past fifteen years) and the apparent failure of special groups to learn and appreciate physics, a group of educators and physicists attempted to develop a course that would not only appeal to potential scientists and technicians but to those who might not be inclined to study physics, such as those with less ability and interest in science. As the course evolved, a number of explicit methods and media were produced to accomplish these ends. A text was written with a moderate density of physical concepts but with lower reading difficulty than other courses. Expanding on the idea of branching in programmed instruction, the text included a number of cognitive modes of learning the same concept (or more advanced concepts), for example, through philosophical explanations, mathematical formulations, historical narratives, and graphic representations. To arouse motivation in students uninterested in science and mathematics, tables, art works, and marginal notes were employed to illustrate concepts and their relations to society and the history of ideas. The text also allowed the student to pursue his own ideas and interests by referencing other course materials, a book of coordinated original readings, laboratory manuals and apparatus, programmed instruction booklets, and film loops. So as not to overwhelm teachers or students with diversity but to allow as many choices as possible, teacher and student guides were produced which describe the organization of the materials and how best to use them for given purposes. It was also hoped that such materials and guides would compensate for poor facilities of some schools and the inadequacies of some physics teachers. Thus two main purposes of the project are to develop methods and media suitable (1) for different students, especially the scientifically disadvantaged, and (2) for different conditions of instruction, especially those less than optimal. (Walberg, 1970, pp. 188-189)

The course was pilot-tested for two years before the summative evaluation. In preparation for the summative evaluation, 57 physics teachers were randomly selected from a nationwide population of physics teachers to teach either Project Physics or the course each was already teaching. Both these groups were acquainted with their roles during the summer before the experiment.

After all courses had been taught, a large battery of both published and project-developed cognitive tests was administered to the students of all the teachers. In addition, six affective instruments were selected or developed and also administered to this national sample. Special studies were made of teacher behavior, enrollment trends in schools where Project Physics was taught, and score comparisons of experimental (Project Physics) and control (other physics courses) groups on the College Board's Advanced Placement Test in physics and the New York Regents' examination in physics.

A series of analyses revealed that Project Physics students scored as high as or significantly higher than the control group on the cognitive tests and scored significantly better on the affective instruments, which assessed the perceived image of physics; attitudes toward and interest in science, especially physics; the desire to learn more about the subject; and desirable qualities of the social environments of learning. It was concluded that the course materials were successful in meeting the objectives as originally set forth and that the course was likely to be effective in raising physics enrollments. (At the time of writing this chapter, these conclusions could not be checked against actual results.)

In this summative evaluation, the important points are that classes using the newly developed materials were compared with classes using other physics courses and that many different instruments were used to assess the outcome of instruction.

The methodology of summative evaluations may be used by the local school system to compare two or more products whose adoption it is considering. All too often, school systems do not put new materials to empirical tests before deciding to adopt them. If the task of curriculum committees were defined as narrowing down the alternatives to two or three, and if a year were allowed in the adoption timetable for empirical testing, better decisions with more widespread consensus might be reached. At the very least, textbook adoption groups and others might find out whether the developers of a product have subjected it to empirical testing at any point in the formative or summative stages of development.

3. User Evaluation: Guidelines for Introducing New Curricula

The Wisconsin Research and Development Center for Cognitive Learning recommends that no new curriculum, or any large segment of it, should be introduced into a school system without trying it out. We further recommend a two-stage evaluation: (1) The instructional materials and related tests and suggestions to teachers should be tried out for a year or two in a small number of schools or classrooms, rather than in all the schools and classrooms of the system. (2) If the evaluation warrants an adoption throughout the system, continuing evaluation should be carried out to make sure that the materials and procedures work well, not only in general, but also as they are adapted by the teachers in the various schools and classrooms. Some materials that work well in the schools in residential or suburban areas do not work well in the inner-city schools, and vice versa.

A committee of the Association for Supervision and Curriculum Development has evolved a number of questions that point up matters to be explored thoroughly by the staff of a school in considering a new curriculum. These are questions that should be answered *before* the staff even attempts to evaluate the curriculum in actual use in a few elementary school buildings or high school classrooms. The three sets of questions related to (1) assessing new projects and their effect on learners, (2) their effect on teachers, and (3) assessment are particularly important in connection with this discussion of evaluation. Study of these questions, which follow, is very likely to be helpful to the teacher or other educational worker in deciding what his role in introducing a new curriculum might be.

STUDY QUESTIONS RELATED TO ASSESSING NEW PROJECTS AND THEIR EFFECT ON LEARNERS

Types of Learners

Are the materials clearly designed for a particular group—for fast, average, slow learners? For a particular age level? Do project materials vary sufficiently to benefit learners who have different cognitive styles (e.g., inquirers and noninquirers, those who work well with symbols and those who work well with concrete objects)? Are the materials more appropriate for boys or for girls?

Effects on Learners

What effect might the new program have on the anxiety levels of learners? What opportunities do learners have to strengthen their intellectual independence? To what extent are learners encouraged to be creative? Are such behaviors restricted by the project materials or services? As a result of the new program, are the pupils likely to become more excited about learning than they have been previously? Are learners encouraged to develop facility with a variety of materials and approaches to learning? What attitudes and values might learners acquire through the project? What kinds of behaviors—cognitive, affective, psychomotor—are learners encouraged to exhibit?

Stability of Student Groups

How will student turnover affect the success of the project? What special arrangements must be made for students who transfer into the school? What prerequisites are required if they are to participate in the new project?

STUDY QUESTIONS RELATED TO ASSESSING NEW PROJECTS AND THEIR EFFECT ON TEACHERS

Demands on Teachers

What new content must the teacher master? What new teaching strategies are required? Are these clearly specified? What programs of teacher preparation will be necessary?

Teacher Characteristics

Are there specific teaching skills demanded; for example, working with large groups, small groups, individuals, audiovisual aids? Is experience an important factor to be considered? Is openness to new ideas essential for teachers in the project? Is teacher personality a significant factor? Must teachers have a great deal of free out-of-class time?

STUDY QUESTIONS RELATED TO ASSESSMENT

Adequacy of Data

Do we have initial data on learners—their achievement, their motivation, their personalities? Do we have initial data on teachers—their strategies, their motivation, their knowledge, their personalities? Do we have these data at many stages during the implementation of the project? Would a model assist us in making a continuing assessment? For example:

T1 (initial appraisal)	*During a Project*	*T2 (final appraisal)*
Set up instruments to assess	Observers analyze the strategies of students, teachers	Set up instruments to assess
students' $\begin{cases} \text{achievement} \\ \text{personality} \\ \text{motivation} \end{cases}$		students' $\begin{cases} \text{achievement} \\ \text{personality} \\ \text{motivation} \end{cases}$
	Assessors analyze materials and their effect on teachers and learners	
teachers' $\begin{cases} \text{satisfaction} \\ \text{strategies} \\ \text{knowledge} \end{cases}$		teachers' $\begin{cases} \text{satisfaction} \\ \text{strategies} \\ \text{knowledge} \end{cases}$

What happens to learners as people and to learners as learners as a result of the project? What happens to teachers as people and to teachers as teachers? Do changes justify the time and funds expended? (Ammons & Gilchrist, 1965, pp. 19-20, 23)

18.5. Ralph Nader, the consumer advocate, has reported that some industrial products, especially some components of automobiles, do not meet minimum standards. Suppose a similar investigation were conducted of textbooks. What do you think would be reported?

18.6. Think of some objective (make it simple) that you would like a few students to attain and also think through the main steps of an instructional program for the students. Refer to Fig. 18.4 and identify the steps in the formative evaluation that are recommended in the figure. With your instructional program in mind, do the steps seem reasonable for publishers and other developers to use? For teachers in developing end-of-unit tests?

18.7. Do you think it would be easier or more difficult to develop and evaluate instructional materials or methods as a member of a teaching team or as an independent teacher? Explain.

18.8. What were the main objectives of Project Physics? Based on the results of the summative evaluation described in this text, how much confidence do you have that Project Physics will achieve its main objectives? (Try to find some users and nonusers and get their reactions.)

18.9. Which of the questions raised in the above quotation do you think should be given highest priority by the school people who select the instructional materials for use in a school system?

NATIONAL ASSESSMENT OF EDUCATION

During recent years, clouds of criticism and controversy have swirled about public education in this country. In response to this widespread concern about the quality of education, the National Assessment of Educational Progress is underway. The plan is to continue the Assessment, which involves annual testing, indefinitely.

Ralph W. Tyler, then director of the Center for Advanced Study in the Behavioral Sciences at Stanford University, and other well-known educators formulated the idea of assessing the quality of American public education and provided the leadership to get it started. (The Carnegie Corporation made grants that financed the initial phases, but the project is now federally supported.) The relationship between the Assessment and Tyler's ideas about evaluation may be inferred from what Tyler wrote:

> The most frequent use of evaluation is to appraise the achievement of individual students. . . . A second use of evaluation is to diagnose the learning difficulties of an individual student or an entire class to provide information helpful in planning subsequent teaching. A third use of evaluation is to appraise the educational effectiveness of a curriculum or part of a curriculum, of instructional materials and procedures, and of administrative and organizational arrangements. . . . There is a fourth use which is to assess the educational progress of large populations in order to provide the public with dependable information to help in the understanding of educational problems and needs and to guide in efforts to develop sound policy regarding education.
>
> . . .
>
> Because education has become the servant of all our purposes, its effectiveness is of general public concern. The educational tasks now faced require many more resources than have thus far been available, and they must be wisely used to produce maximum results. To make these decisions, dependable information about the progress of education is essential; otherwise we scatter our efforts too widely and fail to achieve our goals. Yet we do not now have the necessary comprehensive and dependable data. We have reports on numbers of schools, buildings, teachers, and pupils, and about the moneys expended, but we do not have sound and adequate information on educational results. Because dependable data are not available, personal views, distorted reports, and journalistic impressions are the sources of public opinion and the schools are frequently attacked and frequently defended without having necessary evidence to support either claim. This situation will be corrected only by a careful, consistent effort to obtain valid data to provide sound evidence about the progress of American education. (Tyler, 1966, pp. 1, 2)

Under the National Assessment, specially prepared tests are administered in 10 areas — reading, mathematics, science, music, art, citizenship, literature, social studies, writing, and vocational education. Sampled persons of four age levels — 9, 13, 17, young adult — are being tested on each skill. However, to prevent the testing from becoming burdensome, each student takes only part of the items designed for his age level in only one subject-matter area. By sampling students and then sampling the tests, results will accumulate that may make possible general conclusions about the level of achievement of all individuals of each age group, as shown by all the tests.

The National Assessment is designed also to make available information on the achievements of subpopulations stratified according to four geographic *regions* of the country, four sizes of cities or towns, and two levels of income. Information will not, however, be available broken down in any more detailed categories. For example, it will not be possible to get information about the knowledge, skills, and attitudes of a particular student or about a particular school, city, or state. Also, because of the variety of educational programs in which the subpopulations may be involved, no conclusions about particular methods of instruction will be drawn.

What may the results of the National Assessment tell us? Tyler's early general plan for reporting the Assessment may be inferred from the following:

> In assessing the progress of education, no individual pupil, classroom, or school shows up at all. Instead, a report would indicate that 90 percent (nearly all) of 13-year-old children can comprehend reading paragraphs like these, can solve arithmetic problems like these, can sing songs like these, have citizenship habits like these, and so on. Examples are given of the achievements rather than relative scores. Similarly, the achievements characteristic of 50 percent of the 13-year-old children would be explained and those characteristic of only about 10 percent of the age group. (Tyler, 1965, p. 14).

The first findings of the project, covering science and citizenship, were released in July 1970. The results were reported simply as statistics, with no interpretation. To give just a few examples, these are some of the results in science: Only 22 percent of the 9-year-olds recognized a suitable definition of a scientific theory, though a substantial number were able to use basic scientific apparatus (such as a balance beam); the 13-year-olds did well on questions involving tables and graphs, but had trouble with exercises on molecular theory and chemical reactions; 95 percent of the 17-year-olds could identify a balanced meal, but only 41 percent of them knew the function of the placenta. These are two of the citizenship findings: More than half the 9-year-olds and 80 percent of the 13-year-olds said they would be willing to associate with a companion whose father had been jailed for stealing; 48 percent of 9-year-olds, 71 percent of 13-year-olds, and 92 percent of 17 year-olds could give acceptable reasons for having a government.

After a second cycle of data have been collected, it will be possible to compare the achievements of students of a given age at the two points in time at which the tests were administered. Supposedly, the results will show whether the population sampled at each age is doing better or worse in each particular subject-matter area than that age group was doing at the earlier testing. In other words, one can assess the *progress* of education in the United States.

The National Assessment of American education has met with considerable criticism from diverse individuals and groups. For example, Frymier, actually among the most restrained of the early critics, was much concerned about the national, rather than the state or local, character and control of the effort, the characteristics and quality of the tests developed for the Assessment, and the uses to be made of the information and the related conclusions by the public, including policy-making government officials, rather than by teachers, students, and others directly involved. Frymier summarized his questions in this way:

> In summary, the idea of "national assessment" is not quite four years old. It is predicated upon the possibility of testing a few scattered persons around the country with newly developed instruments to produce new kinds of data about the educational attainments which policy-making groups might use. The idea is exciting in that it outlines a whole new kind of educational feedback. It is frightening in that it is fraught with very real possibilities for undesirable purposes and influence and control.
>
> The questions which arise are tough but real. Should assessment be primarily a national or state or local concern? Can we contrive ways of using assessment data creatively and effectively to assure increasing opportunities for young people to learn? Can we examine the basic assumptions upon which both "national assessment" and "education" rest, then use all of the talents of all of the people to preserve the best of the old while incorporating the best of the new for ever better schools? (Frymier, 1967, pp. 258-259)

In any case, there is likely to be much less criticism in the future because school people are now actively involved in the direction of the Assessment. In 1969, the Education Commission of the States assumed responsibility for the project. The commission, which is composed of state officials and educators, is an organization designed to help the states help themselves in solving problems of public education. The first results of the Assessment were released at an annual meeting of the commission.

Whether or not the National Assessment will be a milestone in education, whether or not it will prove useful in providing the first dependable data about the strengths and weaknesses of American public education as a whole—all this, as of late 1970, remains to be seen. One thing that is definite is that both money and human resources have gone into the Assessment in large amounts. For example, subject-matter experts, test developers, statisticians, and laymen have been drawn together to assure that the content of the tests is meaningful and that the study is conducted with the best technical resources available. Also, a large number of school people are involved in administering the tests. Considering that those responsible for the study have made assurances that the results will be used to improve, rather than weaken, public education, this massive experiment in evaluation deserves the support of the educational community. As with other experiments, a "wait and see" attitude toward evaluating the results and the effects is appropriate.

18.10. Do you agree with the four uses of evaluation as described by Tyler? Do you think it is possible to secure reliable information that would be useful in developing federal or state policies concerned with the support or improvement of public education?

18.11 Public education is supported by federal, state, and local funds (in varying proportions) in all states. Can anything be done that might give taxpayers a better understanding of just what their dollars buy in education? To

what extent should teachers participate in educational policy-making at the
federal, state, or local level?

SUMMARY

Educational evaluation was defined in this chapter as "the process of delineating, obtaining, and providing useful information for judging decision alternatives." Evaluation, then, is a comprehensive activity inter-
twined with other educational processes, including instruction and
materials development.

Three purposes for evaluating pupil performance are: (1) placement of
pupils in the instructional program, (2) monitoring of performance so that
day-to-day adaptations to individual and group needs may be made in the
instructional program, and (3) summary evaluation of individual performance for purposes of reporting to school officials and parents. The discrepancy between individual evaluation according to behavioral criteria in
objective-based instructional programs and traditional forms of reporting
in which pupils are compared with their peers exists in most schools.
Letter grades, either alone or in combination with other reporting procedures, including written comments and conferences, continue to be the
most widespread form of reporting in the United States.

Guidelines assuring the quality of new educational products call for
expert review at various stages of the development process and for empirical testing of the product both in its formative and final stages. Associated with the formative evaluation is a pilot test of the product while it
is still under development. When the criteria set for the product are met
by the participants in the pilot test, the product is prepared for summative evaluation and its counterpart, the larger field test. Summative evaluations frequently are comparative and involve a number of criteria.
School systems developing or adopting new materials can adapt some of
the formative and summative evaluation procedures outlined, including
subjecting the materials to an empirical test under local conditions.

The National Assessment is a comprehensive testing program whose
results are intended to provide information about the competencies of
students of various age levels from both disadvantaged and nondisadvantaged settings in different regions of the country. The results of the initial data collection in two of the 10 subject-matter areas were reported in
July 1970.

SUGGESTIONS FOR FURTHER READING

DYER, H. S. On the assessment of academic achievement. In Ripple, R. E., ed., *Readings in learning and human abilities*. New York: Harper & Row, 2nd ed., 1971.

Procedures are outlined for assessing the level of achievement of students at the
beginning and end of a course.

FRYMIER, J. R. National assessment. In Wilhelms, F., ed., *Evaluation as feedback and guide*. Washington, D.C.: Association for Supervision and Curriculum Development, 1967, pp. 249-259.

Frymier gives the purposes of the national assessment project and offers constructive criticisms concerning it. Among other things the philosophy underlying national assessment involves these points: Education is a national rather than a state or local problem; good data are needed on a nationwide basis; the data are primarily for decision-making by the public rather than by professional educators.

GLOCK, M. D., & MILLMAN, J. The assignment of school marks. In Ripple, R. E., ed., *Readings in learning and human abilities*. New York: Harper & Row, 2nd ed., 1971.

Problems and procedures in grading are identified and discussed.

GROBMAN, H. *Evaluation activities of curriculum projects*. Chicago: Randy McNally, 1968.

This 136-page AERA monograph centers on what to evaluate, whom to evaluate, how to evaluate, and arranging for evaluation. It is more applicable to large-scale curriculum projects than to evaluation which a teacher does independently.

SHELLHAMMER, T. A., ed., *Western Regional Conference on Testing Problems: Proceedings*. Princeton, N. J.: Educational Testing Service, 1968.

This 122-page paperback is comprised solely of five excellent articles on measurement and evaluation related to desegregation, the new college student, national assessment of public education, culture-fair testing, and the effects of college education.

STAKE, R. E., TYLER, R. W., GAGNÉ, R. M., SCRIVEN, M., & OHMANN, J. S. *Perspectives of curriculum evaluation*. Chicago: Rand, McNally, 1967.

This 102-page AERA monograph consists of a series of introductory articles that, in general, indicate the importance of evaluation rather than describing the procedures.

TYLER, R. W., ed. *Educational evaluation: New roles, new means*. National Society for the Study of Education, 68th yearbook. Chicago: University of Chicago Press, 1969, Part II.

This yearbook gives attention to the critical role of evaluation in the development and improvement of educational materials and practices. Chapter 16, pages 370-390, by R. E. Stake and T. Denny, points to the differences between evaluation and educational research as usually conceived and also indicates areas in which evaluation is needed.

Chapter 19 Statistics and Research Design

Tabulating and Graphing Data

frequency distribution table
cumulative distribution
histogram
frequency polygon

Measures of Location and Variability

measures of central tendency
mean, median, mode
partition values
quartile, percentile
measures of variability
range, variance, standard deviation

Statistics and the Interpretation of Scores

normal distribution
standard scores
stanine scores

Sampling and Experimental Procedures

population and sample
simple random sampling
stratified random sampling
null hypothesis
statistical significance of differences

Measures of Relationship

product-moment correlation
ranks and ordered classes

Statistics are essential in many aspects of a teacher's work. A teacher who has at least an elementary knowledge of statistical procedures has acquired a valuable tool that will broaden the scope of his own actions and decisions and also increase his understanding of the actions and decisions of others. Knowledge of statistics, in other words, gives a teacher independence. Such knowledge equips him to act on his own in many situations where otherwise he would simply have to accept information given to him by others and decisions made by others. The truth of these statements becomes apparent in the course of the following descriptions of the three primary ways teachers can and do actually *use* statistics.

First, classroom teachers and other school personnel use simple statistics to interpret data related to the characteristics and achievements of their students. The language of statistics is useful also in communicating such results to students, their parents, and others.

Second, certain statistics are used in describing the characteristics of tests. As noted in Chapter 17, information about both reliability and criterion-related validity of tests is conveyed by a statistic known as the correlation coefficient. Obviously, teachers can better evaluate the tests they construct if they can determine such characteristics of their own tests. This process does require an elementary knowledge of statistics.

Third, most studies carried out in schools become much more valuable when the data collected are subjected to statistical analysis. This is true whether a study is a controlled experiment comparing two methods of instruction or an evaluation of new materials or procedures. It follows that the teacher who understands statistical concepts will find the requests made of him as a participant in a research venture less puzzling. Indeed, with some experience as a participant and mastery of this chapter, he would very likely be able to design and conduct a study himself for his own purposes.

In addition to the specific uses of statistics that have just been described, a teacher will find a more general—but equally rewarding—use for them. A foundation in statistical concepts is of great value to a teacher in understanding reports on student characteristics, test characteristics, evaluation of materials or procedures, and controlled experiments. Obviously, a teacher who fully understands such reports can decide what information in them will be most helpful to him in his *own* teaching and then decide how to apply the information.

It is relevant here to point out that some knowledge of statistical concepts is valuable to a teacher also in his broader role as an informed citizen. Statistics and statistical terms are used and referred to constantly in many vital areas of modern life—government, business, and medicine, to name only three.

It must be apparent that we strongly believe careful study of this chapter is worthwhile. We now turn to the statistical procedures themselves.

Appendix I consists of three tables of data to be used while studying this chapter. Table A[1] presents actual data on 46 fifth-graders in an inner-

---

[1]Table A is referred to so often throughout this chapter that you might find it convenient, if you have ready access to a Xerox copier or similar machine, to make a copy of the table so that you can keep it constantly in view.

city school. Except for column 1, in which the children are numbered according to the alphabetical order of their names, each column contains information pertinent to one characteristic of fifth-grade children. When each child is alike on a characteristic, such as "enrolled in school," the characteristic is called a *constant*; no constant characteristics are included in Table A. When children vary on a characteristic or attribute, that characteristic is called a *variable*; 14 variables are labeled in the headings of columns 2 through 15. These variables are of three kinds:

1. Nominal Variable. Sex is designated as "male" or "female." Variables described by such categories, classes, or labels are known as nominal variables. If numbers are assigned to such categories, they have no mathematical significance. (Although sex is designated by M or F in Table A, often, when data are to be analyzed by a computer, the arbitrary designations 0 or 1 are used instead of letters or words to facilitate electronic data-processing.) The number or proportion of instances of each category is of interest in summarizing nominal data.

2. Ordinal Variable. The only example of an ordinal variable is found in column 5, where each pupil's rank in class according to intelligence is listed. The numbers in this column indicate each individual's position in the series, with 1 designating the highest IQ. Note that ties are handled by averaging the ranks involved: Pupils 2 and 36, who tied for fifteenth and sixteenth place, are therefore both assigned a rank of 15.5. Many statistical procedures apply to rank-order data. Because some of them are simple to use, they can appropriately be applied in the classroom to rank-order data that a teacher has compiled.

3. Interval Variable. The rest of the variables in Table A (columns 3-4 and 6-15) were measured on scales that can be broken into equal intervals. Such scores, known as interval data, lend themselves particularly well to statistical manipulation. When a variable can be measured on an interval scale, the measurements give more precise information than rank-order or nominal data. For instance, consider the intelligence data in three ways: Both the IQ scores and the rank value of each IQ score are included in the table. Each score could also be designated in a nominal way—as above or below average. The first boy's *actual* IQ tells us more about him—is more precise information—than the fact that he has the highest IQ in the group or simply that he is above average. Interval data on a variable, therefore, are the preferred kind, if they can be secured. Scores on classroom tests are interval data.

Most of the statistical and other procedures described in this chapter are applicable to interval data. There is some discussion, however, of the tools used with nominal and ordinal data. A student who has already had courses in statistics may find that he merely needs to scan the chapter to identify any concepts that may be new to him and then study only those portions. The student with little previous work in statistics will find that he must read slowly and perhaps perform some or all of the calculations. It is not necessary to be able to compute the statistics themselves in order to understand the results of a study. It is extremely helpful, however, to have some knowledge of the vocabulary and concepts related to (1) tabulating and graphing data; (2) measures of location and variability; (3) statistics and the interpretation of scores; (4) sampling and experimental procedures; (5) measures of relationship. In the rest of this chapter, therefore, these five aspects of statistics are discussed and explained.

TABULATING AND GRAPHING DATA

Although Table A in Appendix I presents complete information about individuals on the variables listed, it is difficult to form an impression of the group's characteristics, or to relate an individual's performance to that of the group. What is needed is a means of capturing the essence of the data through tabular or graphic representation.

Frequency Distribution Table

The frequency of the occurrence of values of either nominal or interval variables may be summarized and presented in a frequency distribution table. Table 19.1, based on Table A in Appendix I, gives the frequencies for each of the two categories, males and females, for the nominal variable, sex, of the students. Note that the variable (sex) is included in the title of the table and that the categories (males and females) are listed in the table itself. Also, two often used symbols appear: f, indicating the frequency for each category, and N, the total number of cases in the group.

Table 19.1. Frequency Distribution of Sex of Fifth-Grade Subjects

Sex	f
Male	22
Female	24
	$N = 46$

Two-way tables for summarizing categorical information are frequently used as well. By assigning a label of "at or above average" or "below average" to each child's IQ and then ascertaining the number of males and females in each category, we can present the relationship of IQ to sex for this particular group in tabular form—Table 19.2. Note that the subtotals or *marginal frequencies* (22, 24 and 25, 21) are the sums of the two row or column entries and that the total frequency (46) appears in the lower right-hand corner of the table.

When interval data are tabulated, the number of different scores or categories is often so large that it is desirable to group the data into mutually exclusive and exhaustive categories. The term *mutually exclusive* means that a particular score fits into just one category—there is no overlap in categories. An *exhaustive* scheme of categorization provides a category for each score.

Table 19.2 Frequency Distribution of Sex and IQ

| Sex | IQ | | Total |
	At or above average	Below average	
Male	13	9	22
Female	12	12	24
Total	25	21	46

Consider the column of IQ scores in Table A in Appendix I. The scores range from 65 to 137. If we gave each score within the range a line in a frequency distribution table, 73 lines would be needed—hardly an economical way to present information. If, however, the IQ scores are grouped into intervals, as has been done in Table 19.3, the information is more easily understood.

Table 19.3. Frequency Distribution of IQs

Class interval	f	Cumulative f	Cumulative f (percentage)	Real limits of class interval	Midpoint of class interval
133–137	1	46	100.0	132.5–137.5	135
128–132	3	45	97.8	127.5–132.5	130
123–127	2	42	91.3	122.5–127.5	125
118–122	5	40	87.0	117.5–122.5	120
113–117	6	35	76.1	112.5–117.5	115
108–112	3	29	63.0	107.5–112.5	110
103–107	7	26	56.5	102.5–107.5	105
98–102	8	19	41.3	97.5–102.5	100
93– 97	4	11	23.9	92.5– 97.5	95
88– 92	2	7	15.2	87.5– 92.5	90
83– 87	2	5	10.9	82.5– 87.5	85
78– 82	1	3	6.5	77.5– 82.5	80
73– 77	0	2	4.3	72.5– 77.5	75
68– 72	1	2	4.3	67.5– 72.5	70
63– 67	1	1	2.2	62.5– 67.5	65

The first step in developing the frequency distribution in Table 19.3 was to determine the size of the grouping or class interval. Intervals within a particular frequency distribution must be of the same size. Two, three, five, and ten are the most commonly used intervals. In Table 19.3 a class interval of five was chosen (partly for convenience in graphing the information, as explained at the end of this section). Interval size is indicated by the number of score points included in the interval. For instance, the interval 98-102 includes the score points 98, 99, 100, 101, 102. An interval with the whole number limits 98 and 102—its *class limits*—may also be interpreted as extending from 97.5 to 102.5. Known as *real limits*, these boundaries of the class interval 98-102 and other class intervals are speci-

fied in the fifth column of Table 19.3. When a series of numbers is continuous and gradations into fractional parts are implied, the need for exhaustive categories leads to the use of real limits rather than apparent or
class limits. One method of calculating IQ, in fact, does give fractional
numbers, which are usually rounded off before being reported; it is therefore reasonable to state that an IQ of 101 lies between 100.5 and 101.5. To
be precise, 100.5 and 101.5 are the real limits of an IQ of 101.

After the interval size has been selected, an exhaustive list of class
intervals is specified. Note in Table 19.3 that the last interval has a lower
limit of 63, even though the lowest observed score is 65. Because all intervals must be the same size, the lower limit of the lowest interval and the
higher limit of the highest interval may not coincide with the lowest and
highest scores in the distribution. The selection of these lower and higher
limits is arbitrary. A simple way of determining the frequency associated
with each class interval is to tally the scores as they are sequentially presented in Table 19.3. The frequency may then be determined from the
tally marks, which are counted and recorded in the "*f*" column, and a check
made on the accuracy of the coding process by comparing the sum of the
frequencies with the number of scores in the original list in Table A.

Cumulative Distribution

In some situations the data of interest may be the number of persons
whose scores lie within and below a particular class interval. This information is supplied in Table 19.3 in the column labeled "cumulative *f*." At a
glance one can tell how many children have IQs of 97 or below. Note that
because the data are grouped, one cannot determine precisely the number
of pupils whose IQ is 100 or below.

The cumulative frequency is obviously the summation of the entries in
the frequency column, adding from the frequency in the lowest IQ interval upward. For instance, the cumulative frequency (5) associated with
the interval 83-87 is the sum of the frequency for that interval (2) and the
frequencies for all intervals below it (1,0,1,1).

Sometimes the cumulative frequency information is converted into
percentage form. This is readily accomplished by dividing the cumulative
frequency by the total number of subjects. For example, the cumulative
frequency through the 83-87 class interval is 5, which is 10.9 percent of 46
(i.e., 5/46).

Histogram

The information on frequencies in Table 19.3 may be graphically displayed in a histogram — see Fig. 19.1. The vertical axis of the histogram is
marked off in frequency units; the horizontal axis can be marked off in
either class or real limits (real limits are used in this case). As a general
rule, the vertical axis should begin at zero, but the horizontal axis may
begin and end at or slightly beyond the lower and upper limits being used.
In effect, each child is represented by a small square; 46 such squares are

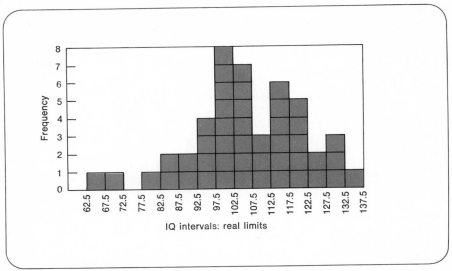

Fig. 19.1. Histogram of fifth-graders' IQs.

enclosed by the heavy lines that form the shape of the histogram. Note that the units on each axis of the graph are labeled and that the histogram is given a title.

Frequency Polygon

A histogram is enlightening when a single distribution is being considered, but it is of limited use in comparing two or more distributions. More appropriate for the latter purpose is the frequency polygon.

The frequency polygon is similar to the histogram in construction. However, the shape of the frequency polygon is determined by connecting the *midpoints* of each class interval at a height appropriate for the frequency in the interval. The horizontal axis is usually labeled in terms of these midpoints rather than by the real limits of the interval. The relationship between the frequency polygon and the histogram is readily seen in Fig. 19.2. Note that the areas under the two "curves," that is, under the frequency polygon and the histogram, are equal; each triangle of area included in the histogram but excluded from the frequency polygon is matched by a new triangular area found only under the frequency polygon. Note also that the line returns to the horizontal axis when the frequency of scores in an interval is zero; this is the case with the interval 73-77. Also, the midpoints of the intervals above the highest and below the lowest intervals with entries appear on the horizontal axis of the graph as the numbers 60 and 140; these represent the intervals 58-62 and 138-142, for which there are, of course, zero frequencies. The outline of a frequency polygon begins and ends on the horizontal axis at the midpoints of the limits beyond the lowest and highest frequency limits.

Graphing Cumulative Frequencies

The information on cumulative frequency and cumulative percentages in Table 19.3 can also be graphed in a manner similar to that used for the frequency polygon, as shown in Fig. 19.3. If one wishes to construct a *cumulative frequency curve*, the horizontal axis of the graph is marked off, however, by the *upper real limits* of the class intervals. The vertical axis is marked off in units that extend to the total N, in this case, 46. By changing the scale on the vertical axis from frequency to percentage units one can construct a *cumulative percentage distribution*. (Both scales appear in Fig. 19.3, although normally only one would be chosen.) If the distribution is smoothed out, an S-shaped curve results that is known as an *ogive*.

When frequency or cumulative distributions are to be graphed, a convention concerning the number of class intervals to be used is generally followed. Graphs are most pleasing in appearance if they have from 10 to 16 intervals. The decisions about number of intervals and interval size should be made together. Take the range of scores and divide by both 10 and 16 to learn the interval size for either extreme option. Given a 73-point range of IQ, the possible interval sizes are whole numbers between 7.3 (73 ÷ 10) and 4.6 (73 ÷ 16). An interval size of 5, 6, or 7 thus would yield a graph with the appropriate number of intervals. Because 5 is a commonly used interval size, this was selected in grouping the data in Table 19.3, and 15 intervals were required in both the table and Figs. 19.1, 19.2, and 19.3.

19.1. Select one column of data from Table A in Appendix I.

a. Find the highest and lowest scores in the column.

Fig. 19.2. Frequency polygon of IQs superimposed on histogram.

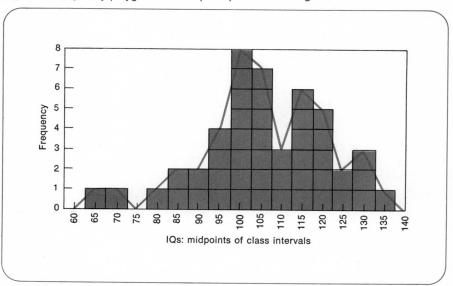

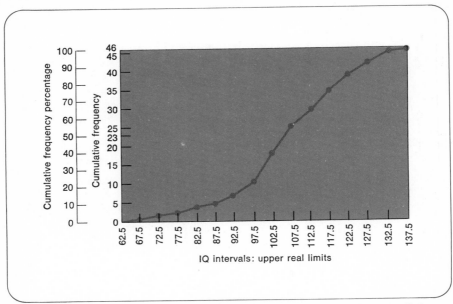

Fig. 19.3. Cumulative distribution of IQs, relating percentage and frequency. Only one vertical scale would ordinarily be used.

b. Decide on an interval size for grouping the data. (Use the procedure suggested in the paragraph immediately preceding this exercise.)

c. Make a table for your data with the headings found in Table 19.3.

d. Represent the data graphically, using a histogram, frequency polygon, and cumulative percentile distribution.

Save your table and graphs for the next set of exercises.

MEASURES OF LOCATION AND VARIABILITY

We often wish to describe a group of individuals in a classroom, school, or experimental situation by such words as "typical" or "average," and for this purpose we use a *measure of central tendency* that indicates where the scores of the group are concentrated. Three measures of central tendency are the *mean, median,* and *mode.* These three statistics are not used interchangeably; they are each appropriate for particular kinds of distributions of scores. Following the discussion of these three statistics, other measures of location (partition values) and measures of variability are described.

Measures of Central Tendency

Mean. The mean is the familiar arithmetic average. In the case of a set of scores, it is calculated by adding all the scores and dividing the total by the number of scores. In effect, the arithmetic mean is the balancing point for the distribution of scores. In a simple case of ungrouped data it is computed as follows. Suppose you wished to find the mean of these five scores: 11, 10, 6, 5, and 3. Their sum, 35, when divided by the number of scores (5), yields a mean of 7. For ungrouped data like this and like that presented in Table A, the formula for computing the mean is given in Computing Guide 19.1.

COMPUTING GUIDE 19.1

Computing the Mean of Ungrouped Data

Let: $\overline{X}$ = the mean
  Σ = the sum of
  X = each score
  N = the number of cases

Formula: $\overline{X} = \dfrac{\Sigma X}{N}$

Example: Find the mean of the 46 IQ scores shown in Table A of Appendix I.
  Step 1: Add the 46 IQs; determine that $\Sigma X = 4876$.
  Step 2: Substitute numbers in the formula and perform the indicated operations:

$$\overline{X} = \frac{4876}{46} = 106.0$$

Note: $\overline{X}$ is read as "*X* bar"; Σ is read as "sigma."

Remember that a set of scores often is grouped into a frequency table, as was done in Table 19.3 for the IQs of the 46 children. When computing the mean from grouped data, it is assumed that all the scores in a class interval lie at the midpoint (*M*) of that interval. The midpoint lies halfway between either the real or the class limits of an interval. By multiplying each midpoint by the frequency, or number of scores in that interval, a product results that is used in computing the mean of the grouped data. This has been done in Table 19.4; note that the first three columns are taken directly from Table 19.3 and that the entries in the fourth column are the product of the entries in the second and third columns. When the products are summed, one is able to proceed to compute the mean for grouped data; this has been done in Computing Guide 19.2.

The fact that Computing Guides 19.1 and 19.2 produce slightly different mean IQs (106.0 and 105.98, respectively) can be easily explained. When data are grouped, precise information is lost; the resulting approximations have produced a mean IQ that is .02 of an IQ point below the raw score mean IQ. If the number of intervals were increased, this approximation would tend to be closer to the true mean IQ. When the number of intervals becomes great enough so that each score is considered individually, the two quantities ΣX and ΣfM become identical, and the two formulas yield identical means.

Table 19.4 Multiplication of Frequency by Class-Interval Midpoint for IQ Grouped Data

Class interval	f	M	fM
133–137	1	135	135
128–132	3	130	390
123–127	2	125	250
118–122	5	120	600
113–117	6	115	690
108–112	3	110	330
103–107	7	105	735
98–102	8	100	800
93– 97	4	95	380
88– 92	2	90	180
83– 87	2	85	170
78– 82	1	80	80
73– 77	0	75	0
68– 72	1	70	70
63– 67	1	65	65
Total	46		4875

Median. The median is the point in a set of continuous measurements on each side of which there is an equal number of cases. If there is an odd number of total cases, the median is the middle-most score. For example, given the scores 8, 10, 2, 6, and 5, the median is 6, as two cases lie above it and two below it. If there is an even number of total cases, the median is the point that lies midway between the two middle-most scores. Given the scores 3, 6, 8, and 12, the median is 7.

COMPUTING GUIDE 19.2

Computing the Mean of Grouped Data

Let: $\overline{X}$ = the mean
Σ = the sum of
f = the frequency in each class interval
M = the midpoint of each class interval
N = the number of cases

Formula: $\overline{X} = \dfrac{\Sigma fM}{N}$

Example: Find the mean of the 46 IQ scores as grouped in Table 19.4.

Step 1: Multiply the midpoint of each class interval by the frequency in that interval.

Step 2: Add the products found in Step 1; determine that $\Sigma fM = 4875$.

Step 3: Substitute numbers in the formula and perform the indicated operations:

$$\overline{X} = \frac{4875}{46} = 105.98$$

   The computation of the median for grouped data is more complicated, but it can readily be accomplished if a histogram or cumulative frequency distribution is available. In either case, the median is a point on the horizontal axis. Using the histogram, one locates the point where a vertical line drawn to the outline defining the histogram divides the area outlined, half to the left and half to the right of the vertical line. This point is easily determined by counting half the squares, starting from either end, thus locating the interval in which the median lies. The histogram already shown appears in Fig. 19.4 with one half of the squares (23) in a darker blue. The median apparently lies in the interval whose real limits are 102.5 and 107.5. Furthermore, because four of the seven rectangles in the column are darker, the median lies 4/7 of the distance between the real limits. Because 4/7 of 5 = 20/7 = 2.86, the median is located at a point 2.86 units above the lower real limit. The median therefore is 105.36. The heavy vertical line in Fig. 19.4 divides the interval 102.5-107.5 into two parts representing 4/7 and 3/7 of the column's area; it also divides the area under the outline of the histogram into two equal parts. Note that the median does not in this case coincide with any score in the distribution.

   When the area approach is used in finding the median, it becomes evident that only the location of the most central scores in the distribution affect this statistic. It is the middle score, or for grouped data the interval in which the middle score lies, that is important. Thus if the child with an IQ of 137 instead had an IQ of 165, the median would not change. If, on the other hand, only four scores lay in the interval 102.5-107.5 and the other three scores were higher, the median would shift from 105.36 to 107.5.

Fig. 19.4. Finding the median on a histogram of fifth-graders' IQs.

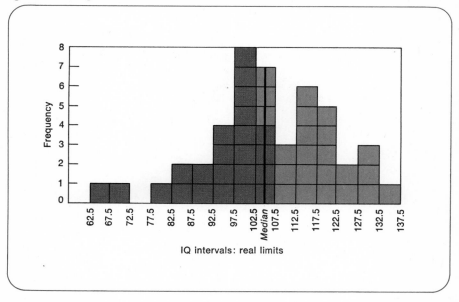

The median may also be conveniently found by using either a cumulative frequency distribution or a cumulative percentage distribution. In either case, the 50 percent or half-way mark on the vertical axis (point A in Fig. 19.5) is identified and a horizontal line (B) is drawn between that point and the distribution curve. At the point where the horizontal line intersects the curve (point C) a vertical line (D) is drawn to the norizontal axis. The point at which the vertical line intersects the horizontal axis (E) is the median. The median is sometimes defined as the point below which 50 percent of the scores lie — this is exactly the definition one would arrive at when finding the median using a cumulative distribution. Note that the results are the same for either method of finding the median for grouped data.

Mode. The mode is the most frequently occurring score in ungrouped data. In grouped data, it is the midpoint of the class interval that includes the greatest number of scores. In Table A, Appendix I, there are two modes in the distribution of IQ: 106 and 119 both occur three times. When the grouped IQ data are considered in Table 19.3, or Figs. 19.1 and 19.2, the mode is 100, because eight IQs occur in the interval whose midpoint is 100.

Relationship Between Mean, Median, and Mode. Using the grouped IQ data in Table 19.3, three measures of central tendency have been calculated and different results obtained for each. In general, unless a distribution has a vertical line of symmetry at its midpoint, the mean, median, and mode do not coincide. Usually, if one is dealing with a symmetric, or near symmetric, distribution, the mean is the proper statistic to communicate the typical value. The mean, however, is affected by all scores in the

Fig. 19.5. Finding the median by using a cumulative distribution graph.

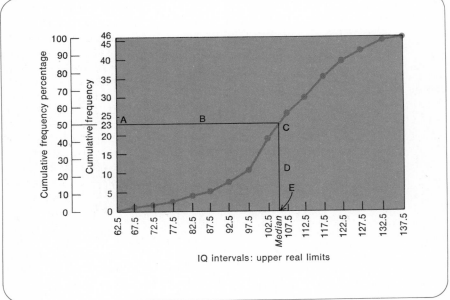

distribution; changing one score would change the mean. If the distribution is not nearly symmetric, the median or mode is a better choice to convey central tendency.

Classroom data may be of either near symmetric or nonsymmetric form. On standardized achievement or intelligence tests, very few students are likely to get perfect scores. The resulting distribution may show a concentration of scores in the middle with a spread of scores at either extreme. In this situation the mean is an appropriate statistic to use in assessing results.

Teachers often construct tests, however, in which many pupils obtain perfect or near perfect scores, and fewer obtain low scores. When scores are clustered at one end of the distribution and spread out with smaller frequencies at the other end, the distribution is called *skewed*. In such cases the median is the preferred statistic.

Finally, there may be two or more peaks or modes in a distribution. If the modes are widely separated, it is better to report each rather than a single summary statistic. The teacher may encounter such data when some of the children have been instructed on the content being tested and others have not. For instance, when the pupils have different instructional backgrounds and a pretest is given, a bimodal distribution may result. Explanations should be sought for such testing results.

Partition Values

A measure of central tendency provides one guidepost in a distribution with which scores can be compared. Other markers can also be defined; these are useful in giving more information than simply "above" or "below" average. Quartiles and percentiles are partition values that are *points* in a distribution that divide the distribution into quarters and hundredths; a pupil's score can then be expressed in relation to these points. If scores are to be reported as falling in the top 10 percent or in the bottom quarter of the group, obviously one needs to know how to calculate the points that demarcate the relevant regions of the distribution. Quartiles and percentiles are quite analogous to the median in computation or in derivation from graphs.

The quartiles (Q_n) are the points in a distribution that divide the *frequencies* into four equal groups, and the percentiles (P_n) into 100 equal groups. The subscript $_n$ refers to the order of these values, starting at the bottom. For example, Q_1, the first quartile, is the point below which one fourth of the cases are; Q_3 is the point below which three fourths of the cases lie; similarly, P_{85} is the point below which are 85 percent of the cases. These points are derived from a cumulative percentage distribution in Fig. 19.6. Notice that the median = Q_2 (second quartile) = P_{50} (fiftieth percentile). Keep in mind that a partition value is a *point* in a distribution and is not necessarily equal to any score or case in the distribution.

Once the points of interest have been identified, one can express any score as being above or below the point. For instance, using Fig. 19.6, we can say that the IQ of child 4 in Table A, Appendix I, is above the first quartile; that of child 5, above the eighty-fifth percentile.

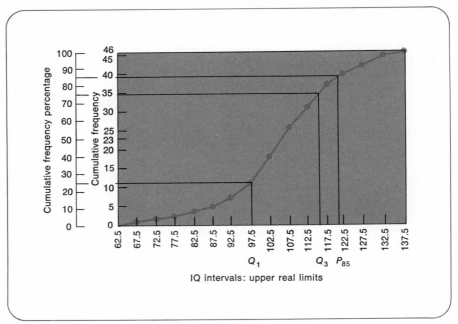

Fig. 19.6. Finding partition values by using a cumulative distribution graph.

If the same partition values are identified for two sets of scores obtained by the same pupils, an individual's performance on the two tests can be compared by using these points. For example, one child might perform above P_{90} in computation and slightly below the class median (P_{50}) in arithmetic concepts.

Measures of Variability

Given a score and the mean, one can merely note the difference between them and the direction of the difference. For instance, on a spelling test a child received a score of 38, and the class mean was 35. Obviously he scored three points above the class mean, but there is no indication whether his score is merely slightly above average or exceptional in his class. Information on the *variability* of the scores is needed to judge how well the pupil performed in relation to other pupils. The extent to which scores are spread out along the scale may be expressed in several ways, including *range*, *variance*, and *standard deviation*.

Range. The range is the simplest measure of variability. It is the difference between the highest and lowest real limits in the distribution; for example, the range of IQ calculated from Table A is $137 - 65 + 1 = 73$, or $137.5 - 64.5 = 73$. The 1 is added in the first computation because real limits are not used as they are in the second computation. If one knew the scores on the spelling test ranged from 15 to 49, one would come to a different conclusion about the pupil who scored 38 than if the range was reported as 29 to 39. Because of the greater variability of scores in the first case, a score of 38 is less outstanding than it is in the second case.

As a statistic, the range has the drawback of taking into account only two extreme scores or measures. A spelling score of 38 could be the second highest score in the class whether the scores ranged from 15 to 49 or 29 to 39. In this situation, assuming the range is 15 to 49, this and the mean of 35 do not give the student enough information to draw a correct conclusion about his performance in relation to those of his peers.

Variance and Standard Deviation. Each score in a distribution affects the mean—changing a single score changes the mean; the same is true of the variance and the standard deviation, which are widely used in describing the way in which scores are dispersed about the mean. The *variance* is defined as the average of the squares of the deviations of the scores from their mean; the *standard deviation* is simply the square root of the variance. It is seldom necessary now to change all raw scores to deviation scores because of the availability of desk calculators and rapid electronic computers. These devices permit computing variance, standard deviation, and many other measures to be described later without grouping the scores. The raw scores are not even put in rank order in most cases but appear as they do in Table A. Computing Guide 19.3 gives the formula (in raw-score units) and the procedure for computing the variance and the standard deviation. Recall that in raw score form, without grouping the data into a frequency table, the mean or $\overline{X} = \Sigma X/N$; note that no new symbols are used in the formula for variance and standard deviation.

The standard deviation is expressed in units comparable to those on the original scale of measurement. For this reason, it is often preferred as a descriptive statistic. Most scores clustering about the midpoint of a distribution lie within one standard deviation of the mean. The two points demarcating this region can be found by adding and subtracting the standard deviation from the mean. For instance, given from Table A in Appendix I the mean IQ of 106 and the standard deviation of approximately 15, scores between 91 (106 − 15) and 121 (106 + 15) lie within one standard deviation of the mean. In fact, 35 of the 46 IQ scores in Table A, or 76 percent, fall within this range; looking ahead to Fig. 19.7, the reader can verify that in a perfectly normal distribution, 68.26 percent of the scores would lie within a standard deviation of the mean. Very few scores lie beyond two standard deviations distance from the mean, that is, below 76 or above 136 in the case of the IQ scores in Table A. Just three scores, in fact, or slightly more than 6 percent, are beyond these limits; in a normal distribution, slightly less than 5 percent of scores are this distant from the mean.

How is the standard deviation used in the classroom? Test results may be reported in terms of the mean and standard deviation. Secondary school pupils can understand the relationship of their score to a graphic representation of actual scores or to a normal distribution which is scaled in standard deviation units. For instance, the child with the spelling score of 38 would form an impression of his relative performance given a

COMPUTING GUIDE 19.3

Computing the Variance and the Standard Deviation of Ungrouped Data

Let: $s^2 =$ the variance
    $s =$ the standard deviation
    $N =$ the number of cases
    $\Sigma X^2 =$ the square of each score, subsequently added together
    $(\Sigma X)^2 =$ the sum of all scores, subsequently squared

Formulas: $s^2 = \dfrac{1}{N-1}\left[\Sigma X^2 - \dfrac{(\Sigma X)^2}{N}\right]$

    $s = \sqrt{s^2}$

Example: Find the variance and standard deviation of the 46 IQ scores in Table A of Appendix I.
    Step 1:   Add all the scores; determine that $\Sigma X = 4876$.
    Step 2:   Square all scores and add them; determine that $\Sigma X_2 = 527{,}104$.
    Step 3:   Substitute numbers in the formula and perform the indicated operations:

$$s^2 = \frac{1}{46-1}\left[527{,}104 - \frac{(4876)^2}{46}\right] =$$

$$\frac{1}{45}(527{,}104 - 516{,}856) = 227.73$$

    Step 4:   Take the square root of s^2 to determine s:

$$s = \sqrt{227.73} = 15.09$$

Note: This guide may be used for grouped data by substituting ΣfM (see Computing Guide 19.2) whenever ΣX now appears in the formula above.

normal curve with the mean of 35 labeled and standard deviations of 7 marked off on the scale. Although teachers do not often calculate the statistic, it is usually reported to the school or teacher when tests are machine-scored, and is thus readily available when published tests are used.

19.2. From one column of data in Table A in Appendix I compute the variance and standard deviation. The computation may be verified by comparing the result with the value of *s* on the last line of the table.

19.3. Use the information about the distribution of IQs in Fig. 19.6 and that in Computing Guide 19.3 to arrange the following points according to how distant they are from the mean. First identify the point that is closest to the mean:

   a. One standard deviation unit above the mean.
   b. Two standard deviation units above the mean.
   c. Three standard deviation units above the mean.
   d. The ninetieth percentile.
   e. The ninety-ninth percentile.
   f. The third quartile.

(You may verify your answer by comparing your list with the standard deviation and percentile scales found in Fig. 19.8.)

19.4. Refer to the table and graphs you made for Exercise 19.1. Calculate the mean, identify the mode or modes, and find the median and Q_1, Q_2, Q_3, and P_{90} through use of a cumulative distribution.

STATISTICS AND THE INTERPRETATION OF SCORES

In Table A in Appendix I the first three measurements are age in months, IQ, and achievement in word meaning. The last child is 121 months old, has an IQ of 110, and has achieved in word meaning at a grade equivalent of 5.9. Because these three measurements are not in comparable units, one cannot compare them. One way to get more comparable scores is to change each set of scores to percentile scores, as already shown. Other methods make use of the fact that scores and other measurements most frequently are normally distributed. Before proceeding with the discussion of statistical means of equating scores, therefore, the student should learn the characteristics of the normal distribution.

The Normal Distribution

The normal curve, illustrated in Fig. 19.7, is a theoretical distribution that is symmetric about the mean. Sometimes referred to, for obvious reasons, as the bell-shaped distribution, it has characteristics that are of great importance in statistics.

Note that, because the curve is symmetric, its mean, median, and mode coincide. Also note that to indicate that its "tails" are theoretically infinitely long, the outline of the distribution does not touch the horizontal axis. Curves as smooth as this one are rarely, if ever, found when data are

Fig. 19.7. Normal distribution with different scales of measurement.

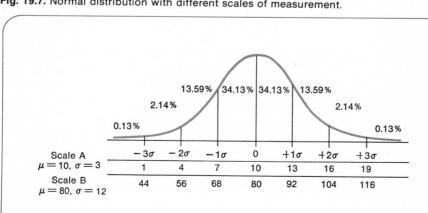

plotted; nevertheless, the frequency with which jagged curves approximate the normal curve is impressive. Many published tests are constructed in such a manner that the distributions of scores are approximately normal. Figure 6.2 shows the curve of the 2904 intelligence scores of the sample used to standardize the 1937 Revised Stanford-Binet Scale; this curve closely approximates a normal distribution. Smaller numbers of scores give a more jagged distribution, such as the one shown in Fig. 19.2.

The idea of normality applies to the shape or form of the distribution but not to the values of any other properties that the distribution may have, such as the mean and the standard deviation. In a theoretical distribution, the mean and the standard deviation are mathematical constants, not values that fluctuate with the sample chosen; they are denoted by the Greek letters mu (μ) and sigma (σ), respectively. One normal distribution may have a mean of 10 and a standard deviation of three, in which case Scale A in Fig. 19.7 would be appropriate; another distribution might have a mean of 80 and a standard deviation of 12, as illustrated in Scale B.

For any amount of deviation from the mean that is expressed in standard deviation units, a normal probability table can be used to ascertain the proportion of the total area under the normal curve up to that deviation or between the mean and that amount of deviation. For example, about 34 percent of the area lies on each side of the mean up to the point one standard deviation away; thus about 68 percent of the area lies between $+1\sigma$ and -1σ, as can be seen in Fig. 19.7. The area between $+2\sigma$ and -2σ includes 95 percent of the total area; thus, only about 5 percent of the area lies beyond ± 2 standard deviation units. Moreover, .997 of the area of a probability curve lies between $+3\sigma$ and -3σ. For standardized tests whose mean and standard deviation are known, the percentile score corresponding to an IQ score can be found simply by using the curve or its tabular representation. The Stanford-Binet Scale, for instance, has a mean of 100 and a standard deviation of 16. A child with an IQ of 132 (two standard deviations above the mean) has a percentile score of approximately 98 (the cumulative percentile representing the area in Fig. 19.7 from the left up to $+2\sigma$), meaning his IQ is higher than that of 98 percent of the population.

Many other types of derived scores are based on the assumption that the raw scores are normally distributed. Strictly speaking, most data do not meet the assumption, but the techniques for converting scores are utilized anyway. The most common of the derived scores are discussed in the following sections.

Standard Scores

Changing a set of raw scores on any test to standard scores, sometimes called "sigma scores" or "z-scores," requires analysis of the entire set of scores. A standard score is derived by dividing the deviation score (the difference between the raw score and the group mean) by the standard deviation for the particular set of test scores. Thus each raw score is expressed as a deviation from the group mean in standard deviation units. Inasmuch as raw scores of the same individuals on different tests can be changed to standard scores, they are useful in comparing measurements on unlike scales and with different variables such as appear in Table A in Appendix I. In other words, standard scores are the means by which the first boy's age, IQ, and achievement in word meaning can be converted to comparable units.

Because raw scores fall below or above the mean, standard scores may be negative or positive. Also, most standard scores fall within the range of +3 to −3 standard deviation units, just as almost all the area under the normal curve falls between these points. The sum of any complete set of standard scores therefore is always zero. Thus, the distribution of the + and − standard scores on any test has a mean of zero and a standard deviation of 1.

Computing Guide 19.4 shows how standard scores are computed. Obtained standard scores like those that result in the guide are very useful. In raw score units boy 46 in Table A in Appendix I had an IQ of 110; his word meaning grade equivalent is 5.9, or fifth grade, ninth month. (These and other grade equivalents reported in Table A were obtained by looking up raw scores on the achievement subtests in tables of norms.) Although boy 46 shows an achievement level in spelling (5.8) that is quite similar to his word meaning achievement, how did he compare in these two tests

COMPUTING GUIDE 19.4

Computing Standard Scores

Let: z = the standard score
   X = the raw score
   $\overline{X}$ = the mean of a group of scores
   s = the standard deviation of a group of scores

Formula: $z = \dfrac{X - \overline{X}}{s}$

Example: Compute the standard scores for boy 46 in Table A of Appendix I for word meaning, spelling, arithmetic computation and science.

   Step 1:   Determine $\overline{X}$ and s for word meaning; in Table A they are given as 4.9 and 1.3, respectively.

   Step 2:   Substitute the proper numbers in the formula and perform the indicated operations for each raw score:

   $z(\text{word meaning}) = \dfrac{5.9 - 4.9}{1.3} = \dfrac{1.0}{1.3} = .77$

   $z(\text{spelling}) = \dfrac{5.8 - 5.2}{1.5} = \dfrac{.6}{1.5} = .40$

   $z(\text{arithmetic computation}) = \dfrac{4.3 - 4.6}{.94} = \dfrac{-.3}{.94} = -.32$

   $z(\text{science}) = \dfrac{9.1 - 5.6}{1.7} = \dfrac{3.5}{1.7} = 2.06$

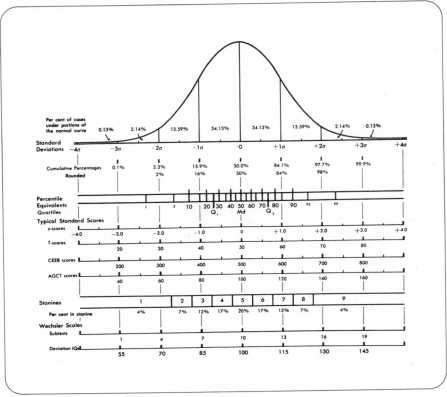

Fig. 19.8. The relationship of some derived scores to the normal distribution. This chart cannot be used to equate scores on one test with scores on another test. For example, both 600 on the CEEB and 120 on the AGCT are one standard deviation above their respective means, but they do not represent "equal" standings because the scores were obtained from different groups. (Adapted from Psychological Corporation, 1955, p. 8)

with the other children in this particular group? The z-scores computed in Guide 19.4 show this boy considerably above the group average in both subjects, but more so in word meaning. In comparison with the other children, he was above the mean on all achievement variables except arithmetic computation, for which he has a negative z-score. In relation to himself, he was highest in science.

Although somewhat time consuming to compute, standard scores do permit meaningful comparisons among the scores obtained by a single group on several tests or among measurements on several variables. This is true because they are expressed in a common unit — the standard deviation unit. If comparisons of z-scores from one test to another are to be made, the groups on which the calculations are based should not have different members.

Scoring schemes commonly encountered which are directly comparable to standard scores include those used to report College Entrance Examination Board scores and Army General Classification Test scores. Each of the measurement scales has a different mean and standard deviation, as indicated in Fig. 19.8.

Stanine Scores

Stanine scores are a form of standard score increasingly used in reporting test results. The following statements about stanines can be verified by consulting Fig. 19.8 (which also shows why "stanine" is a contraction of "standard nine"). The stanine scale is calibrated in half-standard deviation units except at either extreme. A stanine score, however, is a whole number that represents an interval of the scale, rather than a point on it. The average stanine is 5, and the interval it spans extends from .25 standard deviations below the mean to .25 standard deviations above the mean. The stanines 1 and 9 include all scores beyond $\pm 1.75\sigma$.

Achievement test scores may be quickly converted to stanines through tables provided in many test manuals. The chief advantage in using intervals rather than points to report measurements on a scale is that insignificantly small differences between scores are not given undue attention. As has been noted in Chapter 17, the concept of error of measurement suggests that there is unlikely to be a significant difference between an individual's grade equivalent scores of 5.7 and 5.9.

The 10 achievement scores of boy 46 and nine other students are reported in stanines in Table 19.5. (Each child is identified by his serial number.) Note that boy 46's strength in science and weakness in arithmetic computation immediately stand out. The advantages of using such a means of reporting scores to students and parents are twofold: The individual is seen in relation to the class or norm group in all areas, and his performance in various subject matters can be compared. Furthermore, his scores are readily interpreted in terms of percentile ranges. The stanine system is readily explainable to laymen; its use obviates the necessity to deal with meaningless raw scores or the often misinterpreted grade equivalent.

19.5. From Table A in Appendix I select a student whose data you will prepare to report to his parents. In what units will you present it? Choose some pictorial or tabular form in which to present the child's profile. Write a brief explanation of the scale you are using that will be understandable to the parents.

19.6. If achievement tests your class took were machine scorable and you had the option of selecting in what form the scores would be reported, which two of the following would you choose? Explain.
  a. Raw scores
  b. Percentile scores
  c. Standard scores
  d. Grade equivalents

Table 19.5. Stanine Scores of 10 Children with Numbers 37 to 46

Stanine	Percentage in stanine	Word meaning	Paragraph meaning	Spelling	Work skills	Language	Arithmetic computation	Arithmetic concepts	Arithmetic application	Social studies	Science
9	4	40	40	38	41	42		43		39	(46)
8	7	42		41	38 42	40 41	38		38 41	38	40
7	12	(46)	38 41 (46)	39 40 42	40 44		41 43	38 42 (46)		40 42 (46)	38 41
6	17	38 41 43	42 44	(46)	37 39 43	38 44 (46)	40 42	39 41 44	43 (46)		39
5	20	39 44	39 43 45	43 44	45 (46)	39 43	37 39 45	40	39 40 42	41 43	42 43
4	17	37 45		37 45		45	44 (46)		37 44 45	44 45	45
3	12		37			37				37	37 44
2	7							37			
1	4							45			

Note: The circling of 46 was done to aid in observing a profile of the educational achievements for one student.

SAMPLING AND EXPERIMENTAL PROCEDURES

Classroom teachers inevitably are consumers of educational research; often they are participants in it. Occasionally, they are leaders or designers of their own research or evaluation projects. They are consumers in the sense that they read research reports that appear in the professional journals. Results of such research can be used by teachers to improve instruction. Indeed, that is a main reason why studies are done and reports on their results published. For example, a study reported by Ellis Page in the *Journal of Educational Psychology* (see Appendix II) showed that brief positive comments written on pupils' papers can have a facilitating effect on their later learning. A teacher reading the report might decide to write comments, rather than just give letter grades. If a teacher acts on such information, he becomes a consumer of research.

When studies are initiated by school research personnel or professors from colleges or universities, the teacher becomes a research participant. When a teacher designs or carries out his own research or evaluation project, he becomes a researcher.

Classroom teachers, therefore, should be familiar with research methods as consumers, as participants, and as researchers themselves. In this section, some procedures frequently followed by researchers are explained and illustrated with specific examples.

Population and Sample

A sample is a subset or subgroup of an entire group, called a *population*. Sampling is used to save time and money; also, it may provide opportunities for better control than when the whole population is used. Sampling is done in order to generalize from a sample to a population. But, obviously, generalizing from any sample to a population involves uncertainty. If the *amount* of uncertainty or risk of error is known, however, it can be taken into account in assessing the results of a study. This amount can be determined if the sample is selected according to rules that guarantee that every member of the population is ensured a known or determinable chance of being included in the sample. There are many types of sampling designed to achieve this purpose, but only simple random sampling and stratified random sampling are discussed here.

Simple Random Sampling. A simple random sample is one in which the members of a defined population are drawn in such a way that each *one* of the population has an equal chance of being included in the sample, and every possible *combination* of members of the population has the same chance of being included. For example, if the entire population of 17-year-old girls in a city is 5000 and a sample of 500 is desired, each of the 5000 must have an equal chance of being drawn into the sample of 500. Any possible combination of 500 must also have a chance to be drawn into the sample.

A *table of random numbers* is usually used in selecting a simple random sample. Such a table consists of rows and columns of the ten digits in a random order. One selects an arbitrary starting point within the table and moves in any direction, identifying the numbers of interest. For example, if we wished to select randomly one half of the students in Table A to receive some instructional treatment or test, we might look for the first 23 serial numbers between 1 and 46 to appear in a pair of columns in the table. This has been done in Table 19.6, starting where the arrow appears with the number 42, and moving downward. Note that numbers greater than 46 and duplicate numbers are ignored (on line 25 of column 4, "07" is not circled because it appeared previously). The reason for ignoring duplicate numbers is that samples are drawn in education "without replacement." Although it is possible, of course, when using a table of random numbers, to draw the same number more than once, it would make no sense to assign an individual to two different experimental conditions that occurred simultaneously.

Table 19.6. Identification of 23 Serial Numbers Between 1 and 46, Using a Table of Random Numbers

Line/Col.	(1)	(2)	(3)	(4)	(5)	(6)	(7)	(8)
1	10480	15011	01536	0 2 0 1 1	8 1 6 4 7	91646	69179	14194
2	22368	46573	25595	8 5 3 9 3	3 0 9 9 5	89198	27982	53402
3	24130	48360	22527	9 7 2 6 5	7 6 3 9 3	64809	15179	24830
4	42167	93093	06243	6 1 6 8 0	0 7 8 5 6	16376	39440	53537
5	37570	39975	81837	1 6 6 5 6	0 6 1 2 1	91782	60468	81305
6	77921	06907	11008	4 2 7 5 1	2 7 7 5 6	53498	18602	70659
7	99562	72905	56420	6 9 9 9 4	9 8 8 7 2	31016	71194	18738
8	96301	91977	05463	0 7 9 7 2	1 8 8 7 6	20922	94595	56869
9	89579	14342	63661	1 0 2 8 1	1 7 4 5 3	18103	57740	84378
10	85475	36857	43342	5 3 9 8 8	5 3 0 6 0	59533	38867	62300
11	28918	69578	88231	3 3 2 7 6	7 0 9 9 7	79936	56865	05859
12	63553	40961	48235	0 3 4 2 7	4 9 6 2 6	69445	18663	72695
13	09429	93969	52636	9 2 7 3 7	8 8 9 7 4	33488	36320	17617
14	10365	61129	87529	8 5 6 8 9	4 8 2 3 7	52267	67689	93394
15	07119	97336	71048	0 8 1 7 8	7 7 2 3 3	13916	47564	81056
16	51085	12765	51821	5 1 2 5 0	7 7 4 5 2	16308	60756	92144
17	02368	21382	52404	6 0 2 6 8	8 9 3 6 8	19885	55322	44819
18	01011	54092	33362	9 4 9 0 4	3 1 2 7 3	04146	18594	29852
19	52162	53916	46369	5 8 5 8 6	2 3 2 1 6	14513	83149	98736
20	07056	97628	33787	0 9 9 9 8	4 2 6 9 8	06691	76988	13602
21	48663	91245	85828	1 4 3 4 6	0 9 1 7 2	30168	90229	04734
22	54164	58492	22421	7 4 1 0 3	4 7 0 7 0	25306	76468	26384
23	32639	32363	05597	2 4 2 0 0	1 3 3 6 3	38005	94342	28728
24	29334	27001	87637	8 7 3 0 8	5 8 7 3 1	00256	45834	15398
25	02488	33062	28834	0 7 3 5 1	1 9 7 3 1	92420	60952	61280

Note: The table of random numbers was arbitrarily entered where the arrow appears. Since two-digit numbers 46 or lower are of interest, the first two digits in column 4, line 6, are circled because 42 is equal to or less than 46, the highest serial number. Proceeding downward, 69 is not circled because it is greater than 46. When the bottom of the table is reached, one continues with the third and fourth digits in column 4, line 1. When the bottom is again reached, one continues with the last digits in column 4 combined with the first digits in column 5.

Stratified Random Sampling. In this type, the population is divided into subgroups, called "strata," on the basis of one or more characteristics. In educational research two variables frequently used in stratification are IQ and sex. A teaching method in mathematics might be hypothesized to be differentially effective for boys and girls, and for children of high and low IQ. The experimenter would then want to have random samples of pupils of all possible combinations of these variables: high-IQ boys, high-IQ girls, low-IQ boys, and low-IQ girls. Thus, after identifying groups of children in these four categories, he would randomly draw from each group the number of children to be used in the experiment.

Characteristics of Samples

Statistical inference is founded on certain well-known characteristics of samples. Specifically, the descriptive statistics that are associated with a sample vary according to the particular sample drawn. The mean of a sample ($\overline{X}$) is considered an estimate of the population mean (μ), for instance.

Let us define the 46 children listed in Table A as a population of interest, whose characteristics we wish to estimate by sampling. We have already ascertained that the mean IQ in this group is 106. If we were to select 10 different groups of 20 individuals randomly and find the mean IQ for each group, we might end up with $\overline{X}$s either very close to 106 or some distance from it. Table 19.7 lists 10 sample means obtained in such a manner. As can be seen, the means range from 102.1 to 110.1. When these means are arranged in a frequency distribution table or graph, however (Fig. 19.9), it becomes apparent that they cluster around the true mean of the population. In fact, the average of the sample means, if all possible combinations of 20-person samples are drawn, does equal the population mean. The average shown in Table 19.7 comes very close to 106.

If another set of samples were drawn of size 30, we would in all probability find that the sample means tended to be still closer to 106 than in the previous example. In other words, the larger the sample the more likely it is that the sample mean will be closer to the population mean. The standard deviation of the *sampling distribution of means* varies inversely with the size of the samples drawn. In fact, the standard deviation of the sampling distribution is precisely related to the population σ through the formula $\sigma_{\overline{x}} = \sigma/\sqrt{N}$, where N is the number of cases in the sample. This formula may be understood through an example. The standard deviations of the sampling distributions of means of samples sizes 20 and 30 are 2.52 and 1.63, respectively.[2] The theoretical sampling distributions are shown

Table 19.7. Ten Sample Means of IQ, Each Based on a Sample of 20 Children

Subjects	$\overline{x}$
1, 2, 6, 7, 9, 10, 12, 14, 15, 21, 22, 24, 28, 32, 36, 37, 39, 40, 42, 46	110.1
1, 7, 10, 11, 12, 14, 15, 16, 17, 18, 22, 24, 25, 31, 33, 34, 36, 37, 44, 46	104.5
1, 2, 7, 10, 12, 13, 14, 15, 16, 19, 20, 23, 27, 28, 32, 35, 36, 42, 44, 46	104.4
2, 4, 7, 8, 9, 15, 16, 21, 22, 23, 24, 25, 27, 31, 34, 37, 42, 44, 45, 46	102.1
3, 4, 5, 8, 12, 13, 16, 17, 19, 23, 24, 26, 28, 32, 33, 34, 39, 42, 43, 45	107.4
2, 4, 5, 9, 11, 12, 16, 19, 20, 22, 24, 25, 29, 31, 32, 35, 37, 38, 42, 46	106.9
3, 5, 9, 13, 16, 17, 18, 19, 23, 24, 28, 29, 31, 32, 33, 36, 40, 44, 45, 46	108.5
1, 3, 6, 7, 9, 10, 15, 17, 18, 22, 23, 27, 29, 30, 33, 35, 36, 40, 41, 43	104.7
2, 7, 8, 15, 16, 19, 20, 22, 24, 25, 31, 32, 33, 34, 35, 40, 41, 42, 44, 46	106.95
2, 3, 7, 10, 11, 13, 16, 19, 22, 27, 30, 33, 35, 37, 39, 41, 42, 44, 45, 46	105.45
Sum of means	1061.00
Mean of means	106.1

[2]These values are slightly different from those obtained using the formula because the population is finite, and the correct formula is slightly modified.

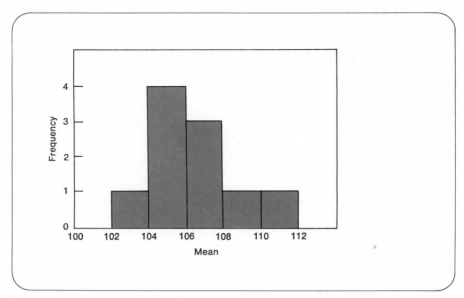

Fig. 19.9. Histogram of 10 sample means drawn from a population whose mean is 106.

in Fig. 19.10 in relation to each other and to the smoothed curve for normally distributed scores with σ equal to 14.9. (The standard deviation for a population, σ, is calculated differently than that for a sample; thus $\sigma = 14.9$ while $s = 15.1$.)

The implication of the preceding discussion is the quite logical one that larger rather than smaller samples give better estimates of the true state of affairs. Next we shall see how the concepts of sampling distributions are used in making inferences.

The Null Hypothesis

An experimental question often is translated from straightforward question form into a declarative statement known as the *null hypothesis*. Suppose we wished to learn the answer to this question: Does spending 10 minutes a week individually with a pupil setting goals for attainment of mathematical objectives positively affect the number of objectives he attains? We could state the problem in terms of two hypothetical outcomes, the first of which is the null hypothesis:

There is no difference in the number of mathematical objectives attained between pupils who have a weekly 10-minute goal-setting conference and those who do not.

There is a difference in the number of mathematical objectives attained between pupils who have a weekly 10-minute goal-setting conference and those who do not.

Each of these hypothetical outcomes can be stated mathematically, as well. We use the symbols μ_g and μ_n to represent the means of the populations of children receiving the goal-setting procedure and those not exposed to it, respectively. Then our hypotheses may be expressed as follows:

$H_0: \mu_g - \mu_n = 0$ or $H_1: \mu_g - \mu_n \neq 0$

Our first hypothesis says that the difference between the two groups is nonexistent. H_0 is called the null hypothesis. H_1, which expresses the experimenter's hunch or anticipated outcome, is known as the *experimental* or *alternative hypothesis*. Answering the question originally posed in plain English is tantamount to making a decision between these two alternatives.

Fig. 19.10. Distributions of normally distributed scores and sampling distributions of means. The mean of all distributions is 106. The broad flat normal distribution is that of scores with a standard deviation 14.9. The most peaked distribution is the sampling distribution of means of size 30 from a finite (limited) population with a standard deviation of 1.63. The slightly less peaked distribution represents the sampling distributions of means of size 20 with a standard deviation of 2.52.

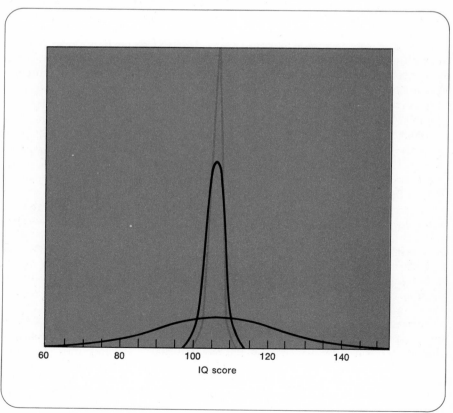

Note that in the mathematical form of expressing the two hypotheses, the symbol μ, rather than $\overline{X}$, was used. The question is whether there is a difference in the populations, *not* in the samples themselves. We have seen that sample means vary depending on exactly who is in each sample. It would be risky to draw a conclusion simply on the basis of the observed differences between two samples.

Nevertheless, the sample means can be used as a *starting point* in answering the question. Using what is known about the standard deviation of the sampling distribution, a range of likely values of the population means for both groups can be determined, and the two ranges compared. Depending on whether or not the ranges overlap, a conclusion can be reached. For instance, if the experimental group attained an average of 18 goals during the period of the experiment, we could assume that the population from which the subjects were drawn would have attained on the average between 15 and 21 if subjected to the experimental treatment. The control group of subjects, on the other hand, might have attained only 11 goals on the average. The range of likely mean values for the entire control population might then be 8 to 14. If the true population value were low for the experimental group (15) and high for the control group (14), we would still be safe in concluding that the groups' means were different. On the other hand, if the control group's observed mean were 13, with likely values of the population mean ranging from 10 to 16, the interval would overlap that of the experimental group (15 to 21), and it is possible that the total control population would have scored higher than the population associated with the experimental treatment. If the ranges do not overlap, the difference between the sample means is said to be *significant* and one rejects the null hypothesis. In other words, one concludes that the data support the alternative hypothesis.

Statistical Significance of Differences

The meaning of the term "likely values" just used needs more elaboration. If 95 out of 100 times the observed mean ($\overline{X}$) were associated with a population whose true mean (μ) fell within a calculated interval, the interval is known as a 95 percent confidence interval. Five percent of the time such an observed mean would be associated with a true mean beyond the limits of the interval. Ninety-nine percent confidence intervals can also be constructed. The likelihood of the true mean lying in such an interval is greater than is that of its being contained in a 95 percent confidence interval; therefore, the range of the 99 percent interval is greater than that of the 95 percent confidence interval.

Actually, when statistical tests of hypotheses are made, a formalized procedure is substituted for the procedure outlined above. A single number is obtained which can be compared with other computed values in a statistical table. If the value obtained would occur by chance, given no real difference, less than 5 percent of the time, the difference between two means is said to be *significant at the .05 level*. If the obtained value is more extreme and would occur by chance less than 1 percent of the time, the difference is significant at the .01 level. Other significance levels commonly used in education include the .10 and .001 levels. Correct statistical procedure calls for the setting of a significance level before the collection of data against which hypotheses are to be tested. In answering the experimental question asked about the effectiveness of goal-setting conferences, we will set a level of .01.

Table B in Appendix I gives the data collected in an experiment designed to answer the goal-setting question. Initially, we shall focus on the data collected after the experiment—that appearing in columns 2 and 4. At the outset of the experiment, two groups of 50 pupils each were randomly selected from the population of interest, third-graders in an inner-city school district. (It is a common experimental procedure to use two groups of the same size.) Because of randomization, we can assume the conference (experimental) and nonconference (control) groups were initially equivalent on many possibly relevant characteristics, including motivation to learn, achievement in mathematics, and intelligence. Sometimes this assumption is tested to see if it is warranted. It is, of course, possible to select randomly a set of children who have relatively high scores, as did the first group in Table 19.7, and another group who end up with a below average mean on some characteristic. However, if the sample is fairly large, differences between the two groups initially are likely to be small and of little or no importance.

The goal-setting procedure was then carried out in conferences with the experimental group for six months. Meanwhile, the control group had some specified or nonspecified treatment—independent reading, for example. Data were then gathered on a *dependent variable* relevant to the hypothesis being tested—the variable in this case was the number of objectives attained during the course of the experiment. Data might also have been collected on other dependent variables, including mathematics achievement on standardized tests and attitude toward mathematics class. Multiple dependent variables are recommended in educational research; we will consider only the first, however, because more than one would complicate the analysis.

The means and standard deviations of the two groups on the postexperimental variable are presented in Table 19.8, as are the standard errors of the means. The standard error of the mean is simply the estimated standard deviation of the sampling distribution of the mean and indicates how the mean might have fluctuated from its reported value had a different sample been drawn.

You will recall that the range of likely values for the population mean may be estimated by using the sample mean. The standard error of the mean is also used in calculating this range. In the last column in Table

Table 19.8. Means and Standard Deviations for Experimental and Control Groups

Group	$\bar{X}$	s	S.E.	99 percent confidence interval
Experimental	17.90	5.09	.727	15.95–19.85
Control	12.34	5.68	.811	10.17–14.51

19.8 the *99 percent confidence intervals* for the means are specified. These intervals are interpreted to mean that 99 percent of the time, data similar to that collected would come from a population whose mean lay within the interval. When 99 percent confidence intervals do not overlap, results are significant at the .01 level.

In our case we see that the intervals do not overlap. This means that it is unlikely that the populations represented by the two means are the same: our experimental procedure succeeded in making the two groups drawn from a single population different. One therefore decides to "reject the null hypothesis" in favor of the alternative. Because we are not 100 percent certain of our conclusion, and never can be when only a sample of evidence is used, we have not *proved* that the alternative hypothesis is correct. We merely note that the evidence supports it.

t-**Tests.** The preceding detailed explanation of significance would not be found in a research report. Rather, the reader might encounter a statement such as the following: "To test for the significance of the difference between the two means, a *t*-test was performed. The results of the analysis ($t = 5.1$, $p < .0001$) lead to rejection of the null hypothesis." The reader unfamiliar with research reports probably would not realize that behind this terse statement are concepts of probability, sampling distributions of the mean, and other ideas not mentioned in the brief overview of statistical inference. Nevertheless, the conclusion reached is no different than that reached in the more fully developed description above. What the researcher did, however, was somewhat different from what is implied in the detailed explanation. He merely substituted values for the observed means and standard deviations in the standard formula for *t*, readily available in a statistics book, and looked up the obtained value in a probability table to determine its likelihood of occurrence by chance. Note that the probability associated with the given *t* exceeds that required to be significant at the .01 level.

Analysis of Variance

The *t*-test described above is appropriate only when two groups are compared or when pairs of scores on the same or matched individuals are at hand. Analysis of variance (ANOVA) is a more generalized procedure for testing the differences among more than two groups. Analysis of variance might be used when simple random sampling has been employed to assign individuals to three or more groups. Analysis of variance is also used when stratified random sampling has been employed to assign individuals to treatments.

A more sophisticated approach to the question about the effectiveness of the goal-setting conference procedure might have taken into account the mathematics achievement levels of the children. One might have hypothesized that the goal-setting procedure would affect high and low achievers differentially, with the low achievers primarily affected.

The way to approach testing of this hypothesis is through stratification of the population into above- and below-average achievers on the basis of a standardized test or teacher ratings, before random selection of the ex-

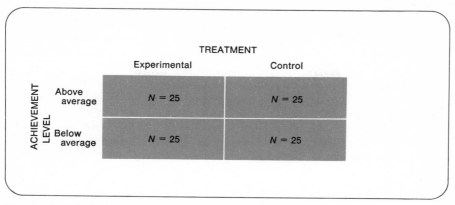

Fig. 19.11. Experimental design for an experiment testing the effectiveness of a goal-setting procedure for above- and below-average achievers in mathematics.

perimental groups. The *experimental design* in Fig. 19.11 might be used. The two dimensions of the figure represent the two experimental or independent variables—treatment and achievement group. There are two "levels" of each independent variable. Notice that the design specifies the N in each *cell*, but that the total number of subjects exposed to each treatment has not changed from the preceding experiment. We will continue to use the .01 significance level established previously.

The results of this experiment may be calculated from the data in Table B of Appendix I if those subjects above the dashed line are treated as above-average achievers and those below the line as below-average achievers. The means are plotted in Fig. 19.12. Notice that on the average the experimental subjects achieved more objectives than the controls, but that the difference was more striking between the two below-average groups.

Information from an analysis of variance is summarized in an ANOVA table, such as Table 19.9. The statistic calculated for each "effect" is F. When the effect is significant, this is noted either by a p-value statement or by an asterisk that is keyed beneath the table. In Table 19.9, three effects are reported. The two *main effects*—achievement group and treatment—correspond to the two nominal variables identified in the experimental design. Both are significant sources of differences in the means. In other words, not only do experimental subjects differ as a group from con-

Table 19.9. Analysis of Variance of Number of Objectives Attained

Source	df	Mean square	F	p
Achievement group	1	219.04	8.50	<.01
Treatment	1	772.84	29.99	<.001
Interaction	1	158.76	6.16	<.05
Error	96	25.77		

trol subjects in the number of objectives attained, but also, above-average achievers differ from below-average achievers in the same way. The interaction term provides an answer to the question of *differential* effectiveness of the treatment for above- and below-average achievers in mathematics. Because it does not meet the significance level set in advance, the null hypothesis is not rejected in connection with interaction. However, a p value of .05 represents a relatively unlikely outcome, given no real difference, and the interaction phenomenon probably deserves more study.

The error term is of less interest, because it is used here to calculate the denominator used in the F-ratio. F is simply the numerical value obtained when the mean square for any effect is divided by the mean square for error. Likewise, degrees of freedom (df) are used in the calculations. F, which is the statistic of interest in an ANOVA table, is calculated for all lines except the last, where the error term appears.

Analysis of Covariance

Let us complicate the hypothesis about the conference procedure further by suggesting that number of objectives attained during the course of the experiment might depend on each pupil's previous record of attainment of objectives. In this case data might be collected *before* the experiment begins to indicate what earlier attainment patterns were during a baseline period, and these data might actually be used in the final analysis. (Note the difference between using baseline data in the analysis and using such data to *form* qualitatively different groups, such as above- and below-average achievers.)

An analysis taking into account both premeasures and dependent measures is known as an *analysis of covariance*; the premeasure in our example, number of objectives attained in the baseline period, is known as the *covariate*. In effect, the final scores on the dependent variable are adjusted to account for preexperimental differences and an analysis of variance performed. The F-test is utilized, and results are reported for an analysis of covariance in the same manner as for an analysis of variance. If the premeasure scores are related to the postmeasure scores, the reported Fs may be higher and the p values more extreme, as is the case in Table 19.10 for the interaction term.

Whereas the interaction term did not meet the .01 significance level set in advance when an analysis of variance was performed, with the anal-

Table 19.10 Analysis of Covariance of Number of Mathematics Objectives Attained with Number of Objectives Attained Before the Experiment as Covariate

Source	df	Mean square	F	p
Achievement group	1	.68	.03	—
Treatment	1	755.61	36.89	< .001
Interaction	1	226.76	11.07	< .01
Error	95	20.48		

ysis of covariance it is significant. The analysis of covariance in this case provides a more sensitive analysis of the data. A significant interaction in this instance means that the treatment is more highly effective for one stratum than the other. Neither the analysis of variance nor analysis of covariance table indicates whether the treatment had greater effect on high or low achievers in mathematics. The unadjusted means plotted in Fig. 19.12 did show, however, that low achievers in mathematics benefited more than high achievers, as was expected.

Note that in Table 19.10 achievement group is not a significant effect, as it was in the analysis of variance table. Because of the high relationship between number of objectives attained during the baseline period and mathematics achievement, the above-mentioned adjustment of scores when analysis of covariance is used eliminates major differences between the two groups on mathematics achievement.

Chi Square. The preceding analyses are most often used in conjunction with interval data. Tests of significance for other kinds of data have also been developed. The most commonly used test for nominal data, the chi square, is discussed here.

Suppose in conjunction with a study of outside reading habits, such as that reported in Chapter 9, pupils were asked the following two questions:

1. Did you read a book last week?
2. Did you see either of your parents reading a book last week?

Fig. 19.12. Mean number of objectives attained by four groups in the goal-setting experiment.

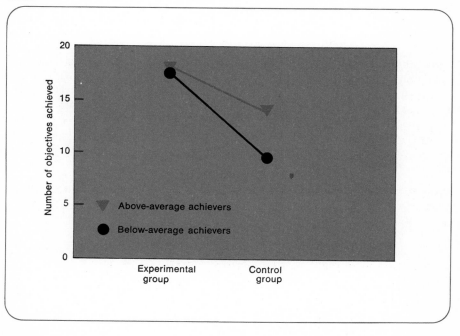

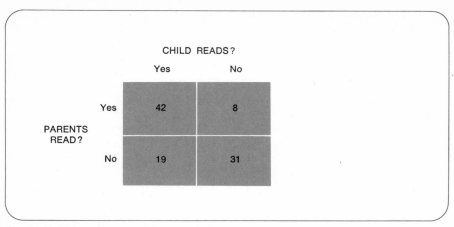

Fig. 19.13. Two-way table of frequencies for computing chi-square test.

Each of the pairs of responses for 100 subjects can be tallied in a two-way table, such as the one in Fig. 19.13 Applying the chi-square test to these frequencies, it is found that the chances are less than one in 1000 that the two variables are independent. In other words, whether the parent reads or not is closely associated with whether the child read a book that week.

The reader should consult any standard statistical reference if he wishes to perform the tests of significance that have been discussed. The intent here is to familiarize the reader with some of the terminology encountered in research reports and its conceptual foundations.

Extrapolating the Results of Research to Another Setting. There is no guarantee that research results reported are important for education or that they can be replicated or repeated in another situation. It is the responsibility of the reader of such reports to evaluate them critically and decide whether the questions posed are of interest and importance and whether the sampling and experimental procedures warrant placing confidence in the findings. Critical factors to keep in mind include the nature of the population, the size of the sample, and the usability or practicality of the procedures. All these factors may not be important for every report, however.

It is suggested that the reader examine the exemplary research report by Ellis Page reprinted (in part) as Appendix II and evaluate it. The following discussion questions are intended to guide the reader in his study of the report.

19.7 Read the report of an educational experiment which appears as Appendix II. (Note that the body of the report relating to points 2, 3, and 4 in the Summary has been omitted.)

a. Identify the population from which the sample of teachers was drawn. What further sampling was done?

b. Why is the author justified in saying in the first paragraph of the method section that one might expect about an equal number of classes at each grade level to be in the sample?

c. The design on which Table 4 is based is a 74 × 3 grid. What are the two dimensions or main effects? Which one is significant? (Note that F is not reported when it is less than one.)

d. What reservations, if any, might you have if the same overall result of the treatment had been reported for an experiment conducted in a single classroom?

e. Do you agree with the author's suggestion that the results can be generalized to the early college years, or would you require the collection of evidence? Would you be willing to generalize the conclusions to the elementary school level?

19.8 If a number of teachers asked to participate in a study refused, the results would be biased—they would apply only to the kind of teacher willing to participate. Would you agree to participate in an experiment in which you were to be randomly assigned to teach a course by one of two methods, if you disliked one of the methods?

19.9 What should the role of the professional teacher be in educational experimentation?

MEASURES OF RELATIONSHIP

One of the important problems facing psychologists and educators is to ascertain the relationships among sets of measurements on the same individuals; for example, the relationship between IQ and achievement, between interest and achievement, between intellectual and psychomotor abilities, between success in school and success in out-of-school activities. *Correlation* is used in measuring and expressing such relationships. It is also used in ascertaining the reliability or criterion-related validity of tests.

The term correlation refers to the relationship between two or more variables, such as height, weight, IQ, and the like. The *coefficient of correlation*, a number between −1.00 and +1.00, indicates the magnitude and direction of the relationship. Which of several methods of calculating a relationship should be used depends primarily on whether the data for the two sets of variables are nominal, ordinal, or interval in nature. Product-moment correlation used with two sets of interval data and a method of determining the relationship in ordered or ranked data are discussed here.

Product-Moment Correlation

The product-moment coefficient of correlation, usually designated by the symbol r, is a widely employed statistic, devised as a measure of relationship between two sets of measurements (variables) on the same subject or between the same measured variable on pairs of subjects. The r can range from −1.00 for a perfect inverse relationship through 0 for no systematic relationship to +1.00 for a perfect direct relationship.

In interpreting a high correlation between two variables, it is incorrect to conclude that one variable *causes* the other, although this possibility exists. In one study it was found that grades earned in a biology course were highly correlated with average number of hours spent studying. It seems reasonable to conclude that more study time causes higher grades. However, it is also possible that the real underlying cause is intelligence, and that amount of time spent studying and grades earned are both influenced by intelligence. The inconclusiveness of correlational research in determining causality is also evident in the arguments marshalled by skeptics who dispute the apparent results of cigarette-lung cancer research.

Another caution is that r cannot be interpreted as a percentage; an r of .60 does not mean 60 percent relationship. Similarly, an r of .60 does not

Fig. 19.14. Scattergram showing the relationship between paragraph meaning and language scores; $r = .89$.

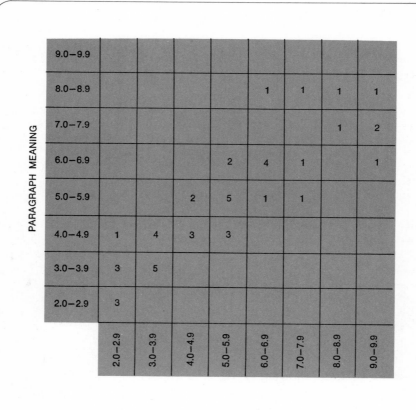

PARAGRAPH MEANING	2.0–2.9	3.0–3.9	4.0–4.9	5.0–5.9	6.0–6.9	7.0–7.9	8.0–8.9	9.0–9.9
9.0–9.9								
8.0–8.9					1	1	1	1
7.0–7.9							1	2
6.0–6.9				2	4	1		1
5.0–5.9			2	5	1	1		
4.0–4.9	1	4	3	3				
3.0–3.9	3	5						
2.0–2.9	3							

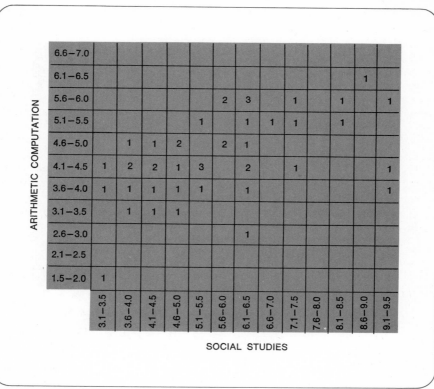

Fig. 19.15. Scattergram showing the relationship between arithmetic computation and social studies scores; $r = .51$.

indicate twice the relationship shown by an r of .30.[3] Also, r is entirely independent of the units in which the two variables are expressed; for example, boys' height in inches can be correlated with their weight in pounds or their carpal age in months.

The meaning of correlation may be brought out more clearly by constructing a scattergram, a table on which the two scores of the same individuals are plotted. Figures 19.14, 19.15, and 19.16 are scattergrams that present graphically the meaning of rs of varying size. Figure 19.14 is for paragraph meaning and language achievement, where $r = .89$; Fig. 19.15 is for arithmetic computation and social studies achievement, where $r = .51$, and Fig. 19.16 is for age and paragraph meaning achievement, where $r = -.03$. To interpret Fig. 19.14, note that three children had second-grade equivalent scores in paragraph meaning and language; similarly, five had third-grade equivalent scores in both areas; all other entries are interpreted the same way. Figure 19.14 shows a positive relationship between the two variables plotted; the higher the language score, the higher the

[3]Squaring correlations results in figures that do enable one to assess their relationship with more validity. This was explained in more detail in Chapter 1, pp. 27-28.

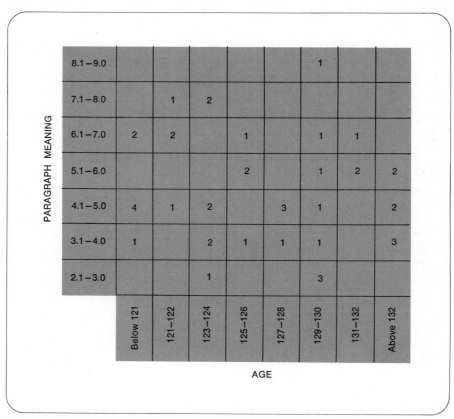

Fig. 19.16. Scattergram showing the relationship between paragraph meaning scores and age in months; $r = -.03$.

paragraph meaning score, and vice versa. If the correlation had been 1.00, instead of .89, every child's set of scores would more nearly have fallen in the eight cells running diagonally from lower left to upper right. (However, this would be strictly true only if the two scales were marked in equal σ units.)

In Fig. 19.15, the correlation coefficient is .51. Notice that many cells with entries are quite distant from a diagonal line from lower left to upper right. For example, two children with below-average computation scores had ninth-grade equivalent scores in social studies. Figure 19.16 shows a correlation of −.03, close to zero, indicating no relationship. Scores are scattered over most of the diagram, with no trend apparent.

The size of negative correlations has the same meaning as that of positive correlations; however, the relationship is inverse. In a scattergram, negatively correlating scores lie along a line going from upper left to lower right. Because a correlation coefficient is a statistic computed from a sample of data, the value varies according to the particular sample drawn. Data from a larger sample of subjects on the average yield correlation coefficients that are closer to the true correlation in the population than data from a smaller sample. The size of the sample must be taken into account in interpreting smaller coefficients; a correlation of .20 may be highly indicative of a small but reliable relationship between two variables if hundreds of cases are taken into account or it may be merely a chance fluctuation from zero, indicative of no relationship, if the data were collected from a small number of subjects.

There are several formulas for computing correlations. If the raw scores are already changed to deviation scores, for example, $x = X - \overline{X}$ and $y = Y - \overline{Y}$, the formula is $r = \Sigma xy / \sqrt{\Sigma(x^2) \Sigma(y^2)}$, where x and y are the deviation scores.

Ordinarily, raw scores are used in conjunction with a desk calculator to compute the correlation between two variables. Computing Guide 19.5, when used in conjunction with columns 3 to 15, excluding 5, in Table A of Appendix I, gives the most common procedure for computing a correlation coefficient. The correlations among the 12 variables with interval data given in Table A have been calculated; they are presented in Table C of Appendix I. The r is .020 between IQ and age and .820 between word meaning and paragraph meaning. Other entries are read in the same way.

COMPUTING GUIDE 19.5

Computing the Product-Moment Coefficient of Correlation Between Two Variables

Let: $r =$ the product-moment correlation coefficient
$N =$ the number of cases
$\Sigma XY =$ the sum of the cross products (a cross product is each person's X score multiplied by his Y score)
$\Sigma X \Sigma Y =$ the sum of all the X scores multiplied by the sum of all the Y scores
$\Sigma X^2 =$ the square of each X score, subsequently added together
$(\Sigma X)^2 =$ the sum of all the X scores, squared
$\Sigma Y^2 =$ the square of each Y score, subsequently added together
$(\Sigma Y)^2 =$ the sum of all the Y scores, squared

Formula: $$r = \frac{N\Sigma XY - \Sigma X \Sigma Y}{\sqrt{[N\Sigma X^2 - (\Sigma X)^2][N\Sigma Y^2 - (\Sigma Y)^2]}}$$

Example: Compute the product-moment correlation between paragraph meaning (X) and language scores (Y) for the 46 children in Table A of Appendix I.
Step 1: Add all the raw scores for X; add all the raw scores for Y. Determine that $\Sigma X = 2354$; $\Sigma Y = 2350$.
Step 2: Square all X scores and add the products; square all Y scores and add the products. Determine that $\Sigma X^2 = 132,218$; $\Sigma Y^2 = 139,008$.
Step 3: Multiply X by Y for each child; add these to determine that $\Sigma XY = 133,538$.

Step 4: Substitute numbers in the formula and perform the indicated operations:

$$r = \frac{(46 \times 133538) - (2354 \times 2350)}{\sqrt{[(46 \times 132218) - (2354)^2][(46 \times 139008) - (2350)^2]}}$$

$$= \frac{610{,}848}{\sqrt{540{,}712 \times 871{,}868}} = \frac{610{,}848}{686{,}607} = .89$$

Association Among Ranks and Ordered Classes

In Table A, IQ scores are also presented as ranks. In cases where two or more children tie for a set of ranks, the average of the ranks is assigned to each. Thus students 2 and 36, who both had IQs of 114, tied for the fifteenth and sixteenth places and were both assigned a rank of 15.5. Teachers often rank a classroom group from highest to lowest on characteristics such as originality and sociability. When a group is ranked on any two characteristics, the relationship between the two sets of ranks may be ascertained by several methods. Kendall's tau (τ) statistic is presented here because it has certain desirable characteristics that other rank statistics do not have and because it can be easily calculated from a scattergram.

Let us suppose 10 exhibits in a science fair are ranked by two judges. The pairs of rankings appearing in Table 19.11 may be readily plotted in a scattergram labeled *across the top and down the left side* from 1 to 10 (see Fig. 19.17). Computation of τ is simply a counting and summing procedure outlined in Computing Guide 19.6.

Table 19.11. Two Judges' Rankings of 10 Science Exhibits

Exhibit	Judge 1	Judge 2
A	2	1
B	1	2
C	5	7
D	3	5
E	6	3
F	4	4
G	8	6
H	7	9
I	9	10
J	10	8

The interpretation of τ is as follows: given two of the subjects or objects ranked, τ is the probability that order of the ranks is the same. A negative τ indicates that an inverse relationship in the order of the ranks is probable. Like r, τ ranges from −1.00 to +1.00.

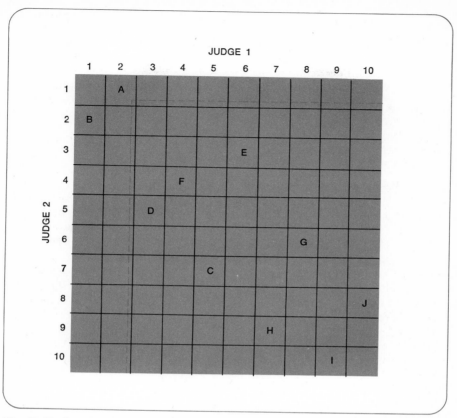

Fig. 19.17. Scattergram showing two judges' rankings of 10 science exhibits (e.g., exhibit C received a rank of 5 from judge 1 and a rank of 7 from judge 2).

COMPUTING GUIDE 19.6

Computing Kendall's Tau Between Two Ranked Variables with No Ties

Let: τ = Kendall's tau
     S_+ = sum of entries to the right and below each entry
     S_- = sum of entries to the left and below each entry

Formula: $\tau = \dfrac{S_+ - S_-}{S_+ + S_-}$

Example: Compute τ between the judges' rankings in Table 19.11.
     Step 1: Make a scattergram such as that illustrated in Fig. 19.17. Be sure the lowest numerical ranks appear in the upper left-hand corner.
     Step 2: Calculate S_+ by counting the number of entries to the right *and* below each entry and summing these numbers. For example, eight entries lie to the right and

below entry A in the space demarcated by dashed lines. Likewise, two entries, I and J, are in a similar relationship to G.

$$S_+ = 8 + 8 + 4 + 5 + 5 + 3 + 2 + 1 = 36$$

Step 3: Calculate S_- by counting the number of entries to the left and below each entry and summing these numbers.

$$S_- = 2 + 2 + 1 + 3 + 1 = 9$$

Step 4: Substitute values for S_+ and S_- in the formula for τ:

$$\tau = \frac{36 - 9}{36 + 9} = \frac{27}{45} = .60$$

When ranks are tied, the same procedure may be applied, but the resulting statistic is known as Kruskal's gamma (γ). In this case, if Table A ranks are being used, the labels in the margins are the ranks that actually appear in the table, including ranks such as 15.5. The statistic can also be used with *ordered* nominal data, such as letter grades. Suppose the relationship between tenth- and eleventh-grade English marks is desired. A scattergram such as the one in Fig. 19.18 is made and the directions in Computing Guide 19.7 are followed. A strong relationship is indicated by $\gamma = .86$.

Fig. 19.18. Scattergram showing the relationship between tenth- and eleventh-grade English marks.

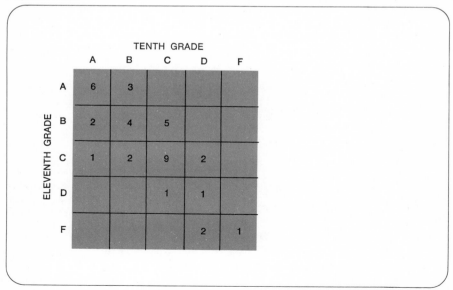

COMPUTING GUIDE 19.7

Computing Kruskal's Gamma Between Variables in Two Ordered Classes

Let: γ = Kruskal's gamma

S_+ = a sum of products as explained in Step 2

S_- = a sum of products as explained in Step 3

Formula: $\gamma = \dfrac{S_+ - S_-}{S_+ + S_-}$

Example: Compute γ between the English marks awarded in grades 10 and 11.

Step 1: Make a scattergram such as that illustrated in Fig. 19.18. Be sure the first numerical class (or rank) in the order appears in the upper left-hand corner. Note that this scattergram differs from that used for Kendall's tau by having more than one entry in a cell.

Step 2: Calculate S_+ by summing the entries to the right and below each cell entry, multiplying the sum by the cell entry, and summing the products for each cell. For the entry in the upper left-hand corner of Fig. 19.18, the sum of cells to the right and below "6" is $4 + 5 + 2 + 9 + 2 + 1 + 1 + 2 + 1 = 27$. This sum is multiplied by 6 to give a product of 162. A product is calculated for each other cell as the table and the products finally are summed.

$$S_+ = 6(27) + 3(21) + 2(18) + 4(16) +$$
$$5(6) + 1(5) + 2(5) + 9(4) +$$
$$2(1) + 1(3) + 1(1) + 2(0) +$$
$$1(0) = 412$$

Step 3: Calculate S_- by summing the entries to the left and below each cell entry, multiplying the sum by the cell entry and summing the products.

$$S_- = 3(3) + 4(1) + 5(3) + 2(1) = 30$$

Step 4: Substitute values for S_+ and S_- in the formula for γ:

$$\gamma = \frac{412 - 30}{412 + 30} = \frac{382}{442} = .86$$

19.10. Construct a scattergram from data in Table A for age and one variable of interest to you. Predict the value of r, and then compute it. You may verify your calculation by referring to Table C.

19.11. Suppose two judges perfectly agreed in ranking the performances of five contestants.

a. What statistic is appropriate to use in this situation?

b. What is its value?

c. Construct the appropriate scattergram and compute the value, verifying your answer to b.

19.12. Rank-order the pupils whose data appears in Table A on one achievement subtest. Using the ranks given for IQ, construct a scattergram using the actual ranks (including fractional ones) assigned and calculate γ. How does the value of γ compare with that given for the correlation (r) between the original data on the two variables? (Look in Table C to determine the value of r.)

SUMMARY

Statistical procedures associated with three kinds of variables — nominal, ordinal, and interval — are described. Distributions of nominal variables are represented in frequency tables or by bar graphs. Ordinal data are usually neither plotted nor graphed. A variety of means is available to represent interval data, including the frequency distribution, cumulative frequency table or graph, histogram, and frequency polygon.

Measures of central tendency include the mean, median, and mode. Other points of interest in a distribution of interval data include the partition values, quartiles and percentiles. These values and the measure of central tendency are all reference points in a distribution to which a particular score can be compared.

The range, standard deviation, and variance are the most commonly used measures of variability. Although the range is easily calculated, it takes into account only the two extreme scores and is thus unstable. The standard deviation is expressed in the same units as the variable measured. The variance is the square of the standard deviation. Both are useful in indicating how scores are dispersed around the mean.

Raw scores are often converted into more meaningful units using certain of the measures of location and variability. Percentile scores and standard scores are commonly used to make scores on different variables comparable. Recently a simple system of derived scores known as stanines has come into widespread use.

Sampling procedures are followed when a limited amount of evidence can be collected from the population of interest. Using a table of random numbers, a sample of subjects is selected at random and data gathered on the sample alone. The fact that sample values fluctuate from the population value means that limited confidence can be placed in the results.

Statistical tests, including the t-test, analysis of variance, and analysis of covariance are formalized procedures for determining the degree of probability that the observed difference between group means would occur by chance. If the probability of the observed difference occurring by chance is very small, the null hypothesis is rejected in favor of the alternative or experimental hypothesis. Whether the t-test, analysis of variance, or analysis of covariance is used depends on the complexity of the experimental design. These tests are used with interval data. Another test of significance, the chi square, is used with nominal data.

The relationship between two variables can be indexed through statistics whose values range from —1.00 to +1.00, indicating, respectively, perfectly inverse and perfectly direct relationships. The product-moment correlation coefficient (r), the best known measure of relationship, is properly used with two sets of interval data. Ordinal data may be related through the use of Kendall's tau; a similar statistic known as Kruskal's gamma can be used for ordinal data with ties or ordered nominal classes. Other measures of relationship exist for special cases, including those where the two variables are not measured on the same type of scale.

SUGGESTIONS FOR FURTHER READING

BRADLEY, J. I., & McCLELLAND, J. N. *Basic statistical concepts: A self-instructional text.* Chicago: Scott, Foresman, 1963.

This 168-page text is truly introductory, starting with relatively simple arithmetic and algebra. The college student who may have had less than two years of high school mathematics should be able to work through the program. There is a close relationship between the topics here and those in Chapter 19.

ELZEY, F. F. *A programed introduction to statistics.* Belmont, Cal.: Brooks/Cole, 1966.

This 376-page programed text assumes a rudimentary knowledge of algebra and includes all the topics covered in Chapter 19, and others.

HEREFORD, C. F., NATALICIO, L., & McFARLAND, S. J., eds. *Statistics and measurement in the classroom.* Dubuque, Ia.: Kendall/Hunt, 1969.

The first six readings in this book discuss statistical concepts at an elementary level.

SPENCE, J. T., UNDERWOOD, B. J., DUNCAN, C. P., & COTTON, J. W. *Elementary statistics.* New York: Appleton-Century-Crofts, 1968.

More information about each topic included in Chapter 19, and other topics, is presented in this book.

Appendixes
To Chapter 19

Appendix I
Three Tables

Table A. Data on 46 Fifth-Graders

Col. No.	Serial number	Sex	Age in months	IQ	IQ rank	Word meaning	Paragraph meaning	Spelling	Word study skills	Language	Arithmetic computation	Arithmetic concepts	Arithmetic application	Social studies	Science
	(1)	(2)	(3)	(4)	(5)	(6)	(7)	(8)	(9)	(10)	(11)	(12)	(13)	(14)	(15)
	1	M	122	137	1.0	73	80	80	68	77	64	63	69	86	85
	2	F	131	114	15.5	51	57	66	62	62	59	65	69	70	60
	3	M	124	118	11.0	52	43	46	70	53	52	52	55	81	60
	4	M	136	98	34.5	49	40	39	39	28	33	50	34	46	52
	5	F	137	119	9.0	52	52	60	62	50	46	46	41	42	44
	6	M	128	106	24.0	52	59	36	67	56	40	52	44	62	36
	7	F	127	113	17.0	67	72	53	73	92	52	43	47	54	56
	8	M	129	99	33.0	32	24	53	34	29	33	39	41	45	38
	9	M	129	106	24.0	47	50	46	48	43	45	48	49	64	75
	10	F	126	108	19.5	49	67	54	57	57	52	57	58	58	56
	11	F	125	107	21.5	27	36	45	40	32	44	36	38	45	39
	12	M	134	82	44.0	27	34	29	29	27	33	27	42	38	45
	13	F	117	94	39.0	42	42	46	62	34	46	57	46	37	42
	14	F	133	103	27.0	42	50	49	57	44	44	41	49	50	42
	15	F	120	65	46.0	27	32	32	20	27	16	33	32	35	29
	16	F	128	101	29.5	44	48	38	34	48	50	48	53	56	56
	17	F	120	96	37.5	56	61	66	63	64	60	71	85	64	65
	18	M	129	105	26.0	49	23	38	24	27	29	50	51	64	57
	19	M	125	115	14.0	56	80	64	62	65	40	65	55	95	95
	20	M	122	106	24.0	52	43	39	48	37	36	59	44	50	46
	21	M	122	117	12.0	56	61	66	63	64	60	71	85	64	65
	22	F	128	107	21.5	67	50	66	48	70	43	55	49	54	65
	23	M	127	86	42.0	33	32	42	20	29	41	29	47	40	38
	24	M	133	119	9.0	56	57	45	57	53	49	61	61	62	85

#	Sex													
25	F	135	89	41.0	37	36	37	39	27	45	45	41	39	40
26	M	131	120	7.0	67	77	66	73	95	59	85	72	95	85
27	F	120	97	36.0	30	48	43	30	32	49	39	44	45	50
28	M	123	98	34.5	46	37	39	20	36	41	41	46	51	58
29	F	123	101	29.5	35	41	52	42	50	38	36	42	51	47
30	M	123	72	45.0	26	21	30	18	22	36	29	29	32	28
31	F	133	100	31.5	44	48	41	33	40	40	46	34	40	46
32	F	126	129	3.0	70	65	66	71	70	41	54	49	67	56
33	F	130	128	4.0	73	84	95	85	92	57	68	85	64	72
34	M	129	96	37.5	39	39	53	57	34	40	50	39	43	43
35	M	130	84	43.0	36	30	35	24	32	43	36	34	39	32
36	M	127	114	15.5	41	47	48	42	37	46	55	51	60	58
37	F	123	102	28.0	44	39	47	58	34	46	29	42	41	42
38	F	130	125	5.0	57	67	88	85	66	58	63	69	81	75
39	M	120	116	13.0	46	49	64	58	50	45	55	49	95	63
40	F	123	132	2.0	75	80	68	76	80	52	52	51	74	81
41	F	132	100	31.5	54	70	71	90	80	56	61	75	56	69
42	F	120	124	6.0	70	61	66	85	95	52	68	53	70	58
43	M	125	119	9.0	56	52	49	63	51	56	76	61	58	56
44	F	130	108	19.5	49	57	52	70	57	43	55	47	52	42
45	F	120	91	40.0	44	48	46	57	41	44	21	46	45	51
46	M	121	110	18.0	59	65	58	53	61	43	68	61	74	91
$\bar{X}$		127	106		4.9	5.2	5.2	5.3	5.1	4.6	5.1	5.1	5.7	5.6
s		4.98	15.1		1.3	1.6	1.5	2.0	2.1	.94	1.4	1.4	1.7	1.7

Note: All scores in columns 6–15 are grade equivalents, usually expressed with a decimal point between the two digits.

Table B. Number of Objectives Attained by Two Groups Before (Baseline) and During an Experiment Using Goal-Setting Procedures

Experimental Group		Control Group	
Baseline period	Experimental period	Baseline period	Experimental period
7	7	17	17
30	22	23	20
26	12	19	13
24	23	33	22
28	19	24	24
39	21	21	17
22	16	26	15
22	22	30	20
25	17	31	15
30	18	15	15
18	13	21	19
32	20	16	8
23	22	13	2
21	14	24	8
20	17	15	12
16	15	20	8
18	10	21	20
29	23	23	16
33	24	21	14
27	18	19	8
16	24	33	21
22	18	25	13
24	17	26	13
22	22	22	11
26	19	25	16
10	10	20	11
11	19	17	13
16	10	22	14
20	18	28	14
15	16	14	7
21	19	7	4
24	20	20	11
5	14	14	17
16	18	17	7
14	16	8	0
15	23	19	14
15	16	29	9
26	18	20	7
20	26	22	5
14	20	10	3
7	11	12	3
19	28	9	14
14	24	14	15
14	16	10	13
10	7	10	14
30	24	22	6
16	25	22	11
8	12	12	17
19	23	14	3
9	9	25	8

Table C. Correlation Matrix Based on Table A

Variable	Name	1 Age	2 IQ	3 Word meaning	4 Paragraph meaning	5 Spelling	6 Word study skills	7 Language	8 Arithmetic computation	9 Arithmetic concepts	10 Arithmetic application	11 Social studies	12 Science
1	Age	1.000											
2	IQ	.020	1.000										
3	Word meaning	-.025	.816	1.000									
4	Paragraph meaning	-.030	.738	.820	1.000								
5	Spelling	-.047	.731	.721	.773	1.000							
6	Word study skills	-.017	.728	.755	.805	.768	1.000						
7	Language	-.049	.723	.873	.890	.790	.820	1.000					
8	Arithmetic computation	-.049	.639	.582	.679	.667	.676	.670	1.000				
9	Arithmetic concepts	-.018	.660	.707	.674	.627	.634	.670	.606	1.000			
10	Arithmetic application	-.072	.559	.612	.688	.738	.625	.677	.773	.751	1.000		
11	Social studies	-.151	.744	.665	.681	.634	.576	.664	.508	.697	.615	1.000	
12	Science	-.054	.683	.725	.762	.639	.526	.677	.546	.666	.678	.810	1.000

Appendix II A Research Report

TEACHER COMMENTS AND STUDENT PERFORMANCE: A SEVENTY-FOUR
CLASSROOM EXPERIMENT IN SCHOOL MOTIVATION[1]

Ellis Batten Page
University of California, Los Angeles[2]

Each year teachers spend millions of hours marking and writing comments
upon papers being returned to students, apparently in the belief that their
words will produce some result, in student performance, superior to that obtained without such words. Yet on this point solid experimental evidence, obtained under genuine classroom conditions, has been conspicuously absent. Consequently each teacher is free to do as he likes; one will comment copiously,
another not at all. And each believes himself to be right.

The present experiment investigated the questions: 1. Do teacher comments
cause a significant improvement in student performance? 2. If comments have
an effect, which comments have more than others, and what are the conditions,
in students and class, conducive to such effect? The questions are obviously
important for secondary education, educational psychology, learning theory,
and the pressing concern of how a teacher can most effectively spend his time.

Previous Related Work

Previous investigations of "praise" and "blame," however fruitful for the
general psychologist, have for the educator been encumbered by certain weaknesses: Treatments have been administered by persons who were extraneous to
the normal class situation. Tests have been of a contrived nature in order to
keep students (unrealistically) ignorant of the true comparative quality of their
work. Comments of praise or blame have been administered on a random basis,

[1]Portions of this paper were read at the National Research Conference of the American
Educational Research Association at San Francisco, March 8, 1958. This research depended
upon cooperation from many persons. Space limitations prevent the listing of their names.
The writer is especially indebted to the teachers who freely donated time and energy after
having been randomly selected. Without their participation the study obviously would have
been impossible.
[2]Where this study was conceived as part of a doctoral dissertation. The study was conducted
in the San Diego City and County Schools while the writer was with San Diego Junior College.

From *Journal of Educational Psychology*, **49**, no. 4 (August 1958), pp. 173-177, 180-181.

unlike the classroom where their administration is not at all random. Subjects have often lacked any independent measures of their performance, unlike students in the classroom. Areas of training have often been those considered so fresh that the students would have little previous history of related success or failure, an assumption impossible to make in the classroom. There have furthermore been certain statistical errors: tests of significance have been conducted as if students were totally independent of one another, when in truth they were interacting members of a small number of groups with, very probably, some group effects upon the experimental outcome.

For the educator such experimental deviations from ordinary classroom conditions have some grave implications, explored elsewhere by the present writer (5). Where the conditions are highly contrived, no matter how tight the *controls*, efforts to apply the findings to the ordinary teacher-pupil relationship are at best rather tenuous. This study was therefore intended to fill both a psychological and methodological lack by *leaving the total classroom procedures exactly what they would have been without the experiment*, except for the written comments themselves.

Method

Assigning the subjects. Seventy-four teachers, randomly selected from among the secondary teachers of three districts, followed detailed printed instructions in conducting the experiment. By random procedures each teacher chose one class to be subject from among his available classes.[3] As one might expect, these classes represented about equally all secondary grades from seventh through twelfth, and most of the secondary subject-matter fields. They contained 2,139 individual students.

First the teacher administered whatever objective test would ordinarily come next in his course of study; it might be arithmetic, spelling, civics, or whatever. He collected and marked these tests in his usual way, so that each paper exhibited a numerical score and, on the basis of the score, the appropriate letter grade A, B, C, D, or F, each teacher following his usual policy of grade distribution. Next, the teacher placed the papers in numerical rank order, with the best paper on top. He rolled a specially marked die to assign the top paper to the *No Comment, Free Comment,* or *Specified Comment* group. He rolled again, assigning the second-best paper to one of the two remaining groups. He automatically assigned the third-best paper to the one treatment group remaining. He then repeated the process of rolling and assigning with the next three papers in the class, and so on until all students were assigned.

Administering Treatments. The teacher returned *all* test papers with the numerical score and letter grade, as earned. No Comment students received nothing else. Free Comment students received, in addition, whatever comment the teacher might feel it desirable to make. Teachers were instructed: "Write anything that occurs to you in the circumstances. There is not any 'right' or 'wrong' comment for this study. A comment is 'right' for the study if it conforms with your own feelings and practices." Specified Comment students, regardless of teacher or student differences, all received comments designated in advance for each letter grade, as follows:

A: Excellent! Keep it up.
B: Good work. Keep at it.

[3]Certain classes, like certain teachers, would be ineligible for a priori reasons: giving no objective tests, etc.

C: Perhaps try to do still better?
D: Let's bring this up.
F: Let's raise this grade!

Teachers were instructed to administer the comments "rapidly and automatically, trying not even to notice who the students are." This instruction was to prevent any extra attention to the Specified Comment students, in class or out, which might confound the experimental results. After the comments were written on each paper and recorded on the special sheet for the experimenter, the test papers were returned to the students in the teacher's customary way.

It is interesting to note that the student subjects were totally naive. In other psychological experiments, while often not aware of precisely what is being tested, subjects are almost always sure that something unusual is underway. In 69 of the present classes there was no discussion by teacher or student of the comments being returned. In the remaining five the teachers gave ordinary brief instructions to "notice comments" and "profit by them," or similar remarks. In none of the classes were students reported to seem aware or suspicious that they were experimental subjects.

Criterion. Comment effects were judged by the scores achieved on the very next objective test given in the class, regardless of the nature of that test. Since the 74 testing instruments would naturally differ sharply from each other in subject matter, length, difficulty, and every other testing variable, they obviously presented some rather unusual problems. When the tests were regarded primarily as *ranking* instruments, however, some of the difficulties disappeared.

A class with 30 useful students, for example, formed just 10 levels on the basis of scores from the first test. Each level consisted of three students, with each student receiving a different treatment: No Comment, Free Comment, or Specified Comment. Students then achieved new scores on the second (criterion) test, as might be illustrated in Table 1, Part A. On the basis of such scores, they were assigned rankings within levels, as illustrated in Table 1, Part B.

If the comments had no effects, the sums of ranks of Part B would not differ except by chance, and the two-way analysis of variance by ranks would be used to determine whether such differences exceeded chance.[4] Then the *sums* of ranks themselves could be ranked. (In Part B the rankings would be 1, 3, and 2 for Groups N, F, and S; the highest score is ranked 3 throughout the study.) And a new test, of the same type, could be made of all such rankings from the 74 experimental classrooms. Such a test was for the present design the better al-

---

[4]The present study employed a new formula,

$$x_r^2 = \frac{6\Sigma(0 - E)^2}{\Sigma 0}$$

which represents a simplification of Friedman's twenty-year-old notation (2). The new form is the classic chi square,

$$\Sigma \frac{(0 - E)^2}{E}$$

multiplied by $6/k$ where k is simply the number of ranks! This conversion was discovered in connection with the present study by a collaboration of the writer with Alan Waterman and David Wiley. Proof that it is identical with the earlier and more cumbersome variation,

$$x_r^2 = \frac{12}{Nk(k + 1)} \Sigma(R_j)^2 - 3N(k + 1),$$

will be included in a future statistical article.

ternative, since it allowed for the likelihood of "Type G errors" (3, pp. 9-10) in the experimental outcome. Still a third way remained to use these rankings. The summation of each column could be divided by the number of levels in the class, and the result was *a mean rank within treatment within class*. This score proved very useful, since it fulfilled certain requirements for parametric data.

Results

Comment vs. No Comment. The over-all significance of the comment effects, as measured by the analysis of variance by ranks, is indicated in Table 2. The first row shows results obtained when students were considered as matched independently from one common population. The second row shows results when treatment groups within classes were regarded as intact groups. In either case the conclusions were the same. The Specified Comment group, which received automatic impersonal comments according to the letter grade received, achieved higher scores than the No Comment group. The Free Comment group, which received individualized comments from the teachers, achieved the highest scores of all. Not once in a hundred times would such differences have occurred by chance if scores were drawn from a common population. Therefore it may be held that the comments had a real and beneficial effect upon the students' mastery of subject matter in the various experimental classes.

It was also possible, as indicated earlier, to use the mean ranks within treatments within classes as parametric scores. The resulting distributions, being normally distributed and fulfilling certain other assumptions underlying parametric tests, permitted other important comparisons to be made. Table 3 shows the mean-ranks data necessary for such comparisons.

The various tests are summarized in Tables 4 and 5. The over-all F test in Table 5 duplicated, as one would expect, the result of the Friedman test, with differences between treatment groups still significant beyond the .01 level. Comparisons between different pairs of treatments are shown in Table 5. All differences were significant except that between Free Comment and Specified Comment. It was plain that comments, especially the individualized comments, had a marked effect upon student performance.

Table 1. Illustration of Ranked Data

Level	Part A (Raw scores on second test)			Part B (Ranks-within-levels on second test)		
	N	F	S	N	F	S
1	33	31	34	2	1	3
2	30	25	32	2	1	3
3	29	33	23	2	3	1
. . .	. . .	. . .	. . .	. . .	. . .	. . .
. . .	. . .	. . .	. . .	. . .	. . .	. . .
. . .	. . .	. . .	. . .	. . .	. . .	. . .
10	14	25	21	1	3	2
Sum:				19	21	20

Note: N is No Comment; F is Free Comment; S is Specified Comment.

Table 2. The Friedman Test of the Overall Treatment Effects

Units considered	N	F	S	df	X_r^2	p
Individual Subjects	1363	1488	1427	2	10.9593	< .01
Class-Group Subjects	129.5	170.0	144.5	2	11.3310	< .01

Table 3. Parametric Data Based Upon Mean Ranks Within Treatments Within Classes

Source	N	F	S	Total
Number of Groups	74	74	74	222
Sum of Mean Ranks	140.99	154.42	148.59	444.00
Sum of Squares of Mean Ranks	273.50	327.50	304.01	905.01
Mean of Mean Ranks	1.905	2.087	2.008	2.000
S.D. of Mean Ranks	.259	.265	.276	
S.E. of Mean Ranks	.030	.031	.032	

Table 4. Analysis of Variance of Main Treatment Effects (Based on Mean Ranks)

Source	Sum of squares	df	Mean square	F	Probability
Between Treatments: N, F, S	1.23	2	.615	5.69	< .01
Between Class-Groups	0.00	73	.000	. . .	
Interaction: T × Class	15.78	146	.108		
Total	17.01	221			

Note: Modeled after Lindquist (3), p. 157 *et passim*, except for unusual conditions noted.

Table 5. Differences Between Means of the Treatment Groups

Comparison	Difference	S.E. of difference	t	Probability
Between N and F	.182	.052	3.500	<.001
Between N and S	.103	.054	1.907	<.05
Between F and S	.079	.056	1.411	<.10(n.s.)

Note: The *t* tests presented are those for matched pairs, consisting of the paired mean ranks of the treatment groups within the different classes. Probabilities quoted assume that one-tailed tests were appropriate.

Summary

Seventy-four randomly selected secondary teachers, using 2,139 unknowing students in their daily classes, performed the following experiment: They administered to all students whatever objective test would occur in the usual course of instruction. After scoring and grading the test papers in their customary way, and matching the students by performance, they randomly assigned the papers to one of three treatment groups. The No Comment group received no marks beyond those for grading. The Free Comment group received whatever comments the teachers felt were appropriate for the particular students and tests concerned. The Specified Comment group received certain uniform comments designated beforehand by the experimenter for all similar letter grades, and thought to be generally "encouraging." Teachers returned tests to students without any unusual attention. Then teachers reported scores achieved on the next objective test given in the class, and these scores became the criterion of comment effect, with the following results.

1. Free Comment students achieved higher scores than Specified Comment students, and Specified Comments did better than No Comments. All differences were significant except that between Free Comments and Specified Comments.

2. When samplings from 12 different schools were compared, no significant differences of comment effect appeared between schools.

3. When the class-groups from six different school years (grades 7-12) were compared, no *conclusive* differences of comment effect appeared between the years, but if anything senior high was more responsive than junior high. It would appear logical to generalize the experimental results, concerning the effectiveness of comment, at least to the early college years.

4. Although teachers believed that their better students were also much more responsive to teacher comments than their poorer students, there was no experimental support for this belief.

When the average secondary teacher takes the time and trouble to write comments (believed to be "encouraging") on student papers, these apparently have a measurable and potent effect upon student effort, or attention, or attitude, or whatever it is which causes learning to improve, and this effect does not appear dependent on school building, school year, or student ability. Such a finding would seem very important for the studies of classroom learning and teaching method.

References

1. Edwards, A. *Experimental design in psychological research.* New York: Rinehart, 1950.
2. Friedman, M. The use of ranks to avoid the assumption of normality implicit in the analysis of variance. *J. Amer. statist. Ass.*, 1937, 32, 675-701.
3. Lindquist, E. F. *Design and analysis of experiments in psychology and education.* Boston: Houghton Mifflin, 1953.
4. McNemar, Q. *Psychological statistics.* (2nd ed.) New York: Wiley, 1955.
5. Page, E. B. Educational research: replicable *or* generalizable? *Phi Delta Kappan*, 1958, 39, 302-304.
6. Page, E. B. The effects upon student achievement of written comments accompanying letter grades. Unpublished doctoral dissertation, Univer. of California, Los Angeles, 1958.

Received March 6, 1958.

References

Aborn, M. (1953) The influence of experimentally induced failure on the retention of material acquired through set and incidental learning. *Journal of experimental psychology*, **45**:225-231.

Allen, R. R., Kauffeld, F. J., & O'Brien, W. R. (1968) *A semiprogramed introduction to verbal argument*. Madison, Wisc.: Wisconsin Research and Development Center for Cognitive Learning.

Allen, W. H. (1967) Media stimulus and types of learning. *Audiovisual instruction*. Washington, D.C.: National Education Association, **12**:27-31.

Allport, G. W. (1955) *Becoming*. New Haven: Yale University Press.

Allport, G. W., Vernon, P. E., & Lindzey, G. (1960) *Study of values*. Boston: Houghton Mifflin.

Almy, M. (1966) *Young children's thinking: Studies of some aspects of Piaget's theory*. New York: Columbia University, Teachers College Press.

Ames, L. B., & Ilg, F. L. (1951) Developmental trends in writing behavior. *Journal of genetic psychology*, **79**:29-46.

Amidon, E. J., & Flanders, N. A. (1963) *The role of the teacher in the classroom: A manual for understanding and improving teachers' classroom behavior*. Minneapolis: Amidon.

Ammons, M. (1969) Objectives and outcomes. In Ebel, R. L., ed., *Encyclopedia of educational research*. New York: Macmillan. Pp. 908-914.

Ammons, M., & Gilchrist, R. S. (1965) In Leeper, R. R., ed., *Assessing and using curriculum content*. Washington, D. C.: Association for Supervision and Curriculum Development.

Ammons, R. B. (1950) Acquisition of a motor skill: III. Effects of initially distributed practice on rotary pursuit performance. *Journal of experimental psychology*, **40**:777-787.

Amrine, M. (1965) The 1967 Congressional inquiry into testing: A commentary. *American psychologist*, **20**:859.

Anderson, C. C. (1962) Developmental study of dogmatism during adolescence. *Journal of abnormal and social psychology*, **65**:132-135.

Anderson, H. H. (1943) Domination and socially integrative behavior. In Barker, R. G., ed., *Child behavior and development*. New York: McGraw-Hill, 457-483.

Anderson, R. C. (1967) Individual differences and problem solving. In Gagné, R. M., ed., *Learning and individual differences*. Columbus, Ohio: Merrill. Pp. 66-89.

Archer, E. J. (1962) Concept identification as a function of obviousness of relevant and irrelevant information. *Journal of experimental psychology*, **63**:616-620.

Archer, E. J. (1966) The psychological nature of concepts. In Klausmeier, H. J., & Harris, C. W., eds., *Analyses of concept learning*. New York: Academic Press. Pp. 37-49.

Archer, E. J., Bourne, L. E., & Brown, F. G. (1955) Concept identification as a function of irrelevant information and instructions. *Journal of experimental psychology*, **49**:153-164.

Association for Supervision and Curriculum Development. (1962) *Perceiving, behaving, becoming.* Washington, D.C.: Association for Supervision and Curriculum Development.

Association for Supervision and Curriculum Development. (1970) *To nurture humaneness: Commitment for the 70's.* Washington, D.C.: Association for Supervision and Curriculum Development.

Atkinson, J. W. (1965) The mainsprings of achievement oriented activity. In Krumboltz, J. D., ed., *Learning and the educational process.* Chicago: Rand McNally. Pp. 25-66.

Atkinson, R. C. (1971) Computerized instruction and the learning process. In Ripple, R. E., ed., *Readings in Learning and Human Abilities.* New York: Harper & Row, 2nd ed.

Atkinson, R. C., & Wilson, H. A. (1968) Computer-assisted instruction. *Science,* 162:73-77.

Atkinson, R. C., & Wilson, H. A., eds. (1969) *Computer-assisted instruction: A book of readings.* New York: Academic Press.

Ausubel, D. P. (1962) A transfer of training approach to improving the functional retention of medical knowledge. *Journal of medical education,* 37:647-655.

Ausubel, D. P. (1963) *The psychology of meaningful verbal learning.* New York: Grune & Stratton.

Ausubel, D. P. (1960) The use of advance organizers in the learning and retention of meaningful verbal learning. *Journal of educational psychology,* 51:267-272.

Ausubel, D. P., & Fitzgerald, D. (1961) The role of discriminability in meaningful verbal learning and retention. *Journal of educational psychology,* 52:266-274.

Ausubel, D. P., & Fitzgerald, D. (1962) Organizer, general background, and antecedent learning variables in sequential verbal learning. *Journal of educational psychology,* 53:243-249.

Ausubel, D. P., & Robinson, F. G. (1969) *School learning: An introduction to educational psychology.* New York: Holt, Rinehart and Winston.

Ausubel, D. P., Schpoont, S. H., & Cukier, L. (1957) The influence of intention on the retention of school materials. *Journal of educational psychology,* 48:87-92.

Back, K. W. (1951) Influence through social communication. *Journal of abnormal and social psychology,* 46:9-23.

Baker, F. B. (1969) *Fortran test analysis program.* Madison, Wisc.: University of Wisconsin Laboratory of Experimental Design.

Baldwin, A. L. (1967) *Theories of child development.* New York: Wiley.

Bandura, A., Ross, D., & Ross, S. A. (1963) Imitation of film-mediated aggressive models. *Journal of abnormal and social psychology,* 66:3-11.

Bandura, A., & Walters, R. H. (1963) *Social learning and personality development.* New York: Holt, Rinehart and Winston.

Barnes, D. (1963) An analysis of remedial activities used by elementary teachers in coping with classroom behavior problems. *Journal of educational research,* 56:544-547.

Barron, F. (1969) *Creative person and creative process.* New York: Holt, Rinehart and Winston.

Beatty, L. S., Madden, R., & Gardner, E. F. (1966) *Manual for administering and interpreting the Stanford diagnostic arithmetic test.* New York: Harcourt, Brace & World.

Beatty, W. H. (1969) *Improving educational assessment and an inventory of measures of affective behavior.* Washington, D.C.: Association for Supervision and Curriculum Development.

Bebell, C. (1968) The educational program. In Morphet, E. L., & Jesser, D. L., eds., *Emerging designs for education: Program, organization, operation and finance. Eight-state project.* 1362 Lincoln Street, Denver, Colorado, Pp. 1-56.

Beberman, M. (1964) An emerging program of secondary school mathematics. In Heath, R. W., ed., *New curricula*. New York: Harper & Row. Pp. 19-34.

Behrendt, D. (1970) Away with tradition. *American education*, 6:18-22.

Bellugi, U., & Brown, R., eds. (1964) The acquisition of language. *Monographs of the society for research in child development*, 29:1-191.

Bennett, G. K., Seashore, H. G., & Wesman, A. G. (1959) *Differential aptitude tests*. New York: Psychological Corporation.

Bereiter, C. (1968) A nonpsychological approach to early compensatory education. In Deutsch, M., Katz, I., & Jensen, A., eds., *Social class, race and psychological development*. New York: Holt, Rinehart and Winston. Pp. 337-346.

Bereiter, C., & Engelmann, S. (1966) *Teaching disadvantaged children in the preschool*. Englewood Cliffs, N.J.: Prentice-Hall.

Berger, E. (1952) Relation between expressed acceptance of self and expressed acceptance of others. *Journal of abnormal and social psychology*, 47:778-782.

Bernstein, B. (1961) Social structure of language and learning. *Educational research*, 3:163-170.

Biemiller, A. (1970) The development of the use of graphic and contextual information as children learn to read. Mimeographed paper.

Bilodeau, E. A., & Bilodeau, I. M. (1961) Motor-skills learning. In *Annual review of psychology*. Stanford, Cal.: Stanford University Press. Pp. 243-280.

Bilodeau, I. M. (1966) Information feedback. In Bilodeau, E. A., ed., *Acquisition of skill*. New York: Academic Press. Pp. 255-296.

Birch, H. G., & Rabinowitz, H. S. (1951) The negative effect of previous experience on productive thinking. *Journal of experimental psychology*, 41:121-125.

Bloom, B. S. (1964) *Stability and change in human characteristics*. New York: Wiley.

Bloom, B. S. (1969) Some theoretical issues relating to educational evaluation. In Tyler, R. W., ed., *Educational evaluation new roles, new means*, 68th yearbook. Part II. National Society for the Study of Education. Chicago: University of Chicago Press. Pp. 26-50.

Bloom, B. S., ed. (1956) *Taxonomy of educational objectives. Handbook I: Cognitive domain*. New York: McKay.

Blount, N. S., Klausmeier, H. J., Johnson, S. L., Fredrick, W. C., & Ramsay, J. G. (1967) *The effectiveness of programed materials in English syntax and the relationship of selected variables to the learning of concepts*, technical report no. 17. Madison, Wisc.: Wisconsin Research and Development Center for Cognitive Learning.

Bonney, M. E., & Powell, J. (1953) Difference in social behavior between sociometrically high and sociometrically low children. *Journal of educational research*, 46:481-495.

Borg, W. R. (1969) *The minicourse as a vehicle for changing teacher behavior: The research evidence*. Berkeley, Cal.: Far West Laboratory for Educational Research and Development.

Borgatta, E. F., ed. (1969) *Social psychology: Readings and perspective*. Chicago: Rand McNally.

Bourne, L. E. (1966) *Human conceptual behavior*. Boston: Allyn & Bacon.

Bowers, D. G., & Seashore, S. E. (1966) Predicting organizational effectiveness with a four-factor theory of leadership. *Administrative science quarterly*, 11:283-293.

Bowman, P. H. (1966) Improving the pupil self-concept. In Strom, R. D., ed., *The inner-city classroom: Teacher behaviors*. Columbus, Ohio: Merrill. Pp. 75-91.

Bradley, J. I., & McClelland, J. N. (1963) *Basic statistical concepts: A self-instructional text*. Chicago: Scott, Foresman.

Bretsch, H. S. (1952) Social skills and activities of socially accepted and unaccepted adolescents. *Journal of educational psychology*, 43:449-458.

Bridges, K. M. (1932) Emotional development in early infancy. *Child development*, 3:324-341.

Brown, W. F., & Holtzman, W. H. (1953) *Survey of study habits and aptitudes.* New York: Psychological Corporation.

Brown, W. N. (1970) Alienated youth. In Frey, S. H., ed., *Adolescent behavior in school.* Chicago: Rand McNally. Pp. 325-334.

Brownell, W. A., & Hendrickson, G. (1950) How children learn information, concepts, and generalizations. *In Learning and instruction,* 49th yearbook. Part I. National Society for the Study of Education. Chicago: University of Chicago Press. Pp. 92-128.

Brownell, W. A., & Moser, H. E. (1949) Meaningful versus mechanical learning: A study in grade III subtraction. *Duke University studies in education,* no. 8. Durham, N.C.: Duke University Press.

Bruce, P. (1958) Relationship of self-acceptance to other variables with sixth grade children oriented in self-understanding. *Journal of educational psychology,* 49:229-238.

Bruner, J. S. (1960) *The process of education.* Cambridge, Mass.: Harvard University Press.

Bruner, J. S., Goodnow, J. J., & Austin, G. A. (1956) *A study of thinking.* New York: Wiley.

Bruner, J. S., Olver, R. R., & Greenfield, P. M. (1966) *Studies in cognitive growth.* New York: Wiley.

Bugental, J. F. T. (1967) *Challenges of humanistic psychology.* New York: McGraw-Hill.

Buros, O. K. (1959) *Fifth mental measurements yearbook.* Highland Park, N.J.: Gryphon Press.

Buros, O. K. (1965) *Sixth mental measurements yearbook.* Highland Park, N.J.: Gryphon Press.

Buros, O. K. (1970) *Personality tests and reviews.* Highland Park, N.J.: Gryphon Press.

Buros, O. K., ed. (1961) *Tests in print.* Highland Park, N.J.: Gryphon Press.

Butler, R. A. (1953) Discrimination learning by rhesus monkeys to visual-exploration motivation. *Journal of comparative and physiological psychology,* 46:95-98.

Butler, R. A. (1954) Incentive conditions which influence visual exploration. *Journal of experimental psychology,* 48:19-23.

Butler, R. A. (1957) The effect of deprivation of visual incentives on visual exploration motivation in monkeys. *Journal of comparative and physiological psychology,* 50:177-179.

Butler, R. A., & Harlow, H. F. (1954) Persistence of visual exploration in monkeys. *Journal of comparative and physiological psychology.* 47:258-263.

Byers, J. L. (1958) An investigation of the goal patterns of academically successful and unsuccessful children in a U.S. history class. Unpublished master's thesis. Madison, Wisc.: University of Wisconsin.

Byers, J. L. (1967) Verbal and concept learning. *Review of educational research,* 37:494-513.

Cahill, H., & Hovland, C. I. (1960) The role of memory in the acquisition of concepts. *Journal of experimental psychology,* 59:137-144.

Calfee, R., Venezky, R., & Chapman, R. (1969) *Pronunciation of synthetic words with predictable and unpredictable letter-sound correspondences,* technical report no. 71. Madison, Wisc.: Wisconsin Research and Development Center for Cognitive Learning.

Campbell, J. A. (1964) CHEM study—An approach to chemistry based on experiments. In Heath, R. W., ed., *New Curricula.* New York: Harper & Row. Pp. 82-93.

Caplan, S. W. (1957) The effect of group counseling on junior high school boys' concepts of themselves in school. *Journal of consulting psychology,* 4:124-128.

Carroll, J. B., (1971a) The future of educational psychology. In Ripple, R. E., ed., *Readings in learning and human abilities*. New York: Harper & Row, 2nd ed.

Carroll, J. B., (1971b) On learning from being told. In Ripple, R. E., ed., *Readings in learning and human abilities*. New York: Harper & Row, 2nd ed.

Carroll, J. B. (1964) Words, meanings, and concepts. *Harvard educational review*, 34:178-202. Also in Ripple, R. E., ed., *Readings in learning and human abilities*. New York: Harper & Row, 2nd ed.

Carter, B. (1967) The teachers give Oklahoma a lesson. In Elam, S., Lieberman, M., & Moskow, M., eds., *Readings on collective negotiations in public education*. Chicago: Rand McNally. Pp. 381-388.

Caspari, E. (1971) Genetic endowment and environment in the determination of human behavior: Biological viewpoint. In Ripple, R. E., ed., *Readings in learning and human abilities*. New York: Harper & Row, 2nd ed.

Cattell, R. B. (1967) Theory of fluid and crystallized intelligence checked at the 5-6 year level. *British journal of educational psychology*, 37:209-224.

Chapman, R., Venezky, R., & Calfee, R. (1970) *Pronunciation of synthetic words with simple and complex letter-sound correspondences*, technical report. Madison, Wisc.: Wisconsin Research and Development Center for Cognitive Learning.

Chapman, R., Venezky, R., & Calfee, R. (1970) Use of simple conditional letter-sound correspondence in children's pronunciation of synthetic words. Madison, Wisc.: Wisconsin Research and Development Center for Cognitive Learning. Mimeographed paper.

Chu, G. C., & Schramm, W. (1968) *Learning from television*. Washington, D.C.: National Association of Educational Broadcasters.

Clancy, N., & Smitter, F. (1953) A study of emotionally disturbed children in Santa Barbara county schools. *California journal of educational research*, 4:209-222.

Clark, C. A., & Walberg, H. J. (1971) The influence of massive rewards on reading achievement in potential urban school dropouts. In Ripple, R. E., ed., *Readings in learning and human abilities*. New York: Harper & Row, 2nd ed.

Cogen, C. (1967) The American Federation of Teachers and collective negotiations. In Elam, S. M., Lieberman, M., & Moskow, M. H., eds., *Readings on collective negotiations in public education*. Chicago: Rand McNally. Pp. 162-172.

Cole, L., & Hall, I. (1970) *Psychology of adolescence*. New York: Holt, Rinehart and Winston.

Coleman, E. G. (1964) Verbal concept learning as a function of instructions and dominance level. *Journal of experimental psychology*, 68:213-214.

Coleman, J. C. (1950) *Abnormal psychology and modern life*. Chicago: Scott, Foresman.

Coleman, J. S., et al. (1966) Equality of educational opportunity. Washington, D.C.: U.S. Government Printing Office.

Commission on Science Education (1963) *Science—A process approach: Part four* (experimental ed.). Washington, D.C.: American Association for the Advancement of Science.

Comprehensive tests of basic skills. (1968) Bulletin of technical data, form Q, no. 1, California Test Bureau. New York: McGraw-Hill.

Conant, J. B. (1959) *The American high school today*. New York: McGraw-Hill.

Conant, J. B. (1961) *Slums and suburbs*. New York: McGraw-Hill.

Cook, W. W., Leeds, C. H., & Callis, R. (1951) *Minnesota teacher attitude inventory*. New York: Psychological Corporation.

Cooley, W. W., & Glaser, R. (1969) The computer and individualized instruction. *Science*, 166:574-582.

Coopersmith, S. (1967) *Antecedents of self-esteem*. San Francisco, Cal.: Freeman.

Corwin, R. G. (1969) Enhancing teaching as a career. *Today's education*, 58:55.

Crawford, T. J. (1956) The effect of emphasizing production typewriting contrasted with speed typewriting in developing production typewriting ability. Doctoral dissertation. Pittsburgh, Pa.: University of Pittsburgh.

Cron, G. W., & Pronko, N. H. (1957) Development of the sense of balance in school children. *Journal of educational research*, 51:33-37.

Cronbach, L. J. (1960) *Essentials of psychological testing*. New York: Harper & Row, 2nd ed.

Cronbach, L. J. (1970) *Essentials of psychological testing*. New York: Harper & Row, 3rd ed.

Cronbach, L. J., & Suppes, P. (1969) *Research for tomorrow's schools: Disciplined inquiry for education*. New York: Macmillan.

Crossman, E. R. (1959) A theory of the acquisition of speedskill. In *Ergonomics*. London: Taylor & Francis. Vol. 2, pp. 153-166.

Crowder, N. A. (1963) On the differences between linear and intrinsic programming. *Phi delta kappan*, 44:250-254.

Cunningham, B. F., & Torrance, E. P. (1965). *Imagi/craft materials*. Boston: Ginn.

Dale, E. (1967) Historical setting of programed instruction. In Lange, P. C., ed., *Programed instruction*, 66th yearbook. Part II. National Society for the Study of Education. Chicago: University of Chicago Press. Pp. 28-54.

Davies, D. R. (1945) The effect of tuition upon the process of learning a complex motor skill. *Journal of educational psychology*, 36: 352-365.

Davis, G. A. (1971) The current status of research and theory in human problem-solving. In Ripple, R. E., ed., *Readings in learning and human abilities*. New York: Harper & Row, 2nd ed.

Davis, G. A. (1969) Training creativity in adolescence: A discussion of strategy. *Journal of creative behavior*, 3:95-104.

Davis, G. A., & Houtman, S. E. (1968) *Thinking creatively: A guide to training imagination*. Madison, Wisc.: Wisconsin Research and Development Center for Cognitive Learning.

Davis, J. K., & Klausmeier, H. J. (in press) Cognitive style and concept identification as a function of complexity and training procedures. *Journal of educational psychology*.

Dean, S. E. (1960) Reporting pupil progress. In Dean, S. E., ed., *Elementary school administration and organization*, U.S. Department of Health, Education and Welfare, Office of Education, bulletin no. 11. Washington, D.C.: U.S. Government Printing Office. Pp. 61-66.

Deese, J. (1967) Meaning and change of meaning. *American psychologist*, 22:641-651.

Deese, J., & Hulse, S. H. (1967) *The psychology of learning*. New York: McGraw-Hill, 3rd ed.

deHirsch, K., Jansky, J. J., & Langford, W. S. (1966) *Predicting reading failure*. New York: Harper & Row.

Dember, W. N. & Earl, R. W. (1957) Analysis of exploratory, manipulatory, and curiosity behaviors. *Psychological review*, 64:91-96.

Dershimer, R. A. (1969) Professional educational organizations. In Ebel, R. L., ed., *Encyclopedia of educational research*. New York: Macmillan. Pp. 1008-1016.

Deutsch, M. (1963) Nursery education: The influence of social programming on early development. *Journal of nursery education*, 18:191-197.

Deutsch, M. (1968) The effects of cooperation and competition upon group process. In Cartwright, D., & Zander, A., eds., *Group dynamics: Research and theory*. New York: Harper & Row. Pp. 461-482.

Deutsch, M. (1969) The disadvantaged child and the learning process. In Borgatta,

E. F., ed., *Social psychology: Readings and perspective*. Chicago: Rand McNally. Pp. 168-179.

Deutsch, M., Katz, I., & Jensen, A. R., eds. (1968) *Social class, race, and psychological development*. New York: Holt, Rinehart and Winston.

Dewey, J. (1933) *How we think*. New York: Heath.

Dewing, R. (1968) Teacher organization and desegregation. *Phi delta kappan*, 50:257-260.

Driezen, S., et al. (1953) The effects of nutritive failure on the growth patterns of white children in Alabama. *Child development*, 24:189-202.

Duncan, C. P. (1951) The effect of unequal amounts of practice on motor learning before and after rest. *Journal of experimental psychology*, 42:257-264.

Duncan, C. P. (1959) Recent research on human problem solving. *Psychological bulletin*, 56:397-429.

Dunn, J. A. (1969) (American Institutes for Research, Palo Alto, California). Accommodation of individual differences in the development of personal programs of study. Paper presented to the American Psychological Association, Washington, D.C.

Dyer, H. S. (1971) On the assessment of academic achievement. In Ripple, R. E., ed., *Readings in learning and human abilities*. New York: Harper & Row, 2nd ed.

Eames, T. H., Douglas, H. B., Guston, G., & King, M. H. (1965) Attitudes and opinions of adolescents. *Journal of education*, 147: 1-43.

Early, C. J. (1968) Attitude learning in children. *Journal of educational psychology*, 59:176-180.

Ebel, R. L., ed. (1969) *Encyclopedia of educational research*. New York: Macmillan.

Editorial. (1969) The schools behind masters of the moon. *Phi delta kappan*, 51:2-7.

Editors, *Education U.S.A.* (June 1970) *TV comes of age in the classroom: The shape of education for 1970-71*. Washington, D.C.: National School Public Relations Association, 12:50-55.

Education Development Center. (1969) *Man: A course of study: A brief review of evaluation findings*. Cambridge, Mass.: Education Development Center.

Eisner, E. W. (1967) Educational objectives—Help or hindrance? *School review*, 75:250-260.

Eisner, E. W. (1969) Instructional and expressive educational objectives: Their formulation and use in curriculum. In American Educational Research Association, *Instructional objectives*. Chicago: Rand McNally. Pp. 1-19.

Elam, S. M., Lieberman, M. F., & Moskow, M. H., eds. (1967) *Readings on collective negotiations in public education*. Chicago: Rand McNally.

Elkind, D., & Sameroff, A. (1970) *Developmental psychology*. In Mussen, P. H., & Rosenzweig, M. R., eds., *Annual review of psychology*. Palo Alto: Cal.: Annual Reviews. Pp. 149-238.

Ellis, H. C. (1965) *The transfer of learning*. New York: Macmillan.

Elzey, F. F. (1966) *A programed introduction to statistics*. Belmont, Cal.: Brooks/Cole.

Engel, M. (1959) The stability of the self concept in adolescence. *Journal of abnormal and social psychology*, 58:211-215.

Eron, L. D. (1969) Relationship of TV viewing habits and aggressive behavior in children. In Sarason, I. G., ed., *Contemporary research in personality*. Princeton, N.J.: Van Nostrand. Pp. 189-192.

Ervin-Tripp, S. (1966) Language development. In Hoffman, L., & Hoffman, M. L., eds., *Review of child development*. New York: Russell Sage Foundation. Pp. 55-105.

Estvan, F. J., & Estvan, E. W. (1959) *The child's world: His social perception*. New York: Putnam.

Fantini, M. O., & Weinstein, G. (1968) *The disadvantaged: Challenge to education.* New York: Harper & Row.

Fehr, H. F. (1966) The teaching of mathematics in the elementary school. In Klausmeier, H. J., & Harris, C. W., eds., *Analyses of concept learning.* New York: Academic Press. Pp. 223-237.

Feldhusen, J. F. (1963) Taps for teaching machines. *Phi delta kappan,* 44:265-267.

Feldhusen, J. F. (1969) A position paper on CAI research and development. A position paper for the Computers in Education project of the ERIC Clearinghouse on Educational Media and Technology. Stanford, Cal.: Stanford University.

Feldhusen, J. F., Check, J., & Klausmeier, H. J. (1961) Achievement in subtraction. *Elementary school journal,* 61:322-327.

Feldhusen, J. F., & Klausmeier, H. J. (1959) Achievement in counting and addition. *Elementary school journal,* 59:388-393.

Feldhusen, J. F., & Klausmeier, H. J. (1962) Anxiety, intelligence and achievement in children of low, average, and high intelligence. *Child development,* 33:403-409.

Feldhusen, J. F., Treffinger, D. J., & Bahlke, S. J. (1970) Developing creative thinking. *Journal of creative behavior,* 4:85-90.

Feldhusen, J. F., Treffinger, D. J., & Elias, R. M. (1970) Prediction of academic achievement with divergent and convergent thinking and personality variables. *Psychology in the schools.*

Ferguson, G. A. (1956) On transfer and the abilities of man. *Canadian journal of psychology,* 10:121-131.

Festinger, L. (1957) *A theory of cognitive dissonance.* Evanston, Ill.: Row, Peterson.

Fey, W. F. (1957) Correlates of certain subjective attitudes toward self and others. *Journal of clinical psychology,* 13:44-49.

Findley, W. G. (1963) Purposes of school testing programs and their efficient development. In Findley, W. G., ed., *The impact and improvement of school testing programs,* 62nd yearbook. Part II. National Society for the Study of Education. Chicago: University of Chicago Press. Pp. 1-27.

Fisher, A. D. (1969) White rites versus Indian rights. *Transaction,* 7:29-33.

Fitts, P. M. (1964) Perceptual motor skill learning. In Melton, A. W., ed., *Categories of human learning.* New York: Academic Press. Pp. 243-285.

Fitts, P. M. (1965) Factors in complex skill training. In Glaser, R., ed., *Training research and education.* New York: Wiley. Pp. 177-197.

Flanagan, J. C. (1967) Project PLAN. Paper given at the Aerospace Education Foundation seminar on education for the 1970s, Washington, D.C. Palo Alto, Cal.: American Institutes for Research.

Flanagan, J. C. (1968) Program for learning in accordance with needs. Paper presented to the American Educational Research Association, Chicago. Palo Alto, Cal.: American Institutes for Research.

Flanders, N. A. (1968) Interaction analysis and inservice training. In Klausmeier, H. J., & O'Hearn, G. T., eds., *Research and development toward the improvement of education.* Madison, Wisc.: Dembar Educational Research Services. Pp. 126-133.

Flanders, N. A. (1969) Teacher effectiveness. In Ebel, R. L., ed., *Encyclopedia of educational research.* New York: Macmillan. Pp. 1423-1437.

Flanders, N. A., Morrison, B., & Brode, E. (1968) Changes in pupil attitudes during the school year. *Journal of educational psychology,* 50:334-338.

Flavell, J. H. (1963) *The developmental psychology of Jean Piaget.* Princeton, N.J.: Van Nostrand.

Flavell, J. H. (1968) Piaget's theory of moral judgment. In Wrightsman, L. S., ed., *Contemporary issues in social psychology.* Belmont, Cal.: Wadsworth. Pp. 23-27.

Fleishman, E. A. (1964) *The structure and measurement of physical fitness.* Englewood Cliffs, N.J.: Prentice-Hall.

Fleishman, E. A. (1967) Individual differences and motor learning. In Gagné, R. M., ed., *Learning and individual differences*. Columbus, Ohio: Merrill. Pp. 165-191.

Fleishman, E. A., & Bartlett, C. J. (1969) Human abilities. In Mussen, P. H., & Rosenzweig, M. R., eds., *Annual review of psychology*. Palo Alto, Cal.: Annual Reviews. Pp. 349-380.

Fleishman, E. A., & Hempel, W. E. (1955) The relation between abilities and improvement with practice in a visual discrimination task. *Journal of experimental psychology*, **49**:301-310.

Fleishman, E. A., & Parker, J. F., Jr. (1962) Factors in the retention and relearning of perceptual-motor skill. *Journal of experimental psychology*, **64**:215-226.

Fox, D. J., & Lorge, I. (1962) The relative quality of decisions written by individuals and by groups as the available time for problem solving is increased. *Journal of social psychology*, **57**:227-242.

Francis, R. J., & Rarick, G. L. (1959) Motor characteristics of the mentally retarded. *American journal on mental deficiency*, **63**:792-811.

Frayer, D. (1969) Effects of number of instances and emphasis of relevant attribute values on mastery of geometric concepts by fourth- and sixth-grade children. Unpublished doctoral dissertation. Madison, Wisc.: University of Wisconsin.

Frayer, D., Fredrick, W. C., & Klausmeier, H. J. (1969) *A schema for testing the level of concept mastery*, working paper no. 16. Madison, Wisc. Wisconsin Research and Development Center for Cognitive Learning.

Fredrick, W. C. (1966) How significant concepts are attained in high school subjects. *North Central Association quarterly*, **40**:340-345.

Fredrick, W. C. (1968) *Information processing and concept learning at grades 6, 8, and 10 as a function of cognitive style*, technical report no. 44. Madison, Wisc.: Wisconsin Research and Development Center for Cognitive Learning.

French, E. G., & Thomas, F. H. (1958) The relation of achievement motivation to problem-solving effectiveness. *Journal of abnormal and social psychology*, **56**:45-48.

Frymier, J. R. (1967) National assessment. In Wilhelms, F., ed., *Evaluation as feedback and guide*. Washington, D.C.: Association for Supervision and Curriculum Development. Pp. 249-259.

Fuller, F. F. (1971) Concerns of teachers: A developmental conceptualization. In Ripple, R. E., ed., *Readings in learning and human abilities*. New York: Harper & Row, 2nd ed.

Gage, N. L. (1965) Desirable behaviors of teachers. *Urban education*, **1**:85-95.

Gage, N. L. (1968) An analytic approach to research on instructional methods. In Klausmeier, H. J., & Harris, C. W., eds., *Research and development toward the improvement of education*. Madison, Wisc.: Dembar Educational Research Services. Pp. 119-125.

Gagné, R. M. (1964) Problem solving. In Melton, A. W., ed., *Categories of human learning*. New York: Academic Press. Pp. 293-317.

Gagné, R. M. (1965a) Educational objectives and human performance. In Krumboltz, J. D., ed., *Learning and the educational process*. Chicago: Rand McNally. Pp. 1-24.

Gagné, R. M. (1965b) *The conditions of learning*. New York: Holt, Rinehart and Winston.

Gagné, R. M. (1966) The learning of principles. In Klausmeier, H. J., & Harris, C. W., eds., *Analyses of concept learning*. New York: Academic Press. Pp. 81-95.

Gagné, R. M. (1967) Instruction and the conditions of learning. In Siegel, L., ed., *Instruction: Some contemporary viewpoints*. San Francisco, Cal.: Chandler. Pp. 291-313.

Gagné, R. M. (1971) Learning hierarchies. *Educational psychologist*, **6**:1-9. Also in

Ripple, R. E., ed., *Readings in learning and human abilites.* New York: Harper & Row, 2nd ed.

Gallagher, J. J. (1958) Social status of children related to intelligence, propinquity, and social perception. *Elementary school journal,* 58:225-231.

Gallagher, J. J. (1965) Expressive thought by gifted children in the classroom. *Elementary English,* 42:559-568.

Gardner, J. W. (1961) *Excellence: Can we be equal and excellent too?* New York: Harper & Row.

Gardner, J. W. (1963) *Self-renewal: The individual and the innovative society.* New York: Harper & Row.

Garrison, K. (1959) A study of student disciplinarian practices in two Georgia high schools. *Journal of educational research,* 53:153-156.

General aptitude test battery. (1959) Washington, D.C.: U.S. Employment Services.

Gephart, W. J. (1969) Editorial. *School research information service quarterly,* 2:2-6.

Gershon, A., Guilford, J. P., & Merrifield, P. R. (1963) *Figural and symbolic divergent-production abilities in adolescent and adult populations.* Report of the psychological laboratory, no. 29. Los Angeles, Cal.: University of Southern California Press

Getzels, J. W. & Jackson, P. W. (1962) *Creativity and intelligence: Explorations with gifted students.* New York: Wiley.

Gideonse, H. D. (1968) An output-oriented model of research and development and its relationship to educational improvement. In Klausmeier, H. J., & O'Hearn, G. T., eds., *Research and development toward the improvement of education.* Madison, Wisc.: Dembar Educational Research Services. Pp. 157-163.

Ginzberg, E., ed. (1961) *Values and ideals of American youth.* New York: Columbia University Press.

Glaser, R. (1965) Toward a behavioral science base for instructional design. In Glaser, R., ed., *Teaching machines and programed learning.* Washington, D.C.: National Education Association. Vol. 2. Pp. 771-809.

Glaser, R., & Taber, J. I. (1961) *Investigations of the characteristics of programed learning sequences.* Pittsburgh, Pa.: Programed Learning Laboratory.

Gleason, G. T., ed. (1967) *The theory and nature of independent learning.* Scranton, Pa.: International Textbook Company.

Glock, M. D., & Millman, J. (1971) The assignment of school marks. In Ripple, R. E., ed., *Readings in learning and human abilities.* Harper & Row, 2nd ed.

Godshalk, F. I., Swineford, F., & Coffman, W. E. (1966) *The measurement of writing ability.* New York: College Entrance Examination Board.

Gold, M. (1968) Power in the classroom. In Cartwright, D., & Zander, A., eds., *Group dynamics: Research and theory.* New York: Harper & Row. Pp. 251-258.

Goldberg, J. (1968) Influence of pupil's attitudes on perception of teachers' behaviors and on consequent school work. *Journal of educational psychology,* 59:1-5.

Goldner, R. H. (1957) Individual differences in whole-part approach and flexibility-rigidity in problem solving. *Psychological monographs,* 71, no. 21 (whole no. 450).

Goodman, K. (1965) A linguistic study of cues and miscues in reading. *Elementary English,* 42:639-643.

Gowan, J. C., Demos, G. O., & Torrance, E. P., eds. (1967) *Creativity: Its educational implications.* New York: Wiley.

Greenberg, I. M. (1969) Project 100,000: The training of former rejectees. *Phi delta kappan,* 50:570-574.

Grinder, R. E. (1971) The growth of educational psychology as reflected in the history of Division 15. In Ripple, R. E., ed., *Readings in learning and human abilities.* New York: Harper & Row, 2nd ed.

Grobman, H. (1968) *Evaluation activities of curriculum projects.* Chicago: Rand McNally.

Grossman, A. (1965) *Data processing for educators.* Chicago: Educational Methods.

Grotelueschen, A., & Sjogren, D. D. (1968) Effects of differentially structured introductory materials and learning tasks on learning and transfer. *American educational research journal,* 5:191-202.

Guilford, J. P. (1958) A system of the psychomotor abilities. *American journal of psychology,* 71:161-174.

Guilford, J. P. (1959) Three faces of intellect. *American psychologist,* 14:469-479.

Guilford, J. P. (1967) *The nature of human intelligence.* New York: McGraw-Hill.

Guilford, J. P. (1968) *Intelligence, creativity, and their educational implications.* San Diego, Cal.: Knapp.

Guilford, J. P. (1971) Intelligence: 1965 model. In Ripple, R. E., ed., *Readings in learning and human abilities.* New York: Harper & Row, 2nd ed.

Guilford, J. P., & Hoepfner, R. (1966) Structure-of-intellect factors and their tests. *Report of the psychological laboratory,* no. 36. Los Angeles, Cal.: University of Southern California Press.

Guthrie, J. T. (1967) Expository instruction versus a discovery method. *Journal of educational psychology,* 58:45-49.

Hall, E. J., Mouton, J. S., & Blake, R. R. (1963) Group problem solving effectiveness under conditions of pooling vs. interaction. *Journal of social psychology,* 59:147-157.

Hall, J. F. (1955) Retroactive inhibition in meaningful material. *Journal of educational psychology,* 46:47-52.

Hamachek, D. E., ed. (1968) *Human dynamics in psychology and education: Selected readings.* Boston: Allyn and Bacon.

Hamachek, D. E. (1969) Characteristics of good teachers and implications for teacher education. *Phi delta kappan,* 50:341-344.

Harding, J., Kutner, B., Proshansky, H., & Chein, I. (1954) Prejudice and ethnic relations. In Lindzey, G., ed., *Handbook of social psychology.* Reading, Mass.: Addison-Wesley. Pp. 1021-1061.

Harlow, H. F. (1949) The formation of learning sets. *Psychological review,* 56:51-65.

Harlow, H. F. (1953) Mice, monkeys, men, and motives. *Psychological review,* 60:23-32.

Harlow, H. F. (1959) Learning set and error factor theory. In Koch, S., ed., *Psychology: A study of a science.* New York: McGraw-Hill. Vol. 2, pp. 492-537.

Harootunian, B., & Tate, M. W. (1960) The relationship of certain selected variables to problem solving ability. *Journal of educational psychology,* 51:326-333.

Harris, F. L., Wolf, M. M., & Baer, D. M. (1969) Effects of adult social reinforcement on child behavior. In Parke, R. D., ed., *Readings in social development.* New York: Holt, Rinehart and Winston. Pp. 124-134.

Harris, T. L. (1969) Reading. In Ebel, R. L., ed., *Encyclopedia of educational research.* New York: Macmillan. Pp. 1069-1104.

Hartshorne, H., & May, M. A. (1928) *Studies in the nature of character: I. Studies in deceit.* New York: Macmillan.

Haslam, W. L., & Brown, W. F. (1968) Effectiveness of study-skill instruction for high school sophomores. *Journal of educational psychology,* 59:223-226.

Havighurst, R. J. (1971) Minority subcultures and the law of effect. In Ripple, R. E., ed., *Readings in learning and human abilities.* New York: Harper & Row, 2nd ed.

Havighurst, R. J. (1966) Overcoming value differences. In Strom, R. D., ed., *The inner-city classroom: Teacher behaviors.* Columbus, Ohio: Ohio State University. Pp. 41-56.

Havighurst, R. J., Bowman, P. H., Liddle, G. P., Matthews, C. V., & Pierce, J. V. (1962) *Growing up in River City.* New York: Wiley.

Havighurst, R. J., & Moorefield, T. E. (1967) The disadvantaged in industrial cities. In Witty, P. A., ed., *The educationally retarded and disadvantaged,* 66th yearbook. Part I. National Society for the Study of Education. Chicago: University of Chicago Press. Pp. 8-20.

Haygood, R. C., & Bourne, L. E. (1964) Forms of relevant stimulus redundancy in concept identification. *Journal of experimental psychology,* 67:392-397.

Hebron, M., & Ridley, F. (1965) Characteristics associated with social prejudice in adolescent boys. *British journal of social and clinical psychology,* 4:92-97.

Heil, L. M., & Washburne, C. (1962) Brooklyn college research in teacher effectiveness. *Journal of educational research,* 55:347-351.

Heilbroner, R. L. (Jan. 3, 1970) Priorities for the seventies. *Saturday review.* Pp. 17-19, 84.

Hellwig, J. (1969) *Introduction to computers and programming.* New York: Columbia University Press.

Hendrickson, G., & Schroeder, W. H. (1941) Transfer of training in learning to hit a submerged target. *Journal of educational psychology,* 32:205-213.

Henry, N. B., ed. (1946) *The measurement of understanding,* 45th yearbook. Part I. National Society for the Study of Education. Chicago: University of Chicago Press.

Hereford, C. F., Natalicio, L., & McFarland, S. J., eds. (1969) *Statistics and measurement in the classroom.* Dubuque, Iowa: Kendall/Hunt.

Hesburgh, T. M. (1969) A national service proposal. *Phi delta kappan,* 51:29-31.

Hess, R., & Goldblatt, I. (1957) The status of adolescents in American society: A problem in social identity. *Child Development,* 28:459-468.

Hesselbart, J. C., D'Arms, T., & Zinn, K. L. (1968) *File oriented interpretive language.* Ann Arbor, Mich.: Center for Research on Learning and Teaching.

Hicklin, W. J. (1962) A study of long-range techniques for predicting patterns of scholastic behavior. Unpublished doctoral dissertation. Chicago: University of Chicago.

Hilgard, E. R. (1964) Postscript: Twenty years of learning theory in relation to education. In Hilgard, E. R., ed., *Theories of learning and instruction,* 63rd yearbook. Part I. National Society for the Study of Education. Chicago: University of Chicago Press. Pp. 416-418.

Hilgard, E. R., Irvine, R. P., & Whipple, J. E. (1953) Rote memorization, understanding, and transfer: An extension of Katona's card-trick experiments. *Journal of experimental psychology,* 46:288-292.

Hilton, E. (1969) Textbooks. In Ebel, R. L., ed., *Encyclopedia of educational research.* New York: Macmillan. Pp. 1470-1478.

Hites, R. W. (1965) Changes in religious attitudes during four years of college. *Journal of social psychology,* 66:51-63.

Hobbs, N. (1969) Helping disturbed children: Psychological and ecological strategies. In Sarason, I. G., ed., *Contemporary research in personality.* Princeton, N.J.: Van Nostrand. Pp. 352-362.

Hoehn, A. J. (1954) A study of social status differentiation in the classroom behavior of nineteen third-grade teachers. *Journal of social psychology,* 39:269-292.

Hoepfner, R., Guilford, J. P., & Bradley, P. A. (1968) *Identification of transformation abilities in the structure of intellect model.* Los Angeles, Cal.: Psychological Laboratory, University of Southern California.

Hoffman, K. I., Guilford, J. P., Hoepfner, R., & Doherty, W. J. (1968) *A factor analysis of the figural-cognition and figural-evaluation abilities.* Los Angeles, Cal.: Psychological Laboratory, University of Southern California.

Hoffman, L. W., & Hoffman, M. L., eds. (1966) *Review of child development research.* New York: Russell Sage Foundation.

Hoffman, M. L., & Saltzstein, H. D. (1969) Parent discipline and child's moral development. In Parke, R. D., ed., *Readings in social development.* New York: Holt, Rinehart and Winston. Pp. 541-561.

Holland, J. L. (1959) Some limitations of teacher ratings as predictors of creativity. *Journal of educational psychology,* 50:219-223.

Holmes, C. C. (1959) An examination of goal-directed behavior in terms of level of aspiration. Unpublished master's thesis. Madison, Wisc.: University of Wisconsin.

Holtzman, W. H., & Brown, W. F. (1968) Evaluating the study habits and attitudes of high school students. *Journal of educational psychology,* 59:404-409.

Hoppe, R. A. (1962) Memorizing by individuals and groups. *Journal of abnormal and social psychology,* 65:64-67.

Horn, J. L. (1971) Intelligence—why it grows, why it declines. In Ripple, R. E., ed., *Readings in learning and human abilities.* New York: Harper & Row, 2nd ed.

Horn, J. L., & Cattell, R. B. (1966) Refinement and test of the theory of fluid and crystallized intelligence. *Journal of educational psychology,* 57:253-270.

Horn, J. L., & Cattell, R. B. (1967) Age differences in fluid and crystallized intelligence. *Acta psychologica,* 26:107-129.

Horrocks, J. (1969) *Psychology of adolescence.* Boston: Houghton Mifflin.

Hovland, C. I., et al. (1957) The effects of commitment on opinion change following communication. In Hovland, C. I., et al., *The order of presentation in persuasion.* New Haven, Conn.: Yale University Press.

Hovland, C. I., Harvey, O. J., & Sherif, M. (1957) Assimilation and contrast effects in reactions to communication and attitude change. *Journal of abnormal and social psychology,* 55:244-252.

Hovland, C. I., & Pritzker, H. A. (1957) Extent of opinion change as a function of amount of change advocated. *Journal of abnormal and social psychology,* 54:257-261.

Howell, W. J. (1950) Work-study skills of children in grades IV-VIII. *Elementary school journal,* 50:384-389.

Hoyt, K. B. (1955) A study of the effects of teacher knowledge of pupil characteristics on pupil achievement and attitudes towards classwork. *Journal of educational psychology,* 46:302-310.

Hudgins, B. B. (1960) Effects of group experience on individual problem solving. *Journal of educational psychology,* 51:37-42.

Hudgins, B. B., Smith, L. M., & Johnson, T. J. (1962) The child's perception of his classmates. *Journal of genetic psychology,* 101:401-405.

Humphreys, L. G. (1951) Transfer of training in general education. *Journal of general education,* 5:210-216.

Hunt, J. M. (1961) *Intelligence and experience.* New York: Ronald.

Huntley, C. W. (1965) Changes in value scores during the four years of college. *General psychology monographs,* 71:349-383.

Huttenlocher, J. (1962) Some effects of negative instances on the formation of simple concepts. *Psychological report,* 11:35-42.

Inhelder, B., & Piaget, J. (1958) *The growth of logical thinking from childhood to adolescence.* New York: Basic Books.

Isaacson, R. L., et al. (1964) Dimensions of student evaluations of teaching. *Journal of educational psychology,* 55:344-351.

Ismail, A. H., & Gruber, J. J. (1967) *Integrated development: Motor aptitude and intellectual performance.* Columbus, Ohio: Merrill.

Jackson, P. (1968) *Life in classrooms.* New York: Holt, Rinehart and Winston.

James, G., & Lott, A. J. (1964) Reward frequency and the formation of positive attitudes toward group members. *Journal of Social Psychology,* **62**:111-115.

Janis, I., & Feshback, S. (1953) Effects of fear-arousing communication. *Journal of abnormal and social psychology,* **48**:78-92.

Jensen, A. R. (1962) Spelling errors and the serial-position effect. *Journal of educational psychology,* **53**:105-109.

Jensen, A. R. (1968) Social class and verbal learning. In Deutsch, M., Katz, I., & Jensen, A. R., eds., *Social class, race and psychological development.* New York: Holt, Rinehart and Winston.

Jensen, A. R. (1969) How much can we boost IQ and scholastic achievement? *Harvard educational review,* **39**:1-123.

Johnson, D. M. (1955) *The psychology of thought and judgment.* New York: Harper & Row.

Johnson, D. M., & Stratton, R. P. (1966) Evaluation of five methods of teaching concepts. *Journal of educational psychology,* **57**:48-53.

Johnson, D. M., & Stratton, R. P. (1971) Evaluation of five methods of teaching concepts. In Ripple, R. E., ed., *Readings in learning and human abilities.* New York: Harper & Row, 2nd ed.

Johnson, R. A., Kast, F. E., & Rosenzweig, J. E. (1967) *The theory and management of systems.* New York: McGraw-Hill, 2nd ed.

Johnson, R. C., & Medinus, G. R. (1965) *Child psychology: Behavior and development.* New York: Wiley.

Johnson, R. C., & Zara, R. C. (1960) Relational learning in young children. *Journal of comparative and physiological psychology,* **53**:594-597.

Jones, D. L. (1968) *Relationships between concept learning and selected ability test variables for an adult population,* technical report no. 51. Madison, Wisc.: Wisconsin Research and Development Center for Cognitive Learning.

Jones, H. E. (1944) The development of physical abilities. In Henry, N. B., ed., *Adolescence,* 43rd yearbook. Part I. National Society for the Study of Education. Chicago: University of Chicago Press. Vol. 43, pp. 100-122.

Jones, R. (1968) *Fantasy and feeling in education.* New York: University Press.

Joyce, B. R., & Harootunian, B. (1967) *The structure of teaching.* Chicago: Science Research Associates.

Judd, C. H. (1908) The relation of special training to general intelligence. *Educational review,* **36**:28-42.

Kagan, J., & Havemann, E. (1968) *Psychology: An introduction.* New York: Harcourt, Brace & World.

Kagan, J., & Moss, H. A. (1962) *Birth to maturity: A study in psychological development.* New York: Wiley.

Kalish, P. W. (1966) *Concept attainment as a function of monetary incentives, competition, and instructions,* technical report no. 8. Madison, Wisc.: Wisconsin Research and Development Center for Cognitive Learning.

Kates, S. L., & Yudin, L. (1964) Concept attainment and memory. *Journal of educational psychology,* **55**:103-109.

Kearney, N. C. (1953) *Elementary school objectives.* New York: Russell Sage Foundation.

Keister, M. E., & Updegraff, R. (1937) A study of children's reactions to failure and an experimental attempt to modify them. *Child development,* **8**:241-248.

Kelley, T. L., Madden, R., Gardner, E. F., & Rudman, H. C. (1964) *Stanford achievement test, directions for administering primary II battery.* New York: Harcourt, Brace & World.

Kelley, T. L., Madden, R., Gardner, E. F., & Rudman, H. C. (1964b) *Stanford achievement test, intermediate II battery, form W.* New York: Harcourt, Brace & World.

Kelly, H., & Woodruff, C. (1956) Members' reactions to apparent group approval of a counternorm communication. *Journal of abnormal and social psychology,* 52:67-74.

Kendler, H. H., & Kendler, T. S. (1956) Inferential behavior in preschool children. *Journal of experimental psychology,* 51:311-314.

Keniston, K. (1965) *The uncommitted: Alienated youth in American society.* New York: Dell.

Kennedy, W. A., & Willcutt, H. A. (1964) Praise and blame as incentives. *Psychological bulletin,* 62:323-353.

Kersh, B. Y., & Wittrock, M. C. (1962) Learning by discovery: An interpretation of recent research. *Journal of teacher education,* 13:461-469.

Keys, A., et al. (1950) *The biology of human starvation.* Minneapolis: University of Minnesota, 2 vols.

Kilpatrick, W. H. (1946) We learn what we live. *New York State education,* 33:535-537.

King, D. J., & Russell, G. W. (1966) A comparison of rote and meaningful learning of connected meaningful material. *Journal of verbal learning and verbal behavior,* 5:478-483.

Kingsley, H. L., & Garry, R. (1957) *The nature and conditions of learning.* Englewood Cliffs, N.J.: Prentice-Hall.

Kittell, J. E. (1957) An experimental study of the effect of external direction during learning on transfer and retention of principles. *Journal of educational psychology,* 48:391-405.

Klausmeier, H. J. (1958) *Teaching in the secondary school.* New York: Harper & Row.

Klausmeier, H. J. (1961) *Learning and human abilities: Educational psychology.* New York: Harper & Row.

Klausmeier, H. J. (1968) The Wisconsin Research and Development Center for Cognitive Learning. In Klausmeier, H. J., & O'Hearn, G. T., eds., *Research and development toward the improvement of education.* Madison, Wisc.: Dembar Educational Research Services. Pp. 146-156.

Klausmeier, H. J., & Check, J. (1962) Retention and transfer in children of low, average, and high intelligence. *Journal of educational research,* 55:319-322.

Klausmeier, H. J., & Davis, J. K. (1969) Transfer of learning. In Ebel, R. L., ed., *Encyclopedia of Educational Research.* New York: Macmillan. Pp. 1483-1493.

Klausmeier, H. J., & Feldhusen, J. (1959) Retention in arithmetic among children of low, average and high intelligence at 117 months of age. *Journal of educational psychology,* 50:88-92.

Klausmeier, H. J., Feldhusen, J., & Check, J. (1959) *An analysis of learning efficiency in arithmetic of mentally retarded children in comparison with children of average and high intelligence.* U.S. Office of Education, cooperative research project no. 153. Madison, Wisc.: University of Wisconsin.

Klausmeier, H. J., & Frayer, D. A. (1969) *Cognitive operations in concept learning,* working paper no. 36. Madison, Wisc.: Wisconsin Research and Development Center for Cognitive Learning.

Klausmeier, H. J., & Harris, C. W., eds. (1966) *Analyses of concept learning.* New York: Academic Press.

Klausmeier, H. J., Harris, C. W., Davis, J. K., Schwenn, E. A., & Frayer, D. (1968) *Strategies and cognitive processes in concept learning,* cooperative research project no. 2850. Madison, Wisc.: University of Wisconsin.

Klausmeier, H. J., Harris, C. W., & Ethnathios, Z. (1962) Relationships between divergent thinking abilities and teacher ratings of high school students. *Journal of educational psychology,* **53**:72-75.

Klausmeier, H. J., Harris, C. W., & Wiersma, W. (1964) *Strategies of learning and efficiency of concept attainment by individuals and groups.* U.S. Office of Education, cooperative research project no. 1442. Madison, Wisc.: University of Wisconsin.

Klausmeier, H. J., & Loughlin, L. J. (1961) Behaviors during problem solving among children of low, average, and high intelligence. *Journal of educational psychology,* **52**:148-152.

Klausmeier, H. J., & Meinke, D. L. (1968) Concept attainment as a function of instructions concerning the stimulus material, a strategy, and a principle for securing information. *Journal of educational psychology,* **59**:215-222.

Klausmeier, H. J., Morrow, R., & Walter, J. E. (1968) *Individually guided education in the multiunit elementary school: Guidelines for implementation.* Madison, Wisc.: Wisconsin Research and Development Center for Cognitive Learning.

Klausmeier, H. J., & O'Hearn, G. T., eds. (1968) *Research and development toward the improvement of education.* Madison, Wisc.: Dembar Educational Research Services. Pp. 132-163. (Selections also cited in Suggestions for Further Reading.)

Klausmeier, H. J., & Wiersma, W. (1965) The effects of IQ level and sex on divergent thinking of seventh grade pupils of low, average, and high IQ. *Journal of educational research,* **58**:300-302.

Klausmeier, H. J., Wiersma, W. W., & Harris, C. W. (1971) Efficiency of initial learning and transfer by individuals, pairs, and quads. In Ripple, R. E., ed., *Readings in learning and human abilities.* New York: Harper & Row, 2nd ed.

Kleinert, E. J. (1969) The Florida migrant. *Phi delta kappan,* **51**:90-93.

Klineberg, O. (1968) Negro-white differences in intelligence test performance—a new look at an old problem. In Wrightsman, L. S., ed., *Contemporary issues in social psychology.* Belmont, Cal.: Wadsworth. Pp. 11-17.

Knapp, C. G., & Dixon, W. R. (1950) Learning to juggle: I. A study to determine the effect of two different distributions of practice on learning efficiency. *Research quarterly of the American Association for Health, Physical Education and Recreation,* **21**:331-336.

Knapp, C. G., & Dixon, W. R. (1952) Learning to juggle: II. A study of whole and part methods. *Research quarterly of the American Association for Health, Physical Education and Recreation,* **23**:398-401.

Knebel, F. (Nov. 18, 1969) The mood of America. *Look.* Pp. 24-25.

Kooi, B., & Schutz, R. (1965) A factor analysis of classroom disturbance intercorrelations. *American educational research journal,* **2**:37-40.

Kopstein, F. F., & Seidel, R. J. (1969) Computer-administered instruction versus traditionally administered instruction: Economics. In Atkinson, R. C., & Wilson, H. A. eds., *Computer-assisted instruction.* New York: Academic Press. Pp. 327-362.

Kounin, J. S., Friesen, W. V., & Norton, A. E. (1966) Managing emotionally disturbed children in regular classrooms. *Journal of educational psychology,* **57**:1-13.

Kounin, J. S., & Gump, P. V. (1958) The ripple effect in discipline. *Elementary school journal,* **62**:158-162.

Kounin, J. S., & Gump, P. V. (1961) The comparative influence of punitive and nonpunitive teachers upon children's concepts of school misconduct. *Journal of educational psychology,* **52**:44-49. Also in Ripple, R. E., ed., *Readings in learning and human abilities.* New York: Harper & Row, 2nd ed.

Kozol, J. (1967) *Death at an early age.* Boston: Houghton Mifflin.

Krathwohl, D. R. (1965) Stating objectives appropriately for program, for curriculum, and for instructional materials development. *Journal of teacher education,* **16**:83-92.

Krathwohl, D. R., Bloom, B. S., & Masia, B. B. (1964) *Taxonomy of objectives: The classification of educational goals. Handbook II: Affective domain.* New York: McKay.

Krech, D., Crutchfield, R., & Ballachey, E. (1962) *Individual in society.* New York: McGraw-Hill.

Kuder, G. G. (1948) *Kuder preference record-vocational, form CH.* Chicago: Science Research Associates.

Kuhlen, R. G., ed. (1968) *Studies in educational psychology.* Waltham, Mass.: Blaisdell.

Kuhlen, R. G., & Houlihan, N. (1969) Adolescent heterosexual interest in 1942 and 1963. In Grinder, R. E., ed., *Studies in adolescence: A book of readings in adolescent development.* New York: Macmillan. Pp. 184-187.

Lambert, S. M. (1967) National Education Association and the real world of education. *National education association journal,* 56:34-36.

Lange, P. C. (1967) Introduction. In Lange, P. C., ed., *Programed instruction,* 66th yearbook. Part II. National Society for the Study of Education. Chicago: University of Chicago Press. Pp. 57-60.

Lazarus, R. (1963) *Personality and adjustment.* Englewood Cliffs, N.J.: Prentice-Hall.

Leeds, C. H. (1954) Teacher behavior liked and disliked by pupils. *Education,* 75:29-36.

Leeper, R. R., ed. (1965) *Assessing and using curriculum content.* Washington, D.C.: Association for Supervision and Curriculum Development.

Leggitt, D. (1934) Measuring progress in working skills in ninth-grade civics. *School review,* 42:676-687.

Lehmann, I. J. (1963) Changes in critical thinking, attitudes, and values from freshman to senior years. *Journal of educational psychology,* 54:305-315.

Lieberman, M. F. (1967) Power and policy in education. In Elam, S. M., Lieberman, M. F., & Moskow, M. H., eds., *Readings on collective negotiations in public education.* Chicago: Rand McNally. Pp. 37-46.

Lieberman, M. F. (1968) Implications of the coming NEA-AFT merger. *Phi delta kappan,* 50:139-144.

Lindvall, C. M. (1967) *Measuring pupil achievement and aptitude.* New York: Harcourt, Brace & World.

Lindvall, C. M., & Bolvin, J. O. (1967) Programmed instruction in the schools: An application of programming principles in "individually prescribed instruction." In Lange, P. C., ed., *Programmed instruction,* 66th yearbook. Part II. National Society for the Study of Education. Chicago: University of Chicago Press. Pp. 217-254.

Lipetz, B. D. (1966) Information storage and retrieval. In Scientific American, eds., *Information.* San Francisco, Cal.: Freeman. Pp. 175-192.

Lippitt, R., & White, R. K. (1958) An experimental study of leadership and group life. In Maccoby, E. E., Newcomb, T. M., & Hartley, E. E., eds., *Readings in social psychology.* New York: Holt, Rinehart & Winston. Pp. 496-511.

Litwin, G. H. (1958) Motives and expectancies as determinants of preference for degrees of risk. Unpublished doctoral dissertation. Ann Arbor, Mich.: University of Michigan.

Lloyd, K. E. (1960) Supplementary report: Retention and transfer of responses to stimulus classes. *Journal of experimental psychology,* 59:206-207.

Loevinger, J., & Wessler, R. (1970) *Measuring ego development: I.* San Francisco: Jossey-Bass.

Lorge, I., & Solomon, H. (1960) Group and individual performance in problem solving related to previous exposure to problem, level of aspiration, and group size. *Behavioral science,* 5:28-38.

Lorge, I., Thorndike, R. L., & Hagen, E. (1964) *Lorge-Thorndike Intelligence Test, form 1, levels A-H.* Boston, Mass.: Houghton Mifflin.

Lott, A. J., & Lott, B. E. (1961) Group cohesiveness, communication level, and conformity. *Journal of abnormal and social psychology*, **62**:408-412.

Lovell, K. (1965) *Educational psychology and children.* London: University of London Press, 8th ed.

Lovell, K. (1968) *Developmental processes in thought.* In Klausmeier, H. J., & O'Hearn, G. T., eds., *Research and development toward the improvement of education.* Madison, Wisc.: Dembar Educational Research Services. Pp. 14-21.

Luchins, A. S. (1942) Mechanization in problem solving: The effect of Einstellung. *Psychological monograph*, **54**, no. 6 (whole no. 248).

Lumsdaine, A. A. (1964) Educational technology, programed learning, and instructional science. In Hilgard, E. R., ed., *Theories of learning and instruction*, 63rd yearbook. Part I. National Society for the Study of Education. Chicago: University of Chicago Press. Pp. 371-409.

Lyman, E. R. (1968) *A descriptive list of PLATO programs, 1960-1968.* CERL report X-2, Computer-Based Education Research Laboratory. Urbana, Ill.: University of Illinois.

McCarthy, D. (1954) Language development in children. In Carmichael, L., ed., *Manual of child psychology.* New York: Wiley, 2nd ed. Pp. 492-630.

McClelland, D. C. (1971) Toward a theory of motive acquisition. In Ripple, R. E., ed., *Readings in learning and human abilities.* New York: Harper & Row, 2nd ed.

Maccoby, E. E. (1966) *The development of sex differences.* Stanford, Cal.: Stanford University Press.

McCurdy, H. G., & Lambert, W. E. (1952) The efficiency of small human groups in the solution of problems requiring genuine cooperation. *Journal of personality*, **20**:478-494.

McDougall, W. P. (1958) Differential retention of course outcomes in educational psychology. *Journal of educational psychology*, **49**:53-60.

McGuigan, F. J., & MacCaslin, E. F. (1955) Whole and part methods in learning a perceptual motor skill. *American journal of psychology*, **68**:658-661.

McKeachie, W. J. (1954) Individual conformity to attitudes of classroom groups. *Journal of abnormal and social psychology*, **49**:282-289.

MacKinnon, D. W. (1962) The nature and nurture of creative talent. *American psychologist*, **17**:484-495. Also in Ripple, R. E., ed., *Readings in learning and human abilities.* New York: Harper & Row, 2nd ed.

Mackworth, J. (1964) Performance decrement in vigilance, threshold, and high-speed perceptual motor tasks. *Canadian journal of psychology*, **18**:209-223.

McLuhan, M. (1967) *The medium is the massage.* New York: Random House.

Madsen, C. H., Becker, W. C., & Thomas, D. R. (1968) Rules, praise, and ignoring: Elements of elementary classroom control. *Journal of applied behavior analysis*, **1**:139-150.

Mager, R. F. (1962) *Preparing instructional objectives.* Palo Alto, Cal.: Fearon.

Mager, R. F. (1968) *Developing attitude toward instruction.* Palo Alto, Cal.: Fearon.

Mager, R. F., & Clark, C. (1963) Explorations in student-controlled instruction. *Psychological reports*, **13**:71-76.

Marckwardt, A. H., ed. (1970) *Linguistics in the schools*, National Society for the Study of Education, 69th yearbook. Part II. Chicago: University of Chicago Press.

Markle, S. M., & Tiemann, P. W. (1969) *Really understanding concepts: Or in frumious pursuit of the jabberwock.* Champaign, Ill.: Stipes.

Marshall, H. H. (1971) Learning as a function of task interest, reinforcement, and social class variables. In Ripple, R. E., ed., *Readings in learning and human abilities.* New York: Harper & Row, 2nd ed.

Maslow, A. H. (1943) A theory of human motivation. *Psychological review*, **50**:370-396.

Maslow, A. H. (1968a) *Toward a psychology of being*. New York: Van Nostrand.

Maslow, A. H. (1968b) Self-actualization and beyond. In Hamachek, D., ed., *Human dynamics in psychology and education: Selected readings*. Boston: Allyn and Bacon. Pp. 173-183.

Mastin, V. E. (1963) Teacher enthusiasm. *Journal of educational research*, **56**:385-386.

Maw, W. H., & Maw, E. W. (1964) *An exploratory investigation into the measurement of curiosity in elementary school children*. U.S. Department of Health, Education and Welfare, Office of Education, cooperative research project no. 801. Washington, D.C.: U.S. Government Printing Office.

Maw, W. H., & Maw, E. W. (1965) Differences in preference for investigatory activities by school children who differ in curiosity level. *Psychology in the schools*, **2**:263-266.

May, F. B. (1961) Creative thinking: A factorial study of seventh-grade children. Unpublished doctoral dissertation. Madison, Wisc.: University of Wisconsin.

Mead, M. (Jan. 10, 1970) Youth revolt: The future is now. *Saturday Review*, 23-25, 113.

Medley, D. M., & Mitzel, H. E. (1963) Measuring classroom behavior by systematic observation. In Gage, N. L., ed., *Handbook of research on teaching*. Chicago: Rand McNally. Pp. 247-328.

Melton, A. W. (1963) Implications of short-term memory for a general theory of memory. *Journal of verbal learning and verbal behavior*, **2**:1-21.

Merrifield, P. R., Guilford, J. P., Christensen, P. R., & Frick, J. W. (1960) A factor-analytic study of problem-solving abilities. *Report of the psychological laboratory*, no. 22. Los Angeles, Cal.: University of Southern California Press.

Merrifield, P. R., Guilford, J. P., & Gershon, A. (1963) The differentiation of divergent-production abilities at the sixth-grade level. *Report of the psychological laboratory*, no. 27. Los Angeles, Cal.: University of Southern California Press.

Meyer, W. J., & Thompson, G. G. (1956) Sex differences in the distribution of teacher approval and disapproval among sixth-grade children. *Journal of educational psychology*, **47**:385-396.

Meyers, C. E., & Dingman, H. F. (1960) The structure of abilities at the preschool ages: Hypothesized domains. *Psychological bulletin*, **57**:514-532.

Miles, D. T., Kibler, R. S., & Pettigrew, L. E. (1967) The effects of study questions on college students' test performances. *Psychology in the schools*, **4**:25-26.

Miles, W. R. (1931) Measures of certain human abilities throughout the life span. *Proceedings of the National Academy of Science*, **17**:627-633.

Miller, G. A., Galanter, E., & Pribram, K. (1960) *Plans and the structure of behavior*. New York: Holt, Rinehart and Winston.

Miller, G. W., & Davis, J. K. (May 1968) *Retention and concept identification as functions of concept complexity, method of presentation, stimulus exposure time, and conditions of recall*, technical report no. 54. Madison, Wisc.: Wisconsin Research and Development Center for Cognitive Learning.

Millman, J., & Johnson, M. (1971) Relation of section variance to achievement gains in English and mathematics in grades 7 and 8. In Ripple, R. E., ed., *Readings in learning and human abilities*. New York: Harper & Row, 2nd ed.

Mischel, W. (1969) Continuity and change in personality. *American psychologist*, **24**:1012-1018.

Mitchell, J. (1959) Goal-setting behavior as a function of self-acceptance, over- and under-achievement, and related personality variables. *Journal of educational psychology*, **50**:93-104.

Mitnick, L. L., & McGinnies, E. (1958) Influencing ethnocentrism in small discussion groups through a film communication. *Journal of abnormal and social psychology*, 56:82-90.

Mitzel, H. E. (1960) Teacher effectiveness. In Harris, C. W., ed., *Encyclopedia of educational research*. New York: Macmillan. Pp. 1481-1486.

Mooney, R. L., & Gordon, L. V. (1950) *Mooney problem check list, 1950 revision*. New York: Psychological Corporation.

Moore, O. K., & Anderson, S. B. (1954) Search behavior in individual and group problem solving. *American sociological review*, 19:702-714.

Morgan, C. T., & Deese, J. (1969) *How to study*. New York: McGraw-Hill, 2nd ed.

Morgan, R. M. (1969) A review of educational applications of the computer including those in instruction, administration and guidance. A series two paper from ERIC at Stanford, ERIC Clearinghouse on Educational Media and Technology at the Institute for Communication Research, Stanford University.

Morrisett, L., & Hovland, C. I. (1959) A comparison of three varieties of training in human problem solving. *Journal of experimental psychology*, 58:52-55.

Moskowitz, R. (1970) Leaving the drug world behind. *American education*, 6: 3-6.

Mussen, P. H., Conger, J. J., & Kagan, J. (1969) *Child development and personality*. New York: Harper & Row, 3rd ed.

Myers, R. E., & Torrance, E. P. (1965a) *Can you imagine? A book of ideas for children of the primary grades*. Boston, Mass.: Ginn.

Myers, R. E., & Torrance, E. P. (1965b) *Invitations to speaking and writing creatively*. Boston, Mass.: Ginn.

National Education Association. (1957) Discipline in the schools. *Research bulletin*, 35:152-155.

National Education Association. (1963) *Schools for the sixties*. New York: McGraw-Hill.

National Education Association. (March 1967) *Research bulletin*.

National Education Association. (1969a) Reporting pupil progress. *Research bulletin*, 75-76.

National Education Association. (1969b) Resolutions, 1969. *Today's education*, 58:42-46, 72, 76, 78-79.

National Education Association. (Oct. 24, 1969c) 17,000 Los Angeles teachers boycott classes to protest rapid deterioration of school system. *National Education Association reporter*. Pp. 1-6.

National Society for the Study of Education. (1950) *Learning and instruction*. 49th yearbook. Part I. Chicago: University of Chicago Press.

Neale, D. C., & Proshek, J. M. (1967) School-related attitudes of culturally disadvantaged elementary school children. *Journal of educational psychology*, 58:238-244. Also in Ripple, R. E., ed., *Readings in learning and human abilities*. New York: Harper & Row, 2nd ed.

Neill, A. S. (1960) *Summerhill: A radical approach to child rearing*. New York: Hart.

Oettinger, A. G., & Marks, S. (1969) *Run, computer, run*. Cambridge, Mass.: Harvard University Press.

Ojemann, R. H. (1971) Should educational objectives be stated in behavioral terms? In Ripple, R. E., ed., *Readings in learning and human abilities*. New York: Harper & Row, 2nd ed.

Ojemann, R. H., & Wilkinson, F. R. (1939) The effect on pupil growth of an increase in teachers' understanding of pupil behavior. *Journal of experimental education*, 8: 143-147.

Ornstein, A. C., & Vairo, P. D., eds. (1969) *How to teach disadvantaged youth*. New York: McKay.

Otto, W., Kamm, K., Peterson, J., Harris, M., & Miles, P. (1970) *Wisconsin Tests of Reading Skill Development: Word attack, level A*. Madison, Wisc.: Wisconsin Research and Development Center for Cognitive Learning.

Otto, W., & Peterson, J. (1969) *A statement of skills and objectives for the Wisconsin prototypic system of reading skill development*, working paper no. 23. Madison, Wisc.: Wisconsin Research and Development Center for Cognitive Learning.

Overstreet, B. W. (1955) The role of the home in mental health. In Henry, N. B., ed., *Mental health in modern education*, 54th yearbook. Part II. National Society for the Study of Education. Chicago, Ill.: University of Chicago Press. Pp. 82-98.

Page, E. B. (1958) Teacher comments and student performance: A seventy-four classroom experiment in school motivation. *Journal of educational psychology*, 49:173-181.

Parker, J. F., Jr., & Fleishman, E. A. (1961) Use of analytical information concerning task requirements to increase the effectiveness of skill training. *Journal of applied psychology*, 45:295-302.

Patterson, C. H. (1966) *Theories of counseling and psychotherapy*. New York: Harper & Row.

Pellegrin, R. J. (1969) *Some organizational characteristics of multiunit schools*, working paper no. 22. Madison, Wisc.: Wisconsin Research and Development Center for Cognitive Learning.

Phi Delta Kappa. (1969) National Study Commission on Evaluation. Mimeograph monograph of report. Bloomington, Ind.: Phi Delta Kappan.

Phillips, J. L. (1969) *The origin of intellect: Piaget's theory*. San Francisco: Freeman.

Piaget, J. (1971a) Development and learning. In Ripple, R. E., ed., *Readings in learning and human abilities*. New York: Harper & Row, 2nd ed.

Piaget, J. (1971b) The development of mental imagery. In Ripple, R. E., ed., *Readings in learning and human abilities*. New York: Harper & Row, 2nd ed.

Plant, W. T. (1958a) Changes in ethnocentrism associated with a four-year college education. *Journal of educational psychology*, 49:162-165.

Plant, W. T. (1958b) Sex, intelligence, and sorority or fraternity membership and changes in ethnocentrism over a two-year period. *Journal of genetic psychology*, 93:53-57.

Plowman, L., & Stroud, J. B. (1942) Effect of informing pupils of the correctness of their responses to objective test questions. *Journal of educational research*, 36:16-20.

Pollert, L. H., Feldhusen, J. F., Van Mondfrans, A. P., & Treffinger, D. J. (1969) Role of memory in divergent thinking. *Psychological reports*, 25:151-156.

Polley, I. (1969) What's right with American education? *Phi delta kappan*, 51:13-15.

Popham, W. J., Atkin, J. M., & Raths, J. (1968) *The instructional objective controversy*. Symposium, Annual Meeting of the American Educational Research Association, Chicago, Ill.

Popham, W. J., Eisner, E., Sullivan, H. J., & Tyler, L. (1969) *Instructional objectives*. Chicago: Rand McNally.

Postman, L. (1964) Short-term memory and incidental learning. In Melton, A. W., ed., *Categories of human learning*. New York: Academic Press. Pp. 145-201.

Pressey, S. L. (1926) A simple apparatus which gives tests and scores—and teaches. *School and society*, 23:373-376.

Pressey, S. L. (1927) A machine for automatic teaching of drill material. *School and society*, 25:549-552.

Pressey, S. L. (1964) Autoinstruction: Perspectives, problems, potentials. In Hilgard, E. R., ed., *Theories of learning and instruction*, 63d yearbook. Part I. National Society for the Study of Education. Chicago: University of Chicago Press. Pp. 354-370.

Proshansky, H., & Newton, P. (1968) The nature and meaning of Negro self-identity. In Deutsch, M., Katz, I., & Jensen, A., eds., *Social class, race and psychological development*. New York: Holt, Rinehart and Winston. Pp. 178-218.

Prusok, R. (1961) Student, student personnel worker, and parent attitudes toward student discipline. *Personnel and guidance journal*, 40:247-253.

Psychological Corporation (1955) *Test Service Bulletin Number 48*. New York: Psychological Corporation.

Radke, M. J., Trager, H. G., & Davis, H. (1949) Social perceptions and attitudes of children. *Genetic psychology monographs*, **40**:327-447.

Rahmlow, H. F. (1969) (American Institutes for Research, Palo Alto, California.) Use of student performance data for improvement of individualized instructional materials. Paper presented to the American Psychological Association, Washington, D.C.

Rand, M. J., & English, F. (1968) Towards a differentiated teaching staff. *Phi delta kappan*, 264-268.

Ranken, H. B. (1963) Effects of name learning on serial learning, position learning, and recognition learning with random shapes. *Psychological reports*, **13**:663-678.

Remmers, H. H., ed. (1963) *Anti-democratic attitudes in American schools*. Evanston, Ill.: Northwestern University Press.

Remmers, H. H., Shemberg, B., & Drucker, A. J. (1953) *SRA youth inventory*. Chicago: Science Research Associates.

Rhine, R. J. (1957) The effect on problem solving of success or failure as a function of cue specificity. *Journal of experimental psychology*, **53**:121-125.

Ringness, T. R. (1968) *Mental health in the schools*. New York: Random House.

Ripple, R. E. (1965) Affective factors influence classroom learning. *Educational leadership*, **22**:476-532, 533.

Ripple, R. E. (1971) American cognitive studies: A review. In Ripple, R. E., ed., *Readings in learning and human abilities*. New York: Harper & Row, 2nd ed.

Ripple, R. E., & May, F. B. (1962) Caution in comparing creativity and IQ. *Psychological reports*, **10**:229-230. Also in Ripple, R. E., ed., *Readings in learning and human abilities*. New York: Harper & Row, 2nd ed.

Ripple, R. E., & Rockcastle, V. N., eds. (1964) *Piaget rediscovered*. Ithaca, N.Y.: Cornell University.

Robertson, N. L., & Engle, C. (1969) Who shall bear the burden of dissent? *School research information service quarterly*, **2**:7-9.

Rogers, C. R. (1971) The place of the person in the new world of the behavioral sciences. In Ripple, R. E., ed., *Readings in learning and human abilities*. New York: Harper & Row, 2nd ed.

Romberg, T. A., & Steitz, J. (1970) *Selection and analysis of mathematics concepts for inclusion in tests of concept attainment*, working paper. Madison, Wisc.: Wisconsin Research and Development Center for Cognitive Learning.

Rorschach, H. (1960) *Rorschach technique*. New York: Grune & Stratton.

Rosenshine, B. (1968) Behavioral correlates of effectiveness in explaining. Unpublished doctoral dissertation. Stanford, Cal.: Stanford University.

Rossman, J. (1931) *The psychology of the inventor*. Washington, D. C.: Inventors.

Ruebush, B. E. (1963) Anxiety. In *Child psychology*, 62nd yearbook. Part I. National Society for the Study of Education. Chicago: University of Chicago Press. Pp. 460-516.

Ryans, D. G. (1960) *Characteristics of teachers: Their description, comparison and appraisal*. Washington, D.C.: American Council on Education.

Sanders, N. M. (1965) *Classroom questions: What kinds?* New York: Harper & Row.

Sarason, I. G. (1968) Verbal learning, modeling and juvenile delinquency. *American psychologist*, **23**:254-266.

Sarason, S., Davidson, K. S., Lighthall, F. F., Waite, R. R., & Ruebush, B. K., (1960) *Anxiety in elementary school children*. New York: Wiley.

Scannell, D. P. (1958) Differential prediction of academic success from achievement test scores. Unpublished doctoral dissertation. Iowa City, Ia.: State University of Iowa.

Schramm, W. (1964) *The research on programed instruction: An annotated bibliography.* Washington, D.C.: U.S. Government Printing Office.

Schramm, W. (1968) Instructional television around the world. In Klausmeier, H. J., & Harris, C. W., eds., *Research and development toward the improvement of education.* Madison, Wisc.: Dembar Educational Research Services. Pp. 89-94.

Schramm, W., Coombs, P. H., Kahnert, F., & Lyle, J. (1967) *The new media: Memo to educational planners.* Paris: UNESCO and International Institute for Educational Planning.

Schroder, H. M., & Hunt, D. E. (1957) Failure-avoidance in situational interpretation and problem solving. *Psychological monograph,* 71:, no. 3 (whole no. 432).

Schroder, H. M., & Rotter, J. B. (1953) Rigidity as learned behavior. *Journal of experimental psychology,* 44:141-150.

Schultz, R. E., & Ohlsen, M. M. (1955) Interest patterns of best and poorest student teachers. *Journal of educational sociology,* 29:108-112.

Schutz, R. E. (1968) Experimentation relating to formative evaluation. In Klausmeier, H. J., Wardrop, J. L., Quilling, M. R., Romberg, T. A., & Schutz, R. E., *Research and development strategies in theory refinement and educational improvement,* theoretical paper no. 15. Madison, Wisc.: Wisconsin Research and Development Center for Cognitive Learning. Pp. 19-22.

Schwab, J. (1969) *College curriculum and student protest.* Chicago, Ill.: University of Chicago Press.

Schwenn, E. A., Sorenson, J. S., & Bavry, J. (1970) *The effect of individual adult-child conferences in the independent reading of elementary school children,* technical report no. 125. Madison, Wisc.: Wisconsin Research and Development Center for Cognitive Learning.

Scriven, M. (1967) The methodology of evaluation. In Tyler, R., Gagné, R. M., & Scriven, M., eds., *Perspectives of curriculum evaluation.* Chicago: Rand McNally. Pp. 39-83.

Sears, P. S. (1940) Levels of aspiration in academically successful and unsuccessful children. *Journal of abnormal and social psychology,* 35:498-536.

Sears, P. S., & Hilgard, E. R. (1964) The teacher's role in the motivation of the learner. In Hilgard, E. R., ed., *Theories of learning and instruction,* 63rd yearbook. Part I. Chicago: University of Chicago Press. Pp. 182-209.

Sequential tests of educational progress: Handbook for essay tests, level I, college. (1957) Princeton, N.J.: Educational Testing Service.

Shannon, J. R. (1940) A comparison of highly successful teachers, failing teachers, and average teachers at the time of their graduation from Indiana State Teachers College. *Education, administration and supervision,* 26:43-51.

Shaw, M. C. (1967) Motivation in human learning. *Review of educational research,* 37:563-582.

Shaycoft, M. F. (1967) *The high school years: Growth in cognitive skills.* Pittsburgh, Pa.: American Institutes of Research.

Shellhammer, T. A., ed. (1968) *Western Regional Conference on Testing Problems: Proceedings.* Princeton, N.J.: Educational Testing Service.

Shepherd, J. (September 20, 1966) The *Look* youth survey. *Look.* Pp. 44-49.

Sheviakov, G. V., & Redl, F. (1944) *Discipline for today's children and youth.* Washington, D.C.: Association for Supervision and Curriculum Development. (Revised by Sybil Richardson, 1956.)

Shoben, E. J., Jr. (1957) Toward a concept of the normal personality. *American psychologist,* 12:183-189.

Shulman, L. S., & Keislar, E. R., eds. (1966) *Learning by discovery: A critical appraisal.* Chicago: Rand McNally.

Siegel, L., ed. (1967) *Instruction: Some contemporary viewpoints.* San Francisco: Chandler.

Simun, P., & Asher, J. W. (1964) The relationship of variables in undergraduate school and school administrators' ratings of first-year teachers. *Journal of teacher education*, 15:293-302.

Skinner, B. F. (1948) *Walden two*. New York: Macmillan.

Skinner, B. F. (1954) The science of learning and the art of teaching. *Harvard educational review*, 24:86-97.

Skinner, B. F. (1968) *The technology of teaching*. New York: Appleton-Century-Crofts.

Slamecka, N. J. (1967) Serial learning and order information. *Journal of experimental psychology*, 74:62-66.

Smith, B. O. (1969) Discipline. In Ebel, R., ed., *Encyclopedia of educational research*. Toronto: Macmillan, 4th ed. Pp. 292-297.

Smith, F., & Miller, G., eds. (1966) *The genesis of language*. Cambridge: MIT Press.

Smith, I. M. (1964) *Spatial ability: Its educational and social significance*. London: University of London Press.

Smith, M. B. (1969) Explorations in competence: A study of Peace Corps teachers in Ghana. In Sarason, I. G., ed., *Contemporary research in personality*. Princeton, N. J.: Van Nostrand. Pp. 21-30.

Sontag, L. W., Baker, C. T., & Nelson, V. L. (1958) Mental growth and personality development: A longitudinal study. *Monograph of the Society for Research in Child Development*, 23:1-143.

Sorenson, J. S., Schwenn, E. A., & Bavry, J. (1970) *The use of individual and group goal-setting conferences as a motivational device to improve student conduct and increase student self-direction: A preliminary study*, technical report no. 123. Madison, Wisc.: Wisconsin Research and Development Center for Cognitive Learning.

Sorenson, J. S., Schwenn, E. A., & Klausmeier, H. J. (1969) *The individual conference: A motivational device for increasing independent reading in the elementary grades*, practical paper no. 8. Madison, Wisc.: Wisconsin Research and Development Center for Cognitive Learning.

Spence, J. T., Underwood, B. J., Duncan, C. P., & Cotton, J. W. (1968) *Elementary statistics*. New York: Appleton-Century-Crofts.

Staats, A. W. (1968) *Language, learning, and cognition*. New York: Holt, Rinehart and Winston.

Staines, J. (1958) The self-picture as a factor in the classroom. *British journal of educational psychology*, 28:97-111.

Stake, R., Tyler, R. W., Gagné, R. M., Scriven, M., & Ohmann, J. S. (1967) *Perspectives of curriculum evaluation*. Chicago: Rand McNally.

Stanley, J. C. (1964) *Measurement in today's schools*. Englewood Cliffs, N.J.: Prentice-Hall, 4th ed.

Stendler, C. B. (1951) Social class differences in parental attitudes toward school at grade I level. *Child development*, 22:36-46.

Stenhouse, L. (1967) *Discipline in schools*. London: Pergamon Press.

Sterrett, M. D., & Davis, R. A. (1954) The permanence of school learning: A review of studies. *Educational administration and supervision*, 40:449-460.

Stevenson, H. W., & Siegel, A. (1971) Effects of instructions and age on retention of filmed content. In Ripple, R. E., ed., *Readings in learning and human abilities*. New York: Harper & Row, 2nd ed.

Stolurow, L. M. (1969a) Programmed instruction. In Ebel, R. L., ed., *Encyclopedia of Educational Research*. New York: Macmillan. Pp. 1017-1022.

Stolurow, L. M. (1969b) Some factors in the design of systems for computer-assisted instruction. In Atkinson, R. C., & Wilson, H. A., eds., *Computer-assisted instruction, a book of readings*. New York: Academic Press. Pp. 65-93.

Stout, R. (1969) Leadership. In Ebel, R. L., ed., *Encyclopedia of educational research*. New York: Macmillan. Pp. 699-706.

Strom, R. D., ed. (1966) *The inner-city classroom: Teacher behaviors.* Columbus, Ohio: Merrill.

Suchman, J. R. (1964) The child and the inquiry process. In Passow, A. H., ed., *Intellectual development: Another look.* Washington, D.C.: Association for Supervision and Curriculum Development. Pp. 59-77.

Suppes, P. (1971) Modern learning theory and the elementary-school curriculum. In Ripple, R. E., ed., *Readings in learning and human abilities.* New York: Harper & Row, 2nd ed.

Swanson, F. J. (1959) Voice mutation in the adolescent male: An experiment in guiding the voice development of adolescent boys in general music classes. Unpublished doctoral dissertation. Madison, Wisc.: University of Wisconsin.

Sweet, Roger C. (1966) *Educational attainment and attitudes toward school as a function of feedback in the form of teachers' written comments,* technical report no. 15. Madison, Wisc.: Wisconsin Research and Development Center for Cognitive Learning.

Symonds, P. M., & Dudek, S. (1956) Use of the Rorschach in the diagnosis of teacher effectiveness. *Journal of projective techniques,* **20**:227-234.

Taba, H. (1965) The teaching of thinking. In *Elementary English.* Champaign, Ill.: National Council of Teachers of English. Vol. 42, pp. 534-542.

Tabachnick, B. R., Weible, E. B., & Frayer, D. A. (1970) *Selection and analysis of social studies concepts for inclusion in tests of concept attainment,* working paper no. 53. Madison, Wisc.: Wisconsin Research and Development Center for Cognitive Learning.

Tagatz, G. E. (1967) Effects of strategy, sex, and age on conceptual behavior of elementary school children. *Journal of educational psychology,* **58**:103-109.

Tagatz, G. E., Walsh, M. R., & Layman, J. A. (1969) Learning set and strategy interaction in concept learning. *Journal of educational psychology,* **60**:488-493.

Taylor, C. W., & Holland, J. L. (1962) Development and application of tests of creativity. *Review of educational research,* **32**:91-102.

Taylor, C. W., Smith, W. R., & Ghiselin, B. (1963) The creative and other contributions of one sample of research scientists. In Taylor, C. W., & Barron, F., eds., *Scientific creativity: Its recognition and development.* New York: Wiley. Pp. 53-76.

Templin, M. (1957) *Certain language skills in children: Their development and interrelationships,* Institute of Child Welfare monograph no. 26. Minneapolis, Minn.: University of Minnesota Press.

Terman, L. M. (1954) The discovery and encouragement of exceptional talent. *American psychologist,* **9**:221-230.

Terman, L. M., & Merrill, M. A. (1937) *Measuring intelligence.* Boston, Mass.: Houghton Mifflin.

Terman, L. M., & Merrill, M. A. (1960) *Revised Stanford-Binet intelligence scales.* Boston, Mass.: Houghton Mifflin.

Thompson, O. (1965) High school students and their values. *California journal of educational research,* **16**:217-227.

Thorndike, E. L. (1913) *The psychology of learning: Educational psychology.* New York: Teachers College Press. Vol. 2.

Thorndike, E. L. (1924) Mental discipline in high school studies. *Journal of educational psychology,* **15**:1-22, 83-98.

Thorndike, R. L. (1950) How children learn the principles and techniques of problem solving. In *Learning and instruction,* 49th yearbook. Part I. National Society for the Study of Education. Chicago: University of Chicago Press. Pp. 192-216.

Tiedeman, H. R. (1948) A study of retention in classroom learning. *Journal of educational research,* **42**:516-531.

Tobias, S. (1971) Dimensions of teachers' attitudes toward instructional media. In

Ripple, R. E., ed., *Readings in learning and human abilities*. New York: Harper & Row, 2nd ed.

Tolor, A., Scarpetti, W. L., & Lane, P. A. (1967) Teachers' attitudes toward children's behavior revisited. *Journal of educational psychology*, 58:175-180. Also in Ripple, R. E., ed., *Readings in learning and human abilities*. New York: Harper & Row, 2nd ed.

Torrance, E. P. (1965) *Rewarding creative behavior: Experiments in classroom creativity*. Englewood Cliffs, N.J.: Prentice-Hall.

Torrance, E. P. (1966) *Torrance tests of creative thinking*. Princeton, N.J.: Personnel Press.

Torrance, E. P. (1967) The Minnesota studies of creative behavior: National and international extensions. *Journal of creative behavior*, 1:137-154.

Travers, R. M. W., McCormick, M. C., Van Mondfrans, A. P., & Williams, F. E. (1964) *Research and theory related to audiovisual information transmission*. U.S. Office of Education, cooperative research project no. 3-20-003. Salt Lake City: University of Utah Bureau of Educational Research.

Traxler, A. E. (1950) Reading growth of secondary-school pupils during a five-year period. Achievement Testing Program in Independent Schools and Supplementary Studies. *Educational records bulletin*, 54:96-107.

Trowbridge, N. (1969) *An approach to teaching a large undergraduate class*. Washington, D.C.: American Documentation Institute, American Society for Informational Sciences.

Tuckman, B. W., & Oliver, W. F. (1968) Effectiveness of feedback to teachers as a function of source. *Journal of educational psychology*, 59:297-301.

Tuckman, J., & Lorge, I. (1962) Individual ability as a determinant of group superiority. *Human relations*, 15:45-51.

Tuddenham, R. D., & Snyder, M. M. (1954) Physical growth of California boys and girls from birth to 18 years. *Child development*, 1:183-364.

Tulving, E. (1968) Organized retention and cued recall. In Klausmeier, H. J., & O'Hearn, G. T., eds., *Research and development toward the improvement of education*. Madison, Wisc.: Dembar Educational Research Services. Pp. 3-13.

Turner, R. L. (1965a) *Acquisition of teaching skills in elementary school settings: A research report*. Bloomington, Ind.: Indiana University School of Education Bulletin, 41:1-94.

Turner, R. L. (1965b) Characteristics of beginning teachers: Their differential linkage with school-system type. *School review*, 73:48-58.

Turner, R. L. (1967) Some predictors of problems of beginning teachers. *Elementary school journal*, 67:251-256.

Tyler, R. W. (1965) Assessing the progress of education. *Phi delta kappan*, 47:13-16.

Tyler, R. W. (1966) The objectives and plans for national assessment of educational progress. *Journal of educational measurement*, 3:1-4.

Tyler, R. W., ed. (1969) *Educational evaluation: New roles, new means*. National Society for the Study of Education, 68th yearbook. Part I. Chicago: University of Chicago Press.

Underwood, B. J. (1965) The representativeness of rote verbal learning. In Melton, A. W., ed., *Categories of human learning*. New York: Academic Press. Pp. 47-78.

Underwood, B. J. (1969) Attributes of memory. *Psychological review*, 76:559-573.

Underwood, B. J., & Ekstrand, B. R. (1968) Linguistic associations and retention. *Journal of verbal learning and verbal behavior*, 7:162-171.

Underwood, B. J., & Freund, J. S. (1968) Effect of temporal separation of two tasks on proactive inhibition. *Journal of experimental psychology*, 78:50-54.

U. S. Employment Services. (1959) *General aptitude test battery*. Washington, D.C.: U. S. Employment Services.

U. S. Government Printing Office. (1968) *How to use ERIC.* GPO 0-310-154, Washington, D.C.: U. S. Government Printing Office.

Van Engen, H., & Parr, R. B. (1969) Using mass communication media to improve arithmetic instruction. *Audio-visual instruction,* 14:34-38.

Van Ness, R. G. (1966) *Principles of data processing with computers.* Elmhurst, Ill.: Business Press.

Veldman, D. J., & Peck, R. F. (1963) Student teacher characteristics from the pupils' viewpoint. *Journal of educational psychology,* 54:346-355.

Venezky, R., Calfee, R., & Chapman, R. (1968) *Skills required for learning to read: A preliminary analysis,* working paper no. 10. Madison, Wisc.: Wisconsin Research and Development Center for Cognitive Learning.

Vernon, P. E. (1950) *The structure of human abilities.* New York: Wiley.

Verplanck, W. S. (1955) The control of content of conversation: Reinforcement of statements of opinion. *Journal of abnormal and social psychology,* 51:668-676.

Verplanck, W. S. (1956) The operant conditioning of human motor behavior. *Psychological bulletin,* 53:70-83.

Walberg, H. J. (1970) A model for research on instruction. *School review,* 78:185-200.

Walberg, H. J., & Anderson, G. J. (1968) Classroom climate and individual learning. *Journal of educational psychology,* 59:414-419.

Wallace, J. (1964) Concept dominance, type of feedback, and intensity of feedback as related to concept attainment. *Journal of educational psychology,* 55:159-166.

Wallach, M. A. (1968) Review of the Torrance Tests of Creative Thinking. *American educational research journal,* 5: 272-281

Wallach, M. A., & Kogan, N. (1971) A new look at the creativity-intelligence distinction. In Ripple, R. E., ed., *Readings in learning and human abilities.* New York: Harper & Row, 2nd ed.

Wallas, G. (1926) *The art of thought.* New York: Harcourt, Brace.

Warner, W. L., Havighurst, R. J., & Loeb, M. B. (1944) *Who shall be educated?* New Haven, Conn.: Yale University Press.

Waterland, J. C. (1956) The effect of mental practice combined with kinesthetic perception when the practice precedes each overt performance of a motor skill. Unpublished master's thesis. Madison, Wisc.: University of Wisconsin.

Wattenberg, W. W. (1966) *Social deviancy among youth,* National Society for the Study of Education, 65th yearbook. Part I. Chicago: University of Chicago Press.

Weber, R. (1968) The study of oral reading errors: A survey of literature. *Reading research quarterly,* 4:96-119.

Wechsler, D. (1949) *Manual, Wechsler Intelligence Scale for Children.* New York: Psychological Corporation.

Wechsler, D. (1955) *Wechsler Adult Intelligence Scale.* New York: Psychological Corporation.

Wechsler, D. (1963) *Wechsler Preschool and Primary Scale of Intelligence.* New York: Psychological Corporation.

Wegner, N., & Zeaman, D. (1956) Team and individual performances on a motor learning task. *Journal of general psychology,* 55:127-142.

Weiner, B. (1969) Motivation. In Ebel, R. L., ed., *Encyclopedia of educational research.* New York: Macmillan. Pp. 878-888.

Weizenbaum, J. (1966) ELIZA—A computer program for the study of natural language communication between man and machine. *Communication of the ACM,* 9:36-45.

Wertheimer, M. (1945) *Productive thinking.* New York: Harper & Row.

West, L. J. (1967) Vision and kinesthesis in the acquisition of typewriting skill. *Journal of applied psychology*, **51**:161-166.

West, L. J. (1969) Business education. In Ebel, R. L., ed., *Encyclopedia of educational research*. Toronto, Ont.: Macmillan. Pp. 105-116.

White, S. H. (1958) Generalization of an instrumental response with variations in two attributes of the CS. *Journal of experimental psychology*, **56**:339-343.

Wickman, K. (1928) *Children's behavior and teachers' attitudes*. New York: The Commonwealth Fund.

Wilhelms, F., ed. (1967) *Evaluation as feedback and guide*. Washington, D.C.: Association for Supervision and Curriculum Development.

Williamson, E. (1956) Preventive aspects of disciplinary counseling. *Educational psychology monograph*, **16**:68-81.

Wilson, A. B. (1963) Social stratification and academic achievement. In Passow, A. H., ed., *Education in depressed areas*. New York: Teachers College Press. Pp. 217-236.

Wilson, W. C. (1963) Development of ethnic attitudes in adolescence. *Child development*, **34**:247-256.

Wing, R. L. (1966) Two computer-based economics games for sixth graders. *The American behavioral scientist*, **10**:31-35.

Wiseman, S. (1959) Trends in educational psychology. *British journal of educational psychology*, **29**:128-135.

Wittrock, M. C. (1963a) Set to learn and proactive inhibition. *Journal of educational research*, **57**:72-75.

Wittrock, M. C. (1963b) Verbal stimuli in concept formation: Learning by discovery. *Journal of educational psychology*, **54**:183-190.

Wittrock, M. C. (January 1965) The learning by discovery hypothesis. Paper presented to the Conference on Learning by Discovery, New York City.

Wittrock, M. C., & Twelker, P. A. (1964) Verbal cues and variety of classes of problems in transfer of training. *Psychological report*, **14**:827-830.

Witty, P. A., ed. (1967) *The educationally retarded and disadvantaged*, National Society for the Study of Education, 66th yearbook. Part I. Chicago: University of Chicago Press.

Wiviott, S. (1970) Bases of classification of geometric concepts used by children of varying characteristics. Unpublished doctoral dissertation. Madison, Wisc.: University of Wisconsin.

Womer, F. B. (1971) Testing programs—Misconceptions, misuse, overuse. In Ripple, R. E., ed., *Readings in learning and human abilities*. New York: Harper & Row, 2nd ed.

Woodrow, H. (1938) The relation between abilities and improvement with practice. *Journal of educational psychology*, **29**:215-230.

Woodruff, A. D. (1962) *Basic concepts of teaching*. San Francisco, Cal.: Chandler.

Woodsworth, J. G. (1965) Some theoretical bases for a psychology of instruction. *Canadian educational research digest*, **5**:14-26.

Woodworth, R. S., & Schlosberg, H. (1954) *Experimental psychology*. New York: Holt, Rinehart & Winston.

Wooton, W. (1964) The history and status of the school mathematics study group. In Heath, R. W., ed., *New curricula*. New York: Harper & Row. Pp. 35-53.

Worthen, B. R. (1968) Discovery and expository task presentation in elementary mathematics. *Journal of educational psychology monograph supplement*, **59**(1,pt.2):1-13. Also in Ripple, R. E., ed., *Readings in learning and human abilities*. New York: Harper & Row, 2nd ed.

Wright, C. E. (1969) Special problems of evaluation activities in an individualized education program. Paper presented to the annual meeting of the American Psychological Association, Washington, D.C.

Yamamoto, K. (1963) Relationships between creative thinking abilities of teachers and achievement and adjustment of pupils. *Journal of experimental education*, 32:3-25.

Yates, F. A. (1966) *The art of memory*. Chicago, Ill.: University of Chicago Press.

Youth fitness test manual. (1965) Washington, D.C.: American Association for Health, Physical Education, and Recreation.

Yuker, H. E. (1955) Group atmosphere and memory. *Journal of abnormal and social psychology*, 51:17-23.

Zeluck, S. (1969) The UFT strike: Will it destroy the AFT? *Phi delta kappan*, **50:** 250-254.

Indexes

Index of Names

Aborn, M., 614
Allen, R. R., 148, 152, 168–170, 173
Allen, W. H., 148, 152
Allport, G. W., 553, 554, 664
Almy, M., 431
American Association for Health, Physical Education, and Recreation, 659
Ames, L. B., 500, 502
Amidon, E. J., 276, 278
Ammons, M., 117, 696
Ammons, R. B., 511
Amrine, M., 660
Anderson, C. C., 531
Anderson, G. J., 283, 296
Anderson, G. L., 389
Anderson, H. H., 292, 293
Anderson, R. C., 491
Anderson, S. B., 447
Archer, E. J., 402, 424, 425
Armstrong, N., 361, 362
Asher, J. W., 243
Association for Supervision and Curriculum Development, 141, 555
Atkin, J. M., 122
Atkinson, J. W., 204, 317, 319, 320, 323–325, 328, 355
Atkinson, R. C., 182, 184, 191, 192
Austin, G. A., 370, 397, 398, 436, 608

Ausubel, D. P., 58–60, 62, 64, 69, 383, 384, 589, 610, 618

Back, K. W., 303
Baer, D. M., 69
Bahlke, S. J., 459
Baker, C. T., 197, 203, 208
Baker, F. B., 652
Baldwin, A. L., 406, 409
Ballachey, E., 520, 539, 540
Bandura, A., 50–53, 55, 68, 506, 523
Barnes, D., 580, 581
Barron, F., 448–450, 452, 474
Bartlett, C. J., 111, 608
Bavry, J., 342, 348
Beatty, W. H., 645, 670
Bebell, C., 119
Beberman, M., 426
Becker, W. C., 338
Behrendt, D., 31, 306
Beilin, H., 550
Bellugi, U., 373
Bennett, G. K., 640
Bereiter, C., 111, 224–226, 228, 239
Berger, E., 562
Bernstein, B., 215, 216
Biemiller, A., 377
Bilodeau, E. A., 513
Bilodeau, I. M., 480, 513
Birch, H. G., 446, 601
Blake, R. R., 447

Index of Subjects

71 72 73 74   7 6 5 4 3 2 1